FOURTH EDITION

COST-BENEFIT ANALYSIS

Concepts and Practice

Anthony E. Boardman

University of British Columbia

David H. Greenberg

University of Maryland Baltimore County

Aidan R. Vining

Simon Fraser University

David L. Weimer

University of Wisconsin–Madison

Prentice Hall

Boston   Columbus   Indianapolis   New York   San Francisco   Upper Saddle River   Amsterdam
Cape Town   Dubai   London   Madrid   Milan   Munich   Paris   Montreal   Toronto   Delhi
Mexico City   Sao Paulo   Sydney   Hong Kong   Seoul   Singapore   Taipei   Tokyo

THE PEARSON SERIES IN ECONOMICS

Abel/Bernanke/Croushore
Macroeconomics*

Bade/Parkin
Foundations of Economics*

Bierman/Fernandez
Game Theory with Economic Applications

Blanchard
Macroeconomics

Blau/Ferber/Winkler
The Economics of Women, Men and Work

Boardman/Greenberg/Vining/Weimer
Cost-Benefit Analysis

Boyer
Principles of Transportation Economics

Branson
Macroeconomic Theory and Policy

Brock/Adams
The Structure of American Industry

Bruce
Public Finance and the American Economy

Carlton/Perloff
Modern Industrial Organization

Case/Fair/Oster
Principles of Economics*

Caves/Frankel/Jones
World Trade and Payments: An Introduction

Chapman
Environmental Economics: Theory, Application, and Policy

Cooter/Ulen
Law & Economics

Downs
An Economic Theory of Democracy

Ehrenberg/Smith
Modern Labor Economics

Ekelund/Ressler/Tollison
Economics*

Farnham
Economics for Managers

Folland/Goodman/Stano
The Economics of Health and Health Care

Fort
Sports Economics

Froyen
Macroeconomics

Fusfeld
The Age of the Economist

Gerber
International Economics

Gordon
Macroeconomics

Greene
Econometric Analysis

Gregory
Essentials of Economics

Gregory/Stuart
Russian and Soviet Economic Performance and Structure

Hartwick/Olewiler
The Economics of Natural Resource Use

Heilbroner/Milberg
The Making of the Economic Society

Heyne/ Boettke/Prychitko
The Economic Way of Thinking

Hoffman/Averett
Women and the Economy: Family, Work, and Pay

Holt
Markets, Games and Strategic Behavior

Hubbard
Money, the Financial System, and the Economy

Hubbard/O'Brien
Economics*

Hughes/Cain
American Economic History

Husted/Melvin
International Economics

Jehle/Reny
Advanced Microeconomic Theory

Johnson-Lans
A Health Economics Primer

Keat/Young
Managerial Economics

Klein
Mathematical Methods for Economics

Krugman/Obstfeld
International Economics: Theory & Policy*

Laidler
The Demand for Money

Leeds/von Allmen
The Economics of Sports

Leeds/von Allmen/Schiming
Economics*

Lipsey/Ragan/Storer
Economics*

Lynn
*Economic Development:
Theory and Practice for
a Divided World*

Melvin
*International Money and
Finance*

Miller
Economics Today*

*Understanding Modern
Economics*

Miller/Benjamin
*The Economics of Macro
Issues*

Miller/Benjamin/North
*The Economics of Public
Issues*

Mills/Hamilton
Urban Economics

Mishkin
*The Economics of Money,
Banking, and Financial
Markets**

*The Economics of
Money, Banking, and
Financial Markets,
Business School
Edition**

Murray
*Econometrics: A Modern
Introduction*

Nafziger
*The Economics of
Developing Countries*

O'Sullivan/Sheffrin/Perez
*Economics: Principles,
Applications and Tools**

Parkin
Economics*

Perloff
Microeconomics*

*Microeconomics: Theory and
Applications with Calculus*

**Perman/Common/
McGilvray/Ma**
*Natural Resources and
Environmental Economics*

Phelps
Health Economics

Pindyck/Rubinfeld
Microeconomics*

**Riddell/Shackelford/Stamos/
Schneider**
*Economics: A Tool for
Critically Understanding
Society*

Ritter/Silber/Udell
*Principles of Money, Banking
& Financial Markets**

Roberts
*The Choice: A Fable of Free
Trade and Protection*

Rohlf
*Introduction to Economic
Reasoning*

Ruffin/Gregory
Principles of Economics

Sargent
*Rational Expectations and
Inflation*

Sawyer/Sprinkle
International Economics

Scherer
*Industry Structure, Strategy,
and Public Policy*

Schiller
*The Economics of Poverty
and Discrimination*

Sherman
Market Regulation

Silberberg
Principles of Microeconomics

Stock/Watson
Introduction to Econometrics

*Introduction to Econometrics,
Brief Edition*

Studenmund
*Using Econometrics: A
Practical Guide*

Tietenberg/Lewis
*Environmental and Natural
Resource Economics*

*Environmental Economics
and Policy*

Todaro/Smith
Economic Development

Waldman
Microeconomics

Waldman/Jensen
*Industrial Organization:
Theory and Practice*

Weil
Economic Growth

Williamson
Macroeconomics

 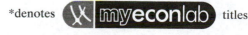

Editorial Director: Sally Yagan
Editor in Chief: Donna Battista
Senior Acquisitions Editor: Adrienne D'Ambrosio
Assistant Editor: Jill Kolongowski
Director of Marketing: Patrice Lumumba Jones
Senior Marketing Manager: Elizabeth A. Averbeck
Marketing Assistant: Ian Gold
Production Project Manager: Clara Bartunek
Creative Art Director: Jayne Conte

Cover Designer: Suzanne Behnke
Rights and Permissions: Michael Joyce
Cover Art: Fotolia
Full-Service Project Management: Mohinder Singh, Aptara®, Inc.
Composition: Aptara®, Inc.
Printer/Binder: Courier/Westford
Cover Printer: Lehigh-Phoenix Color/Hagerstown
Text Font: Times Ten Roman

Credits and acknowledgments borrowed from other sources and reproduced, with permission, in this textbook appear on appropriate page within the text.

Library of Congress Cataloging-in-Publication Data
Cost-benefit analysis: concepts and practice / Anthony E. Boardman ... [et al.]. – 4th ed.
  p. cm. – (Pearson series in economics)
Includes bibliographical references and index.
ISBN-13: 978-0-13-700269-6 (alk. paper)
ISBN-10: 0-13-700269-6 (alk. paper)
1. Cost effectiveness.   I. Boardman, Anthony E.
HD47.4.C669 2011
658.15'54–dc22   2010019030

10 9 8 7 6 5 4 3 2   V013

Prentice Hall
is an imprint of

www.pearsonhighered.com

ISBN 13: 978-0-13-700269-6
ISBN 10:   0-13-700269-6

To
Barbara, Linda, Melanie, and Ulrike

Brief Contents

Contents

PART IV: RELATED METHODS

Preface

Collaborative academic projects often take longer than originally anticipated, not just because of the normal delays of coordinating the efforts of busy people, but also because initially modest goals can become more ambitious as participants delve into their subject. We confess to both these sins with respect to preparing the first edition of this text. Our original plans made in 1990 were very modest. We intended to use an expanded version of the chapter on benefit-cost analysis in the text *Policy Analysis: Concepts and Practice* by David Weimer and Aidan Vining as the conceptual foundation for a collection of cases. Our goal was to produce a book that would be conceptually sound, practically oriented, and easily accessible to both students and practitioners. Though our final product was far different in form and content than we initially planned, we believe that our first edition was such a book.

Our plans evolved for a number of reasons. Perhaps most importantly, through our teaching of undergraduate and graduate students as well as our experiences training government employees, we realized that many topics demanded extended treatment if the essential basics were to be conveyed effectively and if solid foundations were to be laid for further learning of advanced topics. We also decided that fully integrating illustrations and examples with concepts and methods is pedagogically superior to presenting independent cases. The result was a series of chapters that develop conceptual foundations, methods of application, and extensions of cost-benefit analysis through numerous practical examples and illustrations.

Our own use of the book in teaching, as well as comments from other teachers and students, helped us identify several areas for improvement in the second, third, and fourth editions. In addition to adding new material to each edition, we revised and reorganized a number of chapters to make the presentation clearer and more effective.

NEW TO THIS EDITION

Faculty and students will find improvements in presentation and updating of content throughout this new edition. Some of the significant improvements include

- Chapter 3 has been completely rewritten. The revisions include a greater emphasis on welfare and the distributional consequences of changes in surplus, and a new discussion of the implications of indirect taxes.
- Chapter 10 has been updated considerably and simplified. It places more emphasis on cutting-edge discounting methods, especially consumption-based approaches for intragenerational and intergenerational projects.

- Chapter 11 is a new chapter on the important topic of impact prediction. It links the core concepts of cost-benefit analysis presented in the first ten chapters with the monetization methods elucidated in the subsequent chapters.
- Chapter 12 has been simplified and includes new tables.
- Chapter 16 provides an updated catalogue of shadow prices that can serves as a practical resource for using and applying previously estimated values (benefits transfer) in performing new cost-benefit analyses. It contains a new section on pricing global warming emissions.
- Chapter 20 has been considerably simplified and includes new examples of *ex ante-ex post* cost-benefit analyses.

These improvements were made with our three intended audiences in mind. First, we intend this book for use in courses on public-sector decision making offered in graduate programs in public policy analysis, public-sector management, urban planning, public administration, business, economics, public health, and environmental studies. Second, we envision it being used at the undergraduate level either as a primary text for a course on cost-benefit analysis or as a supplementary text for economics courses in public finance, public-sector economics, and policy analysis. Third, we intend it to be useful to policy analysts and public managers as a general introduction and practical guide to cost-benefit analysis, as well as a starting point for exploring advanced topics. In order to be appropriate for these diverse audiences, the fourth edition continues to emphasize clear discussion over formal mathematics, and application over abstract theory. Nevertheless, we think that we cover important, if difficult, conceptual issues in adequate detail both as a framework for thoughtful application and as a basis for further study.

The process of preparing the new edition has been a rewarding one for us. As during preparation of the first three editions, we were forced to think more deeply about some topics that we thought we had already mastered and to develop others with which none of us was very familiar. We did this enjoyably together through numerous exchanges of drafts and during an intensive work session at the University of British Columbia.

FOR INSTRUCTORS

The following supplements are available to adopting instructors. For detailed descriptions, please visit www.pearsonhighered.com/irc/.

Instructor's Resource Center (IRC) Online
(log in at www.pearsonhighered.com/irc/)

Electronic Instructor's Manual

Bibliography

CourseSmart eTextbook

It gets better.   Once you register, you will not have additional forms to fill out, or multiple user names and passwords to remember to access new titles or editions. As a registered faculty member, you can log in directly to download resource files and receive immediate access and instructions for installing course management content to your campus server.

Need help?   Our dedicated support team is ready to assist instructors with questions about the media supplements that accompany this text. Visit http://247pearsoned.custhelp.com for answers to frequently asked questions and toll-free user support phone numbers.

ACKNOWLEDGMENTS

Our project was also made more productive and enjoyable by our many colleagues and students who gave us advice, comments, encouragement, or information. We thank here just a few people who were particularly helpful: Marcus Berliant, Edward Bird, James Brander, Eric Hanushek, Robert Havemen, Stanley Engerman, Doug Landin, Walter Oi, William G. Waters II, and Michael Wolkoff. We thank Roy I. Gobin, George T. Fuller, Ruth Shen, and Larry Karp, who wrote thoughtful reviews of the first edition for the publisher; Ian Davis, John DeWald, Tim Gindling, and Laurie T. Johnson, who offered valuable comments during preparation of the second edition; Terri Sexton and Nachum Sicherman, who offered valuable comments during preparation of the third edition; and Thomas Hopkins and M. Leslie Shiell, who offered valuable comments during preparation of the fourth edition. Haynes Goddard kindly provided helpful suggestions for both the second and third editions. We especially thank Mark Moore, whose joint work with us helped us substantially improve our discussion of the social discount rate, Diane Forbes, who helped with the chapter on shadow prices from secondary sources, and Roger Noll, who made extremely valuable suggestions that prompted many other substantial revisions. Of course, they are not responsible for any errors that remain.

FEEDBACK

The authors and product team would appreciate hearing from you! Let us know what you think about this textbook by writing to economics@pearson.com. Please include "Feedback about Boardman 4e" in the subject line.

   If you have questions related to this product, please contact our customer service department online at http://247pearsoned.custhelp.com.

CHAPTER 1

Introduction to Cost-Benefit Analysis

In the Affair of so much Importance to you, wherein you ask my Advice, I cannot for want of sufficient Premises, advise you what to determine, but if you please I will tell you how. When those difficult Cases occur, they are difficult, chiefly because while we have them under Consideration, all the Reasons pro and con are not present to the Mind at the same time; but sometimes one Set present themselves, and at other times another, the first being out of Sight. Hence the various Purposes or Inclinations that alternately prevail, and the Uncertainty that perplexes us.

To get over this, my Way is, to divide half a Sheet of Paper by a Line into two Columns; writing over the one Pro, and over the other Con. Then during three or four Days Consideration, I put down under the different Heads short Hints of the different Motives, that at different Times occur to me, for or against the Measure. When I have thus got them all together in one View, I endeavor to estimate their respective Weights; and where I find two, one on each side, that seem equal, I strike them both out. If I find a Reason pro equal to some two Reasons con, I strike out the three. If I judge some two Reasons con, equal to some three Reasons pro, I strike out the five; and thus proceeding I find at length where the Balance lies; and if after a Day or two of farther consideration, nothing new that is of Importance occurs on either side, I come to a Determination accordingly. And, tho' the Weight of Reasons cannot be taken with the Precision of Algebraic Quantities, yet, when each is thus considered, separately and comparatively, and the whole lies before me, I think I can judge better, and am less liable to make a rash Step; and in fact I have found great Advantage from this kind of Equation, in what may be called Moral or Prudential Algebra.

—B. FRANKLIN, LONDON, SEPTEMBER 19, 1772[1]

INDIVIDUAL VERSUS SOCIAL COSTS AND BENEFITS

Benjamin Franklin's advice about how to make a decision illustrates many of the important features of cost-benefit analysis (CBA). These include a systematic cataloguing of impacts as benefits (pros) and costs (cons), valuing in dollars (assigning weights), and then determining the *net benefits* of the proposal relative to the status quo (net benefits equal benefits minus costs).

When we as individuals talk of costs and benefits, we naturally tend to consider only our *own* costs and benefits, generally choosing among alternative courses of action according to whichever has the largest individual net benefits. Similarly, in evaluating various investment alternatives, a firm tends to consider only those costs (expenditures) and benefits (revenues) that accrue to it. In CBA we try to consider *all of the costs and benefits to society as a whole,* that is, the *social costs* and the *social benefits.* For this reason, some experts refer to CBA as *social* cost-benefit analysis.

CBA is a policy assessment method that quantifies in monetary terms the value of all consequences of a policy to all members of society. Throughout this book we use the terms *policy* and *project* interchangeably. More generally, CBA applies to policies, programs, projects, regulations, demonstrations, and other government interventions. The aggregate value of a policy is measured by its net social benefits, sometimes simply referred to as the net benefits. The *net social benefits, NSB,* equal the social benefits, *B,* minus the social costs, *C:*

$$NSB = B - C \tag{1.1}$$

Stated at this level of abstraction, it is unlikely that many people would disagree with doing CBA. In practice, however, there are two types of disagreements. First, social critics, including some political economists, philosophers, libertarians, and socialists, have disputed the fundamental utilitarian assumptions of CBA that the sum of individual utilities should be maximized and that it is possible to trade off utility gains for some against utility losses for others. These critics are not prepared to make trade-offs between one person's benefits and another person's costs. Second, participants in the public policy-making process (analysts, bureaucrats, and politicians) may disagree about such practical issues as what impacts will actually occur over time, how to monetize (attach a dollar value to them), and how to make trade-offs between the present and the future.

In this chapter we provide a nontechnical but reasonably comprehensive overview of CBA. Although we introduce a number of key concepts, we do so informally, returning to discuss them thoroughly in subsequent chapters. Therefore, this chapter is best read without great concern about definitions and technical details.

TYPES OF CBA ANALYSES AND THEIR PURPOSES

The broad purpose of CBA is to help social decision making and to make it more rational. More specifically, the objective is to have more efficient allocation of society's resources. As we show in Chapter 3, where markets work well, individual self-interest leads to an efficient allocation of resources. Consequently, government analysts and politicians bear the burden of providing a rationale for any governmental interference with private choice. Economists lump these rationales under the general heading of *market failures.* Where markets fail, there is a *prima facie* rationale for government intervention. However, and this is important to emphasize, it is no more than that. One must be able to demonstrate the superior efficiency of a particular intervention relative to the alternatives, including the status quo. For this purpose, analysts use CBA.

There are two major types of cost-benefit analysis. *Ex ante* CBA, which is just standard CBA as the term is commonly used, is conducted while a project or policy is under consideration, before it is started or implemented. *Ex ante* CBA assists in the decision about whether resources should be allocated by government to a specific project or policy or not. Thus, its contribution to public policy decision making is direct, immediate, and bureau-specific. *Ex post* CBA is conducted at the end of a project. At this time, all of the costs are "sunk" in the sense that they have already been used up to do the project. The value of *ex post* analyses is broader but less immediate as they provide information not only about the particular intervention but also about the "class" of such interventions. In other words, they contribute to "learning" by government managers, politicians, and academics about whether particular classes of projects are worthwhile.

Some CBA studies are performed during the course of the life of a project, that is, *in medias res.* Like *ex ante* analyses, *in medias res* analyses have the potential of directly influencing a decision—whether or not to continue the project. They also provide information that can be used to predict costs and benefits in future *ex ante* analyses.

There is also a fourth type of CBA—one that compares an *ex ante* CBA with an *ex post* (or *in medias res*) CBA *of the same project.* This comparative type of CBA is most useful to policy makers for learning about the efficacy of CBA as a decision-making and evaluative tool. Unfortunately, there are only a few disinterested published examples of this type of CBA. The scarceness of this type of CBA is not as surprising as it may appear because there is relatively little demand for *ex post* or *in medias res* CBAs and, even if one of these studies is done, there may not be an *ex ante* CBA to compare it to.

It is useful to elaborate on the uses of these four types of CBAs. Table 1-1 summarizes the important ways that these four types of cost-benefit analyses aid government decision making.

Project-Specific Decision Making

Ex ante analysis is most useful for deciding whether resources should be allocated to a particular project or program that is under consideration. An *in medias res* analysis of an ongoing project can also be used for decision-making purposes where it is potentially feasible to shift resources to alternative uses. Although such an analysis may lead to discontinuation of service-orientated programs (e.g., government-funded training programs), it will rarely lead to termination of a physical investment project nearing completion, such as a dam or bridge, because a large share of the costs will likely have been incurred, and benefits subsequent to the analysis will usually exceed the remaining costs. However, it can happen. For example, a Canadian Environmental Assessment Panel recommended the decommissioning of a just-completed dam on the basis of an *in medias res* analysis which showed that, with use, future environmental costs would exceed future benefits.[2] Because *ex post* analysis is conducted at the end of the project,

TABLE 1-1   Value of Different Classes of CBA

| Value | Class of Analysis | | | |
	Ex Ante	*In Medias Res*	*Ex Post*	*Ex Ante/Ex Post or Ex Ante/ In Medias Res Comparison*
Resource allocation decision for this project.	Yes—helps to select best project or make "go" versus "no-go" decisions, if accurate.	If low sunk costs, can still shift resources. If high sunk costs, usually recommends continuation.	Too late—the project is over.	Same as *in medias res* or *ex post* analysis.
Learning about actual value of specific project.	Poor estimate— high uncertainty about future benefits and costs.	Better—reduced uncertainty.	Excellent— although some errors may remain. May have to wait long for study.	Same as *in medias res* or *ex post* analysis.
Contributing to learning about actual value of similar projects.	Unlikely to add much.	Good—contribution increases as performed later. Need to adjust for uniqueness.	Very useful— although may be some errors and need to adjust for uniqueness. May have to wait long for project completion.	Same as *in medias res* or *ex post* analysis.
Learning about omission, forecasting, measurement and evaluation errors in CBA.	No	No	No	Yes, provides information about these errors and about the accuracy of CBA for similar projects.

Source: Anthony E. Boardman, Wendy L. Mallery, and Aidan R. Vining, "Learning from *Ex Ante/Ex Post* Cost-Benefit Comparisons: The Coquihalla Highway Example," *Socio-Economic Planning Sciences,* 28(2), 1994, 69–84, Table 1, p. 71. Reprinted with kind permission from Elsevier Science Ltd., The Boulevard, Langford Lane, Kidlington OX5 1GB, UK.

it is obviously too late to reverse resource allocation decisions with respect to that particular project.

Learning about the Net Social Benefits of a Specific Project

In the early stages of a project there is considerable uncertainty about its actual impacts and, consequently, about the true net social benefits. As time goes by, more is known about the impacts, and CBA studies conducted later can estimate the net benefits of the project more accurately. In general, *ex post* studies are more accurate than *in medias res* studies, which in turn are more accurate than *ex ante* studies.

Learning about the Potential Benefits of Similar Projects

Ex post analyses provide information not only about a particular policy intervention but, more importantly, about future similar interventions as well. *Ex post* analyses (and *in medias res* analyses) potentially contribute to learning by political and bureaucratic decision makers, as well as policy researchers, about whether particular kinds of projects are worthwhile. This potential depends crucially on the extent to which the particular project being assessed is being replicated or can serve as a generic model for other projects.[3] CBAs of experiments involving the efficacy of new surgical procedures or new pharmaceutical products usually can be generalized to larger populations. Lessons from other experiments, however, may not be as easily generalized. For example, if the proposed intervention is several orders of magnitude bigger than the experiment, there may be unknown nonlinear scale effects. Also, if the proposed program has a more extended time frame than the experiment, behavioral factors may affect costs or benefits unpredictably.

Learning about the Efficacy of CBA

Comparison of an *ex ante* study with either an *in medias res* or an *ex post* analysis is most useful for learning about the value of CBA itself. Most importantly, a comparison CBA provides information about the accuracy of the earlier *ex ante* CBA which, in turn, provides guidance about the accuracy of future *ex ante* analyses. One study has assessed the accuracy of U.S. regulatory cost estimates (although not of benefits) and found that total costs tend to be overestimated.[4] Information about the predictive ability of CBA is useful for decision-making purposes. Also, comparison studies help analysts understand the reasons for any divergence between predicted and actual benefits or costs. In Chapter 11, we discuss prediction (and valuation) in detail and review some important potential types of errors. Understanding the reasons for these errors helps to reduce them in the future.

THE BASIC STEPS OF CBA: COQUIHALLA HIGHWAY EXAMPLE

CBA may look intimidating and complex. To help make the process of conducting a CBA more manageable, we break it down into nine basic steps, which are listed in Table 1-2. We describe and illustrate these steps using a relatively straightforward example—the construction of a new highway. For each step, we also point out some practical difficulties. The conceptual and practical issues that we broach are the focus of the rest of this book. Do not worry if the concepts are unfamiliar to you; this is a dry run. Subsequent chapters fully explain them.

Imagine that in 1986 a cost-benefit analyst, who works for the Province of British Columbia, Canada, is asked to perform a CBA of a proposed highway between the town of Hope in the south-central part of the Province and Merritt, which is more or less due north of Hope. This highway would be called the Coquihalla Highway. The

TABLE 1-2   The Major Steps in CBA

1. Specify the set of alternative projects.
2. Decide whose benefits and costs count (standing).
3. Identify the impact categories, catalogue them, and select measurement indicators.
4. Predict the impacts quantitatively over the life of the project.
5. Monetize (attach dollar values to) all impacts.
6. Discount benefits and costs to obtain present values.
7. Compute the net present value of each alternative.
8. Perform sensitivity analysis.
9. Make a recommendation.

analyst's CBA is presented in Table 1-3.[5] How did the analyst get these results? What were the difficulties? We will go through each of the nine steps.

1. Specify the set of alternative projects.   Step 1 requires the analyst to specify the set of alternative projects. In this example, the provincial government required the analyst to consider only two alternative four-lane highways, one with tolls and one without. The provincial department of transportation decided that the toll, if applied, would be $40 for large trucks and $8 for cars. Thus, the analyst has a tractable set of alternatives to analyze.

TABLE 1-3   Coquihalla Highway CBA (1986 $ Million)

	No Tolls		With Tolls	
	A *Global Perspective*	B *Provincial Perspective*	C *Global Perspective*	D *Provincial Perspective*
Project Benefits:				
Time and Operating Cost Savings	389.8	292.3	290.4	217.8
Horizon Value of Highway	53.3	53.3	53.3	53.3
Safety Benefits (Lives)	36.0	27.0	25.2	18.9
Alternative Routes Benefits	14.6	10.9	9.4	7.1
Toll Revenues	—	—	—	37.4
New Users	0.8	0.6	0.3	0.2
Total Benefits	494.5	384.1	378.6	334.7
Project Costs:				
Construction	338.1	338.1	338.1	338.1
Maintenance	7.6	7.6	7.6	7.6
Toll Collection	—	—	8.4	8.4
Toll Booth Construction	—	—	0.3	0.3
Total Costs	345.7	345.7	354.4	354.4
Net Social Benefits	148.8	38.4	24.2	−19.7

Source: Adapted from Anthony Boardman, Aidan Vining, and W. G. Waters II, "Costs and Benefits through Bureaucratic Lenses: Example of a Highway Project," *Journal of Policy Analysis and Management,* 12(3) 1993, 532–555, Table 1, p. 537.

In practice, however, there are often difficulties even at this stage. For many projects, including this one, the number of potential alternatives is huge. This highway could vary on many dimensions including the following:

Road surface: It could be surfaced in bitumen or concrete.

Routing: It could take different routes.

Size: It could have two, three, four, or six lanes.

Tolls: The tolls could be higher or lower.

Wild animal friendliness: The highway could be built with or without "elk tunnels."

Timing: It could be delayed until a later date.

Changing the highway on just a few these dimensions would greatly increase the number of alternatives. For example, with four dimensions, each with three possible values, there would be 81 alternatives! Neither decision makers nor analysts can cognitively handle comparisons among such a large number of alternatives. Resource and cognitive constraints mean that analysts typically analyze only a few (less than six) alternatives.[6]

CBA compares the net social benefits of investing resources in one or more particular potential projects with the net social benefits of a project that would be displaced if the project(s) under evaluation were to proceed. The displaced project is often called the *counterfactual.* Usually, the counterfactual is the *status quo,* which means there is no change in government policy (i.e., in this case, no new highway). In Table 1-3 the analyst computes the benefits, costs, and net social benefits if the highway were built (with or without tolls) relative to the benefits, costs, and net social benefits if the highway is not built (the status quo). Thus, one can interpret these benefits, costs, and net benefits as *incremental* amounts.

Sometimes the status quo is not a viable alternative. *If a project would displace a specific alternative, then it should be evaluated relative to the specific displaced alternative.* Thus, if government has committed resources to either a highway project or a rail project, and there is no possibility of maintaining the status quo, then the highway project should be compared with the rail project, not the status quo.

This CBA example pertains to a specific proposed highway. There is no attempt to compare this highway project to alternative highway projects in British Columbia, although one could do so. Rarely does the analyst compare a highway project to completely different types of projects, such as health care, antipoverty, or national defense projects. As a practical matter, full optimization is impossible. The limited nature of the comparisons sometimes frustrates politicians and decision makers who imagine that CBA is a *deus ex machina* that will rank *all* policy alternatives. On the other hand, the weight of CBA evidence can and does help in making broad social choices across policy areas.

2. Decide whose benefits and costs count (standing). Next, the analyst must decide who has *standing*; that is, whose benefits and costs should be included. In this example, the analyst's superiors in the provincial government wanted the CBA to be done from the provincial perspective, but asked the analyst to also take a global perspective. The provincial perspective measures only the benefits and costs that affect British Columbian residents, including costs and benefits borne by the British Columbian government. The global perspective includes the benefits and costs that affect everyone, irrespective of where they reside. Thus, it includes benefits and costs to Americans, Albertans, and even tourists from the United Kingdom. Combining these two perspectives on standing with the no-tolls and with-tolls alternatives gives the four columns in Table 1-3 labeled A through D.

The issue of standing is sometimes contentious. While federal governments usually take only national costs and benefits into account, critics argue that many issues should be analyzed from a global perspective. Environmental issues that fall into this category include ozone depletion, global climate change, and acid rain. At the other extreme, local governments typically want to consider only benefits and costs to local residents and to ignore costs and benefits that occur in adjacent municipalities or are borne by higher levels of government. Our highway example deals with this issue by analyzing costs and benefits from both the global and the British Columbian perspectives.

3. Identify the impact categories, catalogue them, and select measurement indicators. Step 3 requires the analyst to identify the physical impact categories of the proposed alternatives, catalogue them as benefits or costs, and specify the measurement indicator of each impact category. We use the term *impacts* broadly to include both inputs (required resources) and outputs. For this proposed highway, the anticipated benefit impact categories are time saved and reduced vehicle operating costs for travelers on the new highway ("Time and Operating Cost Savings" in Table 1-3); the value of the highway at the end of the discounting period of 20 years ("Horizon Value of Highway"); accidents avoided (including lives saved) due to drivers switching to a shorter, safer new highway ("Safety Benefits"); reduced congestion on alternative routes—the old road ("Alternative Routes Benefits"); revenues collected from tolls ("Toll Revenues"); and benefits accruing to new travelers ("New Users"). The cost impact categories are construction costs ("Construction"), additional maintenance and snow removal ("Maintenance"), toll collection ("Toll Collection"), and toll booth construction and maintenance ("Toll Booth Construction").

Although this list of impact categories appears comprehensive, current critics might argue that some relevant impacts were omitted. At the time of the analysis, health impacts from automobile emissions, impacts on the elk population and other wildlife, and changes in scenic beauty were not considered. Also, the cost of the land was excluded.

From a CBA perspective, analysts are interested only in project impacts that affect the utility of individuals with standing. Impacts that do not have any value to human beings are not counted. (The caveat is that this applies only where human beings have the relevant knowledge and information to make rational valuations.) Politicians often state the purported impacts of projects in very general terms. For example, they might say that a project will promote "community capacity building." Similarly, politicians have a strong tendency to regard "growth" and "regional development" as beneficial impacts. CBA requires analysts to identify explicitly the ways in which the project would make some individuals better off through, for example, improved skills, better education, or higher incomes. Of course, analysts should also include the negative environmental and congestion impacts of growth.

Put another way, in order to treat something as an impact, we have to know there is a cause-and-effect relationship between some physical outcome of the project and the utility of human beings with standing. For some impacts, this relationship is so obvious that we do not think about it explicitly. For example, we do not question the existence of a causal relationship between motor vehicle usage and motor vehicle accidents. For other impacts, however, the causal relationships may not be so obvious. What, if any, is the impact of exhaust fumes from additional vehicle usage on residents' morbidity and mortality? How is this offset by fewer airplane flights? Demonstrating such cause-and-effect relationships often requires an extensive review of scientific and social science research. Sometimes the evidence may be ambiguous. For example, controversy surrounds the effect of chlorinated organic compounds in bleached pulp mill effluent on wildlife. Although a Swedish study found such a link, a later Canadian study found none.[7]

Analysts should be on the lookout for impacts that different groups of people view in opposite ways. Consider, for example, flooded land. Residents of a flood plain generally view floods as a cost because they damage homes, while duck hunters regard them as a benefit because they attract ducks. Even though opposing valuations of the same impact could be aggregated in one category, it is usually more useful to have two impact categories—one for damaged homes and another for recreation benefits.

Specification of impact measurement indicators usually occurs at the same time as specification of the impact categories. There are no particular difficulties in specifying measurement indicators of each impact in this illustration. For example, the number of lives saved per year, the number of person-hours of travel time saved, and the dollar value of gasoline saved are reasonably intuitive indicators. If environmental impacts had been included, then the choice of indicator would have not been so straightforward. For example, the analyst might have to decide whether to use tons of various pollutants or the resultant health effects (e.g., changes in mortality or morbidity).

The choice of measurement indicator depends on data availability and ease of monetization. For example, an analyst may wish to measure the number of crimes avoided due to a policy intervention but may not have any way to estimate this impact. However, the analyst may have access to changes in arrest rates or changes in conviction rates and may be able to use one or both of these surrogates to estimate changes in crime.[8] Bear in mind, however, that all surrogate indicators involve some loss of information. For example, the conviction rate might be increasing while there is no change in the actual crime rate.

4. Predict the impacts quantitatively over the life of the project.   The proposed highway project, like almost all projects, has impacts that extend over time. The fourth task is to quantify all impacts in each time period. The analyst must make predictions for the no-tolls and with-tolls alternatives, for each year, and for each category of driver (trucks, passenger cars on business, passenger cars on vacation) about

- the number of vehicle-trips on the new highway,
- the number of vehicle-trips on the old roads, and
- the proportion of travelers from British Columbia.

With these estimates, knowing the highway is 195 kilometers long and with other information, the analyst can estimate

- the total vehicle operating costs that users save,
- the number of accidents avoided, and
- the number of lives saved.

For example, the analyst estimated the new highway would save 6.5 lives each year:

Shorter distance:
130 vkm × 0.027 lives lost per vkm   = 3.5 lives/year

Safer (4-lane versus 2-lane):
313 vkm × 0.027 lives lost per vkm × 0.33 = 3.0 lives/year

Total lives saved[9]   **= 6.5 lives/year**

Lives would be saved for two reasons. First, the new highway will be shorter than existing alternative routes. It is expected that travelers will avoid 130 million vehicle-kilometers (vkm) of driving each year, and evidence suggests that, on average, there are 0.027 deaths per million vehicle-kilometers. The shorter distance is expected, therefore, to save 3.5 lives per year on the basis of less distance driven. The new highway is also predicted to be safer per kilometer driven. It is expected that 313 million vehicle-kilometers will be driven each year on the new highway. Based on previous traffic engineering evidence, the analyst estimated that the new highway would lower the fatal accident rate by one-third. Consequently, the new highway is expected to save 3.0 lives per year due to being safer. Combining the two components suggests 6.5 lives will be saved each year.

In practice, predicting impacts is very important and very difficult! It is so important in CBA that Chapter 11 is devoted to it (and the related issue of valuation). Prediction is especially difficult where projects are unique, have long time horizons, or relationships among variables are complex. Many of the realities associated with doing steps 3 and 4 are brilliantly summarized by Kenneth Boulding's poem on dam building in the Third World, presented in Exhibit 1-1. Many of his points deal with the omission of impact categories due to misunderstanding or ignorance of cause-and-effect relationships and to prediction errors. He also makes points about the distribution of costs and benefits, which we discuss later.

5. Monetize (attach dollar values to) all impacts. The analyst next has to monetize each of the impacts. To *monetize* means to value in dollars. In the highway example, the analyst has to monetize each unit of time saved, lives saved, and accidents avoided. For this, the analyst needs the monetary value of an hour saved by each type of traveler, the value of a statistical life saved, and the value of an avoided accident. Ideally, these estimates should be specific to British Columbia in 1986. Some of the dollar values used in this CBA were

- leisure time saved per vehicle (25 percent of gross wage times the average number of passengers) = $6.68 per vehicle-hour,
- business time saved per vehicle = $12 per vehicle-hour,
- truck drivers' time saved per vehicle = $14 per vehicle-hour, and
- value of a life saved = $500,000 per life.

These estimates were based on studies conducted prior to 1986. Research over the last twenty years suggests the value of a statistical life saved is much higher, as we discuss in Chapter 16.

EXHIBIT 1-1

A BALLAD OF ECOLOGICAL AWARENESS

The cost of building dams is always underestimated,
There's erosion of the delta that the river has created,
There's fertile soil below the dam that's likely to be looted,
And the tangled mat of forest that has got to be uprooted.

There's the breaking up of cultures with old haunts' and habits' loss,
There's the education programme that just doesn't come across,
And the wasted fruits of progress that are seldom much enjoyed
By expelled subsistence farmers who are urban unemployed.

There's disappointing yield of fish, beyond the first explosion;
There's silting up, and drawing down, and watershed erosion.
Above the dam the water's lost by sheer evaporation;
Below, the river scours, and suffers dangerous alteration.

For engineers, however good, are likely to be guilty
Of quietly forgetting that a river can be silty,
While the irrigation people too are frequently forgetting
That water poured upon the land is likely to be wetting.

Then the water in the lake, and what the lake releases,
Is crawling with infected snails and water-borne diseases.
There's a hideous locust breeding ground when water level's low,
And a million ecologic facts we really do not know.

There are benefits, of course, which may be countable, but which
Have a tendency to fall into the pockets of the rich,
While the costs are apt to fall upon the shoulders of the poor.
So cost-benefit analysis is nearly always sure
To justify the building of a solid concrete fact,
While the Ecologic Truth is left behind in the Abstract.

—KENNETH E. BOULDING

Reprinted with the kind permission of Mrs. Boulding.

Sometimes, the most intuitively important impacts are difficult to value in monetary terms. Valuing environmental impacts is especially contentious. In CBA, the value of an output is typically measured in terms of "willingness-to-pay." As we discuss in Chapter 3, where markets exist and work well, willingness to pay can be determined from the appropriate market demand curve. Naturally, problems arise where markets do not exist or do not work well. Obtaining values for such impact categories can be a life's work. Scholars have spent many person-years trying to determine the appropriate value of a statistical life saved. In practice, most CBA analysts do not reinvent these wheels but instead draw upon previous research: they use "plug in" values whenever possible. Although catalogues of impact values are not comprehensive, considerable progress has been made in this regard as we show in Chapter 16.

If no person is willing to pay for some impact, then that impact would have zero value in a CBA. For example, if construction of a dam would lead to the extermination of a species of small fish, but no one with standing is willing to pay a positive amount to save that species, then the extermination of this fish would have a value of zero in a CBA of the dam.

Some government agencies and critics of CBA are unwilling to attach a monetary value to life or to some other impact. This forces them to use an alternative method of analysis, such as *cost-effectiveness analysis* or *multigoal analysis,* which we discuss in Chapters 2 and 18.

6. Discount benefits and costs to obtain present values.   For a project that has impacts that occur over years, we need a way to aggregate the benefits and costs that arise in different years. In CBA, future benefits and costs are *discounted* relative to present benefits and costs in order to obtain their *present values (PV)*. The need to discount arises for two main reasons. First, there is an *opportunity cost* to the resources used in a project. Second, most people prefer to consume now rather than later. Discounting has nothing to do with inflation per se, although inflation must be taken into account.

A cost or benefit that occurs in year t is converted to its present value by dividing it by $(1 + s)^t$, where s is the social discount rate. Suppose a project has a life of n years and let B_t and C_t denote the benefits and costs in year t, respectively. The present value of the benefits, $PV(B)$, and the present value of the costs, $PV(C)$, of the project are, respectively:

$$PV(B) = \sum_{t=0}^{n} \frac{B_t}{(1 + s)^t} \qquad (1.2)$$

$$PV(C) = \sum_{t=0}^{n} \frac{C_t}{(1 + s)^t} \qquad (1.3)$$

In this highway example the analyst used a real (inflation-adjusted) social discount rate of 7.5 percent. As we discuss in Chapter 10, the choice of the appropriate social discount rate is contentious and is, therefore, a good candidate for sensitivity analysis. For government analysts, the discount rate is usually mandated by a government agency with authority (e.g., the Office of Management and Budget, or the General Accountability Office in the U.S., or the Ministry of Finance or the Treasury Board). However, as we argue in Chapter 10, these rates in other countries, especially in North America. In that chapter, we present the case for a range of rates depending on a few parameters. For most projects that do not have impacts beyond 50 years (it is *intragenerational*), we recommend a real social discount rate of 3.5 percent. If the project is *intergenerational,* then we recommend time-declining discount rates.[10]

7. Compute the net present value of each alternative. The *net present value (NPV)* of an alternative equals the difference between the *PV* of the benefits and the *PV* of the costs:

$$NPV = PV(B) - PV(C) \tag{1.4}$$

The basic decision rule for a single alternative project (relative to the status quo) is simple: *adopt the project if its NPV is positive.* In short, the analyst should recommend proceeding with the proposed project if its $NPV = PV(B) - PV(C) > 0$; that is, if its benefits exceed its costs:

$$PV(B) > PV(C)$$

When there is more than one alternative to the status quo and all the alternatives are mutually exclusive, then the rule is slightly more complicated: *select the project with the largest NPV.* This rule assumes implicitly that at least one *NPV* is positive. If no *NPV* is positive, then none of the specified alternatives are superior to the status quo, which should remain in place.

Earlier we emphasized the net social benefits of a project. We show in Chapter 6 that the *NPV* of a project or policy is identical to the present value of the net social benefits:

$$NPV = PV(NSB) \tag{1.5}$$

Thus, selecting the project with the largest *NPV* is equivalent to selecting the project with the largest *PV* of the net social benefits.

In the highway example, the no-tolls alternatives (columns A and B) have higher *NPV*s than the with-tolls alternatives (columns C and D). Thus, if the analyst were confident in these *NPV*s, she should recommend that the highway should be constructed without tolls. However, it is important to remember that these *NPV*s are estimates and that sensitivity analysis (step 8) should be conducted before making a final recommendation.

Before turning to sensitivity analysis, we discuss decision making in a bit more detail. In fact, there is some confusion about the appropriate decision rule. Both the *internal rate of return,* which is discussed in Chapter 6, and the *benefit-cost ratio,* which is discussed in Chapter 2, have also been proposed as decision rules. This is one area with more heat than light. The *appropriate criterion to use is the NPV rule.* Other rules sometimes give incorrect answers; the *NPV* rule does not.

An obvious caveat about the *NPV* criterion is that it applies only to the actual alternatives specified. Other alternatives might conceivably be better. While the *NPV* criterion results in a *more efficient* allocation of resources, it does not necessarily recommend *the most efficient* allocation of resources. This point is illustrated in Figure 1-1. Consider a set of proposed projects that vary according to the amount of output (Q), which in turn depends on the scale of the project. The benefits and costs associated with alternative scales are represented by the functions $B(Q)$ and $C(Q)$, respectively. The benefits increase as the scale increases, but at a decreasing rate. In contrast, costs increase at an increasing rate. A small-scale project (for example, Q_1) has positive net benefits relative to the status quo, Q_0. As the scale increases, the net benefits increase

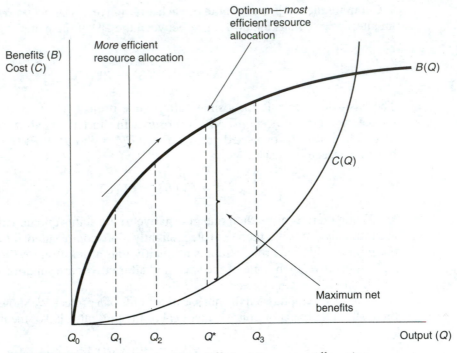

FIGURE 1-1   CBA Seeks More Efficient Resource Allocation

up to the optimal scale, $Q*$.[11] As the scale increases beyond $Q*$, the net benefits decrease. Net benefits are positive as long as the benefit curve is above the cost curve, they are zero where the cost curve and benefit curve intersect, and they are negative for larger-scale projects.

Suppose that the analyst evaluates only two alternative projects (those with output levels, Q_1 and Q_2). Clearly, output level Q_2 is preferred to output level Q_1, which, in turn, is preferred to the status quo, Q_0. The analyst would therefore recommend Q_2. However, as the figure shows, net social benefits are maximized at output level $Q*$. This optimal output level was not recommended because it was not among the set evaluated. As this example illustrates, *use of the NPV criterion leads to a more efficient outcome than the status quo, not necessarily the most efficient outcome.*

The analyst may not have included the optimum output level in the set of alternatives for a number of reasons. The optimum output level may not have been known, even approximately, until after the analysis was performed. Cognitive capacity limitations, often summarized as *bounded rationality* problems, may have hindered the analyst from considering the optimal alternative.[12] Additionally, budgetary or political constraints may have limited the range of alternatives considered.

8. Perform sensitivity analysis. As the foregoing discussion emphasizes, there may be considerable uncertainty about both the predicted impacts and the appropriate monetary valuation of each unit of the impact. For example, the analyst may be uncertain about the predicted number of lives saved and about the appropriate dollar value to place on a statistical life saved. The analyst may also be uncertain about the appropriate social discount rate and about the appropriate level of standing. Sensitivity analysis, which we discuss in Chapter 7, attempts to deal with such uncertainties. As shown in Table 1-3, the analyst performed sensitivity analysis on the standing issue by computing the *NPV*s from both the global perspective and the provincial perspective.

There are practical limits to the amount of sensitivity analysis that is feasible. Potentially, every assumption in a CBA can be varied. In practice, one has to use judgment and focus on the most important assumptions. Although this can mean that CBA is vulnerable to the biases of the analyst, carefully thought-out scenarios are usually more informative than a mindless varying of assumptions.

9. Make a recommendation. Generally, the analyst should recommend adoption of the project with the largest *NPV*. In the highway example, three of the alternative projects had positive *NPV*s and one had a negative *NPV*. The latter indicates that from the British Columbian perspective it would be more efficient to maintain the status quo and not build the Coquihalla highway than to build it and charge tolls. As discussed earlier, the no-tolls alternatives are superior to the with-tolls alternatives. This result gives a flavor of the possibly counterintuitive recommendations that CBA can support. In this case, tolls lower the *NPV* because they deter people from using the highway, and so fewer people enjoy the benefits.[13]

As we have emphasized, however, the *NPV*s are estimated values. Sensitivity analysis, which we have not shown in detail, might suggest that the alternative with the largest expected *NPV* is not necessarily the best alternative in all circumstances.

Finally, it is important to note that analysts make recommendations, not decisions. CBA concerns how resources *should* be allocated; it is *normative*. It does not claim to be a *positive* (i.e., descriptive) theory of how resource allocation decisions are actually made. Such decisions are made in political and bureaucratic arenas. CBA is only one input to this political decision-making process—one that attempts to push it toward more efficient resource allocation. CBA does not always succeed. Politicians are often reluctant to be persuaded by economic arguments. Indeed, the highway was built with tolls, although they were removed in 2008.

BUREAUCRATIC AND POLITICAL "LENSES"[14]

Thus far, we have assumed that CBA is not influenced by bureaucratic or political processes. This approach is appropriate given that CBA concerns how resources should be allocated. In practice, however, CBA frequently gets distorted when bureaucrats or politicians become involved with it. Bureaucrats have a tendency to *see* "costs" and "benefits" differently depending on their position and their agency. Bureaucrats' roles have a strong influence on what they think CBA is, or should be, about. Specifically, their perceptions of what constitutes "benefits" and "costs" are based on whether they are *analysts, spenders,* or *guardians.*[15] These labels are indicative of three different perspectives (lenses) bureaucrats bring to project evaluation in government. The analysts' perspective is standard CBA, which we have already illustrated in Table 1-3. Guardians and spenders have quite different perspectives.

Most government bureaucrats have not taken, and will not take, formal courses in cost-benefit analysis. They believe that what they think is CBA is, in fact, CBA, even if it is not. This section describes the perspectives of guardians and spenders, and shows how these perspectives differ from CBA. This helps clarify what CBA actually is, in contrast to what one may think it is. This section also identifies many of the common mistakes in CBA. These mistakes often vary systematically according to one's background and experiences. Even those trained in CBA may modify their orientation toward those of guardians or spenders as a consequence of the immediacy of their daily bureaucratic roles. If you are in a government job, you should make sure that you are not unconsciously adopting a guardian or spender perspective. We also hope that by understanding these different perspectives, analysts may be better able to communicate with guardians and spenders. Also, guardians and spenders may be better able to communicate with each other. Finally, this section helps students understand better why decisions are often not consistent with CBA—they are often made by guardians or spenders, not analysts.

These bureaucratic lenses are archetypes. In practice, a bureaucrat may not exhibit all of the characteristics associated with a particular lens. From time to time, bureaucrats exhibit schizophrenic tendencies, sometimes adopting one cognitive perspective, sometimes another. Guardians in line agencies are prone to cognitive dissonance because they have dual allegiances. They are likely to be unsure whether they are guardians, spenders, or both. In practice, though, most bureaucrats recognize that they have a tendency to adopt one perspective or another.

Guardians

Guardians are often found in central budgetary agencies, such as the U.S. Office of Management and Budget, and in controllership or accounting functions within line agencies. They tend to have a bottom-line budgetary orientation. Their natural tendency is to equate benefits with revenue inflows to their agency or other governmental coffers (at the same jurisdictional level) and to equate costs with revenue outflows from their agency or other governmental coffers (at the same level). Thus, they engage in *revenue-expenditure analysis.*[16] Guardians have a natural tendency to regard actual CBA as naive, impractical, and, worst of all in their eyes, a tool whereby spenders can justify whatever it is they want to do.

The conceptual lens of "pure" provincial-based guardians can be illustrated by the way they tend to look at the costs and benefits of the Coquihalla Highway, which is shown in Table 1-4. These evaluations of the no-tolls and with-tolls alternatives can be compared to the analyst's evaluations that appear in columns B and D of Table 1-3, respectively.

To guardians, all toll revenues are regarded as benefits, whether paid by the jurisdiction's residents (in this case, the province) or by nonresidents. Construction costs are a cost, because they require an outlay by the provincial government.

TABLE 1-4 Coquihalla Highway from a Provincial Guardian's Perspective (1986 $ Million)

	No Tolls	With Tolls
Revenues ("Benefits"):		
Toll revenues from British Columbia residents	0	112.1
Toll revenues from non–British Columbia residents	0	37.4
	0	149.5
Expenditures ("Costs"):		
Construction	338.1	338.1
Maintenance	7.6	7.6
Toll collection	—	8.4
Toll booth construction	—	0.3
	345.7	354.4
Net Revenue-Expenditure "Benefits"	345.7	204.9

Source: Adapted from Anthony Boardman, Aidan Vining, and W. G. Waters II, "Costs and Benefits through Bureaucratic Lenses: Example of a Highway Project," *Journal of Policy Analysis and Management* 12(3) 1993, 532–555, Table 2, p. 539.

Because guardians seek to minimize net budgetary expenditures, their preference, not surprisingly, is for the with-tolls alternative. Indeed, their gut reaction is to consider raising tolls, irrespective of its effect on levels of use or its impact on social benefits.

How does the guardian's perspective differ from CBA? Most importantly, guardians ignore nonfinancial social benefits, in this case $384.1 million for the no-tolls alternative and $297.3 million for the with-tolls alternative. In general, they ignore impacts valued by consumers and producers such as time saved and lives saved. When guardians are in control of a government service, it is easy to understand why one has to wait so long for the service. Neither your time nor anyone else's figures into their calculations! Similarly, guardians tend to ignore nonfinancial social costs, such as congestion and pollution.

In the Coquihalla Highway example, all social costs happen to represent governmental budgetary costs, and so there is no difference between the CBA cost figures and the guardians' cost figures. In other situations, however, there might be considerable differences between the correct social costs and guardians' costs. Consider, for example, the cost of labor in job-creation programs. Guardians would treat the full financial remuneration to labor as a cost, while CBA analysts would consider only the opportunity cost (such as lost leisure time). Another manifestation of the same mistake concerns the treatment of resources currently owned by the government, such as offices or land. Guardians tend to treat these resources as free because using them for a project does not entail additional budgetary outlay. They ignore the value of these resources in other uses.

Guardians ignore costs not borne by their government. Thus, they ignore the loss suffered by British Columbians from paying tolls and treat all toll revenues as a benefit. In CBA tolls are a transfer from travelers to the government: offsetting costs and benefits result in net benefits of zero. On the other hand, provincial guardians automatically treat subsidies from the federal government as a benefit because they are revenue inflows to their level of government. However, if the federal government has earmarked a certain amount of money to transfer to British Columbia and if funds used for one purpose reduce the amount available for other purposes, then federal funds for this highway should not be treated as a benefit from the provincial perspective.

Finally, guardians generally want to use a high social discount rate. Because of their financial background or their agency's culture, they naturally prefer to use a financial market rate, which is generally higher than the appropriate social discount rate. They also know that using a high discount rate will make it more difficult to justify most projects because costs usually occur before benefits. Thus, they can limit spenders who, in their view, overestimate benefits, underestimate costs, and generally use money less efficiently than the private sector.

Spenders

Spenders are usually in service or line departments. Some service departments, such as transportation, are involved with physical projects, while social service departments, such as health, welfare, or education, make human capital investments. Some service departments, such as housing, make both types of expenditures. The views of spenders are somewhat more varied than those of guardians because the constituencies of particular agencies are more varied. Nevertheless, there are several commonalities.

Most importantly, spenders have a natural tendency to regard expenditures on constituents as benefits rather than as costs. For example, they typically see expenditures on labor as a benefit rather than a cost. Spenders regard themselves as builders or professional deliverers of government-mandated services. As spenders focus on providing projects or services to particular groups in society, we characterize them as engaging in *constituency-support analysis*. Table 1-5 summarizes how spenders in the provincial highway department view the no-tolls and with-tolls alternatives.

TABLE 1-5 Coquihalla Highway from a Provincial Spender's Perspective
(1986 $ Million)

	No Tolls	*With Tolls*
Constituency "Benefits":		
Project Costs (from CBA)	345.7	354.4
Project Benefits (from CBA)	384.1	334.7
	729.8	689.1
Constituency "Costs":		
Toll Revenues from British Columbia Residents	—	112.1
Net Constituency "Benefits"	729.8	577.0

Source: Adapted from Anthony Boardman, Aidan Vining, and W. G. Waters II, "Costs and Benefits through Bureaucratic Lenses: Example of a Highway Project," *Journal of Policy Analysis and Management* 12(3) 1993, 532–555, Table 3, p. 542.

Spenders treat social benefits and monetary payments received by their constituents (residents of British Columbia in this example) as benefits. Thus, time saved, lives saved, and vehicle operating costs saved by British Columbians are benefits. However, they also treat wages received by construction workers who build the highway as a benefit. Thus, spenders think of both project benefits *and* project costs as benefits. With this method of accounting, both the with-tolls and no-tolls highway alternatives generate huge net constituency benefits. In general, spenders tend to support *any* alternative rather than the status quo (no project). Thus, the mistrust of spenders by guardians is perfectly understandable. Guardians and spenders almost always oppose one another in terms of project alternative ranking.

Spenders view monetary outlays by British Columbian highway users (also their constituents) as costs; for example, they treat tolls paid by British Columbians as costs. Table 1-5 shows that spenders favor the no-tolls alternative primarily because a toll is a cost for some of their constituents. Indeed, spenders normally do not favor user fees, unless their agency keeps the toll revenue within its own budget or the payers are not constituents. If spenders could collect and keep the tolls, then they would face a dilemma: tolls would reduce constituency benefits, but would increase the agency's budget. Thus, they would face a trade-off between constituency-support maximization and their budget maximization.[17]

In general, as Robert Haveman and others have pointed out, politicians prefer projects that concentrate benefits on particular interest groups and camouflage costs or diffuse them widely over the population.[18] Spenders have similar preferences. They tend to weight each impact category by the strength of the connection that constituents make between the impact and their agency. They focus on impacts for which their constituents will give them a lot of credit and ignore others. Because people almost always notice expenditures on themselves, such "benefits" are invariably weighted more heavily than social benefits.[19] Thus, for example, construction jobs are more heavily weighted than diffuse social benefits.

Spenders are also similar to politicians in their determination to finish partially completed projects. Congress, for example, decided to complete the Tellico Dam when it was 90 percent complete, even though the incremental costs exceeded the incremental benefits.[20] Presumably, the politicians believed that continuation of the project would bring ongoing political support. Even though sunk costs are, by definition, sunk and it may not be efficient to finish a partially completed project, spenders tend to believe that there are positive constituency-support benefits from completion of projects.

Spenders treat some inputs as neither benefits nor costs. Currently owned government assets may simply be ignored. In support of the Tellico Dam, for example, the Tennessee Valley Authority argued that "since the farm land behind the dam had already been purchased, the value of this land should be considered a sunk cost, even though the land has yet to be flooded and could be resold as farm land if the project was not completed."[21]

Spenders tend to favor large, irreversible, capital-intensive projects, such as urban rail systems, over reversible, less capital intensive projects, such as buses. There are immediate, significant construction job creation benefits. Also, once the infrastructure is in place, it cannot be easily redeployed to other uses, so the system will almost certainly remain in operation, and constituents are guaranteed to receive some benefits. Furthermore, the normally lower operating costs for such projects allow for lower prices and relatively high usage levels, thereby further increasing constituency benefits.

The perspective of spenders concerning market efficiency has a bearing on the way they view many aspects of CBA. To spenders, markets are almost always inefficient. Spenders act as if unemployment is high in all labor markets. They believe that unemployment will be reduced by the number of people used on a government project. Even if some workers switch from other employment, these workers' vacated jobs will be filled by unemployed workers. Thus, even if the job created did not go directly to an unemployed worker, there would eventually be a job created somewhere in the economy for an unemployed worker. Spenders do not recognize that project resources are diverted from other potentially productive uses that might also involve the creation of jobs.

Furthermore, spenders believe there are indirect benefits of creating jobs and making other project expenditures, which are called multiplier effects.[22] In the extreme, spenders have a "Midas touch" view of project evaluation: first declare the expenditures (costs) to be a "benefit" and then increase these benefits by a multiplier. As a result, any government project would be seen as producing benefits greater than costs.

Spenders generally favor using a low (even zero) social discount rate. For some, this is because they are not familiar with the concept of discounting. For others, they know this tends to raise the project's *NPV* and, therefore, the probability of its adoption. Other ways spenders generate support for their projects is to choose a poorly performing counterfactual (a straw man), to lowball cost projections, or to overestimate project usage.[23]

THE DEMAND FOR CBA

CBA was initially used in the U.S. in the 1930s. The Flood Control Act of 1936 required the U.S. Army Corps of Engineers to conduct CBAs for flood control and harbor deepening projects. A big impetus to the use of CBA was given by the Bureau of Budget's Circular A-47 of 1952 and academic work by Otto Eckstein, John Krutilla, and others.[24] In the mid 1960s it was picked up and promoted by Barbara Castle when she was Minister of Transport in the UK. By the end of the 1960s it had spread around the world and was used in both developed and developing countries. Because of its importance in developing countries we devote Chapter 17 to that topic. Now, CBA is used in many different contexts for many different purposes. Many government agencies require CBA of regulatory changes. Other actual or potential uses of CBA include the courts, various progressive interest groups and private corporations.

Government

The U.S. federal government first mandated the general use of CBA in Executive Order 12291, issued by President Reagan in early 1981. This order requires a regulatory impact analysis (RIA) for every major regulatory initiative. (An RIA is essentially a cost-benefit analysis that also takes into account distributional and fairness considerations.) President Clinton confirmed the federal government's commitment to CBA in Executive Order 12866 in 1994. Quite a few U.S. federal laws, such as the Unfunded Mandates Reform Act and the Government Performance and Results Act, specifically mandate some form of *ex ante* analysis.

Nearly all other Western industrialized countries have similar protocols covering broad ranges of programs or specific program areas. For example, Canada's Regulatory Policy requires a CBA of changes to any regulation.

The demand for *ex post* analysis is generally not so explicit; there are usually no mandatory requirements that it be done. However, on occasion, the U.S. Congress does explicitly mandate *ex post* CBA. The Clean Air Act Amendments (1990), for example, require the Environmental Protection Agency to assess the overall benefits and costs of the first 20 years of the Act. The Small Business Regulatory Enforcement Act (1996) also requires retrospective analysis.

Despite the little explicit demand for *ex post* analyses, resource allocation decisions often draw heavily on these analyses. For example, President Clinton's 1993 State of the Union Address emphasized the relationship between *ex post* analyses of specific Head Start programs (i.e., educational programs for low-income preschool children) and his intention to increase funding and expand the scope of such programs. The U.S. federal government has also explicitly induced a form of *ex post* learning by sponsoring and requiring evaluation of a variety of "pilot tests," "demonstration projects," and "social experiments" including, for example, various welfare reform demonstrations that were conducted by different states during the 1980s and 1990s.[25] On a number of occasions the weight of the evidence has led to a policy change.[26] For example, CBAs in the 1960s and 1970s of industry-specific economic regulations showed that the costs of regulation often exceeded the benefits, thereby paving the way for deregulation initiatives in the trucking, airline, and telecommunications industries.[27]

As public officials face citizen resistance to raising taxes or pressure to reduce taxes, they are increasingly forced to ensure that government works more efficiently and effectively. In practice, this provides an impetus toward the increased use of CBA and related methods. Such trends are contemporaneous with greater concern for the environment, which calls for the inclusion of environmental and other social impacts, in addition to government expenditures.

The Courts

Courts of law use CBA or CBA methods in a variety of ways. Perhaps the most notorious has been the use of CBA in the assessment of damages in the Exxon Valdez disaster. Quantitative valuation of the environmental impacts relied heavily on contingent valuation analysis, which we discuss in Chapter 15. The lawsuits continued into 2009, more than 20 years after the disaster itself.

CBA is also used in antitrust cases. Section 9b of the Canadian Competition Act explicitly prohibits the Competition Tribunal from intervening in a merger if the efficiency gains to the merging firms are greater than the potential anticompetitive effect. In effect, this requires determining whether or not the merger is allocatively efficient (i.e., has positive net social benefits).

Environmental and Other Progressive Groups

As mentioned above, the U.S. government and the courts have used CBA extensively to set environmental, health, and safety regulations. However, many environmentalists and other progressive groups prefer to make their arguments on emotional and ethical grounds and are reluctant to conduct CBAs. Recently, Richard Revesz and Michael Livermore argue that such groups will be more effective if they do not "give up on rationality" and perform CBAs. The authors argue that this is necessary if we truly want to protect our natural environment.[28]

CBA, Sustainability, Corporate Social Responsibility, and the Triple Bottom Line

Most private-sector corporations are now paying attention to *sustainability* or their *"triple bottom line"* (i.e., their "social, economic, and environmental" impact), and are being more transparent about such impacts. For a longer time, many companies have been concerned about *corporate social responsibility* (CSR). These terms are not well-defined but overlap considerably. Basically, they mean that firms consider their "social bottom line" and their impact on future generations. In practice, however, firms engage in idiosyncratic behavior and use all sorts of different criteria to measure their "social bottom line." They may measure their carbon footprint, their emissions of carbon and other gasses, or their recycling efforts. Other firms measure different impacts. There are a host of different ways of measuring CSR. However, the basic goal of CSR is to improve the welfare of society as a whole. Since the goal of CBA is to improve net social benefits, this has led some authors to argue that corporations should engage in CBA to measure their CSR.[29] They would likely be for specific projects, rather than on an annual basis, but it would mean the application of a consistent set of principles, instead of the current *ad hoc* approach.

THE COST OF DOING CBA

Although the demand for CBA is increasing, we should keep in mind that it takes many resources (time, skill, and money) to do CBA well, especially where projects are large, complex, and have unique features. The costs of conducting CBA can be very large. For example, Thomas Hopkins reported in 1992 that a CBA of reducing lead in gasoline cost the Environmental Protection Agency (EPA) roughly $1 million.[30] On average, the EPA spent approximately $700,000 for major CBA projects in the 1980s, that is, for the analysis of projects with compliance cost in excess of $100 million annually.[31] Large-scale evaluations of welfare-to-work programs, of which CBA is one component, often ran into millions of dollars.

READERS OF THIS BOOK

This book is primarily for people who want to know how to do CBA. Second, it is for people who want to know how to interpret CBA—in other words, for clients of CBA. Clients can be helped in two ways. In the narrow sense, clients should be well enough informed to judge whether or not a specific CBA has been conducted well. Evidence suggests that U.S. federal agencies, even with extensive budgets, have difficulty performing CBA well. This is certainly also true for other governments with less analytic capacity and smaller budgets. Clients need to be well enough informed to avoid endorsing flawed analysis because there is a growing trend for oversight agencies and external critics to point out and publicize analytic errors.[32]

In the broad sense, clients may have to evaluate CBA studies well enough to have a sense of the weight of evidence in specific policy areas, such as employment training or environmental regulation. In order to do this well, one has to understand the basic principles of CBA.

CONCLUSION

This chapter provides a broad overview of many of the most important issues in CBA. We deal with these issues in detail in subsequent chapters. At this point, do not worry if you can only see CBA "through the glass, darkly." Do not worry if you cannot entirely follow the highway analysis. Our aim was to give you a taste of the practical realities. We think that it is important to provide readers with a sense of these realities before dealing with the technical issues.

CBA is often taught in a way that is completely divorced from political reality. We wish to avoid this mistake. CBA is a normative tool, not a description of how political and bureaucratic decision makers actually make decisions. Because CBA disregards the demands of politicians, spenders, guardians, and interest groups, it is not surprising that there are tremendous pressures to ignore it or, alternatively, to adapt it to the desires of various constituencies or interest groups. In practice, correct CBA is no more than a voice for rational decision making.

EXERCISES FOR CHAPTER 1

1. Imagine that you live in a city that currently does not require bicycle riders to wear helmets. Furthermore, imagine that you enjoy riding your bicycle without wearing a helmet.
   a. From your perspective, what are the major costs and benefits of a proposed city ordinance that would require all bicycle riders to wear helmets?
   b. What are the categories of costs and benefits from society's perspective?
2. The effects of a tariff on imported kumquats can be divided into the following categories: tariff revenues received by the treasury ($8 million), increased use of resources to produce more kumquats domestically ($6 million), the value of reduced consumption by domestic consumers ($13 million), and increased profits received by domestic kumquat growers ($4 million). A CBA from the national perspective would find costs of the tariff equal to $19 million—the sum of the costs of increased domestic production and forgone domestic consumption ($6 million + $13 million). The increased profits received by domestic kumquat growers and the tariff revenues received by the treasury simply reflect higher prices paid by domestic consumers on the kumquats that they continue to consume and, hence, count as neither benefits nor costs. Thus, the net benefits of the tariff are negative (−$19 million). Consequently, the CBA would recommend against adoption of the tariff.
   a. Assuming the Agriculture Department views kumquat growers as its primary constituency, how would it calculate net benefits if it behaves as if it is a spender?
   b. Assuming the Treasury Department behaves as if it is a guardian, how would it calculate net benefits if it believes that domestic growers pay profit taxes at an average rate of 20 percent?

3. (Spreadsheet recommended) Your county is considering building a public swimming pool. Analysts have estimated the present values of the following effects over the expected useful life of the pool:

	PV **(million dollars)**
State grant:	2.2
Construction and maintenance costs:	12.5
Personnel costs:	8.2
Revenue from county residents:	8.6
Revenue from nonresidents:	2.2
Use value benefit to county residents:	16.6
Use value benefit to nonresidents:	3.1
Scrap value:	0.8

The state grant is only available for this purpose. Also, the construction and maintenance will have to be done by an out-of-county firm.

a. Assuming national-level standing, what are the social net benefits of the project?
b. Assuming county-level standing, what are the social net benefits of the project?
c. How would a guardian in the county budget office calculate net benefits?
d. How would a spender in the county recreation department calculate benefits?

NOTES

1. "Letter to Joseph Priestley," in *Benjamin Franklin: Representative Selections, with Introduction, Bibliography and Notes,* Frank Luther Mott and Chester E. Jorgenson (New York: American Book Company, 1936), pp. 348–49.

2. Federal Environmental Assessment Review Office, Oldman River Dam: Report of the Environmental Assessment Panel, Ottawa, Ontario, May 1992.

3. Of course, other criteria may determine whether evaluative research actually gets used. For a review of evaluative research utilization in policy analysis, see David H. Greenberg and Marvin B. Mandell, "Research Utilization in Policymaking: A Tale of Two Series of Social Experiments," *Journal of Policy Analysis and Management* 10(4) 1991, 633–656.

4. Winston Harrington, Richard D. Morgenstern, and Peter Nelson, "On the Accuracy of Regulatory Cost Estimates," *Journal of Policy Analysis and Management* 19(2) 2000, 297–322. See also Henry J. Aaron, "Seeing Through the Fog: Policymaking with Uncertain Forecasts," *Journal of Policy Analysis and Management* 19(2) 2000, 193–206.

5. This example is based on W. G. Waters II and Shane Myers, "Benefit-Cost Analysis of a Toll Highway: British Columbia's Coquihalla," *Journal of Transportation Research Forum* 28(1) 1987, 434–443. This study was not, in fact, conducted at the request of the B.C. government.

6. In practice, individuals can only focus on approximately four to seven alternatives, at best. G. A. Miller, "The Magical Number Seven, Plus or Minus Two: Some Limits on Our Capacity for Processing Information," *Psychological Review* 65(1) 1956, 81–97.

7. These studies are discussed by Robert Williamson, "Pulp Cleanup May Be Waste of Money," *Toronto Globe and Mail,* December 23, 1992, pp. A1, A6.

8. Remember that valuation of the impact at step 5 should be consistent with the chosen measurement indicator. For example, the valuation of an arrest should be lower than the valuation of a conviction so that the analyst would obtain similar estimates of the benefits of reduced crime from using either indicator.

9. Of course, some additional deaths will occur as a result of more people traveling by road. This

additional cost is netted out against the generated traffic benefits.

10. These values are based on those laid out in Mark A. Moore, Anthony E. Boardman, Aidan R. Vining, David L. Weimer, and David H. Greenberg, "Just Give Me a Number! Practical Values for the Social Discount Rate," *Journal of Policy Analysis and Management* 23(4) 2004, 789–812.

11. Note that at the optimum output level, marginal benefits equal marginal costs: $\dfrac{dB}{dQ} = \dfrac{dC}{dQ}$. One can see that the slope of the benefit curve at Q^* equals the slope of the cost curve at Q^*.

12. For the seminal writing on this topic, see Herbert A. Simon, *Models of Man* (New York: Wiley, 1957). Although this problem is unlikely to be of major importance in situations similar to that depicted in Figure 1-1, cognitive factors become an increasingly important issue when (1) project benefits and costs vary simultaneously on many dimensions, (2) the benefit and cost functions are discontinuous or complex (for example, with interaction terms), or (3) there is uncertainty about the interactions or the functional forms.

13. In contrast, as we discuss in Chapter 5, tolls on *congested* highways generally increase net social benefits.

14. This section draws heavily from Anthony Boardman, Aidan Vining, and W. G. Waters II, "Costs and Benefits through Bureaucratic Lenses: Example of a Highway Project," *Journal of Policy Analysis and Management* 12(3) 1993, 532–555.

15. This terminology was introduced by Sanford Borins and David A. Good, "Spenders, Guardians and Policy Analysts: A Game of Budgeting Under the Policy and Expenditure Management System," Toronto, Case Program in Canadian Administration, Institute of Public Administration of Canada, 1987 (revised 1989).

16. Revenue-expenditure analysis is similar to *cash flow analysis* and *budget impact analysis*. Cash flow analysis and budget impact analysis are very helpful for certain purposes, but a problem arises when an analyst does this type of analysis while thinking that she is performing CBA.

17. See, for example, William A. Niskanen, "Bureaucrats and Politicians," *Journal of Law and Economics* 18(3) 1975, 617–643; and André Blais and Stéphane Dion, eds., *The Budget-Maximizing Bureaucrat: Appraisals and Evidence* (Pittsburgh, PA: University of Pittsburgh Press, 1991). For various reasons, senior spenders may be more interested in the discretionary budget or "budget shaping" than in budget maximizing; see Patrick Dunleavy, *Democracy, Bureaucracy and Public Choice* (Englewood Cliffs, NJ: Prentice Hall, 1992). They may, therefore, be willing to support projects that involve considerable "contracting out" and other activities that may not be budget maximizing per se.

18. Robert H. Haveman, "Policy Analysis and the Congress: An Economist's View," *Policy Analysis* 2(2) 1976, 235–250.

19. Barry R. Weingast, et al. refer to this phenomenon as the "Robert Moses effect" after the famous New Yorker who exploited it so effectively. See Barry R. Weingast, Kenneth A. Shepsle, and Christopher Johnsen, "The Political Economy of Benefits and Costs: A Neoclassical Approach to Distributive Politics," *Journal of Political Economy* 89(4) 1981, 642–664, at 648.

20. R. K. Davis, "Lessons in Politics and Economics from the Snail Darter," in *Environmental Resources and Applied Welfare Economics: Essays in Honor of John V. Krutilla,* Vernon K. Smith, ed. (Washington, D.C.: Resources for the Future, 1988), 211–236.

21. Robert D. Behn, "Policy Analysis and Policy Politics," *Policy Analysis* 7(2) 1981, 199–226, at 213, n. 27.

22. One reason why some bureaucrats attach so much importance to multipliers is because they have a basic grounding in input-output analysis, but they do not clearly understand the fundamental distinction between impact analysis and evaluation analysis; see W. G. Waters II, "Impact Studies and the Evaluation of Public Projects," *Annals of Regional Science* 10(1) 1976, 98–103.

23. See, for example, Bent Flyvbjerg Mette Skamris Holm, and Soren Buhl, "Underestimating Costs in Public Works Projects: Error or Lie?" *Journal of the American Planning Association* 68(3) 2002, 279–293; and Linda R. Cohen and Roger G. Noll, eds., *The Technology Pork Barrel* (Washington, D.C.: The Brookings Institution, 1991).

24. For a very brief discussion of the origins of CBA see D. W. Pearce, *Cost-Benefit Analysis* (London: MacMillan, 1971).

25. For summaries of the welfare-to-work evaluations, see Daniel Friedlander, David H. Greenberg, and Philip K. Robins, "Evaluating Government Training Programs for the Economically Disadvantaged," *Journal of Economic Literature* 35(4) 1997, 1089–1855; and Karl Ashworth, Andreas Cebulla, David Greenberg, and Robert Walker, "Meta-Evaluation: Discovering What Works Best in Welfare Provision," *Evaluation* 10(2) 2004, 193–216.

26. See Martha Derthick and Paul J. Quirk, *The Politics of Deregulation* (Washington, D.C.: The Brookings Institution, 1985); and Carol H. Weiss, "Evaluation for Decisions: Is Anybody There? Does Anybody Care?" *Evaluation Practice* 9(1) 1988, 5–20.

27. See Robert Hahn and John A. Hird, "The Costs and Benefits of Regulation: Review and Synthesis," *Yale Journal of Regulation* 8(1) 1991, 233–278.

28. Richard Revesz and Michael Livermore, *Retaking Rationality: How Cost Benefit Analysis Can Better Protect the Environment and Our Health* (New York: Oxford University Press, 2008).

29. Anthony E. Boardman, "Using Social Cost-Benefit Analysis to Measure Corporate Social Responsibility," *Infogas* 5(15) 2009, 6-13 (in Spanish).

30. Thomas D. Hopkins, "Economic Analysis Requirements as a Tool of Regulatory Reform: Experience in the United States," Statement presented to the Sub-Committee on Regulations and Competitiveness Standing Committee on Finance, House of Commons, Ottawa, September 15, 1992, p. 10.

31. U.S. Environmental Protection Agency, EPA's Use of Benefit-Cost Analysis: 1981–1986, EPA-230-05-87-028, Office of Policy, Planning and Evaluation, August 1987, pp. 1–3.

32. See, for example, General Accounting Office (GAO), *Regulatory Reform: Agencies Could Improve Development, Documentation, and Clarity of Regulatory Economic Analyses,* Report to the Committee on Governmental Affairs, U.S. Senate, GAO/RCED-98-142, May 1998; and Robert W. Hahn, Jason K. Burnett, Yee-Ho I. Chin, Elizabeth A. Mader, and Petrea R. Moyle, "Assessing Regulatory Impact Analyses: The Failure of Agencies to Comply with Executive Order 12,866," *Harvard Journal of Law & Public Policy* 23(3) 2000, 859–885.

CHAPTER 2

Conceptual Foundations of Cost-Benefit Analysis

I t seems only natural to think about the alternative courses of action we face as individuals in terms of their costs and benefits. Is it appropriate to evaluate public policy alternatives in the same way? The CBA of the highway sketched in Chapter 1 identifies some of the practical difficulties analysts typically encounter in measuring costs and benefits. Yet, even if analysts can measure costs and benefits satisfactorily, evaluating alternatives solely in terms of their net benefits may not always be appropriate. An understanding of the conceptual foundations of CBA provides a basis for determining when CBA can be appropriately used as a decision rule, when it can usefully be part of a broader analysis, and when it should be avoided.

The goal of *allocative,* or *Pareto, efficiency* provides the conceptual basis for CBA. In this chapter we provide a nontechnical introduction to Pareto efficiency. We then explain its relationship to *potential Pareto efficiency,* which provides the practical basis for actually doing CBA. Our exploration of the roles of Pareto efficiency and potential Pareto efficiency in CBA provides a basis for distinguishing it from other analytical frameworks. It also provides a basis for understanding the various philosophical objections commonly made against the use of CBA for decision making.

CBA AS A FRAMEWORK FOR MEASURING EFFICIENCY

CBA can be thought of as providing a framework for measuring efficiency.[1] Though we develop a more formal definition of efficiency in the following section, it can be thought of as a situation in which resources, such as land, labor, and capital, are deployed in their highest valued uses in terms of the goods and services they create. In situations in which analysts care only about efficiency, CBA provides a method for making direct comparisons among alternative policies. Even when goals other than efficiency are important, CBA serves as a yardstick that can be used to provide information about the relative efficiency of alternative policies. Indeed, analysts rarely encounter situations in which efficiency is not one of the relevant goals. Critical evaluation of these assertions requires a more precise definition of efficiency.

Pareto Efficiency

A simple and intuitively appealing definition of efficiency, referred to as *Pareto efficiency,* underlies modern welfare economics and CBA. *An allocation of goods is*

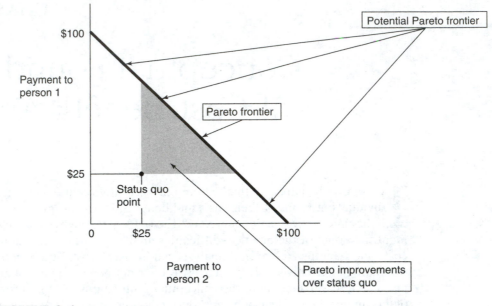

FIGURE 2-1   Pareto Efficiency

Pareto efficient if no alternative allocation can make at least one person better off without making anyone else worse off. An allocation of goods is inefficient, therefore, if an alternative allocation can be found that would make at least one person better off without making anyone else worse off. One would have to be malevolent not to want to achieve Pareto efficiency—why forgo gains to persons that would not inflict losses on others?

Figure 2-1 illustrates the concept of Pareto efficiency in a simple situation involving the allocation of a fixed amount of money between two persons. Imagine that the two persons will receive any total amount of money of up to $100 if they agree on how to split it between themselves. Assume that if they do not agree, then each person receives just $25. The vertical axis measures the amount of money received by person 1, and the horizontal axis measures the amount of money received by person 2. The point labeled $100 on the vertical axis represents the outcome in which person 1 receives the entire $100. Similarly, the point labeled $100 on the horizontal axis represents the outcome in which person 2 receives the entire $100. The line connecting these two extreme points, which we call the *potential Pareto frontier,* represents all the feasible splits between the two persons that allocate the entire $100. Splits involving less than $100 lie within the triangle formed by the potential Pareto frontier and the axes. The one labeled ($25, $25) is such a point. This point represents the status quo in the sense that it gives the amounts the two persons receive if they do not reach an agreement about splitting the $100. The segment of the potential Pareto frontier that gives each person at least as much as the status quo is called the *Pareto frontier.*

The lightly shaded triangle formed by the lines through the status quo point and the Pareto frontier represents all the alternative allocations that would make at least one of the persons better off than the status quo without making the other worse off. The existence of these points, which are feasible alternatives to the status quo that make at least one person better off without making the other worse off, means that the status quo is not Pareto efficient. Movement to any one of these points is called a *Pareto improvement*. Any Pareto improvement that does not lie on the potential Pareto frontier would leave open the possibility of further Pareto improvements and thus not provide a Pareto-efficient allocation. Only on the potential Pareto frontier is it impossible to make a feasible reallocation that makes one person better off without making the other person worse off.

It should be clear that the segment of the potential Pareto frontier that guarantees at least $25 to each person represents all the Pareto efficient allocations relative to the status quo. Each of these points makes a Pareto improvement over the status quo and leaves no opportunity for further improvements. The segment of the potential Pareto frontier that represents actual Pareto improvements depends upon the status quo. In other words, implicit in the concept of Pareto efficiency are the initial starting positions of the members of society. We return later to the significance of the difference between the potential and actual Pareto frontiers in our discussion of criticisms of CBA.

Net Benefits and Pareto Efficiency

The link between positive net social benefits (henceforth, net benefits) and Pareto efficiency is straightforward: *if a policy has positive net benefits, then it is possible to find a set of transfers, or "side payments," that makes at least one person better off without making anyone else worse off.* A full understanding of this link requires some reflection on how one measures benefits and costs in CBA. In particular, as illustrated in Figure 2-2, it requires one to consider willingness to pay (WTP) as the method for valuing the outputs of a policy and opportunity cost as the method for valuing the resources required to implement the policy. Though we develop these important concepts more fully in the next three chapters in the context of market exchange, the simple introductions that follow provide the basis for understanding the link between net benefits and Pareto efficiency.

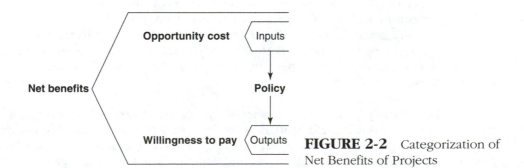

FIGURE 2-2 Categorization of Net Benefits of Projects

Willingness to Pay.   Consider a proposed policy that would produce outputs of relevance to three people. Assume that these people make honest revelations of their assessments of the values of the outputs. Through a series of questions, we elicit the payments that each person would have to make or to receive under the policy so that he would be indifferent between the status quo and the policy with the payments. So, for example, imagine that person 1 honestly reveals that she would be indifferent between the status quo and paying $100 to have the policy implemented. Similarly, person 2 might say that he is indifferent between the status quo and paying $200 to have the policy implemented. These values are the WTP of persons 1 and 2 for the policy. Unlike persons 1 and 2, assume that person 3 does not like the impacts of the proposed policy and would have to receive a payment of $250 if the policy were implemented to feel just as well off as he did under the status quo; this $250 is the amount that would have to be given to the person in conjunction with the proposed policy so that he is indifferent between it and the status quo. The negative of this amount ($-$250) would be the WTP of person 3 for the policy. As the policy in effect takes something away from person 3, the amount is called the person's *willingness to accept.* In this stylized example, the distinction between willingness to pay and willingness to accept is purely semantic. However, the distinction has substantive importance when one actually seeks to measure WTP through survey methods, because, as discussed in Chapters 15 and 18, people often demand larger payments to accept small decrements in some good than they are WTP to obtain small increments of exactly the same size. For now, we use WTP inclusively, assuming that its elicitation appropriately takes account of whether people perceive policies as giving them something or as taking away something.

The algebraic sum of these willingness-to-pay values is the appropriate measure of the net benefits of the impacts of the policy. In this example, the willingness-to-pay amounts can be divided into $300 of benefits ($100 + $200) accruing to persons 1 and 2 and $250 of costs ($-$250) accruing to person 3. The net benefits are thus positive and equal to $50. If these were the only three persons affected by the policy, and if the policy required no resources to implement, then the $50 would be the appropriate measure of net benefits from the perspective of CBA. Simple implementation of the policy would not be Pareto efficient because person 3 would be made worse off with respect to the status quo.

Yet, we can easily imagine altering the policy so that it would be Pareto efficient. For example, imagine that person 3 receives $75 from person 1 and $175 from person 2 as part of the policy. Now person 1 is better off than the status quo ($100 of benefits minus $75 given to person 3), person 2 is better off ($200 of benefits minus $175 given to person 3), and person 3 is no worse off ($250 of costs from the policy minus $250 of benefits in the form of compensation from persons 1 and 2).

The key point is that if, and only if, the aggregate net benefits of the policy as measured by the WTP of all affected individuals are positive, then there exist sets of contributions and payments that would make the policy a Pareto improvement over the status quo.

Opportunity Cost.   The implementation of policies almost always requires the use of some inputs that could be used to produce other things of value. For example, implementing a policy to build a bridge across a river would require the use of labor, steel, concrete, construction machinery, and land that could be used to produce other things of value to people. The concept of opportunity cost is used in CBA to place a dollar value on the inputs required to implement policies. *The opportunity cost of using an input to implement a policy is its value in its best alternative use.* Opportunity cost measures the value of what society must forgo to use the input to implement the policy.

Return to the example of the three persons whose aggregate WTP for the policy was $50. Imagine that the policy requires inputs that have an opportunity cost of $75. That is, if the policy were implemented, then some other members of society would have to give up goods valued at $75. In this case, the policy does not generate enough net benefits to the three persons to allow them to compensate those who must forgo the $75 of goods—the net benefits to society as a whole are negative $25 ($50 of net benefits to the three persons minus $75 in opportunity costs to the rest of society). Thus, the policy could not be made Pareto efficient because it does not produce enough benefits to permit all those who bear costs to be compensated fully. If the opportunity cost were only $20 instead of $75, then net benefits to society would be $30 and it would be possible to compensate all those who bear costs so that no one is made worse off, and some people are made better off, by the policy. In general, if the net benefits of a policy are positive, then it is potentially Pareto improving.

USING CBA FOR DECISION MAKING

The connection between net benefits and Pareto efficiency should now be clear. *As long as analysts value all impacts in terms of willingness to pay and value all required inputs in terms of opportunity costs, then the sign of the net benefits indicates whether it would be possible to compensate those who bear costs sufficiently so that no one is made worse off and at least one person is better off.* Positive net benefits indicate the potential for compensation to make the policy Pareto efficient; negative net benefits indicate the absence of this potential.

One could imagine the following decision rule for CBA: adopt only policies that are actually Pareto efficient. In other words, only policies that yield positive benefits after providing full compensation to all those who bear costs would be adopted so that there would be no losers, only winners. Although conceptually this is appealing, such a rule would be extremely difficult to apply in practice for a number of reasons. First, it would place great informational burdens on analysts not just to measure aggregate costs and benefits, which can often be inferred from observing prices and quantities in markets, but also to measure costs and benefits for each person, a task that would generally render CBA too costly to use. Second, once the distribution of costs and benefits at the individual level were known, the administrative costs of actually making specific transfers for each government policy would almost certainly be high. Third, it is difficult to operate a practical system of compensation payments that does not distort the investment and work behavior of households. Fourth, the requirement that everyone be fully compensated would create a strong incentive for people to find ways to overstate the costs and understate the benefits that they expect to receive from policies, complicating the already difficult task of inferring how much each person is willing to pay for the outputs produced by the policy. The "actual Pareto efficiency" principle in practice would thus result in society forgoing many policies that offer positive net benefits and the diversion of much effort toward the seeking of unjustified compensation.

Potential Pareto Efficiency

CBA utilizes an alternative decision rule with somewhat less conceptual appeal, but much greater feasibility, than the actual Pareto efficiency rule. It is based on what is known as the *Kaldor-Hicks criterion:* a policy should be adopted if and only if those who will gain could fully compensate those who will lose and still be better off.[2] The Kaldor-Hicks criterion provides the basis for the *potential Pareto efficiency rule,* or, more commonly, the *net benefits criterion: adopt only policies that have positive net benefits.* As long as net benefits are positive, it is at least possible that losers could be compensated so that the policy potentially could be Pareto improving. In terms of Figure 2-1, any point on the potential Pareto frontier would pass the potential Pareto efficiency rule, while only those points on the potential Pareto frontier that guarantee at least $25 to each person (the heavily shaded segment of the potential Pareto frontier) pass the actual Pareto efficiency rule.

In practice, the assessment of whether particular policies increase efficiency depends on whether they represent *potential Pareto improvements.* That is, do the policies provide sufficient net gains so that all losers could be compensated? Potential Pareto efficiency is achieved only when all potential Pareto improvements have been exhausted.

Several justifications, aside from feasibility, are commonly offered in defense of the potential Pareto efficiency rule. First, by always choosing policies with positive net benefits, society maximizes aggregate wealth. This indirectly helps those who are worse off in society because richer societies have greater capability for helping their poorest members and, if redistribution is a normal good (that is, other things being equal, people want more of it as their wealth increases), members of society have a greater willingness to help.[3] Second, it is likely that different policies will have different sets of winners and losers. Thus, if the rule is consistently applied to government activity, then costs and benefits will tend to average out across people so that each person is likely to realize positive net benefits from the full collection of policies. Third, as we discuss later in this chapter, the rule stands in contrast to the incentives in representative political systems to give too much weight to costs and benefits that accrue to organized groups and too little weight to costs and benefits that accrue to unorganized interests. Its use in public discourse may thereby reduce the chances that Pareto-inefficient policies will be adopted. Fourth, if a more equal distribution of wealth or income is an important goal, then it is possible to address it directly through transfers after a large number of efficiency-enhancing policies have been adopted. In other words, redistribution, at least in theory, can be done "wholesale" with a single redistribution program rather than "retail" in each particular program.

Application of the Decision Rule in Practice

Two polices can be thought of as independent if the adoption of one does not influence the costs and benefits of the other. When all relevant projects are independent, the CBA decision rule is simple: *adopt all policies that have positive net benefits.* A more

TABLE 2-1 Choosing Efficient Projects and the Use of Net Benefits versus Benefit-Cost Ratios

	Costs (millions of dollars)	Benefits (millions of dollars)	Net Benefits (millions of dollars)	Benefits/Costs
No project	0	0	0	—
Project A	1	10	9	10
Project B	10	30	20	3
Project C	4	8	4	2
Project D	3	5	2	1.7
Projects C and D	7	21	14	3
Project E	10	8	−2	0.8

(1) No constraints: Choose A, B, and combination C and D (net benefits equal $43 million).
(2) All projects mutually exclusive: Choose B (net benefits equal $20 million).
(3) Total costs cannot exceed $10 million: Choose A and combination C and D (net benefits equal $23 million).
Source: Adapted from David L. Weimer and Aidan R. Vining, *Policy Analysis: Concepts and Practice,* 5th ed. (Upper Saddle River, NJ: Pearson Prentice Hall, 2011), Figure 16.2.

general version of the rule applies in situations involving multiple policies that may enhance or interfere with each other: *choose the combination of policies that maximizes net benefits.* Physical, budgetary, and other constraints may limit the combinations of policies that are feasible.

Consider the list of projects in Table 2-1. Interpret the costs and benefits as being expressed in terms of present values, so that they can be directly compared with dollars of current consumption. Note that projects C and D are shown as synergistic. That is, the net benefits from adopting both together exceed the sum of the net benefits from adopting each one independently. Such might be the case if project C were a dam that created a reservoir that could be used for recreation as well as hydroelectric power and D were a road that increased access to the reservoir. Of course, projects can also interfere with each other; for instance, the dam might reduce the benefits of a downstream recreation project. The important point is that care must be taken to determine interactions among projects so that the combinations of projects providing the greatest net benefits in aggregate can be readily identified.

Suppose we could choose any combination of projects; then we should simply choose all those with positive net benefits—namely, projects A, B, and combination C and D.

Suppose now the policies are mutually exclusive. For example, we cannot drain a swamp to create agricultural land and simultaneously preserve it as a wildlife refuge. When all the available policies are mutually exclusive, efficiency is maximized by choosing the one with the largest net positive benefits—project B, with net benefits of $20 million. Assume, however, that all projects are mutually exclusive, except C and D, which can be built together to obtain synergistic gains. By taking the combination of C and D to be a separate project, we can consider all the projects on the list to be mutually exclusive. Looking down the column labeled "Net Benefits," we see that project B still offers the largest net benefits and therefore should be the one selected, but the combination of C and D offers the next highest net benefits.

Analysts often compare programs in terms of *benefit-cost ratios.* Note that project B, which offers the largest net benefits, does not have the largest ratio of benefits to costs. Project A has a benefit-cost ratio of 10, while project B has a benefit-cost ratio of only 3. Nevertheless, project B should be selected because it offers larger net benefits than project A. This comparison shows how the benefit-cost ratio can sometimes confuse the choice process when the projects under consideration are of different scale (that is, project B involves substantially higher costs than project A). Furthermore, the benefit-cost ratio is sensitive to whether negative WTP (willingness to accept) amounts are subtracted from benefits or added to costs. For example, imagine that the cost of $10 million for project B was opportunity costs and the benefits of $30 million consisted of $40 million for one group and −$10 million for another. Treating the negative WTP as a cost rather than as a negative benefit would leave the net benefits unchanged but lower the benefit-cost ratio from 3 to 2. Thus, benefit-cost ratios are subject to manipulation. For these reasons, *we recommend that analysts avoid using benefit-cost ratios and rely instead on net benefits to rank policies.*

Return to Table 2-1 and interpret the listed costs as public expenditures exactly equal to opportunity costs and the listed benefits as the willingness-to-pay values for all project effects. Now assume that, while none of the projects are mutually exclusive in a physical sense, total public expenditures (costs) cannot exceed $10 million because of a budget constraint that is binding for political reasons. If project B is selected, then the budget constraint is met, and net benefits of $20 million result. If project A and the combination of projects C and D are selected instead, then the budget constraint is also met, but net benefits of $23 million result. No other feasible combination offers larger net benefits. Thus, under the budget constraint, net benefits are maximized by choosing projects A and the combination of C and D.

FUNDAMENTAL ISSUES RELATED TO WILLINGNESS TO PAY

Three sets of fundamental issues arise with respect to the interpretation of WTP as a measure of benefits in the assessment of the efficiency of policies. First, a theoretical limitation in the aggregation of willingness-to-pay amounts across individuals opens the possibility that the net benefits criterion will not lead to fully satisfactory rankings of policies. Second, normative issues arise because of the dependence of WTP on the distribution of wealth in society. Third, normative issues also arise with respect to the issue of *standing,* which concerns whose WTP counts in the aggregation of benefits.

The Theoretical Limitation of Willingness to Pay as Basis for Social Orderings

Although using net benefits as a basis for choosing efficient public policies is intuitively appealing, its implementation through the aggregation of the willingness-to-pay amounts of the members of society confronts a fundamental theoretical limitation: ranking policies in terms of net benefits does not guarantee a transitive social ordering of the policies.

A *transitive* ordering requires that if X is preferred to Y, and Y is preferred to Z, then X is preferred to Z. The logic of transitivity seems so clear that it is usually taken as an axiom of rationality in the preferences of individuals. We would certainly be

TABLE 2-2   Cyclical Social Preferences under
Pairwise Majority Rule Voting

Preference Ordering	Voter 1	Voter 2	Voter 3
First Choice	X	Z	Y
Second Choice	Y	X	Z
Third Choice	Z	Y	X

(1) Pairwise Voting Outcomes: X *versus* Y, X *wins;* Y *versus* Z,
Y *wins;* X *versus* Z, Z *wins.*
(2) Implied Social Ordering: X *is preferred to* Y, Y *is preferred
to* Z, *but* Z *is preferred to* X!

skeptical about the mental state of someone who tells us she prefers apples to oranges, and she prefers oranges to peaches, but she prefers peaches to apples. This violation of transitivity implies a cyclical, and therefore ambiguous, ordering of the alternatives. Clearly, transitivity is a desirable property of any preference ordering.

If every member of a society has transitive preferences, does it follow that reasonable procedures for aggregating their preferences will always produce a transitive social ordering? An example makes clear that the answer is no. Consider a common aggregation procedure: majority rule voting over pairs of alternatives. Imagine that society consists of three voters who have preferences over three alternatives, X, Y, and Z, as displayed in Table 2-2. Specifically, voter 1 prefers X to Y to Z, voter 2 prefers Z to X to Y, and voter 3 prefers Y to Z to X. If the voters express their sincere preferences in each round of voting, then we would find that given the choice between X and Y, voters 1 and 2 (a majority) would vote for X because they each prefer it to Y. Similarly, given the choice between Y and Z, a majority would vote for Y. Yet in a choice between X and Z, a majority would vote for Z. Thus, the implied social ordering is intransitive because X is preferred to Y, Y is preferred to Z, but Z is preferred to X!

Is the possibility of obtaining an intransitive social ordering peculiar to the use of pairwise majority rule voting to produce rankings alternatives? Surprisingly, it can result from any rule for creating a social ordering that satisfies certain minimal requirements. We cannot expect any rule for creating a social ranking of policy alternatives to be fully satisfactory. In 1951, Kenneth Arrow proved that any *social choice rule* that satisfies a basic set of fairness conditions can produce an intransitive social ordering.[4] *Arrow's theorem* applies to any rule for ranking alternatives in which two or more persons must rank three or more alternatives. It requires any such scheme to satisfy at least the following conditions to be considered fair: First, each person is allowed to have any transitive preferences over the possible policy alternatives (*axiom of unrestricted domain*). Second, if one alternative is unanimously preferred to a second, then the rule for choice will not select the second (*axiom of Pareto choice*). Third, the ranking of any two alternatives should not depend on what other alternatives are available (*axiom of independence*). Fourth, the rule must not allow any one person dictatorial power to impose his or her preferences as the social ordering (*axiom of nondictatorship*). Arrow's theorem states that any fair rule for choice (one that satisfies the four previous axioms) will not guarantee a transitive *social ordering* of policy alternatives. That is, it is possible that individual preferences are such that the social ordering will be cyclical. Thus, unless the net benefit rule, which is a social choice rule, violates one of the axioms, it cannot guarantee a transitive social ordering of policies.

In order to ensure that the use of WTP in the implementation of the net benefit rule will produce a transitive social ordering of policies, some restrictions, violating the axiom of unrestricted domain, must be placed on the preferences that individuals are allowed to hold.[5] Economic models commonly assume that individual preferences are represented by utility functions (numerical representations of preference orderings) that exhibit positive but declining marginal utility; that is, other things equal, incremental consumption of any good increases utility but not by as much as the previous incremental unit. Unfortunately, this relatively weak restriction of the domain of preferences (it rules out preferences that cannot be represented by such utility functions) is not enough to guarantee that the net benefit rule based on WTP will *always* produce a transitive social ordering. Two additional restrictions are required: (1) The utility functions of individuals must be such that the individual demand curves that they imply can be aggregated into a market demand curve with the sum of individual incomes as an argument, and (2) all individuals must face the same set of prices.[6] The first restriction is quite strong in that it requires each individual's demand for each good to increase linearly with increasing income and have the same rate of increase for each individual. The second restriction, generally satisfied when all goods are traded in markets, may be violated when policies allocate quantities of goods to individuals who cannot resell them in markets.

The necessity of restricting the allowed preferences of individuals to guarantee a transitive social ordering from the use of WTP in the implementation of the net benefits criterion makes clear that it is an imperfect criterion for assessing the relative efficiency of alternative policies.[7] Of course, analysts can avoid this theoretical problem by assuming that the preferences of individual consumers conform to restrictive assumptions consistent with the existence of an appropriate aggregate demand function. Alternatively, analysts can avoid it by assuming that policies affect the price of only a single good. Indeed, as discussed in the next three chapters, analysts seeking to estimate WTP typically work with an aggregate, or market, demand schedule for a single good, implicitly assuming away price effects in the markets for other goods.

Despite its theoretical imperfection as a measure of efficiency, WTP is an intuitively appealing and practical concept for guiding the implementation of the net benefits criterion. As discussed next, however, its dependence on the distribution of wealth raises a serious normative concern about its use.

Dependence of Willingness to Pay on the Distribution of Wealth

The willingness of a person to pay to obtain a desired policy impact will tend to be higher the greater the wealth that she or he has available. Consequently, the sum of the willingness of persons to pay, the benefit measure in CBA, depends on their levels of wealth. If the distribution of wealth in society were to be changed, then it would be likely that the sum of individuals' willingness-to-pay amounts would change as well, perhaps altering the ranking of alternative policies in terms of their net benefits.

The dependence of net benefits on the distribution of wealth would not pose a conceptual problem if losers from adopted policies were *actually* compensated so that the adopted polices would produce actual, rather than potential, Pareto improvements. From a utilitarian perspective, Pareto improvement guarantees that the sum of utilities of individuals in society increases. In application of the potential Pareto principle, however, it is possible that an adopted policy could actually lower the sum of utilities if people with different levels of wealth had different *marginal utilities of money*.[8] As an illustration, consider a policy that gives $10 of benefits to a person with high wealth and inflicts $9 of costs on a person with low wealth. If the low-wealth person's marginal utility of money is higher than that of the high-wealth person, then it is possible that the utility loss of the low-wealth person could outweigh the utility gain of the high-wealth person. Thus, while the Pareto principle allows us to avoid interpersonal utility comparisons by guaranteeing increases in aggregate utility for policies with positive net benefits, the potential Pareto principle does not do so.

The implication of the dependence of WTP on wealth is that the justification for the potential Pareto principle weakens for policies that concentrate costs and benefits on different wealth groups. Policies with positive net benefits that concentrate costs on low-wealth groups may not increase aggregate utility; moreover, policies with negative net benefits that concentrate benefits on low-wealth groups may not decrease aggregate utility. However, if the potential Pareto principle is consistently applied and adopted policies do not produce consistent losers or winners, then the overall effects of the policies taken together will tend to make everyone better off. Hence, concerns about reductions in aggregate utility would be unfounded.

Critics of CBA sometimes question the validity of the concept of Pareto efficiency itself because it depends on the status quo distribution of wealth. Returning to Figure 2-1, note that the location of the Pareto frontier would change if the location of the status quo point were changed. Some have advocated the formulation of a social welfare function that maps the utility, wealth, or consumption of all individuals in society into an index that ranks alternative distributions of goods.[9] In this broader framework incorporating distributional values, an efficient policy is one that maximizes the value of the social welfare function. But how does society determine the social welfare function? Unfortunately, Arrow's theorem, as well as practical difficulties in obtaining needed information, precludes the formulation of a social welfare function through any fair collective choice procedure.[10] In practice, it must therefore be provided subjectively by the analyst.[11] We believe that it is usually better to keep the subjective distributional values of analysts explicit by comparing policies both in terms of efficiency and the selected distributional criteria, as illustrated in the discussion of multigoal analysis and distributionally weighted CBA later in this chapter. As an alternative, analysts can report net benefits by wealth or income group as well as for society as a whole.

Dependence of Net Benefits on Assumptions About Standing

The question of whose WTP should count in the aggregation of net benefits has come to be known as the issue of standing.[12] It has immediate practical importance in at least three contexts: the jurisdictional definition of society, the exclusion of socially unacceptable preferences, and the inclusion of the preferences of future generations. A recognition of social constraints, rights, and duties often helps answer the question of standing.

Jurisdictional Definition of Society.   The most inclusive definition of society encompasses all people, no matter where they live or to which government they owe allegiance. Analysts working for the United Nations or some other international organization might very well adopt such a universalistic, or global, perspective. Yet for purposes of CBA, most analysts define society at the national level. The basis for this restriction in jurisdiction is the notion that the citizens of a country share a common constitution, formal or informal, that sets out fundamental values and rules for making collective choices. In a sense, they consent to being a society. Furthermore, they accept that the citizens of other countries have their own constitutions that make them distinct polities.

The distinction between universal and national jurisdiction becomes relevant in the evaluation of policies whose impacts spill over national borders. For example, if U.S. analysts adopt the national-level jurisdiction as defining society, then they would not attempt to measure the willingness of Canadian residents to pay to avoid pollution originating in the United States that exacerbates acid rain in Canada. Of course, the willingness of U.S. citizens to pay to reduce acid rain in Canada should be included in the CBA, though in practice, it would be very difficult to measure.

As in the highway example discussed in Chapter 1, a similar issue arises with respect to subnational units of government. As an illustration, consider a city that is deciding whether to build a bike path. Assume that a CBA from the national perspective (giving standing to everyone in the country) predicts that the project will generate $1 million in benefits (which all accrue to city residents) and $2 million in costs (which are also borne by city residents), thereby resulting in negative $1 million in net benefits (or $1 million in net costs). Also assume, however, that through an intergovernmental grants program the national government will repay the city's $2 million of costs resulting from this particular project. The grant appears to the city residents as a $2 million benefit offsetting $2 million in local costs. Thus, from the perspective of the city, the bike path generates $1 million in net benefits rather than $1 million in net costs.

One can make an argument that the city should treat its residents as the relevant society and, hence, should not give standing to nonresidents. The city government has a charter to promote the welfare of its residents. The city by itself can do relatively little to affect national policy—even if it does not take advantage of all the opportunities offered by the national government, other cities probably will. Furthermore, analysts who do not adopt the city's perspective, but instead employ only the broader national perspective, risk losing influence, a possibility of special concern to analysts who earn their living by giving advice to the city.

Adopting the subnational perspective, however, makes CBA a less valuable decision rule for public policy. We believe that *analysts should ideally conduct CBA from the national perspective*. They may, of course, also conduct a parallel CBA from the subnational perspective as a response to the narrower interests of their clients. If major impacts spill over national borders, then the CBA should be done from the global as well as the national perspective.

Jurisdictional Membership.   Deciding the jurisdictional definition of society leaves open a number of questions about who should be counted as members of the jurisdiction. For example, almost all analysts agree that citizens of their country, whether living domestically or abroad, should have standing. With respect to noncitizens in their country, most analysts would probably give standing to those who were in the country legally. Less consensus exists with respect to the standing of other categories of people: should illegal aliens have standing? What about the children of illegal aliens?

One source of guidance for answering these types of questions is the system of legally defined rights.[13] For example, a ruling by the courts that the children of illegal aliens are entitled to access publicly funded education might encourage the analyst to give these children standing in CBA. Reliance on legally defined rights to determine standing, however, is not always morally acceptable. It would not have been right to deny standing in CBA to slaves in the antebellum United States, nonwhites in apartheid South Africa, or Jews in Nazi Germany simply because they lacked legal rights. Therefore, legal rights alone cannot fully resolve the issue of standing in CBA. They provide a presumption, but one that analysts may sometimes have an ethical responsibility to challenge. Democratic regimes usually provide mechanisms for challenging such presumptions, but often with personal cost to individual analysts.

One other issue of membership deserves brief mention. CBA is anthropocentric. *Only the willingness of people to pay counts.* Neither flora nor fauna have standing. That is not to say that their "interests" have no representation. Many people are willing to pay to preserve a species, and some are even willing to pay to preserve individual animals or plants. As discussed in Chapter 9, it is conceptually correct within the CBA framework to take account of these willingness-to-pay amounts, though doing so effectively is very often beyond our analytical reach.

Exclusion of Socially Unacceptable Preferences. People sometimes hold preferences that society seeks to suppress through widely supported legal sanctions. For instance, although some people would be willing to pay for the opportunity to have sexual relations with children, most countries attempt to thwart the expression of such preferences through strict criminal penalties. Should such socially unacceptable preferences be given standing in CBA?

One approach to answering this question adds duties and prohibitions to legal rights as sources of guidance about social values. Together they can be thought of as social constraints that should be taken into account in CBA just as the analyst takes into account physical and budgetary constraints.[14] Clear and widely accepted legal sanctions may help identify preferences that should not have standing.

An important application arises in estimating the net benefits of policies that are intended to reduce the amount of criminal behavior in society. Some analysts count reductions in the monetary returns to crime as a cost borne by criminals, offsetting the benefits of reduced criminal activity enjoyed by their victims.[15] As the returns from crime are illegal and widely viewed as wrong, however, the social constraint perspective argues against treating them in this manner.

The issue of the standing of preferences can be especially difficult for analysts to resolve when they are dealing with foreign cultures. Consider, for instance, the CBA of a program to bring water to poor communities in Haiti.[16] Analysts found that husbands had negative willingness to pay amounts for the time that their wives saved from easier access to water. By contemporary standards in most urban settings, people would generally regard these preferences as unworthy. Yet in the cultural context of rural Haiti at the time, they were consistent with prevailing norms. Should these preferences of husbands have standing? In practice, lack of data to estimate willingness-to-pay amounts for this sort of impact usually spares analysts from having to answer such difficult questions.

Inclusion of the Preferences of Future Generations. Some policies adopted today, such as the disposal of nuclear wastes or the restoration of wilderness areas, may have impacts on people not yet born. Though we believe that these people should have standing in CBA, there is no way to measure their WTP directly because they are not yet here to express it.[17] How serious a problem does this pose for CBA?

The absence of direct measures of the willingness of future generations to pay for policy impacts generally poses few problems for two reasons. First, because few policies involve impacts that appear only in the far future, the WTP of people alive today for the effects during their lifetimes can be used to some extent to predict how future generations will value them. Second, as most people alive today care about the well-being of their children, grandchildren, and great-grandchildren, whether born or yet to be born, they are likely to include the interests of these generations to some extent in their own valuations of impacts. Indeed, because people cannot predict with certainty the place that their future offspring will hold in society, they are likely to take a very broad view of future impacts.

In Chapters 9 and 10, we return to the question of the standing of future generations when we discuss existence value and the social discount rate.

CONCERNS ABOUT THE ROLE OF CBA IN THE POLITICAL PROCESS

The most vocal critics of CBA fear that it subverts democratic values. Some see the monetizing of impacts as a profane attempt to place a price on everything. Others see CBA as undermining democracy. Though these fears are largely unfounded, they deserve explicit consideration by advocates of CBA.

Does CBA Debase the Terms of Public Discourse?

A number of objections have been raised to the effort made in CBA to value all policy impacts in terms of dollars: Pricing goods not normally traded in markets—for example, life itself—decreases their perceived value by implying that they can be compared to goods that are traded in markets; pricing such goods reduces their perceived value by weakening the claim that they should not be for sale in any circumstance; and pricing all goods undercuts the claim that some goods are "priceless."[18] The language and conceptual frameworks that people use almost certainly affect the nature of debate to some extent. It is not clear, however, how influential the technical concepts of economics are in actually shaping public discourse. In any event, the correct interpretation of how nonmarket goods are monetized largely undercuts the charge that CBA debases public discourse.

Consider the issue of the monetization of the value of life. On the surface it may appear that economists are implying that a price can be put on someone's life. A closer look, which we provide in Chapters 14 and 16, indicates that the value of life estimated by economists is a measure of how much people are willing to pay to reduce

---
EXHIBIT 2-1

Does wealth produce happiness? Surveys conducted within countries consistently find that rich people (say those in the top quarter of the income distribution) on average report being happier than poorer people (say those in the bottom quarter of the income distribution). Yet, if one looks at either of these groups over time, one discovers that its absolute level of happiness is roughly constant despite the fact that economic growth has made it richer. Similarly, comparing the happiness of the rich (or poor) across countries generally shows similar levels of happiness despite substantial differences in the overall levels of wealth between the countries. What explains this puzzle? Richard Layard suggests two psychological effects that move up the norm to which people compare their own circumstances as societies become wealthier: habituation and rivalry. Habituation involves getting used to things we have—an initial feeling of happiness from acquisition tends to evaporate as we get used to having the good. Rivalry involves comparing one's situation to those in a reference group—happiness depends on relative position.

These phenomena raise concerns about interpreting changes in social surplus as changes in aggregate happiness. A policy that increased everyone's income would certainly pass the net benefits test. Yet extreme habituation might quickly return everyone to their initial levels of utility, or extreme rivalry would result in no utility gains at all because no one's relative position changes!

Source: Adapted from Richard Layard, "Happiness: Has Social Science a Clue?" Lionel Robbins Memorial Lectures, London School of Economics, Lecture 1: Income and Happiness: Rethinking Economic Policy, March 3, 4, and 5, 2003.

their risk of death; in other words, it is the value of a *statistical life,* the WTP to avoid risks that will result in one less death in a population. Although it may not be appropriate to place a dollar value on the life of any particular person, it is appropriate to use the value of a statistical life in assessing proposed policies that change the risk of death that people face.

Every day people voluntarily make trade-offs between changes in the risk of death and other values: driving faster to save time increases the risk of being involved in a fatal traffic accident; eating fatty foods is pleasurable but increases the risk of fatal heart disease; skiing is exhilarating but risks fatal injury. Is it inappropriate to take account of these preferences in valuing the impacts of public policies? Most economists would answer no. Indeed, valuing statistical lives seems less problematic than attempting to place a dollar value on a specific person by estimating the person's forgone future earnings, the procedure employed by courts in cases of wrongful death.

Does CBA Undermine Democracy?

Some critics of CBA charge that it undermines democracy by imposing a single goal, efficiency, in the assessment of public policies. Their charge would be justified if the appropriate comparison were between a world in which public policy is determined solely through democratic processes that gave equal weight to all interests and a world in which public policy is determined strictly through the application of CBA. But this is an inappropriate comparison for two reasons. First, actual governmental processes fall far short of "ideal democracy." Second, at most, CBA has modest influence in public policy making.[19]

The interests of vocal constituencies, often those who can organize themselves in anticipation of obtaining concentrated benefits or avoiding concentrated costs, typically receive great attention from those in representative governments who wish to be reelected or advance to higher office. Less vocal constituencies usually have their interests represented less well. The interests of many of these less vocal constituencies are often better reflected in CBA. For example, CBA takes account of the individually small, but in aggregate large, costs borne by consumers because of government price-support programs that raise prices to the benefit of a small number of well-organized agricultural producers. But CBA rarely serves as the decisive decision rule for public policy. Indeed, it is difficult to identify important public policies selected *solely* on the basis of CBA.

A realistic assessment of representative democracy and the current influence of CBA should allay concerns that the latter is subverting the former. To the extent it is influential, CBA probably contributes to more democratic public policy by paying attention to diffuse interests typically underrepresented in a representative democracy. It would have to become much more influential before it could possibly be viewed as undermining democratic processes. Despite our hopes that the readers of this book will help make the use of CBA more prevalent, we have no concerns about it being too influential in the near future.

LIMITATIONS OF CBA: OTHER ANALYTICAL APPROACHES

It is important for analysts to realize the limitations of CBA. Two types of circumstances make the net benefits criterion an inappropriate decision rule for public policy. First, technical limitations may make it impossible to quantify and then monetize all relevant impacts as costs and benefits. Second, goals other than efficiency are relevant to the policy. For example, some policies are intended to affect the equality of outcomes or opportunity. Nevertheless, even when the net benefits criterion is not appropriate as a decision rule, CBA usually provides a useful yardstick for comparing alternative policies in terms of efficiency along with other goals.

Technical Limitations to CBA

CBA in its pure form requires that all impacts relevant to efficiency be quantified and made commensurate through monetization. Only when all the costs and benefits are expressed in dollars can the potential Pareto principle be applied through the calculation of net benefits. Limitations in theory, data, or analytical resources, however, may make it impossible for the analyst to measure and value all impacts of a policy as commensurate costs and benefits. Nonetheless, it may still be desirable to do a qualitative cost-benefit analysis or, if all but one important effect can be monetized, to switch from CBA to cost-effectiveness analysis. A brief description of each of these alternative approaches follows.

Qualitative CBA.   The advice given by Benjamin Franklin at the beginning of Chapter 1 can be thought of as a prescription for qualitative CBA. In conducting qualitative CBA, the analyst typically monetizes as many of the impacts as possible and then makes qualitative estimates of the relative importance of the remaining costs and benefits. Consider, for instance, a program to plant trees along an urban highway. The cost of the program, which consists only of the expenditures that must be made to hire a contractor to plant and to maintain the trees, can be directly monetized. The benefits, however, include a number of effects that are likely to be difficult to monetize: the visual pleasure the trees give to motorists, the reduction of noise in adjoining neighborhoods, and the filtering of pollutants from the air. With sufficient resources, the analyst would be able to monetize these benefits through a variety of techniques such as surveys of motorists and comparisons with the effects of other noise-reduction programs on property values. But because the program involves relatively small costs, it is unlikely that such efforts would be justified. Instead, a reasonable approach would be to list these benefits with rough estimates of their order of magnitude.

Analysts who lack the time, data, or other resources needed to value all relevant impacts directly may be able to make use of estimates found in other cost-benefit analyses or economic research. For example, most analysts doing CBA do not directly estimate people's WTP for reductions in mortality risk. Instead, as discussed in Chapters 13, 14, and 16, they rely on econometric studies investigating how people trade such things as changes in wages for changes in levels of risk.

When possible, analysts should quantify the impacts of the policy; that is, they should estimate the numeric values of the nonmonetized impacts. For example, consider analysis of a proposed regulation to restrict commercial fishing practices so that fewer dolphins will be killed per ton of tuna harvested. The regulation produces a benefit because some people have a positive willingness to pay for dolphin deaths avoided. Actually monetizing, that is, measuring the WTP, is a difficult task that might not be feasible for the analyst conducting the CBA. Even if monetization is infeasible, however, it is useful to attempt to predict the number of dolphins saved by the regulation. Doing so increases the usefulness of the qualitative CBA for others by conveying the magnitude of the impact of the regulation. Additionally, the client or other users of the analysis may be able to provide estimates of the willingness of people to pay for each dolphin saved so that (fully monetized) CBA becomes feasible.

Analysts often face a more complicated choice than simply whether to quantify a category of costs or benefits. Empirical measures can have varying degrees of accuracy, ranging from precise estimates in which we have great confidence to imprecise estimates in which we have little confidence. The decision to quantify, and with what degree of effort, should reflect the value of the increased precision that can be obtained and the costs of obtaining it. In other words, we should make such decisions within a CBA framework!

Cost-Effectiveness Analysis.   Analysts can often quantify impacts but not monetize them all. If the analysts are unable or unwilling to monetize the major benefit, then cost-effectiveness analysis may be appropriate. Because not all of the impacts can be monetized, it is not possible to estimate net benefits. The analysts can, however, construct a ratio involving the quantitative, but nonmonetized, benefit and the total dollar costs. A comparison allows the analyst to rank policies in terms of the cost-effectiveness criterion. However, unlike the net benefits criterion of CBA, it does not directly allow the analysts to conclude that the highest-ranked policy contributes to greater efficiency.

Return to the qualitative CBA of the fishing regulation discussed earlier. Suppose that, except for the benefit from avoided dolphin deaths, all the impacts could be monetized to a net cost of c dollars. If the number of avoided dolphin deaths were n_d, then the analyst could construct an effectiveness-cost ratio for the regulation, n_d/c, which can be interpreted as the average number of dolphins saved per dollar of cost borne. (Alternatively, the analyst could construct the cost-effectiveness ratio as c/n_d, which can be interpreted as the average dollar cost per dolphin saved.) Now imagine a number of alternative regulations, each of which involves different net costs and a different number of dolphins saved. A cost-effectiveness ratio can be calculated for each of these programs to facilitate comparison across alternative regulations.

Using cost-effectiveness analysis for decision making usually requires that some additional information be brought to bear. If the objective is to save as many dolphins as possible at a net cost of no more than c^*, then the analyst should select the most effective regulation from among those with net costs of less than c^*. Alternatively, if the objective is to save at least n_d^* dolphins, then the analyst should select the regulation with the lowest cost from among those regulations saving at least n_d^*. This is not necessarily the alternative with the best cost-effectiveness ratio. For example, if $n_d^* = 1,000$, one would choose a regulation that saved 1,000 dolphins at a cost of $1 million ($1,000 per dolphin saved) over an alternative regulation that saved 500 dolphins at a cost of $50 thousand ($100 per dolphin saved).

Analysts often encounter situations in which they or their clients are unable or unwilling to monetize impacts such as human lives saved, injuries avoided, and the acres of old-growth forest preserved. Because cost-effectiveness analysis may be useful in these situations, we consider it in greater depth in Chapter 18.

The Relevance of CBA when Goals Other than Efficiency Matter

One goal, efficiency, underlies CBA. The general public, politicians, and even economists, however, very often consider goals reflecting other values to be relevant to the evaluation of public policies proposed to solve social problems. Although efficiency almost always is one of the relevant goals in policy analysis, other goals, such as equality of opportunity, equality of outcome, expenditure constraints, political feasibility, and national security, for instance, may be as, or even more, important. Indeed, the spenders and guardians we met in Chapter 1 behave as if they are responding to goals other than efficiency. When goals in addition to efficiency are relevant, as well as when efficiency is the only goal, but relevant impacts cannot be confidently monetized, *multigoal analysis* provides the appropriate framework. In the special case in which efficiency and equality of outcome are the only relevant goals, *distributionally weighted* CBA may be an appropriate technique.

Multigoal Analysis.   The most general analytical framework is multigoal analysis. At the heart of multigoal analysis lies the notion that all policy alternatives should be compared in terms of all the relevant goals. Though multigoal analysis can be prescribed as a number of distinct steps,[20] three of its aspects are especially important. First, the analyst must move from relevant social values to general goals to specific impact categories that can be used as yardsticks for evaluating alternative policies. For example, the value

TABLE 2-3 Evaluation Matrix Worksheet for Alternative Family Aid Policies

Goals	Impact Categories	Policy A (status quo)	Policy B	Policy C
Efficiency	Labor earnings Investment in human capital Administrative costs			
Quality of life of poorest families	Number of families below poverty line Number of one-parent families Educational achievement of family members			
Political feasibility	Probability of adoption of required legislation			

of human dignity may imply a goal of improving equality of opportunity, which might be expressed as quantifiable impacts such as increasing participation in higher education and expanding workforce participation. Second, the analyst must evaluate each alternative policy, including the status quo, with respect to each of the impacts. Third, as no policy alternative is likely to dominate the others in terms of improvement in all the goals, the analyst usually can only make a recommendation to adopt one of the alternatives by carefully considering and making a subjective judgment concerning the trade-offs in the achievement of goals it offers relative to the other alternatives.

As a simple example, consider a multigoal analysis of alternative income transfer policies intended to help poor families. The analyst might construct the worksheet shown in Table 2-3 as a checklist for keeping track of the relevant goals. Increasing efficiency and improving the quality of life of poor families are both appropriate substantive goals. The former captures the aggregate gain or loss to society from transfers; the latter captures that portion of the gain or loss accruing to the poorest families. The goal of achieving political feasibility might be added to take account of the fact that a consensus on the relative importance of the substantive goals among politicians is unlikely. In this example, it can be thought of as an instrumental goal that is valuable not for its own sake but because it helps achieve the substantive goals. The major efficiency impacts are likely to be work disincentives for the recipients of aid and the real resource costs of administering the aid policy. If both of these impacts could be monetized, then the criterion for measuring efficiency would simply be the sum of the net benefits of these two impacts as measured in CBA. If either one of them could not be monetized, however, then efficiency would be stated in terms of the two impacts. The goal of improving the quality of life of poor families would probably be expressed in terms of such impacts as reducing the number of families below the poverty line, reducing the number of one-parent families, and increasing the educational achievement of family members.

The impact associated with the additional goal of political feasibility might be the change in the probability of passage of legislation required to implement the policy.

Before selecting among the alternative policies, the analyst should fill in all the cells of a matrix like the one shown in Table 2-3. Each cell would contain a prediction of the effect of a particular policy in terms of a particular impact category. By filling in all the cells, the analyst seeks to gain a comprehensive comparison of the alternatives across all the impact categories, and hence across their related goals.

Note that one can think of CBA, qualitative CBA, and cost-effectiveness analysis as special cases of multigoal analysis. In the case of CBA, there is one goal (efficiency) with one criterion (net benefits) so that the evaluation matrix has only one row, and the choice among alternatives is trivial (simply select the policy with the largest net benefits). In the case of qualitative CBA, there is also one goal, but because all relevant impacts cannot be monetized, it corresponds to several criteria, one for each impact. In the case of cost-effectiveness analysis, the goal of efficiency is often combined with some other goal such as satisfying a constraint on monetary costs or achieving some target level of reduction in the quantified but nonmonetized impact.

Distributionally Weighted CBA.   If both efficiency and equality of income are relevant goals and their relative importance can be quantified, then distributionally weighted CBA provides an alternative decision rule to the maximization of net benefits. Instead of considering aggregate net benefits as in standard CBA, net benefits are calculated for each of several relevant groups distinguished by income, wealth, or some similar characteristic of relevance to a distributional concern. As discussed in more detail in Chapter 19, the net benefits of each group are multiplied by a weighting factor, selected by the analyst to reflect some distributional goal, and then summed to arrive at a number that can be used to rank alternative policies.

The major problem analysts encounter in doing distributionally weighted CBA is arriving at an appropriate and acceptable set of weights. One general approach, which takes as a desirable social goal increasing equality of wealth, involves making the weights inversely proportional to wealth (or income) to favor policies that tend to equalize wealth (or income) in the population.[21] Another general approach, which takes as a desirable social goal the raising of the position of the least advantaged in society, involves placing a higher weight on the net benefits of those with incomes or wealth below some threshold levels than on those with incomes or wealth above the threshold. As reasonable arguments can be made in support of each of these approaches, the absence of a consensus about appropriate weights is not surprising.[22]

Obviously, developing weights that allow a single quantitative criterion for ranking alternative policies makes the choice among policy alternatives easier. Yet this ease is achieved only by making an assumption that forces efficiency and equality of outcomes to be fully commensurate. Dissatisfaction with the strong assumption required to do this has led a number of analysts to suggest that distributionally weighted CBA should always be done in conjunction with standard CBA to make clearer the efficiency implications of the selected weights.[23] In doing so, the study becomes, in effect, a multigoal analysis, raising the question of whether an explicit treatment of efficiency and equality as separate goals might not be a more appropriate framework when both efficiency and distributional concerns are important. Cost-effectiveness analysis

—— **EXHIBIT 2-2** ——

A study by the Congressional Budget Office to assess three alternatives for reducing U.S. consumption of gasoline listed the following criteria:

This study weighs the relative merits of tightening CAFE standards, raising the federal gasoline tax, and creating a cap-and-trade program against several major criteria:

Cost-Effectiveness. Reducing gasoline consumption would impose costs (both monetary and nonmonetary) on various producers and consumers. A cost-effective policy would keep those costs to a minimum.

Predictability of Gasoline Savings. How reliably would the policy bring about the desired reduction in gasoline consumption?

Effects on Safety. How would the policy alter the number and severity of traffic accidents?

Effects on Other External Costs Related to Driving. Reducing gasoline consumption would affect not only the United States' energy security and carbon emissions but other driving-related external costs (ones whose full weight is borne by society at large rather than by an individual). Those external costs include traffic congestion, the need for highway construction and maintenance, and emissions of air pollutants besides carbon dioxide.

In addition to those factors, the three policy options would have other implications that policymakers may care about—such as their effects on people at different income levels and in different parts of the country and their impact on the amount of revenue collected by the federal government. (Summary, p.1)

One could imagine turning the analysis into a CBA by monetizing the effects on safety and the effects on other external costs related to driving and treating predictability of gasoline savings through sensitivity analysis. As monetizing the distributional concerns would be difficult, a multigoal analysis with the CBA assessing efficiency and a separate treatment of distributional impacts could be useful.

Source: Adapted from Congressional Budget Office, *Reducing Gasoline Consumption: Three Policy Options*, November 2002 (www.cbo.gov/ftpdocs/39xx/doc3991/11-21-GasolineStudy.pdf).

might also provide a more reasonable approach than distributionally weighted CBA by posing the question in terms of achieving the most desirable redistribution possible for some fixed level of net cost.[24]

CONCLUSION

CBA is a method for determining if proposed policies could potentially be Pareto improving: positive net benefits make it possible, in the sense of making available resources to compensate those who bear costs so that some people are made better off without making anyone else worse off. Willingness to pay and opportunity cost are the guiding principles for measuring costs and benefits. Much of the rest of this book deals with how to make use of the concepts in practice.

Part II sets out the conceptual foundations for CBA in more depth. It begins by reviewing supply and demand analytics (Chapter 3), and then uses these analytics to show how information revealed in markets can be used to estimate willingness to pay and opportunity cost (Chapters 4 and 5). Subsequent chapters consider how to take account of policy effects that accrue in different time periods (Chapters 6 and 10) or with uncertainty (Chapters 7 and 8) and impacts on goods that have value beyond their direct use (Chapter 9).

Part III considers empirical approaches for predicting and valuing policy impacts. After considering general issues in prediction and valuation in Chapter 11. three chapters demonstrate estimation methods based on observed behavior. Policy demonstrations sometimes provide information of direct relevance to CBA, especially in terms of predicting policy impacts (Chapter 12). More often, however, analysts face the task of making inferences about demand schedules from data revealed in markets (Chapter 13) or through other behaviors (Chapter 14). In some circumstances, especially those arising in the context of environmental policy, the unavailability of data from observed behavior forces analysts to rely on survey responses as a basis for estimation (Chapter 15). Analysts can often make use of existing research to find values needed to monetize impacts as costs and benefits (Chapter 16), though some special care must be taken in transferring these values to CBAs of policies in developing countries (Chapter 17).

Part IV further develops two of the analytical methods introduced in this chapter that can be used as alternatives to CBA: cost-effectiveness analysis (Chapter 18) and distributionally weighted cost-benefit analysis (Chapter 19).

EXERCISES FOR CHAPTER 2

1. Many experts claim that, although VHS came to dominate the video recorder market, Betamax was a superior technology. Assume that these experts are correct, so that, all other things equal, a world in which all video recorders were Betamax technology would be Pareto superior to a world in which all video recorders were VHS technology. Yet it seems implausible that a policy that forced a switch in technologies would be even potentially Pareto improving. Explain.

2. Let's explore the concept of willingness to pay with a thought experiment. Imagine a specific sporting, entertainment, or cultural event that you would very much like to attend—perhaps a World Cup match, the seventh game of the World Series, a Rolling Stones concert, or a Kathleen Battle performance.
   a. What is the most you would be willing to pay for a ticket to the event?
   b. Imagine that you won a ticket to the event in a lottery. What is the minimum amount of money that you would be willing to accept to give up the ticket?
   c. Imagine that you had an income 50 percent higher than it is now, but that you didn't win a ticket to the event. What is the most you would be willing to pay for a ticket?
   d. Do you know anyone who would sufficiently dislike the event that they would not use a free ticket unless they were paid to do so?
   e. Do your answers suggest any possible generalizations about willingness to pay?

3. How closely do government expenditures measure opportunity cost for each of the following program inputs?
   a. Time of jurors in a criminal justice program that requires more trials.
   b. Land to be used for a nuclear waste storage facility that is owned by the government and located on a military base.
   c. Labor for a reforestation program in a small rural community with high unemployment.
   d. Labor of current government employees who are required to administer a new program.
   e. Concrete that was previously poured as part of a bridge foundation.

4. Three mutually exclusive projects are being considered for a remote river valley: Project R, a recreational facility, has estimated benefits of $10 million and costs of $8 million; project F, a forest preserve with some recreational facilities, has estimated benefits of $13 million and

costs of $10 million; project W, a wilderness area with restricted public access, has estimated benefits of $5 million and costs of $1 million. In addition, a road could be built for a cost of $4 million that would increase the benefits of project R by $8 million, increase the benefits of project F by $5 million, and reduce the benefits of project W by $1 million. Even in the absence of any of the other projects, the road has estimated benefits of $2 million.

    a. Calculate the benefit-cost ratio and net benefits for each possible alternative to the status quo. Note that there are seven possible alternatives to the status quo: R, F, and W, both with and without the road, and the road alone.

    b. If only one of the seven alternatives can be selected, which should be selected according to the CBA decision rule?

5. An analyst for the U.S. Navy was asked to evaluate alternatives for forward-basing a destroyer flotilla. He decided to do the evaluation as a CBA. The major categories of costs were related to obtaining and maintaining the facilities. The major category of benefit was reduced sailing time to patrol routes. The analyst recommended the forward base with the largest net benefits. The admiral, his client, rejected the recommendation because the CBA did not include the risks to the forward bases from surprise attack and the risks of being unexpectedly ejected from the bases because of changes in political regimes of the host countries. Was the analyst's work wasted?

6. Because of a recent wave of jewelry store robberies, a city increases police surveillance of jewelry stores. The increased surveillance costs the city an extra $500,000 per year, but as a result, the amount of jewelry that is stolen falls. Specifically, without the increase in surveillance, jewelry with a retail value of $1 million would have been stolen. This stolen jewelry would have been fenced by the jewelry thieves for $600,000. What is the net social benefit resulting from the police surveillance program?

7. (Spreadsheet recommended.) Excessive and improper use of antibiotics is contributing to the resistance of many diseases to existing antibiotics. Consider a regulatory program in the United States that would monitor antibiotic prescribing by physicians. Analysts estimate the direct costs of enforcement to be $40 million, the time costs to doctors and health professionals to be $220 million, and the convenience costs to patients to be $180 million (all annually). The annual benefits of the program are estimated to be $350 million in avoided resistance costs in the United States, $70 million in health benefits in the United States from better compliance with prescriptions, and $280 million in avoided resistance costs in the rest of the world. Does the program have positive net benefits from the national perspective? If not, what fraction of benefits accruing in the rest of the world would have to be counted for the program to have positive net benefits?

NOTES

1. Unless otherwise stated, we intend efficiency to mean *allocative efficiency,* as defined in this section. A broader interpretation of efficiency, which we discuss in a later section, is the maximization of a specific social welfare function that explicitly ranks alternative allocations.

2. Nicholas Kaldor, "Welfare Propositions of Economics and Interpersonal Comparisons of Utility," *Economic Journal* 49(195) 1939, 549–552; and John R. Hicks, "The Valuation of the Social Income," *Economica* 7(26) 1940,

105–124. The principle can also be stated as suggested by Hicks: Adopt a policy if and only if it would not be in the self-interest of those who will lose to bribe those who will gain not to adopt it.

3. Those who are worse off in society may or may not have been the ones who have borne the net costs of public policies. This argument thus shifts the focus from fairness with respect to particular policies to the relative position of those in society who are worse off for whatever reason.

4. Kenneth Arrow, *Social Choice and Individual Values,* 2nd ed. (New Haven, CT: Yale University Press, 1963). For a treatment that can be followed with minimal mathematics, see Julian H. Blau, "A Direct Proof of Arrow's Theorem," *Econometrica* 40(1) 1972, 61–67.

5. For an overview, see Charles Blackorby and David Donaldson, "A Review Article: The Case Against the Use of the Sum of Compensating Variation in Cost-Benefit Analysis," *Canadian Journal of Economics* 23(3) 1990, 471–494.

6. Charles Blackorby and David Donaldson, "Consumers' Surpluses and Consistent Cost-Benefit Tests," *Social Choice and Welfare* 1(4) 1985, 251–262.

7. Even if one does not demand that the potential Pareto principle always produce a transitive social ordering of policies, the most commonly used measure of willingness to pay, *compensating variation,* can produce what are called *Scitovsky reversals* (Tibor Scitovsky, "A Note on Welfare Propositions in Economics," *Review of Economic Studies* 41(1) 1941, 77–88). Compensating variation, which is discussed in Appendix 4A, is the change in income that would be needed to make the consumer indifferent between the new policy with the income change and the old policy without it. For example, if the price of a good increases, it is the amount of income needed to compensate consumers so that they would be indifferent between the original price and the new price with the compensation. A Scitovsky reversal results when the sum of compensating variations for a group of individuals is positive for a move from one Pareto efficient policy to another *and* is also positive for a move from the new policy back to the original policy! More generally, the sum of compensating variations can be positive for moves among Pareto-efficient allocations, so that it being positive is a necessary but not a sufficient condition for a potential Pareto improvement (Blackorby and Donaldson, "A Review Article: The Case Against the Use of the Sum of Compensating Variation in Cost-Benefit Analysis," 471–494).

8. The marginal utility of money is how much a person's utility changes for a small increase in the person's wealth. Economists generally assume declining marginal utility of money. That is, as a person's wealth increases, each additional dollar produces smaller increases in utility.

9. Abram Bergson [as Burk], "A Reformulation of Certain Aspects of Welfare Economics," *Quarterly Journal of Economics* 52(2) 1938, 310–334.

10. Tibor Scitovsky, "The State of Welfare Economics," *American Economic Review* 51(3) 1951, 301–315; and Kenneth Arrow, *Social Choice and Individual Values,* 2nd ed. (New Haven, CT: Yale University Press, 1963).

11. One could imagine asking a sample of members of society to value alternative states of the world resulting from alternative policies, including the situations of other people. In this way, their willingness to pay would include the value they place on the distributional impacts of policies. Unfortunately, implementing such surveys is very difficult.

12. The seminal work is Dale Whittington and Duncan MacRae Jr., "The Issue of Standing in Cost-Benefit Analysis," *Journal of Policy Analysis and Management* 5(4) 1986, 665–682.

13. Richard O. Zerbe Jr., "Comment: Does Benefit Cost Analysis Stand Alone? Rights and Standing," *Journal of Policy Analysis and Management* 10(1) 1991, 96–105.

14. For a development of the notion of social constraints in CBA, see William N. Trumbull, "Who Has Standing in Cost-Benefit Analysis?" *Journal of Policy Analysis and Management* 9(2) 1990, 201–218; and Richard O. Zerbe Jr., "Is Cost-Benefit Analysis Legal? Three Rules," *Journal of Policy Analysis and Management* 17(3) 1998, 419–456. For a more general treatment of institutional constraints and social welfare, see Daniel W. Bromley, *Economic Interests and Institutions: The Conceptual Foundations of Public Policy* (New York: Basil Blackwell, 1989).

15. David A. Long, Charles D. Mallar, and Craig V. D. Thornton, "Evaluating the Benefits and Costs of the Job Corps," *Journal of Policy Analysis and Management* 1(1) 1981, 55–76.

16. For a discussion of this case from the perspective of a number of issues of standing of preferences, see Duncan MacRae Jr. and Dale Whittington, "Assessing Preferences in Cost-Benefit Analysis: Reflections on Rural Water Supply Evaluation in Haiti," *Journal of Policy Analysis and Management* 7(2) 1988, 246–263.

17. See Daniel W. Bromley, "Entitlements, Missing Markets, and Environmental Uncertainty," *Journal of Environmental Economics and Management* 17(2) 1989, 181–194.

18. Steven Kelman, "Cost-Benefit Analysis: An Ethical Critique," *Regulation* January/February 1981, 33–40.

19. Alan Williams, "Cost-Benefit Analysis: Bastard Science? And/Or Insidious Poison in the Body Politick?" *Journal of Public Economics* 1(2) 1972, 199–226; and Aidan R. Vining and David L. Weimer, "Welfare Economics as the Foundation for Public Policy Analysis: Incomplete and Flawed but Nevertheless Desirable," *Journal of Socio-Economics* 21(1) 1992, 25–37.

20. For a detailed presentation of multigoal analysis, see David L. Weimer and Aidan R. Vining, *Policy Analysis: Concepts and Practice,* 5th ed. (Upper Saddle River, NJ: Pearson Prentice Hall, 2011), Chapter 15.

21. For a demonstration of the application of various measures of vertical and horizontal equality, see Marcus C. Berliant and Robert P. Strauss, "The Horizontal and Vertical Equity Characteristics of the Federal Individual Income Tax," in *Horizontal Equity, Uncertainty, and Economic Well-Being,* Martin David and Timothy Smeeding, eds. (Chicago: University of Chicago Press, 1985), 179–211.

22. The fact that people routinely donate to charities suggests that, other things equal, most people would be willing to pay something to obtain a distribution of wealth that is more favorable to the currently poor. Ironically, CBA provides a conceptual way to place a dollar value on alternative distributions of wealth: the sum of the willingness of the individual members of society to pay for moving from the status quo distribution of wealth to an alternative one. Unfortunately, it is usually impractical to elicit willingness-to-pay amounts of this sort.

23. For example, Harberger proposes that a dual test be applied: The policy should have positive weighted and unweighted net benefits. Arnold C. Harberger, "On the Use of Distributional Weights in Social Cost-Benefit Analysis," *Journal of Political Economy* 86(2, part 2) 1978, S87–120.

24. For an excellent development of this approach, see Edward M. Gramlich and Michael Wolkoff, "A Procedure for Evaluating Income Distribution Policies," *Journal of Human Resources* 14(3) 1979, 319–350.

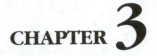

Microeconomic Foundations of Cost-Benefit Analysis

Microeconomic theory provides the basic technical foundations for CBA. This chapter begins with a review of the major concepts of microeconomic theory as they apply to the measurement of social costs and benefits. Most of these concepts should be at least somewhat familiar from your previous exposure to economics. After that we move to welfare economics, which concerns the normative evaluation of markets and of policies. We explain how to use microeconomic theory to assess benefits, costs, and net social benefits in CBA.

For purposes of simplicity, we assume the presence of perfect competition throughout this chapter. Specifically, we assume that there are so many buyers and sellers in the market that no one can individually affect prices, that buyers and sellers can easily enter and exit the market, that the goods sold are homogeneous (i.e., identical), that there is an absence of transaction costs, that information is perfect, and that private costs and benefits are identical to social costs and benefits (i.e., there are no externalities). Chapter 4 considers how to measure benefits and costs when some of these assumptions do not hold; that is, various forms of market failure are present.

DEMAND CURVES

An individual's *ordinary demand curve* (schedule) indicates the quantities of a good that the individual wishes to purchase at various prices. The market demand curve is the horizontal sum of all individual demand curves. It indicates the aggregate quantities of a good that all individuals in the market wish to purchase at various prices.

In contrast, a market *inverse demand curve,* which is illustrated by line D in Figure 3-1, has price as a function of quantity. The vertical axis (labeled Price) can be interpreted as the highest price someone is willing to pay for an additional unit of the good. A standard assumption in economics is that demand curves slope downward. The rationale for this assumption is based on the principle of *diminishing marginal utility*; each additional unit of the good is valued slightly less by each consumer than the preceding unit. For that reason, each consumer is willing to pay less for another unit than for the preceding unit. Indeed, at some point, each consumer would be unwilling to pay anything for an additional unit; his or her demand would be sated.

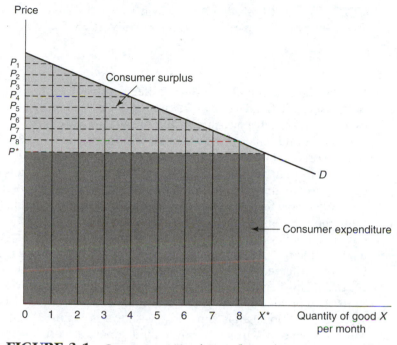

FIGURE 3-1 Consumers' Total Benefits and Consumer Surplus

In Figure 3-1 one member of society is willing to pay a price of P_1 for one unit of good X. Also, there is a person (possibly the same person who is willing to pay P_1 for the first unit) who would pay P_2 for a second unit of good X, and there is someone who would pay P_3 for a third unit of X, and so forth.[1] Each additional unit is valued at an amount given by the height of the inverse demand curve. The sum of all these willingness to pay amounts equals the total willingness to pay (WTP) for the good by all the members of society. It is approximately equivalent to summing the unit-wide rectangles under the demand curve. For X^* units it equals the area under the inverse demand curve from the origin to X^*, which is represented by the sum of the light and dark shaded areas.

As stated in Chapter 2, WTP is an appropriate measure of the benefit of a good or service. Since, P_1 measures the marginal benefit of the first unit, P_2 measures the marginal benefit of the second unit, and so on, the sum of X^* marginal benefits measures the *total benefits* (B) society would obtain from consuming X^* units of good X.[2] Thus, the area under the demand curve, which consists of the sum of the lightly and darkly shaded areas, measures the *total benefits* (B) society would receive from consuming X^* units of good X.

Consumer Surplus and Changes in Consumers' Surplus

In a competitive market consumers pay the market price, which we denote as P^*. Thus, consumers spend P^*X^*, represented by the darkly shaded area, to consume X^* units. The *net benefit* to consumers equals the total benefits (B) less consumers' actual expenditures

(P^*X^*). This lightly shaded area, which equals the area below the demand curve but above the price line, is called *consumer surplus (CS):*

$$CS = B - P^*X^* \qquad \qquad \textbf{(3.1)}$$

Consumer surplus (sometimes called *consumers' surplus*) is one of the basic concepts used in CBA. Under most circumstances, changes in consumer surplus can be used as a reasonable measure of the benefits to consumers of a policy change. In the appendix to this chapter, we examine the circumstances under which changes in consumer surplus do provide close approximations to willingness-to-pay values and the circumstances under which they do not. The major conclusion is that, in most instances, such approximations are sufficiently accurate for CBA purposes.

To see how the concept of consumer surplus can be used in CBA, suppose that initially the price and quantity consumed are given by P^* and Q^*, respectively, and then consider a policy that results in a price change. For example, as shown in Figure 3-2(a), a policy that reduces the price of good X from P^* to P_1 would result in a benefit to consumers (an increase in consumer surplus) equal to the area of the shaded trapezoid P^*ABP_1. This benefit results because existing consumers pay a lower price for the X^* units they previously purchased, and some consumers gain from the consumption of $X_1 - X^*$ additional units. Similarly, as shown in Figure 3-2(b), a policy that increases the price of good X from P^* to P_2 would impose a "cost" on consumers (a loss in consumer surplus) equal to the area of the shaded trapezoid P_2ABP^*.

Suppose that a policy results in a price decrease, as in Figure 3-2(a). Let $\Delta P = P_1 - P^* < 0$ denote the change in price and let $\Delta X = X_1 - X^* > 0$ denote the change in the

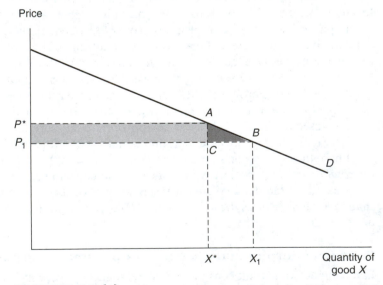

FIGURE 3-2(a)   Change in Consumer Surplus Due to a Price Decrease

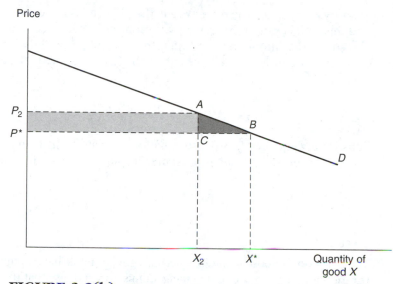

FIGURE 3-2(b)   Change in Consumer Surplus Due to a Price Increase

quantity of good X consumed. If the demand curve is linear, then the change in consumer surplus, ΔCS, can be readily computed by the following formula:

$$\Delta CS = -(\Delta P)(X^*) - \tfrac{1}{2}(\Delta X)(\Delta P) \qquad (3.2)$$

If the price of X increases by $\Delta P = P_2 - P^* > 0$, as in Figure 3-2(b), the quantity of good X consumed changes by $\Delta X = X_2 - X^* < 0$ and if the demand curve is linear, then the change in consumer surplus, ΔCS, can also be readily computed from equation (3.2). In fact, this formula usually provides a good approximation to the change in consumer surplus even if the demand curve is not linear.

Sometimes the analyst may not know the demand curve and, therefore, may not know directly how many units will be demanded after a price change, but she may know the (own) *price elasticity of demand*, E_d. The price elasticity of demand is defined as the percentage change in quantity demanded that results from a 1 percent increase in price. Formally:[3]

$$E_d = \frac{P}{X}\frac{dX}{dP} \qquad (3.3a)$$

Because demand curves slope downward, the price elasticity of demand is always negative. All things being equal, as the slope of the demand curve *increases* (i.e., it becomes steeper—more negative), the elasticity *decreases* (become more negative). This is cumbersome. To simplify, we follow economists' usual practice of talking about an elasticity as if it were positive, in effect taking the absolute value. We say that the elasticity *increases* as the slope of the ordinary demand curve *increases*. Also, the more responsive quantity is to a change in price, we say that demand is more elastic. Noneconomists may find this a bit confusing at first, but everyone soon gets used to it.

Given the initial price and quantity, P^* and X^*, and defining ΔX and ΔP as the changes in quantities and prices, then the price elasticity of demand approximately equals:

$$E_d = \frac{P^*}{X^*} \frac{\Delta X}{\Delta P} \qquad (3.3b)$$

Substituting equation (3.3b) into equation (3.2) and rearranging provides the following expression for the change in consumer surplus due to a price change:

$$\Delta CS = -X^* \Delta P - \frac{E_d X^* (\Delta P)^2}{2P^*} \qquad (3.4)$$

Taxes

Taxes are very important in CBA because governments have to finance their projects, and taxation is a main source of financing. Let us now suppose that the price increase from P^* to P_2 shown in Figure 3-2(b) results from a government-imposed excise tax, where each unit of X is taxed by an amount equal to the difference between the old and the new price $(P_2 - P^*)$. In this case, the rectangular part of the trapezoid in Figure 3-2(b), P_2ACP^*, represents the tax revenue collected. It can be viewed as a *transfer* from consumers of X to the government. It is called a transfer because, from the perspective of society as a whole, its net impact is zero: consumers pay the tax, but this cost is offset by an identical benefit received by the government.[4]

The triangular part of the trapezoid, ABC, is a cost of the tax, however. It represents lost consumer surplus for which there is no offsetting benefit accruing to some other part of society. This pure loss in consumer surplus is an example of *deadweight loss*.[5] It results from a distortion in economic behavior from the competitive equilibrium. The tax causes some consumers to purchase less output than they would in the absence of the tax because, inclusive of the tax, the price now exceeds those consumers' WTP. Those consumers, who in the absence of the tax would collectively have purchased $X^* - X_2$ units of the good, and received the consumer surplus represented by the triangular area, ABC, lose this consumer surplus.

It follows from equation (3.4) that the deadweight loss resulting from a price change is given approximately by:

$$\Delta DWL = -\frac{E_d X^* (\Delta P)^2}{2P^*} \qquad (3.5)$$

If the change in price is due to a unit tax, t, then the deadweight loss is:

$$\Delta DWL = -\frac{E_d X^* t^2}{2P^*} \qquad (3.6)$$

There will always be a deadweight loss if a government imposes a tax on a good sold in a competitive market. Of particular interest is the amount of the *leakage,* which equals the ratio of the deadweight loss due to the tax to the amount of tax revenue collected. If the price increase in Figure 3-2(b) is due to a tax, the leakage equals area ABC divided by area P_2ACP^*, which equals:

$$\text{Leakage} = -\frac{E_d t}{2P^*(1 + \Delta X/X^*)} \qquad (3.7)$$

If the change in output is relatively small, then the following simple formula provides a very slight overestimate of the leakage:

$$\text{Leakage} = -\frac{E_d t}{2P^*} \qquad (3.8)$$

The implications of this result for CBA are discussed later in this chapter in the section on government surplus.

SUPPLY CURVES

In CBA, as Chapter 2 pointed out, costs are opportunity costs. Figure 3-3 presents a standard U-shaped *marginal cost (MC)* curve for an individual firm, where costs are opportunity costs. This curve pertains to costs in the short run, when at least one factor of production, for example capital, is fixed. We later consider the long run where all factors

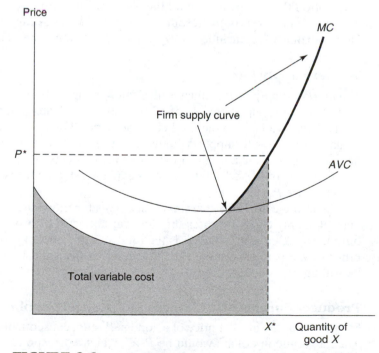

FIGURE 3-3 Individual Firm's Supply Curve

of production can vary. As is well known, the *MC* curve passes through the firm's *average variable cost (AVC)* curve at its lowest point, as shown in Figure 3-3. The rising part of the *MC* curve reflects *diminishing marginal returns*—the phenomenon that, given at least one fixed factor of production (say, capital), diminishing factor returns must eventually occur as output expands and increasing amounts of the variable factors of production (say, labor) are used with the fixed factor(s), or it reflects rising opportunity costs of a variable factor of production as more units of that factor are employed.

Just as the demand curve indicates the marginal benefit of each additional unit of a good consumed, the supply curve indicates the marginal cost of each additional unit of the good produced. Thus, the area under the firm's marginal cost curve represents the firm's *total variable cost* (*VC*) of producing a given amount of good X, say X^*.

The upward-sloping segment of the firm's marginal cost curve above the firm's *AVC* corresponds to the *firm's supply curve* in a competitive market. If the price were lower than the firm's average variable cost, then the firm could not cover its average variable cost and would shut down, rather than produce any output. At a price above average variable cost, however, the upward-sloping segment of the marginal cost curve determines how much output the firm will produce at any given price. For example, at a price of P^*, the firm would maximize profit by producing at X^*. If it produced more output than X^*, it would take in less in additional revenue than the additional cost it would incur. If it produced less output than X^*, it would lose more in revenue than it would save in costs.

As indicated in Chapter 2, the concept of opportunity cost is critical to CBA. The cost of a policy or project reflects the opportunity costs incurred by various members of society to implement the policy. Consequently, the cost curve in Figure 3-3 is drawn under the assumption that the owners of all the resources the firm uses are paid prices equal to the opportunity costs of the resources. For such factors as capital and entrepreneurship, the opportunity cost include a *normal return*,[6] reflecting their best alternative use.[7]

Market Supply Curve

The *market supply curve*, which is illustrated in Figure 3-4, can be derived by summing horizontally the supply curves of all the individual firms in a market. It indicates the total supply available to the market at each price. For example, at price P_1 firms in aggregate are willing to supply X_1 units. Because individual firm supply curves are based on marginal cost, the market supply curve also reflects marginal cost. For example, the marginal cost of the X_1th unit is P_1. This explains why the firms are willing to supply X_1 units at price P_1.

As in the case of the marginal cost curves for individual firms, the area under the market supply curve indicates the total variable cost of producing a given amount of output, say X^*. The area $0abX^*$ is the total variable cost of supplying X^* units. Put another way, it is the minimum total revenue that firms must receive before they would be willing to produce output X^*.

Producer Surplus and Changes in Producer Surplus

Suppose that the market price of a good is P^* and, consequently, firms supply X^* units. Their revenue in dollars would be P^*X^*, which corresponds to the rectangular area $0P^*bX^*$ in Figure 3-4. Their total variable cost (*TVC*) would be $0abX^*$, the darkly

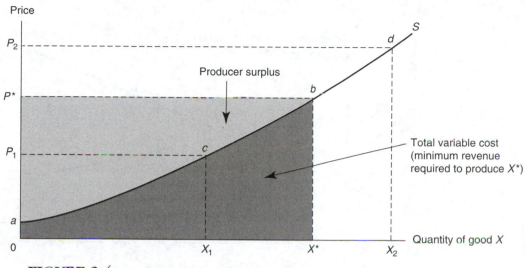

FIGURE 3-4   Market Supply Curve

shaded area in Figure 3-4. The difference between these two areas, the lightly shaded area aP^*b, is called *producer surplus (PS)*:

$$PS = P^*X^* - TVC \tag{3.9}$$

Producer surplus measures the benefit going to firms (or their factors of production). It equals the difference between actual revenues and the minimum total revenue that firms in the market represented in Figure 3-4 must receive before they would be willing to produce X^* units at a price of P^*.

Producer surplus is the supply-side equivalent to consumer surplus. Just as changes in prices resulting from government policies have impacts on consumers that can be valued in terms of changes in consumer surplus, price changes also result in impacts on producers that can be valued in terms of changes in producer surplus. For example, referring again to Figure 3-4, a decrease in the market price from P^* to P_1 decreases producer surplus by P^*bcP_1 to P_1ca, and an increase in price from P^* to P_2 increases producer surplus by P_2dbP^* to P_2da.

SOCIAL SURPLUS AND ALLOCATIVE EFFICIENCY[8]

Let us now look at the market as a whole. In the absence of impacts on government, the sum of consumer surplus and producer surplus is called *social surplus (SS)*; sometimes it is called *total surplus:*

$$SS = CS + PS \tag{3.10}$$

Social surplus is illustrated in Figure 3-5, which depicts both a market demand curve and a market supply curve in the same graph. In this graph, which once again is drawn under the assumption of perfect competition, equilibrium occurs at a price of P^* and a

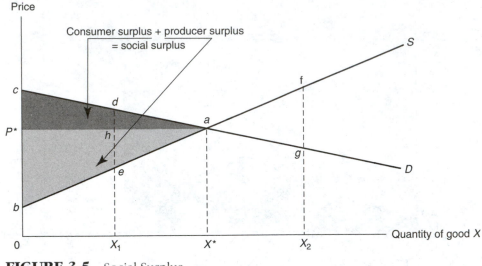

FIGURE 3-5   Social Surplus

quantity of X^*. Consumer surplus is the area caP^*, producer surplus is the area P^*ab, and social surplus is the sum of these areas, cab.

Now, net social benefits equals the difference between total consumer benefits and total producer costs. Total consumer benefits equal the area under the demand curve, caX^*0, while total costs equal total variable costs, the area under the supply curve, baX^*0.[9] The difference is the area cab. This formulation makes it clear that social surplus equals net social benefits.

Remembering that the demand curve reflects marginal benefits (MB) and the supply curve reflects marginal cost (MC), at the competitive equilibrium demand equals supply and marginal benefits equals marginal cost. Therefore, net social benefits are maximized.[10] Thus, in a well-functioning, perfectly competitive market net social benefits and social surplus are maximized. The outcome is *Pareto efficient*: it is not possible to make someone better off without making someone else worse off. We also say that it is *allocatively efficient (or economically efficient)* because social surplus is maximized. The fact that a competitive equilibrium is economically efficient is referred to as the first fundamental theorem of welfare economics, clearly reflecting its importance.

In a perfectly competitive market, anything that interferes with the competitive process will reduce allocative efficiency. Suppose, for example, government policy causes output to be restricted to X_1, due, for example, to output quotas. At least some people will be worse off relative to output level X^*. The loss in social surplus at X_1 would equal the triangular area dae—the area between the demand curve (MB) and the supply curve (MC) from X_1 to X^*. Similarly, the loss in social surplus at X_2 would equal the triangular area afg—the area between the demand curve and the supply curve from X^* to X_2. These deadweight losses reflect reductions in social surplus relative to what would be attained in a competitive market (at X^*). Any government policy that moves the market away from the perfectly competitive equilibrium increases deadweight loss and reduces social surplus. Thus, it is only in the presence of market failures that government should consider intervening in a market. Such market failures, however, provide only a *prima facie* reason to intervene. One must do CBA to decide whether to intervene. Potentially, a government policy that moves a distorted market toward the perfectly competitive equilibrium produces net social benefits by increasing social surplus and reducing deadweight loss.

For policy purposes, it is important to note the relationship between price and allocative efficiency. Allocative efficiency is maximized in Figure 3-5 at a price of P^* and a quantity of X^*. At the equilibrium point, *a*, the price paid by consumers equals the marginal cost of producing the good. *Allocative efficiency can be obtained only when the price paid by consumers for a good equals the marginal social cost to society of producing the good.*[11] This important result can be used to formulate efficient pricing policies.

Profits and Factor Surplus

The above formula that measures producer surplus, equation (3.9), is not entirely satisfactory two reasons. First, the formula excludes firms' *fixed costs*. Thus far we have focused on short-term effects where some factors of production were fixed. While some government policies do not change firms' fixed costs, other policies do change them. For example, if the government makes a one-time purchase of concrete to build a road extension, the fixed costs of the firms that provide the concrete would probably not change and the above formulas would apply. On the other hand, for a large, long-term project, such as the Three Gorges Dam in China, all the factors of production (including the number of concrete trucks) would vary. In this situation, changes in fixed costs should be included in the measure of social surplus. We need a way to do this. Note, by the way, if as is usual we focus on annual benefits and annual costs, then the fixed costs may have to be amortized over their useful life or the life of the project. Second, whether or not we include fixed costs, but especially if we do include them, it is easier for most people to think about *profits* than producer surplus.

Fortunately, there is an easy way to deal with both of these concerns. Producer surplus equals *profits* (π) plus *Ricardian rents* going to factors of production, which we call *factor surplus (FS)*.[12] An example of a Ricardian rent is the return going to a particularly productive plot of land in a competitive agricultural market. The farmer may rent this land in which case the rents go to the landlord from whom he rents it or he may own the land in which case he gets them. Or, in a market with minimum wages, rents may go to workers. In either case, we can rewrite equation (3.10) as:

$$SS = CS + \pi + FS \qquad \textbf{(3.11a)}$$

The incremental net social benefit (ΔSS) of a change in policy is given by:

$$\Delta SS = \Delta CS + \Delta \pi + \Delta FS \qquad \textbf{(3.11b)}$$

Much of Canadian competition policy concerns whether proposed mergers should be allowed to go ahead. In these cases, the effect on employees, ΔFS, is assumed to be zero, and the key issue boils down to whether the potential reduction in consumer surplus, ΔCS, is more than offset by increases in profits, $\Delta \pi$. A firm making this argument in a merger hearing is said to be using the "efficiency defense."[13]

GOVERNMENT SURPLUS AND ALLOCATIVE EFFICIENCY

Thus far we have considered the effects of policies on consumers and producers. There is a third important sector in society—government. Impacts on government must also be included. Specifically we should include the net budget impacts on government, which is called *government surplus (GS)*. Financial inflows to government from taxes increase government surplus while financial outflows from expenditures decrease government surplus. When government surplus is not zero, social surplus becomes:

$$SS = CS + PS + GS \qquad (3.12a)$$

The incremental net social benefit (ΔSS) of a change in policy is given by:

$$\Delta SS = \Delta CS + \Delta PS + \Delta GS \qquad (3.12b)$$

In a competitive market, the *net social benefit of a project equals the net government revenue plus the resulting change in the sum of consumer surplus and producer surplus.* Often, government incurs all of the costs of a project and enjoys none of the financial benefits, for example, it may build rent-free housing for disabled people. To simplify, and consistent with our assumption of perfect competition, it is reasonable to assume in this situation that there is no change in producer surplus. The benefit is the change in consumer surplus, the cost is net government expenditure, and the net social benefit equals the benefits minus the costs. That is, $B = \Delta CS$, $C = -\Delta GS$, and $\Delta SS = NSB = B - C$.

Now suppose that government builds housing but charges a maket rent. As before, we assume that there is no change in producer surplus. There are two ways to compute the change in social surplus (or net social benefits). One way measures the benefit as the change in consumer surplus and the cost as the change in government expenditure (i.e., construction costs plus operating costs), as above. The rent paid is a transfer—a cost to consumers but a benefit to government. *The net effect of a transfer is zero. Thus, it may be ignored in the calculation of net social benefits. In fact, including the rent paid to government as part of government surplus would be a mistake.*

An alternative way to compute the NSB involves gross benefits. The *gross benefit* to consumers (B) equals the area under the inverse demand curve. From equation (3.1), $B = \Delta CS + $ Rents. The total cost to society equals the sum of the rents paid by consumers and the project expenditures paid by government. Therefore, the net social benefits are given by $NSB = B - C = \Delta CS - $ Construction costs—Operating expenses, which is the same as before.

This example makes it clear that there are often different ways to calculate net social benefits. In this example, it is possible to measure gross benefits that include consumer expenditures (e.g., rent) if this transfer is also included in the costs. Alternatively, one can focus on changes in consumer surplus, producer surplus and government surplus as expressed in equation (3.12b).

To illustrate direct estimation of equation (3.12b), suppose that initially the perfectly competitive market shown in Figure 3-6 is in equilibrium at a price of P^* and a quantity of X^*. Now suppose that a law is passed guaranteeing sellers a price of P_T. Such a policy has been utilized in otherwise competitive agricultural markets in the United States, such as those for corn and cotton, and is known as *target pricing*. At a

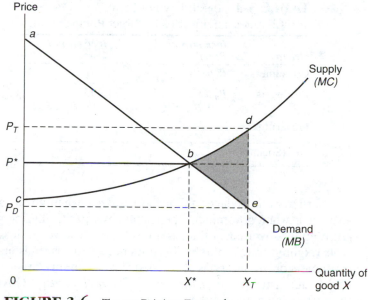

FIGURE 3-6   Target Pricing Example

target price of P_T, sellers desire to sell a quantity of X_T. However, buyers are willing to pay a price of only P_D for this quantity, so this becomes the effective market price. Under target pricing, the gap between P_T and P_D is filled by subsidies paid to sellers by the government. As the marginal cost of producing X_T exceeds marginal benefit for this quantity of good X, a social surplus loss (deadweight loss), corresponding to area bde, results from the policy.

Distributional Implications

The target pricing policy affects buyers, sellers, and the government differently. The incremental benefit, incremental cost, and change in social surplus (net benefit) to each of the three affected groups, and to society as a whole, are presented in a *social accounting ledger* in Table 3-1. Because buyers pay a price of only P_D under the policy, total consumer surplus increases from area abP^* to area aeP_D, a gain of P^*beP_D. Sellers receive an effective price of P_T, causing total producer surplus to increase from area P^*bc to area P_Tdbc, a gain of P_TdbP^*. Government provides subsidies represented by area P_TdeP_D. Subtracting the GS cost from the CS and PS gains, as suggested by equation (3.12), gives a deadweight loss resulting from the policy equal to area bde. Estimates of the actual social cost of agricultural price supports in the U.S. are provided in Exhibit 3-1.

As shown in the right hand column of Table 3-1, the government subsidy (P_TdeP_D) can be broken down into three areas: the consumer surplus gain, the producer surplus gain, and the deadweight loss. While area bde represents the net social loss from the policy, the remainder of the subsidy represent transfers from taxpayers to buyers and sellers. Because the benefits and costs associated with transfers are fully offsetting, they have no net impact on the change in social surplus as defined above in equation (3.12b).

TABLE 3-1   Breakdown of Incremental Benefits, Incremental Costs, and Changes in Surpluses in Target Pricing Example

Group	Incremental Benefit	Incremental Cost	Change in Surplus
Consumers	P^*beP_D		P^*beP_D
Producers	$P_T dX_T O$ $- P^*bX^*O$	$bdX_T X^*$ $- P_T deP_D$	$P_T dbP^*$
Government			$-P_T deP_D$
Net (Social)			$-bde$

Earlier we introduced the idea of *leakage* when government raises funds. It may also occur when government spends money. Specifically, the proportion of each dollar given up by government that, as a result of a deadweight loss (and any administrative costs required to raise the funds), does not accrue as transfers to any other group (i.e., consumers or producers) is also called leakage. In this target pricing example, which ignores administrative costs, the leakage is $bde/P_T deP_D$. Obviously, 1 - leakage equals the proportion of the government subsidy that is transferred to consumers or producers.

Marginal Excess Tax Burden

Most government policies and projects require government expenditure. This expenditure has to be financed in some way. In this chapter, we have shown that an excise tax on a good usually results in deadweight loss. Taxes on individuals also generally result in a deadweight loss. Indeed, social surplus is usually (but not always) lost when government taxes consumers, taxpayers, or producers.

EXHIBIT 3-1

The magnitudes of the inefficiencies of agricultural price supports in the United States have at times been very large. For example, Gordon C. Rausser estimated the economic impacts of price support programs for wheat, corn, cotton, peanuts, and dairy products during the mid-1980s. He estimated additional annual costs to consumers of between $3.27 billion and $4.57 billion, annual transfers to producers of between $12.8 billion and $14.9 billion, and annual costs to taxpayers of between $13.5 billion and $15.7 billion. The annual net social cost of these effects on consumers, producers, and taxpayers was between $1.9 billion and $7.4 billion. That is, the social surplus loss of these policies was several billion dollars annually.

The Federal Agricultural Improvement and Reform Act of 1996, the so-called Freedom to Farm Act, called for phasing out price supports by 2002. Beginning in 1998 with falling world agricultural prices, Congress began reversing the phase-out of price supports. By fiscal year 2001 direct government subsidies to farmers had risen to $20 billion annually.

Sources: Adapted from Gordon C. Rausser, "Predatory Versus Productive Government: The Case of U.S. Agricultural Policies," *Journal of Economic Perspectives* 6(3) 1992, 133–157; and David Orden, "Reform's Stunted Crop: Congress Re-Embraces Agricultural Subsidies," *Regulation* 25(1) 2002, 26–32.

Because there are numerous sources of deadweight loss in addition to taxes, economists refer to the deadweight loss that results specifically from a tax as *excess tax burden*. The change in deadweight loss resulting from raising an additional dollar of tax revenue is called the *marginal excess tax burden* (METB). The size of the METB depends on the magnitude of the behavioral response to a tax change, for example, the extent to which consumer purchases change due to an excise tax or the change in work hours due to a tax on earnings.[14] Exhibit 3-2 presents a hypothetical, but not implausible, illustration of computing the average social cost of taxing higher-income households and redistributing the money to lower-income households. In this illustration, it costs, on average, $1.63 to transfer each dollar (i.e., the METB = 0.63). Our suggested estimates of the METB, which vary according to the nature of the tax, are given in Chapter 16.

Allocative Efficiency and the METB

Because raising government revenue through taxation inevitably involves a deadweight loss, changes in government revenue do not fully capture their efficiency implications. A program that costs the government a dollar actually costs society in aggregate (1 + METB). Similarly, a program that yields a dollar of government revenue allows it to avoid a dollar of taxation and therefore benefits society in aggregate (1 + METB). Taking this efficiency effect into account, equation (3.12) becomes:

$$SS = CS + PS + (1 + METB)GS \qquad \textbf{(3.13a)}$$
$$\Delta SS = \Delta CS + \Delta PS + (1 + METB)\Delta GS \qquad \textbf{(3.13b)}$$

In other words, in order to measure the allocative efficiency impacts of a project and to compute its net social benefits, government project expenditures and revenues should be multiplied by one plus the marginal excess tax burden.

EXHIBIT 3-2

The following table, which was adopted with modifications from a study by Edgar Browning, is based on a hypothetical society with only five households. The idea is to tax everyone to obtain $1,350 in additional revenue and then distribute this equally to everyone. In effect, as shown in column 6, $270 is transferred from the two richest households to the two poorest households. As shown in column 8, however, the real incomes of the two poorest households increase by $240 in aggregate, whereas the real incomes of the three richest households decrease by $390. Thus, it costs society $390/$240 = $1.63 in lost income for every dollar transferred, ignoring administrative costs.

For purposes of the illustration, it is assumed that all households initially work 2,000 hours a year and face a marginal tax rate of 40 percent. Thus, as indicated in column 2, the gross before-tax hourly wage rate of household A is $5 ($10,000/2,000), but its after-tax net wage rate is only $3 ($5 × 0.6). The gross and net hourly wage rates for the remaining four households may be similarly computed. It is further assumed that the compensated labor supply elasticity for all households is 0.15, a value that is consistent with empirical estimates presented in Chapter 12. In other words, it is assumed that a 1 percent change in net wages, holding income constant,

(continued)

will cause households to change their hours worked by 0.15 percent.

Suppose now that the government introduces a separate income tax of 1 percent that increases each household's marginal tax rate from 40 to 41 percent. This reduces each household's net after-tax wage rate by 1.67 percent (i.e., 0.01/0.60 = 0.0167). As a consequence, hours worked fall by 0.25 percent (0.15 × 0.0167 × 0.0025), or 5 hours per year. Hence, as shown in column 3, earnings also fall by 0.25 percent.

Net additional tax revenue is given in column 4. For example, household A initially paid taxes of $4,000 ($10,000 × 0.4), while after the new income tax, it paid taxes of about $4,090 ($9,975 × 0.41), an increase of approximately $90. The total of $1,350 in additional tax revenue is divided equally, and $270 is distributed to each household. The net transfer (column 5 − column 4) is given in column 6.

Column 7 presents the total change in disposable income, which is obtained by adding columns 3 and 6. The net incomes of the three richest households have been reduced by $570 in aggregate, while the net incomes of the two poorest families have been increased by a total of only $195. But all families are now working less and enjoying more leisure. Assuming that the value of additional leisure equals the after-tax net wage rate, household A receives a leisure gain valued at $15 ($3 × 5 hours), household B receives a leisure gain valued at $30 ($6 × 5 hours), and so forth. The total change in real income (including the value of the gain in leisure) is given in column 8. The real incomes of households A and B increase by $240 in aggregate, while the incomes of households C, D, and E decrease by $390.

The Marginal Cost of Redistribution

Household (1)	Initial (Gross) Earnings (2)	Net Change in Earnings (3)	Additional Tax Revenue* (4)	Transfer (5)	Net Transfer (6)	Change in Disposable Income (7)	Change in Real Income (8)
A	10,000	−25	90	270	180	155	170
B	20,000	−50	180	270	90	40	70
C	30,000	−75	270	270	0	−75	−30
D	40,000	−100	360	270	−90	−190	−130
E	50,000	−125	450	270	−180	−305	−230
Total	150,000	−375	1,350	1,350	0	−375	−150

*These figures are rounded to the nearest $10.
Source: Adapted from Edgar K. Browning, "The Marginal Cost of Redistribution," *Public Finance Quarterly* 21(1) 1993, 3–32, Table 1 at p. 5. Reprinted by permission of Sage Publications, Inc.

MEASURING CHANGES IN WELFARE

This chapter focuses on allocative efficiency and the measurement of net social benefits. Welfare, however, concerns allocative efficiency and *equity*. Conceptually, it is straightforward to generalize equation (3.13b) so that it measures changes in welfare:

$$\Delta W = \gamma_c \Delta CS + \gamma_p \, \Delta \pi + \gamma_f \Delta FS + \gamma_g \Delta GS \qquad (3.14)$$

━━━━━━━━━━━━━ **EXHIBIT 3-3** ━━━━━━━━━━━━━

Boardman and colleagues estimated the welfare gains from the privatization of Canadian National (CN) Railway in 1995. This was one of the largest rail privatizations in history. A unique feature of the study is that the authors were able to create a more credible counterfactual than in other privatization studies based on cost data from Canadian Pacific Railway (CP). Boardman and colleagues argued that the benefit to consumers (shippers) was zero because a variety of evidence suggests that privatization had no impact on CN's or CP's prices or output. The sole factor of production of interest was employees. Employment decreased at CN following privatization, but the rate of decrease in employment was slower after 1992 than before 1992 (when the privatization was announced). Following privatization, wages and salaries at CN increased faster than at CP. Thus, there is no clear evidence that employees were better or worse off as a result of privatization. Attention focused on firms (and their shareholders) and the Canadian government. Using their preferred estimate of the counterfactual, Boardman and colleagues estimated that the increase in profits to foreign (non-Canadian) shareholders was $4.46 billion, the increase in profits to Canadian shareholders was $3.69 billion, and the increase in government surplus (to the Canadian government) was $6.90 billion. Following usual practice in CBA and assigning equal welfare weights to profits and governments (i.e., $\gamma_p = \gamma_g = 1$) implies that the net social benefit equals $15.06 billion. Assuming that only Canadians have standing suggests that the net social benefit to Canadians was $10.59 billion ($6.90 billion + $3.69 billion). As noted in the text, however, there are efficiency arguments for setting $\gamma_g = 1 +$ METB. Boardman and colleagues also argue that there are efficiency arguments for setting $\gamma_p = 1 +$ *shadow price of capital*, a topic that we discuss in detail in Chapter 10. They suggest $\gamma_g = 1.4$ and $\gamma_p = 1.16$, implying that the net benefit to Canadians of the privatization of CN equaled $13.94 billion.

Source: Anthony E. Boardman, Claude Laurin, Mark A. Moore, and Aidan R. Vining, "A Cost-Benefit Analysis of the Privatization of Canadian National Railway," *Canadian Public Policy* 35(1) 2009, 59–83.

where $\gamma_c, \gamma_p, \gamma_f,$ and γ_g are welfare weights for consumers, producers, factors of production, and government, respectively. These parameters can reflect efficiency or equity considerations.[15] If $\gamma_c = \gamma_p = \gamma_f = 1$ and $\gamma_g = 1 +$ METB, then equation (3.14) becomes equation (3.13b), and it measures net social benefits. This can be justified on allocative efficiency grounds. Any other set of weights requires consideration of equity. This issue is discussed in more detail in Chapter 19. Some studies have used equation (3.14) to measure changes in welfare due to privatization as is illustrated in Exhibit 3-3.

CONCLUSIONS

The objective of CBA is more efficient allocation of resources. This chapter has reviewed the major principles from microeconomics and welfare economics that provide the technical foundation for cost-benefit analysis. The key concept is that in conducting a CBA one must estimate the changes in social surplus that result when new policies, programs, or projects are implemented. The change in social surplus, provides a measure of the change in allocative efficiency (or net social benefits). Social surplus is often expressed as the sum of consumer surplus, producer surplus, and government surplus. However, projects have to be financed and are often financed by taxes, and all taxes create a deadweight loss. To account for the efficiency impacts of taxes, government inflows or outflows should be multiplied by 1 + METB.

This chapter assumes that markets are initially perfectly competitive. Chapters 4 and 5 make use of the concepts introduced in this chapter to develop measures of benefits and costs that are conceptually appropriate under numerous different circumstances.

Consumer Surplus and Willingness to Pay

Earlier in this chapter, we asserted that under most circumstances, estimates of changes in consumer surplus, as measured by demand curves, can be used in CBA as reasonable approximations of individuals' WTP to obtain or to avoid the effects of policy changes. In this appendix, we examine the circumstances under which measured changes in consumer surplus do in fact provide a close approximation to WTP and the circumstances under which they do not. For purposes of illustration, we specifically focus on the link between the amount of money a consumer would be willing to pay to avoid a given price increase and estimates based on the demand curve of the loss in the consumer's surplus resulting from the price increase.

Compensating Variation

The maximum amount of money that consumers would be willing to pay to avoid a price increase is the amount required to return them to the same level of utility they enjoyed prior to the change in price, an amount called *compensating variation*. If the consumers had to spend any more than the value of their compensating variation, then they would be worse off paying to avoid the increase than allowing it to occur. If they could spend any less, then they would be better off paying to avoid the increase, rather than allowing it to occur. Hence, for a loss in consumer surplus resulting from a price increase to equal the consumers' WTP to avoid the price increase, it has to correspond exactly to the compensating variation value associated with the price increase.

These assertions are most readily demonstrated by an indifference curve analysis. Such an analysis is presented in Figure 3A-1(a). This diagram represents a consumer who faces a

world with only two goods, X and Y. The straight lines in the diagram are budget constraints. The particular budget constraint that the consumer faces depends upon the consumer's income level and on the relative prices of goods X and Y. The greater the consumer's income, the more of X and Y the consumer can afford and, consequently, the greater the distance the budget constraint will be from the origin, 0. Thus, for example, the budget constraint JK represents a higher income level than the budget constraint GI, and the budget constraint GH represents a higher income level than the budget constrain LK. The slope of the consumer's budget constraint indicates how many additional units of Y can be obtained if one less unit of X is purchased. Thus, holding everything else constant, the slope of the budget constraint is negative and depends upon the price of X relative to the price of Y. Consequently, if the price of X rises relative to that of Y, the consumer's budget constraint will become more steeply sloped, changing, for example, from budget constraint GH to budget constraint GI. As can be seen, such a change means that a larger number of units of Y can be purchased in exchange for each unit of X that the consumer gives up.

The curved lines in Figure 3A-1(a) are *indifference curves*. All points along a single indifference curve represent combinations of goods X and Y that provide the consumer with equal levels of utility. Thus, the consumer is indifferent between points b and d on U_0 or points a and c on U_1. The further an indifference curve is from the origin, the greater the level of utility. Thus, the consumer would prefer any point on indifference curve U_1 (e.g., point a) to any point on indifference curve U_0 (e.g., point b). This is not surprising in this case because more of both good X and good Y would be consumed at point a than at point b.

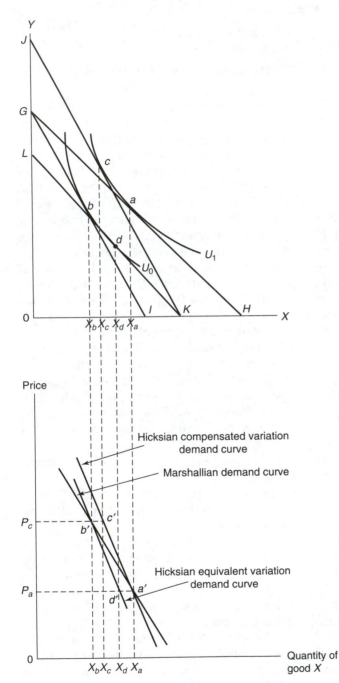

FIGURE 3A-1(a) Indifference Curve Analysis of a Price Change

FIGURE 3A-1(b) Demand Curve Analysis of Price Change

The indifference curves in Figure 3A-1(a) are negatively sloped because any movement along an indifference curve definitionally represents a situation whereby an increase in the consumption of one good is offset by a sufficient reduction in the consumption of the other good such that the consumer's level of utility is left unchanged.[1] Were the individual to consume either more of both goods or less of both goods, the level of utility would obviously change.

The fact that the indifference curves are convex in shape (i.e., they bend inward toward the origin) reflects diminishing marginal utility—as the consumer consumes more of one good, she becomes increasingly less willing to give up consumption of an additional unit of the other good. For example, the convex shape of indifference curve U_0 implies that at point *b* the consumer would be willing to give up more units of *Y* in order to consume one additional unit of *X* than she would at point *d*.

Now let us assume that good *X* in Figure 3A-1(a) is a product on which the consumer spends only a small fraction of her total income, for example, movie tickets, and good *Y* is a composite good on which the consumer spends the rest of her income. Under these circumstances, good *Y* is a reasonable approximation of the consumer's total money income. Consequently, the slope of a budget constraint in the figure would indicate the price of good *X*, that is, the amount of money income (i.e., good *Y*) the consumer would have to give up to obtain one more unit of *X*.

Assume that the consumer initially faces budget constraint *GH*. She will then choose point *a* on indifference curve U_1. Point *a* represents an equilibrium because the consumer cannot increase her utility by moving to any alternative point and, hence, has no incentive to do so.[2] Now assume that as a result of a government policy, the price of good *X* is doubled.[3] This changes the consumer's equilibrium to point *b* on a more steeply sloped budget constraint, *GI*, and a lower indifference curve, U_0. Thus, the consumer's consumption of good *X* falls from X_a to X_b.[4]

If the consumer were paid a lump sum of money sufficient to compensate her entirely for the price increase in *X*, then this payment would shift the budget constraint in a parallel movement from *GI* to *JK*, allowing her to move back to the original indifference curve, U_1. However, the consumer would now choose point *c* (rather

than *a*) and would consume X_c of the good (rather than X_a). As the vertical distance between the two parallel budget constraints (i.e., the difference between points *G* and *J* on the vertical axis) represents the amount of good *Y* (that is, money income) that the consumer would have to be paid in order to lose no utility as a result of the price increase, this distance measures the compensating variation associated with the price increase.

As asserted previously, this compensating variation value is the maximum amount that the consumer would be willing to pay to avoid the price increase. To see this, suppose that the price increase occurs and that the consumer is fully compensated for it. Now imagine that if she is willing to pay all the compensation she received—that is, the full value of her compensating variation—the price increase will be revoked. Will she accept or reject this offer? She will, in fact, be indifferent to it. If she accepts the offer, then she will return to her initial equilibrium at point *a* on indifference curve U_1; if she rejects it, then she will remain at point *c*, which is also on U_1. Thus, the compensation value represents the maximum amount the consumer would be willing to pay to avoid the price increase. If she could pay a bit less to revoke the price increase, then she would definitely do so. If she had to pay a bit more, then she would prefer to accept the increase.

Income and Substitution Effects

Given the information contained in Figure 3A-1(a), the total effect of the increase in the price of *X* on the consumer's demand for good *X* (i.e., the change from X_a to X_b) can be decomposed into two separate effects: a *compensated substitution effect* and an *income effect*.[5] The compensated substitution effect is represented in Figure 3A-1(a) as the change in demand from X_a to X_c. It allows us to examine the effect of a change in the price of *X* on the demand for *X* if the individual were exactly compensated for any losses of utility she suffers as a result of the price increase and, as a consequence, remained on indifference curve U_1. The compensated substitution effect always causes the demand for a good to change in the opposite direction from a change in the price of the good. For example, holding the consumer's level of utility constant, an increase in the price of good X causes her to substitute some of the now relatively less expensive good Y for good X. Hence, as shown in the figure, X_c is smaller than X_a.

The income effect is represented in Figure 3A-1(a) as the change in demand from X_c to X_b and results because the increase in the price of good X reduces the consumer's disposable income. If, as the figure implies, X is a *normal good*—that is, if purchases of the good and disposable income are positively related—then the consumer will purchase less of it. Hence, X_b is smaller than X_c. Thus, like the substitution effect, the income effect associated with the price increase will also cause the consumer to reduce her demand for the good.

Demand Curves

Because the slopes of the budget constraints in Figure 3A-1(a) indicate both the old and the new prices of good X and the points tangent to these budget constraints with indifference curves indicate the amount of the good that the consumer wants at each price, the figure provides information about two points along the consumer's demand curve for X. Indeed, as we know the quantity of output the consumer would demand after the price increase, both if her utility were held constant and if it were not, we can determine the location of pairs of points along two different demand curves. These two pairs of points appear in Figure 3A-1(b) as points a' and c' and as points a' and b', respectively. (Ignore the third pair of points, d' and b', for the moment.) We can approximate the demand curves with straight lines by simply drawing straight lines between the two points in each pair.

The line in Figure 3A-1(b) that connects points a' and b' is a conventional demand schedule of the sort usually emphasized in textbooks. This demand curve, which is known as a *Marshallian*

demand curve, incorporates both the substitution and income effects associated with changes in the price of good X. Statistical efforts by economists to estimate relations between the price of a good and quantities purchased, which are discussed in Chapter 12, are usually attempts to estimate Marshallian demand curves empirically, as this work typically involves trying to hold income, other prices, and other factors constant.

The demand curve in Figure 3A-1(b) that connects points a' and c' keeps utility constant as the price of good X changes and, thus, incorporates only the compensated substitution effect associated with price changes. This demand curve is sometimes called the *utility compensated* or the *Hicksian compensated variation demand curve.* Because Hicksian demand curves are unaffected by income effects, they are usually, as is the case in Figure 3A-1(b), more steeply sloped than Marshallian demand schedules. Unlike Marshallian demand curves, Hicksian demand curves usually cannot be directly estimated using statistical techniques. However, it is often possible to indirectly estimate them by first estimating the Marshallian demand curve and then, in effect, netting out the income effect.[6]

Equivalence of Consumer Surplus and Compensating Variation

Movements up the Hicksian compensated variation demand curve, for example, from P_a to P_c, are equivalent to allowing the price to increase while compensating the consumer with a lump-sum payment of just sufficient size to permit her to remain on her original indifference curve. This lump-sum payment can be measured graphically as either the vertical distance between the two parallel budget constraints in Figure 3A-1(a) (i.e., as the difference between money income at points G and J) or as the change in consumer surplus indicated by the Hicksian compensated variation demand curve in Figure 3A-1(b) (the area $P_a a'c'P_c$). Thus, the change in consumer surplus resulting from a price change measured with a Hicksian compensated variation demand schedule exactly equals the consumer's compensating variation; that is, the maximum amount the consumer would be willing to pay to avoid the price increase.

Hence, it is Hicksian compensated variation demand curves that permit measurement of the compensating variation associated with price changes. To the extent these two demand curves differ, using a Marshallian compensated variation demand curve to measure consumer surplus will result in a biased estimate of compensating variation and, therefore, of WTP. As can be seen from Figure 3A-1(b), the two alternative demand curves do produce different measures of consumer surplus, one that differs by the triangular area $a'b'c'$. For a price increase, the change in consumer surplus is smaller if measured with the Marshallian demand schedule than with a Hicksian compensated variation demand curve; for a price reduction, it is larger.

As previously suggested, the difference between the two types of demand curves is that the Marshallian curve incorporates the income effects associated with price changes, as well as the substitution effects, while the Hicksian curve incorporates only the latter. Thus, the biased estimate of WTP that results from using Marshallian rather than Hicksian demand curves to measure consumer surplus depends upon the size of the income effect associated with a price change. *Usually this income effect and, hence, the bias are small and can be safely ignored in CBA.*[7] This, at least, is the case if the price change is moderate and the good in question accounts for a fairly small part of total consumption. Thus, CBAs of government policies that affect corn, cotton, tobacco, and gasoline prices will generally be little affected by use of Marshallian rather than Hicksian demand curves. However, *the bias could be of some importance for a CBA of a government policy that would result in large price changes in such consumption goods as housing or automobiles or in large changes in wage rates.* Consequently, except for a few instances when it clearly seems inappropriate to do so, throughout the rest of this book we shall assume that the income effects associated with various policy changes are sufficiently small that consumer sur-

pluses that are measured by using Marshallian demand schedules provide reasonable approximations of WTP.

Equivalent Variation as an Alternative to Compensating Variation

In those situations in which the bias should not be ignored, there is an alternative to compensating variation for measuring the welfare effects of price changes that should be used instead because it has more desirable properties: namely, *equivalent variation.*[8]

In terms of Figure 3A-1(a), equivalent variation is the amount of money, GL, that if paid by the consumer would cause her to lose just as much utility as the price increase. If she could pay a bit less, then she would not be as bad off as the price increase makes her. If she had to pay a bit more, then she would be even worse off.

Using the equivalent variation approach, the income effect is represented in Figure 3A-1(a) as the change in demand from X_a to X_d, while the substitution effect is represented as the change in demand from X_d to X_b. Note that, as in the case of the compensating variation approach, both effects that result from the price increase cause the quantity of the good demanded to fall as long as the good is a normal good. Also note that the compensating variation approach measures the substitution effect by holding utility constant at its level *before* the price change was made, while the equivalent variation approach measures the substitution effect holding utility constant *after* the price change. In both cases, however, a Hicksian demand curve can be derived because, holding utility constant, the old and the new prices of good X and the quantity demanded at both prices are all known. Thus, the Hicksian compensated variation demand curve is represented in Figure 3A-1(b) by the line that connects points a' and c' and the Hicksian equivalent variation demand curve is represented by the line that connects points d' and b'. Neither of the Hicksian demand curves are affected by income effects; hence, they are more steeply sloped than the Marshallian demand curve. Compensating variation is represented in Figure 3A-1(b) by the area $P_a a'c'P_c$ and equivalent variation by the area $P_a d'b'P_c$.

As indicated by Figure 3A-1(b), the compensating variation that results from the price increase is larger than the change in consumer surplus measured with the Marshallian demand curve (by the triangular area $a'b'c'$), while the resulting equivalent variation is smaller (by area $b'd'a'$). The opposite would be true in the case of a price decrease. The size of these differences, as previously discussed, depends on the size of the income effect resulting from the change in prices. If they are large, then it is equivalent variation that should ideally be used to measure the change in welfare resulting from a price change, rather than either Marshallian consumer surplus or compensating variation. This is often, but not always, possible if a measure of Marshallian consumer surplus is available.[9]

EXERCISES FOR CHAPTER 3

1. A person's demand for gizmos is given by the following equation:

    $$q = 6 - 0.5p + 0.0002I$$

    where q is the quantity demanded at price p when the person's income is I. Assume initially that the person's income is $40,000.
    a. At what price will demand fall to zero? (This is sometimes called the choke price because it is the price that chokes off demand.)
    b. If the market price for gizmos is $10, how many will be demanded?
    c. At a price of $10, what is the price elasticity of demand for gizmos?
    d. At a price of $10, what is the consumer surplus?
    e. If price rises to $12, how much consumer surplus is lost?
    f. If income were $60,000, what would be the consumer surplus loss from a price rise from $10 to $12?

2. At the current market equilibrium, the price of a good equals $40 and the quantity equals 10 units. At this equilibrium, the price elasticity of supply is 2.0. Assume that the supply curve is linear.
    a. Use the price elasticity and market equilibrium to find the supply curve. (Hint: the supply curve has the following form: $q = a + (\Delta q/\Delta p)p$. First, find the value of $\Delta q/\Delta p$; then, find the value of a.)
    b. Calculate the producer surplus in the market.
    c. Imagine that a policy results in the price falling from $40 to $30. By how much does producer surplus fall?
    d. What fraction of the lost producer surplus is due to the reduction in the quantity supplied and what fraction is due to the fall in price received per unit sold?

3. (This question pertains to Appendix 3-1; instructor-provided spreadsheet recommended.) Imagine a person's utility function over two goods, X and Y, where Y represents dollars. Specifically, assume a Cobb-Douglas utility function:

    $$U(X,Y) = X^a Y^{(1-a)}$$

    where $0 < a < 1$.
    Let the person's budget be B. The feasible amounts of consumption must satisfy the following equation:

    $$B = pX + Y$$

where p is the unit price of X and the price of Y is set to 1.

Solving the budget constraint for Y and substituting into the utility function yields:

$$U = X^a(B - pX)^{(1-a)}$$

Using calculus, it can be shown that utility is maximized by choosing:

$$X = aB/p$$

Also, it can be shown that the area under the Marshallian demand curve for a price increase from p to q yielding a change in consumption of X from x_p to x_q is given by:

$$\Delta CS = [aB\ln(x_q) - px_q] - [aB\ln(x_p) - px_p] - (q - p)x_q$$

When $B = 100$, $a = 0.5$, and $p = .2$, $X = 250$ maximizes utility, which equals 111.80. If price is raised to $p = .3$, X falls to 204.12.

a. Increase B until the utility raises to its initial level. The increase in B needed to return utility to its level before the price increase is the compensating variation for the price increase. (It can be found by guessing values until utility reaches its original level.)

b. Compare ΔCS, as measured with the Marshallian demand curve, to the compensating variation.

NOTES

1. One can envision deriving an inverse demand curve through an auction in which bids are taken on the first unit of a good offered for sale, then on the second unit, then the third unit, and so forth, with successively lower bids obtained for each additional unit of the good that is offered. This kind of auction is called a Dutch auction. Although now done electronically, in years past it was common in Holland to have a mechanical "clock" with hands that started at the bid made on the previous unit and swept through successively lower bids until stopped by an individual who wished to make a bid.

2. The total benefit (B) from consuming X^* units can be obtained by integrating under the (inverse) demand curve, $P(x)$, from the origin to X^*:

$$B = \int_0^{X^*} P(x)\,dx$$

Since the inverse demand curve measures marginal benefits, MB, we can also write:

$$B = \int_0^{X^*} MB(x)\,dx$$

3. If the absolute value of E_d is greater than 1 and, hence, the percentage change in quantity demanded is greater than the percentage change in price, then demand is said to be *elastic*. On the other hand, if the absolute value of E_d is less than

1 and, hence, the percentage change in quantity demanded is smaller than the percentage change in price, then demand is said to be *inelastic*. If the value approaches infinity (i.e., the demand curve is horizontal), then demand is said to be *perfectly elastic*, while if the value is 0 (the demand curve is vertical), then demand is said to be *completely inelastic*. The use of elasticity estimates in conducting CBAs is further described in Chapter 13.

4. The government is not, of course, the ultimate beneficiary of the tax revenues. However, if it simply returned this revenue to consumers, then consumers in aggregate would be compensated for their greater expenditures on the units of the good that they continue to purchase.

5. More generally, with a downward sloping demand (marginal benefit) curve, $MB(x)$, and an upward sloping supply (marginal cost) curve, $MC(x)$, the deadweight loss (DWL) may be defined more formally:

$$DWL = \int_{x^*}^{x_1} (MB(x) - MC(x))\,dx, \quad \text{if } x^* < x_1$$

$$DWL = \int_{x_2}^{x^*} (MB(x) - MC(x))\,dx, \quad \text{if } x_2 < x^*$$

6. By normal return, we simply mean the risk-adjusted market price or rate of return that each

unit of a resource commands under perfect competition.

7. Thus, because we are presently assuming the existence of perfect competition and well-functioning markets, social opportunity costs, as we have defined them, correspond to private economic costs. In the absence of perfect competition (or, if externalities exist), private economic costs may differ from the costs that using resources imposes on society. These latter costs, *social opportunity costs*, are the relevant cost measure for purposes of CBA. The use of shadow pricing to obtain appropriate measures of social opportunity costs when markets are distorted is discussed in Chapter 4.

8. For an accessible discussion of the topics covered in this section and elsewhere in this chapter, and a history of the development of the concept of consumer surplus, see James R. Hines Jr., "Three Sides of Harberger Triangles," *Journal of Economic Perspectives* 13(2) 1999, 167–188.

9. Of course, total costs equal total variable costs plus fixed costs. Here, for simplicity, we assume fixed costs are zero.

10. By definition, $NSB(x) = B(x) - C(x)$. To obtain the value of X that maximizes NSB we differentiate with respect to X and set the result equal to zero:

$$\frac{dNSB}{dX} = \frac{dB}{dX} - \frac{dC}{dX} = 0$$

Which implies

$$\frac{dB}{dX} = \frac{dC}{dX}$$

Thus, net social benefits are maximized when marginal benefit equals marginal cost.

11. In this discussion, we are assuming that marginal (private) costs equal marginal social costs. In Chapter 4, we consider situations where marginal (private) costs do not equal marginal social costs—for example, when externalities exist.

12. For a clear discussion of the distinction between producer surplus, rents and profits see Margaret F. Sanderson and Ralph A. Winter, "Profits Versus Rents in Antitrust Analysis: An Application to the Canadian Waste Services Merger," *Antitrust Law Journal* 70(2) 2002, 485–511.

13. Thomas W. Ross and Ralph A. Winter, "The Efficiency Defense in Merger Law: Economic Foundations and Recent Canadian Developments," *Antitrust Law Journal* 72(2) 2004, 471–503.

14. In some cases, as we discuss in Chapter 4, taxes may increase social surplus. For example, if prior to being taxed a good was overconsumed due to a negative externality, then the introduction of a tax could increase allocative efficiency by reducing the overconsumption. In this case the METB would be negative. More generally, the efficiency implications of interventions depend on the distortions already in the market. For example, Charles Ballard demonstrates that when labor markets for low-income groups are distorted by high effective marginal tax rates, redistributing through wage subsidies can actually result in efficiency gains. Charles L. Ballard, "The Marginal Efficiency Cost of Redistribution," *American Economic Review* 78(5) 1988, 1019–1033.

15. One can argue that these parameters are not unity on distributional (equity) grounds as well as efficiency grounds. For this argument applied to γ_g see, for example, Joel Slemrod and Shlomo Yitzhaki, "Integrating Expenditure and Tax Decisions: The Marginal Cost of Funds and the Marginal Benefits of Projects," *National Tax Journal* 54(2) 2001, 189–201.

APPENDIX NOTES

1. The slope of an indifference curve is called the marginal rate of substitution, where the marginal rate of substitution $\left.\frac{dX}{dP}\right|_{\overline{U}} < 0$ and $\overline{U}$ indicates that utility is being held constant.

2. At equilibrium, the marginal rate of substitution equals the ratio of the price of good X to the price of good Y.

3. Thus, in Figure 3A-1(a), $0I = (1/2)0H$ or $I = H/2$.

4. Depending on the slopes of the indifference curves, the consumption of good Y could either

increase or decrease. As shown in Figure 3A.1(a), it slightly decreases in this particular example.

5. In calculus notation, this decomposition can be represented as follows:

$$\frac{dX}{dP} = \frac{dX}{dP}\Big|_{\overline{U}} - X\frac{dX}{dP}\Big|_{\overline{P}}$$

This equation is known as the *Slutsky equation.* The first term to the right of the equal sign is the substitution effect, where utility is held constant. The second term is the income effect, where prices are held constant, and X is the amount of the good consumed prior to the price change.

6. One way of doing this first requires obtaining estimates of the relation between quantity purchased and prices and the relation between quantity purchased and income and then (as implied by the preceding note) using the Slutsky equation to derive the income-compensated (rather than the utility-compensated) relation between prices and quantity purchased. In practice, however, it is not always feasible to estimate the relation between quantity purchased and income and, hence, to use the Slutsky equation.

7. For analyses of the size of the bias, see Ian J. Irvine and William A. Sims, "Measuring Consumer Surplus with Unknown Hicksian Demands," *American Economic Review* 88(1) 1998, 314–322; Robin W. Boadway and Neil Bruce, *Welfare Economics* (Oxford, UK: Basil Blackwell Ltd., 1984), 216–219; Julian M. Alston and Douglas M. Larson, "Hicksian vs. Marshallian Welfare Measures: Why Do We Do What We Do?" *American Journal of Agricultural Economics* 75(3) 1993, 764–769; Jerry A. Hausman, "Exact Consumer's Surplus and

Deadweight Loss," *American Economic Review* 71(4) 1981, 662–676; and Robert D. Willig, "Consumer's Surplus Without Apology," *American Economic Review* 66(4) 1979, 589–597.

8. Specifically, using compensating variation is only theoretically correct if consumers have homothetic preferences (i.e., the slopes of all indifferent curves are constant along any ray from the origin), which implies that each good in a consumer's utility function has an income elasticity of one. Equivalent variation does not require a similarly restrictive assumption. See George W. McKenzie, *Measuring Economic Welfare: New Methods* (New York: Cambridge University Press, 1983). Also see Marco Becht, "The Theory and Estimation of Individual and Social Welfare Measures," *Journal of Economic Surveys* 9(1) 1995, 53–87; and the references therein.

    Although equivalent variation is an appropriate measure of the welfare change resulting from a price increase or decrease, it has been argued that either compensating surplus or equivalent surplus is more appropriately used when the quantity of a good, rather than its price, increases or decreases. In this appendix, we focus on price rather than quantity changes. For a discussion of when each of the welfare change measures is most appropriately used, as well as a useful graphical presentation of each, see V. Kerry Smith and William H. Desvousges, *Measuring Water Quality Benefits* (Boston: Kluwer-Nijhoff Publishing, 1986), Chapter 2.

9. A fairly simple procedure for using the Slutsky equation to approximate the Hicksian measures of consumer surplus is described by Irvine and Sims ("Measuring Consumer Surplus . . ."). Also, see appendix note 6.

CHAPTER 4

Valuing Benefits and Costs in Primary Markets

A cost-benefit analysis of a project or a change in government policy sums all the benefits resulting from the project or policy and subtracts all the associated costs. Doing this requires that the values of all these benefits and costs are measured in monetary terms. Although this is often difficult to accomplish in practice, in principle it would be relatively straightforward if the changes in consumer surplus and producer surplus resulting from a change in government policy, as well as the policy's effects on government revenues, could be determined. Under most circumstances, as indicated in Chapter 3, it is changes in these values that provide conceptually correct measures of the monetary value of a government policy's benefits and costs.

This chapter and the next illustrate how changes in consumer surplus, producer surplus, and net government revenues could be readily estimated if all the pertinent market demand and supply curves were known. This chapter focuses on demand and supply curves in *primary markets,* while Chapter 5 examines demand and supply curves in *secondary markets.* Primary markets refer to markets that are directly affected by a policy or project; for example, if a city builds a new subway system, the primary markets are the market for public transportation and the market for materials used to build the subway. Secondary markets are markets that are indirectly affected—for example, the market for gasoline if some commuters switch from driving to riding the new subway.

The chapter begins with a brief discussion of why real CBA studies often fail to use conceptually correct measures of benefits and costs and what the implications are of this. We then examine how the effects of government policies in primary markets can be valued. In doing so, we emphasize the concept of willingness to pay (WTP) and, thus, demand curves and consumer surplus. We next describe the valuation of resources purchased in primary markets as inputs for government projects, stressing the concept of opportunity costs and, hence, the use of supply curves and producer surplus. *Throughout this chapter we ignore the marginal excess tax burden.*

This chapter also provides brief explanations of common types of market failures including monopoly, externalities, information asymmetries, public goods, and addictive goods. The reason for discussing market failures is that their presence provides the *prima facie* rationale for most, although not all, proposed government interventions that are assessed through CBA. If markets worked perfectly, then Pareto efficiency would be obtained without government intervention: a set of prices would arise that distributes resources to firms and goods to individuals in such a way that it would not be possible to

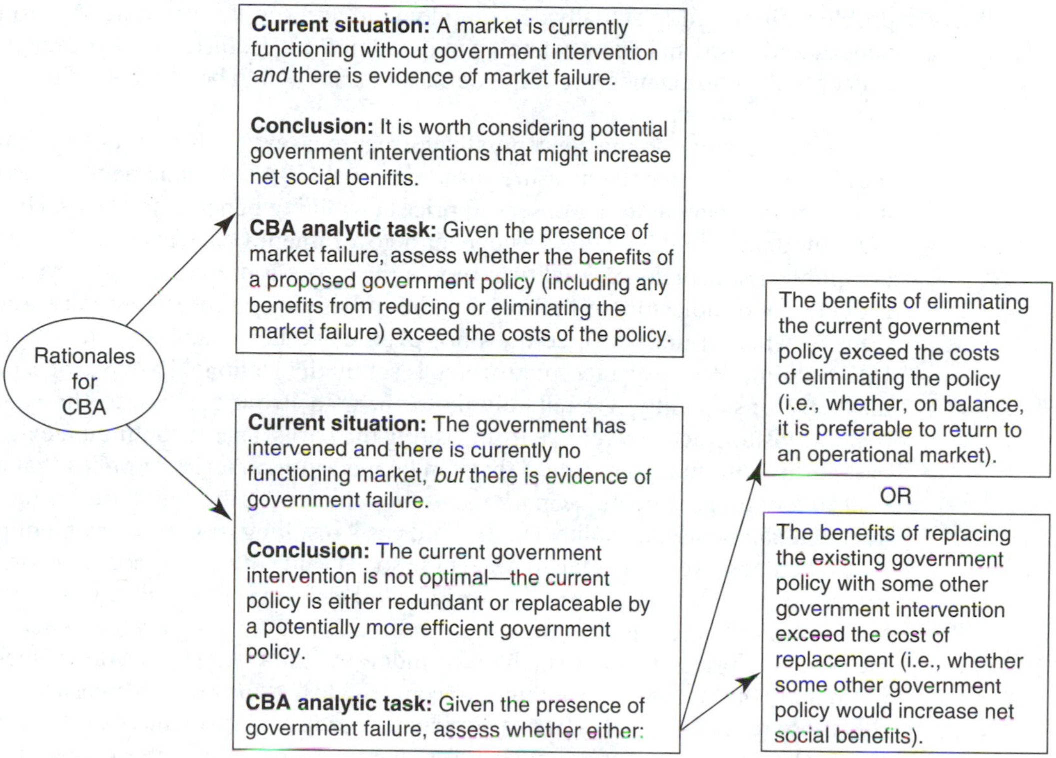

Current situation: A market is currently functioning without government intervention *and* there is evidence of market failure.

Conclusion: It is worth considering potential government interventions that might increase net social benifits.

CBA analytic task: Given the presence of market failure, assess whether the benefits of a proposed government policy (including any benefits from reducing or eliminating the market failure) exceed the costs of the policy.

Rationales for CBA

The benefits of eliminating the current government policy exceed the costs of eliminating the policy (i.e., whether, on balance, it is preferable to return to an operational market).

OR

Current situation: The government has intervened and there is currently no functioning market, *but* there is evidence of government failure.

Conclusion: The current government intervention is not optimal—the current policy is either redundant or replaceable by a potentially more efficient government policy.

CBA analytic task: Given the presence of government failure, assess whether either:

The benefits of replacing the existing government policy with some other government intervention exceed the cost of replacement (i.e., whether some other government policy would increase net social benefits).

FIGURE 4-1   How to Consider Market and Government Failure in CBA

find a reallocation that would make at least one person better off without also making at least one other person worse off. Furthermore, as shown in Chapter 3, such an outcome would maximize net social benefits. It is only when markets fail that allocative efficiency grounds exist for government interventions. However, no more than a *prima facie* case exists. It is up to CBA to demonstrate that a specific intervention is worthwhile from society's perspective. CBA may also be used to assess existing government policies. In this case, the analyst is essentially attempting to determine whether the current policy is inefficient and, therefore, exhibits "government failure."[1]

Figure 4-1 summarizes the analytic steps to follow depending on whether the analyst observes market failure, government failure, or both.

PRACTICAL VERSUS CONCEPTUALLY CORRECT MEASURES OF BENEFITS AND COSTS

In most CBAs, the measures of benefits and costs actually used differ somewhat from the conceptually correct measures. One purpose of examining the conceptually correct measures of the benefits and costs of a government policy is so they can serve as a benchmark against which the measures used in actual CBAs can be compared. So that we can focus on this objective in this and the next chapter, we ignore the practical problems inherent in actually deriving demand and supply curves needed to measure benefit and costs, an issue we take up in detail in Part III. Instead, we focus on how the conceptually correct measures of benefits and costs would be obtained *if* the necessary curves were known.

Before turning to the conceptually correct measures, it is helpful to examine why they often differ from the measures used in actual CBAs. A fundamental reason is that it is often convenient to use observed prices in valuing benefits and costs. However, as illustrated later in this chapter, whenever a government policy involves the production of a public good, or an externality or monopoly power is present, market prices may not provide good indicators of the social value of benefits or costs. There are other situations in which a market price does not even exist. For example, persons entering a U.S. National Park pay a fee, but this fee is set by the National Park Service, not by the market. Consequently, it is unlikely that it bears a strong relation to the value of the benefits visitors actually receive from visiting the parks. Thus, a continuum exists. At one end of this continuum are values that can be measured in terms of prices that are set in well-functioning, competitive markets. At the other end is the complete absence of markets that can be used to value benefits and costs resulting from a government policy.

When observed prices fail to reflect the social value of a good accurately or observed prices do not exist, an approach called *shadow pricing* is often used to measure some benefits or costs. That is, analysts adjust observed prices or assign values when appropriate observed prices do not exist, thereby finding in "the shadows," needed values that are not readily observable. They attempt to come as close as possible to measuring the value that those receiving benefits from a government project place on them or the lost value to those who incur costs. For example, prices charged by paper factories may understate the true social cost of paper if the production process generates pollution. Given such circumstances, an analyst conducting a CBA may adjust the market price upward to account for the negative externality resulting from the pollution. Another important example of shadow pricing is the considerable effort that economists have put into attempting to place an appropriate value on human life. Also, economists have also put much work into trying to determine the social value of recreational areas such as public parks. We indicate many other situations in this chapter when shadow pricing is required and at several junctures suggest approaches that can be taken toward obtaining shadow prices. In Chapters 14–17, we describe these and other techniques to obtain shadow prices in more detail.

Although numerous shadow pricing techniques exist, it is still frequently the case that the measures of benefits and costs used in actual studies differ from their conceptually correct counterparts. There are several reasons for this:

1. As discussed in Chapter 11, errors are sometimes made in CBA. In some instances, for example, the distinction between the measure being used and the conceptually correct measure is sufficiently subtle that it is inadvertently overlooked. In such instances, those conducting the study may be unaware that their results are incorrect and thus do not attempt to use appropriate shadow pricing techniques.
2. It is often difficult to derive an appropriate shadow price. In some studies, consequently, the difference between the actual and the correct measure may be potentially serious, but it is technically infeasible or beyond the time and resources avail-

able to those conducting the study to do much about it. In the most extreme instances, even determining the conceptually correct measures of value is so complex and daunting as to put it beyond the grasp of analysts. Even when shadow prices are used, the resulting measures of benefits and costs may vary from their conceptually correct counterparts. When this is the case, it is at least incumbent upon those conducting the study to point out why and how the study results may be biased.

3. There may be reason to think that the differences between the actual and the correct measures are sufficiently minor such that the study results are not much affected. In such instances, shadow pricing may not be necessary.

VALUING OUTCOMES: WILLINGNESS TO PAY (WTP)

The valuation of policy outcomes should be based on the concept of WTP. Some people like a policy impact and are willing to pay for it. Other people do not like the same impact and are willing to pay to avoid it. *Benefits are the sums of the maximum amounts people would be willing to pay to gain outcomes that they view as desirable; costs are the sums of the maximum amounts that people would be willing to pay to avoid outcomes they view as undesirable.*[2] Estimating changes in social surpluses that occur in relevant markets enables us to take account of these costs and benefits. In the discussion that follows, we distinguish between changes in surplus that take place in efficient markets and those that occur in inefficient or distorted markets where market or government failures are found. This discussion also focuses on *gross benefits*, rather than *net benefits*, because it usually ignores the inputs the government must purchase to carry out policies. Measurement of the social cost of these resources is discussed in the following section. Net benefits would be obtained by subtracting the costs of these inputs from gross benefits. Thus, as used in this section, the word "costs" refers to negative changes resulting from a policy, not the expenses on inputs the government must purchase to carry out the policy.

Valuing Benefits in Efficient Markets

Valuation of gross benefits is relatively straightforward when a policy affects the supply curves of goods in efficient markets. Under these circumstances, the rule is as follows: *the gross social benefits of a policy equal the net government revenue generated by the policy (exclusive of project costs) plus the resulting changes in consumer surplus and producer surplus.*

We examine two common situations where this rule is applicable. First, we consider policies that directly affect the quantity of a good available to consumers. For example, a publicly operated childcare center shifts the supply curve to the right, as it results in more child care being offered to consumers at each price. This often (but not always) reduces prices, resulting in benefits to consumers. Second, we consider policies that shift the supply curve down by altering the price or availability of some input used to produce the good. An example is deepening a harbor so that it accommodates larger ships, thus reducing the cost of transporting bulk commodities to and from the port for shipping companies. This results in direct reductions in costs to producers.

Direct Increases in Supply Available to Consumers.   Figure 4-2 shows the gross benefits that result when a project directly increases the available supply of a good in a

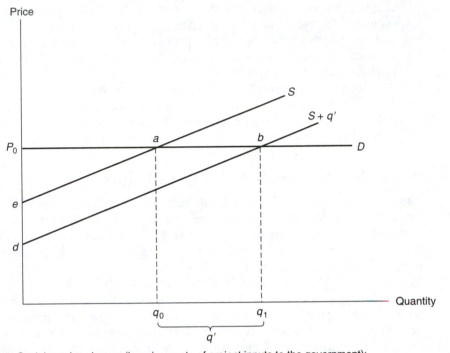

Social surplus change (ignoring costs of project inputs to the government):
Project (a): Direct increase in supply of q'—gain of project revenue equal to area of rectangle $q_0 a b q_1$
Project (b): Supply schedule shift through cost reduction for producers—gain of trapezoid *abde*

FIGURE 4-2   Measuring Benefits in an Efficient Market with No Price Effects

well-functioning market, but the increase is so small that the price of the good is unaffected. If the government sells the additional units of the good at the market price, then it may be treated like other competitors in an efficient market. Hence, as shown in the figure, it faces a horizontal demand curve, D, for the good at the market price, P_0. If the project directly adds a quantity, q', to the market, then the supply curve as seen by consumers shifts from S to $S + q'$.[3] Because the demand curve is horizontal, the price of the good and, hence, consumer surplus and producer surplus are unaffected by the shift in the supply curve. However, if consumers purchase the additional units of the good, the government receives revenue equal to P_0 times q', the area of rectangle $q_0 a b q_1$. The rectangle $q_0 a b q_1$ also, of course, represents a cost to those consumers who purchase the good. This "cost," however, is exactly offset by benefits that these persons enjoy in consuming the good and, consequently, can be ignored in our analysis. Therefore the revenues received by the government are the only gross benefits that accrue from the project selling q' units in the market.

If the government adds a sufficiently large quantity of a good to a market so that the price of the good is reduced, however, then consumers will benefit. Figure 4-3 illustrates this possibility by showing a downward-sloping demand curve, D. The intersection of the demand curve and the supply curve, S, indicates the equilibrium price, P_0, prior to the

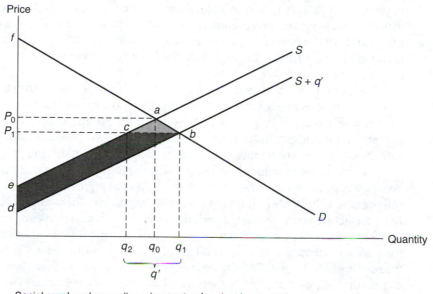

Social surplus change (ignoring costs of project inputs to the government):
Project (a): Direct increase in supply of q'—gain of triangle *abc* plus project revenue equal
        to area of rectangle q_2cbq_1.
Project (b): Supply schedule shift through cost reductions for producers—gain of trapezoid *abde*

FIGURE 4-3   Measuring Benefits in an Efficient Market

project. The equilibrium price of the good falls to P_1 after the government provides the q' units of the good. This time, because of the reduction in the price facing consumers, there is a gain in consumer surplus corresponding to the area of trapezoid P_0abP_1. Because private-sector suppliers continue to operate on the original supply curve, S, the output they sell falls from q_0 to q_2, and they suffer a loss of producer surplus equal to the area of trapezoid P_0acP_1. Thus, the net gain in surplus among private actors (consumers and producers) equals the area of triangle *abc*, which is lightly shaded. In addition, the government receives revenues from the project equal to the area of rectangle q_2cbq_1. The sum of project revenues and the gain in social surplus in the market equals area q_2cabq_1, which is the total gross benefit from the project selling q' units in the market.

What benefits would accrue if q' units of the good were instead distributed free to selected consumers? If the price of the good does not change, as in the situation depicted in Figure 4-2, then the answer is straightforward: as a result of receiving q' units of the good free, consumers gain surplus equal to the area of rectangle q_0abq_1, an area that exactly corresponds to the revenues that would have accrued had the project's output been sold.

The answer is more complex if the q' units of the good are distributed free, but the increase in supply causes its price to fall. This situation is shown in Figure 4-3. Under these circumstances, if the q' units are given only to those consumers who would have valued these units at P_1 or higher, then the project's gross benefit measure is again exactly the same as it would have been had the output been sold. As before, the reduction in price from P_0 to P_1 results in an increase in social surplus equal to area *abc*. With free distribution, however, no revenue accrues to the project. Instead, as a result of receiving q' units of the good free, consumers enjoy an additional surplus equal to the area of rectangle q_2cbq_1. Thus, total gross benefits from the project once again equal the area of trapezoid q_2cabq_1.

It is more likely, however, that if q' units of the good are distributed for free, some would go to consumers who are located below point *b* on the market demand curve shown in Figure 4-3. In other words, some units would be distributed to some consumers in greater quantities than they would have purchased at price P_1. If these consumers keep the excess units, then area q_2cabq_1 overestimates the project's benefit because these persons value their marginal consumption of these units at less than P_1. Area q_2cabq_1 approximates project benefits, however, if recipients of the excess units sell them to others who would have been willing to buy them at a price of P_1 (provided the transaction costs associated with the sale of the excess units are zero).

Suppose, for example, that a project provides previously stockpiled gasoline free to low-income consumers during an oil supply disruption (an in-kind subsidy). Some low-income households will find themselves with more gasoline than they would have purchased on their own at price P_1; therefore, they will try to sell the excess. Doing so will be relatively easy if access to the stockpiled gasoline is provided through legally transferable coupons; it would obviously be more difficult if the gasoline had to be physically taken away by the low-income households. If the gasoline coupons could be costlessly traded among consumers, then we would expect the outcome to be identical to one in which the gasoline is sold in the market and the revenue given directly to low-income consumers.

Reductions in Costs to Producers. We now turn to a different type of public-sector project: one, such as harbor deepening, which lowers the private sector's cost of supplying a market. Figure 4-3 can again be used to analyze this situation. In this case, however, the supply curve shifts to $S + q'$, not because the project directly supplies q' to the market, but rather because reductions in marginal costs allow private-sector firms to offer q' additional units profitably at each price.[4] As in the case of direct supply of q', the new equilibrium price is P_1. Thus, the gain in consumer surplus corresponds to the area of trapezoid P_0abP_1. The change in producer surplus corresponds to the difference in the areas of triangle P_0ae (the producer surplus with supply curve S) and triangle P_1bd (the producer surplus with supply curve $S + q'$). Area P_1ce is common to the two triangles and therefore cancels. Hence, producers enjoy a net gain in surplus equal to area *ecbd* minus area P_0acP_1. Adding this gain to the gain in consumer surplus, area P_0abP_1, means that the net gain to consumers and producers resulting from the project equals the area of trapezoid *abde*. (That is, area *ecbd* + area P_0abP_1 − area P_0acP_1 = area *ecbd* + area *abc* = area *abde*.[5]) Because no project revenue is generated, area *abde* alone is the gross benefit of the project. Notice that because we once again ignore expenditures the government incurs in purchasing inputs needed to undertake the project, we are again measuring gross benefits rather than net benefits.

Revenues as a Measure of Gross Benefits in Efficient Markets. To private-sector producers of goods or services, project revenues are a natural measure of gross benefits. However, while revenues figure prominently in the computation of producer surplus, they generally do not equate to gross consumer benefits. There are, however, two situations in which it is appropriate to use revenues as gross benefits.

The first situation, which is discussed above, occurs when the government sells a good in an undistorted market without affecting the market price. For example, a government may have surplus office equipment that it sells in sufficiently small quantities that the market price of office equipment does not change. The assumption of a negligible effect on price is more reasonable for goods traded in large, national markets than for goods traded in small, local markets. It is also more reasonable for homogeneous goods, such as surplus equipment, than for heterogeneous goods, such as land, which may differ in desirability from one parcel to another.

Second, revenues can be used as a measure of gross consumer benefits when changes in consumer surplus are zero. This may occur when a project exports all of its output. The North East Coal Development Project, which we discuss in Chapter 6, provides an example. The primary beneficiaries (besides the Canadian federal government) were the mining and transportation companies. Their producer surplus increase is legitimately computed as the difference between their additional revenues and their additional costs, that is, as their incremental profits. However, as this project would supply coal to Japanese customers only, Table 6-5 does not include any consumer surplus benefits for Canadians. The consumer surplus would accrue to foreigners and, therefore, should not be counted in the CBA if the analyst takes a Canadian perspective.

In practice, government often sells goods when markets are distorted or when the sale has an impact on the price of the good. For example, electricity may not be available to residents of a remote town unless the government sponsors the construction of an electric power transmission line. Here, introduction of electricity effectively reduces the price from infinity to the user fee charged. In these situations, government or firm revenues are an especially poor measure of gross benefits.

Valuing Benefits in Distorted Markets

If market or government failures distort the relevant product market, then project benefits should continue to be measured as changes in consumer surplus plus producer surplus resulting from the project plus net government revenues generated by the project. However, complications arise in determining the correct surplus changes. We illustrate these complications by examining five different types of market failures: monopoly, information asymmetry, externalities, public goods, and addictive goods. We do not attempt to provide a comprehensive discussion of market failures in this chapter, just an overview. For a comprehensive discussion, we recommend a book by David Weimer and Aidan Vining, which is cited in the first endnote.[6]

Monopoly.   It is useful to examine monopoly first because it is an excellent example of a topic introduced in Chapter 3: a deviation from the competitive equilibrium that results in a deadweight loss and, hence, reduces social surplus.[7] One key to understanding monopoly is to recognize that because, by definition, a monopolist is the only firm in its market, it views the market demand curve as the demand curve for its output.

Because market demand curves slope downward, if the monopolist sells all its output at the same price, then it can sell an additional unit of output only by reducing the price on every unit it sells. Consequently, the monopolist's marginal revenue—the

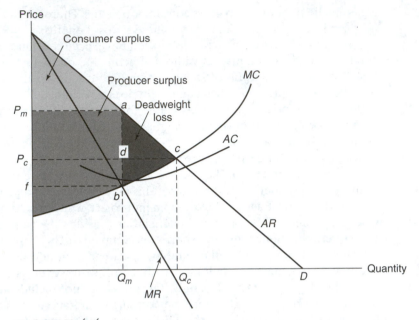

FIGURE 4-4 Monopoly

additional revenue it receives for each additional unit of output it sells—is less than the selling price of that unit. For example, if a monopolist could sell four units of output at a price of $10 but must reduce its price to $9 in order to sell five units, its revenue would increase from $40 to $45 as a result of selling the fifth unit. Therefore, the $5 in marginal revenue it receives from the fifth unit is less than the $9 selling price of the unit. Thus, as shown in Figure 4-4, the monopolist's marginal revenue curve, denoted *MR*, is located below its demand curve, denoted *AR*.

Given this situation, the monopolist would maximize profit by producing at Q_m, where its marginal cost equals its marginal revenue. The price it can charge is determined by what people are willing to pay for those units, which is given by the demand curve it faces. At the output level Q_m it would set its price equal to P_m.

As before, the social surplus generated by the output produced and sold by the monopolist is represented graphically by the area between the demand curve, which reflects the marginal benefit to society, and the marginal cost curve that is to the left of the intersection of the marginal revenue and marginal cost curves. This is the sum of consumer surplus plus producer surplus. The consumer surplus, which is captured by buyers, is the lightest shaded area above the price line. The producer surplus, which is captured by the monopolist, is the darker shaded area below the price line.

Although the term *monopolist* is sometimes used pejoratively, in a CBA any increase in producer surplus received by a monopolist that results from a government policy is counted as a benefit of the policy. The rationale is that owners of monopolies, like consumers and the owners of competitive firms, are part of society; therefore, benefits accruing to them "count."[8]

Notice that, unlike the perfectly competitive case, social surplus is not maximized if the monopolist is left to its own devices. This is because the monopolist maximizes profits, not net social benefits. Net social benefits are maximized at point c on Figure 4-4, where the marginal cost curve intersects the marginal benefit curve (demand curve). The "lost" social surplus, which is called the deadweight loss of monopoly, is represented in Figure 4-4 by the darkly shaded triangular area *abc*. Were it possible for the government to break up the monopoly into a large number of competing firms, each firm would produce where price equals MC.[9] In Figure 4-4 this occurs where industry output and price are Q_c and P_c, which are sometimes referred to as the "competitive" output and price. If this competitive outcome resulted, two things would happen: first, the deadweight loss would disappear and social surplus would increase by the area *abc*. In CBA, this would count as a benefit of the government's actions. Second, because the competitive price, P_c, is less than the monopolistic price, P_m, consumers would capture that part of the monopolist's producer surplus that is represented by the rectangular area $P_m a d P_c$. In CBA, this is viewed as a transfer.

Natural Monopoly.   So far, we have been focusing on a general form of monopoly. We now turn to a specific type of monopoly: *natural monopoly*. The essential characteristic of a natural monopoly is that it enjoys *economies of scale* over a wide range of output. Usually, its fixed costs are very large relative to its variable costs; public utilities, roads, and bridges all provide good examples. As shown in Figure 4-5, these large fixed costs cause average costs to fall over a large range of output. Put another way, and as shown in Figure 4-5, (long run) average costs exceed (long run) marginal costs over what we term the *relevant range of output,* which is the range between the first unit of output and the amount consumers would demand at a zero price, Q_0.

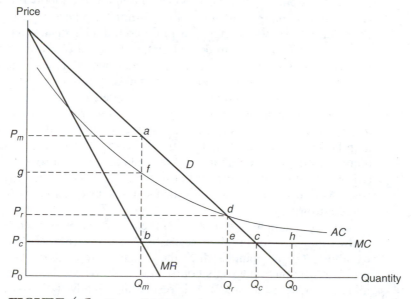

FIGURE 4-5   Natural Monopoly

In principle, marginal costs could be rising or falling over the relevant output range, but for the sake of simplicity, we have drawn the marginal cost curve as horizontal. The important point is that (long run) marginal costs are less than (long run) average costs over the relevant range, so that average costs fall over the relevant range of output as output increases. As a result, one firm, a natural monopoly, can provide a given amount of output at a lower average cost than could two or more firms.

In these circumstances, it is reasonable for the government to permit a monopoly to exist. If it does, however, it must decide whether to regulate the monopoly, and if it regulates it, what type of policies to invoke. To make our discussion of these policies as concrete as possible, we will assume that the natural monopoly represented in Figure 4-5 is a road and that output is the number of cars that travel the road. Although most roads are built under government contract and operated by the government, they could instead be built and operated by private-sector firms under various regulatory frameworks. In fact, several roads have been built by private companies or public–private partnerships over the past 200 years.[10]

The government could follow one of four policies. The first is simply to allow the road-operating authority, whether a private-sector firm or a government agency, to maximize profits. As discussed previously, profits are maximized at output Q_m, where marginal cost equals marginal revenue. The road-operating authority could obtain this output level by charging a toll (i.e., a price) set at P_m. However, under this policy, output is restricted below the competitive level of Q_c, and willingness to pay, P_m, exceeds marginal costs, P_c. This results in a deadweight loss equal to area *abc*. The policy is also unattractive politically because it typically permits substantial monopoly profits, corresponding to area $P_m afg$.

An alternative policy that is often used in regulating natural monopolies is to require the road-operating authority to set its price at P_r, where the average cost curve crosses the demand curve. This policy eliminates monopoly profits by transferring social surplus from the road-operating authority to persons using the road. It also expands output, increasing social surplus and reducing deadweight loss from area *abc* to area *dec*. Thus, as compared to allowing the road-operating authority to maximize profits, society receives a benefit from the policy that corresponds to area *adeb*. But deadweight loss is not completely eliminated. In other words, society could potentially benefit still further if output could be expanded.

The third policy alternative does this by requiring the road construction and operating authority to set its price at P_c, where the marginal cost curve intersects the demand curve—in other words, by requiring competitive market pricing. This completely eliminates the deadweight loss, thereby maximizing net social benefits. But a problem exists with this policy: price is below average costs; hence, revenues no longer cover costs. As a result, tax money must be used to subsidize the road construction and operating authority.

The fourth policy alternative is the one most often used in the case of roads: to allow free access, or in other words, to charge a zero price. In this case, output would expand to Q_0, the point at which the demand curve intersects the horizontal axis. The problem with this policy is that output expands to a level at which marginal costs exceed marginal benefit (i.e. WTP). This results in a deadweight loss equal to the triangular area chQ_0. Moreover, because no tolls are collected directly from road users, the entire construction and operating costs of the road must be paid through government subsidies obtained from taxes.

Information Asymmetry.   The term *information asymmetry* implies that information about a product or a job may not be equal on both sides of a market. For example, sellers may have more information concerning how well made or safe a product is than buyers, doctors may know more about needed care than patients, or employers may know more about job-related health risks than their workers.

The implications of information asymmetry are easy to show in a diagram. To do this, we focus on the case in which sellers of a product have more information than buyers. Such a situation is represented in Figure 4-6, which shows two demand curves. One of these curves, D_i, represents how many units of the product buyers would desire if they had full information concerning it, while the other demand curve, D_u, indicates how many units they actually desire, given their lack of full information.[11] In other words, the two demand curves represent, respectively, consumers' WTP with and without full information concerning the product. They indicate that if buyers had full information, their WTP would be lower.[12]

Figure 4-6 shows that there are two effects of information asymmetry. First, by raising the price and the amount of the good purchased, information asymmetry increases producer surplus and reduces consumer surplus, resulting in a transfer from consumers to sellers. This transfer is shown by the trapezoidal area $P_u acP_i$. Second, by increasing the amount of the good sold relative to the full information case, information asymmetry results in a deadweight loss, which is shown as the triangular area abc.

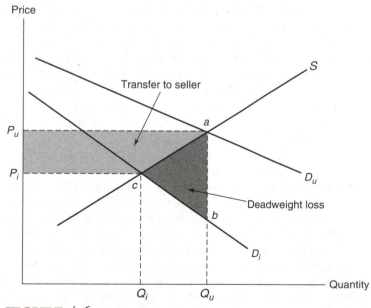

FIGURE 4-6   Information Asymmetry

These two effects, especially the second one, suggest a rationale for the government to intervene by providing the missing information. If the government does this effectively, society will benefit because deadweight loss is reduced. In addition, there will be a transfer of surplus (back) from sellers to buyers. However, there are also costs associated with the government obtaining and disseminating information. These costs, which do not explicitly appear in the diagram, may be sizable.[13] Hence, for a government information program to have positive net benefits, and not just positive gross benefits, the deadweight loss associated with the lack of information in the absence of government intervention must usually be substantial.

It is useful to discuss the circumstances under which information asymmetry is sufficiently important that the benefits from government intervention are likely to exceed the costs. This largely depends upon two factors: first, the ease with which consumers can obtain the information for themselves; and second, whether third parties that could provide the missing information are likely to arise through market forces. To discuss these factors, it is helpful to distinguish among three types of products: (1) search goods, (2) experience goods, and (3) post-experience goods.[14]

Search goods are products with characteristics that consumers can learn about by examining them prior to purchasing them. For example, a student who needs a notebook for a class can go to the bookstore and easily learn pretty much everything he or she wants to know about the characteristics of alternative notebooks. Under such circumstances, information asymmetry is unlikely to be serious.

Experience goods are products about which consumers can obtain full knowledge, but only after purchasing and experiencing them. Examples are tickets to a movie, a meal at a new restaurant, a new television set, and a house. At least to a degree, information asymmetry concerning many such products takes care of itself. For example, once consumers have been to a restaurant, they acquire some information concerning the expected quality of the meal should they eat there again. Warranties, which are typically provided for televisions and many other major consumer durables, serve a similar purpose. In addition, market demand for information about experience goods often prompts third parties to provide information for a fee. This reduces information asymmetry. For example, newspaper reviews provide information about movies and restaurants; in the United States, *Consumer Reports* provides information about many goods; and inspection services examine houses for perspective buyers.

In the case of *post-experience goods,* consumption does not necessarily reveal information to consumers. Government intervention to reduce information asymmetry associated with post-experience goods is most likely to be efficiency-enhancing because learning through individual action does not always occur. Examples of this situation include adverse health effects associated with a prescription drug and a new automobile with a defective part. Employee exposure to an unhealthy chemical at work is similar. In these cases, information asymmetry may persist for long periods of time, even after the health of some people has been ruined. Moreover, because the needed information is often expensive to gather and individuals may be unwilling to pay for it, third parties may not provide the necessary information. Under these circumstances, there may be a strong rationale for government intervention.

Externalities.   An *externality* is an effect that production or consumption has on third parties—people not involved in the production or consumption of the good. It is a by-product of production or consumption for which there is no market. Indeed, externalities are sometimes referred to as the problem of "missing markets." Examples include pollution caused by a factory and the pleasure derived from a neighbor's beautiful garden. Externalities may occur for a wide variety of reasons. For example, some result because a particular type of manufacturing technology is used (e.g., air pollution caused by smokestack industry). Others arise because of interdependencies (or synergies) between producers and consumers or different groups of producers (e.g., beekeepers who unintentionally provide pollination services for nearby fruit growers). Still other externalities occur because of networks (e.g., the larger the number of persons who purchase a particular type of automobile, the greater the number of qualified service garages available to each owner). Because the number of externalities is enormous, a careful CBA should first be conducted before the government intervenes to correct any specific externality.[15]

We first examine a negative externality (i.e., one that imposes social costs) and then a positive externality (i.e., one that produces benefits). Figure 4-7 illustrates a market in which the production process results in a negative externality, such as air or water pollution. The supply curve, S^*, reflects only the private marginal costs incurred by the suppliers of the good, while the second supply curve, $S^\#$, incorporates the costs that the negative externality imposes on third parties, as well as the private marginal costs incurred by suppliers. The vertical distance between these two curves, measured over the quantity of the good purchased, can be viewed as the amount those subjected to the negative externality would be willing to pay to avoid it. In other words, it represents the costs imposed by the externality on third parties. The length of this distance

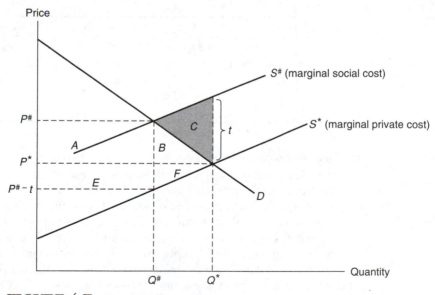

FIGURE 4-7   Negative Externality

depends in part upon whether the market somehow compensates third parties for the negative externality. For example, it would be smaller if homeowners were able to purchase their houses at lower prices because of pollution in their neighborhood than if they were not.

Figure 4-7 indicates that, if left to its own devices, the market sets too low a price for the good ($P^* < P^{\#}$) because it fails to take account of the cost to third parties of producing the good. As a result, too much output is produced ($Q^* > Q^{\#}$). This causes deadweight loss, which is represented by the shaded triangular area labeled C. This deadweight loss reflects the fact that for each unit of additional output produced in excess of $Q^{\#}$, marginal social costs (shown by the supply curve $S^{\#}$) increasingly exceed marginal social benefits (shown by the demand curve D).

The standard technique for reducing deadweight loss resulting from negative externalities is to impose taxes.[16] For example, the suppliers of the good represented in Figure 4-7 could be required to pay a tax, t, on each unit they sell, with the tax set equal to the difference between marginal social costs and marginal social benefits (shown in the figure as the vertical distance at Q^* between the two supply curves). As production costs would now include the tax, the supply curve of sellers, S^*, would shift upward to $S^{\#}$. Consequently, the price paid by consumers would increase from P^* to $P^{\#}$, the net price received by producers would fall from P^* to $P^{\#} - t$, and output produced and sold would fall from Q^* to $Q^{\#}$. Note that pollution associated with the good would be reduced, but not completely eliminated, because the good would continue to be produced, although in smaller amounts.[17]

Figure 4-7 implies that the benefits and costs of the government's tax policy are distributed unequally among different groups in the economy. These are displayed in the following social accounting ledger.

	Benefits	Costs
Consumers of good		$A + B$
Producers of good		$E + F$
Third parties	$B + C + F$	
Government revenue	$A + E$	
Social benefit	C	

Because the policy causes consumers to pay a higher price for less of the good, they lose surplus equal to areas A and B. Similarly, because the tax causes producers to sell less of the good but increases their production costs, they lose producer surplus equal to areas E and F. On the other hand, because of the reduction in production of the good and, hence, in pollution, third parties receive benefits from the policy equal to areas B, C, and F. Finally, the government receives tax revenues equal to areas A and E. Because areas A, B, E, and F represent transfers from one group to another, only area C can be counted as a gain to society as a whole from the tax policy. This area corresponds to the deadweight loss eliminated by the tax policy. To compute the *net* social benefit of the tax, the cost of administering it would have to be subtracted from the reduction in deadweight loss.

Now let us look at an example of a positive externality, a program that subsidizes the purchase of rodent extermination services in a poor neighborhood. One mechanism for doing this is to provide residents with vouchers that are worth a certain number of dollars, $v, for each unit of extermination services they purchase. After subtracting the face value of these vouchers from what they charge neighborhood residents for their services, exterminators would then be reimbursed the face value of the voucher by the government.

By increasing the use of extermination services, such a program may result in a positive externality: the fewer the rodents in the neighborhood, the easier it is for residents in adjoining neighborhoods to control their own rodent populations. This situation is illustrated in Figure 4-8, where the market demand curve, D_M, is shown as understating the social demand curve, D_S. The area between these two demand curves represents the WTP for the extermination voucher program by residents of adjoining neighborhoods, assuming they had knowledge of the potential benefits from the program to them. Thus, the market equilibrium price, P_0, and quantity, q_0, are both too low from the social perspective, resulting in deadweight loss equal to $C + F + H$.

What are the social benefits of a program that distributes vouchers worth $v per unit of extermination service to the residents of a poor neighborhood? As implied by Figure 4-8, when the vouchers become available, residents of the poor neighborhood

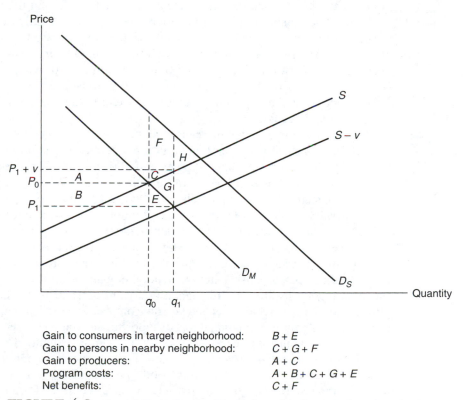

Gain to consumers in target neighborhood:	$B + E$
Gain to persons in nearby neighborhood:	$C + G + F$
Gain to producers:	$A + C$
Program costs:	$A + B + C + G + E$
Net benefits:	$C + F$

FIGURE 4-8 Social Benefits for Direct Supply of a Good with a Positive Externality

face a supply curve that is below the original market supply curve, S, by \$$v$. As a consequence of a voucher-induced shift in the supply curve, neighborhood residents increase their purchases of extermination services from q_0 to q_1, paying an effective price of P_1. Consumers in the targeted neighborhood enjoy a surplus gain equal to the area of trapezoid $B + E$; producers, who now receive a higher supply price of $P_1 + v$, enjoy a surplus gain equal to the area of trapezoid $A + C$; and people in the surrounding neighborhoods, who enjoy the positive externality, gain surplus equal to the area of parallelogram $C + G + F$, the area between the market and social demand curves over the increase in consumption. The program must pay out \$$v$ times q_1 in subsidies, which equals the area of rectangle $A + B + C + G + E$. Subtracting this program cost from the gains in social surplus in the market yields gross program benefits: the area of trapezoid $C + F$.[18] This benefit results because the program succeeds in eliminating part (although not all) of the deadweight loss in the market for extermination services.

Public Goods.   Once produced, public goods—for example, flood control projects or national defense—are available for everyone. No one can or, indeed, should be excluded from enjoying their benefits. In this sense, public goods may be regarded as a special type of positive externality. Similar to other positive externalities, private markets, if left to their own devices, tend to produce less public goods than is socially optimal. Pure public goods have two key characteristics: they are nonexcludable, and they are nonrivalrous.

A good is nonexcludable if it is impossible, or at least highly impractical, for one person to prevent others from consuming it. If it is supplied to one consumer, it is available for all consumers, a phenomenon sometimes called *jointness in supply*. For example, it would be very difficult for a user of the light emitted from a particular streetlight to prevent others from using that light. In contrast, most private goods are excludable. For instance, a purchaser of a hamburger can exclude others from taking a bite unless overcome by physical force.

The reason nonexcludability causes market failure is easy to see. Once a nonexcludable good such as street lighting or national defense exists, it is available for everyone to use. Because people cannot be excluded from using it, a *free-rider problem* results. As a consequence, there is not sufficient incentive for the private sector to provide it. Usually it must be publicly provided, if it is going to be provided at all.

Nonrivalry implies that one person's consumption of a good does not prevent someone else from also consuming it; consequently, more than one person can obtain benefits from a given level of supply at the same time. For example, one person's use of a streetlight to help him see at night does not diminish the ability of another person to use the same light. But if one person eats a hamburger, another cannot consume the same hamburger. The hamburger is rivalrous; a streetlight is nonrivalrous. Thus, unlike the hamburger, even if it were feasible to exclude a second person from using street lighting, it would be inefficient to do so because the marginal cost of supplying lighting to the second person is zero.

The reason nonrivalry causes market failure can be examined by contrasting how a *total marginal benefit curve,* a curve that reflects the incremental benefits to consumers from each additional unit of a good that is available for their consumption, is derived for a rivalrous good with how such a curve is derived for a nonrivalrous good. To do this graphically as simply as possible, we assume that there are only two potential consumers of each of the two goods. Thus, Figure 4-9a displays two graphs: one for

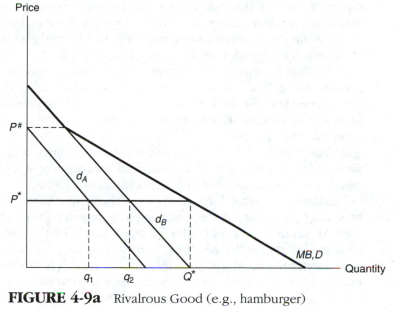

FIGURE 4-9a   Rivalrous Good (e.g., hamburger)

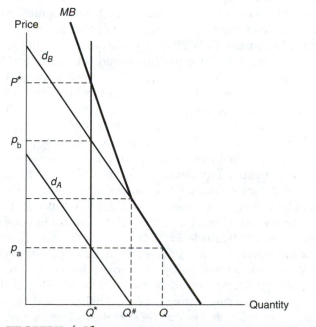

FIGURE 4-9b   Nonrivalrous Good (e.g., streetlight)

the rivalrous good (hamburger) and one for the nonrivalrous good (streetlight). Each graph contains three curves: a demand curve representing consumer A's WTP (d_A), a demand curve representing consumer B's WTP (d_B), and a total marginal benefit (MB) curve, which is derived from the demand curves for the two consumers.

The total marginal benefit curve for the rivalrous good is equivalent to a market demand curve. To derive this curve, the two demand curves for individual consumers are summed horizontally. For example, at a price of P^*, consumer A would want to consume q_1 and consumer B would want q_2 of the good. Total market demand for the good at a price of P^* is equal to $q_1 + q_2$, a total of Q^*. Thus, WTP for (or equivalently, marginal benefits from) the last unit of the total of Q^* units consumed is P^*. Notice that until the price falls below $P^\#$, the marginal benefit curve would correspond to B's demand curve because A would not demand any of the good.

In contrast, the total marginal benefit curve for the nonrivalrous good is derived by adding the demand curves for individual consumers vertically rather than horizontally. At an output level of Q^*, for example, total WTP (i.e., the total marginal benefits from the last unit of the good that is made available) is equal to $p_a + p_b$ or P^*. Notice that at output levels above $Q^\#$, consumer A's WTP falls to zero and, consequently, the marginal benefit curve corresponds to consumer B's demand curve.

The reason the demand curves for individual consumers must be summed horizontally in the presence of rivalry and vertically in its absence can be clarified through use of a numerical example. If at a price of $2 consumer B wanted to buy two hamburgers and consumer A one hamburger, then total demand would equal three hamburgers—the horizontal sum of demands at a particular price. But if at a price of $1,000, B wanted two streetlights on the block on which he and A both lived, but A wanted only one, then two streetlights would completely satisfy the demands of both. Thus, the total demand for a nonrivalrous good cannot be determined by summing the quantity of the good each consumer desires at a given price. It must be determined instead by summing each consumer's WTP for a given quantity of the good. Hence, although A and B have a different WTP for the two streetlights, their total WTP for the two streetlights can be determined by adding A's WTP for two lights to B's.

The distinction between how the total demand for rivalrous and nonrivalrous goods is determined has an important implication. In the case of the rivalrous good, consumers will reveal to the market how much they want. For example, if the price of hamburgers is set at P^*, consumer A will actually purchase q_1 of the good and consumer B will actually purchase q_2. But in the case of a nonrivalrous good, no market mechanism exists that causes consumers to reveal how many units they would purchase at different prices. For example, if the price of streetlight is at p_b, consumer B would be willing to purchase Q^* of the good. But if B did that, A would not purchase any because, as a result of B's purchase, he could consume all he wanted. In other words, A would free ride on B. Because of this free-rider problem, B might refuse to make any purchase until A agreed to make some sort of contribution.[19]

When only a small group of people is involved, they may be able to work out the free-rider problems caused by the nonexcludability and nonrivalry of public goods through negotiations. For example, a neighborhood association might make arrangements for installing and paying for streetlights. But too much or too little of the good may be produced. For example, if consumers A and B are to be charged for streetlights on the basis of their WTP, each will probably try to convince the other that they place a low value on streetlights regardless of how they actually value them. It is therefore difficult to determine where the total marginal benefit curve for a public good is located, even if only a small group of people is involved. When a large group of people share a good that is nonexcludable and nonrivalrous, such as national defense, negotiations become impractical. Consequently, if the good is going to be produced at all, the government must almost certainly intervene by either producing the good itself or subsidizing its production.

Because streetlighting is both nonrivalrous in consumption and nonexcludable, it is close to being a pure public good. Other goods may be either nonrivalrous or nonexcludable, but not both. For example, an uncrowded road is essentially nonrivalrous in nature. One person's use of it does not keep another from using it. Yet, it is excludable. Individuals could be required to pay a toll to use it. Thus, it is sometimes called a *toll good*. Fish in international waters provide an example of a good that is rivalrous but nonexcludable. Fish and fishers move around so it is difficult to preclude fishers from catching a particular type of fish, for example, tuna. But if a fisher catches a tuna, then that tuna is no longer available to other fishers. This type of good is called an *open access resource*. Goods that are either nonrivalrous or nonexcludable, but not both, exhibit some, but not all of the characteristics of public goods. However, for the sake of brevity, we have focused on pure public goods, which are both nonrivalrous and nonexcludable. Examples of goods that are close to being pure public goods are streetlights, flood control, national defense, and crime deterrence resulting from police patrolling the streets.

As suggested by the preceding analysis, because of both nonrivalry and nonexcludability, actual markets for pure public goods are unlikely to exist. However, marginal benefit and marginal cost curves, which are analogous to market demand and supply curves, do exist. We have already shown how to derive a marginal benefit curve for a public good. And, as in the case of a private good, the marginal cost curve for a public good simply reflects the costs of producing each incremental unit of the good. Social welfare is maximized when marginal benefits equal marginal costs, while deadweight loss results at either smaller or larger output amounts. However, because of the absence of a true market, little or none of a pure public good would be produced without government intervention, or at least some sort of negotiation process. Thus, in the absence of government intervention or negotiations, society would forgo social surplus resulting from consumption of the good. Even if the government does intervene or negotiations do take place, there is nonetheless no guarantee that output of the good will be at the point where marginal benefits equal marginal costs because the marginal benefit curve for a pure public good is inherently unknowable. As a consequence, too much or too little of it may be produced. However, as described in Chapter 15, techniques exist that can be used to obtain information about WTP for public goods.

Intrapersonal Externalities: Consumption under Addiction. For some people, the consumption of a particular good today increases their demand for its consumption in the future. For example, exposure to classical music during childhood may contribute to a demand for such music in adulthood. Economic models of addictive goods assume that the amount demanded at any time depends on the amount of previous consumption. *Rational addiction* occurs when consumers fully take account of the future effects of their current consumption.[20] If current consumption is myopic or fails to take account of future risks, then addiction is not rational. For example, some children may fail to anticipate the consequences of tobacco addiction during their adulthood or some adults may fail to anticipate the risk that their casual gambling may become a disruptive compulsion. Such cases involve *negative intrapersonal externalities*—harm imposed by current consumers on their future selves.

The presence of negative intrapersonal externalities brings into question the appropriateness of using changes in consumer surplus measured under market demand curves as the basis for assessing the benefits of alternative policies. On the one hand, the demand curve reveals the marginal willingness of the market to pay for additional units of the good. On the other hand, the satisfaction from addictive consumption may not actually make consumers better off—it avoids the pain of abstinence but does not provide as much happiness as would alternative consumption in a nonaddicted state. The stated desire and costly efforts made by many adult smokers to quit smoking suggests that they perceive benefits from ending their addiction. In other words, they wish they had not been addicted by their younger selves.

A plausible approach to measuring consumer surplus in the presence of undesirable addiction involves assessing consumer surplus using unaddicted demand curves.[21] Figure 4-10 illustrates the approach taking as an example addicted, or so-called problem, gamblers. It shows two demand curves: D_A, the demand curve for gambling in the presence of the addiction, and D_R, the demand curve for the same group of addicted gamblers if they were instead like the majority of recreational gamblers who enjoy gambling but do not have a strong compulsion to gamble that leads them to regret

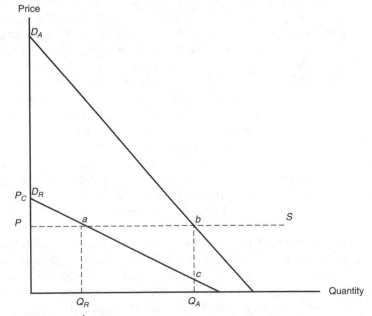

FIGURE 4-10 Consumer Surplus in the Presence of Gambling Addiction

their gambling behaviors. The quantity of gambling demanded by these addicted gamblers at price P is Q_A. If they were not addicted, however, then they would consume only Q_R at that price. Q_A minus Q_R is the excess consumption due to the addiction. Consumption up to level Q_R involves a positive consumer surplus of PaP_C. The consumption from Q_R to Q_A involves expenditures of $Q_R abQ_A$ but consumer value equal to only $Q_R acQ_A$ as measured under their recreational demand curve, resulting in a loss equal to area abc. Overall, participation in this market by these addicted gamblers yields consumer surplus equal to $PaP_C - abc$. If a policy resulted in these addicted gamblers becoming unaddicted recreational gamblers, then a surplus gain of abc would result.

The Australian Productivity Commission applied this approach to estimate consumer surplus losses and gains from the Australian gambling industry. It estimated a consumer surplus gain for recreational gamblers (97.9% of all gamblers) to be between AU$2.7 billion and AU$4.5 billion annually but a consumer surplus loss of almost AU$2.7 billion annually for problem gamblers (2.1% of all gamblers).[22]

VALUING INPUTS: OPPORTUNITY COSTS

Public policies usually require resources (i.e., inputs) that could be used to produce other goods or services instead. Public works projects such as dams, bridges, highways, and subway systems, for example, require labor, materials, land, and equipment. Similarly, social service programs typically require professional employees, computers, telephones, and office space; wilderness preserves, recreation areas, and parks require at least land. Once resources are devoted to these purposes, they obviously are no longer available to produce other goods and services. Almost all public policies incur opportunity costs. Conceptually, these costs equal the value of the goods and services that would have been produced had the resources used in carrying them out been used instead in the best alternative way. These opportunity costs, as seen in Chapter 3, are represented by areas under supply curves. These areas are the theoretically appropriate measures of the costs of the inputs.

As a practical matter, the most obvious and natural way to measure the value of the resources used by a project is simply as the direct budgetary outlay needed to purchase them. Under certain circumstances, the direct budgetary outlay is also identical to the conceptually appropriate opportunity cost measure, but under other circumstances, it is not. To determine when it is and is not permissible to use budgetary outlays, we compare the conceptually appropriate measure of costs with the direct budgetary outlay measure of costs in three alternative market situations: (1) when the market for a resource is efficient (i.e., there are no market failures) and purchases of the resource for the project will have a negligible effect on the price of the resource; (2) when the market for the resource is efficient, but purchases for the project will have a noticeable effect on prices; and (3) when the market for the resource is inefficient (i.e., there is a market failure). As will be seen, in the first of these situations, budgetary expenditures usually accurately measure project opportunity costs; in the second situation, budgetary outlays often only slightly overstate project opportunity costs; and in the third situation, expenditures may substantially overstate or understate project opportunity costs.

Before beginning, it may be helpful to make a general point concerning opportunity costs: the relevant determination is what must be given up today and in the future, *not* what has already been given up. The latter costs are *sunk* and, unlike variable costs, are not represented by the areas under supply curves. In CBA, the extent to which costs are sunk depends importantly on whether an *ex ante, ex post,* or *in medias res* analysis is being conducted. For instance, suppose that you are asked to evaluate a decision to complete a bridge after construction has already begun. What is the opportunity cost of the steel and concrete that is already in place? It is not the original expenditure made to purchase them. Rather, it is the value of these materials in their current best alternative use. This value is most likely measured by the maximum amount for which the steel and concrete could be sold as scrap. Conceivably, the cost of scrapping the materials may exceed their value in any alternative use so salvaging them would not be justified. Indeed, if salvage is still necessary, perhaps for environmental or other reasons, then the opportunity cost of the materials will be negative (and thus counted as a benefit, an avoided cost) when calculating the net gains of continuing construction. In situations where resources that have already been purchased have exactly zero scrap value (the case of labor already expended, for instance), the costs are entirely sunk and are not relevant to decisions concerning future actions.

Measuring Opportunity Costs in Efficient Markets with Negligible Price Effects

Perfectly Elastic Supply Curves.   An example of this is when a government agency running a training program for unemployed workers purchases pencils for trainees. Assuming an absence of failures in the market for pencils, and that the agency buys only a small proportion of the total pencils sold in the market, the agency is realistically viewed as facing a horizontal supply curve for pencils. Thus, the agency's purchases will have a negligible effect on the price of pencils; it can purchase additional pencils at the price they would have cost in the absence of the training program.

This situation is depicted in Figure 4-11. If a project purchases q' units of the input factor represented in the diagram (e.g., pencils), the demand curve, D, would shift horizontally to the right by q'. As implied by the horizontal supply curve, marginal costs remain unchanged and, hence, the price remains at P_0. The area under the supply curve represents the opportunity cost of the factor and P_0 is the opportunity cost of one additional unit of the factor. Consequently, the opportunity cost to society of the q' additional units of the factor needed by the project is simply the original price of the factor times the number of units purchased (i.e., P_0 times q'). In Figure 4-11, this is represented by the shaded rectangle abq_1q_0. Thus, the amount that the agency must pay to purchase additional pencils equals the opportunity cost of the resources used to produce them. In other words, if the q' units of the factor were not used for purposes of the project, then P_0 times q' worth of goods could be produced elsewhere in the economy.

What is important about the situation just described is that the social cost of the units of the factor needed by the project, the shaded rectangular area in Figure 4-11, is identical to the budgetary outlay required to purchase the units; both are equal to P_0 times q'. Because most factors have neither steeply rising nor declining marginal cost curves, *it is often reasonable to presume that expenditures required for project inputs*

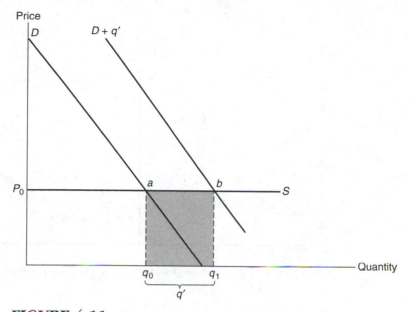

FIGURE 4-11 Opportunity Costs with No Price Effects

equal their social costs. This is the case when the quantity of the resource purchased makes only a small addition to the total demand for the resource, and where, in addition, there is no reason to suspect the existence of significant market failures.

Perfectly Inelastic Supply Curves. In contrast to pencils, let us now examine a government purchase of a parcel of land for a park. We assume that, unlike the pencils, the quantity of land in a specified area is fixed at A acres. Thus, the government faces a vertical rather than horizontal supply curve. In addition, we assume that if the government does not purchase the land, it will be sold in one-acre parcels to private buyers who will build houses on it.

This situation is represented in Figure 4-12, where S is the supply curve and D the private-sector demand curve. If the owners of the land sell it in the private market, they receive the amount represented by the rectangle $PbA0$. Now let us assume that the government secures all A units of the land at the market price through its eminent domain powers, paying owners the market price of P. Thus, the government's budgetary cost is represented in Figure 4-12 by area $PbA0$.

Here, however, the government's budgetary outlay understates the opportunity cost of removing the land from the private sector. The reason is that the potential private buyers of the land lose consumer surplus (triangle aPb in Figure 4-12) as a result of the government taking away their opportunity to purchase land, a real loss that is not included in the government's purchase price. The full cost of the land if it is purchased by the government is represented in Figure 4-12 by all of the area under the demand curve to the left of the vertical supply curve, area $abA0$, not only the rectangular area below the price line.[23]

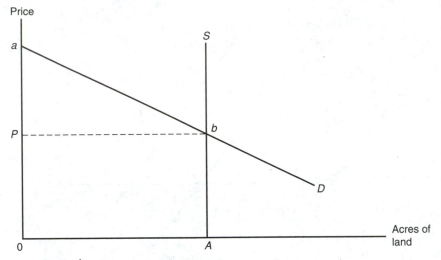

FIGURE 4-12   Opportunity Costs with Inelastic Supply Curve

Measuring Opportunity Costs in Efficient Markets with Noticeable Price Effects

It is possible that even when a resource required by a project is purchased in an essentially efficient market, such a large quantity is required that its price is bid up. This could occur, for example, if the construction of a very large dam requires massive amounts of concrete. In such a situation, the project should be viewed as facing an upward-sloping supply curve for the resource input. Such a supply curve is illustrated in Figure 4-13. In this example, project purchases of q' units of the resource would shift the demand curve, D, to the right. Because the supply curve, S, is upward sloping, the equilibrium price rises from P_0 to P_1, indicating that the large purchase causes the marginal cost of the resource to rise. The price increase causes the original buyers in the market to decrease their purchases from q_0 to q_2. However, total purchases, including those made by the project, expand from q_0 to q_1. Thus, the q' units of the resource purchased by the project come from two distinct sources: (1) units bid away from their previous buyers, and (2) additional units sold in the market.

Total project expenditures on the resource are equal to P_1 times q'. In Figure 4-13, these expenditures are represented by areas $B + C + G + E + F$, which together form a rectangle. Unlike the case where the price of the resource does not change, however, this expenditure does not correspond to the opportunity cost of using q' units of the resource. The price change must be taken into account in computing the opportunity cost. In doing this, the general rule is that *opportunity cost equals expenditure less (plus) any increase (decrease) in consumer surplus or producer surplus occurring in the factor market*. In other words, budgetary outlays on a resource do not equal opportunity costs when the outlays cause a change in consumer surplus or producer surplus in the market for the resource.

To understand why, first look at the areas labeled A and B in Figure 4-13. These two areas represent a decrease in the consumer surplus of the original buyers because of the price increase. However, sellers gain more in producer surplus as a result of the price in-

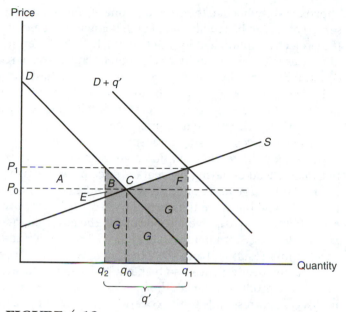

FIGURE 4-13 Opportunity Costs with Price Effects

crease than the original buyers lose—a gain represented by areas $A + B + C$. Part of the gain in producer surplus, the area represented by $A+B$, merely offsets the loss in consumer surplus and, hence, is a transfer from buyers to sellers. However, area C represents a gain in producer surplus that partially offsets the social cost resulting from increased government expenditure on the resource.[24] To measure the social cost of the project's purchase of the resource, this net gain in producer surplus must be subtracted from the project's total budgetary outlay on the resource, areas $B + C + G + E + F$. Thus, the net social cost of the project's purchase of q' units of the resource is represented by areas $B + G + E + F$. The effects of the purchase are summarized in the following social accounting ledger.[25]

	Benefits	Costs
Original buyers		$A + B$
Sellers	$A + B + C$	
Project expenditures		$B + C + G + E + F$
Net social cost		$B + G + E + F$

The basic point is that when prices change the budgetary outlay does not equal the social cost. In the example shown in Figure 4-13, they differ by area C. As an examination of the figure suggests, however, unless the rise in prices is quite substantial, this area will be small relative to total budgetary cost. This suggests that in many instances budgetary outlay will provide a good approximation of true social cost.

If the price of an input does go up substantially, however, then the budgetary cost must be adjusted for CBA purposes. If the demand and supply curves are linear (or approximately linear), then the amount of this adjustment, which is the area represented by C, can be readily calculated. It equals the amount of the factor purchased for the project, q', multiplied by $1/2(P_1 - P_0)$, half the difference between the new and the old prices.[26] The opportunity cost of purchasing the resource for the project can also be computed directly by multiplying the amount purchased by the average of the new and old prices, $1/2(P_1 + P_0)(q')$.[27] The average of the new and old prices is a shadow price; it reflects the social opportunity cost of purchasing the resource more accurately than either the old price or the new price alone.

The social cost of using a resource for a project or program does not necessarily depend upon the mechanism that a government uses to obtain it. Suppose, for example, that instead of paying the market price for q' units of the resource represented in Figure 4-13, the government instead first orders supplying firms to increase their prices to the original buyers in the market from P_0 to P_1, thereby causing sales to these buyers to fall from q_0 to q_2. Next suppose that the government orders these firms to supply q' units to the government at the additional cost required to produce them. The social surplus loss resulting from the price increase to the original buyers is area $B + E$, which is the deadweight loss attributable to the increase in price. The social opportunity cost of producing the additional q' units of the resource for the government, which in this case corresponds to the government's budgetary expenditure, is the trapezoidal area $G + F$. Thus, the total social cost that results from the government's directive is $B + G + E + F$. This social cost is exactly the same as the social cost that results when the government purchases the resource in the same manner as any other buyer in the market. Notice, however, that this time the government's budgetary outlay, $G + F$, is smaller, rather than larger, than the social opportunity cost of using the resource.

Measuring Costs in Inefficient Markets

As indicated in Chapter 3, in an efficient market, price equals marginal social cost. Whenever price does not equal marginal social cost, allocative inefficiency results. A variety of circumstances can lead to inefficiency: absence of a working market, market failures (e.g., public goods, externalities, natural monopolies, markets with few sellers, and information asymmetries), and distortions due to government interventions (such as taxes, subsidies, regulations, price ceilings, and price floors). Any of these distortions can arise in factor markets, complicating the estimation of opportunity cost.

Because of space limitations, it is possible to examine only three distortions here. First, we consider the situation in which the government purchases an input at a price below the factor's opportunity cost. Second, we examine the case in which the government hires from a market in which there is unemployed labor. Third, we explore the situation in which the government purchases inputs for a project from a monopolist. In each of these situations, shadow pricing is needed to measure accurately the opportunity cost of the input.

Purchases at Below Opportunity Costs. Consider a proposal to establish more courts so that more criminal trials can be held. Budgetary costs include the salaries of judges and court attendants, rent for courtrooms and offices, and perhaps expenditures for additional correctional facilities (because the greater availability of trial capacity leads to more imprisonment). For these factors, budgetary costs may correspond well to social opportunity costs. However, the budget may also include payments to jurors, payments that typically just cover commuting expenses. If any compensation is paid to jurors for their time, then it is usually set at a nominal *per diem* not related to the value of their time as reflected, perhaps, by their wage rates. Thus, budgetary outlay to jurors almost certainly understates the opportunity cost of jurors' time. Consequently, some form of shadow pricing is necessary. A better estimate of jurors' opportunity cost is, for example, their commuting expenses plus the number of juror-hours times either the average or the median pre-tax hourly wage rate for the locality. The commuting expenses estimate should include the actual resource costs of transporting jurors to the court, not just out-of-pocket expenses. The hourly pre-tax wage rate times the hours spent on jury duty provides a measure of the value of goods forgone because of lost labor, although several criticisms of it are discussed in Chapter 14.

Hiring Unemployed Labor.   We have stressed that assessing opportunity costs in the presence of market failures or government interventions requires a careful accounting of social surplus changes. Analysis of the opportunity cost of workers hired for a government project who would otherwise be unemployed illustrates the kind of effort that is required.

Let us examine the opportunity costs of labor in a market in which minimum wage laws, union bargaining power, or some other factor creates a wage floor that keeps the wage rate above the market-clearing level and, consequently, there is unemployed labor.[28] Notice that we are focusing here on a very specific form of unemployment: that which occurs when the number of workers who desire jobs at the wage paid in a particular labor market exceed the number of workers employers are willing to hire at that wage. Workers who are unemployed for this reason are sometimes said to be *in surplus*. We focus on surplus workers so that we can examine their opportunity costs when they are hired for a government project. This issue is of particular importance because there are government projects that are specifically designed to put surplus workers to work and numerous other projects that are likely to hire such workers. Of course, there are other forms of unemployment than the type considered here. For example, some persons are briefly unemployed while they move from one job to another.

Before discussing how the opportunity cost of surplus labor might be measured, it may be useful to consider more explicitly the extent to which the labor hired to work on a government project reduces the number of unemployed workers.[29] Consider, for example, a project that hires 100 workers. How many fewer workers will be unemployed as a result? In considering this question, it is important to recognize that the project does not have to hire directly from the ranks of the unemployed. Even if the project hires 100 previously employed persons, this will result in 100 job vacancies, some of which may be filled by the unemployed. If the unemployment rate for the type of workers hired for the project (as determined by their occupation and geographic location) is very high (say, over 10 or 15%), the number of unemployed workers may fall by nearly 100. But if the unemployment rate for the workers is low (say, below 5%), most of the measured unemployed are probably between jobs rather than in surplus. As a consequence, the project is likely to cause little reduction in the number of persons who are unemployed. Instead the project will draw its workforce from those

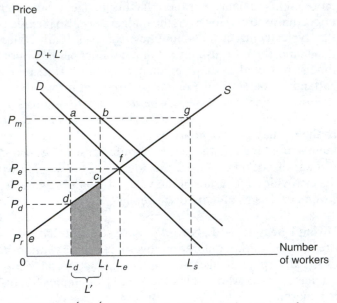

FIGURE 4-14 Opportunity Costs with a Price Floor

employed elsewhere or out of the labor force. At rates of unemployment between 5 and 10 percent, the reduction in the number of unemployed persons will probably be well under 100 but substantially above zero.

Figure 4-14 depicts a situation in which a government project reduces unemployment. In this figure, the pre-project demand curve for labor, D, and the supply curve for labor, S, intersect at P_e, the equilibrium price in the absence of the wage floor, P_m. At the wage floor, L_s, workers desire employment, but only L_d workers are demanded so that $L_s - L_d$ workers are in surplus and thus unemployed. Now imagine that L' workers are hired for a government project at a wage of P_m. This shifts the demand curve to the right by L'. As long as L' is less than the number of unemployed laborers, the price remains at the floor.

We now consider five alternative measures of the social cost of hiring the L' unemployed workers. All five of these measures are subject to criticism. Indeed, it is not obvious that, as a practical matter, it is possible to obtain an accurate value of the social cost of hiring the unemployed. However, some of the alternative measures described here are far better approximations of the true social cost than others.

1. **Measure A.** It is sometimes suggested that because the unemployed are not working, there are zero opportunity costs in putting them to work. This treats the unemployed, however, as if their time is valueless. This is clearly inappropriate on two grounds. First, many unemployed persons are in fact engaged in productive enterprises such as job search, child care, and home improvements. Second, even if they were completely at leisure, leisure itself has value to those who are enjoying it. Consequently, few, if any, unemployed persons are willing to work at a zero wage. Indeed, the supply curve in Figure 4-14 represents the value that various individuals, both those who are employed and those who are unemployed, place on

their time when they are not employed. For example, an individual located at point f would only be willing to accept employment at a price of P_e or greater. Thus, P_e provides a measure of the value that this person places on his or her time. In other words, his or her opportunity cost of giving up leisure time to work is P_e. Similarly, individuals located on the supply curve at points c and d value their time at P_c and P_d, respectively. No individual is willing to work at a price below P_r, and, as P_r has a positive value, Figure 4-14 implies that the opportunity cost of hiring the unemployed must be above zero.

2. **Measure B.** Figure 4-14 indicates that total budgetary expenditure on labor for this project is P_m times L', which equals the area of rectangle abL_tL_d. This budgetary outlay for labor, however, is likely to overstate substantially the true social cost of hiring workers for the project. As implied by the supply curve in Figure 4-14, although employed workers are paid a price of P_m, most would be willing to work for less. This difference between the value they place on their time, as indicated by the supply curve, and P_m, the price they are actually paid while employed, is producer (i.e., worker) surplus, which may be viewed as a transfer to the workers from the government agency hiring them. To obtain a measure of the social cost of hiring workers for the project, this producer surplus must be subtracted from the budgetary expenditure on labor. Measure B fails to do this.

3. **Measure C.** As the project expands employment in the market represented by Figure 4-14 from L_d to L_t, one might assume that the trapezoid $abcd$ represents producer surplus enjoyed by the newly hired. Given this assumption, one would subtract area $abcd$ from area abL_tL_d to obtain a measure of the social cost of hiring workers for the project. Thus, the social cost would be measured as the shaded trapezoid cdL_dL_t, the area under the supply curve between L_d and L_t. This shaded area would equal the opportunity cost of the newly hired workers—that is, the value of the time they give up when they go to work.

4. **Measure D.** One shortcoming of measure C is that it is implicitly based on an assumption that all the unemployed persons hired for the project value their time at less than P_c and at greater than P_d. In other words, this approach assumes that these workers are all located between points c and d on the supply curve. However, there is no basis for such an assumption. Indeed, it is quite likely that some of the hired unemployed persons value their time at well above P_c and that others value their time at well under P_d. In fact, the figure implies that unemployed persons who value their time as low as P_r and as high as P_m would be willing to work on the project because the project would pay them a price of P_m. Thus, perhaps, a better assumption is that the unemployed persons who would actually get hired for the project are distributed more or less equally along the supply curve between points e and g, rather than being confined between points d and c. This assumption implies that the unemployed persons who are hired for the project value their time by no more than P_m, by no less than P_r, and, on average, by $1/2(P_m + P_r)$. Thus, the social cost of hiring L' workers for the project would be computed as equal to $1/2(P_m + P_r)(L')$.

5. **Measure E.** One practical problem with using measure D in an actual CBA is that the value of P_r, the lowest price at which any worker represented in Figure 4-14 would be willing to accept employment, is unlikely to be known. Given this, some

assumption about the value of P_r must be made. One possible, and perhaps not unreasonable, assumption is that the supply curve passes through the origin and, hence, the value of P_r equals zero. The fact that the probabilities of illness, divorce, and suicide all increase with unemployment, while job skills deteriorate, suggest that P_r could, in practice, be very low for at least some unemployed persons. If we once again assume that the unemployed persons who are hired for the project are distributed more or less equally along the supply curve between the point at which it intersects the vertical axis and point g, then this implies that the unemployed persons who are hired for the project value their time by no more than P_m, by no less than zero, and, on average, by $\frac{1}{2}(P_m + 0) = \frac{1}{2}P_m$. Hence, the social cost of hiring workers for the project would be computed as $\frac{1}{2}P_m(L')$. Note that the estimate provided by this computation is equal to half the government's budgetary outlay. While this cost estimate would be smaller and almost certainly less accurate than that computed using measure D, it is usually easier to obtain.

Given our preceding argument that nonwork time has a positive value, measure E is probably best viewed as providing an easily obtainable lower-bound estimate of the true project social costs for labor, while the project budgetary cost for labor, measure B, provides an upper-bound estimate.

Purchases from a Monopoly.　We now turn to a final example of measuring the social cost of project or program purchases in an inefficient market—the purchase of an input supplied by a monopoly. In this circumstance, a government agency's budgetary outlay overstates the true social costs resulting from the purchase. This overstatement occurs because the price of the input exceeds the social cost of producing it. As a consequence, a substantial share of the revenues a monopolist receives are transfers or *monopoly rents*. Thus, in principle, a CBA should not use the budgetary outlay as a measure of social cost.

Figure 4-15 illustrates a government agency's purchase of an input from a monopoly. Prior to the purchase, the input is produced at level Q_1, where the monopolist's marginal cost and marginal revenue curves intersect. The price at Q_1, as determined by the demand curve, is P_1. Now, as a result of the agency's purchase of Q' units, the monopolist's demand curve and marginal revenue curve shift to the right. The price of the input increases to P_2 and the quantity sold increases to Q_2. At the new higher price, the agency purchases a quantity equal to the distance between Q_3 and Q_2, while the original buyers in the market reduce the quantity they purchase by an amount equal to the distance between Q_1 and Q_3.

As in our previous examples, the direct budgetary cost of the agency's purchase equals the price times the quantity purchased: $P_2(Q_2 - Q_3)$. In Figure 4-15, this is represented by the rectangle between Q_3 and Q_2 and bounded by P_2 (i.e., areas $A + C + G + E$). However, these budgetary costs overstate the true social cost. To find the true social cost of the agency's purchase, one must examine the effects of the purchase on the monopolist and the original buyers of the input, as well as on the agency's revenues.

Because the monopolist sells more of the input at higher prices, its producer surplus increases. This increase has two parts: (1) that resulting from the higher price the monopolist now receives for the units that it previously sold (which is represented in

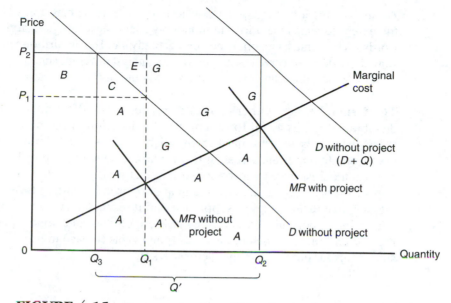

FIGURE 4-15 Opportunity Costs When Buying from a Monopoly

Figure 4-15 by areas $B + C + E$), and (2) that resulting from the additional units that the monopolist now sells (area G). Thus, as can be seen from the figure, part of the cost to the agency, areas $C + G + E$, is a transfer to the monopolist.

Original buyers in the market are clearly worse off as a result of the agency's purchase because they now have to pay a higher price for the input. In measuring their loss of consumer surplus, it is the original demand curve that is pertinent because this is the curve that reflects the original buyers' WTP for the input. Thus, the total loss in consumer surplus by the original buyers, all of which is a transfer to the monopolist, is equal to areas $B + C$.

The following distributional accounting ledger summarizes the effects of the purchase:

	Benefits	Costs
Original buyers		$B + C$
Monopolistic seller	$B + C + G + E$	
Project expenditures		$A + C + G + E$
Net social cost		$A + C$

The major conclusion of this analysis is that in the case of input purchases from a monopolist, budgetary expenditures are larger than the social costs. The reason is that the price the monopoly charges exceeds the marginal cost of producing the input. Consequently, in conducting a CBA, the government's budgetary cost should, in principle, be adjusted downward through shadow pricing. In practice, however, the error that would result from using the unadjusted budgetary expenditures would often not be very large.

As an examination of Figure 4-15 suggests, the size of the bias, areas $G + E$, depends on the extent to which the price the monopoly charges exceeds its marginal costs—in other words, on how much monopoly power it actually has. This, in turn, depends on how steeply sloped the demand curve is. Thus, before an analyst develops shadow prices, a sometimes difficult undertaking, he or she should ask whether it is really necessary to do so.

The General Rule.   Other market distortions also affect opportunity costs in predictable ways. It is useful to summarize the direction of the bias created by some of these distortions. In factor markets in which supply is taxed, direct expenditure outlays overestimate opportunity cost; in factor markets in which supply is subsidized, expenditures underestimate opportunity cost. In factor markets exhibiting positive externalities of supply, expenditures overestimate opportunity cost; in factor markets exhibiting negative externalities of supply, expenditures underestimate opportunity costs. To determine opportunity costs in such cases, apply the rule: opportunity cost equals direct expenditures on the factor minus (plus) gains (losses) in producer surplus or consumer surplus occurring in the factor market.

CONCLUSIONS

This chapter has shown that the benefits and costs associated with government programs and projects are appropriately determined by valuing the resulting changes in net government revenue flows, producer surplus, and consumer surplus. Even when the relevant demand and supply curves are known, great care must be exercised in order to measure the changes appropriately, especially when the relevant markets are distorted. Two types of relevant markets were considered: the market in which the policy intervention takes place and factor markets where the government purchases the inputs required by the program or project. These markets, primary markets, are the ones that are directly affected by a particular policy. Markets that are indirectly affected— secondary markets—are the focus of the following chapter.

EXERCISES FOR CHAPTER 4

1.   Consider a low-wage labor market. Workers in this market are not presently covered by the minimum wage, but the government is considering implementing such legislation. If implemented, this law would require employers in the market to pay workers a $5 hourly wage. Suppose all workers in the market are equally productive, the current market-clearing wage rate is $4 per hour, and that at this market-clearing wage there are 600 employed workers. Further suppose that under the minimum wage legislation, only 500 workers would be employed and 300 workers would be unemployed. Finally, assume that the market demand and supply curves are linear and that the market reservation wage, the lowest wage at which any worker in the market would be willing to work, is $1.

   Compute the dollar value of the impact of the policy on employers, workers, and society as a whole.

2.   Suppose the government is considering an increase in the toll on a certain stretch of highway from $.40 to $.50. At present, 50,000 cars per week use that highway stretch; after the toll is imposed, it is projected that only 40,000 cars per week will use the highway stretch.

a. Assuming that the marginal cost of highway use is constant (i.e., the supply curve is horizontal) and equal to $.40 per car, what is the net cost to society attributable to the increase in the toll? (Hint: the toll increase will cause the supply curve, not the demand curve, to shift.)

b. Because of the reduced use of the highway, the government would reduce its purchases of concrete from 20,000 tons per year to 19,000 tons per year. Thus, if the price of concrete were $25 per ton, the government's cost savings would be $25,000. However, the government's reduced demand for concrete causes its market price to fall from $25 to $24.50 per ton. Moreover, because of this reduction in price, the purchases of concrete by nongovernment buyers increase by 300 tons per year. Assuming that the factor market for concrete is competitive, can the government's savings of $25,000 be appropriately used as the measure of the social value of the cost savings that result from the government purchasing less concrete? Or would shadow pricing be necessary?

3. A country imports 3 billion barrels of crude oil per year and domestically produces another 3 billion barrels of crude oil per year. The world price of crude oil is $90 per barrel. Assuming linear curves, economists estimate the price elasticity of domestic supply to be 0.25 and the price elasticity of domestic demand to be 0.1 at the current equilibrium.

a. Consider the changes in social surplus that would result from imposition of a $30 per barrel import fee on crude oil that would involve annual administrative costs of $250 million. Assume that the world price will not change as a result of the country imposing the import fee, but that the domestic price will increase by $30 per barrel. Also assume that only producers, consumers, and taxpayers within the country have standing. Determine the quantity consumed, the quantity produced domestically, and the quantity imported after the imposition of the import fee. Then estimate the annual social net benefits of the import fee.

b. Economists have estimated that the marginal excess burden of taxation in the country is 0.25 (see Chapter 3). Reestimate the social net benefits assuming that 20 percent of the increase in producer surplus is realized as tax revenue under the existing tax system. In answering this question, assume that increases in tax revenues less the cost of administrating the import fee are used to reduce domestic taxes.

c. The reduction in the country's demand for imports may affect the world price of crude oil. Assuming that the import fee reduces the world price from $90 to $80 per barrel, and thus, the after-tax domestic price is $80 + $30 = $110 per barrel, a net increase in domestic price of $20 per barrel, repeat the analysis done in parts a and b.

4. (Instructor-provided spreadsheet recommended.) A proposed government project in a rural area with 100 unemployed persons would require the hiring of 20 workers. The project would offer wages of $12 per hour. Imagine that the reservation wages of the 100 unemployed fall between $2 and $20.

a. Estimate the opportunity cost of the labor required for the project assuming that the government makes random offers to the 100 unemployed until 20 of them accept jobs. (First, generate a list of the reservation prices of 100 persons according to the formula $2 + $18u$ where u is a random variable distributed uniformly [0,1]. Second, work down the list to identify the first 20 workers with reservation wages less than $12. Third, sum the reservation wages of these 20 workers to get the opportunity cost of the labor used for the project.)

b. Estimate the opportunity cost of the labor required for the project assuming that the government can identify and hire the 20 unemployed with the lowest reservation wages.

c. Repeat part a 15 times to get a distribution for the opportunity cost and compute its standard deviation.

NOTES

1. For a detailed examination of government failures, see David L. Weimer and Aidan R. Vining, *Policy Analysis: Concepts and Practice*, 5th ed. (Upper Saddle River, NJ: Pearson Prentice Hall, 2011), Chapter 8.

2. As mentioned in Chapter 1, sometimes a policy outcome that people would be willing to pay to avoid is referred to as a negative benefit, rather than as a cost. These two terms can be viewed as equivalent.

3. A change in price only causes a movement along the supply curve, a change in quantity supplied. But a project that provides more of a good increases the supply of the good, resulting in a shift of the supply curve.

4. This assumes, of course, that the market is sufficiently competitive and the firms in it are sufficiently efficient that all of the cost savings are passed on to consumers in the form of a price decrease.

5. An alternative method of measuring the gain in social surplus is simply to compare total social surplus with and without the project. In the absence of the project, total social surplus would be represented by the triangular area *fae*, while in the presence of the project, total social surplus would be represented by the triangular area *fbd*. Subtracting the smaller triangle from the larger triangle, we again find that the net gain in social surplus equals the trapezoidal area *abde*.

6. For a theoretical treatment of externalities, public goods, and club goods, see Richard Corres and Todd Sandler, *The Theory of Externalities, Public Goods and Club Goods* (New York: Cambridge University Press, 1986).

7. There are, of course, other types of markets in which individual firms have market power—for example, those characterized by oligopoly or monopolistic competition. We focus on markets characterized by monopoly, and especially natural monopoly, because government intervention is most likely to occur in these markets.

8. Of course, foreign-owned firms, regardless of whether they are competitive or monopolistic, usually would not be given standing. Therefore, their benefits would not be counted in a CBA.

9. There are, of course, alternative policies that the government might adopt in response to the

10. monopoly. For example, it might tax the monopolist's profits, regulate the prices the monopolist charges, or operate it as a state-owned enterprise.

11. For a survey of recent infrastructure of public-private partnerships (P3s) in the United States and Canada, see Aidan R. Vining, Anthony E. Boardman, and Finn Poschmann, "Public-Private Partnerships in the US and Canada: 'There are No Free Lunches'," *Journal of Comparative Policy Analysis* 7(3) 2005, 199–220. This article discusses a number of road projects including the Dulles Greenway in Virginia, SR 91 Express Lanes in Orange County, Highway 407 outside Toronto, and the Confederation Bridge that links Prince Edward Island to the mainland of Canada.

12. In principle, it is possible that D_u could be to the left of D_i, rather than to the right of it as shown in Figure 4-6. This would occur if instead of desiring more of the product in the absence of information concerning it than they would with the information, consumers desire less of it. In practice, however, such situations are unlikely to continue for long because strong incentives would exist for sellers to eliminate such information asymmetry by providing buyers with the needed information, thereby increasing their demand for the product. When the actual demand curve is to the right of the fully informed demand curve, the incentive, in contrast, is for sellers to withhold the information.

13. The two demand curves are drawn closer together at high prices rather than at low prices to imply that at higher prices buyers would go to more trouble to obtain additional information about the product than they would at lower prices. Whether or not this is actually the case, however, is not essential to the analysis.

14. This is discussed more fully in Aidan R. Vining and David L. Weimer, "Information Asymmetry Favoring Sellers: A Policy Framework," *Policy Sciences* 21(4) 1988, 281–303.

15. For a more extensive discussion of these three types of products, see Vining and Weimer, "Information Asymmetry Favoring Sellers: A Policy Framework."

16. For an entertaining discussion of possible misuses of the term "externality" and when intervention may or may not be appropriate for

correcting externalities, see Virginia Postrel, "External Cost: The Dangers of Calling Everything Pollution," *Reason*, 1999.

16. This tax can be levied either in the traditional manner—that is, on the good itself—or, alternatively, by the government issuing transferable permits that, in effect, tax effluents emitted by firms, rather than the goods they produce. Under the latter approach, which is currently being used in the United States to control sulphur dioxide emissions, firms that have found ways to control their pollution relatively inexpensively can sell their permits to pollute to firms for which pollution control would be relatively more costly.

17. Indeed, when, as in the case illustrated in Figure 4-7, the tax is levied on the good, there is no special incentive for firms to reduce the amount of pollution resulting from their production process. However, when the effluent itself is taxed—for example, through use of the transferable pollution permits discussed in the previous endnote—such incentives do exist.

18. In this example, gross program benefits only differ from net program costs by the administrative costs required to operate the program. Also notice that in the context of the example the rule that gross project benefits equal changes in social surplus plus net revenues generated by the project continues to hold once it is recognized that in this instance net revenues are actually negative.

19. The free-rider problem is also closely linked to difficulties in remedying problems resulting from externalities. For example, because clean air is both nonrivalrous and nonexcludable, in the absence of government intervention, limited incentives exist for the private sector to produce clean air by reducing air pollution.

20. Gary S. Becker and Kevin M. Murphy, "A Theory of Rational Addiction," *Journal of Political Economy* 96(4) 1988, 675–700.

21. Independent developments of this approach can be found in Fritz L. Laux, "Addiction as a Market Failure: Using Rational Addiction Results to Justify Tobacco Regulation," *Journal of Health Economics* 19(4) 2000, 421–437; and Australian Productivity Commission, *Australia's Gambling Industries*, Inquiry Report No. 10, 26 1999, Appendix C, 11–13. Available at www.pc.gov.au/ inquiry/gambling/finalreport/index.html.27.

22. Australian Productivity Commission, *Australia Gambling Industries,* Chapter 5, p. 24.

23. If the government were to purchase only a small part of the fixed supply of land on the open market, its budgetary outlay would very closely approximate the opportunity cost of removing the land from the private sector. In this case, the government's entry into the market would bid up the price of the land slightly, crowding potential private-sector land buyers who are just to the left of point b on the demand curve out of the market. These buyers would lose a negligible amount of surplus. In addition, those private-sector buyers who remain in the market would pay a slightly higher price. Hence, surplus would be transferred between these buyers and the sellers of the land.

24. There is a natural tendency for those who are promoting a particular government project (e.g., a dam or a recreational area) to emphasize the potential benefits to those who must supply resources to the project. Our analysis suggests that in well-functioning markets these benefits only occur if the price of these resources increases, and even then, part of the benefits to the suppliers of the resources is offset by increases in costs to the original buyers of the resources. Note, however, that the analysis is based on the assumption that the resources used in the project would be fully employed even in the absence of the project. As will be seen later in this chapter, if this assumption does not hold, additional project benefits can then accrue to suppliers of resources.

25. Kerry Krutilla emphasizes the importance of using a social accounting ledger (which he calls a "Kaldor-Hicks" tableau) in CBA in order to reveal fully program or project effects on all the affected stakeholder groups. Depending on the circumstances, the tableau Krutilla suggests can become can become fairly elaborate. Chapter 19 further considers the distribution of project costs and benefits among stakeholder groups. Kerry Krutilla, "Using the Kaldor-Hicks Tableau Format for Cost-Benefit Analysis and Policy Evaluation," *Journal of Policy Analysis and Management* 24(4) 2005, 864–875.

26. This formula is based on a bit of geometry. The triangular area C equals one-half the rectangular area from which it is formed, $B + C + F$. Thus, area C is equivalent to $1/2(P_1 - P_0)(q')$.

27. This amount is derived as follows:

$$P_1q' - \tfrac{1}{2}(P_1 - P_0)q' = \tfrac{1}{2}(P_0 + P_1)(q').$$

28. For a discussion of various forms of wage rigidity that result in unemployment, see Ronald G. Ehrenberg and Robert S. Smith, *Modern Labor Economics: Theory and Public Policy,* 7th ed. (Reading, MA: Addison Wesley Longman, Inc., 2000), Chapter 15.

29. For more detailed discussions of these issues, see Robert H. Haveman, "Evaluating Public Expenditure Under Conditions of Unemployment," in *Public Expenditure and Policy Analysis,* 3rd ed., Robert H. Haveman and Julius Margolis, eds. (Boston: Houghton Mifflin Company, 1983), 167–182; and E. J. Mishan, *Cost-Benefit Analysis*, 4th ed. (London: Unwin Hyman, 1988), 325–329.

Valuing Benefits and Costs in Secondary Markets

In conducting CBAs of government policies, there is a natural tendency to list as many effects of the policies as one's imagination permits. For example, an improvement in public transportation in a particular city may increase bus usage and reduce car usage. It may also reduce downtown pollution and congestion. In addition, it may reduce the demand for automobile repairs, parking places, and gasoline.

To assess these effects, one must first determine which occur in primary markets and which occur in secondary markets. Primary markets refer to markets that are directly affected by a policy, while secondary markets are markets that are indirectly affected. The changes in bus usage previously mentioned clearly occur in the primary market for public transportation. The reductions in pollution and congestion also can be thought of as occurring in the primary market for public transportation, though these particular impacts are in the external, or missing, part of that market. Any effect that occurs in a primary market should be accounted for in a CBA. On the other hand, effects on the demand for auto repairs, parking places, and gasoline occur in secondary markets and, as will be seen, often can (and indeed should) be ignored in conducting CBA. This last group of effects is often referred to as *secondary, second-round, spillover, side, pecuniary,* or *indirect effects.*

While Chapter 4 examined the benefits and costs of government policies that occur in primary markets, this chapter focuses on policy impacts in secondary markets. As in Chapter 4, we distinguish between efficient and distorted markets. In addition, the chapter takes a brief look at the special implications of secondary market effects for local communities, as the benefits of such effects are often touted by advocates of local infrastructure projects such as sports stadiums and convention centers.

VALUING BENEFITS AND COSTS IN EFFICIENT SECONDARY MARKETS

Complements and Substitutes

Secondary market effects result because government policies affect the prices of goods in primary markets, and this, in turn, noticeably affects the demand for other goods. These latter goods are referred to as *complements* and *substitutes.*

Consider the following example. Stocking a lake near a city with fish lowers the effective price of access to fishing grounds for the city's residents. They not only fish more often, but they also demand more bait and fishing equipment. We say that access

115

to fishing grounds and fishing equipment are complements because a decrease (increase) in the price of one will result in an increase (decrease) in the demand for the other. In contrast, fishing is a substitute for golfing because as the price of fishing goes down (up), the demand for golfing goes down (up).

If government policies affect the demand for goods in secondary markets, then prices in these secondary markets may or may not change as a result. We first discuss the simpler situation in which prices do not change. We then analyze the more complex situation in which prices do change in secondary markets.

Efficient Secondary Market Effects without Price Changes

Because most goods have substantial numbers of complements and substitutes, many government projects cause effects in large numbers of secondary markets. Accounting for all these effects would impose an enormous burden on analysts. Fortunately, however, such effects can often be ignored in CBA without substantially biasing the estimates of net benefits. When can we ignore secondary market effects? *We can, and indeed should, ignore impacts in undistorted secondary markets as long as changes in social surplus in the primary market resulting from a government project are measured **and** prices in the secondary markets do not change.* The reason for this is that in the absence of price adjustments in secondary markets in response to price changes in primary markets, impacts are typically fully measured as surplus changes in primary markets. Measuring the same effects in both markets will, therefore, result in double counting. Thus, for example, if prices of fishing equipment do not change, then the increased consumption of fishing equipment is not relevant to the CBA of a project that increases access to fishing grounds.

A closer look at the fishing example should make the rule for the treatment of secondary markets clearer. For simplicity, we assume that the price of fishing equals the marginal social cost of fishing and that this marginal social cost is constant. This, in turn, implies that no producer surplus or externalities exist in the primary market (e.g., highway congestion does not result because of increased travel to the newly stocked lake).

Figure 5-1(a) shows the market for "fishing days." Prior to the stocking of the nearby lake, the effective price of a day of fishing (largely the time costs of travel) was P_{F_0}, the travel cost to a lake much further away. Once fishing is available at the nearby lake, the effective price falls to P_{F_1} and, as a consequence, the number of days spent fishing by local residents rises from q_{F_0} to q_{F_1}. The resulting increase in social surplus equals the area of trapezoid $P_{F_0}abP_{F_1}$, the gain in consumer surplus. We measure this gain in consumer surplus using the demand schedule for fishing, D_F. As is customary in textbooks, this demand schedule should be viewed as the relation between price and quantity that would exist in the primary market if the prices of all secondary goods were held constant. Later we discuss the importance of this assumption.

Now consider the market for fishing equipment. The decline in the effective price of fishing days shifts the demand schedule for fishing equipment from D_{E_0} to D_{E_1} as shown in Figure 5-1(b). If the supply schedule is perfectly elastic, which is likely when the local market accounts for only a small fraction of regional or national demand, then the shift in demand will not increase the price of fishing equipment.

Does this shift in demand for fishing equipment represent a change in consumer welfare that should be counted in a CBA of the fish-stocking project? In other words, should the gap between the old and new demand schedules that is above the price line

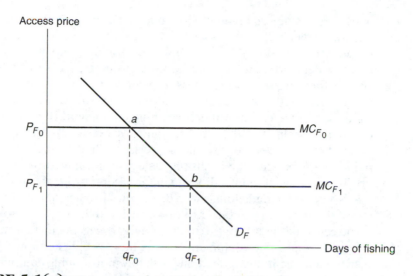

FIGURE 5-1(a) Primary Market: Market for Fishing Days

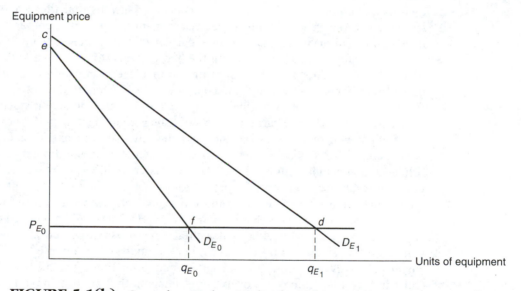

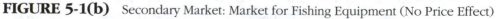

FIGURE 5-1(b) Secondary Market: Market for Fishing Equipment (No Price Effect)

be counted as an additional increase in consumer surplus? It is tempting to treat the increase in consumer surplus from efP_{E_0} to cdP_{E_0} in panel (b) as an additional increase in social benefits that should be added to $P_{F_0}abP_{F_1}$ in panel (a), but this should *not* be done. As discussed next, doing so would result in double counting. As long as price does not change in the equipment market as a result of stocking the lake, the social surplus change in the fishing market measures the entire benefit from the stocking project.

To see this, first consider fishers who already own all the fishing equipment they need at the time the lake is stocked and, hence, presently contribute no demand to the market for fishing equipment. The value that these persons place on their existing fishing equipment will tend to increase as a result of stocking the nearby lake. However, because they are not in the market for new fishing equipment, the gap between the old and new demand schedules for new fishing equipment does not reflect this increase. Of course, these persons' willingness to pay (WTP) for fishing days will presumably be higher than it otherwise would have been as a result of the fact that they will not have to make further expenditures for fishing equipment. But any additional increase in consumer surplus that these fishers enjoy as a result of already owning fishing equipment at the time the nearby lake is stocked will already be reflected by the primary market demand schedule for fishing days, which will be further to the right than it otherwise would be. It cannot show up in the secondary market for fishing equipment.

Now consider individuals who do not own fishing equipment at the time the lake is stocked but are now induced to make such purchases. The gap between the two demand schedules in Figure 5-1(b) accurately reveals the increased value that these persons place on fishing equipment. That is, these people are now willing to pay more for fishing equipment, and indeed they will buy more fishing equipment. It is the only way they can fully realize surplus gains from the stocking project. But this expenditure is not an additional benefit from the stocking project. Just like the fishers who already own fishing equipment, the increase in consumer surplus that these persons receive from the stocking project is fully reflected by the primary market demand schedule for fishing days. This includes any consumer surplus that they receive from their purchases of fishing equipment. Thus, counting the gap between the two demand schedules in panel (b) as benefits and also counting the increase in consumer surplus shown in panel (a) as benefits would result in counting the same benefits twice.

Persons who do not own fishing equipment at the time the lake is stocked would be even better off if, like the current owners of fishing equipment, they did not have to buy new equipment in order to take advantage of the newly stocked lake. Thus, everything else being equal, WTP for fishing days is presumably greater among those who already own fishing equipment than among those who must purchase it. The increase in consumer surplus that results from the stocking project for both groups, even if different from one another, will be fully reflected in the primary market demand schedule for fishing days.

It is important to stress that secondary market effects can be ignored only if social surplus in the primary market is measured directly. As discussed in greater detail in Chapter 14, in situations in which cost-benefit analysts are unable to measure social surplus changes in primary markets, they may infer them instead from the demand shifts in secondary markets. For example, imagine that analysts have no information about the demand schedule for fishing days, but they do know how the demand schedule for fishing equipment will change. With no direct measure of the benefits from stocking the lake, they might use the difference between the social surplus in the fishing equipment market after the project (based on demand schedule D_{E_1}) and the social surplus in the equipment market prior to the project (based on demand schedule D_{E_0}). They would then apply some sort of scaling factor to correct for the underestimation that results from the fact that not all the consumer surplus from fishing will be reflected in the equipment market. (Because some fishers will use old equipment and collect their own bait, their surplus will not appear in the equipment market. Moreover, equipment and bait comprise only some of the inputs to fishing.)

Efficient Secondary Market Effects with Price Changes[1]

The situation is more complex when the supply schedule in the secondary market is upward sloping. To see this, we examine the effect of stocking the lake on the demand for golfing. In Figure 5-2a, panel (a) once again shows the demand for fishing days, while panel (b) now shows the demand for golfing days. As before, the reduction in the price of fishing days from P_{F_0} to P_{F_1} as a result of stocking the lake causes an increase in social surplus equal to the area $P_{F_0}abP_{F_1}$ (for the moment ignore demand schedules D_{F_1} and D^*).

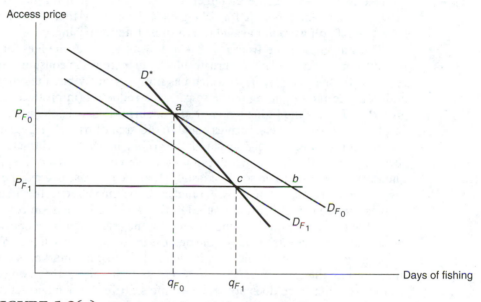

FIGURE 5-2(a)   Primary Market: Market for Fishing Days

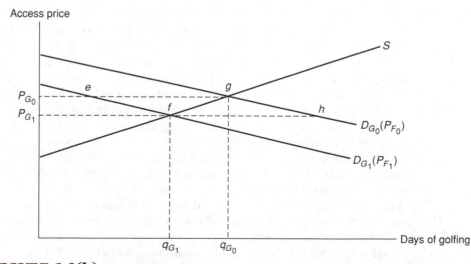

FIGURE 5-2(b)   Secondary Market: Market for Golfing Days (Price Effects)

As fishing and golf are presumed to be substitutes, a reduction in the price of fishing days from P_{F_0} to P_{F_1} would cause the demand for golfing to fall. Thus, the demand schedule for golfing in panel (b) would shift to the left from D_{G_0} to D_{G_1}. As previously emphasized, by itself this shift does not represent a change in consumer surplus that is not already fully accounted for in measuring the change in consumer surplus in the primary market. Golfers are obviously not made worse off by stocking the lake, although some may now place a lower valuation on golf. Instead, by itself, the shift in demand merely indicates that in the absence of golf, the consumer surplus gains from stocking the lake would have been even larger. The existence of golf is reflected in the location of D_{F_0}, the demand schedule for fishing days, which is farther to the left than it would have been if golf were not available as a substitute for fishing.

The shift of demand from D_{G_0} to D_{G_1}, however, causes the fees for golf course use to fall from P_{G_0} to P_{G_1}. This, in turn, results in an increase in consumer surplus, one represented by the area $P_{G_0}efP_{G_1}$, which has not previously been taken into account. In addition, the fall in golfing fees also causes a reduction in producer surplus equal to area $P_{G_0}gfP_{G_1}$. As the reduction in producer surplus exceeds the increase in consumer surplus, a net loss in social surplus equal to the area of triangle *efg* results.[2]

Should this loss in social surplus in the golfing market be subtracted from the social surplus gain in the fishing market in measuring net gains from the project? It is frequently unnecessary to do so. The reason is that the increase in consumer surplus gain in the fishing market is often likely, in practice, to be measured as the area $P_{F_0}acP_{F_1}$ rather than as the area $P_{F_0}abP_{F_1}$. If measured in this way, the increase in consumer surplus in the fishing market would be understated by the triangular area *abc*, but this triangle closely approximates triangle *efg*, the net loss in social surplus in the golfing market.

To see why the consumer surplus gain in the fishing market is often, in practice, measured as the area $P_{F_0}acP_{F_1}$ rather than as the area $P_{F_0}abP_{F_1}$, one must recognize that our fishing story does not end with the shift in the demand schedule in the secondary market. If golf and fishing are substitutes, the reduction in golf course fees will cause people to switch from fishing to golf, and the demand for fishing days will fall. This is shown in panel (a) as a leftward shift in the demand schedule for fishing days from D_{F_0} to D_{F_1}. By itself, this shift does not cause any further changes in social surplus; because we have assumed that the supply of fishing days is perfectly elastic, prices in the market for fishing days are unaffected. Note, however, that by drawing a line between the original and the final equilibrium points in panel (a) of Figure 5-2—that is, between points *a* and *c*—one can derive a special type of demand schedule, D^*.

This demand schedule, which is sometimes called an *observed* or *equilibrium demand schedule*,[3] indicates what the demand for fishing days will be once prices in other markets, including the market for golfing days, have fully adjusted to the change in prices in the market for fishing days. Thus, D^* differs from the demand schedules D_{F_0} and D_{F_1}, which, as mentioned earlier, indicate the number of fishing days demanded at each price for fishing days, *holding the prices of all other goods constant*. As it is frequently difficult statistically to hold the prices of secondary goods constant while measuring the relation between price and quantity demanded in a primary market, empirically estimated demand schedules—the ones actually observed and available for use in a CBA—often more closely resemble equilibrium demand schedules such as D^* than "textbook-style" demand schedules such as D_{F_0} and D_{F_1}.[4]

Thus, the equilibrium demand schedule, D^*, is the one that is often used in practice to obtain a measure of the increase in social surplus resulting from the reduction in the price of fishing days. However, the resulting measure, $P_{F_0}acP_{F_1}$, understates the true measure of the gain in social surplus in the primary market, $P_{F_0}abP_{F_0}$, by the triangular area abc. But, as previously suggested, area abc provides a good approximation of area efg in panel (b),[5] the area that should be subtracted from area $P_{F_0}acP_{F_1}$ to obtain an accurate measure of the overall net gains from stocking the lake. In other words, area abc represents part of the benefits from the fish-stocking project and area efg an approximately offsetting cost of the project. Hence, by using the equilibrium demand schedule to measure the change in social surplus, we incorporate social surplus changes that occur in the market for golfing days, as well as those that occur in the market for fishing days. We do not have to obtain separate measures of the surplus changes that occur in secondary markets.[6]

This is important because it illustrates an important general point: by using an equilibrium demand schedule for the primary market—the type of demand schedule that is often empirically estimated, and thus available—one can capture the effects of policy interventions in both the primary market in which they were initiated *and* in all secondary markets. Thus, we can restate our earlier rule concerning project impacts in secondary markets: *we should ignore effects in undistorted secondary markets, regardless of whether there are price changes, if we are measuring benefits in the primary market using empirically measured demand schedules that do not hold prices in secondary markets constant.*

VALUING BENEFITS AND COSTS IN DISTORTED SECONDARY MARKETS

Unfortunately, use of equilibrium demand schedules in primary markets misses some of the relevant effects that occur in distorted secondary markets—that is, in secondary markets in which prices do not equal social marginal costs. To see why, examine Figure 5-3, a slightly altered version of panel (b) of Figure 5-1. This new figure is based on the assumption that because of negative externalities the market price of fishing equipment, P_{E_0}, underestimates the marginal social cost by x cents. (Think of the equipment as lead sinkers, some of which eventually end up in the lake, where they poison ducks and other wildlife. The x cents would then represent the value of the expected loss of wildlife from the sale of another sinker.) In this case, the expansion of consumption involves a social surplus loss equal to x times $q_{E_1} - q_{E_0}$, which is represented in Figure 5-3 by the shaded rectangle. This loss, which is not reflected at all by market demand or supply schedules in the fishing market, should be subtracted from the benefits occurring in that market in order to obtain an accurate measure of net gains from the program.

Another type of distortion in secondary markets is imposed by the presence of taxes. For example, Figure 5-4 illustrates local produce markets for beef and chicken, which are substitutes for one another. For simplicity, the supply schedules in both markets are assumed to be perfectly elastic. In the absence of any taxes on these products, the price of beef (the primary good) would be P_B and the price of chicken (the secondary good) would be P_C.

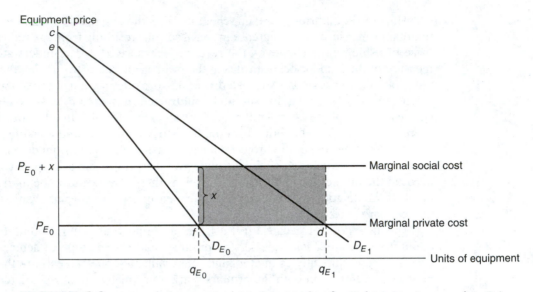

FIGURE 5-3 Distorted Secondary Market: Market for Fishing Equipment (No Price Effect)

For purposes of our illustration, let us assume that chicken is currently subject to a tax of t_C cents per pound, but beef is not presently taxed. In this situation, the existing demand schedules for beef and chicken are represented by D_{B_0} and D_{C_0}, respectively. As panel (b) of Figure 5-4 indicates, the tax on chicken provides the government with revenue equal to area T but reduces consumer surplus by areas $T + U$. Thus, the tax on chicken results in deadweight loss equal to the triangular area U.

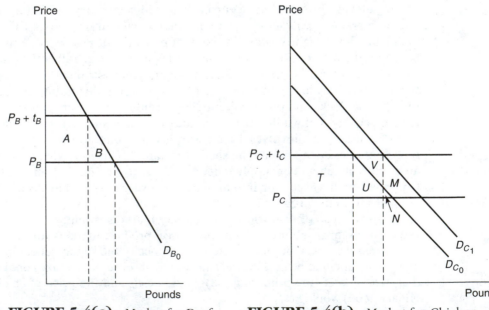

FIGURE 5-4(a) Market for Beef   **FIGURE 5-4(b)** Market for Chicken

Now assume that the government is considering imposing a tax of t_B cents per pound on beef. As indicated in panel (a), if the new tax is adopted, the government will collect revenue represented by area A, but consumers of beef will lose surplus equal to the areas $A + B$. Consequently, imposition of the new tax will result in deadweight loss in the beef market equal to area B.

The increase in the market price of beef shifts the demand schedule for chicken, a substitute, from D_{C_0} to D_{C_1}. For reasons discussed previously, this shift does not represent a change in consumer surplus. Indeed, the deadweight loss in the market for chicken remains the same, although it does shift from area U to areas $M + N$. However, the shift causes an increase in the sale of chickens, as consumers substitute chicken for beef, resulting in an increase in tax revenues collected by the government. This increase, which is represented in panel (b) by area $U + V$, is a benefit from the tax imposed on beef that could conceivably more than offset the deadweight loss occurring in the beef market. The various effects of the tax on beef are summarized in the following social accounting ledger:

	Benefits	Costs
Consumers	—	$A + B$
Government revenue	$A + U + V$	—
Social benefit and costs	$U + V$	B

Notice that while *all* of the change in consumer surplus takes place in the primary market, increases in tax revenues occur in both markets.

The important lesson from this illustration is that, unlike situations in which there are no distortions in secondary markets, benefits and costs of a policy intervention cannot be fully measured by observing only the effects that occur in primary markets. Effects that occur in distorted secondary markets should, in principle, be valued separately. A method for doing this is described in Exhibit 5-1. Yet, in practice and as indicated in the exhibit, it is usually very difficult to do so. Estimation problems usually preclude accurate measurement of welfare changes that occur in secondary markets. Estimating own-price effects (how quantity demanded changes as the price of the good changes) is often difficult; estimating cross-price effects (how the quantity demanded of good Y changes as the price of good Z changes) is more difficult yet. Consequently, we are rarely very confident of predictions of demand shifts in secondary markets. Moreover, when secondary markets are distorted, it is also difficult to measure the size of the distortions. (Recall the x-cent loss of wildlife from the sale of another sinker. How is the value of x to be estimated?) But such measures are usually needed if program effects in distorted secondary markets are to be taken into account.

Fortunately, price changes in most secondary markets are likely to be small. Most pairs of goods are neither strong complements nor strong substitutes. Hence, large price changes in the primary markets are usually necessary to produce noticeable demand shifts in the secondary markets. Thus, even when secondary markets are distorted, ignoring these markets may result in relatively little bias to CBA.

──────── **EXHIBIT 5-1** ────────

It is sometimes both desirable and feasible to build models of closely linked markets to estimate changes in social surplus. They are commonly referred to as *computable general equilibrium* (CGE) models, but this is a misnomer—they take account of a small set of the many markets that make up an economy and thus might be more accurately called computable multi-market equilibrium models. Considering multiple markets rather than limiting analysis to the equilibrium demand schedule in the primary market is appropriate when markets are not neatly separable because of externalities in consumption or production.

One application of CGE models is to assessing policy changes in markets for heterogeneous goods with production externalities. For example, what is commonly referred to as the oil market involves the extraction of crude oils of various qualities in various locations, their transportation to refineries employing different technologies to produce petroleum products in various locations, and the sale of these petroleum products in various regional markets. George Horwich, Hank Jenkins-Smith, and David Weimer use such a model to assess the efficiency of various public policy responses to oil supply disruptions.

Constructing, calibrating, and using industry-level CGE models are demanding tasks that require substantial resources and thus often are not worth developing for purposes of a single CBA. For example, a proper CBA of changes in the capacity of O'Hare International Airport would require a model that takes account of the network externality inherent in the airline system—delays originating at O'Hare propagate to flights into and out of other U.S. airports. Creating a CGE model of the U.S. airline industry would likely be too costly a task for analysts doing a one-time study of a proposed O'Hare expansion but might be an appropriate investment for the Federal Aviation Administration to provide as a tool for assessing the net benefits of any proposed airport expansions.

Despite the difficulty of creating useful CGE models, they are being increasingly used in policy analysis. For example, Thomas Nechyba has developed models of public education to take into account the effect of school outcomes on residential choice and the consequences of residential choice on student body composition and tax revenues, important factors in schooling outcomes.

───

Sources: George Horwich, Hank Jenkins-Smith, and David L. Weimer, "The International Energy Agency's Mandatory Oil-Sharing Agreement: Tests of Efficiency, Equity, and Practicality." In George Horwich and David L. Weimer, eds., *Responding to International Oil Crises* (Washington, D.C.: American Enterprise Institute for Public Policy Research, 1988), 104–133; Thomas J. Nechyba, "What Can Be (and What Has Been) Learned from General Equilibrium Simulation Models of School Finance?" *National Tax Journal* 54(2) 2003, 387–414.

INDIRECT EFFECTS OF INFRASTRUCTURE PROJECTS

Public infrastructure projects that improve transportation or communications, such as road building or harbor deepening, may substantially reduce the cost of production in some industries. These reductions in costs may have indirect effects in markets for consumption goods by reducing the prices at which the goods are sold. These indirect effects are similar but not quite the same as the secondary market effects that are the main topic of this chapter. In the case of secondary markets, a government policy influences prices in a primary market, which in turn influences demand in secondary markets in which goods that are complements of or substitutes for the primary market good are sold. In the case of an indirect effect, a government infrastructure project reduces the production costs of firms by reducing their expenditures on various inputs, and this direct effect of the project causes indirect effects by reducing prices in markets in which the goods produced by the firms are sold.

Although the two situations differ, both raise a similar question: can the change in social surplus that results from the government's policy be adequately measured by focusing on the market in which the intervention takes place? In both cases the answer is similar: it can if the markets that are indirectly affected are not seriously distorted.[7]

We have already demonstrated this point when secondary market effects occur. To illustrate this in the case of indirect effects that result from public expenditures on infrastructure improvement, consider the harbor-deepening project that was discussed in Chapter 4. The direct effect of the project on shippers that use the harbor is a gain in surplus that is represented by area P_0abP_1 in Figure 4-3. However, the shippers do not necessarily keep this entire gain. Competitive pressures will likely result in firms paying lower prices for productive inputs that are shipped through the harbor. This, in turn, will cause cost curves in the markets in which these firms sell their goods to shift downward and to the right. If prices in these markets fall as a result, then consumer surplus will increase.

In competitive markets for these goods, this indirect gain in consumer surplus is already captured by the direct surplus gain represented by area P_0abP_1 in Figure 4-3.[8] The reason is that some of the surplus gains initially enjoyed by shippers are ultimately passed on to the buyers of consumption goods through the reductions in the prices of these goods. If markets where the indirect effects occur are distorted, however, then some of the changes in surplus in these markets may not be captured by surplus changes in the market where the direct effects take place. For example, the price reductions may engender increases in sales in markets with both positive and negative externalities. If so, third parties will enjoy an increase in surplus when positive externalities are present and will suffer a decrease in surplus when negative externalities exist. These changes are not reflected by the direct changes in surplus.

SECONDARY MARKET EFFECTS FROM THE PERSPECTIVE OF LOCAL COMMUNITIES

Advocates of localized recreational facilities—for example, advocates of new sports stadiums, museums, and parks—frequently contend that major benefits will occur in secondary markets. For example, they predict that the demand for the services of local restaurants, hotels, and other businesses will increase. In addition, they often claim that such projects result in *multiplier effects*; that is, as purchases from nearby businesses increase, these businesses will, in turn, also spend their newly gained revenues nearby, and this, in turn, will generate still more revenues that will be spent locally, and so forth.

As long as secondary markets in a community are not distorted, one should be very cautious in counting revenues from local projects that are generated by secondary market effects and multiplier effects as project benefits. There are several reasons for exercising this caution.

First, absent market distortions, these revenues are relevant only when standing is restricted to some group smaller than society as a whole, such as to residents of a specific geographic area. As discussed in this chapter, when society is broadly defined, such claims cannot be justified unless the secondary market is distorted. For example, in evaluating the fish-stocking project from the narrow perspective of the local county, one might count as a benefit increases in revenues received by local businesses resulting from nonresidents buying fishing equipment in the county or frequenting local hotels or restaurants. From the broader social or national perspective, however, these expenditures simply represent a transfer from nonresidents to residents because they occur only as a result of consumers shifting their spending from one geographic area to another.

Second, when standing is restricted to residents of a local community, any social surplus gains that accrue to nonresidents as a result of a local project can no longer be counted as project benefits. For example, surplus gains enjoyed by sports team fans or owners who reside outside the community no longer count. Thus, the case for a local project could actually be stronger if standing is not restricted to the local community than if it is.

Third, as indicated earlier in this chapter, even if the demand for local products and services increases as a result of a local project, suppliers do not receive increases in surplus unless prices increase. Even when prices do increase, the resulting increase in producer surplus is at least partially offset because consumers who are residents of the local community must now pay more for goods and services and, as a result, lose consumer surplus. However, some residents may value the growth that occurs in the local economy in and of itself. Moreover, expansions in local businesses may provide some opportunities for taking advantage of economies of scale and, therefore, could produce benefits in the form of lower production costs.

Fourth, localized multiplier effects generally tend to be relatively small because local businesses are often owned by nonresidents. Moreover, many of the purchases by local businesses are made outside the local area. Thus, expenditures made within a local area readily dissipate elsewhere, and this becomes increasingly true as standing is restricted to a smaller geographic area.

It is only when secondary markets are distorted that effects in these markets can potentially generate important benefits for the community. However, negative impacts can also occur, such as increases in pollution and congestion that result when nonresidents use local roads to reach a recreational facility. Local projects are most likely to generate significant positive benefits in secondary markets when local rates of unemployment are high or other local resources are idle and substantial barriers to resource mobility exist. Under such circumstances, increases in demand in secondary markets and the multiplier effects that accompany these demand increases could significantly reduce levels of unemployment and increase the utilization of other idle resources such as empty buildings. The utilization of idle resources such as empty buildings has very low opportunity costs, and as discussed in Chapter 4, large increases in surplus accrue to many unemployed workers when they are hired. However, as also pointed out in Chapter 4, it is only when the rate of unemployment is fairly high that a substantial fraction of those hired are likely to be drawn from the ranks of the unemployed.

CONCLUSION

Most of the key concepts from Chapters 4 and 5 are summarized in Table 5-1. As the table indicates, changes in social surplus serve as the basis for measuring the costs and benefits of policies. The concept of opportunity cost helps us value the inputs that policies

TABLE 5-1 Rules for Measuring Social Benefits and Costs of Government Interventions

Type of Intervention	Efficient Markets	Inefficient Markets
Purchases from factor markets. (Concept: value costs as the opportunity cost of the purchased resources.)	If supply schedule is flat, value cost as direct budgetary expenditure. (Example: purchase of materials from a competitive national market.) If supply schedule is not flat, value cost as direct budgetary expenditure less (plus) any increase (decrease) in social surplus in market. (Example: purchases of materials from a competitive local market.)	Value costs as direct budgetary expenditure less (plus) any increase (decrease) in social surplus in market. (Examples: hiring unemployed labor; purchases of materials from a monopoly.)
Changes in costs to consumers or producers in primary markets. (Concept: value benefits as WTP for the change and costs as WTP to avoid the change.)	Value change as net change in social (i.e., consumer and producer) surplus plus (less) any increase (decrease) in government revenues. (Example: government provision of goods and services to consumers or producers.)	Value change as net change in social (i.e., consumer, producer, and third-party) surplus plus (less) any increase (decrease) in government revenues. (Example: tax or subsidy in market with externality.)
Changes in quantities exchanged in secondary markets as a result of government intervention in primary or factor markets. (Concept: commodities exchanged in secondary markets are typically complements of or substitutes for commodities exchanged in primary markets; most impacts in secondary markets can be valued in primary markets.)	If prices do not change in secondary market, ignore secondary market impacts. If prices do change, but benefits in primary market are measured using a demand schedule with other market prices held constant, then social surplus changes in the secondary market will always represent reductions in social surplus that should be subtracted from changes in the primary market. But if benefits in the primary market are measured using a demand schedule that does not hold other prices constant, ignore secondary market impacts. (Example: price changes in primary market cause demand schedule shifts in competitive secondary market.)	Costs or benefits resulting directly from increases in the size of the distortion should, in principle, be measured. Other impacts in secondary market should be ignored if prices do not change. (Example: price changes in primary market causes the demand schedule to shift in a secondary market with an externality.)

These rules pertain only to measuring impacts of government interventions on society as a whole. Issues concerning standing are ignored in the rules.

divert from other uses; the concept of WTP helps us value policy outputs. The key to valuing outputs is to identify the primary markets in which they occur. When the outputs are not traded in organized markets, ingenuity is often needed to infer supply and demand schedules (remember the market for "fishing days"). For this purpose, various shadow pricing techniques, such as those discussed in Part III of this book, are often needed. Costs and benefits that occur in undistorted secondary markets are typically very difficult to value, but generally need not and, indeed, should not be added to costs and benefits that are measured in primary markets. Doing so will usually result in double counting.

The rules that appear in Table 5-1 cannot be used without first determining the type of market in which the various potential impacts of a project or program occur—primary, secondary, or factor market—and then determining whether the market is efficient or inefficient. In practice, this is sometimes difficult. To illustrate the sorts of judgments that must be made in practice, we conclude by listing selected impacts of a hypothetical street-widening project that would substantially increase traffic along the route and ask the reader to consider what type of market each occurs in and, hence, whether each should be included in a cost-benefit analysis of the project. Our own judgment concerning each, which is based on the assumption that surplus gains by those who drive on the street are measured using an equilibrium demand schedule for trips, appears in Exhibit 5-2.

1. The increased traffic would cause vibrations that crack the walls of adjacent houses.
2. Profits of gasoline at filling stations that are located along the route would increase.
3. The property values of these stations would also increase.
4. Traffic on adjacent streets would decline. Therefore, the remaining motorists would experience quicker and cheaper journeys.
5. Air pollution along the route would increase.
6. The increased auto traffic would require the city to hire three more police officers to enforce traffic regulations.
7. The greater number of motorists would lead to an increased number of traffic violations, and the resulting fines would mean that the city receives increased revenue.
8. Fewer people would ride buses; as a consequence the bus company would lay off 10 bus drivers.
9. Widening the road would necessitate cutting down a number of trees. These trees would then be sold to a nearby sawmill.

EXHIBIT 5-2

1. The cracked walls in houses that would result from the increased traffic are a negative externality. Although the externality would occur in the secondary market for housing, it should be taken into account in the study.

2. The increased purchases of gasoline would occur in a secondary market. If this market is not seriously distorted (e.g., by externalities or monopoly power), then the increase in gasoline purchases should be ignored because any

effects on surplus will be captured by measuring surplus in the primary market. (Notice, however, that doing this neglects the fact that it is the owners of the filling stations, rather than automobile drivers, who receive the increase in surplus from increased purchases of gasoline; it also ignores the possibility that filling station owners who are located on other streets may face reductions in surplus.)

3. The property market is also a secondary market. Hence, these effects should be ignored.

4. The decrease in traffic on adjacent streets can be viewed as a reduction in a negative externality—congestion—that distorts a secondary market (the adjacent streets are presumably substitutes for the street that would be widened). This is a real benefit that should be taken into account.

5. Air pollution is a negative externality that distorts the primary market. Hence, it should be taken into account.

6. The hiring of three additional police officers would take place in a factor market for labor and can be viewed as a direct cost of the project.

7. The increase in traffic fines would simply be a transfer between motorists and the city and,

except for their distributional implications, can be ignored.

8. The 10 laid off bus drivers would lose their jobs because the demand schedule in the secondary market for public transportation would shift to the left. Unless this market or the factor markets that serve this market are distorted, the shift in demand can be ignored. Examples of such distortions are the loss of monopoly profits by the bus company or the inability of the bus drivers to find new jobs because of high rates of unemployment. Otherwise, the bus drivers would simply find new jobs at a similar level of compensation, implying that widening the road would have no effect on the social value of the output they produce.

9. The benefits and costs of cutting down the trees and selling them to a sawmill can be assessed independently of the street-widening project. If the benefits from cutting down the trees exceed the costs, then the trees should be cut regardless of whether the street-widening project is undertaken. However, if the costs exceed the benefits, then the costs and benefits of cutting the trees should be included in the CBA of the street-widening project.

EXERCISES FOR CHAPTER 5

1. Recall exercise 2 from Chapter 4 in which an increase in the toll on a highway from $.40 to $.50 would reduce use of the highway by 10,000 cars per week.
   a. Because of the reduced use of the highway, demand in the secondary market for subway rides increases. Assuming that the price of subway rides is set equal to the marginal cost of operating the subway and marginal costs are constant (i.e., the supply schedule is horizontal), and no externalities result from the reduced use of the highway and the increased use of the subway, are there additional costs or benefits due to the increased demand for subway rides? Why or why not?
   b. Because of the reduced use of the highway, demand in the secondary market for gasoline falls by 30,000 gallons per year. There is a stiff tax on gasoline, one that existed prior to the new toll. Assuming that the marginal cost of producing gasoline is $1 per gallon, that these marginal costs are constant (i.e., the supply schedule is horizontal), that no externalities result from the consumption of gasoline, and that the gasoline tax adds 30 percent to the supply price, are there any additional costs or benefits due to this shift? If so, how large are they?

2. Recall exercise 3 from Chapter 4 in which a country imposes an import fee on the crude oil it imports. Assume that prior to the imposition of the import fee, the country annually consumed 900 million short tons of coal, all domestically mined, at a price of $66 per short ton.

How would the CBA of the import fee change if, after imposition of the import fee, the following circumstances are assumed to result from energy consumers switching from crude oil to coal?

   a. Annual consumption of coal rises by 40 million short tons, but the price of coal remains unchanged.

   b. Annual consumption of coal rises by 40 million short tons and the price of coal rises to $69 per short ton. In answering this question, assume that the prices of other goods, including coal, were not held constant in estimating the demand schedule for crude oil.

   c. Annual consumption of coal rises by 40 million short tons and the price of coal rises to $69 per short ton. In answering this question, assume that the prices of other goods, including coal, were held constant in estimating the demand schedule for crude oil. Also assume that the demand schedule for coal is completely inelastic.

   d. The market price of coal underestimates its marginal social cost by $15 per short ton because the coal mined in the country has a high sulphur content that produces smog when burned. In answering this question, assume that the annual consumption of coal rises by 40 million short tons, but the price of coal remains unchanged.

3. Recall exercise 3 from Chapter 4 in which a country imposes an import fee on the crude oil it imports. Imagine that all the crude oil imports to the country are made by ships owned by its nationals. The Association of Petroleum Shippers argues that the reduction in imports resulting from the import fee will drive down the price of shipping services and thereby inflict a loss on them. The Committee for Energy Independence, which favors the import fee, argues that the reduction in shipping prices will benefit consumers of shipping services. Which argument is correct? In preparing an answer, make the following assumptions: the import fee will reduce the quantity of imported crude oil from 3 billion to 2.5 billion barrels per year; the reduction in barrels shipped will drive per-barrel shipping costs down from $4 per barrel to $3 per barrel; and the elasticity of demand in the shipping market at the new equilibrium ($3, 2.5 billion barrels) is -0.3. Also assume that the shipping market is undistorted and that the prices of other goods, including shipping services, were held constant in estimating the demand schedule for crude oil.

4. (Instructor-provided spreadsheet recommended.) Consider an individual's utility function over two goods, q_m and q_s, where m indicates the primary market in which a policy will have its effect and s is a related secondary market:

$$U = q_m + \alpha q_s - (\beta_m q_m^2 + \gamma q_m q_s + \beta_s q_s^2)$$

where α, β_m, β_s, and γ are parameters such that $\beta_m > 0$, and $\beta_s > 0, \beta_m < (1 - \gamma q_s)/2q_m$, $\beta_s < (1 - \gamma q_m)/2q_s$, and $\gamma < p_m \beta_s / p_s + p_s \beta_m / p_m$. For purposes of this exercise, assume that $\alpha = 1, \beta_m = 0.01, \beta_s = 0.01$, and $\gamma = -0.015$. Also assume that the person has a budget of $30,000 and the price of q_m, p_m, is $100 and the price of q_s, p_s, is $100. Imagine that the policy under consideration would reduce p_m to $90.

    The provided spreadsheet has two models. Model 1 assumes that the price in the secondary market does not change in response to a price change in the primary market. That is, p_s equals $100 both before and after the reduction in p_m. Step 1 solves for the quantities that maximize utility under the initial p_m. Step 2 solves for the quantities that maximize utility under the new p_m. Step 3 requires you to make guesses of the new budget level that would return the person to her original level of utility prior to the price reduction—keep guessing until you find the correct budget. (You may wish to use the Tools|Goal Seek function on the spreadsheet instead of engaging in iterative guessing.) Step 4 calculates the compensating variation as the difference between the original budget and the new budget. Step 5 calculates the change in the consumer surplus in the primary market.

Model 2 assumes that $p_s = a + bq_s$. Assume that $b = 0.25$ and a is set so that at the quantity demanded in step 2 of model 1, $p_s = 100$. As no analytical solution for the quantities before the price change exists, step 1 requires you to make guesses of the marginal utility of money until you find the one that satisfies the budget constraint for the initial p_m. Step 2 repeats this process for the new value of p_m. Step 3 requires you to guess both a new budget to return the person to the initial level of utility and a marginal utility of money that satisfies the new budget constraint. A block explains how to use the Tools|Goal Seek function to find the marginal utility consistent with your guess of the new budget needed to return utility to its original level. Step 4 calculates the compensating variation. Step 5 calculates the change in the consumer surplus in the primary market and bounds on the change in consumer surplus in the secondary market.

Use these models to investigate how well the change in social surplus in the primary market approximates compensating variation. Note that as utility depends on consumption of only these two goods, there are substantial income effects. That is, a price reduction in either of the goods substantially increases the individual's real income. Getting started: the values in the spreadsheet are set up for a reduction in p_m from \$100 to \$95. Begin by changing the new primary market price to \$90 and resolving the models.

NOTES

1. For a helpful analysis that uses a somewhat different approach than the one presented in this section but reaches very similar conclusions, see Herbert Mohring, "Maximizing, Measuring, and Not Double Counting Transportation-Improvement Benefits: A Primer on Closed- and Open-Economy Cost-Benefit Analysis," *Transportation Research* 27(6) 1993, 413–424.

2. As advocates of a policy often claim benefits in secondary markets, it is ironic that demand shifts in undistorted secondary markets that cause price changes always involve losses in social surplus. This can be seen by using panel (b) in Figure 5-2 to illustrate the case of an outward shift in demand in a secondary market, as well as the case of an inward shift in demand. Simply take D_{G_1} as the original demand schedule and D_{G_0} as the post-project demand schedule. Using the post-project demand schedule for measuring social surplus changes, we see that the price increase from P_{G_1} to P_{G_0} results in a producer surplus increase equal to the area of trapezoid $P_{G_1}fgP_{G_0}$ and a consumer surplus loss equal to the area of $P_{G_1}hgP_{G_0}$ so that social surplus falls by the area of triangle *fgh*.

3. See Richard E. Just, Darrell L. Hueth, and Andrew Schmitz, *Applied Welfare Economics and Public Policy* (Englewood Cliffs, NJ: Prentice Hall, 1982), Chapter 9.

4. For greater detail concerning this point, see Just, Hueth, and Schmitz, *Applied Welfare Economics and Public Policy*, 200–213.

5. Indeed, under certain assumptions, areas *abc* and *efg* will almost exactly equal one another. The most important of these assumptions is that the price changes in the two markets represented in Figure 5-2 are small and that no income effects result from these price changes. If there are no income effects, there will be symmetry in substitution between the two goods. In other words, their cross-substitution effects will be equal. That is, $\partial q_F / \partial P_G = \partial q_G / \partial P_F$. Given this equality, $\Delta P_F \Delta q_F \approx \Delta P_G \, \Delta q_G$. Hence, area *abc* approximately equals area *efg*. Typically, income effects do occur as a result of price changes, but as discussed in Appendix 3A, these effects tend to be small for most goods. Consequently, one would anticipate that area *abc* would generally closely approximate area *efg*.

6. Separate measures would have to be obtained, however, to examine how benefits and costs were distributed among various groups. For example, area *abc* is a gain to consumers, while area *efg* is a loss to producers. To the extent these two areas are equal, they represent a transfer of surplus from producers to consumers. In addition, surplus corresponding to area $P_{G_0}efP_{G_1}$ is also transferred from producers to consumers.

7. For a detailed analysis of the secondary market effects of transportation and land use projects, see David M. Newberry, "Spatial General Equilibrium and Cost-Benefit Analysis" in *Cost-Benefit Analysis: Environmental and Ecological Perspectives,* K. Puttaswamaiah, editor, New Brunswick, NJ: Transaction Publishers, 2002, pp. 1–18.

8. For a formal demonstration of this assertion, see Jan Rouwendal, "Indirect Welfare Effects of Price Changes and Cost-Benefit Analysis," unpublished paper (Amsterdam: Tinbergen Institute, 2002).

CHAPTER 6

Discounting Benefits and Costs in Future Time Periods

Both private and public decisions can have important consequences that extend over time. When consumers buy houses, automobiles, or education, they generally expect to derive benefits and incur costs over a number of years. When the government builds a dam, subsidizes job training, regulates carbon dioxide emissions, or leases the outer continental shelf for oil exploration, it also sets in motion impacts that extend over many years. Often, analysts have to compare projects with benefits and costs that arise in different time periods. Formally, they have to make intertemporal (across time) comparisons. To do this, analysts discount future costs and benefits so that all costs and benefits are in a common metric—the present value. They can then measure and compare the net social benefits of each policy alternative using the net present value criterion.

This chapter deals with the practical techniques needed to compute the net present value of a project (or policy). It assumes that the social discount rate, the rate at which analysts should discount the future benefits and costs of a project, is known. As we discuss in Chapter 10, some controversy remains over the appropriate value of the social discount rate. In practice, though, oversight agencies, such as the Office of Management and Budget in the United States, Her Majesty's Treasury in the United Kingdom, or the Treasury Board in Canada, often specify the discount rate that analysts should use.

The sections of this chapter cover the following topics: the basics of discounting, compounding and discounting over multiple years, the timing of benefits and costs, comparing projects with different time frames, real versus nominal dollars, relative price changes, long-lived projects and calculating horizon values, time-declining discounting, and sensitivity analysis in discounting.

Appendix 6A presents some shortcut formulas for calculating the present value of annuities and perpetuities. The topics covered in this chapter are essentially uncontroversial. Readers who are familiar with the time value of money and capital budgeting techniques may want to skip this chapter.

THE BASICS OF DISCOUNTING

Projects with Lives of One Year

Technically speaking, discounting takes place over *periods* rather than years. However, because the discounting period is a year in almost all public-sector applications, and it is easier to think of years rather than periods, we generally use the term years.

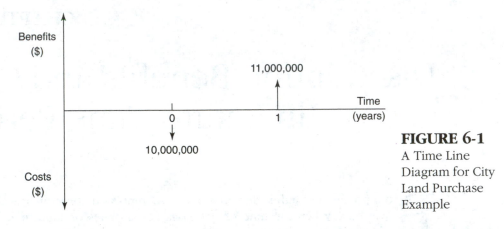

FIGURE 6-1
A Time Line
Diagram for City
Land Purchase
Example

In this section, we consider projects that last for exactly one year. In the following section we consider projects that last for longer than one year. Suppose, for example, a city government has the opportunity to buy a parcel of land for $10 million. Also suppose that if it buys the land, then the land will be sold for $11 million one year from now. Should the city buy the land now?

Before proceeding, it is worth noting that it is often useful to lay out the annual benefits and costs of a project on a *time line*, as shown in Figure 6-1. The horizontal axis represents time measured in years. Benefits appear above the time line and costs are below it. Although a time line might seem unnecessary for this simple example, this tool clarifies the timing of the benefits and costs of a project and is particularly useful when the timing of impacts is more complicated.

To decide whether to buy the land, the city should compare the land purchase project, which has a cost of $10 million now and a benefit of $11 million in one year to the best alternative—in this case, the *status quo* (not buy the land, invest the money). There are three ways to do this, each of which gives the same answer.

Future Value Analysis.   This method compares the amount the city will receive in the future if it engages in the project with the amount it will receive in the future if it invests the money. Suppose that if the city does not buy the land, it will invest the money in Treasury bills (T-bills) at an interest rate of 5 percent.[1] If it invests in T-bills, then it will have $10.5 million in one year—the principal amount of $10 million plus interest of $500,000. This amount, $10.5 million, is called the *future value (FV)* of the T-bills because it represents the amount the city will have in a future period if it buys them. The city can compare this future value with the future value it will receive if it invests in the land, $11 million, and choose the alternative that has the highest future value. In this example, the city should buy the land.

In general, the future value in one year of some amount X (available today) is given by the following formula:

$$FV = X(1 + i) \tag{6.1}$$

where, i is the annual rate of interest. The concept of future value is intuitively appealing to anyone who has ever had a savings account. For example, if one invests $1,000 in a savings account at 4 percent, one will have $1,000(1 + 0.04) = $1,040 in a year. As is evident from equation (6.1), the future value increases as the interest rate increases.

Note that interest rates are often stated as percentages, such as 5 percent. This corresponds to an interest rate, i, equal to 0.05.

Present Value Analysis.   We now switch from future values to present values. Present value analysis compares the current equivalent value of the project, which is called its *present value (PV)*, with the current equivalent value of the best alternative project, given prevailing interest rates. The present value of buying the land that will be worth $11 million in one year's time, given that the city could invest its money at 5 percent, is found by setting FV = $11,000,000, X = PV, and i = 0.05 in equation (6.1):

$$PV(1 + 0.05) = \$11,000,000$$

Solving this equation for PV gives:

$$PV = \frac{\$11,000,000}{1.05} = \$10,476,190$$

In contrast, the present value of the best available alternative, buying the T-bills now, is $10 million.[2] Comparing these two present values shows that the city would be $476,190 better off in present value terms if it bought the land.

In general, if the prevailing interest rate is i, then the present value of an amount received in one year, Y, is given by:

$$PV = \frac{Y}{1 + i} \tag{6.2}$$

As is evident from equation (6.2), the present value decreases as the interest rate increases.

Net Present Value Analysis.   This method calculates the present values of all the benefits and costs of a project, including the initial investment, and sums them to obtain the *net present value (NPV)* of that project. For the land purchase example, the NPV is the difference between the present value of the land if the city buys it and the current cost of the land:

$$NPV = \$10,476,190 - \$10,000,000 = \$476,190$$

These calculations are represented graphically on a time line in Figure 6-2. As the NPV of buying the land is positive, the city should buy the land. It will be $476,190 better off in present value terms if it invests in this project.

By definition, the NPV of a project equals the difference between the present value of the benefits, $PV(B)$, and the present value of the costs, $PV(C)$:

$$NPV = PV(B) - PV(C) \tag{6.3}$$

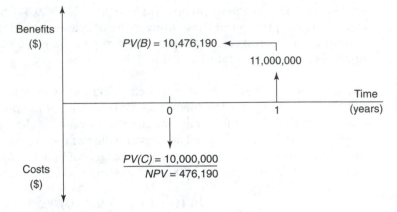

FIGURE 6-2 *NPV* of Buying the Land

As discussed in Chapter 1, the *NPV* method provides a simple criterion for deciding whether to undertake a project. If the *NPV* of a project is positive, then one should proceed with it; if the *NPV* is negative, then one should not. The positive *NPV* decision rule assumes implicitly that no other alternative with a higher *NPV* exists. *If there are multiple, mutually exclusive alternatives, then one should select the alternative with the highest* NPV.

The foregoing example assumes that the city has $10 million available that could be used either to buy the land or to invest at interest rate *i*. Sometimes analysts calculate *NPV*s of projects for which the government does not have all the cash immediately available and has to borrow some funds. *Implicitly, analysts assume that the government can borrow or lend funds at the same interest rate i. Under this assumption it does not matter whether the government currently has the money or not: the* NPV *rule still holds.* In Chapter 10 we discuss how the source of funding for a project may affect the choice of the discount rate. However, even in these situations, analysts should select the project with the largest *NPV*.

COMPOUNDING AND DISCOUNTING OVER MULTIPLE YEARS

We now generalize these results to apply to projects with impacts that occur over many years. Again, we first discuss future values, then present values, and finally net present values.

Future Value over Multiple Years. Suppose that the city could invest the $10 million for five years with interest at 5 percent per annum. Using equation (6.1), at the end of the first year the city would have $10 million × 1.05 = $10.5 million. In order to calculate the interest in future years, we need to know if there is simple interest or compound interest.

If there is *simple interest*, then each year interest is paid only on the original principal amount, and the city would receive interest of $500,000 per year. The future value would be $12.5 (the initial $10 million plus five years of interest of $0.5 million).

TABLE 6-1   Investment of $10 Million with Interest Compounded Annually at 7 Percent

Year	Beginning of Year Balance ($ millions)	Annual Interest ($ millions)	End of Year Balance ($ millions)
1	10.000	0.700	10.700
2	10.700	0.749	11.449
3	11.449	0.801	12.250
4	12.250	0.858	13.108
5	13.108	0.918	14.026

However, if interest is compounded annually, then, in effect, $10.5 million would be invested at the beginning of the second year which, again using equation (6.1), would grow to $10.5 million × 1.05 = $11.025 million at the end of the second year. Notice that the interest in the second year, $0.525 million, is more than the interest in the first year, $0.500 million. With *compound interest*, interest is earned on the principal amount *and* on the interest that has been reinvested (*interest on the interest*). This process is called *compounding interest*. Henceforth, we shall always assume that interest is compounded annually, unless explicitly stated otherwise.

Table 6-1 illustrates that when interest is compounded annually, the future value can grow quickly—much more quickly than under simple interest. For example, at an interest rate of 7 percent compounded annually, the original capital amount increases by more than 40 percent after only five years. Under simple interest the *FV* would increase by only 35 percent. Over longer periods (10 years or more), the divergence between compound interest and simple interest becomes quite large. This gap increases with time, thereby lending credence to the adage of many pension fund sales agents who exhort young adults "to invest early and leave it alone."

In general, if an amount, denoted by X, is invested for n years and interest is compounded annually at rate i, then the future value is:[3]

$$FV = X(1 + i)^n \qquad \qquad \textbf{(6.4)}$$

For example, if $10 million is invested for four years with interest compounded annually at 7 percent, then the future value is:

$$FV = \$10(1 + 0.07)^4 = \$13.108 \text{ million}$$

The term $(1 + i)^n$, which gives the future value of $1 in n years at annual interest rate i, compounded annually, is called the *compound interest factor*. In this example, the compound interest factor is 1.3108.[4] Most finance textbooks include an appendix of compound interest factors. Many pocket calculators and electronic spreadsheets have this function. Different sources may give slightly different answers due to rounding error. In practice, though, these rounding errors are not material.

Present Value over Multiple Years.   Suppose that a government agency wants to undertake an organizational restructuring in three years that is expected to cost $100,000 at that time. If the interest rate is 6 percent, then the amount needed now to yield $100,000 in three years, denoted by PV, can be found by substituting into equation (6.4):

$$PV (1 + 0.06)^3 = \$100,000.$$

Solving this equation for PV gives:

$$PV = \frac{\$100,000}{(1 + 0.06)^3} = \frac{\$100,000}{1.19102} = \$83,962$$

Consequently, the government agency would need $83,962 now to have $100,000 in three years.

In general, the present value of an amount received in n years, denoted Y, with interest compounded annually at rate i is:

$$PV = \frac{Y}{(1 + i)^n} \qquad (6.5)$$

The term $1/(1 + i)^n$ is called the *present value factor*, or the *discount factor*. It equals the present value of $1 received in n years when the interest rate is i, compounded annually. For example, the present value factor in the foregoing example equals $1/(1 + .06)^3 = 0.8396$. Again, these factors are available in most finance textbooks, on calculators, and in computer spreadsheet programs.

The process of calculating the present value of a future amount is called *discounting*. As is evident from equation (6.5), the present value of a future amount is less than the future amount itself—it is discounted. The amount of the discount increases as the interest rate increases and as the number of years increases. Comparing equations (6.4) and (6.5) shows that discounting is the reverse of compounding.[5]

If a project yields benefits in many periods, then we can compute the present value of the whole stream of benefits by adding the present values of the benefits received in each period. Specifically, if B_t denotes the benefits received in period t for $t = 0, 1, \ldots, n$, then the present value of the stream of benefits, denoted $PV(B)$, is:

$$PV(B) = \frac{B_0}{(1 + i)^0} + \frac{B_1}{(1 + i)^1} + \cdots + \frac{B_{n-1}}{(1 + i)^{n-1}} + \frac{B_n}{(1 + i)^n}$$

$$PV(B) = \sum_{t=0}^{n} \frac{B_t}{(1 + i)^t} \qquad (6.6)$$

Similarly, if C_t denotes the costs incurred in period t for $t = 0, 1, \ldots, n$, then the present value of the stream of costs, denoted $PV(C)$, is:

$$PV(C) = \sum_{t=0}^{n} \frac{C_t}{(1 + i)^t} \qquad (6.7)$$

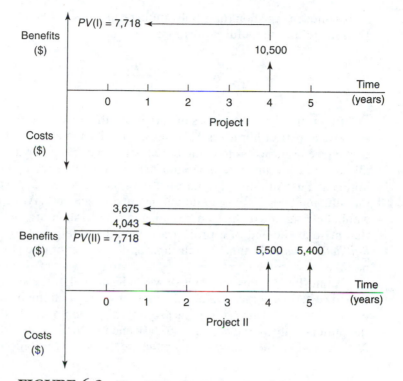

FIGURE 6-3   Time Lines for Project I and Project II

To illustrate the use of equation (6.6), consider a government agency that has to choose between two alternative projects. Project I yields a benefit of $10,500 four years from now, whereas project II yields $5,500 four years from now and an additional $5,400 five years from now. Assume the interest rate is 8 percent. Which is the better project? The present values of the projects follow:

$$PV(\text{I}) = \frac{\$10{,}500}{(1 + 0.08)^4} = \$7{,}718$$

$$PV(\text{II}) = \frac{\$5{,}500}{(1 + 0.08)^4} + \frac{\$5{,}400}{(1 + 0.08)^5} = \$4{,}043 + \$3{,}675 = \$7{,}718$$

In this example, the present values of the two projects happen to be identical. Thus, one would be indifferent between them. Time lines for these two projects are shown in Figure 6-3.

Net Present Value of a Project.   We have now introduced all of the material on basic discounting needed for CBA. As discussed earlier, the *NPV* of a project is the difference between the present value of the benefits and the present value of the costs, as represented in equation (6.3). Substituting equations (6.6) and (6.7) into equation (6.3) gives the following useful expression:

$$NPV = \sum_{t=0}^{n}\frac{B_t}{(1 + i)^t} - \sum_{t=0}^{n}\frac{C_t}{(1 + i)^t} \tag{6.8}$$

To illustrate the mechanics of computing the *NPV* of a project using this formula, suppose a district library is considering purchasing a new information system that would give users access to a number of online databases for five years. The benefits of this system are estimated to be $100,000 per annum, including both cost savings to the library and user benefits. The information system costs $325,000 to purchase and set up initially, and $20,000 to operate and maintain each year. After five years, the system would be dismantled and sold, resulting in a net cash inflow of $20,000. Such amounts that arise at the end of a project are sometimes referred to as a *terminal value* or *liquidation value*. Assume that the appropriate discount rate is 7 percent and there are no other costs or benefits.

A time line for this project is shown in Figure 6-4. It shows the timing of each benefit and cost, their present values, the present value of all the benefits, the present value of all the costs, and the *NPV* of the project. The present value of the benefits is $424,280; the present value of the costs is $407,004; and the *NPV* of the project is $17,276. As the *NPV* is positive, the library should purchase the new information system.

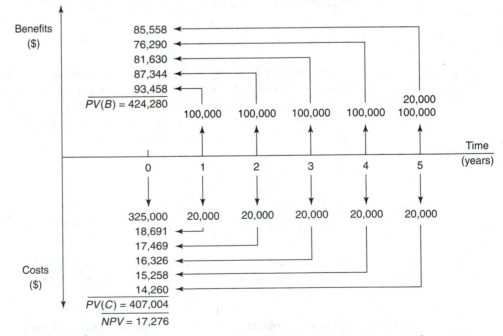

FIGURE 6-4 Time Line of the Benefits and Costs of the Library Information System

TABLE 6-2 The Net Present Value of the Library Information System

Year	Event	Annual Benefits	Annual Costs	Annual Net Benefits
0	Purchase and install	0	325,000	−325,000
1	Annual benefits and costs	100,000	20,000	80,000
2	Annual benefits and costs	100,000	20,000	80,000
3	Annual benefits and costs	100,000	20,000	80,000
4	Annual benefits and costs	100,000	20,000	80,000
5	Annual benefits and costs	100,000	20,000	80,000
5	Liquidation	20,000	0	20,000
	PV	$424,280	$407,004	$17,276

An alternative way to compute the *NPV* of a project is to compute the present value of the annual *net (social) benefits*. Let $NB_t = B_t - C_t$ denote the annual net social benefits that arise in year t ($t = 0, 1, 2, \ldots, n$). It follows from equation (6.8) that the NPV *of a project equals the present value of the net benefits:*[6]

$$NPV = \sum_{t=0}^{n} \frac{NB_t}{(1 + i)^t} \qquad (6.9)$$

To illustrate that equations (6.8) and (6.9) produce the same *NPV*, Table 6-2 contains the annual benefits, annual costs, and annual net benefits of the library information system project. Using equation (6.9), the present value of the net benefits of the project is $17,276, as shown in the last column of Table 6-2. This is the same value as the *NPV* obtained earlier by taking the difference between the present value of the benefits and the present value of the costs.

In many respects, tables and time lines are substitutable. They both present key information succinctly, and they facilitate computation of project *PV*s and *NPV*s. Neither is necessary. Analysts can experiment with them and use them whenever they are helpful. For complicated projects it is often useful to start with a time line to indicate precisely when impacts occur and then enter the data into a spreadsheet to compute the *PV*s and the *NPV*s.

One special situation is worth discussing briefly. In some projects, all of the costs occur at the beginning ($t = 0$) and only benefits occur in the ensuing years ($t = 1, 2, \ldots, n$). In this situation, equation (6.8) simplifies to:

$$NPV = \sum_{t=0}^{n} \frac{B_t}{(1 + i)^t} - C_0$$

Continuous Compounding. Throughout this chapter we assume that interest is compounded once per period, with a period being a year. In practice, interest on mortgages, savings accounts and other investments is often compounded more than once per period. It may be compounded semiannually, monthly, or even daily. Sometimes, interest is compounded continuously.[7] In general, the present value of a future amount declines as the frequency of discounting increases. However, the difference between assuming interest is compounded once per period and assuming it is compounded continuously is not great. For example, under the assumption of continuous compounding, the *PV* of the benefits of the library information system would be $421,374, the *PV* of the costs would be $406,456, and the *NPV* would be $14,918.

TIMING OF BENEFITS AND COSTS

The compounding and discounting formulae presented above assume that all benefits and costs occur at the end of each period (year). Impacts are assumed to arise immediately ($t = 0$), or at the end of the first year ($t = 1$), or at the end of the second year ($t = 2$), and so on. For many projects, this is a reasonable assumption. Furthermore, when most of the costs occur early in the project and most of the benefits occur late in the project, this assumption is conservative, in the sense that the *NPV*s are lower than they would be if they were computed under alternative assumptions.

To illustrate this point, reconsider the library information system example, but now assume that the annual benefits of $100,000 all occur at the beginning of each year instead of at the end of each year, and assume the timing of all other benefits and costs is unchanged. A time line under these assumptions is given in Figure 6-5. The present value of the benefits increases by $28,702 from $424,280 to $452,982, and the *NPV* of the project increases by $28,702 from $17,276 to $45,978. Clearly, the *NPV* of a project can vary considerably according to the assumptions made about the timing of benefits and costs.

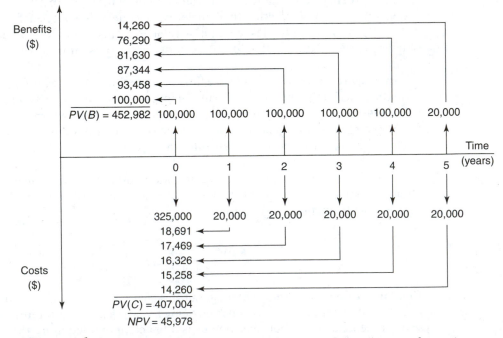

FIGURE 6-5 Time Line of the Benefits and Costs of the Library Information System Assuming User Benefits Occur at the Beginning of Each Year

When costs or benefits actually occur over the course of a year, a more appropriate approach is to treat them as if they occurred in the middle of that year. So, for instance, if the $100,000 in benefits and $20,000 in operating costs were distributed throughout each of the five years of the library project, one would discount these benefits and costs at times $t = 0.5, 1.5, 2.5, 3.5$, and 4.5. If, as before, the installation costs of $325,000 occurred at the beginning of the first year of the project ($t = 0$) and the liquidation benefit of $20,000 arose at the end of the fifth year ($t = 5$), then the *NPV* of the project would be $28,562.

COMPARING PROJECTS WITH DIFFERENT TIME FRAMES

In principle, projects should always be compared over the same discounting period so that they have the same opportunity to accumulate costs and benefits. Projects with different time frames are not directly comparable.

Suppose that a government-owned electric utility company is considering two new alternative sources of power. One is a large hydroelectric dam (*HED*), which would last 75 years; the other is a cogeneration plant (*CGP*), which would last 15 years. After considering all relevant social benefits and costs, and assuming a discount rate of 8 percent, the *NPV* of the 75-year hydroelectric project is $30 million and the *NPV* of the 15-year cogeneration project is $24 million. Is the hydroelectric project preferable simply because it has the larger *NPV*? The answer is no. These projects are not comparable because they have different life spans. The cogeneration project could be "rolled over" five times within the life of the hydro project.

There are two methods for evaluating projects with different time frames: the *roll-over method* and the *equivalent annual net benefit method*. They always lead to the same conclusion, as we now illustrate.

Roll-Over Method

Suppose that the utility decides to build the cogeneration power plant. Further suppose that in 15 years time it builds another new cogeneration plant; in 30 years it builds another one; and it builds another again in 45 and 60 years. If so, the length of these five sequential cogeneration plants will be the same as the length of the 75-year hydroelectric project. This makes the projects directly comparable.[8]

The *NPV* of five back-to-back cogeneration power plants, denoted 5CGP, is:

$$NPV(5CGP) = \$24,000,000 + \frac{\$24,000,000}{(1 + 0.08)^{15}} + \frac{\$24,000,000}{(1 + 0.08)^{30}}$$

$$+ \frac{\$24,000,000}{(1 + 0.08)^{45}} + \frac{\$24,000,000}{(1 + .008)^{60}} = \$34.94 \text{ million}^9$$

As this *NPV* is higher than the *NPV* of the hydroelectric project, the utility should select this option.

Equivalent Annual Net Benefit Method

An often easier way to compare projects of unequal lengths is to use the *equivalent annual net benefit (EANB) method*. The *EANB* of a project equals its *NPV* divided by the *annuity factor* that has the same term and discount rate as the project itself (i.e., the present value of an annuity of $1 per year for the life of the project, discounted at the rate used to calculate the *NPV*):

$$EANB = \frac{NPV}{a_i^n} \tag{6.10}$$

where, a_i^n is the annuity factor, defined by equation (6A.2). The *EANB* is the amount which, if received each year for the life of the project, would have the same *NPV* as the project itself. This process is called *amortization*: the cost of the project is amortized over n years. The *EANBs* for the hydroelectric and the cogeneration projects equal:[10]

$$EANB(HED) = \$30/12.461 = \$2.407 \text{ million}$$
$$EANB(CGP) = \$24/8.559 = \$2.804 \text{ million}$$

The *EANB* of the cogeneration project is $2.804 million, which implies that this project is equivalent to an annuity of $2.804 million per year for 15 years. In contrast, the net benefit of the hydroelectric alternative is equivalent to an annuity of $2.407 million per year for 75 years. If one could continuously replace each project at the end of its life with a similar project, then the cogeneration project would yield net annual benefits equivalent to a perpetuity of $2.804 million per year, and the hydroelectric project would yield annual net benefits equivalent to a perpetuity of $2.407 million per year. Consequently, the cogeneration alternative is preferable, assuming replacement of both types of plant is possible at the end of their useful lives.

An Additional Advantage of the Cogeneration Project

In fact, if the utility chooses the cogeneration project at the beginning, then it may not be desirable to replace it with an identical cogeneration plant in 15 years. At that time a more efficient alternative is likely to be available. In contrast, if the utility builds the hydroelectric project, then it is probably locked in for 75 years. Thus, the cogeneration project has an additional benefit because of its flexibility in allowing the introduction of more efficient technology as it becomes available during the 75-year period. Chapter 7 discusses such benefits, called quasi-option value, in more depth. Here it is sufficient to recognize that the shorter project has an additional benefit that is not incorporated in the *EANB* calculation.

INFLATION AND REAL VERSUS NOMINAL DOLLARS

Conventional private-sector financial analysis measures revenues, expenditures, net income, assets, liabilities and cash flows in terms of historical monetary units. Such units are referred to as *nominal dollars* (sometimes called *current dollars*). However, if you have ever listened to an older person reminisce, then you probably know that a dollar purchased more in 1986 than it does now—"a dollar's not worth a dollar anymore!" For example, nominal per capita disposable personal income in the United States was approximately 2.345 times higher in 2006 than in 1986 ($32,049 versus $13,665), but the average person could not buy 2.3 times as many goods and services in 2006 as in 1986.[11] The purchasing power of a dollar declines with price inflation. In order to control for the declining purchasing power of a dollar due to inflation, we convert nominal dollars to *real dollars* (sometimes called *constant dollars*).

To obtain real dollar measures, analysts *deflate* nominal dollars. There are a number of possible deflators. Usually, the *deflator* is based on the market price of a basket of goods and services purchased by consumers, that is, based on consumer prices: sometimes analysts use the gross domestic product (GDP), which is broader and reflects the price of all goods and services in the economy, including the public sector. The choice of whether to use a consumer price deflator or the GDP deflator depends on whether the impacts of a project are concentrated on consumers or are much broader. In practice, most CBA studies use a consumer price deflator, especially when calculating consumer surplus. Some studies use a GDP deflator when calculating producer surplus.

In the U.S. the most-often-used deflator reflecting consumer prices is the *Consumer Price Index* (CPI). The most commonly-used variant is the all-items CPI for all urban consumers, CPI-U, which is published by the Bureau of Labor Statistics and is summarized in Table 6-3 for the period 1980–2009.[12] Currently, the base year (when the CPI = 100) is the period 1982–1984. The CPI is expressed as the ratio of the cost of purchasing a standard basket of market goods in a particular year to the cost of purchasing the same (or very similar) basket of goods in the base year, multiplied by 100. For example, the CPI for 1980 was 82.4, which implies that the cost of a basket of goods in 1980 was 82.4 percent of the cost of a similar basket of goods in 1982–1984.

Returning to our example where average incomes increased 2.345 times from 1986 and 2006, Table 6-3 shows that average market prices increased 1.84 times (201.6/109.6) from 1986 to 2006. Therefore, on average, people were about 27.5 percent ((2.345 − 1.84)/1.84) better off in 2006 than in 1986 in terms of how much more market goods and services they could consume.[13]

In order to convert amounts measured in nominal dollars for some year into amounts measured in real dollars for the base year (1982–1984), we simply divide by the CPI for that year (divided by 100). For example, the average real income of people in 1986 measured in 1982–1984 dollars was $12,468 ($13,665/1.096), and the average real income of people in 2006 measured in 1982–1984 dollars was $15,897 ($32,049/2.016), again showing an increase of 27.5 percent.

To convert amounts from base year dollars to, say, 2003 dollars, they are simply multiplied by the CPI for 2003 (divided by 100). Thus, the average real disposable incomes of people in 1986 and 2006, expressed in 2003 dollars, were $22,941 and $29,250, respectively.

More generally, as the preceding example illustrates, to convert amounts expressed in year *a* nominal dollars into amounts expressed in year *b* real dollars, the year *a* dollar amounts are divided by the CPI for year *a* and multiplied by the CPI for year *b*. Fortunately for analysts in the U.S., the following government website contains an inflation calculator that does this automatically: http://www.bls.gov/data/inflation_calculator.htm.

Problems with Indices Based on Consumer Prices

Although the CPI is the most widely used price index in the U.S., it is subject to a number of criticisms. Its value matters considerably to those many people who receive

TABLE 6-3   The U.S. Consumer Price Index (CPI)
All Urban Consumers—All items 1982–84 = 100

Year	Average Annual CPI	% Change	Year	Average Annual CPI	% Change
1980	82.4	13.5	1995	152.4	2.8
1981	90.9	10.3	1996	156.9	3.0
1982	96.5	6.2	1997	160.5	2.3
1983	99.6	3.2	1998	163.0	1.6
1984	103.9	4.3	1999	166.6	2.2
1985	107.6	3.6	2000	172.2	3.4
1986	109.6	1.9	2001	177.1	2.8
1987	113.6	3.6	2002	179.9	1.6
1988	118.3	4.1	2003	184.0	2.3
1989	124.0	4.8	2004	189.9	2.7
1990	130.7	5.4	2005	195.3	3.4
1991	136.2	4.2	2006	201.6	3.2
1992	140.3	3.0	2007	207.3	2.8
1993	144.5	3.0	2008	215.3	3.8
1994	148.2	2.6	2009	214.5	−0.4

Source: ftp://ftp.bls.gov/pub/special.requests/cpi/cpiai.txt

payments linked to it. Many pensions, for example, are adjusted each year (usually upward) according to the increase in the CPI. The return to holders of index-linked bonds also depends on the value of the CPI.

Most academic economists believe that the CPI overstates the rate of increase in market prices.[14] In the mid-1990s, a commission set up by the Senate Finance Committee and chaired by Michael Boskin estimated that in the United States the CPI overestimated the increase in the cost of living by about 1 percentage point per annum, with a range between 0.8 percentage points and 1.6 percentage points.[15] As a result, people receiving entitlements linked to the CPI were, in effect, receiving more than was necessary to keep their purchasing power constant.

The main reason why the CPI might be biased upward is because it does not accurately reflect consumers' *current* purchases of goods.[16,17] This is sometimes called the *commodity substitution effect*. When the price of a good rises, consumers change their spending patterns and buy similar, but less expensive, products. As this switch to less expensive goods is not immediately picked up by the CPI, it overestimates the cost of living.[18] One version of this argument is sometimes called the discount stores effect. While government statisticians are visiting the same older, relatively expensive stores, consumers are switching to newer, cheaper discount stores. A similar problem occurs when pharmaceutical patents expire. Some consumers switch to new generic drugs, which are often as effective as patented drugs, but are considerably less expensive. These generic drugs did not exist previously and so are not included in the sample basket. This *"new goods" problem* applies also to new "high-tech" goods, such as iPads or BlackBerry phones, which improve our quality of life and are often cheaper than older substitutes, but are also not included in the basket. A second type of problem concerns quality improvements to existing products. The CPI does not reflect changes in product quality, such as safer and more reliable cars. The U.S. government has corrected the CPI for some of these problems. In 1998, it under took some major revisions that reduced the estimated bias to about 0.65 percent per annum.[19]

The downward bias in consumer price indices is probably not as large in other countries as in the U.S. For example, Allan Crawford estimates that the bias was about one-half a percentage point per annum in 1998 in Canada.[20] One reason why it was lower in Canada than the United States is that the base basket of goods has been updated every 4 years in Canada versus approximately every 10 years in the United States. Also, the Canadian index attaches a lower weight to medical services.

The United Kingdom has two main consumer-focused indices: the UK Consumer Price Index (also abbreviated by CPI) and the Retail Prices Index (RPI).[21] The UK's CPI is the main measure of inflation for macroeconomic policy purposes, currently targetted at 2 percent. It is constructed in a way that is consistent across the European Union and thereby allows inflation to be compared across the EU. The RPI is the more familiar index, going back to 1947, and is used for indexation of pensions, state benefits, and index-linked gilts (short-term government bonds). The weights in the UK's CPI and the RPI are updated annually. In general, the RPI index is considerably more variable over time than the CPI index.

Analyzing Future Benefits and Costs in CBA

Analysts may work with project benefits and costs in either real dollars or nominal dollars. Also, they may use either a real interest rate or a nominal interest rate. Care must be taken to ensure that the units of measurement of benefits and costs are consistent with the units of measurement of the discount rate. *If benefits and costs are measured in nominal dollars, then the analyst should use a nominal discount rate; if benefits and costs are measured in real dollars, then the analyst should use a real discount rate*. Both methods result in the same numerical answer.[22]

In the private sector, it is more natural to work in nominal dollars. Interest rates and other market data are expressed in nominal dollars; *pro forma* income and cash flow projections are usually made in nominal dollars; and the tax system is based on nominal amounts. However, for the analysis of public policy projects, *it is usually easier and more intuitively appealing to express all benefits and costs in real dollars and to discount using a real discount rate*. Returning to our library example, it makes more sense to think about the current and future annual cost savings to the library at today's prices than in future inflated prices. Similarly, it is easier to think about user benefits in terms of the number of hours of use at today's value per hour than to think about them in terms of future valuations. If one expects that user benefits will increase over time, for example, due to more people using the system or because each person uses it more often, then the projected real annual benefits will increase. This would be immediately clear if annual benefits were measured in real dollars. If, alternatively, annual benefits were expressed in nominal dollars, then it would not be immediately obvious whether increases were due to real increases in benefits or were due to inflation.

If the analyst prefers to work in real dollars, but benefits, costs, or the interest rate are expressed in nominal dollars, then nominal dollar amounts must be converted to real dollars. This requires an estimate of *expected inflation throughout the life of the project*, denoted *m*. To convert future impacts (benefits or costs) measured in nominal dollar to real dollars *we use the formula for computing present values, equation (6.5), but discount at rate m:*[23]

$$Real\ cost\ or\ benefit_t = \frac{Nominal\ cost\ or\ benefit_t}{(1 + m)^t}$$

For example, if a city could invest $10 million for five years at 7 percent, the nominal future value would be $14.026 million; see Table 6-1. However, with an expected inflation rate of 4 percent throughout the period, the real future value would be $14.026/(1.04)^5 = $11.53 million.

Suppose we begin with $1 today. With a nominal interest rate, *i* , we would receive $(1 + i)$ one year from now. However, if the inflation rate is *m*, then $(1 + i)$ received one year from now would buy only as much as $(1 + i)/(1+m)$ does today, using the formula immediately above or equation (6.2). The real interest rate, *r* , is therefore defined by $(1 + r) = (1 + i)/(1 + m)$. Rearranging this expression gives the following equation, which we use to *convert a nominal interest rate, i, to a real interest rate, r, with an inflation rate, m:*[24]

$$r = \frac{i - m}{1 + m} \tag{6.11}$$

For example, if the nominal interest rate is 7 percent and inflation is 4 percent, then the real interest rate is $(.07-.04)/1.04 = 0.0288$, or 2.88 percent. Note that if the City could invest $10 million for 5 years at a real interest rate of 2.88 percent then it would have $10(1.0288)^5 = $11.53 million in real terms, the same amount we computed above. If inflation is quite low (*m* is small), then the real interest rate *approximately* equals the nominal interest rate minus the rate of inflation: $r \approx i - m$. For example, if the nominal interest rate is 7 percent and inflation is 4 percent, then the real interest rate is approximately 3 percent.

In order to convert benefits or costs from real dollars to nominal dollars, analysts can use the formula for computing future values, equation (6.4), but compound at the rate of inflation, m. To convert a real interest rate to a nominal interest rate, solve equation (6.11) for i.

Estimates of Expected Inflation

Moving from nominal interest rates to real interest rates or from nominal dollars to real dollars, or vice versa, requires an estimate of the *expected* rate of inflation *during the life of the proposed project*. For convenience, some analysts use the current annual rate of increase in the CPI, but this could be extremely inaccurate, especially for longer projects. It would be better to use one of four other alternative methods.

One option is to use an inflation forecast from a published source such as reputable investment firm, branches of the federal government, a Federal Reserve Bank, or the Organisation for Economic Co-operation and Development (OECD). Each week *The Economist* presents the latest changes in consumer prices in many countries and includes a forecast of the change in the current year's consumer prices. Each month it provides a forecast for the following year for major industrialized countries.

A second alternative is to use a readily accessible survey measure of inflationary expectations. Three such measures are available in the United States: the Livingston Survey of professional economists, the University of Michigan Survey of Consumers, and the Survey of Professional Forecasters (SPF).[25] Most of these sources provide short-term forecasts. However, SPF respondents have provided 10-year-ahead inflation forecasts of the CPI since 1991. Dean Croushore found that the Livingston Survey and the SPF underestimated inflation during the 1970s (by over 7 percent some years), but more recent estimates were not biased.[26] Lloyd Thomas compared the one-year predictive performance of these three surveys and two simple naive alternatives. He found that all of the surveys performed better than the naive models, with the median Michigan consumer survey forecast performing best.[27]

Probably the best approach is to use the inflation expectations implied by the price of *inflation-indexed government bonds*. This type of bond is called a *Treasury Inflation Protected Security* (TIPS) in the United States, an *index-linked gilt* in the United Kingdom, or a *real return bond* in Canada. The semi-annual coupon payments and the final principal payment are linked to the inflation rate in each country. An estimate of expected inflation during the life of a project is provided by taking the difference between the nominal yield on conventional bonds that have the same term as the project and the real yield on real-return bonds with the same term. Suppose, for example, that the life of the project is 20 years. If the nominal yield on a conventional bond that matures in 20 years is currently 6 percent, and the real yield on a 20-year index-linked bond is 2 percent, then the expected annual rate of inflation over this 20-year period is about 4 percent.

One advantage of this approach is that it is usually much easier to find bonds that have the same maturity length as the project of interest than to find a survey whose inflationary expectations pertain to the same period as the project. A second advantage is that by comparing inflationary expectations for one period to those for a different period, one can estimate inflation during the intervening period. For example, if the expected average annual inflation rate is 5 percent per annum for the next 5 years, but only 4 percent per annum for the next 4 years, then one can compute the expected inflation during the fifth year (9.1 percent).

A fourth approach is to infer inflationary expectations from *inflation swaps*. However, we will not discuss this more complicated method as it should, in theory, provide the same estimates as using inflation-indexed bonds. Matthew Hurd and Jon Rellen explain this method in detail and discuss discrepancies between the results obtained from this method and using inflation-indexed bonds.[28]

A Simple Example of Handling Inflation: Garbage Trucks

A practical example illustrates the basic technique of handling inflation and moving from market interest rates, which are nominal rates, to real interest rates. Consider a

TABLE 6-4　The Net Present Value of Investment in New Garbage Trucks

Year	Event	Annual Benefits and Costs (in real dollars)	Annual Benefits and Costs (in nominal dollars)
0	Truck purchase	−500,000	−500,000
1	Annual savings	100,000	104,000
2	Annual savings	100,000	108,160
3	Annual savings	100,000	112,486
4	Annual savings	100,000	116,986
4	Truck liquidation	200,000	233,972
	NPV	66,812[a]	66,812[b]

[a]*Using a real discount rate of 1.923 percent.*
[b]*Using a nominal discount rate of 6 percent.*

city that uses a rural landfill to dispose of solid refuse. By adding large trucks to the refuse fleet, the city would save $100,000 in real disposal costs during the first year and the same amount in each successive year. The trucks would be purchased today for $500,000 and would be sold after four years when the city will open a resource recovery plant that will obviate the need for landfill disposal. The current market value of four-year-old trucks of the same type and quality as the city might buy is $200,000. The city can currently borrow money at a market interest rate of 6 percent. Analysts expect that inflation will be 4 percent during the next four years. Should the city buy the trucks? As usual, the answer should be yes if the *NPV* is positive. Is it?

Using Real Dollars

The annual benefits and costs in real dollars are given in column 3 of Table 6-4. It is assumed that the annual savings are the same in real terms each year. This assumption is based on several implicit assumptions, for example, that the amount of time operators drive the trucks remains constant and vehicle operating costs and operator wages increase with inflation. As benefits and costs are expressed in real dollars, we need to use a real discount rate. Since the market interest rate is 6 percent and inflationary expectations are 4 percent, the real interest rate equals $(.06 − .04)/1.04 = 0.0192$, or 1.92 percent, using equation (6.11). Applying this real discount rate to the real annual benefits and costs yields an *NPV* equal to $66,812. Thus, as long as no alternative equipment configuration offers a greater *NPV*, the city should purchase the larger trucks.

Using Nominal Dollars

If analysts take the market interest rate facing the city as the appropriate discount rate, which is a nominal rate, then they must predict future costs and benefits in nominal dollars. To convert amounts in real dollars to nominal dollars, we simply inflate them by the expected rate of inflation, m. The right-hand column of Table 6-4 shows the anticipated benefits and costs of this project in nominal dollars, assuming a 4 percent annual inflation rate. Notice that the city expects to receive $233,972 when it sells the trucks at the end of the fourth year. This is called the *nominal liquidation value* of the trucks.

Discounting the benefits and costs measured in nominal dollars using a nominal interest rate of 6 percent gives an *NPV* of the project equal to $66,812, as shown in the 4th column of Table 6-4. Thus, the two methods give exactly the same answer.

RELATIVE PRICE CHANGES

The preceding section discusses how to handle general price increases due to inflation. It assumes relative prices do not change. This section discusses how to handle relative price changes.

The importance of relative price changes is illustrated by a CBA of a development project in British Columbia to supply coal to Japanese customers, which is summarized in Table 6-5.[29] The second, third, and fourth columns contain the proposed project's benefits, costs, and net benefits, respectively, according to a CBA prepared by the provincial government of British Columbia (roughly equivalent to a state government in the United States).[30] Overall, the net benefits were estimated to be $330 million. The main beneficiaries of this project were expected to be the Canadian National Railway (CNR), which was the state-owned railway company at that time, and the Canadian federal government, which would receive corporate taxes.[31] The mining sector was also expected to benefit in terms of increased profits (producer surplus). While the British Columbian government was expected to benefit from royalties and higher corporate taxes, it would pay for the Tumbler Ridge Branchline extension. Previously unemployed workers in British Columbia and the rest of Canada were expected to enjoy benefits worth $25 million. Notice that this analysis does not include any consumer surplus benefits because it was conducted from the perspective of British Columbia, and all of the coal would be exported.

The fifth column contains the expected net benefits to each sector if the price of coal were to fall to 90 percent of the base price. Under this assumption, the aggregate net benefits would fall by $264 million from $330 million to $66 million, a substantial change. The sixth column shows the expected net benefits to each sector if the price of coal were to fall to 90 percent of the base price and Japanese customers cut back their purchases of coal to 90 percent of their expected orders. Under this assumption, the overall net benefits would fall by $449 million from $330 million to −$119 million.[32] Thus, fairly small changes in relative prices and quantities purchased would have a huge impact on the *NPV* of this project.

Under the base case scenario the main anticipated "winners" were the CNR, the federal government of Canada and, to a lesser extent, the mining sector. If the price of coal fell by 10 percent, then the mining sector would lose money. Also, the residents of British Columbia would switch from being marginal "winners" to marginal "losers," largely because royalties and corporate taxes would decrease while the costs of highways and the Tumbler Ridge Branchline would be fixed. If the price and quantity levels were to fall to 90 percent of the anticipated levels, then the mining sector would lose badly.

TABLE 6-5 CBA of North East Coal Development Project

	Benefits ($ million)	Costs ($ million)	Net Benefits Base Case ($ million)	Net Benefits 90% Base Price ($ million)	Net Benefits 90% Base Price and Quantity ($ million)
Mining Sector	3,316	3,260*	56	−146	−240
Transport Sector					
Trucking	33	33	0	0	0
Canadian National Railway	504	358	146	146	121
B.C. Railway	216	202	15	15	6
Port Terminal	135	150	−15	−15	−23
Analysis and Survey	11	11	0	0	0
British Columbia**					
Royalties	77	0	77	69	62
Corporate Taxes	154	0	154	125	107
Producer Surplus (Labor)	25	0	25	25	25
Environment	10	5	5	5	5
Highways***	0	88	−88	−88	−88
Tumbler Ridge Branchline	91	267	−176	−176	−185
Canada					
Corporate Taxes	132	0	132	107	92
Highways, Port Navigation	0	26	−26	−26	−26
Producer Surplus (Labor)	25	0	25	25	25
Totals	4,729	4,400	330	66	−119

*Includes taxes and royalties.
**Excluding impacts included elsewhere.
***Highways, electric power, townsite.
Source: Based on W. G. Waters II, "A Reanalysis of the North East Coal Development," (undated), Tables 2 & 3. All figures in millions of 1980 dollars, assuming a real discount rate of 10 percent with the discounting period ending in 2003 and no terminal value.

LONG-LIVED PROJECTS AND HORIZON VALUES

Earlier we stated that analysts should discount benefits and costs using equation (6.8) or, equivalently, equation (6.9). These equations imply that all of the impacts attributable to the project occur during the first *n* years. Subsequent benefits and costs are assumed to equal zero.

Even though a project may be finished from an engineering or administrative perspective after a relatively short period of time, the benefits (and some costs) may continue to flow from the project for many years. In England, for example, cars travel on roads that were laid out by the Romans more than 18 centuries ago. The Great Wall of China continues to generate tourism benefits even though it was built to discourage particularly unwelcome "visitors" many centuries ago. The same issue also arises in human capital investment programs, especially training and health programs. For example, preschool training programs may benefit participants throughout their entire lives, years after they completed the program; some benefits may even accrue to their children. All of these impacts should be included in a CBA. However, in practice, it is often not clear how to handle costs and benefits that arise far in the future.

If benefits or costs occur indefinitely then the *NPV* can be calculated using equations (6.8) or (6.9) with *n* replaced with infinity, ∞. For example, one could use:

$$NPV = \sum_{t=0}^{\infty} \frac{NB_t}{(1+i)^t} \qquad (6.12)$$

Alternatively, one could discount net benefits (or benefits and costs) over the first *k* years, the *discounting horizon*, and include a second term that equals the present value of all subsequent net benefits, which is denoted $PV(H_k)$:[33]

$$NPV = \sum_{t=0}^{k} \frac{NB_t}{(1+i)^t} + PV(H_k) \qquad (6.13)$$

H_k is called the *horizon value*. It equals the present value *at the end of the discounting horizon* of all subsequent net benefits. This amount has to be converted to its present value at time zero. Suppose that the useful life of a highway is 20 years and the horizon value of the highway in 20 years is $100 million. Further suppose that the discount rate is 3.5 percent, then $PV(H_k)$ equals $50.3 million.

It is practical to use equation (6.12) if it is reasonable to assume that the net benefits are constant or grow or decline indefinitely at a constant rate; see Appendix 6A. Analysts might prefer to use equation (6.13) if they are more confident about predicting costs and benefits during the "near future" (the first *k* periods) than the "far future." The first k years might perhaps be the *useful life* of the project, and one might be able to specify and estimate reasonably confidently the benefits and costs in each of these years. The present value of all subsequent impacts (those in the "far future") is reduced to a single number.

When using horizon values, the length of the discounting period, *k*, is arbitrary in theory.[34] In practice, it is usually determined by the nature of each project. For example, analysts often use a 20-year discounting period for highways because they tend to last about 20 years before they require major repairs. Sometimes the discounting period ends when an intervention ends and the remaining assets are liquidated. In this situation, the horizon value is sometimes referred to as the terminal value or the liquidation value. Notice that many short-lived projects have horizon values. For example, the library information project had a horizon value even though it lasted only five years. Some projects have negative horizon values. For example, there may be costs associated with decommissioning the site used for a World Exposition, the Olympic Games, or a nuclear power plant.

Alternative Methods for Estimating Horizon Values

A variety of methods exist for estimating horizon values, although none may be entirely satisfactory. One method is based on simple projections, another uses scrap values or liquidation values, a third uses (economic) depreciated values, a fourth is based on initial construction costs, and a fifth assumes the horizon value is zero.

Horizon Value Based on Simple Projections.   One method estimates the horizon value based on simple extrapolations of benefits and costs (or net benefits). This is similar to estimating equation (6.12), but it distinguishes between the "near future" and the "far future." Consider, for example, the construction of a new dike and suppose the annual net benefits have been calculated for the first 35 years. It is necessary to estimate the horizon value after 35 years. One possibility is to make an assumption about the growth in future net benefits. Suppose analysts expect net benefits will be $1 million in the thirty-sixth year and will grow at 1.5 percent per annum indefinitely. Using equation (6A.7) in Appendix 6A, the formula for the present value of a perpetuity that grows at a constant rate, and an interest rate of 8 percent, the horizon value at the end of the *thirty-fifth year* is $1/(0.080 - 0.015) million = $15.38 million. The present value of this horizon value is $1.04 million.

There is strong evidence that, for medium- to long-term periods, simple forecasting models predict better than more complicated models. Thus, this method may estimate the *NPV* of the project at least as well as more complicated direct estimation of equation (6.10). For many government projects, especially training programs, it is reasonable to assume that the annual net benefits decay at a constant rate after some date.

Horizon Value Based on Salvage Value or Liquidation Value.   The remaining assets may be sold at the end of some project, and the value of these assets may be used as the horizon value (also called the terminal value, scrap value, residual value, liquidation value, or salvage value in this context). For example, a school board may buy some buses, operate them for a specific period of time, and then sell them at their market value. This liquidation value may be used as the horizon value.

This method is appropriate when no other social costs or benefits arise beyond the discounting period, when there is a well-functioning market in which to value the asset, and when the market value reflects the asset's social value (i.e., there are no externalities). For example, the library information system example assumes that the net social benefits of the equipment at liquidation is $20,000 (plus dismantling costs). However, if the equipment could be used in schools where its social value (less new setup costs) would be more than $20,000 (plus dismantling costs), then a higher horizon value should be used.

In practice, it is difficult to determine the liquidation value of some government assets. Clearly, there is often no market for a used highway, and even if there were, the market value would probably not reflect the discounted value of future net social benefits.

Horizon Value Based on Its Depreciated Value.   The third method recognizes that the current value of an asset equals the present value of its future net benefits. However, instead of estimating the stream of future benefits and costs, this method estimates the value of an asset by subtracting its depreciation from its initial value, where its depreciation is calculated based on empirical market studies of similar assets.

The value of most assets decline at a geometric rate; that is, the value in one year is a constant proportion of the value in the previous year. The depreciation rate is high for assets with short lives, such as tires, motor vehicles, and medical equipment, and is low for assets with long lives, such as steam turbines, warehouses, railroad structures, and water systems. Barbara Fraumeni describes the methodology used by the Bureau of Economic Analysis (BEA) for calculating depreciation and presents a comprehensive summary of the depreciation rates and service lives of many assets.[35]

Of course, one should make adjustments where appropriate. For example, if the asset will be used more heavily or maintained more poorly than normal, then one should raise the depreciation rate and reduce the horizon value. One should also ensure that the depreciated value reflects the anticipated future use of the asset. For example, an aircraft may have a fairly high depreciated value, but if it is in mothballs and nobody will fly it, then the social benefits may be much less, possibly zero.

It is important to emphasize that we are referring to real (i.e., economic) depreciation, not accounting depreciation. There is often a substantial difference between the two. Economic depreciation concerns the decline in the economic value of an asset over time. In contrast, accounting depreciation, also called capital cost allowance (CCA), is often largely determined by tax or reporting requirements. The tax authority may allow companies to write off all of an investment in one year take (100 percent CCA), even though the investment itself may yield benefits that extend over decades. Thus, the depreciated accounting value may bear no relationship to the actual economic usefulness of an asset. *Accounting depreciation should never be included as a cost (expense) in CBA.*

Horizon Value Based on the Initial Construction Cost. This method estimates the horizon value as a fraction of the initial construction cost. In the highway example in Chapter 1, for example, the horizon value of the highway was assumed to equal 75 percent of the initial construction cost: 0.75 × $338.1 million = $253.58 million.[36] However, the 75 percent figure is quite arbitrary. It may bear no relationship to the future net social benefits. Thus this method, while simple, is not intuitively appealing.

Setting the Horizon Value Equal to Zero. A final method chooses a fairly long discounting period and ignores subsequent benefits and costs. In effect, this is a special case of the first method we discussed—it is equivalent to assuming that after k periods the net benefits in each subsequent period are zero. This is often a reasonable assumption in private-sector decision making because project evaluation requires only the consideration of private benefits and costs that may approach zero fairly quickly. The social impacts of government projects, however, may last many years. Analysts may incorrectly omit important benefits or costs if they use a time horizon that is too short.

Reprise of Horizon Values

The analyst must decide on both the discounting period and the method for calculating the horizon value. These may be interdependent. If, for example, the analyst is going to assume the horizon value is zero, then he or she should use a relatively long discounting period. If the analyst is using one of the other methods, then it makes sense to discount over the project's useful life. Analysts may try to check their results by calculating the horizon value in several different ways. Because of uncertainty concerning the actual magnitude of the horizon value, *sensitivity analysis* is often conducted by selecting alternative horizon values and seeing how this affects the findings.

A further consideration is that for some very long-lived projects analysts should use time-declining discount rates. We now turn to that issue.

TIME-DECLINING DISCOUNTING

Thus far this chapter has assumed that the discount rate is constant, that is, it does not vary over time. This is reasonable for most projects because most projects have "short" discount periods. However, some projects, including those that affect climate change, have impacts that last a very long time. In such circumstances many authors have proposed the use of time-declining discount rates. In Chapter 10 we suggest that for long-lived projects, benefits and costs should be discounted at 3.5 percent for the first 50 years, at 2.5 percent for years 50–100, 1.5 percent for years 100–200, 0.5 percent for years 200–300, and 0.0 percent for years more than 300 in the future.

It is important to understand how this works. Suppose that a project has a cost of $1 million today and a benefit of $1 billion in 400 years time. Assuming continuous discounting, the *PV* of the benefit would be $1 billion $[(e^{-0.035*50}) * (e^{-0.025(100-50)}) * (e^{-0.015(200-100)}) * (e^{-0.005(300-200)})]$, which is approximately $6,737,945, yielding a project *NPV* of $5,737,947. Note that we discount at 0 percent from year 400 to 300. We then discount at 0.5 percent from year 300 to 200, then take the resulting value in year 200 and discount it back to year 100 at 1.5 percent, then take the resulting value in year 100 and discount it back to year 50 at 2.5 percent and so on. This is equivalent to applying a single, constant rate of 1.26 percent over 400 years.

SENSITIVITY ANALYSIS IN DISCOUNTING

This chapter assumes that the rate (or rates with time declining discounting) that should be used to discount future benefits and costs is known. However, for reasons discussed in Chapter 10, there are significant differences of opinion about the correct value of the social discount rate. Also, there may be some uncertainty about the magnitude of the horizon value. Because the discount rate and the horizon value often determine the sign of the *NPV* and, therefore, whether a project should be adopted, analysts frequently conduct sensitivity analyses with respect to these two parameters.

Varying the Discount Rate and the Horizon Value

As discussed more fully in Chapter 7, the most straightforward way to perform sensitivity analysis is to vary each parameter about which there is uncertainty and recalculate the *NPV*. This is easy to do on a spreadsheet. If the policy recommendations are robust (i.e., the *NPV* remains either positive or negative) under all plausible values of the parameters, we can have greater confidence that the recommendations are valid.

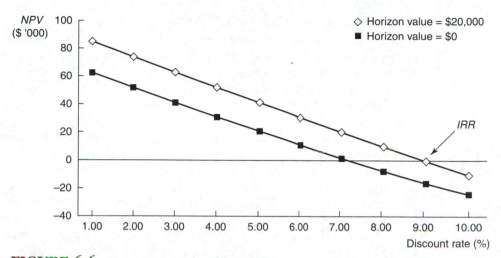

FIGURE 6-6 Sensitivity Analysis: *NPV* of the Library Information System as a Function of the Discount Rate and the Horizon Value

Figure 6-6 plots the *NPV* of the library project against the discount rate for two different horizon values, one of $20,000 and the other $0. As the discount rate increases, the *NPV* of the project decreases. This common pattern arises for investment projects whose costs occur early and whose benefits occur late. A higher discount rate results in a lower *NPV* because the future benefits are discounted more than the more immediate costs.

The top curve corresponds to a horizon value of $20,000. If the discount rate equals 7 percent, then the *NPV* equals $17,276, as shown in Figure 6-4 and Table 6-2. The *internal rate of return (IRR)*, or *breakeven discount rate,* is 8.9 percent, which can be read off the graph where the *NPV* = 0 or found exactly by trial and error.[37] As long as the horizon value equals $20,000 and the appropriate discount rate is less than 8.9 percent, the project offers a positive *NPV* and should be adopted; if the appropriate discount rate is more than 8.9 percent, then the project has a negative *NPV* and should not be adopted.

If the horizon value equals zero, then the curve shifts down by the discounted value of $20,000. As this value decreases as the discount rate increases, the curve shifts down less for high interest rates than for low interest rates. Thus, it is flatter than the curve with a horizon value of $20,000. Although the *NPV* is smaller at every interest rate if the horizon value equals zero, it is still positive as long as the discount rate is less than 7.35 percent. Most analysts agree that the appropriate real social discount rate is less than 7.35 percent; see Chapter 10. Consequently, we can be reasonably confident that if the project goes ahead it will have a positive *NPV*.

Of course, we could also compute the *breakeven horizon value*—the horizon value at which the *NPV* equals zero. Assuming the appropriate discount rate is 7 percent, the project would break even if the present value of the horizon value were −$3,016 and, therefore, if the horizon value were −$4,230. This implies the city would just break even on the project if it *cost* $4,230 to dismantle the project at the end.

Using the Internal Rate of Return as a Decision Rule

As mentioned above, the discount rate at which the *NPV* is zero is called the internal rate of return *(IRR)*. The *IRR* of the library information system project is 8.9 percent, which implies that this project is equivalent to a project of similar size that provides annual benefits equal to 8.9 percent of the original amount for five years (the length of the project) and returns all of the initial invested capital at the end of the fifth year.

The *IRR may* be used for selecting projects *when there is only one alternative to the status quo*. If the *IRR* of a project is greater than the appropriate social discount rate, then one should proceed with the project; if the *IRR* is less than the appropriate social discount rate, then one should not proceed with it. In this example, the library should proceed with the project because the *IRR* of 8.9 percent is greater than the appropriate social discount rate of 7 percent. The basic idea, which we discuss in depth in Chapter 10, is that society should only invest in projects that earn a higher return than could be earned by investing the resources elsewhere. In other words, the appropriate discount rate should reflect the opportunity cost of the funds.

There are, however, a number of potential problems with using the *IRR* for decision making. First, it may not be unique; that is, there may be more than one discount rate at which the *NPV* is zero. This problem may arise when annual net benefits change more than once from positive to negative (or vice versa) during the discounting period. Second, *IRR*s are percentages (i.e., ratios), not dollar values. Therefore, they should not be used to select one project from a group of projects that differ in size. This scale problem always arises with the use of ratios, including benefit-cost ratios, cost-effectiveness ratios, and *IRR*s. Nonetheless, if it is unique, the *IRR* conveys useful information to decision makers or other analysts who want to know how sensitive the results are to the discount rate.[38]

CONCLUSION

This chapter presents the main issues concerning the mechanics of discounting. It assumes that the appropriate discount rate is known. In fact, determination of the appropriate discount rate to use in CBA is a somewhat contentious issue, which we discuss in Chapter 10.

Shortcut Methods for Calculating the Present Value of Annuities and Perpetuities

In many practical situations the benefits or costs of a project can be treated as annuities or perpetuities. If so, there are some relatively easy ways to calculate the present values.

An *annuity* is an equal, fixed amount received (or paid) each year for a number of years. A *perpetuity* is an annuity that continues indefinitely. Suppose, for example, that in order to finance a new state highway, a state government issues $100 million worth of 30-year bonds with an interest rate of 7 percent paid annually.

The annual interest payments of $70,000 are an annuity. If at the end of *each* 30-year period the state government refinances the debt by issuing another 30-year bond that also has an interest rate of 7 percent, then the annual interest payments of $70,000 would continue indefinitely, which is a perpetuity.

Sometimes an annuity grows or declines at a constant rate. Equations (6.6) or (6.7) could be used to compute its present value, but this can be extremely time consuming. Computing the PV of a perpetuity in this way can be even more time consuming. Fortunately, some simple formulas enable analysts to compute PVs of annuities or perpetuities easily.

Present Value of an Annuity

The library information system problem contains two annuities: the annual benefits of $100,000 per year for five years, which we refer to as annuity A1, and the annual costs of $20,000 per year for five years, which we refer to as annuity A2. From Figure 6-4 we see that the present value of A1 is $410,020 and the present value of A2 is $82,004. But there is an easier way to obtain the present values.

Using equation (6.6), the present value of an annuity of $A per annum (with payments received at the end of each year) for n years with interest at i percent is given by:

$$PV = \sum_{t=1}^{n} \frac{A}{(1 + i)^t}$$

This is the sum of n terms of a geometric series with the common ratio equal to $1/(1 + i)$. Consequently,

$$PV = Aa_i^n \qquad \textbf{(6A.1)}$$

where

$$a_i^n = \frac{1 - (1 + i)^{-n}}{i} \qquad \textbf{(6A.2)}$$

The term a_i^n, which equals the present value of an annuity of $1 per year for n years when the interest rate is i, is called an *annuity factor*. Tables of annuity factors are contained in most finance textbooks and are also built into many calculators and computer spreadsheets.

Returning to our library example, the present value of annuity A1 computed using equations (6A.1) and (6A.2) is:

$$PV(A1) = \$100,000 \times \frac{1 - (1 + 0.07)^{-5}}{0.07}$$

$$PV(A1) = \$100,000 \times 4.1002$$

$$PV(A1) = \$410,020$$

Similarly,

$$PV(A2) = \$20,000 \times 4.1002 = \$82,004$$

Although this example dealt with only a five-year annuity, it is easy to compute the present value of annuities that extend over much longer periods.

When working with annuities it is important to get the timing of the cash flows exactly right. Equation (6A.1) assumes that the benefits or costs occur at the end of each period (year), with the first payment occurring one year from now. This type of annuity is called an *ordinary annuity*. An *annuity due* is an annuity with payments that occur at the beginning of each period (year). Many spreadsheets allow one to easily compute the present values of ordinary annuities and of annuities due. If the spreadsheet (or calculator) computes only ordinary annuities, then one can calculate the *PV* of an annuity due for *n* years by computing the *PV* of an ordinary annuity for *n*−1 years and adding the value of the initial payment or receipt made today.

A *deferred annuity* is an annuity whose first payment is deferred until after the first year. Suppose, for example, a government agency is considering refinancing some of its debt. Currently, it is scheduled to make debt payments of $150,000 per year for seven years with the first payment in three years. Assuming interest rates are 8 percent, what is the present value of this obligation? A time line for this problem is shown in Figure 6A-1. The first step is to treat the seven annual payments as an ordinary annuity and compute its present value as of the beginning of year 2 using equations (6A.1) and (6A.2) or a calculator. This *PV* is $780,956. The second step, recognizing that this amount is the value of an ordinary annuity *in two years' time*, is to discount the $780,956 back two years to obtain the present value of $669,543.

It is informative to note that the *present value of an annuity decreases as the interest rate increases, and vice versa*. This is a partial explanation for why bond prices rise as interest rates fall.

Another important observation is that when there is a relatively constant annuity stream, *annuity payments received after about the twentieth year add little to the present value when interest rates are 10 percent or higher*. Thus, private companies are often reluctant to make very long-term investments such as reforestation.

Present Value of a Perpetuity

A *perpetuity* is an annuity that continues indefinitely. Taking the limit of equation (6A.2) as *n* goes to infinity, the annuity factor reduces to $1/i$, if $i > 0$. Consequently, the present value of an amount, denoted by A, received (at the end of) each year in perpetuity is given by:

$$PV = \frac{A}{i} \qquad \text{if } i > 0 \qquad \textbf{(6A.3)}$$

To provide some intuition for this formula, suppose that a municipality has an endowment of

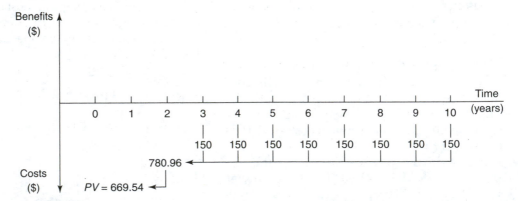

FIGURE 6A-1 Present Value of $150 per Year (in Thousands) for Seven Years, Starting in Three Years

$10 million. If interest rates are 6 percent, then this endowment will provide annual interest payments of $600,000 indefinitely. More generally, if the municipality has an endowment of X and if the interest rate is i, then the perpetual annual income from the endowment, denoted by A, is given by $A = iX$. Rearranging this equation shows the present value of the perpetual annuity is given by $X = A/i$, which is equation (6A.3).

Equation (6A.3) is easy to apply. For example, the present value of a perpetuity of $150,000 per year when interest rates are 8 percent is:

$$PV = \frac{\$150,000}{0.08} = \$1,875,000$$

When interest rates are 10 percent, the present value of a perpetuity is especially easy to calculate: it simply equals the perpetuity multiplied by 10. For example, the present value of a perpetuity of $150,000 per year is $1,500,000 when interest rates are 10 percent.

The Present Value of an Annuity that Grows or Declines at a Constant Rate

Sometimes a project's benefits (or costs) grow at a constant rate. Let B_t denote the annual benefits in year t. If the annual benefits grow after the first year at a constant rate, g, then the benefits in year t will be:

$$B_t = B_{t-1}(1 + g) = B_1(1 + g)^{t-1} \quad t = 2, \ldots, n$$
$$\textbf{(6A.4)}$$

Under these circumstances, and if $i > g$, then the present value of the total benefits—the stream over n years—can be shown to be:[1]

$$PV(B) = \frac{B_1}{(1 + g)} a_{i_0}^n \quad \textbf{(6A.5)}$$

where $a_{i_0}^n$ is defined by equation (6A.2) and:

$$i_0 = \frac{i - g}{1 + g}, \quad i > g \quad \textbf{(6A.6)}$$

Comparing equation (6A.1) with (6A.5) shows that the PV of a benefit stream that starts at B_1 in year 1 and grows at a constant rate g for $n - 1$ additional years, when the interest rate is i, equals the PV of an annuity of $B_1/(1 + g)$ for n years when the interest rate is i_0, where i_0 is given by equation (6A.6).

To illustrate how to calculate the present value of a stream of benefits that grows at a constant rate, return again to the library example. Suppose we now assume that, due to increased use, the annual use benefits grow at 2 percent per annum *after the first year* (and, as before, $i = 0.07$). From equation (6A.5), the present value of this stream of benefits equals the present value of an annuity of $100,000/1.02 = $98,039 per annum for five years, discounted at the following rate:

$$i_0 = \frac{i - g}{1 + g} = \frac{0.07 - 0.02}{1.02} = 0.049$$

which amounts to $425,636.[2] In contrast, when the annual benefits are constant ($100,000/yr.), the present value equals $410,020, a difference of $15,614. This increase would be carried straight to the bottom line because the NPV would also increase by $15,614; in fact, the NPV almost doubles from $17,276 to $32,890. This example illustrates that even quite small growth rates can have large impacts on NPVs.

If the growth rate is small, then $B_1/(1 + g) \cong B_1$ and $i_0 \cong i - g$. Therefore, from equation (6A.5), the present value of a benefits stream that starts at B_1 and grows at rate g for $n - 1$ additional years approximately equals the present value of an annuity of B_1 for n years discounted at rate $i - g$, as long as $i > g$. This approximation makes it clear that when benefits grow at a positive rate, the annuity is discounted at a lower rate, which will yield a higher PV. On the other hand, if the benefits are declining at a constant rate, then the annuity is discounted at a higher rate, which will yield a lower PV.

To illustrate this approximation, the present value of a stream of benefits that starts at

$100,000 per year and grows at 2 percent per annum for four additional years with $i = 0.07$ is approximately equal to the present value of an annuity of $100,000 per year for five years discounted at $i - g = 5$ percent, which equals $432,948.[3] This value is slightly higher than the correct amount of $425,634, but it is within 2 percent of the right answer and it is easier to calculate.

Equation (6A.5) only holds if the interest rate exceeds the growth rate: $i > g$. If $i \leq g$, then it should not be used. Importantly, though, it can always be used if g is negative, that is, if benefits decline at a constant rate. Of course, equation (6A.5) pertains to costs that change at a constant rate as well as to benefits that change at a constant rate.

Present Value of Benefits (or Costs) that Grow or Decline at a Constant Rate in Perpetuity

If the initial benefits, B_1, grow indefinitely at a constant rate g and if the interest rate equals i, then the PV of the benefits is found by taking the limit of equation (6A.5) as n goes to infinity, which gives:

$$PV(B) = \frac{B_1}{i - g} \quad \text{if } i > g \quad \textbf{(6A.7)}$$

Some finance students may recognize this model as the Gordon growth model, which is also called the dividend growth model. This model can be used to value a stock that yields a constant flow of dividends that grow at a constant rate. As before, this formula holds only if $i > g$.

EXERCISES FOR CHAPTER 6

1. A highway department is considering building a temporary bridge to cut travel time during the three years it will take to build a permanent bridge. The temporary bridge can be put up in a few weeks at a cost of $740,000. At the end of three years, it would be removed and the steel would be sold for scrap. The real net *costs* of this would be $81,000. Based on estimated time savings and wage rates, fuel savings, and reductions in risks of accidents, department analysts predict that the benefits in real dollars would be $275,000 during the first year, $295,000 during the second year, and $315,000 during the third year. Departmental regulations require use of a real discount rate of 4 percent.
   a. Calculate the present value of net benefits assuming that the benefits are realized at the end of each of the three years.
   b. Calculate the present value of net benefits assuming that the benefits are realized at the beginning of each of the three years.
   c. Calculate the present value of net benefits assuming that the benefits are realized in the middle of each of the three years.
   d. Calculate the present value of net benefits assuming that half of each year's benefits are realized at the beginning of the year and the other half at the end of the year.
   e. Does the temporary bridge pass the net benefits test?
2. A government data processing center has been plagued in recent years by complaints from employees of back pain. Consultants have estimated that upgrading office furniture at a net cost of $425,000 would reduce the incidence and severity of back injuries, allowing the center to avoid medical care that currently costs $68,000 each year. They estimate that the new furniture would also provide yearly benefits of avoided losses in work time and employee comfort worth $18,000. The furniture would have a useful life of five years, after which it would have a scrap value equal to 10 percent of its initial net cost. The consultants made their estimates of avoided costs assuming that they would be treated as occurring at the beginning of each year.

In its investment decisions, the center uses a nominal discount rate of 9 percent and an assumed general inflation rate of 3 percent. It expects the inflation rate for medical care will run between 3 and 6 percent but is uncertain as to the exact rate. In other words, it is uncertain as to whether the cost of medical care will inflate at the same rate as other prices or rise 3 percentage points faster. Should the center purchase the new furniture?

3. A town's recreation department is trying to decide how to use a piece of land. One option is to put up basketball courts with an expected life of 8 years. Another is to install a swimming pool with an expected life of 24 years. The basketball courts would cost $180,000 to construct and yield net benefits of $40,000 at the end of each of the 8 years. The swimming pool would cost $2.25 million to construct and yield net benefits of $170,000 at the end of each of the 24 years. Each project is assumed to have zero salvage value at the end of its life. Using a real discount rate of 5 percent, which project offers larger net benefits?

4. The environmental protection agency of a county would like to preserve a piece of land as a wilderness area. The current owner has offered to lease the land to the county for 20 years in return for a lump sum payment of $1.1 million, which would be paid at the beginning of the 20-year period. The agency has estimated that the land would generate $110,000 per year in benefits to hunters, bird watchers, and hikers. Assume that the lease price represents the social opportunity cost of the land and that the appropriate real discount rate is 4 percent.
   a. Assuming that the yearly benefits, which are measured in real dollars, accrue at the end of each of the 20 years, calculate the net benefits of leasing the land.
   b. Some analysts in the agency argue that the annual real benefits are likely to grow at a rate of 2 percent per year due to increasing population and county income. Recalculate the net benefits assuming that they are correct.

5. Imagine that the current owner of the land in the previous exercise was willing to sell the land for $2 million. Assuming this amount equaled the social opportunity cost of the land, calculate the net benefits if the county were to purchase the land as a permanent wildlife refuge. In making these calculations, first assume a zero annual growth rate in the $110,000 of annual real benefits; then assume that these benefits grow at a rate of 2 percent per year.

6. Instructor-provided spreadsheet recommended New City is considering building a recreation center. The estimated construction cost is $12 million with annual staffing and maintenance costs of $750,000 over the 20-year life of the project. At the end of the life of the project, New City expects to be able to sell the land for $4 million, though the amount could be as low as $2 million and as high as $5 million. Analysts estimate the first-year benefits (accruing at the end of the year of the first year) to be $1.2 million. They expect the annual benefit to grow in real terms due to increases in population and income. Their prediction is a growth rate of 4 percent, but it could be as low as 1 percent and as high as 6 percent. Analysts estimate the real discount rate for New City to be 6 percent, though they acknowledge that it could be a percentage point higher or lower.
   a. Calculate the present value of net benefits for the project using the analysts' predictions.
   b. Investigate the sensitivity of the present value of net benefits to alternative predictions within the ranges given by the analysts.

NOTES

1. T-bill is an abbreviation of Treasury bill. A T-bill is a short-term bond issued by the Treasury Department of the U.S. government.
2. $PV = \$10,500,000/1.05 = \$10,000,000$.
3. At the end of the first year, one would have $FV = X(1 + i)$. At the end of the second year, one would have $FV = [X(1 + i)](1 + i) = X(1 + i)^2$, and so on.
4. There is a handy rule for computing approximate future values called the "rule of 72." Capital roughly doubles when the interest rate (expressed in percentage points) times the number of years

equals seventy-two: $100 \times i \times n = 72$. For example, if the interest rate is 8 percent, then your capital doubles in $72/8 = 9$ years. Similarly, in order to double your capital in 10 years, you need an interest rate of at least $72/10 = 7.2$ percent.

5. The following equation summarizes the relationship between discounting and compounding:

$$PV = \frac{FV}{(1+i)^n}$$

where PV is the present value and FV is the future value.

6. $NPV = \sum_{t=0}^{n} \frac{B_i}{(1+i)^t} - \sum_{t=0}^{n} \frac{C_t}{(1+i)^t}$

$= \sum_{t=0}^{n} \frac{B_t - C_t}{(1+i)^t} = \sum_{t=0}^{n} \frac{NB_t}{(1+i)^t}$

7. If interest is compounded continuously, then the present value of $\$Y$ received in n years time with interest rate i is given by:

$$PV = \frac{Y}{e^{in}}$$

where $e = \lim_{n \to \infty} \left(1 + \frac{1}{n}\right)^n$ is the base of the natural logarithm, which equals 2.71828 to five decimal places. For example, the present value of $\$100,000$ received in five years with interest at 7 percent, compounded continuously, is:

$$PV = \frac{\$100,000}{e^{0.07 \times 5}} = \frac{\$100,000}{1.419} = \$70,469$$

8. If project A were two-thirds the length of project B, then the analyst should compare three project As back-to-back with two project Bs back-to-back.

9. The difference between the NPV of five back-to-back cogeneration plants and the NPV of only one cogeneration plant is $\$10.94$ million. In effect, we would have arrived at the same figure if we had evaluated building only one cogeneration plant, but assigned a horizon value with a present value of $\$10.94$ million to this project.

10. The annuity factor for the hydroelectric project is the present value of an annuity of $\$1$ per year for 75 years using an interest rate of 8 percent, which, using equation (6A.2) or a calculator, equals 12.461. Similarly, the annuity factor for the cogeneration project equals the present value of $\$1$ per annum for 15 years at an interest rate of 10 percent.

11. Bureau of Labor Statistics, November 2007, "The U.S. Economy to 2016: Slower Growth as Boomers Begin to Retire," *Monthly Labor Review*, Table 4, available at http://www.bls.gov/emp/empmacro04.htm.

12. The most recent CPI figures for the United States as well as CPI figures back to 1913 are available from the Bureau of Labor Statistics at its web site: *www.bls.gov*. The most recent CPI figures for Canada are available from Statistics Canada at its web site: *www.statcan.ca*. For long, term historical Canadian data, see F. H. Leacy, ed., *Historical Statistics of Canada* (Ottawa, Ontario: Statistics Canada, 1983). For the latest statistics for the United Kingdom see the Office for National Statistics' web site at http://www.statistics.gov.uk/default.asp. Another useful website for the U.S. is www.bls.gov/data/inflation_calculator.htm, which provides.

13. An alternative way to obtain this result follows. A person with an average disposable income of $\$13,665$ in 1986 would be able to purchase the same basket of goods in 2006 as a person on an income of $\$25,136$ ($\$13,665 \times 201.6/109.6$). Because the average disposable income was $\$32,049$ in 2006, we can conclude that effective (i.e., real) average disposable incomes increased by ($\$32,049 - \$25,136$)/$\$25,136 = 0.275$, or 27.5 percent over this period.

14. Some economists argue that the CPI understates inflation; see, for example, John Williams' Shadow Government Statistics at http://www.shadowstats.com/.

15. See Michael J. Boskin, Ellen R. Dulberger, Robert J. Gordon, Zvi Griliches and Dale W. Jorgenson, *Toward a More Accurate Measure of the Cost of Living*, Final Report to the Senate Finance Committee from the Advisory Committee to Study the Consumer Price Index. (Washington, D.C.: Senate Finance Committee, 1996).

16. For more detail see Brent R. Moulton, "Bias in the Consumer Price Index: What Is the Evidence?" *Journal of Economic Perspectives* 10(4) 1996, 159–177 and Allan Crawford, "Measurement Biases in the Canadian CPI: An Update," *Bank of Canada Review* Spring 1998, 39–56.

17. For practical reasons the CPI is a Laspeyres index, which uses the quantities of each good consumed in a previous period to compute expenditures in the current period.

18. See Zvi Griliches and Iain Cockburn, "Generics and New Goods in Pharmaceutical Price Indexes," *American Economic Review* 84(5) 1994, 1213–1232.
19. For more information about the 1998 CPI revisions see http://www.bls.gov/cpi/cpi1998.htm.
20. See Allan Crawford, "Measurement Biases in the Canadian CPI: An Update."
21. There are three main differences between the CPI and the RPI. The first concerns the goods. The CPI covers the full range of consumer purchases made by households, excluding council tax and most owner-occupier housing costs, such as mortgage interest payments, which are included in the RPI. Other items included in the RPI but not in the CPI include vehicle excise duty and trade union subscriptions. Items included in the CPI but not in the RPI include unit trust and stockbroker charges, overseas students' university fees and accommodation costs. The second key difference is that the CPI has a broader population base: the RPI (unlike the CPI) excludes households in the top 4 percent of income and some pensioners. The third key difference is the weights: the CPI weights are based on household expenditure from the National Accounts, while the RPI uses the Expenditure and Food Survey. Fourth, the aggregation formulae are different. For more information see Rob Pike, Measuring inflation, Office for National Statistics, available at http://www.statistics.gov.uk/elmr/07_08/downloads/ELMR_Jul08_Pike.pdf.
22. Recall that the *NPV* for a project is given by equation (6.8), and suppose that these benefits, B_t, and costs, C_t, are in nominal dollars and i is the nominal interest rate. Let b_t denote real benefits, c_t denote real costs, and suppose the rate of inflation is m, then, using equation (6.4), $B_t = b_t(1 + m)^t$ and $C_t = c_t(1 + m)^t$. Consequently,

$$NPV = \sum_{t=0}^{n} \frac{B_t - C_t}{(1 + i)^t} = \sum_{t=0}^{n} \frac{(b_t - c_t)(1 + m)^t}{(1 + i)^t}$$

Now, to simplify, set $1/(1 + r) = (1 + m)/(1 + i)$, which gives:

$$NPV = \sum_{t=0}^{n} \frac{b_t - c_t}{(1 + r)^t}$$

As we discuss later, we can interpret r as the real interest rate.

23. The expected CPI in t periods in the future equals $(1 + m)^t$ times the current CPI. Therefore, dividing the future amounts measured in nominal dollars by $(1 + m)^t$, in accordance with equation (6.5), is exactly the same as the method implied at the end of the previous subsection for converting amounts expressed in year b dollars into amounts expressed in year a dollars, namely: dividing by the expected CPI in t periods in the future and multiplying by the CPI for the current year.
24. This relationship is known as the Fisher effect. An alternative derivation follows. Suppose that we invest $1 for a year, the real rate of return is r and the rate of inflation during the year is m, then the we would have $\$(1 + r)(1 + m)$ in a year. Thus, the nominal rate of return i is:

$$i = (1 + r)(1 + m) - 1, \text{ or}$$
$$(1 + i) = (1 + r)(1 + m)$$

Rearranging this expression also gives equation (6.11).

25. For the Livingston survey data and more information about this survey see http://www.phil.frb.org/research-and-data/real-time-center/livingston-survey/. For more information about the SPF see http://www.phil.frb.org/research-and-data/real-time-center/survey-of-professional-forecasters/, and for more information about the University of Michigan's Survey of Consumers see http://research.stlouisfed.org/fred2/series/MICH/.
26. Dean Croushore, 2006, "An Evaluation of Inflation Forecasts from Surveys Using Real-Time Data," Federal Reserve Bank of Philadeplphia, Working Paper 06-19.
27. Lloyd B. Thomas Jr., "Survey Measures of Expected U.S. Inflation," *Journal of Economic Perspectives* 13(4) 1999, 125–144.
28. See http://www.bankofengland.co.uk/publications/quarterlybulletin/qb060101.pdf.
29. An initial study was prepared by the government of British Columbia, "A Benefit-Cost Analysis of the North East Coal Development," (Victoria, B.C.: Ministry of Industry and Small Business, 1982). Subsequent analysis was conducted by W. W. Waters, II, "A Reanalysis of the North East Coal Development," (Working paper, University of British Columbia, undated).
30. The initial study made shadow price adjustments for foreign exchange earnings. These are excluded from Table 6-5 because, according to Bill Waters, the author of the re-analysis, they are probably inappropriate.

31. Like many studies, this study ignores the marginal excess tax burden.

32. This scenario of declining prices and declining quantities sold is quite plausible for this project. The major Japanese customers were simultaneously encouraging development of Australian and other sources. If these alternative sources came on line at the same time, there would be a worldwide excess supply, internationally determined coal prices would fall, and demand for B.C. coal would fall.

33. Comparing equation (6.13) with equation (6.12) implies:

$$PV(H_k) = NPV - \sum_{t=0}^{k}\frac{NB_t}{(1+i)^t} = \sum_{t=k+1}^{\infty}\frac{NB_t}{(1+i)^t}$$

34. For example,

$$NPV = \sum_{t=0}^{20}\frac{NB_t}{(1+i)^t} + PV(H_{20})$$
$$= \sum_{t=0}^{30}\frac{NB_t}{(1+i)^t} + PV(H_{30})$$

35. Barbara M. Fraumeni, "The Measurement of Depreciation in the U.S. National Income and Product Accounts," *Survey of Current Business* 77(7) 1997, 7–23.

36. This is the value 20 years after the highway was completed, which was 21.5 years after the decision to build the highway in 1986. Consequently,

according to the method, the present value of the horizon value was $53.3 million.

37. By definition, the internal rate of return can be found by setting the left-hand side of equations (6.8) or (6.9) equal to zero and solving for i. In practice, this can be quite difficult. It is usually easier to enter the data into a spreadsheet and use trial and error.

38. If expenditures equal social costs and if the total amount of expenditures is constrained, then ranking projects on the basis of the IRR criterion may maximize the total *NPVs*. For example, if three projects cost a *total* of $1 billion and, in addition, each has a higher IRR than a fourth project that costs $1 billion by itself, then the first three projects will also have a larger *combined NPV* than the *NPV* of the fourth project. In effect, the IRR provides an estimate of the average annual net benefit per unit of (constrained) expenditure. Problems with ranking project in terms of their IRRs only arise when the total expenditure on the projects with the highest IRRs does not exactly equal the total amount available. Even if the first, second, and third projects have higher IRRs than the fourth project, the fourth project *may* still have a higher *NPV* than the three smaller projects combined if its total cost is larger (but still no more than $1 billion). In any constrained project choice setting, the optimal set of projects can be found by using linear programming.

APPENDICES NOTES

1. $PV(B) = \sum_{t=1}^{n}\frac{B_1(1+g)^{t-1}}{(1+i)^t} = \sum_{t=1}^{n}\frac{B_1}{(1+g)}\left(\frac{1+g}{1+i}\right)^t$

   Setting $i_0 = (i-g)/(1+g)$ implies $1/(1+i_0) = (1+g)/(1+i)$. Therefore,

   $PV(B) = \sum_{t=1}^{n}\frac{B_1}{(1+g)}\left(\frac{1}{(1+i_0)^t}\right) = \frac{B_1}{(1+g)}a_{i_0}^n$

2. Alternatively, substituting equation (6A.2) into equation (6A.5) gives the following formula for computing the *PV* of the benefits:

   $PV(B) = \frac{B_1}{(1+g)}\left(\frac{1-(1+i_0)^{-n}}{i_0}\right)$

Therefore, for this example:

$PV(B) = \frac{\$100,000}{(1+0.02)} \times \frac{1-(1-0.049)^{-5}}{0.049}$
$= \$98,039 \times 4.3415 = \$425,636$

3. That is:

$PV(B) = \sum_{t=1}^{n}\frac{B_1}{(1+i-g)^t} = \sum_{t=1}^{5}\frac{\$100,000}{(1+0.07-0.05)^t}$
$= \$432,948$

Dealing with Uncertainty: Expected Values, Sensitivity Analysis, and the Value of Information

Cost-benefit analysis often requires us to predict the future. Whether it is desirable to begin a project depends on what we expect will happen after we have begun. But, as mere mortals, we rarely are able to make precise predictions about the future. Indeed, in many situations analysts can be certain that circumstances largely beyond their clients' control, such as epidemics, floods, bumper crops, or fluctuations in international oil prices, will greatly affect the benefits and costs that would be realized from proposed policies. How can analysts reasonably take account of these uncertainties in CBA?

In this chapter, we consider three topics relevant to uncertainty: *expected value* as a measure reflecting risks, *sensitivity analysis* as a way of investigating the robustness of net benefit estimates to different resolutions of uncertainty, and the *value of information* as a benefit category for CBA and as a guide for allocating analytical effort. Expected values take account of the dependence of benefits and costs on the occurrence of specific contingencies, or "states of the world" to which analysts are able to assign probabilities of occurrence. Sensitivity analysis is a way of acknowledging uncertainty about the values of important parameters in our predictions—it should be a component of almost any CBA. When analysts have opportunities for gaining additional information about costs or benefits, they may be able to value the information by explicitly modeling the uncertainty inherent in their decisions. A particular type of information value, called *quasi-option value,* is relevant when assessing currently available alternatives that have different implications for learning about the future.

EXPECTED VALUE ANALYSIS

One can imagine several types of uncertainty about the future. At the most profound level, one might not be able to specify the full range of relevant circumstances that may occur. Indeed, the human and natural worlds are so complex that one cannot hope to anticipate every possible future circumstance. Yet, in many situations of relevance to one's daily life and public policy, it is reasonable to characterize the future in terms of a number of distinct contingencies. For example, in deciding whether to take an umbrella to work, one might reasonably divide the future into two contingencies: Either it will or will not rain sufficiently to make the umbrella useful. Of course, other relevant contingencies can be imagined as well—it will be a dry day, but one may or may not be the victim of an attempted mugging in which the umbrella would prove valuable in self-defense! Yet, if these additional contingencies are very unlikely, it is often reasonable to leave them out of one's model of the future. Modeling the future as a set of relevant contingencies involves yet another narrowing of uncertainty: How likely are each of the contingencies? If one is willing to assign probabilities of occurrence to each of the contingencies, then uncertainty about the future becomes a problem of dealing with risk. In relatively simple situations, risk can be readily incorporated into CBA through expected value analysis.

Contingencies and their Probabilities

Modeling uncertainty as risk begins with the specification of a set of *contingencies* that, within the simplified model of the world being employed, are *exhaustive* and *mutually exclusive*. Contingencies can be thought of as possible events, outcomes, or states of the world such that one and only one of the relevant set of possibilities will actually occur. What makes a set of contingencies the basis of an appropriate model for conducting a CBA of a policy?

One important consideration is that the contingencies capture the full range of likely variation in net benefits of the policy. For example, in evaluating an oil stockpile for use in the event of an oil price shock sometime in the future, one would want to consider at least two contingencies: There never will be an oil price shock (a situation in which the policy is likely to result in net losses), and there will be a major price shock (a situation in which the policy is likely to result in net gains).

Another consideration is how well the contingencies represent the possible outcomes between the extremes. In some circumstances, the possible contingencies can be listed exhaustively so that they are fully representative. More often, however, they sample an infinite number of possibilities. In these circumstances, each contingency can be thought of as a *scenario,* which is just a description of a possible future. Do the specified contingencies provide a sufficient variety of scenarios to convey the possible futures adequately? If so, then the contingencies are representative.

Figure 7-1 illustrates the representation of a continuous scale with discrete contingencies. The horizontal axis gives the number of inches of summer rainfall in an agricultural region. The vertical axis gives the net benefits of a water storage system, which increase as the amount of rainfall decreases. Imagine that an analyst represents uncertainty about rainfall with only two contingencies: "excessive" and "deficient." The excessive contingency assumes 22 inches of rainfall, which would yield zero net benefits from the storage system. The deficient contingency assumes zero inches of rainfall, which would yield $4.4 million in net benefits. If the relationship between rainfall and net benefits follows the straight line labeled *A*, and all the rainfall amounts between 0 and 22 are equally likely, then the average of net benefits over the full continuous range would be $2.2 million. If the analyst assumed that each of the contingencies were equally likely, then the average over the two contingencies would also be $2.2 million, so that using two scenarios would be adequately representative.[1]

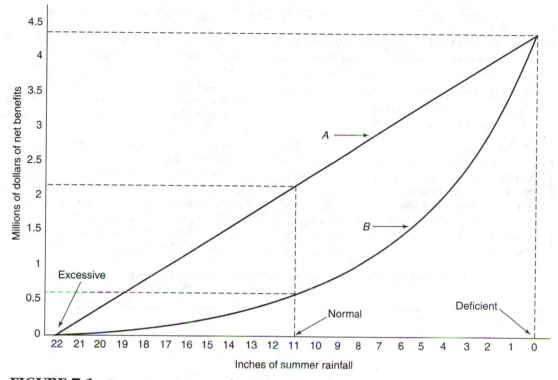

FIGURE 7-1   Representativeness of Contingencies

Now imagine that the net benefits follow the curved line labeled *B*. Again assuming that all rainfall amounts between 0 and 22 inches are equally likely, the average of net benefits over the full continuous range would only be about $1.1 million, so that using only two contingencies would grossly overestimate the average net benefits from the storage system.[2] Adding "normal" as a contingency that assumes 11 inches of rainfall and averaging net benefits over all three contingencies yields net benefits of $1.6 million, which is more representative than the average calculated with two contingencies but still considerably larger than the $1.1 million calculated over the full continuous range. Even more contingencies are desirable. For example, moving to five equally spaced contingencies gives an average of $1.3 million, which is much closer to the average over the continuous range.[3]

Once we have specified a tractable but representative set of contingencies, the next task is to assign probabilities of occurrence to each of them. To be consistent with the logical requirement that the contingencies taken together are exhaustive and mutually exclusive, the probabilities that we assign must each be nonnegative and sum to exactly 1. Thus, if there are three contingencies, C_1, C_2, and C_3, we must assign corresponding probabilities p_1, p_2, and p_3 such that $p_1 + p_2 + p_3 = 1$.

The probabilities may be based solely on historically observed frequencies; on subjective assessments by clients, analysts, or other experts based on a variety of

--- **EXHIBIT 7-1** ---

Being explicit about contingencies, their probabilities, and their consequences can help structure complex decision problems. Consider the following letter that President Abraham Lincoln wrote to Major General George B. McClellan on February 3, 1862:

My dear Sir:

You and I have distinct, and different plans for a movement of the Army of the Potomac—yours to in be down the Chesapeake, up the Rappahannock to Urbana, and across land to the terminus of the Railroad on the York River—, mine to move directly to a point on the Railroad South West of Manassas.

If you will give me satisfactory answers to the following questions, I shall gladly yield my plan to yours.

First. Does not your plan involve a greatly larger expenditure of time and money than mine?

Second. Wherein is a victory more certain by your plan than mine?

Third. Wherein is a victory more valuable by your plan than mine?

Fourth. In fact, would it not be less valuable, in this, that it would break no great line of the enemy's communications, while mine would?

Fifth. In case of disaster, would not a safe retreat be more difficult by your plan than by mine?

Yours truly, Abraham Lincoln

Source: John G. Nicolay and John Hay, eds., *Abraham Lincoln: Complete Works, Volume Two* (New York: The Century Company, 1894), 120.

information and theory; or on both. For example, return to the contingencies in Figure 7-1: agriculturally "excessive," "normal," and "deficient" precipitation in a river valley for which a water storage system has been proposed. The national weather service may be able to provide data on average annual rainfall over the last century that allows an analyst to estimate the probabilities of the three levels of precipitation from their historical frequencies. If such data were not available, then the analyst would have to base the probabilities on expert opinion, comparison with similar valleys in the region for which data are available, or some other subjective assessment. As such subjective assessments are rarely made with great confidence, it is especially important to investigate the sensitivity of the results to the particular probabilities chosen.

Calculating the Expected Value of Net Benefits

The specification of contingencies and their respective probabilities allows us to calculate the *expected net benefits* of a policy. We do so by first predicting the net benefits of the policy under each contingency and then taking the weighted average of these net benefits over all the contingencies, where the weights are the respective probabilities that the contingencies occur. Specifically, for n contingencies, let B_i be the benefits under contingency i, C_i be the costs under contingency i, and p_i be the probability of contingency i occurring. Then the expected net benefits, $E[NB]$, are given by the formula:

$$E[NB] = p_1(B_1 - C_1) + \cdots + p_n(B_n - C_n) \qquad (7.1)$$

which is just the expected value of net benefits over the n possible outcomes.[4]

EXHIBIT 7-2

In their evaluation of alternative government oil stockpiling programs in the early 1980s, Glen Sweetnam and colleagues at the U.S. Department of Energy modeled the uncertainty surrounding oil market conditions with five contingencies: *slack market*—oil purchases for the U.S. stockpile of up to 1.5 million barrels per day (mmb/d) could be made without affecting the world oil price; *tight market*—oil purchases increase the world price at the rate of $3.60 per mmb/d; *minor disruption*—loss of 1.5 mmb/d to the world market (e.g., caused by a revolution in an oil-exporting country); *moderate disruption*—loss of 6.0 mmb/d to the world market (e.g., caused by a limited war in the Persian Gulf); *major disruption*—loss of 12.0 mmb/d to the world market (e.g., caused by a major war in the Persian Gulf). For each of the 24 years of their planning horizon, they assumed that the probabilities of each of the contingencies occurring depended only on the contingency that occurred in the previous year. For each year, they calculated the social surplus in the U.S. oil market conditional on each of the five market contingencies and change in the size of the stockpile.

The model they constructed allowed them to answer the following questions: For any current market condition and stockpile size, what change in stockpile size maximizes the present value of expected net benefits? How much storage capacity should be constructed? How fast should it be added? The model and the answers it provided were influential in policy debates concerning expansion of the U.S. stockpile, the Strategic Petroleum Reserve.

Sources: Adapted from Glen Sweetnam, "Stockpile Policies for Coping with Oil-Supply Disruptions," in George Horwich and Edward J. Mitchell, eds., *Policies for Coping with Oil-Supply Disruptions* (Washington, D.C.: American Enterprise Institute for Public Policy Research, 1982), 82–96. On the role of the model in the policy-making process, see Hank C. Jenkins-Smith and David L. Weimer, "Analysis as Retrograde Action: The Case of Strategic Petroleum Reserves," *Public Administration Review* 45(4) 1985, 485–494.

When facing complicated risk problems, analysts often find it useful to model them as *games against nature*. A game against nature assumes that nature will randomly, and nonstrategically, select a particular state of the world. The random selection of a state of the world is according to assumed probabilities. The selection is nonstrategic in the sense that nature does not alter the probabilities of the states of the world in response to the action selected by the analysts. A game against nature in *normal form* has the following elements: *states of nature* and their *probabilities of occurrence*, *actions* available to the decision maker facing nature, and *payoffs* to the decision maker under each combination of state of nature and action.

Table 7-1 shows the analysis of alternatives for planetary defense against asteroid collisions as a game against nature in normal form. It considers three possible states of nature over the next 100 years: exposure of Earth to collision with an asteroid larger than one kilometer in diameter, which would have enough kinetic energy to impose severe regional or even global effects on society (10 on the Torino Scale); exposure of Earth to collision with an asteroid smaller than one kilometer but larger than 20 meters in diameter, which would have severe local or regional effects on society (8 or 9 on the Torino Scale); and no exposure of Earth to an asteroid larger than 20 meters in diameter. The game shows three actions: build a forward-based asteroid defense, which would station nuclear devices sufficiently deep in space to give a good possibility of

TABLE 7-1   A Game against Nature: Expected Values of Asteroid Defense Alternatives

State of Nature	Exposure to a Collision with an Asteroid Larger Than One Kilometer in Diameter	Exposure to a Collision with an Asteroid between 20 Meters and 1 Kilometer in Diameter	No Exposure to Collision with an Asteroid Larger Than 20 Meters in Diameter	
Probabilities of states of nature (over next century)	.001	.004	.995	
Actions (alternatives)	**Payoffs (net costs in billions of 2000 dollars)**			*Expected Value*
Forward-based asteroid defense	5,060	1,060	60	69
Near-Earth asteroid defense	10,020	2,020	20	**38**
No asteroid defense	30,000	6,000	0	54

Choose near-Earth asteroid defense: Expected net cost = $38 billion.

their timely use in diverting asteroids from collision courses with Earth; build a near-Earth asteroid defense, which would be less expensive but not as effective as the forward-based defense; and build no asteroid defense.

Although actually estimating the payoffs for this game would be a monumental and controversial analytical task, Table 7-1 displays some hypothetical figures. The payoffs, shown as the present value of net costs over the next century, range from $30 trillion (Earth is exposed to a collision with an asteroid larger than one kilometer in diameter in the absence of any asteroid defense) to $0 (Earth is not exposed to collision with an asteroid larger than 20 meters and no defense system is built). Note that estimating the costs of a collision between Earth and an asteroid would itself involve expected value calculations that take account of size, composition, and point of impact of the asteroid. The $30 trillion figure is about half the world's annual sum of gross domestic products.

The last column of Table 7-1 shows expected values for each of the three alternatives. The expected value for each alternative is calculated by summing the products of its payoff conditional on states of nature with the probabilities of those states. For example, the expected value of payoffs (present value of net costs) for no asteroid defense is:

$$(0.001)(\$30,000 \text{ billion}) + (0.004)(\$6,000 \text{ billion}) + (0.995)(\$0) = \$54 \text{ billion}$$

Similar calculations yield $69 billion for forward-based asteroid defense and $38 billion for near-Earth asteroid defense. As the maximization of expected net benefits is equivalent to minimizing expected net costs, the most efficient alternative is near-Earth asteroid defense. Alternatively, one could think of near-Earth asteroid defense as offering expected net benefits of $16 billion relative to no defense ($54 billion in expected net costs minus $38 billion in expected net costs equals $16 billion in expected net benefits), while forward-based asteroid defense offers negative $15 billion in expected net benefits relative to no defense ($54 billion in expected net costs minus $69 billion in expected net costs equals negative $15 billion in expected net benefits).

In CBA, it is common practice to treat expected values as if they were certain amounts. For example, imagine that a perfect asteroid defense system would have a present value cost of $100 billion under each of the states of nature. In this case, assuming accurate prediction of costs, the $100 billion *would be certain* because it does not depend on which state of nature actually results. CBA generally treats a certain amount such as this as fully commensurate with expected values, even though the latter will not actually result in its expected value. In other words, although the expected net cost of no asteroid defense is $54 billion, assuming an accurate prediction of payoffs, the actually realized net cost will be $30 trillion, $6 trillion, or $0. If the perfect defense system cost $54 billion, then CBA would rank it and no defense as equally efficient.

Treating expected values as if they were certain amounts implies that the person making the comparison has preferences that are *risk neutral*. A person has risk neutral preferences when he or she is indifferent between certain amounts and lotteries with the same expected payoff. A person is *risk averse* if he or she prefers the certain amount and is *risk seeking* if he or she prefers the lottery. Buying insurance, which offers a lower expected payoff than the certain premium charged, indicates risk aversion; buying a lottery ticket, which offers a lower expected value than its price, indicates risk seeking.

Chapter 8 considers the appropriateness of treating expected values and certain equivalents as commensurate (e.g., risk neutrality). It explains that doing so is not conceptually correct in measuring willingness to pay in circumstances in which individuals face uncertainty. Nevertheless, it argues that, in practice, *treating expected values and certain amounts as commensurate is generally reasonable when either the pooling of risk over the collection of policies, or the pooling of risk over the collection of persons affected by a policy, will make the actually realized values of costs and benefits close to their expected values.* For example, a policy that affects the probability of highway accidents involves reasonable pooling of risk across many drivers (some will have accidents, others will not) so that realized values will be close to expected values. In contrast, a policy that affects the risk of asteroid collision does not involve pooling across individuals (either everyone suffers from the global harm if there is a collision or no one does if there is no collision), so that the realized value of costs may be very far from their expected value. As discussed in Chapter 8, such unpooled risk may require an adjustment to expected benefits called *option value*.

Decision Trees and Expected Net Benefits

The basic procedure for expected value analysis, taking weighted averages over contingencies, can be directly extended to situations in which costs and benefits accrue over multiple years, as long as the risks in each year are independent of the realizations of risks in previous years. Consider, for example, a CBA of a dam with a 20-year life. Assume that the costs and benefits of the dam depend only on the contingencies of below-average rainfall and above-average rainfall in the current year. Additionally, if the analyst is willing to make the plausible assumption that the amount of rainfall in any year does not depend on the rainfall in previous years, then the analyst can simply calculate the present value of expected net benefits for each year and calculate the present value of this stream of net benefits in the usual way.

The basic expected value procedure cannot be so directly applied when either the net benefits accruing under contingencies or the probabilities of the contingencies depend on the contingencies that have previously occurred. For example, above-average rainfall in one year may make the irrigation benefits of a dam less in the next year because of accumulated ground water. In the case of a policy to reduce the costs of earthquakes, the probability of a major earthquake may change each year depending on the mix of earthquakes that occurred in the previous year.

Such situations require a more flexible framework for handling risk than basic expected value analysis. *Decision analysis* provides the needed framework.[5] Though it takes us too far afield to present decision analysis in any depth here, we sketch its general approach and present simple illustrations that demonstrate its usefulness in CBA. A number of book-length treatments of decision analysis are available for those who wish to pursue this topic in more depth.[6]

Decision analysis can be thought of as a *sequential, or extended form, game* against nature. It proceeds in two basic stages. First, one specifies the logical structure of the decision problem in terms of sequences of decisions and realizations of contingencies using a diagram, called a *decision tree*, that links an initial decision (the trunk) to final outcomes (branches). Second, using *backward induction,* one works from final outcomes back to the initial decision, calculating expected values of net benefits across contingencies and pruning dominated branches (i.e., eliminating branches with lower expected values of net benefits).

Consider a vaccination program against a particular type of influenza that involves various costs.[7] The costs of the program result from immunization expenditures and possible adverse side effects; the benefits consist of the adverse health effects that are avoided if an epidemic occurs. This flu may infect a population over the next two years before sufficient immunity develops worldwide to stop its spread. Figure 7-2 presents a simple decision tree for a CBA of this vaccination program. The tree should be read from left to right to follow the sequence of decisions, denoted by □, and random selections of contingencies, denoted by (○). The tree begins with a decision node, the square labeled 0 at the extreme left. The upper bough represents the decision to implement the vaccination program this year; the lower bough represents the decision not to implement the program this year.

Upper Bough: The Vaccination Program.   Follow the upper bough first. If the program is implemented, then it will involve direct administrative costs, C_a, and the costs of adverse side effects, such as contracting the influenza from the vaccine itself, suffered by those who are vaccinated, C_s. Note that C_s, like most of the other costs in this example, is itself an expected cost based on the probability of the side effect, the cost to persons suffering the side effect, and the number of persons vaccinated. The solid vertical line on the bough can be thought of as a toll gate at which point the program costs, $C_a + C_s$, are incurred. A chance node, represented by a circle, appears next. Either the influenza infects the population (the upper branch, which occurs with probability P_1 and results in costs $C_{e|v}$, where the subscript should be read as "epidemic occurs given that the vaccination program has been implemented"), or the influenza does not infect the population (the lower branch, which occurs with probability $1 - P_1$ and results in zero costs at that time). If the influenza does occur, then the population will be immune

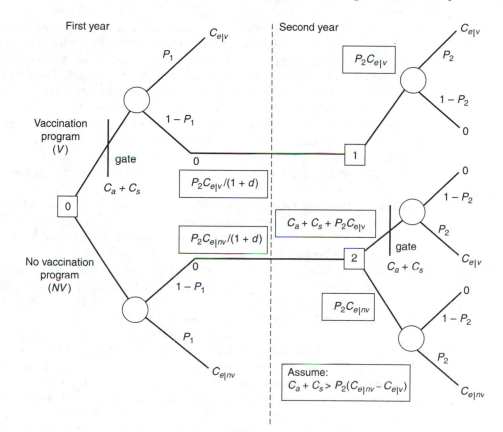

First year

Second year

$C_{e|v}$

P_1

$P_2 C_{e|v}$

P_2

$C_{e|v}$

$1 - P_2$

$1 - P_1$

Vaccination
program
(V)

gate

0

1

0

$C_a + C_s$

$P_2 C_{e|v}/(1 + d)$

0

0

0

$1 - P_2$

$C_a + C_s + P_2 C_{e|v}$

P_2

$P_2 C_{e|nv}/(1 + d)$

2

gate

$C_{e|v}$

No vaccination
program
(NV)

0

$C_a + C_s$

$1 - P_1$

0

$P_2 C_{e|nv}$

$1 - P_2$

P_1

P_2

Assume:

$C_{e|nv}$

$C_a + C_s > P_2(C_{e|nv} - C_{e|v})$

$C_{e|nv}$

FIGURE 7-2   Decision Tree for Vaccination Program Analysis

in the next year. Thus, the upper branch does not continue. If the influenza does not occur, then there is still a possibility that it might occur in the next year. Therefore, the lower branch continues to the second year, where the square labeled 1 notes the beginning of the second year. It leads directly to another chance node that specifies the two contingencies in the second year: The influenza infects the population (the upper sub-branch, which occurs with probability P_2 and results in costs $C_{e|v}$), or the influenza does not infect the population (the lower subbranch, which occurs with probability $1 - P_2$ and results in zero costs).[8] We assume that P_2 is known at the time of the initial decision.[9]

Lower Bough: No Vaccination Program.   We now return to the initial decision node and follow the lower bough representing no vaccination program in the first year. Initially there is no cost associated with this decision. A chance node follows with two branches: Either the influenza infects the population (the lower branch, which occurs with probability P_1 and results in costs $C_{e|nv}$), or the influenza does not infect the population (the upper branch, which occurs with probability $1 - P_1$ and results in zero costs).[10] If the influenza does occur, then there is no need to consider the next year. If it does not occur, then the tree continues to decision node 2: Either implement the vaccination program in the second year (the upper subbranch crossing the gate where program costs $C_a + C_s$ are incurred) or do not implement it (the lower subbranch).

If the program is implemented, then a chance node occurs: The influenza infects the population (the lower twig, which occurs with probability P_2 and results in costs $C_{e|v}$), or the influenza does not infect the population (the upper twig, which occurs with probability $1 - P_2$ and results in zero costs). We complete the tree by considering the parallel chance node following the decision not to implement the program in the second year: The influenza infects the population (the lower twig, which occurs with probability P_2 and results in costs $C_{e|nv}$), or the influenza does not infect the population (the upper twig, which occurs with probability $1 - P_2$ and results in zero costs).

Solving the Decision Tree.   To solve the decision problem, we work from right to left, replacing chance nodes with their expected costs and pruning off parallel nodes that are dominated. Consider the chance node following decision node 1. Its expected cost, calculated by the expression $P_2C_{e|v} + (1 - P_2)0$, equals $P_2C_{e|v}$.

Now consider the chance nodes following decision node 2. The lower chance node, following a decision not to implement the vaccination program, has an expected cost of $P_2C_{e|nv}$. The upper chance node has an expected cost of $P_2C_{e|v}$, to which must be added the certain payment of program costs so that the full expected cost of implementing the vaccination program in the second year is $C_a + C_s + P_2C_{e|v}$. We can now compare the expected cost of the two possible decisions at node 2: $P_2C_{e|nv}$ versus $C_a + C_s + P_2C_{e|v}$. To illustrate, assume that program costs are greater than the expected cost reduction from the vaccine, that is, $C_a + C_s > P_2(C_{e|nv} - C_{e|v})$, then $P_2C_{e|nv}$ is smaller than $C_a + C_s + P_2C_{e|v}$ so that not implementing the program dominates implementing it. (If this were not the case, then the lower branch would be unequivocally dominated by the upper branch.[11]) We can now prune off the upper subbranch. If we reach decision node 2, then we know that we can obtain expected second-year costs of $P_2C_{e|nv}$.

At decision node 0 the expected costs of implementing the vaccination program (i.e., following the upper bough) consist of direct costs plus the expected costs of the following chance node, which now has the payoffs $C_{e|v}$ if there is an epidemic and the discounted expected value of node 1, $P_2C_{e|v}/(1 + d)$ if there is not an epidemic. Note that because this latter cost occurs in the second year, it is discounted using rate d. Thus, the present value of expected costs from implementing the vaccination program is given by:

$$E[C_v] = C_a + C_s + P_1C_{e|v} + (1 - P_1)P_2C_{e|v}/(1 + d) \qquad (7.2)$$

where the last term incorporates the expected costs from the second year.

The expected costs of not implementing the vaccination program are calculated in the same way: The payoff if there is not an epidemic becomes the discounted expected costs from decision node 2, $P_2C_{e|nv}/(1 + d)$; the payoff if there is an epidemic is still $C_{e|nv}$. Therefore, the expression:

$$E[C_{nv}] = P_1C_{e|nv} + (1 - P_1)P_2C_{e|nv}/(1 + d) \qquad (7.3)$$

gives the present value of expected costs of not implementing the program.

The final step is to compare the present values of expected costs for the two possible decisions at node 0. We prune the bough with the larger present value of expected costs. The remaining bough is the optimal decision.

As an illustration, suppose that we have gathered data suggesting the following values for parameters in the decision tree: $P_1 = .4$, $P_2 = .2$, $d = .05$, $C_{e|v} = .5C_{e|nv}$ (the vaccination program cuts the costs of influenza by half), $C_a = .1C_{e|nv}$ (the vaccination costs 10 percent of the costs of the influenza), and $C_s = .01C_{e|nv}$ (the side-effect costs are 1 percent of the costs of the influenza). For these values, $E[C_v] = .367C_{e|nv}$ and $E[C_{nv}] = .514C_{e|nv}$. Therefore, the vaccination program should be implemented in the first year because $E[C_v] < E[C_{nv}]$.

Calculating Expected Net Benefits of the Vaccination Program. Returning explicitly to CBA, we can recognize the benefits of the vaccination program as the costs it avoids. Thus, the present value of expected net benefits of the vaccination program is simply $E[C_{nv}] - E[C_v]$, which in the numerical illustration presented in the preceding paragraph equals $0.147C_{e|nv}$. In Chapter 8, we return to the question of the appropriateness of expected net benefits as a generalization of net benefits in CBA.

Extending Decision Analysis. Decision analysis can be applied to both public- and private-sector issues, and it can be used to structure much more complicated analyses than the CBA of the vaccination program. Straightforward extensions include more than two alternatives at decision nodes, more than two contingencies at chance nodes, more than two periods of time, and different probabilities of events in different periods. For example, analyses of the U.S. oil stockpiling program typically involve trees so large that they can only be fully represented and solved by computers.[12] Even in less complex situations, however, decision analysis can be very helpful in showing how risk should be incorporated into the calculation of expected net benefits.

SENSITIVITY ANALYSIS

Whether or not we structure a CBA explicitly in terms of contingencies and their probabilities, we always face some uncertainty about the magnitude of the impacts we predict and the values we assign to them. Our basic analysis usually submerges this uncertainty by using our most plausible estimates of these unknown quantities. These estimates comprise what is called the *base case*. The purpose of sensitivity analysis is to acknowledge the underlying uncertainty. In particular, it should convey how sensitive predicted net benefits are to changes in assumptions. If the sign of net benefits does not change when we consider the range of reasonable assumptions, then our results are robust, and we can have greater confidence in them.

Large numbers of unknown quantities, the usual situation in CBA, make the brute force approach of looking at all combinations of assumptions unfeasible. For example, the vaccination program analysis, which we further develop in the next section, involves 17 different uncertain numerical assumptions. If we looked at just three different values for each assumption, there would still be over 129 million different combinations of assumptions to consider.[13] Even if we could compute net benefits for all these combinations, we would still face the daunting task of sorting through the results and communicating them in an effective way.

Instead, we illustrate three more manageable approaches to doing sensitivity analysis. First, we demonstrate *partial sensitivity analysis:* How do net benefits change as we vary a single assumption while holding all others constant? Partial sensitivity is most appropriately applied to what the analyst believes to be the most important and uncertain assumptions. It can be used to find the values of numerical assumptions at which net benefits equal zero, or just break even. Second, we consider *worst- and best-case analysis:* Does any combination of reasonable assumptions reverse the sign of net benefits? Analysts are generally most concerned about situations in which their most plausible estimates yield positive net benefits, but they want to know what would happen in a worst case involving the least favorable, or most conservative, assumptions. Third, we present *Monte Carlo sensitivity analysis:* What distribution of net benefits results from treating the numerical values of key assumptions as draws from probability distributions? The mean and variance, or spread, of the distribution of net benefits convey information about the riskiness of the project.

A Closer Look at the Vaccination Program Analysis

We illustrate these techniques by considering a more detailed specification of the costs relevant to the decision analysis of the hypothetical vaccination program presented in Figure 7-2. This program would vaccinate some residents of a county against a possible influenza epidemic.[14]

Consider the following general description of the program. Through an advertising and outreach effort by its Department of Health, the county expects to be able to recruit a large fraction of older residents in poor health who are at high mortality risk from influenza, and a much smaller fraction of the general population, for vaccination. As the vaccine is based on a live virus, some fraction of those vaccinated will suffer an adverse reaction that, in effect, converts them to high-risk status and gives them influenza, a cost included in the side effects of the vaccine, C_s. As the vaccine does not always confer immunity, often because it is not given sufficiently in advance of the exposure to the influenza virus, its effectiveness rate is less than 100 percent. Everyone who contracts the influenza must be confined to bed rest for a number of days. Analysts can value this loss as the average number of hours of work lost times the average wage rate for the county, although this procedure might overestimate the opportunity costs of time for older persons and underestimate the cost of the unpleasantness of the influenza symptoms for both younger and older persons. They can place a dollar value on the deaths caused by the influenza by multiplying the number of expected deaths times the dollar value of life. The various numerical assumptions for the analysis appear in Table 7-2. Notice, for example, that the base case value used for each saved life is $3 million. That is, it is assumed that people make decisions about how much value they place on changes in risks of death as if they valued their lives at $3 million.

The benefits of vaccination arise through two impacts. First, those effectively vaccinated are immune to the influenza. Thus, the program targets persons with high mortality risk because they benefit most from immunity. Second, through what is known as the *herd immunity* effect, a positive externality, vaccinated persons reduce the risks of

TABLE 7-2 Base-Case Values for Vaccination Program CBA

Parameter	Value [Range]	Comments
County Population (N)	380,000	Total population in the county
Fraction High Risk (r)	.06 [.04, .08]	One-half population over age 64
Low-Risk Vaccination Rate (v_l)	.05 [.03, .07]	Fraction of low-risk persons vaccinated
High-Risk Vaccination Rate (v_h)	.60 [.40, .80]	Fraction of high-risk persons vaccinated
Adverse Reaction Rate (α)	.03 [.01, .05]	Fraction vaccinated who become high risk
Low-Risk Mortality Rate (m_l)	.00005 [.000025, .000075]	Mortality rate for low-risk infected
High-Risk Mortality Rate (m_h)	.001 [.0005, .002]	Mortality rate for high-risk infected
Herd Immunity Effect (θ)	1.0 [.5, 1.0]	Fraction of effectively vaccinated who contribute to herd immunity effect
Vaccine Effectiveness Rate (e)	.75 [.65, .85]	Fraction of vaccinated who develop immunity
Hours Lost (t)	24 [18, 30]	Average number of work hours lost to illness
Infection Rate (i)	.25 [.20, .30]	Infection rate without vaccine
First-Year Epidemic Probability (p_1)	.40	Chance of epidemic in current year
Second-Year Epidemic Probability (p_2)	.20	Chance of epidemic next year
Vaccine Dose Price (q)	$9/dose	Price per dose of vaccine
Overhead Cost (o)	$120,000	Costs not dependent on number vaccinated
Opportunity Cost of Time (w)	$12/hour	Average wage rate (including benefits) in the county
Value of Life (L)	$3,000,000	Assumed value of life
Discount Rate (d)	.05	Real discount rate
Number High-Risk Vaccinations (V_h)	13,680	High-risk persons vaccinated: $v_h r N$
Number Low-Risk Vaccinations (V_l)	17,860	Low-risk persons vaccinated: $v_l(1-r)N$
Fraction Vaccinated (v)	.083	Fraction of total population vaccinated: $rv_h + v_l(1-r)$

infection to those not vaccinated—this is the reason why some low-risk persons are recruited for vaccination to increase the total fraction of the population that is vaccinated.[15] These two effects cause the expected costs of the epidemic with vaccination, $C_{e|v}$, to be less than the expected costs of the epidemic without the vaccination program, $C_{e|nv}$.

TABLE 7-3   Formulas for Calculating the Net Benefits of Vaccination Program

Variable	Value (millions of dollars)	Formula
C_a	0.404	$o + (V_h + V_l)q$
C_s	3.111	$\alpha(V_h + V_l)(wt + m_h L)$
$C_{e\|nv}$	57.855	$i[rN(wt + m_h L) + (1 - r)N(wt + m_l L)]$
$C_{e\|v}$	36.014	$(i - \theta ve)\{(rN - eV_h)(wt + m_h L) + [(1 - r)N - eV_l](wt + m_l L)\}$
EC_v	22.036	$C_a + C_s + p_1 C_{e\|v} + (1 - p_1)p_2 C_{e\|v}/(1 + d)$
EC_{nv}	29.754	$p_1 C_{e\|nv} + (1 - p_1)p_2 C_{e\|nv}/(1 + d)$
$E[NB]$	7.718	$EC_{nv} - EC_v$

Table 7-3 relates the specific numerical assumptions in Table 7-2 to the parameters in Figure 7-2. From Table 7-3, we see that the direct program costs, C_a, depend on the overhead (i.e., fixed) costs, o, and cost per vaccination, q, times the number of vaccinations given $(V_h + V_l)$. The costs of side effects, C_s, depend on the adverse reaction rate, α, the number vaccinated, and the cost per high-risk infection, $wt + m_h L$, where wt is the opportunity cost of lost labor and $m_h L$ is the cost of loss of life. The epidemic's costs without the vaccination program, $C_{e\|nv}$, depend on the infection rate, i, the number of high-risk susceptibles, rN, the number of low-risk susceptibles, $(1 - r)N$, and the costs per high- and low-risk infections. Finally, the cost of the epidemic with the vaccination program, $C_{e\|v}$, depends on the postvaccination infection rate, $i - \theta ve$, the number of high-risk individuals remaining susceptible, $rN - eV_h$, the number of low-risk individuals remaining susceptible, $(1 - r)N - eV_l$, and the costs per low- and high-risk infections. Working through these formulas in Table 7-3 yields expected net benefits equal to $7.718 million for the base-case assumptions presented in Table 7-2.

Partial Sensitivity Analysis.   An important assumption in the analysis is the probability that the epidemic occurs. In the base case, we assume that the probability of the epidemic in the next year, given no epidemic in the current year, p_2, is one-half the probability of the epidemic in the current year, p_1. To investigate the relationship between net benefits and the probability of epidemic, we vary p_1 (and, hence, p_2) holding all other base-case values constant. Specifically, we vary p_1 from 0 to 0.5 by increments of 0.05. We thereby isolate the marginal partial effect of changes in probability on net benefits.

The results of this procedure are displayed as the line labeled $L = \$3$ million in Figure 7-3. This label reminds us of another base-case assumption, the value of life equals $3 million, which we vary next. Because the equations underlying the calculation of net benefits were embedded in a spreadsheet on a personal computer, it was easy to generate the points needed to draw this line by simply changing the values of p_1 and recording the corresponding net benefits.

As expected, this line is upward sloping: the higher the probability of the epidemic, the larger the net benefits of the vaccination program. Note that for values of p_1 less than about 0.11, net benefits become negative (i.e., it lies below the solid horizontal

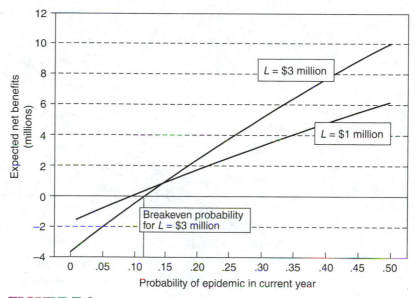

FIGURE 7-3 Expected Net Benefits of Vaccination

line). In other words, if we think that the probability of the epidemic in the current year is less than 0.11, and we are willing to accept the other base-case assumptions, then we should not implement the program. The probability at which net benefits switch sign is called the *breakeven value*. Finding and reporting breakeven values for various parameters is often a useful way to convey their importance.

The line labeled $L = \$1$ million repeats the procedure changing the base-case assumption of the value of life from $3 million per life to $1 million per life.[16] The graph thus conveys information about the impact of changes in two assumptions: Each line individually gives the marginal impact of epidemic probability; looking across lines conveys information about the impact of changes in the assumed value of life. As this illustration suggests, we can easily consider the sensitivity of net benefits to changing two assumptions at the same time by constructing families of curves in a two-dimensional graph. Although computers make it feasible to produce graphs that appear three-dimensional, the added information that these graphs convey is sometimes difficult to interpret.

Figure 7-4 considers one more example of partial sensitivity analysis. It repeats the investigation of the marginal impact of epidemic probability on net benefits for two different assumptions about the size of the herd immunity effect, θ. The upper curve is for the base case that assumes a full herd immunity effect ($\theta = 1$). The lower curve assumes that only one half of the effect occurs ($\theta = .5$), perhaps because the population does not mix sufficiently uniformly for the simple model of herd immunity assumed in the base case to apply. (Both cases return to the base-case assumption of $3 million per life saved.) Note that the breakeven probability rises to over 0.16 for the weaker herd immunity effect. Of course, we could instead give primary focus to the herd immunity effect by graphing net benefits against the size of the herd immunity effect, holding epidemic probability constant.

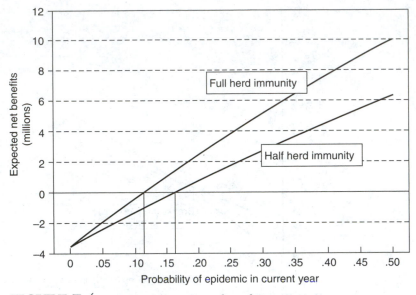

FIGURE 7-4   Expected Net Benefits of Vaccination

A thorough investigation of sensitivity ideally considers the partial marginal impacts of changes in each of the important assumptions. However, there is a "chicken and egg" problem: Identifying the important assumptions often cannot be done before actually doing the sensitivity analysis because importance depends on the marginal response of net benefits to changes in assumptions, as well as the plausible range of the assumptions. In the analysis of the vaccination program, for example, partial sensitivity analysis might well be warranted for most of the assumptions presented in Table 7-2.

Worst- and Best-Case Analysis.   The base-case assumptions, which generally assign the most plausible numerical values to unknown parameters, produce an estimate of net benefits that we think is most representative. In the vaccination program example, these assumptions yield fairly large positive net benefits. We can put a plausible lower bound on net benefits by considering the least favorable of the *plausible range* of values for each of the assumptions. In this way, we can calculate a pessimistic prediction of net benefits. Also, we can calculate an optimistic prediction of net benefits by using the most favorable assumptions. As we discuss later in the chapter, information usually has value in decision making to the extent it can potentially lead us to make a different choice. Therefore, worst-case analysis is generally most valuable when the expected net benefits are positive; best-case analysis is generally most valuable when the expected net benefits are negative. It should be kept in mind, however, that if the ranges are plausible, then the probability of actually realizing net benefits as extreme as either the worst or the best case gets very small as the number of parameters gets large.

Worst-case analysis acknowledges that society, or specific decision makers, may be risk averse. That is, they often care not just about expected net benefits, the appropriate consideration in most cases, but also about the possible "downside." Furthermore, as we point out in Chapters 1 and 11, there are often cognitive limitations and bureaucratic incentives to generate optimistic forecasts. Worst-case analysis provides a useful check against these biases.

As a demonstration of worst-case analysis, we take the lower end of each of the ranges presented in Table 7-2 for $r, v_l, v_h, m_l, m_h, \theta, e, t$, and i, and the higher end of the range for α. For example, we assume that r, the fraction of the population at high mortality risk, equals .04 rather than the base-case value of .06. (For the time being, we keep p_1, p_2, q, o, w, L, and d at their base-case values.) With worst-case assumptions, net benefits fall to $0.101 million. Though still positive, this more conservative estimate is almost two orders of magnitude (10^2) less than under the base-case assumptions.

Return to the question of the sensitivity of net benefits to the probability of epidemic. The breakeven probability rises from about 11 percent under the base-case assumptions to almost 37 percent under the more conservative worst-case assumptions. In other words, expected net benefits would no longer be positive if we assessed the probability of an epidemic to be only somewhat less likely than 0.4, the assumed value under the base case.

Care must be taken in determining which are the most conservative assumptions. Under the base-case assumptions, for example, net benefits increase as our assumed value of life increases. Under the conservative assumptions, however, net benefits decrease as the value of life increases. This reversal in the direction of the marginal impact of the value of life occurs because the higher rate of adverse reactions, α, under the conservative case is sufficiently large so that the expected number of deaths is greater with the vaccination program (1.8 deaths) than without it (1.7 deaths).

More generally, caution is warranted when net benefits are a nonlinear function of a parameter. In such cases, the value of the parameter that either minimizes or maximizes net benefits may not be at the extreme of its plausible range. Close inspection of partial sensitivity graphs generally gives a good indication of the general nature of the relationship, though these graphs can sometimes be misleading because they depend on the particular assumed values of all other parameters. A more systematic approach is to inspect the functional form of the model used to calculate net benefits. When a nonlinear relationship is present, extreme values of assumptions may not necessarily result in extreme values of net benefits. Indeed, inspection of Table 7-3 indicates that net benefits are a quadratic function of vaccination rates v_l and v_h because they depend on $C_{e|v}$, which involves the product of direct effects and the herd effect. Under the base-case assumptions, for instance, net benefits would be maximized if all high-risk persons were vaccinated and 46 percent of low-risk persons were vaccinated. As these rates are well above those that could realistically be obtained by the program, we can reasonably treat the upper and lower bounds of vaccination rates as corresponding to extreme values of net benefits.

If the base-case assumptions generate negative net benefits, then it would have been reasonable to see if more optimistic, or best-case, assumptions produce positive net benefits. If the best-case prediction of net benefits is still negative, then we can be very certain that the policy should not be adopted. If it is positive, then we may want to see if combinations of somewhat less optimistic assumptions can also sustain positive net benefits.

Monte Carlo Sensitivity Analysis.   Partial- and extreme-case sensitivity analyses have two major limitations. First, they may not take account of all the available information about assumed values of parameters. In particular, if we believe that values near the base-case assumptions are more likely to occur than values near the extremes of their plausible ranges, then the worst and best cases are highly unlikely to occur because they require the joint occurrence of a large number of independent low-probability events. Second, these techniques do not directly provide information about the variance, or spread, of the statistical distribution of realized net benefits. If we cannot distinguish between two policies in terms of expected values of net benefits, then we may be more confident in recommending the one with the smaller variance because it has a higher probability of producing realized net benefits near the expected value.

Monte Carlo analysis provides a way of overcoming these problems. The name suggests the casinos of that famous gambling resort. It is apt because the essence of the approach is playing games of chance many times to elicit a distribution of outcomes. Monte Carlo analysis has played an important role for many years in the investigation of statistical estimators whose properties cannot be adequately determined through mathematical techniques alone. The falling opportunity cost of computing, especially the greater availability of flexible spreadsheet software for microcomputers, makes Monte Carlo analysis feasible for most practicing policy analysts. As it is a method that effectively takes account of uncertainty about assumed parameters in complex analyses, it should be in every analyst's tool kit. *Indeed, it should be routinely used in CBA*.

The basic steps for doing Monte Carlo analysis are as follows. First, specify probability distributions for all the important uncertain quantitative assumptions. For the Monte Carlo analysis of the vaccine program, we focus on the ten parameters with expressed ranges in Table 7-2. If we do not have theory or empirical evidence that suggests a particular distribution, then it is sometimes reasonable to specify a uniform distribution over the range. That is, we assume that any value between the upper and lower bound of plausible values is equally likely. For example, we assume that the distribution of the fraction of the population at risk, r, is uniformly distributed between 0.04 and 0.08. Often, though, we believe that values near the most plausible estimate should be given more weight. For example, assume that analysts believe that hours lost due to influenza follow a normal distribution. They could then center it at the best estimate of 24 hours and set the standard deviation at 3.06 so that there is only a 5 percent chance of values falling outside the plausible range of 18 to 30 hours. (See Appendix 7A for a brief discussion of working with probability distributions on spreadsheets.) As discussed in Chapter 13, analysts can sometimes estimate unknown parameters statistically using regression analysis. They might then wish to use their 95 percent confidence intervals as their ranges. Commonly used regression models allow analysts to approximate the distribution of an unknown parameter as normal with mean and standard deviation given by their empirical estimates.

Second, we execute a trial by taking a random draw from the distribution for each parameter to arrive at a set of specific values for computing realized net benefits. For example, in the case of the vaccination program analysis, analysts have to determine which contingencies occur in each of the two periods. To determine if an epidemic occurs in the current year, they take a draw from a Bernoulli distribution with probability p_1 of yielding "epidemic" and $(1 - p_1)$ of yielding "no epidemic." That is, it is as if we were to flip a coin that has a probability of p_1 of landing with "epidemic" face up. Almost all spreadsheets allow users to take draws from random

── **EXHIBIT 7-3** ──

Influenza vaccination programs are usually targeted to those in high-risk groups, such as infants, the elderly, and people with compromised immune systems. Is vaccination of healthy workers cost-beneficial? Kristin L. Nichols attempts to answer this question with a cost-benefit analysis. Benefits of vaccination include avoided lost work days, hospitalizations, and deaths. Costs include the costs of the vaccination and lost work days, hospitalizations, and deaths from side effects. She employed Monte Carlo analysis to estimate net benefits. Noting that previous studies reported that managers generally took fewer sick days than other personnel, she built a negative correlation between sick days and wage rate, two of the important parameters, into the Monte Carlo trials. She estimated the mean value of net benefits to be $18.27 (2010 dollars) with a 95 percent confidence interval ranging from $44.10 in positive net benefits to $2.92 in negative net benefits. In order to assess the relative importance of various assumed parameters to net benefits, she regressed the net benefits from each trial on the randomly drawn values of the parameters. Net benefits were most sensitive to the illness rate, the work absenteeism rate due to influenza, and the hourly wages. In addition, a poor match between the vaccine and the circulating virus strain gave negative net benefits. Not surprisingly, the 95 percent confidence interval from the Monte Carlo analysis was much tighter than the best/worst-case range of positive net benefits of $233.15 to negative net benefits of $28.45.

Source: Adapted from Kristin L. Nichol, "Cost-Benefit Analysis of a Strategy to Vaccinate Healthy Working Adults Against Influenza," *Archives of Internal Medicine* 161(5) 2001, 749–759.

variables uniformly distributed between 0 and 1—a draw from the uniform distribution produces an outcome within this range that is as likely to occur as any other outcome in the range. Thus there is a p_1 probability of a value between zero and p_1 occurring. To implement a draw from a Bernoulli distribution that has a probability of p_1 of yielding "epidemic," one simply compares the draw from the uniform distribution to p_1: If the random draw from the uniform distribution is smaller (larger) than p_1, then assume that an epidemic does (not) occur in the current year; if an epidemic does not occur in the current year, then follow a similar procedure to determine if an epidemic occurs in the second year. Three mutually exclusive realizations of net benefits are possible:

$$\text{Epidemic in neither year:} \quad NB = -(C_a + C_s)$$
$$\text{Epidemic in current year:} \quad NB = -(C_a + C_s) + (C_{e|nv} - C_{e|v})$$
$$\text{Epidemic in next year:} \quad NB = -(C_a + C_s) + (C_{e|nv} - C_{e|v})/(1 + d)$$

where the value of NB depends on the particular values of the parameters drawn for this trial.

Note that these estimates of NB no longer involve expectations with respect to the contingencies of epidemics, though the cost estimates themselves are expected values. For each random draw, only one combination of contingencies can actually occur. (The epidemic poses a collective risk to the population, while the costs result from the realizations of independent risks to individuals in the population.)

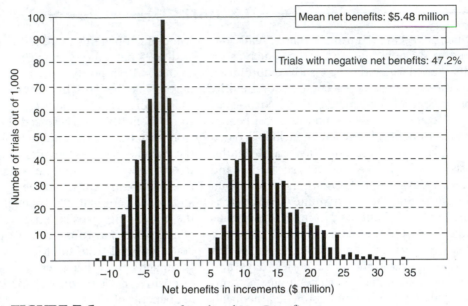

FIGURE 7-5 Histogram of Realized Net Benefits

Third, we repeat the trial described in the second step many times to produce a large number of realizations of net benefits. The average of the trials provides an estimate of the expected value of net benefits. An approximation of the probability distribution of net benefits can be obtained by breaking the range of realized net benefits into a number of equal increments and counting the frequency with which trials fall into each one. The resulting *histogram* of these counts provides a picture of the distribution. The more trials that go into the histogram, the more likely it is that the resulting picture gives a good representation of the distribution of net benefits. Underlying this faith is the law of large numbers, which tells us that, as the number of trials approaches infinity, the frequencies will converge to the true underlying probabilities.

Figure 7-5 presents a histogram of 1,000 replications of random draws from the bracketed assumptions in Table 7-2. The assumed distributions are all uniform except that for hours lost, w, which follows a normal distribution, and whether or not the epidemic occurs, which, although a Bernoulli distribution, is implemented with the readily available uniform distribution. The height of each bar is proportional to the number of trials that had net benefits falling in the corresponding increment.

The average of net benefits over the 1,000 trials is $5.48 million. This differs from our base-case calculation of $7.72 million because the base-case value of the herd immunity factor, θ, was set at 1 rather than at the middle of the plausible range. Repeating the Monte Carlo procedure with the herd immunity factor set to 1 yields an average of realized net benefits of $7.47 million, which is almost identical to the base-case calculation of expected net benefits.[17]

The histogram provides a visual display of the entire distribution of net benefits so that its spread and symmetry can be easily discerned. The trials themselves can be used to calculate directly the sample variance, standard deviation, and other summary statistics describing net benefits.

The most striking feature of the histogram is that it portrays a bimodal distribution. If an epidemic occurs in either year, then the vaccination program has positive net benefits and it is as if we are drawing only from the right-most hump of the distribution. If an epidemic occurs in neither year, then the vaccination program has negative net benefits and it is as if we are drawing from the left-most hump of the distribution. The assumed probabilities of epidemic in the two years lead us to expect positive net benefits 52 percent of the time $[p_1 + (1 - p_1)\,p_2]$, which is close to the 52.8 percent of trials with positive net benefits in the Monte Carlo analysis.

The Monte Carlo results presented in Figure 7-5 treated several parameters as if they were certain. Most important, they treated the values of time and life and the discount rate as certain. As suggested in Chapter 16, we are in fact uncertain about these values. One approach would be to repeat the Monte Carlo analysis treating these parameters as random variables as well. In effect, we would be mixing uncertainty about predicted effects with uncertainty over how we value those effects. In some situations, this may be appropriate, but here it would probably be clearer to distinguish between these two types of uncertainty. To take account of our uncertainty about how we should value effects, we can simply repeat the original Monte Carlo analysis for a number of combinations of the fixed. It is usually best to handle uncertainty about the appropriate discount rate in this way. Our results would be a collection of histograms like Figure 7-5 that would provide the basis for assessing how sensitive our assessment of net benefits is to changes in these values.

INFORMATION AND QUASI-OPTION VALUE

The various analytical techniques developed in the previous sections provide a basis for assessing uncertainty about information (assumed or measured parameters) in CBA. In this section we demonstrate the use of games against nature to place value on information itself. We use the normal form to illustrate the basic concepts. We then use decision trees to explicate a particular information value, the quasi-option value, that arises in the context of delaying irreversible decisions to allow time for the gathering or revelation of information about the future.

Introduction to the Value of Information

The value of information in the context of a game against nature answers the following question: by how much would the information increase the expected value of playing the game? As an example of how to answer this question, return to the asteroid defense game presented in Table 7-1. Imagine that scientists have proposed developing a detection device that would allow them to determine with certainty whether the Earth would be exposed to a collision with a large asteroid (diameter greater than one kilometer) in the next 100 years. What is the maximum investment that should be made to develop this device?

If the device were to be built, then it would tell us which of two possible futures were true: First, with a probability of .001, it would tell us that there would be a collision with a large asteroid. Second, with a probability of .999, it would tell us that there

---

EXHIBIT 7-4

Research and development projects typically have very uncertain costs and benefits when they are initiated. Based on an assessment of detailed case studies of six research and development projects (Supersonic Transport, Applications Technology Satellite Program, Space Shuttle, Clinch River Breeder Reactor, Synthetics Fuels from Coal, and Photovoltaics Commercialization), Cohen and Noll concluded: "The final success of a program usually hinges on a few key technical objectives and baseline economic assumptions about demand or the cost of alternative technologies, or both. The results of the research that addressed the key technical issues, and realizations a few years after that pro-

gram was started of the key unknown economic parameters, typically made the likely success of a project very clear" (p. 82).

For example, Susan Edelman prepared CBAs of the supersonic transport project with the information that would have been available to conscientious analysts in each of a number of years. She reports that the plausible range of benefit-cost ratios fell from 1.97 to 4.97 in 1963 to 1.32 to 1.84 in 1971. They declined as it became clear that either higher operating costs or reduced loads would result from failures to achieve technical objectives and that operations over land would likely be restricted to reduce the impacts of sonic booms on people (pp. 112–121).

Source: Adapted from Linda R. Cohen and Roger G. Noll, eds., *The Technology Pork Barrel* (Washington, D.C.: The Brookings Institution, 1991).

---

would be no collision with a large asteroid. Each of these two futures implies a different game against nature. These are shown in Table 7-4.

Game One, shown on the left side of Table 7-4, results if the detection device indicates that the Earth will be exposed to collision with a large asteroid. Not surprisingly, in this game the best action is to choose forward-based asteroid defense, which has the smallest net costs of the three actions ($5,060 billion). Game Two, shown on the right side of Table 7-4, results if the detection device indicates that the Earth will not be exposed to collision with a large asteroid. As exposure to collision with a large asteroid is ruled out, the probabilities of the other two possible states of nature are adjusted upward so that they sum to 1 (.004004 and .995996). In this game, the best action is to choose no asteroid defense, which has the smallest net costs of the three actions ($24.02 billion).

Prior to developing the detection device, we do not know which of these two games it will give us to play. We do know, however, that it will indicate Game One with probability .001 and Game Two with probability .999. Thus we can compute an expected net cost over the two games as (.001)($5,060 billion) + (.999)($24.02 billion) = $29.06 billion. In order to place a value on the information provided by the device, we compare the expected net cost of the optimal choice in the game without it ($38 billion as shown in Table 7-1) with the expected net cost resulting from optimal choices in the games with it ($29.06 billion). The difference between these net costs ($38 billion − $29.06 billion) equals $8.94 billion, which is the value of the information provided by the device. Consequently, as long as the detection device cost less than $8.94 billion, it would be efficient to develop it.

TABLE 7-4 Reformulated Games against Nature: Value of Device for Detecting Large Asteroids

State of Nature	Game One p = .001 Exposure to a Collision with an Asteroid Larger Than 1 Kilometer in Diameter	Game Two p = .999 Exposure to a Collision with an Asteroid between 20 Meters and 1 Kilometer in Diameter	No Exposure to Collision with an Asteroid Larger Than 20 Meters in Diameter
Probabilities of states of nature (over next century)	1	.004004	.995996

Actions (alternatives)	Payoffs (net costs in billions of 2000 dollars)	Expected Value	Payoffs (net costs in billions of 2000 dollars)		Expected Value
Forward-based asteroid defense	5,060	**5,060**	1,060	60	64.01
Near-Earth asteroid defense	10,020	10,020	2,020	20	28.01
No asteroid defense	30,000	30,000	6,000	0	**24.02**

Game One: Choose forward-based asteroid defense: Expected net cost = $5,060 billion.
Game Two: Choose no asteroid defense: Expected net cost = $24.02 billion.
Expected net cost of decision with detection device: (.001)($5,060 billion) + (.999)($24.02 billion) = $29.06.
Value of information provided by detection device: $38 billion − $29.06 billion = $8.94 billion.

Note that the value of the information derives from the fact that it leads to different optimal decisions. The optimal choice without the device is near-Earth asteroid defense. The optimal choice with the device is either forward-based asteroid defense if collision exposure is confirmed or no asteroid defense if the absence of collision exposure is confirmed.

In practice, analysts rarely face choices requiring them to value perfect information of the sort provided by the asteroid detection device. They do, however, routinely face choices involving the allocation of resources—time, energy, budgets—toward reducing uncertainty in the values of the many parameters used to calculate net benefits. For example, a statistical estimate based on a random sample size of 600 will be much more precise than one based on a sample of 300. How can the analyst determine if the investment in the larger sample size is worthwhile?

In a CBA involving many assumed parameters, Monte Carlo analysis may provide especially useful information. For example, suppose an agency is deciding whether it is worthwhile to invest analytical resources in conducting a study that would reduce the estimate of the variance of hours lost from the influenza described in the previous section. One could replicate the analysis presented in Figure 7-5 with a smaller assumed variance of hours lost and compare the resulting distribution of net benefits to that resulting with the larger variance. A necessary condition for the investment of analytical resources to be worthwhile is a meaningful change in the distribution of realized net benefits.

Quasi-Option Value

It may be wise to delay a decision if better information relevant to the decision will become available in the future. This is especially the case when the costs of returning to the status quo once a project has begun are so large that the decision is effectively irreversible. For example, consider the decision of whether to develop a virgin wilderness area. We may be fairly certain about the costs and benefits of development to the current generation. We may be very uncertain of the opportunity cost to future generations of losing the virgin wilderness, however. If information will become available over time that would reduce our uncertainty about how future generations will value the wilderness area, then it may be desirable to delay a decision about irreversible development so that we have the opportunity to incorporate the new information into our decision. The expected value of information gained by delaying an irreversible decision is called *quasi-option value*.[18]

Quasi-option value can be quantified by explicitly formulating a multiperiod decision problem that allows for the revelation of information about the value of options in later periods.[19] Although some environmental analysts see quasi-option value as a distinct benefit category for policies that preserve unique assets such as wilderness areas, scenic views, and animal species, it is more appropriately thought of as a correction to the calculation of expected net benefits through an inappropriate one-period decision problem. As the calculation of quasi-option value itself requires specification of the proper decision problem, *whenever quasi-option value can be quantified, the correct expected net benefits can and should be calculated directly.*

As background for an illustration of quasi-option value, Table 7-5 sets out the parameters for a CBA of alternatives for use of a wilderness area. The value of net benefits from full development (*FD*) and limited development (*LD*) are measured relative to no development (*ND*) for two contingencies. Under the contingency labeled "Low Value," which will occur with a probability p, future generations place the same value as current generations on preservation of the wilderness area. Under the contingency labeled "High Value," which will occur with a probability $1 - p$, future generations place a much higher value than current generations on preservation of the wilderness area. If the Low Value contingency occurs, then *FD* yields a positive present value of net benefits equal

TABLE 7-5   Benefits and Costs of Alternative Development Policies Assuming No Learning

	Preservation Contingencies	
	Low Value	*High Value*
Full development (*FD*)	B_F	$-C_F$
Limited development (*LD*)	B_L	$-C_L$
No development (*ND*)	0	0
Probability of contingency	p	$1 - p$
Expected value of full development:	$E[FD] = pB_F - (1 - p)C_F$	
Expected value of limited development:	$E[LD] = pB_L - (1 - p)C_L$	
Expected value of no development:	$E[ND] = 0$	
Adopt full development if:	$pB_F - (1 - p)C_F > pB_L - (1 - p)C_L$ and $pB_F - (1 - p)C_F > 0$	

to B_F and LD yields a positive present value of net benefits equal to B_L. That is, after taking account of all costs and benefits, the present value of net benefits for FD and LD are the positive amounts B_F and B_L, respectively. If instead the High Value contingency occurs, then FD yields a negative present value of net benefits equal to $-C_F$ and LD yields a negative present value of net benefits equal to $-C_L$, where C_F and C_L are net costs and therefore signed negative to be the present value of net benefits. Assume that $B_F > B_L > 0$ and $C_F > C_L > 0$ so that FD yields greater net benefits under the Low Value contingency and greater net costs under the High Value contingency than LD.

Imagine that we conduct a CBA assuming that no learning will occur over time. That is, we assume that no useful information will be revealed in future periods. The expected net benefits of FD equal $pB_F - (1 - p)C_F$; the expected net benefits of LD equal $pB_L - (1 - p)C_L$; and the expected net benefits of ND equal 0. We would simply choose the alternative with the largest expected net benefits.

Now consider the case of *exogenous learning*. That is, we assume that after the first period we discover with certainty which of the two contingencies will occur. Our learning is exogenous in the sense that the information is revealed to us no matter what actions we take.

Figure 7-6 presents a decision tree for the case of exogenous learning. The square box at the extreme left-hand side of the figure represents our initial decision. If we

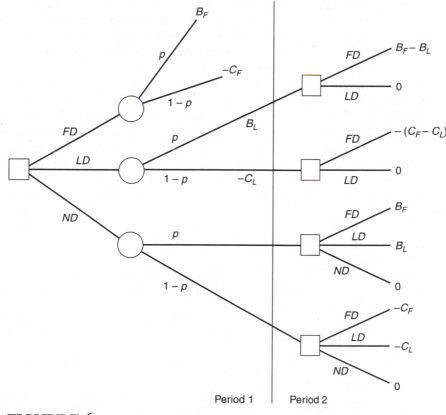

FIGURE 7-6 Exogenous Learning

select *FD*, then we have the same expected value as in the case of no learning—we have made an irreversible decision and, hence, learning has no value because we have no decision left to make in period 2. If we select either *LD* or *ND* in the first period, then we do have a decision left to make in period 2 after we know which contingency has occurred. The expected values of the *LD* and *ND* decisions in period 1 can be found by the method of backward induction introduced in the vaccine example developed earlier in the chapter.

Consider *LD* first. If the Low Value contingency is revealed at the beginning of period 2, then the optimal decision will be to complete the development to obtain net benefits $B_F - B_L$. The present value of this amount is obtained by discounting at rate d. It is then added to BL, the period 1 net benefits, to obtain the net benefits of *LD* conditional on the Low Value contingency occurring. If the High Value contingency is revealed at the beginning of period 2, then the optimal decision is to forgo further development so that the net benefits conditional on the High Value contingency occurring consist only of the $-C_L$ realized in period 1. Multiplying these conditional net benefits by their respective probabilities yields the expected net benefits for limited development in period 1 of $p[B_L + (B_F - B_L)/(1 + d)] - (1 - p)C_L$. Note that it differs from the expected value in the no-learning case by the expected net benefits of the period 2 option, $p(B_F - B_L)/(1 + d)$, which is the quasi-option value of *LD*.

Next consider the decision *ND* in period 1. If the Low Value contingency is revealed at the beginning of period 2, then the optimal decision is *FD*, which has a present value of $B_F/(1 + d)$. If the High Value contingency is revealed at the beginning of period 2, then the optimal decision is *ND*, which has a present value of 0. Consequently, the expected net benefits from choosing *ND* in period 1 are $pB_F/(1 + d)$, which equal the quasi-option value of *ND*.

The middle column of Table 7-6 summarizes the expected values of the period 1 alternatives for the case of exogenous learning.

Figure 7-7 presents a decision tree for the case of endogenous learning. Unlike the case of exogenous learning, information is generated only from development itself. For example, the value placed on preservation by future generations may depend on the risk that development poses to a species of bird that feeds in the wilderness area during its migration. The effect of limited development on the species may provide enough information to permit a reliable prediction of the effect of full development. If no

TABLE 7-6   Expected Values for Decision Problems: Quasi-Option Values (QOV) Measured Relative to No Learning Case

	No Learning	*Exogenous Learning*	*Endogenous Learning*
$E[FD]$	$pB_F - (1-p)C_F$	$pB_F - (1-p)C_F$ $QOV = 0$	$pB_F - (1-p)C_F$ $QOV = 0$
$E[LD]$	$pB_L - (1-p)C_L$	$p[B_L + (B_F - B_L)/(1+d)]$ $- (1-p)C_L$ $QOV = p(B_F - B_L)/(1+d)$	$p[B_L + (B_F - B_L)/(1+d)]$ $- (1-p)C_L$ $QOV = p(B_F - B_L)/(1+d)$
$E[ND]$	0	$pB_F(1+d)$ $QOV = pB_F/(1+d)$	0 $QOV = 0$

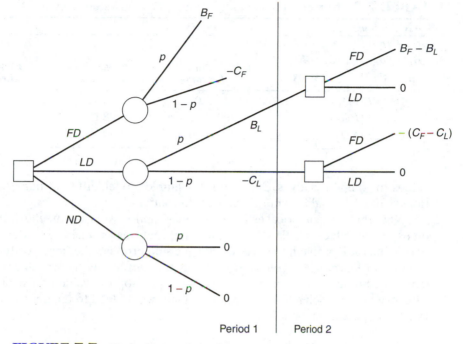

FIGURE 7-7 Endogenous Learning

development is undertaken, then no new information will be available at the beginning of the second period. If full development is undertaken, then new information will be generated but there will be no decision for it to affect.

As shown in the last column of Table 7-6, the expected net benefits for the *FD* and *LD* alternatives in the case of endogenous learning are identical to those for the case of exogenous learning. The expected net benefits of *ND* are zero, however, because there will be no new information to alter the decision not to develop in the future.

Table 7-7 compares the different learning cases for a specific set of parameter values. If we specify the decision problem as one of no learning, then *FD* has the largest expected net benefits. Imagine that instead we specify the decision problem as the exogenous learning case. Now *ND* has the largest expected net benefits. Furthermore, relative to the case of no learning, the quasi-option value of *ND* is $46.3 million (46.30 − 0) and the quasi-option value of *LD* is $23.15 million (28.15 − 5). Now imagine that we specify the decision problem as the case of endogenous learning. *LD* has the largest expected net benefits. Relative to the case of no learning, the quasi-option value of *LD* is $23.15 million (28.15 − 5), and the quasi-option value of *ND* is 0 (0 − 0).

This simple numerical illustration conforms to the common wisdom about quasi-option value: *It tends to be large for no development in cases of exogenous learning and large for limited development in cases of endogenous learning.* It is important to keep in mind, however, that the illustration is based on very stylized models of learning. Differently specified models could yield different rankings and different quasi-option

TABLE 7-7   Numerical Illustration of Quasi-Option Value ($ million)

Assumptions:		No Learning	Exogenous Learning	Endogenous Learning
$B_F = 100$ $C_F = 80$				
$B_L = 50$ $C_L = 40$				
$p = .5$ $d = .08$				
	$E[FD]$	10.00	10.00	10.00
	$E[LD]$	5.00	28.15	28.15
	$E[ND]$	0.00	46.30	0.00

values for the alternatives. Even with this simple model, different numerical assumptions could lead to different rankings of alternatives.

Note that our numerical estimates of quasi-option values in the illustration depend on expected values calculated by comparing what was assumed to be the correct two-period decision problem to a one-period decision problem that incorrectly fails to take account of learning. Of course, if we knew the correct decision problem, then there would be no need to concern ourselves with quasi-option value as a separate benefit category because solving the decision problem would lead to the appropriate calculations of expected net benefits.

Quasi-Option Value in Practice

How should we treat quasi-option value in practice? Two heuristics seem warranted. First, *quantitative quasi-option values should be based on an explicit decision problem that structures the calculation of the expected net benefits.* An explicit decision problem focuses attention on the key assumptions that determine the magnitude of quasi-option value. It also makes it unnecessary to consider quasi-option value as a distinct benefit category. Second, *when insufficient knowledge is available to formulate a decision problem for explicitly calculating the magnitude of quasi-option value, it should be discussed as a possible source of bias rather than added as an arbitrary quantitative adjustment to expected net benefits.* As with other biases, one can ask the question: How big would quasi-option value have to be to affect the ranking of policies?

CONCLUSIONS

Uncertainty is inherent to some degree in every CBA. Through expected value analysis, we attempt to average over the possible contingencies to arrive at expected net benefits as a plausible prediction of net benefits. In situations not explicitly involving risk, we often assume parameter values that are more appropriately thought of as draws from probability distributions rather than as certainties. The purpose of sensitivity analysis is to determine how net benefits change if these parameters deviate from their assumed values. Partial sensitivity analysis, the most commonly used approach, focuses attention on the consequences of alternative assumptions about key parameters. Extreme-case analysis examines whether combinations of plausible assumptions exist that reverse the sign of net benefits. Monte Carlo analysis attempts to estimate the distribution of net benefits by explicitly treating assumed parameter values as random variables. It is especially useful when the risk of the policy is of particular concern and the parameters have nonuniform distributions or the formula for the calculation of net benefits involves the parameters in other than simple sums. While the nature of the policy under consideration and the resources available to the analysts attempting to estimate its benefits and costs determine the appropriate form of sensitivity analysis, every CBA should be subjected to tests of its sensitivity to the assumptions it employs.

Explicit decision analysis frameworks, including games against nature in both normal and extensive form, provide a basis for assessing the value of information in risky circumstances. It allows an explicit calculation of quasi-option value, which is sometimes treated as a separate benefit category in CBAs. Quasi-option values take account of the value of being able to act upon future information. As solving a correctly specified decision problem naturally incorporates quasi-option values, they need not be treated as distinct benefits. Quantitative claims about quasi-option values should be based on an explicit decision problem.

Doing Monte Carlo Sensitivity Analysis with a Simple Spreadsheet

Spreadsheets greatly reduce the labor needed to conduct sensitivity analysis. Usually the calculation of net benefits can be organized so that partial sensitivity analysis can be done by simply changing the value of a single spreadsheet cell. Although specialized software is available for doing Monte Carlo analysis, such as Crystal Ball (Decisioneering, Inc.) for use with Excel and DATA (TreeAge, Inc.) for decision analysis, with a bit of effort it can be done with any simple spreadsheet that provides a random number generator.

Generating Random Variables

Most spreadsheets provide a function for generating random variables that are distributed uniformly from 0 to 1. [In Excel, the function is RAND(); in Quattro Pro, the function is @RAND.] To generate uniform random variables with other ranges, one simply multiplies the draw from the random variable uniformly distributed from 0 to 1 by the desired range and then adds the minimum value. So, for example, to get the appropriate random variable for the fraction of high-risk persons in the population, r in Table 7-2, use the following formula: $.04 + (.08 - .04)z$ where z is the uniform random variable with range 0 to 1.

Some other distributions can be generated directly from the uniform distribution. For example, to obtain a triangular distribution between zero and one, simply take one-half of the sum of two independent draws from a uniform distribution over zero to one. To obtain draws from an exponential distribution, one would simply take the natural logarithm of the uniformly distributed random variable and multiply it by the negative of the desired expected value of the exponential distribution. The most

useful distribution, the normal, can also be generated in most spreadsheets by combining functions for the inverse of the cumulative normal distribution and the uniform distribution. [In Excel, the formula for generating a draw from a standard normal distribution is NORMSINV(RAND()) and the formula for Quattro Pro is @NORMSINV(@RAND).]

The standardized normal distribution can be given any expected value and variance through simple transformations: Add a constant equal to the desired expected value and multiply by the square root of the desired variance. A range of 3.92 standard deviations includes 95 percent of the area of the normal distribution. To get the random variable we used in the Monte Carlo analysis for hours lost, t in Table 7-2, we added 24 to the standardized normal and multiplied it by $(30 - 18)/3.92$ so that there was only a 5 percent chance that a value of t would be generated outside the range 18 to 30.

Most books on mathematical statistics indicate how random variables distributed as chi-square, Student's t, F, and multivariate normal can be generated using combinations of normally distributed random variables. Similarly, the gamma distribution and the discrete Poisson distribution can be generated from exponential distributions. Discussion of these methods here would take us too far afield.

Steps in Monte Carlo Sensitivity Analysis

Once procedures have been developed for generating appropriately distributed random variables, doing Monte Carlo analysis is straightforward, although, depending on the capabilities of the spreadsheet and the hardware upon which it operates, perhaps somewhat tedious. A simple approach follows.

First, construct a row of appropriate random variables and the formulas that use them to compute net benefits. The last cell in the row should contain net benefits.

Second, copy the entire row a number of times so that the last column of the resulting block contains different realizations of net benefits. Most spreadsheet and hardware arrangements should be able to handle blocks of more than 1,000 rows without memory or time problems.

Third, analyze the accumulated realizations in the last column along the lines of Figure 7-5, calculating the mean and standard deviation, and plotting as a histogram.

EXERCISES FOR CHAPTER 7

1. The initial cost of constructing a permanent dam (i.e., a dam that is expected to last forever) is $425 million. The annual net benefits will depend on the amount of rainfall: $18 million in a "dry" year, $29 million in a "wet" year, and $52 million in a "flood" year. Meteorological records indicate that over the last 100 years there have been 86 "dry" years, 12 "wet" years, and 2 "flood" years. Assume the annual benefits, measured in real dollars, begin to accrue at the end of the first year. Using the meteorological records as a basis for prediction, what are the net benefits of the dam if the real discount rate is 5 percent?

2. Use several alternative discount rate values to investigate the sensitivity of the present value of net benefits of the dam in exercise 1 to the assumed value of the real discount rate.

3. The prevalence of a disease among a certain population is .40. That is, there is a 40 percent chance that a person randomly selected from the population will have the disease. An imperfect test that costs $250 is available to help identify those who have the disease before actual symptoms appear. Those who have the disease have a 90 percent chance of a positive test result; those who do not have the disease have a 5 percent chance of a positive test. Treatment of the disease before the appearance of symptoms costs $2,000 and inflicts additional costs of $200 on those who do not actually have the disease. Treatment of the disease after symptoms have appeared costs $10,000.

The government is considering the following possible strategies with respect to the disease:

S1. Do not test and do not treat early.

S2. Do not test and treat early.

S3. Test and treat early if positive and do not treat early if negative.

Find the treatment/testing strategy that has the lowest expected costs for a member of the population.

In doing this exercise, the following notation may be helpful: Let D indicate presence of the disease, ND absence of the disease, T a positive test result, and NT a negative test result. Thus, we have the following information:

$$P(D) = .40, \text{ which implies } P(ND) = .60$$

$$P(T|D) = .90, \text{ which implies } P(NT|D) = .10$$

$$P(T|ND) = .05, \text{ which implies } P(NT|ND) = .95$$

This information allows calculation of some other useful probabilities:

$$P(T) = P(T|D)P(D) + P(T|ND)P(ND) = .39 \text{ and } P(NT) = .61$$

$$P(D|T) = P(T|D)P(D)/P(T) = .92 \text{ and } P(ND|T) = .08$$

$$P(D|NT) = P(NT|D)P(D)/P(NT) = .07 \text{ and } P(ND|NT) = .93$$

4. In exercise 3 the optimal strategy involved testing. Does testing remain optimal if the prevalence of the disease in the population is only .05? Does your answer suggest any general principle?

5. (Use of a spreadsheet recommended for parts a through e and necessary for part f.) A town with a population of 164,250 persons who live in 39,050 households is considering introducing a recycling program that would require residents to separate paper from their household waste so that it can be sold rather than buried in a landfill like the rest of the town's waste. Two major benefits are anticipated: revenue from the sale of waste paper and avoided tipping fees (the fee that the town pays the owners of landfills to bury its waste). Aside from the capital costs of specialized collection equipment, household containers, and a sorting facility, the program would involve higher collection costs, inconvenience costs for households, and disposal costs for paper that is collected but not sold. The planning period for the project has been set at eight years, the expected life of the specialized equipment.

The following information has been collected by the town's sanitation department:

Waste Quantities: Residents currently generate 3.6 pounds of waste per person per day. Over the last 20 years, the daily per capita amount has grown by about 0.02 pounds per year. Small or no increases in the last few years, however, raise the possibility that levels realized in the future will fall short of the trend.

Capital Costs: The program would require an initial capital investment of $1,688,000. Based on current resale values, the scrap value of the capital at the end of eight years is expected to be 20 percent of its initial cost.

Annual Costs: The department estimates that the separate collection of paper will add an average of $6/ton to the cost of collecting household waste. Each ton of paper collected and not sold would cost $4 to return to the landfill.

Savings and Revenues: Under a long-term contract, tipping fees are currently $45 per ton with annual increases equal to the rate of inflation. The current local market price for recycled paper is $22 per ton but has fluctuated in recent years between a low of $12 per ton and a high of $32 per ton.

Paper Recovery: The fraction of household waste made up of paper has remained fairly steady in recent years at 32 percent. Based on the experience of similar programs in other towns, it is estimated that between 60 and 80 percent of paper included in the program will be separated from other waste and 80 percent of the paper that is separated will be suitable for sale, with the remaining 20 percent of the collected paper returned to the waste stream for landfilling.

Household Separation Costs: The sanitation department recognized the possibility that the necessity of separating paper from the waste stream and storing it might impose costs on households. An average of 10 minutes per week per household of additional disposal time would probably be needed. A recent survey by the local newspaper, however, found that 80 percent of respondents considered the inconvenience of the program negligible. Therefore, the department decided to assume that household separation costs would be zero.

Discount Rate: The sanitation department has been instructed by the budget office to discount at the town's real borrowing rate of 6 percent. It has also been instructed to assume that annual net benefits accrue at the end of each of the eight years of the program.

a. Calculate an estimate of the present value of net benefits for the program.

b. How large would annual household separation costs have to be per household to make the present value of net benefits fall to zero?

   c. Assuming that household separation costs are zero, conduct a worst-case analysis with respect to the growth in the quantity of waste, the price of scrap paper, and the percentage of paper diverted from the waste stream.

   d. Under the worst-case assumptions of part c, how large would the average yearly household separation costs have to be to make the present value of net benefits fall to zero?

   e. Investigate the sensitivity of the present value of net benefits to the price of scrap paper.

   f. Implement a Monte Carlo analysis of the present value of net benefits of the program.

6. Imagine that, with a discount rate of 5 percent, the net present value of a hydroelectric plant with a life of 70 years is $25.73 million and that the net present value of a thermal electric plant with a life of 35 years is $18.77 million. Rolling the thermal plant over twice to match the life of the hydroelectric plant thus has a net present value of ($18.77 million) + ($18.77 million)/$(1 + 0.05)^{35}$ = $22.17 million.

     Now assume that at the end of the first 35 years, there will be an improved second 35-year plant. Specifically, there is a 30 percent chance that an advanced solar or nuclear alternative will be available that will increase the net benefits by a factor of three, a 60 percent chance that a major improvement in thermal technology will increase net benefits by 50 percent, and a 10 percent chance that more modest improvements in thermal technology will increase net benefits by 10 percent.

   a. Should the hydroelectric or thermal plant be built today?

   b. What is the quasi-option value of the thermal plant?

NOTES

1. A more realistic assumption (e.g., rainfall amounts closer to the center of the range are more likely) would not change this equality as long as the probability density function of rainfall is symmetric around 11 inches.

2. Assuming that rainfall is distributed uniformly over the range, the expected value of net benefits is simply the area under curve *B* from 22 inches to 0 inches. See note 4 on how to calculate this area for any distribution of rainfall.

3. The representativeness is very sensitive to the particular shape of the probability density function of rainfall. The use of two contingencies would be even less representative if amounts of rainfall near 11 inches were more likely than more extreme amounts.

4. In the case of a continuous underlying dimension, such as price, the expected value of net benefits is calculated using integration, the continuous analog of addition. Let $NB(x)$ be the net benefits given some particular value of x, the underlying dimension. Let $f(x)$ be the probability density function over x. Then,

$$E[NB] = \int NB(x)f(x)dx$$

where the integration is over the range of x.

5. The term *decision analysis* was originally used to include both choice under risk (statistical decision analysis) and games against strategic opponents (game theory). Now it is commonly used to refer only to the former.

6. We recommend Howard Raiffa, *Decision Analysis: Introductory Lectures on Choices under Uncertainty* (Reading, MA: Addison-Wesley, 1969); Morris H. DeGroot, *Optimal Statistical Decisions* (New York: McGraw-Hill, 1970); Robert L. Winkler, *Introduction to Bayesian Inference and Decision* (New York: Holt, Rinehart and Winston, 1972); and Robert D. Behn and James W. Vaupel, *Quick Analysis for Busy Decision Makers* (New York: Basic Books, 1982) as general introductions. For more direct application to CBA, see Miley W. Merkhofer, *Decision Science and Social Risk Management: A Comparative Evaluation of Cost-Benefit Analysis, Decision Analysis, and Other Formal Decision-Aiding Approaches* (Boston: D. Reidel Publishing Company, 1987).

7. Although this example is hypothetical, it captures the essence of the problem facing public health officials in confronting the N1H1 virus in 2009 and 2010. For an analysis of the issues that arose in the Swine Flu episode in the 1970s, see

Richard E. Neustadt and Harvey V. Fineberg, *The Swine Flu Affair: Decision-Making on a Slippery Disease* (Washington, D.C.: U.S. Government Printing Office.

8. Note that in this example the probability of an epidemic in the second year is conditional on whether an epidemic occurred in the first year. If an epidemic has occurred in the first year, then the population gains immunity and there is zero probability of an epidemic in the second year. If an epidemic has not occurred, then there is some probability, p_2, that one will occur in the second year.

9. Instead, we might have allowed the estimate of P_2 to be adjusted after information was revealed, or gathered, during the first year. If this were the case, then we might use *Bayes' theorem* to update the initial beliefs about P_2 in the face of the new information. Bayes' theorem provides a rule for updating subjective probability estimates on the basis of new information. Let A and B be events. A basic axiom of probability theory is that:

$$P(A \text{ and } B) = P(A|B)P(B) = P(B|A)P(A)$$

where $P(A \text{ and } B)$ is the probability of both A and B occurring, $P(A)$ is the probability of A occurring, $P(B)$ is the probability of B occurring, $P(A|B)$ is the conditional probability that A occurs given that B has occurred, and $P(B|A)$ is the conditional probability of B occurring given that A has occurred. It follows directly from the axioms that:

$$P(A|B) = P(B|A)P(A)/P(B)$$

which is the simplest statement of Bayes' rule.

Its application is quite common in diagnostic tests. For example, we may know the frequency of a disease in the population, $P(A)$, the probability that a test will yield a positive result if randomly given to a member of the population, $P(B)$, and the conditional probability that, given the disease, the test will be positive, $P(B|A)$. We would thus be able to calculate, $P(A|B)$, the conditional probability that someone with a positive test has the disease.

Discussions of Bayes' rule can be found in almost any introductory text on probability and statistics. For a more advanced treatment, see

S. James Press, *Bayesian Statistics: Principles, Models, and Applications* (New York: John Wiley and Sons, 1989).

10. Note the assumption that the probability of the influenza reaching the population, p_1, is independent of whether or not this particular population is vaccinated. This would not be a reasonable assumption if the vaccination were to be part of a national program that reduced the chances that the influenza would reach this population from some other vaccinated population.

11. In this particular problem, it will never make sense to wait until the second year to implement the program if it is going to be implemented at all. If, however, the risk of side effects were expected to fall in the second year, say, because a better vaccine would be available, then delay could be optimal. In terms of the decision tree, we could easily model this alternative scenario by using different values of C_s in the current and next years.

12. For a discussion of the application of decision analysis to the stockpiling problem, see David L. Weimer and Aidan R. Vining, *Policy Analysis: Concepts and Practice*, 4th ed. (Upper Saddle River, NJ: Pearson Prentice Hall, 2005), Chapter 17.

13. Calculating the number of combinations: $3^{17} = 129,140,163$.

14. For examples of CBA applied to hepatitis vaccine programs, see Josephine A. Mauskopf, Cathy J. Bradley, and Michael T. French, "Benefit-Cost Analysis of Hepatitis B Vaccine Programs for Occupationally Exposed Workers," *Journal of Occupational Medicine* 33(6) 1991, 691–698; Gary M. Ginsberg and Daniel Shouval, "Cost-Benefit Analysis of a Nationwide Neonatal Inoculation Programme against Hepatitis B in an Area of Intermediate Endemicity," *Journal of Epidemiology and Community Health* 46(6) 1992, 587–594; and Murray Krahn and Allan S. Detsky, "Should Canada and the United States Universally Vaccinate Infants against Hepatitis B?" *Medical Decision Making* 13(1) 1993, 4–20.

15. Call the basic reproductive rate of the infection R_0. That is, each primary infection exposes R_0 individuals to infection. If i is the fraction of the population no longer susceptible to infection because of previous infection, then the actual reproductive rate is $R = R_0(1 - i - v)$, where v

is the fraction of the population effectively vaccinated. If R falls below 1, then the infection dies out because, on average, each infection generates less than one new infection. Assuming that the population is homogeneous with respect to susceptibility to infection and that infected and non-infected individuals uniformly mix in the population, a rough estimate of the ultimate i for the population is given by the formula $i = 1 - (1/R_0) - v$ where $1 - 1/R_0$ is the estimate of the infection rate in the absence of the vaccine. For an overview, see Roy M. Anderson and Robert M. May, "Modern Vaccines: Immunisation and Herd Immunity," *The Lancet* 8690(March) 1990, 641–645; and Joseph W. G. Smith, "Vaccination Strategy," in Philip Selby, ed., *Influenza, Virus, Vaccines, and Strategy* (New York: Academic Press, 1976), 271–294.

16. The L = $3 million and L = $1 million lines cross because lives are at risk both from the vaccination side effects and from the epidemic. At low probabilities of epidemic, the expected number of lives saved from vaccination is negative so that net benefits are higher for lower values of life. At higher probabilities of epidemic, the expected number of lives saved is positive so that net benefits are higher for higher values of life.

17. In general, if the calculation of net benefits involves sums of random variables, using their expected values yields the expected value of net benefits. If the calculation involves sums and products of random variables, then using their expected values yields the expected value of net benefits only if the random variables are uncorrelated. In the Monte Carlo approach, correlations among variables can be taken into account by drawing parameter values from either multivariate or conditional distributions rather than from independent univariate distributions as in this example. Finally, if the calculation involves ratios of random variables, then even independence (i.e., an absence of correlations) does not guarantee that using their expected values will yield the correct expected value of net benefits. In this latter situation, the Monte Carlo approach is especially valuable because it provides a way of estimating the correct expected net benefits.

18. The concept of quasi-option value was introduced by Kenneth J. Arrow and Anthony C. Fisher, "Environmental Preservation, Uncertainty, and Irreversibility," *Quarterly Journal of Economics* 88(2) 1974, 312–319.

19. Jon M. Conrad, "Quasi-Option Value and the Expected Value of Information," *Quarterly Journal of Economics* 44(4) 1980, 813–820; and Anthony C. Fisher and W. Michael Hanemann, "Quasi-Option Value: Some Misconceptions Dispelled," *Journal of Environmental Economics and Management* 14(2) 1987, 183–190.

20. The concept of quasi-option value also applies to private sector investments involving large initial costs that cannot be recovered if abandoned. For overviews, see Robert S. Pindyck, "Irreversibility, Uncertainty, and Investment," *Journal of Economic Literature* 29(3) 1991, 1110–1148; Avinash Dixit and Robert Pindyck, *Investment Under Uncertainty* (Princeton, NJ: Princeton University Press, 1994); Gilbert E. Metcalf and Donald Rosenthal, "The 'New' View of Investment Decisions and Public Policy Analysis: An Application to Green Lights and Cold Refrigerators," *Journal of Policy Analysis and Management* 14(4) 1995, 517–531; and Anthony Edward Boardman and David H. Greenberg, "Discounting and the Social Discount Rate," in Fred Thompson and Mark T. Green, eds., *Handbook of Public Finance* (New York: Marcel Dekker, 1998), 269–318.

CHAPTER 8

Option Price and Option Value

In the actual practice of CBA in circumstances involving significant risks, analysts almost always apply the Kaldor-Hicks criterion to expected net benefits. They typically estimate changes in social surplus conditional on particular contingencies occurring, and then they compute an expected value over the contingencies as demonstrated in Chapter 7. Economists, however, now generally consider *option price,* the amount that individuals are willing to pay for policies prior to the realization of contingencies, to be the theoretically correct measure of willingness to pay in circumstances of uncertainty. Whereas social surplus can be thought of as an *ex post* measure of welfare change in the sense that individuals value policies as if contingencies have already occurred, option price is an *ex ante* welfare measure in the sense that consumers value policies without knowing which contingency will actually occur. These measures generally differ from one another. In this chapter, we consider the implications of the common use of expected social surplus, rather than option price, as the method for measuring benefits.

The central concern of this chapter is the conceptually correct measure of willingness to pay in circumstances in which individuals face uncertainty. Individuals may face uncertainties about their demand for a good, the supply of a good, or both. With respect to demand, one may be uncertain about one's future income, utility function (tastes), and the prices of other goods. For example, one's utility from skiing may depend on the sturdiness of one's knees, a physical condition that cannot be predicted with certainty. With respect to supply, one may be uncertain about the future quantity, quality, or price of a good. For example, the increase in the quality of fishing that will result from restocking a lake with game fish depends on such circumstances as weather and spills of toxic chemicals, and thus is uncertain to some degree.

In contrast to Chapter 7, we limit our attention to uncertainties of direct relevance to individuals. We ignore uncertainties that are not of direct individual relevance, but instead arise because analysts must make predictions about the future to estimate measures of WTP. In the context of the CBA of the vaccination program discussed in Chapter 7, for example, the probability of epidemic, the probability an unvaccinated individual will be infected, the probability a vaccinated individual will be infected, and the probability a vaccinated individual will suffer a side effect are exactly the types of uncertainties considered in this chapter. The analyst's uncertainties about the magnitude of these probabilities, the appropriate shadow price of time, or the number of people who will choose to be vaccinated were adequately addressed in the discussion of sensitivity analysis presented in Chapter 7. Although these analytical uncertainties are usually of greatest practical concern in CBA, we seek here to provide the conceptual foundation required for understanding the appropriate measure of costs and benefits when individuals face significant uncertainties. We are especially interested in how to assess government policies that increase or reduce the uncertainties that individuals face.

This chapter has three major sections. The first introduces option price and clarifies its relationship to expected surplus. The second section introduces the concept of *option value,* the difference between option price and expected surplus, and reviews the theoretical literature that attempts to determine its sign. Although sometimes thought of as a conceptually distinct category of benefits, option value is actually an adjustment to measured benefits to account for the fact that they are usually measured in terms of expected surplus rather than in terms of option prices. The third section provides a general assessment of the appropriateness of the use of expected surplus as a proxy for option price.

EX ANTE WTP: OPTION PRICE[1]

Viewing benefits (or costs) in terms of the willingness of individuals to pay to obtain desirable (or avoid undesirable) policy impacts provides a clear perspective on the appropriateness of treating expected net benefits as if they were certain amounts. By identifying the conceptually correct method for valuing uncertain costs and benefits, we can better understand the circumstances under which the use of expected net benefits is more or less appropriate.

There is now a near consensus among economists that the conceptually correct way to value the benefits of a policy in circumstances involving risk is to sum the *ex ante* amounts that the individuals affected by the policy would be willing to pay to obtain it.[2] To see this, imagine that each person, knowing the probabilities of each of the contingencies that would occur under the policy, would give a truthful answer to the following question: *Prior to knowing which contingency will actually occur, what is the maximum amount that you would be willing to pay to obtain the policy?* Each individual's answer to this question is what economists call the person's *option price* for the policy. If we think of the policy as a lottery having probabilities of various payoffs to the person, then the individual's option price is a *certainty equivalent* of the lottery—that is, an amount the person would pay for a ticket without knowing the payoff (or contingency) that is actually realized. (It is called a certainty equivalent because the amount paid for a lottery ticket is certain even if the payoff is not.)

By summing the option prices of all persons, we obtain the aggregate benefits of the policy, which can then be compared to its opportunity cost in the usual way. If the opportunity cost is not dependent on which contingency actually occurs, then we have fully taken account of risk by comparing the aggregate WTP, which is independent of the contingency that actually occurs, with the certain opportunity cost.

Illustrations of Option Price

To illustrate the concept of option price, return to the asteroid defense policies set out in Table 7-1 in the previous chapter. Assume that the United Nations wishes to evaluate forward-based asteroid defense from the perspective of humankind. Analysts might employ a contingent valuation survey of the sort described in

Chapter 15. It would require surveyors to explain to each person (or more likely to a representative of each household) the possible contingencies (exposure to collision with an asteroid larger than one kilometer diameter, exposure to collision with an asteroid between 20 meters and one kilometer in diameter, and no exposure to collision with an asteroid larger than 20 meters in diameter), the probabilities of each contingency, and the consequences to the Earth under each contingency with and without forward-based asteroid defense. Each person would then be asked questions to elicit the maximum amount that he or she would be willing to pay to have forward-based asteroid defense. These amounts would be summed over all earthlings to arrive at the social benefits of forward-based asteroid defense. As this sum represents aggregate WTP before people know which contingency occurs, and therefore is the WTP irrespective of which one actually occurs, it can be thought of as a certainty equivalent. Let us assume that the social net benefits, the sum of individual option prices, equaled $100 billion. The net benefits of forward-based asteroid defense would then be calculated as this amount minus the certain program costs of $60 billion, or $40 billion.

Recall that in actual CBA, analysts more commonly measure benefits by first estimating the social surplus under each contingency and then taking the expected value of these amounts using the probabilities of the contingencies. For example, the information in Table 7-1 indicates that the expected benefits of forward-based asteroid defense relative to no program to be −$15 billion. (The expected value of net costs of no program, $54 billion, minus the expected value of net costs of forward-based asteroid defense, $69 billion.) Thus, in this example, the expected surplus would underestimate net benefits by $55 billion ($40 billion minus −$15 billion). This difference between option price and expected surplus is the option value of forward-based asteroid defense. In this case, the option value can be thought of as an additional "insurance benefit" of the program. It is the maximum amount beyond expected benefits that individuals are willing to pay to have the defense program available to reduce the risk of the catastrophic consequences that would result from an undefended collision with a large asteroid.

In general, how does this expected surplus measure compare to the option price? Assuming that individuals are risk averse, *expected surplus can either underestimate or overestimate option price depending on the sources of risk.* For an individual who is risk averse and whose utility function depends only on income, expected surplus will underestimate option price for policies that reduce income risk and overestimate option price for policies that increase income risk. In order to understand how these possibilities can arise, it is necessary to look more carefully at the relationship between option price and expected surplus from the perspective of an individual consumer. The following diagrammatic expositions illustrate cases where option price exceeds expected surplus (a temporary dam) and expected surplus exceeds option price (a bridge).

Table 8-1 shows the contingent payoffs for building a temporary dam that provides water for irrigation. With or without the dam, the farmer can be viewed as facing two contingencies: It rains a lot or it does not rain very much. If it is wet, then he will always produce more crops than if it is dry. Without the dam, the farmer would receive an income of $100 if it rains a lot and only $50 if it does not rain very much. As a result of the dam, his income will increase by $50 if it is dry but by only $10 if it is wet. These $50 and $10 figures are the surplus that the farmer receives from the dam under each

TABLE 8-1   Example of a Risk-Reducing Project

| Contingency | Policy | | Probability of Contingency |
	Dam	No Dam	
Wet	110	100	.5
Dry	100	50	.5
Expected value	105	75	
Variance	25	625	

Surplus point:	$U(110 - S_w) = U(100)$ implies $S_w = 10$
	$U(100 - S_d) = U(50)$ implies $S_d = 50$
Expected surplus:	$E(S) = .5S_w + .5S_d = 30$
Expected utility of no dam:	$EU = .5U(100) + .5U(50)$
Willingness-to-pay locus:	(s_w, s_d) such that
	$.5U(110 - s_w) + .5U(100 - s_d) = EU$
Option price:	$.5U(110 - OP) + .5U(100 - OP) = EU$
	$EU = 4.26$ and $OP = 34.2$
	for $U(c) = \ln(c)$, where c is net income
Comparison:	$OP > E(S)$

contingency. In expected value terms, assuming that the dry and wet contingencies are equally likely, this surplus equals $30. This $30 expected surplus figure corresponds to the measure of benefits that is used in CBA when option price is not estimated.[3]

Notice that this example assumes that the dam will store water that can be used for irrigation purposes if it is dry. Consequently, the dam will do more for the farmer if it turns out to be dry than if it turns out to be wet. As a result, his income depends much less on which contingency actually occurs once the dam is built than it did without the dam. In other words, the dam reduces the income risk faced by the farmer by reducing the variation in his income. A useful summary measure of this reduction in income risk is provided by the effect of the dam on the variance of the farmer's income, which is $625 without the dam but only $25 with the dam.[4]

To determine the farmer's benefits from the dam, we first calculate his expected utility, EU, without the dam. We then find his option price, which is the maximum amount he would be willing to pay for the dam or, equivalently, the amount that gives him the same expected utility as he would have without the dam. To compute these amounts, we need to know the farmer's utility function. Normally, we would not have this information, which is why, in practice, expected surplus rather than option price is normally used to determine net benefits. For purposes of our illustration, however, we assume that the farmer's utility is given by the natural log of his income as shown in Table 8-1.

The curved line in Figure 8-1 shows this utility function. In the absence of a dam, the farmer realizes income of $50 dollars if it is dry and $100 if it is wet. Because the probabilities of wet and dry are each one-half, the expected utility without the dam can be found as the point midway between the utilities of these no-dam

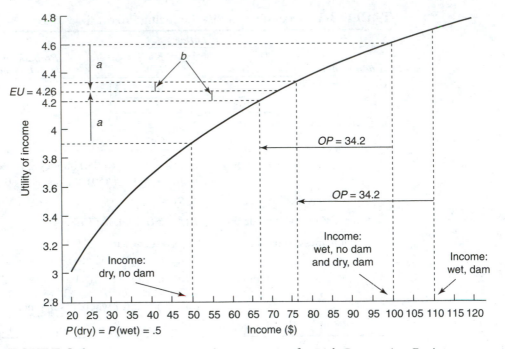

FIGURE 8-1 Utility Function and Option Price for Risk-Decreasing Project

incomes. The point on the vertical axis labeled $EU = 4.26$ is exactly a units of utility away from each of the contingent utilities. As it is midway between them, it equals the expected utility. If the dam is built, then the farmer receives an income of $100 if it is dry and $110 if it is wet. The option price for the dam is the maximum amount of income the farmer would be willing to give up to have the dam—in other words, the amount that would allow him to obtain the same expected utility with the dam as he would obtain without it. The arrows marked $OP = 34.2$ shift the contingent incomes with the dam by subtracting $34.20 from each so that the net contingent incomes are $65.80 and $75.80. The utilities of these net incomes are each b units of utility away from 4.26 so that their expected utility equals the expected utility of no dam. Thus, either no dam or a dam with a certain payment of $34.20 gives the farmer the same expected utility.

The farmer's option price for the dam of $34.20 exceeds his expected surplus of $30. Thus, if the opportunity cost of the project were $32 and the farmer were the only beneficiary, then the common practice of using expected surplus would result in rejecting building the dam when, in fact, the option price indicates that building the dam would increase the farmer's utility.

Figure 8-2 provides an alternative graphical representation of the relationship between expected surplus and option price for the farmer. The vertical axis indicates the farmer's willingness-to-pay amounts if it is dry; the horizontal axis represents his willingness-to-pay amounts if it is wet. Thus, point A represents his surplus under each contingency.

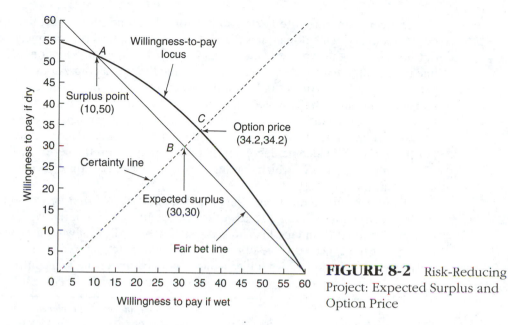

FIGURE 8-2 Risk-Reducing Project: Expected Surplus and Option Price

There is a slightly different way to view point *A*. Imagine that before the government will build the dam the farmer would be required to sign a contract, Contract *A*, that stipulates that he will pay the government an amount equal to $\$X_w$ if it turns out to be wet and an amount equal to $\$X_d$ if it turns out to be dry. This is called a *contingent contract* because its terms depend on events that will not be known until sometime in the future. Although the government is unlikely to require a contingent contract in practice, it is a useful device for thinking about how much the farmer values the dam or, in other words, his benefits from the dam. These benefits correspond to the maximum value that the government could assign to $\$X_w$ and $\$X_d$ and still get the farmer to sign Contract *A*, $10 and $50, respectively. The farmer would be willing to sign at these amounts because he would be exactly back to the situation he faced without the dam, when his income equaled $100 if it rained and $50 if it was dry. In other words, $10 and $50 are his maximum WTP under Contract *A*.

Notice that because the $10 payment if it is wet and the $50 payment if it is dry put the farmer back to where he would be without the dam, they measure the surplus he receives but not the utility he receives because the dam reduces the income risk he faces. If the farmer makes these payments, then his income variability would be exactly what it was without the dam. To examine the change in income risk resulting from the dam, imagine now that the government is also willing to let the farmer choose an alternative contract, Contract *B*, that allows him to pay the same amount, $30, regardless of which contingency actually occurs. If the government does this, then the expected value of the payment it will receive would be equal under the two contracts. However, Contract *B* would place the farmer on a line that bisects the origin of Figure 8-2. This line is called the *certainty line* because payment amounts along it are the same regardless of which contingency actually occurs. Thus, any point along this line, including *B*, represents a certainty equivalent.

The certainty line intersects another line. This one passes through the surplus point, but every point along it has the same expected value. For example, in the case of our illustration, the expected value would always be equal to $30 along this line. This line is called the *fair bet line*. To see why, imagine flipping a coin. A payoff of $10 if you get heads and $50 if you get tails would have exactly the same expected value as $20 if you get heads and $40 if you get tails. Thus, the slope of the fair bet line, −1, is equal to the negative of the ratio of the probabilities of the contingencies. As one moves along the fair bet line toward the certainty line, the expected value always remains the same, but the variation in income decreases. Finally, at point B on the certainty line, the payoff is equal regardless of which contingency, heads or tails, actually occurs.[5] In our example, this payoff is $30.

We now return to our farmer and the dam and ask whether he would be indifferent between signing Contract A, under which he must pay $10 if it is wet and $50 if it is dry, and Contract B, under which he must pay $30 regardless of whether it is wet or dry, noting that the expected value of his income would be equal under the two contracts. To answer this, we look at what his income would be under the two contracts:

Contingency	Probability	Income under Contract A	Income under Contract B
Wet	.5	$100	$80
Dry	.5	$50	$70
EV		$75	$75

Although the expected value of income under the two contracts would be identical, the variation in income between the two contingencies is obviously much less under Contract B. Thus, by comparing Contracts A and B, we can examine the effect of the dam on the risk facing the farmer, while holding the expected value of his income constant. If the farmer is risk averse and, hence, would prefer a more stable to a less stable income from year to year, then he will not be indifferent between the two contracts but will prefer B to A because he will face less risk with B than with A.

Now, recall that at point A in Figure 8-2 the farmer was willing to sign a contract that would require him to pay $10 if it is wet and $50 if it is dry and that the expected value of these payments was $30. Because the farmer prefers point B to point A, this suggests that in order to reach the certainty line, the farmer would be willing to sign a contract requiring him to pay a certainty equivalent greater than $30. The maximum such amount that he would pay is represented by point C in Figure 8-2, a point that is farther northeast along the certainty line than point B. Point C represents the farmer's option price, the maximum amount that he would be willing to pay for *both* the increase in expected income and the reduction in income risk resulting from the dam. In other words, it incorporates the full value of the dam to the farmer. Conceptually, it is the correct measure of benefits that the farmer would receive from the dam. But in CBAs, it is point B, the expected value of the surpluses resulting from the dam, that is typically predicted. While point B captures the effect of the dam on expected income, it does not incorporate the effect of the dam on income variability or risk.

TABLE 8-2 Example of a Risk-Increasing Project

Contingency	Policy Bridge	Policy No Bridge	Probability of Contingency
No earthquake	200	100	.8
Earthquake	100	80	.2
Expected value	180	96	
Variance	1600	64	

Surplus point:	$U(200 - S_n) = U(100)$ so $S_n = 100$ $U(100 - S_e) = U(80)$ so $S_e = 20$
Expected surplus:	$E(S) = .8S_n + .2S_e = 84$
Expected utility of no bridge:	$EU = .8U(100) + .2U(80)$
Willingness-to-pay locus:	(s_n, s_e) such that $.8U(200 - s_n) + .2U(100 - s_e) = EU$
Option price:	$.8U(200 - OP) + .2U(100 - OP) = EU$ $EU = 4.56$ and $OP = 71.1$ for $U(c) = \ln(c)$, where c is net income
Comparison:	$OP < E(S)$

Although the farmer would prefer point B to point A, he would be indifferent between points A and C. Indeed, a curve drawn between these points is very similar to an indifference curve. This curve, the *willingness-to-pay locus*,[6] shows all of the combinations of contingent payments for the dam that give the farmer the same expected utility with the dam as without it.[7] It is based on knowledge of the probabilities of the contingencies prior to knowing which one will actually occur.

If the option price lies farther to the northeast along the certainty line than does the certain project cost, then the project would increase the farmer's welfare.

Table 8-2 describes a policy involving constructing a bridge in an area where the probability of an earthquake is 20 percent. The bridge would increase the expected value of income that the individual described in the table receives, but at the same time, it would make her income more dependent on whether or not a quake actually occurs. In other words, the bridge increases the income risk facing the individual. Consequently, as shown in the table, the expected surplus of $84 exceeds the option price of $71.10. Thus, if the opportunity cost of the bridge were a certain $75 and the person were the only beneficiary, then the option price indicates that building it would reduce her expected utility if she actually had to pay the opportunity cost of its construction. Hence, the bridge should not be built, even though the expected surplus from building it is positive.

This situation is illustrated in Figure 8-3. The bridge can be viewed as initially placing the individual at point D. Once again, we can imagine the government requiring the individual to sign a contingent contract, Contract D. In this case, the individual would

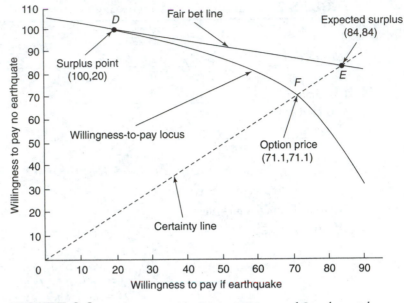

FIGURE 8-3   Risk-Increasing Project: Expected Surplus and Option Price

be willing to pay up to $100 in the event that there is not a quake but only $20 if there is a quake. By signing such a contract, she would be no worse off than she was without the bridge.

We have taken account of the fact that the bridge would increase expected surplus but not the fact that it would also affect income risk. Thus, as before, we imagine that the government is also willing to sign a different contract, Contract E, as long as the expected value of the payments continues to equal $84, their expected value under Contract D.

Which contract would she prefer? If she is risk averse, she would prefer Contract D to Contract E because, in the following table even though the expected value of her income is identical under the two contracts, her income would be subject to less risk:

Contingency	Probability	Income under Contract D	Income under Contract E
No quake	.8	$100	$116
Quake	.2	$80	$16
EV		$96	$96

Because a risk-averse individual would prefer Contract D to Contract E, her willingness to pay locus for the bridge would be below her fair bet line. Consequently, her option price, which is represented by point F, is less than $84. As in the previous illustration, the individual would be indifferent between points D and F, but not between points D and E.

Is Option Price the Best Measure of Benefits?

The illustrations previously described demonstrate that, in general, option price does not equal expected surplus in circumstances of uncertainty. In the first illustration, option price was larger than the expected value; in the second illustration, it was smaller. We have implicitly taken option price to be the correct benefit measure. Is this generally the case? The answer to this question requires a clearer specification of the institutional environment of policy choice.

The key consideration concerns the availability of insurance against the risks in question. *If complete and actuarially fair insurance is unavailable against the relevant risks, then option price is the conceptually correct measure of benefits.* Insurance is complete if individuals can purchase sufficient coverage to eliminate their risks entirely. It is actuarially fair if its price depends only on the true probabilities of the relevant contingencies. In the case of two contingencies, with the probability of contingency 1 equal to p and the probability of contingency 2 equal to $1 - p$, actuarially fair insurance would allow the individual to trade contingent income in contingency 1 for contingent income in contingency 2 at a price of $p/(1 - p)$. For example, if p equals .2, then the price of insurance equals .25 (.2/.8), so that to increase income in contingency 1 by $100, the individual would have to give up $25 in contingency 2. Graphically, the availability of actuarially fair insurance means that individuals could move along the fair bet lines toward the certainty lines shown in Figures 8-2 and 8-3 through purchases of insurance.

Complete and actuarially fair insurance is rarely available in the real world.[8] The problem of *moral hazard,* the changes in risk-related behavior of insurees induced by insurance coverage, encourages profit-maximizing insurers to limit coverage through copayments.[9] Insurers may be unwilling to provide full insurance against losses to unique assets that cannot be easily valued in markets.[10] *Adverse selection* occurs when insurees have better information about their true risks than do insurers. Adverse selection may result in either the combining of low- and high-risk persons in the same price pool or the limiting of the extent of coverage to induce high risks to reveal themselves.[11] The pooling of high- and low-risk persons implies that at least one of the groups receives an actuarially unfair price; limiting available coverage to high-risk persons means that complete insurance is unavailable. Routine administrative costs, as well as efforts to control moral hazard and adverse selection, inflate prices above the actuarially fair levels. Limited pools of insurees or uncertainty about the magnitudes of risks may require a further increment in prices to reduce the risk of bankruptcy.[12] Finally, some risks are so highly correlated across individuals that risk pooling does not sufficiently reduce aggregate risk to allow actuarially fair prices.[13] In order to manage the risk of going bankrupt, insurers facing correlated risks must charge an amount above the actuarially fair price to build a financial cushion or buy reinsurance to guard against the possibility of having to pay off on many losses at the same time.

Imagine that, despite these practical limitations, complete and actuarially fair insurance were available for the risk in question. It would then be possible for the sponsor of the project to trade the contingent surplus amounts for a certain payment by purchasing sufficient insurance to move along the fair bet line, which represents actuarially fair insurance, to the certainty line. In this way, a certain payment corresponding to the expected surplus could be achieved. For example, returning to Figure 8-3, the project sponsor could guarantee a certain payment of $84, which is larger than the option price of \$71.10. Notice, however, that if the option price exceeds the expected surplus (the situation illustrated in Figure 8-2), then the latter will understate the conceptually correct measure of project benefits, even if complete and actuarially fair insurance can be purchased. In general, therefore, *if complete and actuarially fair insurance is available, then the larger of option price or expected surplus is the appropriate measure of benefits.*

This generalization ignores one additional institutional constraint: It is not practical to specify contingency-specific payments that would move an individual from his or her contingent surplus point to other points on his or her willingness-to-pay locus. The impracticality may arise from a lack of either information about the shape of the entire willingness-to-pay locus or the administrative capacity to write and execute contingent contracts through taxes and subsidies whose magnitudes depend on the occurrence of events. Yet, if such contracts were administratively feasible *and* the analyst knew the entire willingness-to-pay locus, then the policy could be designed with optimal contingent payments so that the person's postpayment contingent surpluses would have the greatest expected value, which could then be realized with certainty through insurance purchases.

Figure 8-4 illustrates this possibility. In the absence of payments, the person realizes either S_1 or S_2 depending on which contingency occurs. If, in addition to the direct

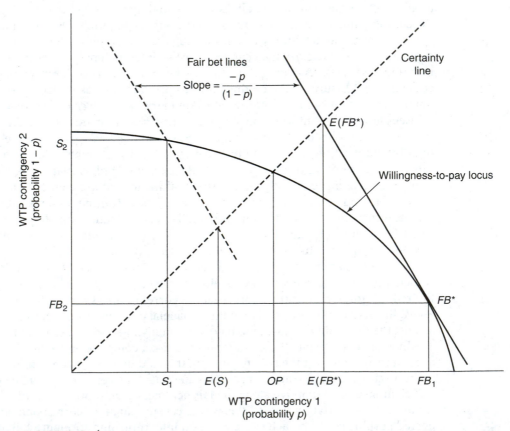

FIGURE 8-4 Option Price and the Maximum Expected Value of Willingness to Pay

effects of the policy, the person were given a payment equal to $FB_1 - S_1$ if contingency 1 occurred or paid a fee of $S_2 - FB_2$ if contingency 2 occurred, then the person's post-payment contingent surpluses would be given by point FB^*. Because FB^* is the point of tangency between the willingness-to-pay locus and a fair bet line, it has the largest expected value of any point on the willingness-to-pay locus. Starting at this point, complete and actuarially fair insurance would allow the policy sponsors to move along the fair bet line to the certainty line. The resulting certain payment, $E(FB^*)$ would be the maximum certain amount of benefit produced by the payment-adjusted policy.[14]

Thus, *in the exceedingly unlikely circumstance that optimal contingent payments are feasible **and** complete and actuarially fair insurance is available, the expected value of the point on the willingness-to-pay locus that is just tangent to the fair bet line is the appropriate measure of benefits.*

In summary, if the policy under consideration involves costs that are certain and complete and actuarially fair insurance is unavailable, then option price is the appropriate measure of benefits because it allows us to compare certain willingness-to-pay amounts with certain costs. In practice, however, option prices are difficult to measure. Indeed, as will be evident from the discussion of option values in the next section, very specific assumptions about the nature of risks must be made to be able to determine whether option price is larger or smaller than the commonly measured expected surplus.

DETERMINING THE BIAS IN EXPECTED SURPLUS: SIGNING OPTION VALUE

Early attempts to apply CBA to recreational resources such as national parks raised uneasiness about the appropriateness of expected surplus as a benefit measure. In a seminal article dealing with the issue, Burton Weisbrod pointed out that estimates of the benefits of preserving a national park based solely on the benefits accruing to actual visitors do not capture its value to those who anticipate visiting it sometime in the future but actually never do.[15] He argued that these nonvisitors would be willing to pay something to preserve the option of visiting. He called this amount *option value*, which has been interpreted by many as a separate benefit category of relevance to valuing assets, such as natural resources, that offer opportunities for future consumption.

CBA requires a more precise definition of option value, however.[16] The key to formulating it lies in the recognition that option price fully measures a person's *ex ante* willingness to pay for a policy in the presence of uncertainty about the benefits that will accrue *ex post*. The uncertainty may arise from a variety of sources, including not only uncertainty about the demand the person will actually have for the goods produced by the policy if it is implemented (Weisbrod's point), but also uncertainty about the quantities, qualities, and prices of the goods, as well as the prices of other goods. Because, even with such uncertainties, it is a full measure of willingness to pay, option price includes option value.

It is now standard to define *option value* as the difference between option price and expected surplus:

$$OV \equiv OP - E[S] \tag{8.1}$$

where *OV* is option value, *OP* is the option price, and *E[S]* is expected surplus. For example, the option value for the dam presented in Table 8-1 is $4.20, the option price of $34.20 minus the expected surplus of $30. The option value of the bridge presented in Table 8-2 is −$12.90, the option price of $71.10 minus the expected surplus of $84.

Rearranging the equation defining option value gives the practical interpretation of option value as an adjustment to expected surplus required to make it equal to option price:

$$OP = E[S] + OV \qquad\qquad (8.2)$$

where the left-hand side is the certain amount a person is willing to pay, the conceptually correct measure of benefits, and the right-hand side consists of expected surplus, which is what is typically measurable, and option value, which is the amount that would have to be added to expected surplus to make it equal to option price. Though it may seem natural to interpret option value as a distinct benefit category, it is probably better to interpret it as the bias in estimated benefits resulting from measurement by expected surplus rather than option price. Unfortunately, either interpretation requires caution because the sign, let alone the magnitude, of option value is often difficult to determine.

Determining the Sign of Option Value

The sign of option value may be positive or negative, depending on a variety of assumptions concerning the source and nature of risk, the characteristics of the policy being analyzed, and the underlying structure of individual utility. With only a few exceptions, the sign of option value has proven to be theoretically ambiguous. This raises the issue of the usefulness of the concept of option value for even determining the direction of bias when expected surplus is used as an approximation of option price.

The earliest studies (see Appendix 8A) attempted to determine the sign of option price when the change in the price or quantity of the good being valued is certain but the demand for the good is uncertain. For example, in the earliest effort to sign option value, Charles J. Cicchetti and A. Myrick Freeman III assumed that there is some probability that a person will have positive demand for the good.[17] Their conclusion that option price is always positive when demand is uncertain was later contradicted by Richard Schmalensee, who showed that the sign was ambiguous under general assumptions.[18]

Subsequent efforts to sign option value without making specific assumptions about individuals' utility functions have produced an unequivocal result only with respect to uncertainty in income. Specifically, in valuing a certain change in the price or quantity of a normal good (quantity demanded increases with increases in income), option value will be negative for a risk-averse person with uncertain income because the change in price or quantity of the good accentuates the income uncertainty. Conversely, in valuing a certain change in the price or quantity of an inferior good (quantity demanded decreases with increases in income), option value will be positive for a risk-averse person. As CBA typically involves valuing normal goods, this general result cautions against the tendency to think of option value as a positive adjustment to expected surplus.

EXHIBIT 8-1

In 1980 Richard G. Walsh, John B. Loomis, and Richard A. Gillman combined survey and recreational use data in an effort to estimate the willingness of Colorado households to pay for increments of land designated for wilderness. They estimated that residents of the state were willing to pay a total of $41.6 million annually for 2.6 million acres. Approximately $6.0 million, or almost 15 percent, of this total was option value.

Source: Adapted from Richard G. Walsh, John B. Loomis, and Richard A. Gillman, "Valuing Option, Existence, and Bequest Demands for Wilderness," *Land Economics* 60(1) 1984, 14–29.

On the other hand, with the imposition of a variety of different restrictive assumptions, it appears that for risk-averse persons, uncertainty about the quantity, quality, or price of a normal good (supply-side uncertainty) will usually result in a positive option value. For example, Douglas M. Larson and Paul R. Flacco show that if the demand for a normal (inferior) good is linear, semilog, or loglinear in price, then option price is positive (negative) for uncertainty in the price or quality of the good being valued.[19] They also show that uncertainty about the prices of other goods and tastes—demand-side uncertainty—similarly yields positive (negative) option values for normal (inferior) goods for these demand functions.[20]

Overall, the theoretical studies of option value suggest the following general heuristic: *With risk-averse individuals and normal (inferior) goods, treat option value as negative (positive) for income uncertainty, positive (negative) for other demand-side uncertainties, and generally positive (negative) for supply-side uncertainties.* Of course, the assumed sign of option value should be consistent with the specific assumptions employed. So, for example, if the empirically estimated demand for a normal good employs a loglinear functional form with a positive income elasticity, then option value would be negative for income uncertainty, positive for other demand-side uncertainties, and positive for supply-side uncertainties.

It should not be surprising that in view of the difficulty in establishing the sign of option value, even less progress has been made in putting bounds on its size relative to expected surplus. Calculations by V. Kerry Smith suggest that the size of option value relative to expected surplus is likely to be greater for assets that have less perfect substitutes.[21] Larson and Flacco derived expressions for option value for the specific demand functions that they investigated, but the implementation of these expressions is computationally very difficult.[22] Consequently, it is generally not possible to quantify option value using the information from which estimates of expected surplus are typically made.

RATIONALES FOR EXPECTED SURPLUS AS A PRACTICAL BENEFIT MEASURE

Although option price is generally the conceptually correct measure of benefits in circumstances of uncertainty, analysts most often estimate benefits in terms of expected surpluses. As indicated in the preceding discussion of option value, determining even the sign of the bias that results from the use of expected surplus rather than option price is not always possible. In this section we consider the reasonableness of expected surplus as a practical benefit measure.

We present two arguments often made in defense of the use of expected surplus. One argument is based on the consideration of benefits at the aggregate social level. Another argument applies at the level of the individual policy when people face independent risks so that realized net benefits are likely to be close to expected net benefits. We consider each of these arguments in turn.

Expected Values and Aggregate Social Benefits

If society were risk neutral, then choosing policies that individually maximized expected net benefits would be efficient in the sense of maximizing the expected value of society's entire portfolio of policies.[23] If we assume that projects spread costs and benefits broadly over a large population, then the effect of any particular project on the net income of any person is likely to be small. Even if people are risk averse, their preferences can be reasonably approximated as being risk neutral for such small changes in income. Therefore, aggregation of individual preferences would lead to risk neutrality at the social level so that expected surplus would be an appropriate measure of benefits.[24]

The variable magnitudes and uneven distribution of costs and benefits that often arise from public policies undercut this line of argument, however. Policies of great import may involve large costs and benefits that remain significant at the individual level, even when spread over a large population. Policies that are targeted at specific groups, such as the unemployed, or at geographical regions often impose substantial costs on and produce substantial benefits for specific individuals. Thus, because social risk neutrality is a questionable assumption, this aggregate-level argument for the use of expected surplus is weak.

A related line of argument is based on the assumption that society holds a fully diversified portfolio of policies that allows it to self-insure against the risk of any particular project. In other words, society is able to pool risk across projects so that it effectively has complete and actuarially fair insurance. (As previously noted, insurance is complete if it is available against all risks; it is actuarially fair if it is offered at a premium equal to the expected values of the risks.) As discussed earlier, with the availability of such insurance, the larger of option price and expected surplus is the appropriate benefit measure. Thus, benefits would always be at least as large as expected surplus so that any project with positive expected net benefits would be potentially Pareto improving. Of course, the comparison of mutually exclusive policies in terms of expected surpluses could be misleading if any of the projects have option prices larger than expected surpluses.

It is worth noting that this version of the argument does not rely on the collection of policies effectively averaging costs and benefits across individuals as does the first version of the argument. Rather, it relies on an averaging of aggregate net benefits across policies so that the potential Pareto criterion can be met overall, if not at the level of the individual project.

The weakness of this argument is that diversification does not eliminate all risk. A portfolio of policies as broad as even the whole stock market would still involve some systematic risk. For example, imagine adding independent policies with positive expected net benefits to the portfolio. Although the variance of the average net benefits of the policies would approach zero, the variance in total net benefits would actually increase. The variance in total net benefits means that society cannot guarantee that it will realize the total expected value of net benefits. As diversification does not permit fully effective self-insurance, it does not provide a fully satisfactory rationale for the practical use of expected net benefits.

Expected Values and Pooling Risks across Individuals: Collective and Individual Risk

We next consider the possibility of risk pooling at the level of the individual policy. It is important to make a distinction between collective risk and individual risk.

By *collective risk,* we simply mean that the same contingency will result for all individuals in society. For example, in the context of doing a CBA for a nuclear power plant, the contingencies might be "no accident" and "nuclear accident"—everyone in the geographic area experiences the same realized contingency. The actual realized net benefits can differ substantially from the expected net benefits because all individuals share either the favorable or the unfavorable outcome, rather than the weighted average of the two. In such circumstances, the world does not offer us a "middle" outcome corresponding to the expected value. Realized net benefits will, therefore, differ substantially from expected net benefits.

In contrast, consider the case of a large number of individuals who have identical preferences and who face the same probabilities of realizing each of the contingencies, but the contingency that each individual realizes is independent of the contingency realized by any other individual. This is a case of *individual risk.* This might occur, for instance, in the context of evaluating an automobile safety device using a model of traffic accidents in which there is some probability that a driver will have a potentially fatal accident for each mile driven. Multiplying the expected net benefits for one individual by the number of individuals yields a measure of total expected net benefits for the policy that can appropriately be treated as approximately certain. The reason is that in circumstances of individual risk with large numbers of individuals exposed to the risk, the proportion of individuals realizing each contingency approximates the probability associated with that contingency. In other words, the averaging process tends to produce realizations of total net benefits close to those calculated by the expected value procedure.

This averaging is analytically equivalent to the availability of actuarially fair insurance—it effectively translates, through a movement along a fair bet line, any contingent surplus point to a point on the certainty line. Thus, *in cases of individual risk, the larger of option price and expected surplus is the appropriate benefit measure.* As with complete diversification, the use of expected surplus as a benefit measure would guarantee that adopted policies were potentially Pareto improving but would not necessarily lead to the adoption of the most efficient policies in comparisons of mutually exclusive alternatives.

Reprise: Expected Surplus as a Practical Measure

How reasonable is the use of expected surplus as a practical benefit measure? Although social risk neutrality argues for expected surplus as the correct benefit measure, its underlying assumptions are not plausible. Somewhat more plausibly, diversification across policies argues for expected surplus as a conservative measure of benefits. That is, benefits can be no smaller than expected surplus. The pooling of individual risks among those affected by a policy argues convincingly for treatment of expected surplus as a conservative measure of benefits. Overall, these arguments suggest that when neither option prices nor option values can be estimated, and risks are individual rather than collective, analysts can reasonably use expected surplus as an approximate measure of benefits. When dealing with cases involving collective risk, they should take special care to consider the potential bias in this approach.

CONCLUSIONS

We rarely have much opportunity to infer option prices directly from observable behavior, though insurance premiums and self-protection investments may convey some useful information about people's WTP for reductions in risk. Contingent valuation surveys provide an alternative approach for directly eliciting option prices through structured conversations with respondents, but they are prone to the problems we discuss in Chapter 15. Consequently, we often have no alternative but to predict policy effects under the specified contingencies, value them with shadow price estimates from observed market behavior, and calculate expected net benefits. In cases of individual risk, it is unlikely that this procedure will result in an overestimation of net benefits. In cases of collective risk, however, these expected net benefits may either understate or overstate the conceptually correct benefits based on option price by an amount called the option value. Unfortunately, confidently signing, let alone quantifying, option price is often not possible.

APPENDIX 8A

Signing Option Value

The following table shows the progression of theoretical investigations of the sign of option value.

Study	Assumptions and Conclusions	Comments
Douglas M. Larson and Paul R. Flacco, "Measuring Option Prices from Market Behavior," *Journal of Environmental Economics and Management* 22(2) 1992, 178–198.	(1) Linear, semilog, or loglinear demand functions; uncertainty in own-price, other prices, quality, or tastes: Option value positive for normal goods; option price negative for inferior goods. (2) Linear demand, uncertainty about income, normal or inferior goods: Option value is zero. (3) Semilog or loglinear demand; uncertainty about income; normal or inferior goods: Option value is negative.	Assumption of specific functional forms for demand allow signing of option value for nonincome uncertainty. Linear demand implies risk neutrality; semilog and loglinear demands imply risk aversion for normal goods and risk seeking for inferior goods.
Richard C. Hartman and Mark L. Plummer, "Option Value under Income and Price Uncertainty," *Journal of Environmental Economics and Management* 14(3) 1987, 212–225.	(1) Uncertainty in income: Option value is negative for normal goods. (2) Uncertainty in own-price and other prices: Sign of option value is ambiguous.	General in the sense that preferences may depend on contingencies.
Mark L. Plummer and Richard C. Hartman, "Option Value: A General Approach," *Economic Inquiry* 24(3) 1986, 455–471.	(1) Uncertainty in income and risk aversion: Option value is negative for normal goods. (2) Uncertainty in quality and risk aversion: Option value is positive for normal goods. (3) Uncertainty in tastes and risk aversion: Option value ambiguous for more than two contingencies.	Sign of option value for uncertain parameter depends on signs of the changes in surplus and marginal utility with respect to the parameter.
A. Myrick Freeman III, "The Sign and Size of Option Value," *Land Economics* 60(1) 1984, 1–13.	(1) Uncertainty in demand due to exogenous factors and risk aversion: Option value is positive. (2) If probability of demand is low, expected consumer surplus is large, and person is highly risk averse, then option value may be large.	Depends on assumption that marginal utilities and attitudes toward risk independent of exogenous factors; demonstrated for only two contingencies.
Richard C. Bishop, "Option Value: An Exposition and Extension," *Land Economics* 58(1) 1982, 1–15.	(1) Uncertainty in demand: Sign of option value is ambiguous. (2) Uncertainty in supply (price uncertainty): Option value is positive.	Supply-side case demonstrated for only two contingencies.
Richard Schmalensee, "Option Demand and Consumer's Surplus: Valuing Price Changes under Uncertainty," *American Economic Review* 62(5) 1972, 813–824.	Uncertainty in demand: Sign of option value is ambiguous.	Sign depends on risk aversion and whether surplus is measured by equivalent or compensating variation.

Charles J. Cicchetti and A. Myrick Freeman III, "Option Demand and Consumer Surplus: Further Comment," *Quarterly Journal of Economics* 85(3) 1971, 528–539.

Uncertainty in demand: Option value is positive.

Overly strong assumptions imply the same utility results under each contingency.

EXERCISES FOR CHAPTER 8

1. A large rural county is considering establishing a medical transport unit that would use helicopters to fly emergency medical cases to hospitals. Analysts have attempted to estimate the benefits from establishing the unit in two ways. First, they surveyed a random sample of residents to find out how much they would be willing to pay each year for the unit. Based on responses from the sample, the analysts estimated a total willingness to pay of $8.5 million per year. Second, the analysts estimated the dollar value of the improvements in health outcomes and avoided medical costs of users of the unit to be $6.2 million per year. Taking the analysts' estimates at face value, specify the following:
   a. The aggregate of individuals' annual option prices for the unit.
   b. The annual total expected gain in social surplus from use of the unit.
   c. The annual aggregate option value for the unit.

2. Imagine that we want to value a cultural festival from the point of view of a risk-averse person. The person's utility is given by $U(I)$ where I is her income. She has a 50 percent chance of being able to get vacation time to attend the festival. If she gets the vacation time, then she would be willing to pay up to S to attend the festival. If she does not get the vacation time, then she is unwilling to pay anything for the festival.
   a. What is her expected surplus from the cultural festival?
   b. Write an expression for her expected utility if the festival does not take place.
   c. Write an expression incorporating her option price, OP, for the festival if the festival takes place. (To do this, equate her expected utility if the festival takes place to her expected utility if the festival does not take place. Also, assume that if the festival does take place, then she makes a payment of OP whether or not she is able to attend the festival.)
   d. Manipulate the expression for option price to show that the option price must be smaller than her expected surplus. (In doing this, begin by substituting $0.5S - e$ for OP in the equation derived in part c. Also keep in mind that because the person is risk averse, her marginal utility declines with income.)
   e. Does this exercise suggest any generalizations about the benefits of recreational programs when individuals are uncertain as to whether they will be able to participate in them?

3. (Spreadsheet required.) Imagine that a rancher would have an income of $80,000 if his county remains free from a cattle parasite but only $50,000 if the county is exposed to the parasite. Further imagine that a county program to limit the impact of exposure to the parasite would reduce his income to $76,000 if the county remains free of the parasite but increase it to $70,000 if the county is exposed to the parasite. Assume that there is a 60 percent chance of exposure to the parasite and that the rancher's utility is the natural logarithm of his income. What is the rancher's option price for the county program? (Set up the appropriate equation and solve through iterative guessing.)

NOTES

1. Our discussion in this section is based on Daniel A. Graham, "Cost-Benefit Analysis Under Uncertainty," *American Economic Review* 71(4) 1981, 715–725; V. Kerry Smith, "Uncertainty, Benefit-Cost Analysis, and the Treatment of Option Value," *Journal of Environmental Economics and Management* 14(3) 1987, 283–292; and Charles E. Meier and Alan Randall, "Use Value Under Uncertainty: Is There a 'Correct' Measure?" *Land Economics* 67(4) 1991, 379–389. The latter is the best overview of this topic despite a pedagogically relevant typographical error (the slope of the fair bet line is misstated in several diagrams).

2. Measuring benefits by persons' *ex ante* willingness to pay assumes that they correctly assess and process risks. Lack of information about risks, or biases in processing the information, muddies the comparison between this approach and the expectational approach if the latter involves more accurate risk assessments. For overviews, see Colin F. Camerer and Howard Kunreuther, "Decision Processes for Low Probability Risks: Policy Implications," *Journal of Policy Analysis and Management* 8(4) 1989, 565–592, and W. Kip Viscusi, *Fatal Trade-offs: Public and Private Responsibilities for Risk* (New York: Oxford University Press, 1992).

3. Formally, let m_i be the person's wealth under contingency i and let Z be an indicator of whether or not the policy under consideration is adopted ($Z = 0$ if not adopted; $Z = 1$ if adopted). The person's utility under contingency i can be written as $U(m_i, Z)$. The person's surplus (willingness to pay) for the project given that contingency i occurs, S_i, satisfies the equation:

$$U(m_i - S_i, 1) = U(m_i, 0)$$

The expected value of the person's contingent surpluses is $E(S) = p_1 S_1 = p_2 S_2$ in the case of two contingencies with probabilities p_1 and p_2, respectively.

4. Variance is defined as: $\text{Var}[X] = E\{(X - E[X])^2\}$. For a discrete random variable with possible outcomes x_i, $i = 1, 2, \ldots n$,

$$E[X] = \Sigma x_i p(x_i) \text{ and } \text{Var}[X] = \Sigma (x_i - E[X])^2 p(x_i)$$

where $p(x_i)$ is the probability of the ith outcome occurring.

In the case of the payoffs from the dam given in Table 8-1:

$$E[X] = (.5)(F110) + (.5)(100) = 105$$
$$\text{and Var}[X] = (.5)(110 - 105)^2$$
$$+ (.5)(100 - 105)^2$$
$$= 25$$

5. The intersection of the fair bet line and the certainty line corresponds to the solution of the following equations:

$$E(S) = p_1 x_1 + p_2 x_2 \text{ (expected value line)}$$
$$x_1 = x_2 \text{ (certainty line)}$$
$$p_1 = 1 - p_2$$

where x_1 defines the location of points on the vertical axis and x_2 defines the location of points on the horizontal axis. Solving these equations gives $E(S) = x$, where x is the point of intersection.

6. Two aspects of the relation among the fair bet line, the certainty line, and the willingness-to-pay locus are worth noting. First, if insurance were available in unlimited quantity at an actuarially fair price, then the person could actually move from any point on the willingness-to-pay locus along the fair bet line to the certainty line by buying insurance. The near consensus that option price is the appropriate benefit measure is based on the reasonable assumption that complete and actuarially fair insurance markets generally do not exist in the real world. Second, a fair bet line can be drawn through any point. Thus, for example, if we wanted to know which point on the willingness-to-pay locus has the largest expected value, then we would find the point that is just tangent to a fair bet line.

7. Continuing with the notation from note 3, points on the willingness-to-pay locus, (w_1, w_2), satisfy the following equation:

$$p_1 U_1(m_1 - w_1, 1) + p_2 U_2(m_2 - w_2, 1) = EU$$

where $EU = p_1 U_1(m_1, 0) + p_2 U_2(m_2, 0)$ is the person's expected utility without the project.

8. For a general introduction to the theory of insurance, see Isaac Ehrlich and Gary S. Becker, "Market Insurance, Self-Insurance, and Self-Protection," *Journal of Political Economy* 80(4) 1972, 663–648.

9. Mark V. Pauly, "The Economics of Moral Hazard: Comment," *American Economic Review* 58(3) 1968, 531–537.

10. Philip J. Cook and Daniel A. Graham, "The Demand for Insurance and Protection: The Case of Irreplaceable Commodities," *Quarterly Journal of Economics* 91(1) 1977, 141–156.

11. One way to get high-risk persons to reveal themselves is to offer two insurance options: one that gives full coverage at a premium that is actuarially fair for high risks and another that gives only limited coverage at a premium that is actuarially fair for low risks. If the level of coverage under the latter option is sufficiently low, then high risks will be better off revealing themselves to get the full coverage. The result is a so-called *separating equilibrium* in which both risk groups honestly reveal themselves. The information is gained, however, at the cost of limiting coverage to low-risk persons. See Michael Rothschild and Joseph Stiglitz, "Equilibrium in Competitive Insurance Markets: An Essay on the Economics of Imperfect Information," *Quarterly Journal of Economics* 90(4) 1976, 629–650. An extension of the Rothschild-Stiglitz model, which incorporates contracting costs, allows for the possibility that low-risk persons receive more favorable coverage. See Joseph P. Newhouse, "Reimbursing Health Plans and Health Providers: Efficiency in Production Versus Selection," *Journal of Economic Literature* 34(3) 1996, 1236–1263.

12. J. David Cummins, "Statistical and Financial Models of Insurance Pricing and the Insurance Firm," *Journal of Risk and Insurance* 58(2) 1991, 261–301.

13. Jack Hirshleifer and John G. Riley, *The Analytics of Uncertainty and Information* (New York: Cambridge University Press, 1992).

14. The difference between $E[FB^*]$ and $E[S]$ is called the *option premium*. Unlike option value, it is always nonnegative. See Dennis C. Cory and Bonnie Colby Saliba, "Requiem for Option Value," *Land Economics* 63(1) 1987, 1–10. Unfortunately, the extreme assumptions of complete and actuarially fair insurance, knowledge of the entire willingness-to-pay locus, and the feasibility of contingent-specific payments give the notion of option premium little practical relevance to CBA.

15. Burton A. Weisbrod, "Collective Consumption Services of Individual Consumption Goods," *Quarterly Journal of Economics* 78(3) 1964, 71–77.

16. The possibility of double counting benefits with this formulation was soon pointed out by Millard F. Long, "Collective-Consumption Services of Individual-Consumption Goods," *Quarterly Journal of Economics* 81(2) 1967, 351–352.

17. Charles J. Cicchetti and A. Myrick Freeman III, "Option Demand and Consumer Surplus: Further Comment," *Quarterly Journal of Economics* 85(3) 1971, 528–539.

18. Richard Schmalensee, "Option Demand and Consumer's Surplus: Valuing Price Changes under Uncertainty," *American Economic Review* 62(5) 1972, 813–824. Robert Anderson later showed that the contradictory results arose because of additional assumptions made by Cicchetti and Freeman that had the unattractive consequence of guaranteeing the option buyer a certain utility level no matter which contingency arose. Robert J. Anderson Jr., "A Note on Option Value and the Expected Value of Consumer's Surplus," *Journal of Environmental Economics and Management* 8(2) 1981, 187–191.

19. Douglas M. Larson and Paul R. Flacco, "Measuring Option Prices from Market Behavior," *Journal of Environmental Economics and Management* 22(2) 1992, 178–198.

20. Larson and Flacco, "Measuring Option Prices from Market Behavior." As discussed in Chapter 13, empirical estimation of demand equations usually involves at least income and own-price as explanatory variables for quantity. If the sign of the estimated coefficient of income is positive (negative), then the good is normal (inferior).

21. V. Kerry Smith, "A Bound for Option Value," *Land Economics* 60(3) 1984, 292–296.

22. Their expressions require not only estimates of the parameters of the demand equations, but also fairly complicated expectations over the parameters that are treated as uncertain.

23. To say that society is risk neutral implies that there is a social welfare function that ranks alternative distributions of goods among individuals. That is, it gives a "score" to each possible distribution such that a distribution with a higher score is preferred by society to a distribution with a lower score. Aggregation of individual preferences, however, cannot guarantee a social welfare function that satisfies minimally desirable properties as noted in Chapter 2. Again, see Tibor Scitovsky, "The State of Welfare Economics," *American Economic Review* 51(3) 1951, 301–315. More generally, see Kenneth J. Arrow, *Social Choice and Individual Values*, 2nd ed. (New Haven, CT: Yale University Press, 1963).

24. Kenneth J. Arrow and Robert C. Lind, "Uncertainty and the Evaluation of Public Investment Decisions," *American Economic Review* 60(3) 1970, 364–378.

Existence Value

Within the CBA framework, people's willingness to pay (WTP) for a policy change comprehensively measures its social benefits. Though analysts sometimes elicit willingness-to-pay amounts through contingent valuation surveys (see Chapter 15), they prefer to make inferences about them from observations of people's behaviors (see Chapters 12, 13, and 14). Observed changes in consumption of a good whose price or quantity is affected by the policy change allow WTP to be estimated. For many, perhaps most, applications of CBA, analysts can reasonably assume that such estimates capture the entire WTP. Yet in some applications of CBA, especially those involving changes to unique environmental resources, people may be willing to pay for the existence of "goods" that they themselves will never actually "consume." Correctly conceptualizing and measuring such *existence values* poses a challenge to the application of CBA.

In this chapter, we consider existence value as an additional category of benefit. It is often grouped with option value and quasi-option value under the heading of *nonuse* or *passive use* benefits. As discussed in Chapters 7 and 8, however, option and quasi-option values are better thought of as adjustments to standard benefit measures to take account of various aspects of uncertainty rather than as distinct categories of benefits. In contrast, existence value is another meaningful benefit category, though one that poses problems of definition and measurement.[1] After framing existence value as a special benefit category, we discuss the theoretical and empirical problems analysts face in measuring it.

ACTIVE AND PASSIVE USE VALUE

The notion that people may place a value on the very existence of "unique phenomena of nature" that they neither visit, nor ever anticipate visiting, was introduced into the CBA literature almost 30 years ago by John V. Krutilla.[2] Consider, for example, a unique wilderness area. Hunters might be willing to pay to preserve the area because it either lowers the price of or increases the quality of hunting. Naturalists might be willing to pay to preserve the area because it provides a desirable area for hiking or bird-watching. Nearby residents may be willing to pay to preserve the area because they enjoy its scenic beauty and it prevents commercial development that they find undesirable. People who enjoy nature films may be willing to pay to preserve the area because it provides a unique setting for filming rare species. All of these people value the area because they make use of it in some way. Yet one can imagine that some people might be willing to pay to preserve the area even though they do not use it in any of these ways. In commonly used terminology, these people are said to derive *nonuse value* from the wilderness area. Note that while it might make sense to think about these people as additional people, they may not be, that is, some people may derive both use value and nonuse value from an asset.

While most economists accept the general idea that people may derive value from mere knowledge of the existence of unique assets such as scenic wilderness, animal species, or works of art, clearly defining nonuse value is a complicated issue, and there is not yet a clear consensus on its precise meaning.

One complication is the difficulty of drawing a sharp line between use and nonuse. In terms of standard consumer theory, any good that a person values is an argument in his or her utility function. The good need not involve any observable activity by the person to secure its value. The quantity of a pure public good such as national defense, for instance, is "consumed" by individuals, however passively. Existence value can also be thought of as a pure public good.[3] It is nonrivalrous—the value one person derives from it does not diminish the values derived by others. It is nonexcludable—no one can be excluded from deriving value from the quantity of the good, which is provided commonly to all. Viewed as a public good, it seems more appropriate to describe existence value as *passive use* rather than nonuse.

Yet, how passive must the "consumption" be in order to distinguish use from nonuse? It is probably safe to say that merely thinking about the good does not constitute use as the term is commonly understood. What about discussing the good with other people? Consumption now involves observable behavior, the consumption of a complementary good, time, but most economists would probably consider it nonuse. Consuming films and photography books based on the good, however, probably crosses the line between use and nonuse because it leaves a behavioral trace in the markets for these complementary goods. These distinctions hinge not just on the intrinsic attributes of the good, but also on our ability to observe and value behavior. Thus, in actual application, distinguishing between use and nonuse is not just a purely conceptual issue.

A second complication, which we consider in more detail in Appendix 9A, arises because individuals derive both use and nonuse value from a given asset. A person's WTP for preservation of a wilderness area may be motivated by the anticipation of hunting *and* the pleasure of knowing that future generations will be able to enjoy it as well. While the person's total WTP, or as it is often called in this context *total economic value,* is conceptually clear, the division between these two categories of value is ambiguous because the order of valuation is generally relevant. One ordering is to elicit first the person's WTP for use and then, taking this amount as actually paid, to elicit the person's WTP for nonuse. The other possible ordering is to elicit first the person's WTP for nonuse and then, taking this amount as actually paid, elicit the person's WTP for use. The orderings should yield the same total WTP, but they probably will yield different values for use and nonuse. Obviously, the ordering problem blurs the boundary between use and nonuse.

A third complication has to do with differences in the way quantity changes affect use and nonuse benefits. In general, nonuse benefits tend to be less quantity sensitive than use benefits. For example, consider a species of mammal that will remain viable as long as its population exceeds 20,000. Someone may very well have a nonuse value for the existence of this species that is the same for total populations of either 25,000 or 25 million because either level of population is large enough to avoid extinction. Hikers who wish to see this species in its natural habitat, however, may have a use value that is substantially higher for a larger population because it offers a greater likelihood of an encounter with the species.

Finally, the nonuse category raises issues of motivation that are typically avoided by economists. If nonuse does not leave a behavioral trace, then its value can normally only be discovered empirically through stated rather than revealed preferences, in other words, by contingent valuation surveys, which are discussed in Chapter 15. Sometimes economists may be able to find behavioral traces outside of normal market transactions. For example, especially at the local level, binding referenda on the provision of public goods are sometimes held. By relating percentages of affirmative votes to district-level property values or incomes, it may be possible to make inferences about WTP. Nonetheless, most empirical estimates of nonuse values rely on stated rather than revealed preferences.

A theory about the motivations behind nonuse value can help guide the formulation and interpretation of questions for eliciting stated preferences. For example, a possible motivation for nonuse value is altruism toward either current people or future generations. Yet, it makes a difference whether the altruism is either individualistic or paternalistic. A concern about the general utility levels of others can be described as *individualistic altruism;* a concern about the consumption of specific goods by others is *paternalistic altruism.* For example, giving money to homeless alcoholics is consistent with individualistic altruism, while contributing to a program that gives them only meals is consistent with paternalistic altruism. If the analyst believes that individualistic altruism is the motivation for existence value, then it is important that respondents be given sufficient context to understand the implications of provision of the good on the overall wealth of others. Because the targets of altruism generally bear some share of the costs of the provided goods, individualistic altruism generally results in lower existence values than paternalistic altruism.[4] For example, altruism might motivate someone to want to bequeath the current world climate to subsequent generations. If the altruism is paternalistic rather than altruistic, then, in determining WTP for current policies, the person ignores the possibility that members of future generations might prefer some climate change and a higher endowment of capital to no climate change and a lower endowment of capital.

With these caveats in mind, we present Table 9-1 as a way of thinking about existence value as a benefit category within the broader framework of benefit categories.[5] The distinction between use benefit and nonuse benefit partially reflects our ability to measure them.

Consider first benefits that arise from active use of a good. The most obvious benefit category is *rivalrous consumption* of goods, such as trees for wood products, water for irrigation, and grasslands for cattle grazing. As markets usually exist for rivalrous goods, they are the category most amenable to valuation through the estimation of demand schedules and consumer surplus.

The other use categories are for nonrivalrous goods. Those consumed onsite, such as hiking and bird-watching that do not interfere with other users or uses, are labeled *direct nonrivalrous consumption.* Though rarely traded in markets, such goods often can be valued by observing the travel and time costs people are willing to bear to consume

TABLE 9-1 Taxonomy of Benefits: Possible Partitioning of WTP

Type of Use	Benefit Category	Example
Active Use	Rivalrous consumption	Logging of old-growth forest
	Nonrivalrous consumption: direct	Hiking in wilderness
	Nonrivalrous consumption: indirect	Watching a film of wilderness area
Passive Use (nonuse)	Option value	Possibility of visiting wilderness area in the future
	Pure existence value: good has intrinsic value	Perceived value of natural order
	Altruistic existence value: gift to current generation	Others hiking in wilderness
	Altruistic existence value: bequest to future generation	Future others hiking in wilderness

them (see Chapter 14.) In alternative taxonomies of benefits, this category is sometimes labeled *nondestructive consumption*.

Indirect nonrivalrous consumption takes place offsite. For example, a person may derive value from watching a film about wildlife in a particular wilderness area. Expenditures of time and money on offsite nonrivalrous consumption provide some information for estimating its value, though much less reliably than for the other use categories.

Consider next passive use benefits. Four categories can be distinguished in terms of motivation. The first category, *option value,* was discussed in Chapter 8. It is the amount that someone is willing to pay to keep open the option of use, active or passive, in the future. It is only passive in the sense that it would not be fully captured by estimates of WTP based on observations of active use.

The other categories pertain to different types of existence value. The second category, *pure existence value,* arises because people believe the good has intrinsic value apart from its use. For example, some people might be willing to pay to preserve a wilderness area because they think that it is right that some natural habitats exist for rare animal species.

The remaining two categories are based on altruism. Some people may be willing to pay to preserve a wilderness area, for example, because they get pleasure from knowing that it is used by others. Generally, the motivation for such *altruistic existence value* is paternalistic in the sense that it is driven by the desire for others to consume this particular good, rather than by the desire to increase their consumption overall. It may be based on the belief that exposure to nature, art, or historical sites is intrinsically good or perhaps on the desire to share with others a type of experience one has found to be emotionally enriching. When the altruism is directed toward future generations, the good is said to have a *bequest value*. People get pleasure from knowing that those not yet born will be able to use (and not use!) the good. Just as people often wish to leave their children a share of the wealth they have accumulated, they may want to bequeath them access to unique goods as well.

The distribution of benefits across these categories obviously depends on the specific attributes of the project being evaluated. By their very nature, projects involving the conservation of wilderness areas are likely to derive a high fraction of their benefits from nonuse values. For example, based on survey data, K. G. Willis estimated existence values for three nature sites of special scientific interest in Great Britain.[6] Consumer surplus associated with use of the sites appeared to account for only about 10 to 12 percent of people's total WTP. Option value accounted for a comparable percentage. The remaining portion of WTP consisted of existence (pure and bequest) value. Only if the nonuse benefits were included did conservation of these areas appear to have positive net benefits.

THE MEASUREMENT OF EXISTENCE VALUE

Despite the difficulty economists have in clearly defining existence value as a benefit category, few economists would deny that sometimes people are willing to pay a total amount for the preservation of assets that exceeds their WTP for their use or anticipated possible future use. Yet, some economists believe that the method of measurement currently available, the contingent value survey, lacks sufficient reliability for existence values to be reasonably included in CBA. Because we consider contingent valuation in detail in Chapter 15, our discussion here raises only the general issues most relevant to the measurement of existence value.

Directly Eliciting Total Economic Value

One way to avoid some of the conceptual problems in defining existence value is to measure WTP for a policy change holistically rather than disaggregating it into component parts. In the context of contingent valuation, the analyst poses questions aimed at getting respondents to state their WTP amounts based on consideration of *all* their possible motivations for valuing policy changes. The total economic value revealed through this *structured conversation* is each respondent's benefit from the policy change.

The viability of this approach obviously depends on the analyst's ability to structure a meaningful conversation. The analyst must convey a full description of the policy effect being valued. Considerably more context must be provided in the valuation of effects on passive than active use. People typically know their own current levels of use as a starting point for valuing marginal changes. They are less likely to know the total stock of a good that has nonuse value to them. Yet their valuation of marginal changes in the good is likely to depend on how much they think is currently available. For example, people who think that a particular species lives only in one particular wilderness area are likely to place a much higher value on the preservation of that area than if they knew that the species lived in several other already protected areas. Indeed, one can imagine that, given enough information and time for reflection, some people may place a zero or negative value on the existence of more of some good when its quantity is above some threshold. One may place a negative value on policies that increase the number of deer in an area if, for instance, their number is already so large as to threaten the survival of other species.

Existence value based on altruism poses special problems. When individuals are concerned only about their own consumption, it is reasonable to separate costs from benefits. Each can be estimated separately and combined to find net benefits. Altruistic

EXHIBIT 9-1

Public opinion and economic analysis frequently conflict in the evaluation of public subsidies for the construction and operation of stadiums for professional sports teams. Valid CBAs of sports stadiums based only on use benefits almost never find positive social net benefits, especially if conducted from the national perspective. One possible exception is the baseball stadium built for the Baltimore Orioles at Camden Yards, which appears to have increased average attendance from 30 thousand to 45 thousand per game. Further, approximately 70 percent of the increase in attendance consists of residents from outside Maryland, suggesting the possibility of positive net benefits if the CBA were conducted from a state rather than a national perspective.

Bruce W. Hamilton and Peter Kahn conducted a detailed CBA from the perspective of the residents of Maryland. They reported the following annual benefits and costs:

Annual Benefits:		$3.36 million
Job creation	$0.48 million	
Out-of-stadium incremental taxes	$1.25 million	
Incremental admission tax	$1.20 million	
Sales tax on incremental stadium spending	$0.43 million	
Annual Costs:		$14.00 million
Annual Net Benefits:		$10.64 million

The net cost of the stadium to Maryland taxpayers is $10.64 million per year, which is equivalent to about $14.20 per Baltimore household per year. Hamilton and Kahn note that building the stadium was probably necessary to keep the Orioles from eventually moving to another city, and that citizens of Maryland, even if they never attend Orioles games, may place a value on the stadium because they get pleasure from simply having the Orioles in Baltimore. Hamilton and Kahn call these values "public consumption benefits," which can be thought of as passive use benefits, consisting of some combination of option value and existence value. Only if the annual value of public consumption benefits exceed $10.64 million would Oriole Park at Camden Yards pass the net benefits test.

Source: Adapted from Bruce W. Hamilton and Peter Kahn, "Baltimore's Camden Yards Ballparks," in Roger G. Noll and Andrew Zimbalist, eds., *Sports, Jobs, and Taxes: The Economic Impact of Sports Teams and Stadiums* (Washington, D.C.: The Brookings Institution, 1997), 245–281. Corrections to original provided by Bruce W. Hamilton.

values, however, may depend on the distribution of both costs and benefits. Respondents thus need to know who is likely to use the good being valued and who is likely to bear the costs of preserving it. Failure to include the latter may inflate existence values if it leads to respondents not taking into account all the effects on others.

Let us assume that these concerns, along with the more general problems of contingent valuation discussed in Chapter 15, are adequately addressed so that analysts can be confident that they have correctly elicited individuals' total economic value for the policy change under consideration. If their sample of respondents included all the people with standing, then these total valuations would suffice for completing the CBA. Often, however, analysts wish to combine benefits estimated from behavioral data with existence value estimates from a relatively small sample drawn from people with standing. As already noted, partitioning respondents' total WTP into use and nonuse values is sensitive to the ordering of categories. If nonuse values from the sample are to be added to use values estimated by other methods to get total economic benefits, then it is important that questions be asked so as to elicit nonuse values after respondents have considered and reported their use values.

In contrast to use, nonuse does not occur in easily defined geographic markets. Aggregate existence values are very sensitive to the geographic assumptions made in extrapolating from survey samples to the population with standing.[7] People appear to place a higher existence value on resources in closer proximity.[8] Using average existence values estimated from local samples to obtain aggregate existence values for a more geographically extensive population may be inappropriate. Indeed, the question of geographic extrapolation appears to be one of the most controversial aspects of the use of existence values in damage assessment cases.[9]

As a final point, note that as long as the structured conversation leads respondents to consider all the sources of uncertainty relevant to their valuation of the policy change, their total WTP amount is an option price. It is thus fully inclusive of option value so that no adjustments for uncertainty are required.

Behavioral Traces of Existence Value?

Many economists would be more comfortable measuring existence value through the observation of related behavior. As a pure public good, however, its behavioral trace is likely to be so weak that considerable ingenuity will be required to find ways of measuring it through nonconversational methods. Nevertheless, the history of the development of increasingly sophisticated methods for measuring benefits offers some hope that a way will be found.

Bruce Madariaga and Kenneth McConnell suggest one line of investigation.[10] They note that people are willing to pay to join such organizations as the Nature Conservancy and the Audubon Society. Some part of their membership fees can be thought of as voluntary contributions for a public good, the preservation of wilderness areas. Ways of making inferences about existence values from the patterns of contributions to such organizations have yet to be developed. Doing so is complicated by the problem of *free riding*—some who benefit from the public good will not voluntarily contribute to its provision.

More sophisticated models of individual utility may also provide some leverage on the measurement of existence value. Douglas Larson notes that public goods are sometimes complements of, or substitutes for, private goods.[11] If investigators are willing to impose assumptions about the form of the demand for market goods and the nature of the complementarity between market goods and existence values, then they may be able to make inferences about the magnitudes of the existence values from observation of the consumption of the market goods. Larson also suggests that explicitly treating time as a constraint in utility maximization may open up possibilities for measurement based on people's allocations of time. For example, the time people spend watching films or reading books about habitats of endangered species might, with sufficient cleverness, provide a basis for estimating their existence values for the habitats.

Should Existence Value Be Included in CBA?

A growing number of efforts to estimate existence values through surveys can be found in the literature.[12] The particular estimates are often controversial.[13]

Should existence values be used in CBA? The answer requires a balancing of conceptual and practical concerns. On the one hand, recognizing existence values as pure public goods argues for their inclusion. On the other hand, given the current state of practice, estimates of existence values are very uncertain. This trade-off suggests the following heuristic: *Although existence values for unique and long-lived assets should be estimated whenever possible, costs and benefits should be presented with and without their inclusion to make clear how they affect net benefits.* When existence values for such assets cannot be measured, analysts should supplement CBA with discussion of their possible significance for the sign of net benefits.

CONCLUSION

As CBA is increasingly applied to environmental policies, concern about existence values among analysts will almost certainly grow. Unless methods of measurement improve substantially, however, deciding when and how to include existence values in CBA will continue to be difficult. By being aware of the limitations of these methods, analysts can be better producers and consumers of CBA.

Expenditure Functions and the Partitioning of Benefits

Policies that have multiple effects pose conceptual problems for the aggregation of benefits. In most situations, we approximate willingness-to-pay by summing the changes in social surplus associated with each of the effects. In general, however, this procedure tends to overestimate total economic value (*TEV*). In this appendix, we introduce some notation for formally representing the measurement of utility changes from policies with multiple effects with expenditure functions, an analytical approach commonly used in more theoretical treatments of social welfare.[1] A stylized numerical example follows to show the ambiguity in the partitioning of benefits among the various effects.

Imagine that a person has a budget B and also has a utility function U that depends on the quantities of goods $X_1, X_2, \ldots, X_n$. Assume that the prices of these goods are $p_1, p_2, \ldots, p_n$, respectively. The problem facing the consumer is to choose the quantities of the goods that maximize U such that $p_1 X_1 + p_2 X_2 + \ldots + p_n X_n \leq B$. Let U^* be the maximum utility that the person can obtain given B and the prices of the goods. We can construct an expenditure function, $e(p_1, p_2, \ldots, p_n; U^*)$, which is defined as the minimum dollar amount of budget necessary to obtain utility U^* at the given prices. Obviously, for the original set of prices that we used to find U^*, $e(p_1, p_2, \ldots, p_n; U^*) = B$.

Assume that we instituted a policy that *increased* the price of the first good from p_1 to q_1. Associated with this new price is the expenditure function $e(q_1, p_2, \ldots, p_n; U^*) = B'$, where B' is greater than B because the person must be given more budget to keep the utility equal to U^* in the face of the higher price. A measure of the consumer surplus loss from the price increase is given by:

$$e(q_1, p_2, \ldots, p_n; U^*) - e(p_1, p_2, \ldots, p_n; U^*)$$

which equals $B' - B$. This amount equals the compensating variation for the price change as discussed in the appendix to Chapter 3.[2]

Imagine now that X_1 and X_2 are goods, perhaps existence value and hiking, provided to the person by a particular wilderness area. How would we use the expenditure function to value the wilderness area, given the original budget and set of prices?

We want to know how much compensation we would have to give to the person to restore his or her utility level to U^* after making X_1 and X_2 equal zero. In terms of the expenditure function, we do this by setting p_1 and p_2 sufficiently high so that the person's demand for X_1 and X_2 is "choked off" at zero quantities. Assume that p_{1c} and p_{2c} choke off demand. To get the *TEV* of the wilderness area to the individual, we calculate how much additional budget we would have to give the person to return him or her to the original utility level:

$$\begin{aligned} TEV = {} & e(p_{1c}, p_{2c}, \ldots, p_n; U^*) \\ & - e(p_1, p_2, \ldots, p_n; U^*) \end{aligned}$$

which is an unambiguous and correct measure of the person's willingness-to-pay for the wilderness area.

Now consider how we might partition *TEV* into its two components associated with X_1 and X_2. One way would be to first value X_1 and then X_2. We can express this by adding and subtracting $e(p_1, p_{2c}, \ldots, p_n; U^*)$ to the equation for *TEV* to get the following equation:

$$\begin{aligned} TEV = {} & [e(p_{1c}, p_{2c}, \ldots, p_n; U^*) \\ & - e(p_1, p_{2c}, \ldots, p_n; U^*)] \\ & + [e(p_1, p_{2c}, \ldots, p_n; U^*) \\ & - e(p_1, p_2, \ldots, p_n; U^*)] \end{aligned}$$

where the first line represents the WTP to obtain X_1 at price p_1 and the second line represents the WTP to obtain subsequently X_2 at price p_2.

The other possible partition is to first restore X_2 at price p_2 and then restore X_1 at price p_1. It is expressed by the following equation:

$$
\begin{aligned}
TEV = &[e(p_{1c}, p_{2c}, \ldots, p_n; U^*) \\
&- e(p_{1c}, p_2, \ldots, p_n; U^*)] \\
&+ [e(p_{1c}, p_2, \ldots, p_n; U^*) \\
&- e(p_1, p_2, \ldots, p_n; U^*)]
\end{aligned}
$$

where the first line represents the WTP to obtain X_2 at price p_2 and the second line represents the WTP to subsequently obtain X_1 at price p_1.

These alternative partitionings generally will not yield the same WTP amounts for X_1 and X_2. Typically, the WTP for a good will be greater if the good is introduced in the partitioning sequence earlier rather than later. The rough intuition behind this result is that a good will be relatively less valuable at the margin if it is added to an already full bundle of goods.

If one can measure *TEV* directly, then this ambiguity in partitioning is of little concern.[3] In most circumstances, however, analysts attempt to construct *TEV* from independent estimates of separate benefit categories. In terms of expenditure functions, what is commonly done can be expressed as follows:

$$
\begin{aligned}
TB = &[e(p_{1c}, p_{2c}, \ldots, p_n; U^*) \\
&- e(p_1, p_{2c}, \ldots, p_n; U^*)] \\
&+ [e(p_{1c}, p_{2c}, \ldots, p_n; U^*) \\
&- e(p_{1c}, p_2, \ldots, p_n; U^*)]
\end{aligned}
$$

where the first line is the compensating variation for making only X_1 available, the second line is the compensating variation for making only X_2 available, and *TB* is the total estimated benefits. In general, *TB* does not equal *TEV*. *TB* systematically overestimates *TEV*. The overestimation tends to increase as the number of benefit components increases.[4]

We next illustrate these concepts with the stylized numerical example presented in Table 9A-1. The model assumes that the person's utility, U, depends on three goods: E, the size of the wilderness area (existence); X, a particular use of the wilderness area such as hiking; and Z, a composite good that represents all goods other than E and X. It also depends on the parameter Q, an index of the quality of the wilderness area. The person has a budget of $B = 100$ and faces prices for E, X, and Z of $p_e = \$.50, p_x = \$1$, and $p_z = \$2$, respectively.[5] The quantities of E, X, and Z that maximize utility for the parameter values listed in the table can be found through numerical methods to be $E = 9.89$, $X = 30.90$, and $Z = 32.08$.[6] The utility from this combination of goods, U^*, equals 38.93.

The expenditure function follows directly. Obviously, the budget that gives $U^* = 38.93$ is just the budget of \$100 in the optimization. Therefore, we can write the expenditure function for the initial position as:

$$
e(p_e = 0.5, p_x = 1, p_z = 2; Q = 1;
$$
$$
U^* = 38.93) = 100
$$

Before illustrating the partitioning problem, it may be helpful to consider how expenditure functions can be used to find compensating variations for independent policy effects. Consider, for instance, how one can find the compensating variation for a reduction in the price of X from \$1 to \$.50. The procedure involves finding the expenditure function:

$$
e(p_e = 0.5, p_x = 0.5, p_z = 2;
$$
$$
Q = 1; U^* = 38.93) = 63.25
$$

by asking what budget amount would allow the person to obtain the original utility at the lower price. The compensating variation for the price reduction is just the difference between the values of the expenditure function with the lower price, \$63.25, and the value of the original expenditure function, \$100. That is, the person would be indifferent between facing the original price of \$1 with a budget of

TABLE 9A-1 An Illustration of the Benefits Partitioning Problem

Utility function	$U(E, X, Z; Q) = QE^\gamma + QX^\beta + Z^\theta$ where E is the quantity of wilderness that exists, X is the use level of the wilderness, Z is a market good, and Q is an index of quality of the wilderness
Budget constraint	$B = p_e E + p_x X + p_z Z$ where B is the available budget, and p_e, p_x, and p_z are the respective prices of E, X, and Z
Optimization problem	Maximize $L = U + \lambda [B - p_e E - p_x X - p_z Z]$ where λ is the marginal utility of money
Numerical assumptions	$Q = 1; \gamma = 0.5; \beta = 0.75; q = 0.9; p_e = 0.5; p_x = 1; p_z = 2; B = 100$ $E = 9.89; X = 30.90; Z = 32.08; \lambda = .318$
Solution values	$U(9.89, 30.90, 32.08; 1) = 38.93 = U^*$ $e(p_e, p_x, p_z; Q; U^*) = e(0.5, 1, 2; 1; 38.93) = 100$
Expenditure functions	Wilderness area not available: $e(\infty, \infty, 2; 1; 38.93) = 116.95$ Wilderness existence, no use: $e(0.5, \infty, 2; 1; 38.93) = 111.42$ Wilderness use only: $e(\infty, 1, 2; 1; 38.93) = 105.04$
Existence-use partition *TEV = 16.95*	Existence value $= e(\infty, \infty, 2; 1; 38.93) - e(0.5, \infty, 2; 1; 38.93)$ $\qquad = 116.95 - 111.42 = 5.53$ Use value $= e(0.5, \infty, 2; 1; 38.93) - e(0.5, 1, 2; 1; 38.93)$ $\qquad = 111.42 - 100 = 11.42$
Use-existence partition *TEV = 16.95*	Use value $= e(\infty, \infty, 2; 1; 38.93) - e(\infty, 1, 2; 1; 38.93)$ $\qquad = 116.95 - 105.04 = 11.91$ Existence value $= e(\infty, 1, 2; 1; 38.93) - e(0.5, 1, 2; 1; 38.93)$ $\qquad = 105.04 - 100 = 5.04$
Independent summation *TB = 17.44*	Existence value $= e(\infty, \infty, 2; 1; 38.93) - e(0.5, \infty, 2; 1; 38.93)$ $\qquad = 116.95 - 111.42 = 5.53$ Use value $= e(\infty, \infty, 2; 1; 38.93) - e(\infty, 1, 2; 1; 38.93)$ $\qquad = 116.95 - 105.04 = 11.91$

$100 and facing the reduced price of $.50 with a budget of $63.25. Therefore, the willingness-to-pay for the price reduction is the difference between $100 and $63.25, or $36.75.

Now consider how one could value a policy that would increase the quality index, Q, by 10 percent. The expenditure function for the quality improvement relative to the initial position is:

$$e(p_e = 0.5, p_x = 1, p_z = 2; Q = 1.1;$$
$$U^* = 38.93) = 94.45$$

which indicates that the compensating variation for the quality improvement is −$5.55 ($94.45 − $100), indicating that the original utility could be obtained with a smaller budget.

Returning to the initial position, let us now consider the total value of wilderness, TEV, and the two ways of partitioning it between existence and use. We choke off consumption of E and X by setting their prices at infinity. This yields the expenditure function:

$$e(p_e = \infty, p_x = \infty, p_z = 2; Q = 1;$$
$$U^* = 38.93) = 116.95$$

which implies that the wilderness area has a total value of $16.95 ($116.95 − $100). If we partition first by existence and then by use, we calculate:

$$e(p_e = 0.5, px = \infty, p_z = 2;$$
$$Q = 1; U^* = 38.93) = 111.42$$

which implies an existence value of $5.53 ($116.95 − $111.42) and a use value of $11.42 ($111.42 − $100).[7] If instead we partition first by use and then by existence, we calculate:

$$e(p_e = \infty, p_x = 1, p_z = 2; Q = 1;$$
$$U^* = 38.93) = 105.04$$

which implies a use value of $11.91 ($116.95 − $105.04) and an existence value of $5.04 ($105.04 − $100).[8] Thus, we see that the sequence of valuation makes a difference: Existence value and use value are each larger when they are valued first rather than second.[9]

Finally, consider the independent summation of benefits. Existence is valued as in the existence-use sequence and use is valued as in the use-existence sequence. Thus, we would estimate the total economic value of the wilderness to be $17.44 ($5.53 + $11.91), which exceeds the correct compensating variation by $.49 ($17.44 − $16.95).

In summary, the partitioning of benefits between existence and use is conceptually ambiguous when the same individuals derive both values from a policy change. More generally, policies that affect people's utilities in multiple ways are prone to overestimation of WTP when each effect is valued independently as a separate benefit category.

EXERCISES FOR CHAPTER 9

1. Imagine a wilderness area of 200 square miles in the Rocky Mountains. How would you expect each of the following factors to affect people's total WTP for its preservation?
   a. The size of the total wilderness area still remaining in the Rocky Mountains
   b. The presence of rare species in this particular area
   c. The level of national wealth
2. An analyst wishing to estimate the benefits of preserving a wetland has combined information obtained from two methods. First, she surveyed those who visited the wetland—fishers, duck hunters, and bird-watchers—to determine their WTP for these uses. Second, she surveyed a sample of residents throughout the state about their WTP to preserve the wetland. This second survey focused exclusively on nonuse values of the wetland. She then added her estimate of use benefits to her estimate of nonuse benefits to get an estimate of the total economic value of preservation of the wetland. Is this a reasonable approach? (Note: In responding to this question assume that there was virtually no overlap in the persons contacted in the two surveys.)

NOTES

1. Put another way, and in the context of the discussion in Chapter 8, existence value is part of option value. That is, option value includes use value and nonuse value. We simply ignored existence value in Chapter 8.
2. John V. Krutilla, "Conservation Reconsidered," *American Economic Review* 57(4) 1967, 777–786 at 784. For a discussion of the importance of this article, see V. Kerry Smith, "Krutilla's Legacy: Twenty-First Century Challenges for Environmental Economics," *American Journal of Agricultural Economics* 86(5) 2004, 1167–1178.
3. Charles Plourde, "Conservation of Extinguishable Species," *Natural Resources Journal* 15(4) 1975, 791–797.
4. Bruce Madariaga and Kenneth E. McConnell, "Exploring Existence Value," *Water Resources Research* 23(5) 1987, 936–942.
5. For an alternative framework, see R. Kerry Turner, Jouni Paavola, Philip Cooper, Stephen Farber, Valma Jessamy, and Stavros Georgiou, "Valuing Nature: Lessons Learned and Future Research Directions," *Ecological Economics* 46(3) 2003, 493–510 at 495 (Table 1).

6. K. G. Willis, "Valuing Non-Market Wildlife Commodities: An Evaluation and Comparison of Benefits and Costs," *Applied Economics* 22(1) 1990, 12–30.

7. For an overview, see V. Kerry Smith, "Nonmarket Valuation of Environmental Resources," *Land Economics* 69(1) 1993, 1–26.

8. Ronald J. Sutherland and Richard G. Walsh, "The Effect of Distance on the Preservation Value of Water Quality," *Land Economics* 61(3) 1985, 281–291; and Ian J. Bateman and Ian H. Langford, "Non-Users' Willingness to Pay for a National Park: An Application and Critique of the Contingent Valuation Method," *Regional Studies* 31(6) 1997, 571–582.

9. Raymond J. Kopp and V. Kerry Smith, "Benefit Estimation Goes to Court: The Case of Natural Resource Damage Assessment," *Journal of Policy Analysis and Management* 8(4) 1989, 593–612.

10. Bruce Madariaga and Kenneth E. McConnell, "Exploring Existence Value," *Water Resources Research* 23(5) 1987, 936–942.

11. Douglas M. Larson, "On Measuring Existence Value," *Land Economics* 69(1) 1992, 116–122.

12. Richard G. Walsh, John B. Loomis, and Richard A. Gillman, "Valuing Option, Existence, and Bequest Demands for Wilderness," *Land Economics* 60(1) 1984, 14–29; K. G. Willis, "Valuing Non-Market Wildlife Commodities: An

Evaluation and Comparison of Benefits and Costs," *Applied Economics* 22(1) 1990, 13–30; Thomas H. Stevens, Jaime Echeverria, Ronald J. Glass, Tim Hager, and Thomas A. More, "Measuring the Existence Value of Wildlife: What Do CVM Estimates Really Show?" *Land Economics* 67(4) 1991, 390–400; John B. Loomis and Douglas S. White, "Economic Benefits of Rare and Endangered Species: Summary and Meta-Analysis," *Ecological Economics* 18(3) 1996, 197–206; John Loomis, "Estimating Recreation and Existence Values of Sea Otter Expansion in California Using Benefit Transfer," *Coastal Management* 34(4), 2006, 387-404.

13. See, for example, Donald H. Rosenthal and Robert H. Nelson, "Why Existence Value Should Not Be Used in Cost-Benefit Analysis," *Journal of Policy Analysis and Management* 11(1) 1992, 116–122; and Raymond J. Kopp, "Why Existence Value Should Be Used in Cost-Benefit Analysis," *Journal of Policy Analysis and Management* 11(1) 1992, 123–130. One practical problem is that the estimates of values are quite sensitive to the empirical model used, see, for example, Aurelia Bengochea-Morancho, Ana M. Fuertes-Eugenio, and Salvador del Saz-Salazar, "A Comparison of Empirical Models to Infer the Willingness to Pay in Contingent Valuation," *Ecological Economics* 30(1), 2005, 235–244.

APPENDIX NOTES

1. A more formal treatment can be found in Alan Randall, "Total and Nonuse Values," in John B. Braden and Charles D. Kolstad, eds., *Measuring the Demand for Environmental Quality* (New York: North-Holland, 1991), 303–321. The original analysis of the importance of the sequence of valuation can be found in J. R. Hicks, *A Revision of Demand Theory* (Oxford, UK: Clarendon Press, 1956), 169–179.

2. Though we use compensating variation as a measure of the dollar value of utility here because we find it most intuitive (as discussed in the appendix to Chapter 3), equivalent variation, which measures welfare changes relative to the utility level after the price change, is generally considered a superior money metric for utility because

it provides an unambiguous ordinal measure for ranking price changes.

If $U\sim$ is the utility after the price change, then the equivalent variation is:

$$e(q_1, p_2, \ldots, p_n; U\sim) - e(p_1, p_2, \ldots, p_n; U\sim)$$

where $e(q_1, p_2, \ldots, p_n; U\sim) = B$.

Compensating and equivalent variation typically differ by a small amount due to income effects. In the case of quantity changes of public goods, however, the size of their difference also depends on the availability of close substitutes for the public good. See W. Michael Hanemann, "Willingness-to-Pay and Willingness-to-Accept: How Much Can They Differ?" *American Economic Review* 81(3) 1991, 635–647.

3. Of course, the value of *TEV* will depend on whether it is measured in terms of compensating variation or equivalent variation.

4. John P. Hoehn and Alan Randall, "Too Many Proposals Pass the Benefit Cost Test," *American Economic Review* 79(3) 1989, 544–551.

5. If *E* is a public good, then we would interpret p_e as the tax per unit of *E* that the person pays. As everyone would have to consume the same quantity, the person would not be able to choose the value of *E* so that the optimization of utility would be over only *X* and *Z*.

6. The partial derivatives of *L* with respect to *E*, *X*, *Z*, and λ give four equations in four unknowns. Although these *first-order conditions* cannot be solved analytically, they can be rearranged so that *E*, *X*, and *Z* are each expressed as a function of λ and parameters. A solution can be found by guessing values of λ until a value is found that implies values of *E*, *X*, and *Z* that satisfy the budget constraint.

7. If we assume that *E* is fixed at its initial level, the more realistic case in evaluating an existing wilderness area, then the existence value equals only $5.47. It is smaller than in the example because the person does not have the opportunity to purchase more *E* when *X* is not available. This assumption changes neither the *TEV* nor the existence value as estimated by the use-existence partition.

8. It may seem strange to partition in this way because one would normally think of existence as being a prerequisite for use. Some types of uses, however, could be provided without maintaining existence value. For example, through stocking it may be possible to provide game fishing without preserving a stream in its natural form.

9. Using equivalent variation rather than compensating variation as the consumer surplus measure leads to the following:

$$e(p_e = \infty, p_x = \infty, p_z = 2; Q = 1; U\~ = 33.81) = 100.00$$
$$e(p_e = 0.5, p_x = 1, p_z = 2; Q = 1; U\~ = 33.81) = 84.10$$
$$e(p_e = \infty, p_x = 1, p_z = 2; Q = 1; U\~ = 33.81) = 89.00$$
$$e(p_e = 0.5, p_x = \infty, p_z = 2; Q = 1; U\~ = 33.81) = 94.68$$
$$TEV_{ev} = 100.00 - 84.10 = 15.90$$

Existence-use partition:	existence value = 100.00 − 94.68 = 5.32
	use value = 94.68 − 84.10 = 10.58
Use-existence partition:	use value = 100.00 − 89.00 = 11.00
	existence value = 89.00 − 84.10 = 4.90
Independent summation:	existence value = 100.00 − 94.68 = 5.32
	use value = 100.00 − 89.00 = 11.00

$$TB_{ev} = 16.32$$

CHAPTER 10

The Social Discount Rate[1]

W hen evaluating government policies or projects, analysts must decide on the appropriate weights to apply to policy impacts that occur in different years. Given these weights, denoted by w_t, and estimates of the real annual net social benefits, NB_t, the estimated net present value (NPV) of a project is given by:[2]

$$NPV = \sum_{t=0}^{n} w_t NB_t \qquad (10.1)$$

In effect, the weights make costs, benefits, or net benefits that occur in the future commensurable with (i.e., comparable to) costs, benefits, or net benefits realized by society today so that we can aggregate them to obtain a single measure of the value of a project, the NPV. This chapter deals with theoretical issues pertaining to the selection of an appropriate *set of weights* to use in equation (10.1).

Discounting reflects the generally accepted idea that resources available at some future date are worth less today than the same amount available right now. This is for two basic reasons. First, through investment, a given amount of currently available resources can be transformed into a greater amount of resources in the future. This reflects the opportunity cost of the resources. Second, people are impatient: they prefer to consume a given amount of resources now rather than in the future. For these two reasons, it is generally accepted that the weights decline over time: $0 \leq w_n \leq w_{n-1} \leq \cdots \leq w_1 \leq w_0 = 1$. However, there is less agreement about the specific values of the weights.

These weights are referred to as *social discount factors*. To see this, note that equation (10.1) is a more general version of equations (6.8) and (6.9), the formulas for calculating the NPV of a project that were introduced in Chapter 6. These equations are equivalent if, for all t:

$$w_t = \frac{1}{(1 + i)^t} \qquad (10.2)$$

The term on the right-hand side of equation (10.2) is, in general, called a discount factor. If i (>0) is the real social discount rate (SDR), then it is called a social discount factor. The social discount factor for period t measures the social value of one dollar of net benefit arising at that time relative to the same amount arising now (time zero).

Selecting a set of weights (social discount factors) to use in equation (10.1) is equivalent to selecting the real SDR. If equation (10.2) holds then $w_t = \frac{w_{t-1}}{(1 + i)}$, where $t > 0$ and $w_0 = 1$. In this case, the weights decline geometrically: the weight in one period is proportional to the weight in the previous period and this relationship is constant over time. The rate of decline in the weights equals i, the SDR.[3] The assumption that the SDR is constant is appropriate for intra-generational projects. However, later in this chapter we relax this assumption and discuss situations in which it is more reasonable to assume that the weights do not decline at a constant rate; rather, there are *time-declining discount rates*.

It is possible to do CBA without knowing the theoretical issues pertaining to the choice of the social discount rate. Indeed, as we discuss near the end of this chapter, the Office of Management and Budget or some similar government agency usually prescribes the discount rate that should be used by government agencies. However, while you might therefore be able to compute the *NPV*, you would not be able to give advice or answer questions about the choice of the discount rate you were using unless you read this chapter.

It is generally accepted that society's choices, including the choice of weights, should be based on individuals' choices. But there are three fundamental unresolved issues. The first issue is whether observed market interest rates can be used to represent how individuals weight future consumption relative to present consumption. The second issue is whether society's choices today should reflect the wishes of individuals from unborn future generations in addition to individuals who are alive today. The third issue is whether society attaches the same value to a unit of investment as to a unit of consumption. Different views on these issues lead to different methods for estimating the SDR and to different values (or set of values) of the SDR.

The next section of this chapter shows that the choice of the SDR does matter: a different social discount rate leads to a different policy recommendation. We then present the theory behind the appropriate SDR. We begin with a simple two-period model with no taxes and no market failures. In this situation, the choice of SDR would be obvious and would equal the market interest rate. However, in the absence of perfect markets, there are a number of plausible market interest rates upon which to base the SDR. To resolve this problem we adopt an alternative approach that derives the consumption rate of interest (CRI)—the rate at which society is willing to trade current consumption for future consumption—from an optimal growth model. Traditionally, though, the value of the SDR was based on market interest rates. We discuss the merits of different market-based rates, the circumstances under which each is most applicable, and provide our best judgment about their specific values. Private-sector investment returns are generally higher than the CRI. To avoid a misallocation of resources when using the CRI, positive or negative investment flows should be multiplied by the shadow price of capital prior to discounting. The next section discusses problems with using market-based rates to derive the SDR and proposes values of the CRI based on the optimal growth model. The final major issue concerns intergenerational discounting. Again, we discuss the main issues and present our recommended values. Finally, we contrast our recommended rates with actual practice.

One issue that invariably arises in the discussion of the social discount rate is the treatment of risk and uncertainty. One approach is to add a risk premium to the discount rate to reflect the risk. We do not favor this approach. In our view, the best way to handle risk is to use certainty equivalents, as discussed in Chapter 8. Thus, throughout this chapter, we assume that benefits and costs are measured in terms of certainty equivalents.[4] The key issue is to determine the rate at which analysts should discount certainty equivalents that arise in different years.

DOES THE CHOICE OF DISCOUNT RATE MATTER?

The choice of the SDR is one of the most important topics in CBA. Its importance has recently been driven home in the debate over the *Stern Review* on the economics of climate change.[5] This widely reported study argues that current policies could lead to the cost of climate change amounting to 5% of global gross domestic product (GDP) each year, now and forever. Accordingly, it argues for an immediate current sacrifice of 1% of global GDP. However, William Nordhaus argues that this conclusion is based on "an extreme assumption about discounting" and that if "we substitute more conventional discount rates used in other global-warming analyses . . . the *Review's* dramatic results disappear."[6] Although the SDR does not have as dramatic an impact on most policy questions as it does on global warming, it nearly always plays an important role in determining the present value of the net benefits of public investments and, therefore, on the recommended policy alternative.

Different discount rates can lead to different policy recommendations. To see how the value of the SDR can change the ranking of projects, consider a government agency with a budget of only $100,000 that can be spent on one of three potential projects. The annual net benefits of these projects are shown in Table 10-1. Choosing the lower discount rate (2 percent) would favor project *C*, while the higher discount rate (10 percent) would favor project *B*. Thus, the ranking of projects depends crucially on the choice of discount rate.

Generally, a low discount rate favors projects with the highest total benefits, irrespective of when they occur, because all of the social discount factors (weights) are close to 1 (i.e., high). Increasing the discount rate applies smaller weights to benefits or costs that occur further in the future and therefore weakens the case for projects with benefits that are back-end loaded (such as project *C*) and strengthens the case for projects with benefits that are front-end loaded (such as project *B*).

TABLE 10-1   Annual Net Benefits and Net Present Values for Three Alternative Projects

Year	Project A	Project B	Project C
0	−80,000	−80,000	−80,000
1	25,000	80,000	0
2	25,000	10,000	0
3	25,000	10,000	0
4	25,000	10,000	0
5	25,000	10,000	140,000
NPV ($i = 2\%$)	37,836	35,762	46,802
NPV ($i = 10\%$)	14,770	21,544	6,929

THE THEORY BEHIND THE APPROPRIATE SOCIAL DISCOUNT RATE

Welfare economics frames policy choices as an attempt to maximize social welfare – an aggregation of the well-being or utility of the individuals that make up the society. It also generally assumes that well-being depends ultimately on consumption (of both privately consumed goods and services, such as food, as well as public goods, such as environmental goods). As individuals, we tend to prefer immediate consumption benefits to those occurring in the future. More formally we have a positive *marginal rate of time preference*. Also, we face an opportunity cost of forgone interest when we spend dollars today rather than invest them for future use, given that the *marginal rate of return on private investment* is positive. These considerations provide a basis for deciding how costs and benefits realized by society in the future should be discounted.

This section first introduces the concept of an individual's marginal rate of time preference. We then show that in a simple two-period model with perfect markets, every individual's marginal rate of time preference would equal the market interest rate. In this case the choice of the SDR would be obvious. We then generalize the model to a small, isolated country and introduce production. The main results still hold in perfect markets: The social marginal rate of time preference, the rate of return on investment, and the market interest rate would all be equal. Again, the value of the SDR would be obvious. Then we show that, due to taxes, risk and transaction costs, the three rates listed above are unlikely to be equal in a real economy. In these circumstances, the choice of SDR would not be clear. For this reason, and due to other problems that occur in basing the value of the SDR on market interest rates (which we discuss later), we examine an alternative theoretical approach for deriving the SDR that is based on optimal growth in consumption model.

An Individual's Marginal Rate of Time Preference

Most of us would not be willing to lend someone $100 today in return for a promise of payment of $100 in a year's time, even if there were no inflation. We generally value $100 today more than the promise of $100 next year in real terms, even if we are certain that the promise will be carried out. Perhaps $90 is the most that we would be willing to lend today in return for a promise of payment of $100 in a year's time. Economists refer to our preference to consume sooner rather than later as *time preference*. The rate at which an individual makes marginal trade-offs is called an individual's *marginal rate of time preference* (MRTP).

The concept of time preference can be easily understood in the context of borrowing and lending. Imagine that you are a graduate student who will receive a stipend of $10,000 this year and $15,000 next year. Your rich uncle offers to give you some money and asks if you would rather have $1,000 this year or $1,200 next year. Suppose that you are indifferent between the gifts; that is, you are just willing to sacrifice $200 additional consumption next year in order to consume the extra $1,000 this year rather than next year.[7] In this case, you would have an MRTP of 20 percent. Put another way, your MRTP tells us that you require more than 20 percent more next year in order to decrease your current consumption by a small amount.

Absent a rich uncle, you might be able to consume more today through borrowing. Although many banks may not be interested in lending you money because they fear you may not pay them back, let us assume that your local credit union will lend you money at an annual interest rate of 10 percent. That is, you can borrow $1,000 if you promise to pay back this amount plus $100 in interest next year. If you were willing to give up $200 to get an additional $1,000 immediately from your uncle, then you would surely take advantage of the loan that requires you to give up only $100 in consumption next year in order to consume $1,000 more this year.

Once you take out the loan, you will have $11,000 to spend this year and $13,900 to spend next year. Now that you have reduced the gap between what you have to spend this year relative to next year, you probably have an MRTP of less than 20 percent. After taking out the loan you may now, if given the choice, prefer a gift of $1,200 next year over a gift of $1,000 this year. If so, this indicates your MRTP is now less than 20 percent. This example illustrates that your MRTP changes as you shift consumption from one year to another year.

Equality of Discount Rates in Perfect Markets

As long as you can borrow as much as you like, you can shift consumption from the future to the present until your MRTP falls to the rate of interest you must pay. If banks offer a rate of interest in excess of your MRTP, then you will happily save now and defer some consumption to the future. For example, if you are indifferent between an additional $1,000 today and an additional $1,050 next year but can deposit $1,000 for one year to obtain an additional $1,060 next year, then you would want to make the deposit. Only when the rate of interest you earn just equals your MRTP will you be indifferent between spending or depositing an additional dollar.

In a perfectly competitive capital market every individual's MRTP equals the market interest rate. To see this, suppose that a consumer's utility is a function of consumption over two years: C_1 denotes consumption in this year (year 1) and C_2 denotes consumption in next year (year 2). The consumer maximizes her utility, denoted by $U(C_1, C_2)$, subject to a budget constraint in which T denotes the present value of total income available to be spent over the two years and i denotes the market interest rate:

$$\text{Max } U(C_1, C_2) \tag{10.3}$$

$$\text{s.t. } C_1 + \frac{C_2}{1 + i} = T \tag{10.4}$$

This problem is represented graphically in Figure 10-1.

The curves labeled U^1 and U^2 are *indifference curves*. Each curve represents combinations of current and future consumption that provide the individual with the same level of utility. Thus, the individual is indifferent between any two points on an indifference curve. All points on the curve U^2 are preferred to all points on the curve U^1; that is, the preference directions are north and east.

The slope of each indifference curve is negative, reflecting the fact that consumers require more consumption in the next period in order to give up consumption in this period. If you are indifferent between an additional $1,000 today and an additional $1,050 next year, for example, then the slope of your indifference curve equals $-1,050/1,000 = -1.05$. The absolute value of the slope of the indifference curve measures the rate at which an individual is indifferent between substituting current

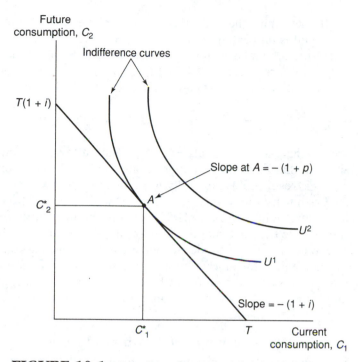

FIGURE 10-1 Equality of MRTP and the Market Interest Rate

consumption for future consumption and is called the consumer's *marginal rate of substitution* (MRS) between consumption this year and consumption next year.

In this example, the individual wants 5 percent more next year in order to defer consumption; therefore his or her marginal rate of time preference equals 0.05. *In general, if you require $1 + p$ more units in the future in order to give up one unit of current consumption, then the slope of your indifference curve is $-(1 + p)$; your marginal rate of substitution is $1 + p$; and your marginal rate of time preference is p.* In the relevant range, $p > 0$ and the slope of the indifference curve is greater than 1 in absolute value.

As consumption in the current period increases, the indifference curve becomes flatter, indicating that the consumer requires relatively smaller additional amounts of future consumption in order to forgo a given amount of current consumption. Put another way, as current consumption increases, the consumer's marginal rate of substitution and the consumer's marginal rate of time preference decrease.

The individual receives all of his or her income in the first period and can invest all or part of it at interest rate i.[8] Thus, the individual could spend all of his or her income in year 1, which means $C_1 = T$ and $C_2 = 0$; the individual could spend all of it in year 2, in which case $C_1 = 0$ and $C_2 = (1 + i)T$; or he or she could consume at any other point on the budget constraint represented by the straight line with slope $-(1 + i)$. Each additional unit of consumption in period 1 costs $(1 + i)$ units of consumption in period 2 and each additional unit of consumption in period 2 costs $1/(1 + i)$ units of consumption in period 1.

To determine the optimal consumption level, we find the point at which the budget constraint is tangential to an indifference curve. This occurs at point A in Figure 10-1 where the optimal consumption levels are denoted C_1^* and C_2^*. At this point the slope of the indifference curve, $-(1 + p)$, equals the slope of the budget constraint.

Rewriting the budget constraint, equation (10.4), thus:

$$C_2 = T(1 + i) - (1 + i)C_1 \qquad\qquad (10.5)$$

implies that its slope equals $-(1 + i)$.[9] Thus at the optimum consumption level, point $A, p = i$, that is, the market interest rate equals the consumer's MRTP.[10]

This result holds generally in perfect markets where individuals can borrow or lend as much as they want to and have "well-behaved" preference functions.[11] *Every individual would have an MRTP equal to the market interest rate.* Because all consumers face the same market interest rate, all consumers would have the same MRTP. Everyone is willing to trade current and future consumption at the same rate. Because this rate equals the market interest rate, it would be natural to use the market interest rate as the social discount rate. Later we discuss the appropriateness of using market interest rates as the social discount rate when markets are not perfect.

A Simple Two-Period Model with Production

We now present a more general two-period model that pertains to a group of individuals in a hypothetical country. We assume that this country does not trade with another country. Moreover, as before, we ignore taxes and transaction costs associated with making loans (although we come back to them later). Consequently, anyone who wants a loan can borrow the desired amount at the market interest rate. In addition, except when explicitly indicated otherwise, we ignore market failures, such as externalities and information asymmetry, which could cause private and social discount rates to diverge from one another.

The economy of our hypothetical country is depicted in Figure 10-2. The horizontal axis indicates consumption during the current period and the vertical axis indicates consumption during the future period. The major difference between this model and the previous model is that this model incorporates production. The curve labeled *CPF* is a consumption possibility frontier that represents all the combinations of current and future consumption that are feasible if the country utilizes its resources efficiently.

Suppose that at the beginning of the first period, the country has T units worth of resources, which can be allocated between current consumption and investment. As before, there are two extremes. At one extreme, which is represented by point T on the horizontal axis, "society" (i.e. the country's citizens in aggregate) could consume all T units in the current period, invest none, and therefore have no future consumption. At the other extreme, society could consume no units in the current period, invest all T units, and consume S units in the future period, which is represented by point S on the vertical axis. Note that $S > T$, which implies a positive rate of return on all resources invested in the current period.

Point X represents a more realistic intermediate position where current consumption equals C_t^* and future consumption equals C_{t+1}^*. At this point, society would relinquish for investment $I_t = T - C_t^*$ units of potential consumption in the current period.

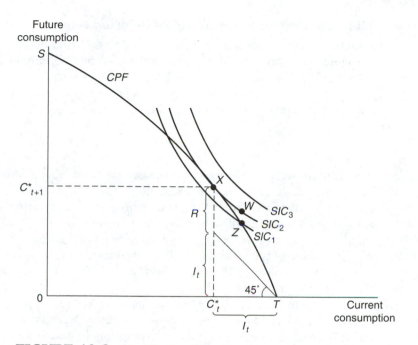

FIGURE 10-2   The Optimal Levels of Consumption and
Investment in a Two-Period Model

In the future period society would consume $C^*_{t+1} = I_t + R$ units, where I_t represents the amount invested in the first period and R represents the return on this investment. Future consumption can be partitioned into two components by drawing a 45° line from point T to the line between X and C^*_t on Figure 10-2. The lower segment corresponds to I_t and the upper segment corresponds to R.

Implicitly, there is a portfolio of investment projects. The investment, I_t, can be thought of as a number of small investments that sum to I_t. The average rate of return on these investments, which we denote as r, equals R/I_t. This average return is higher than the marginal return on (a small) investment at X, denoted r_x. To see this, note that when viewed from below, the *CPF* curve is concave (i.e., it bows outward). This implies that as the economy moves along its *CPF* curve from T toward S and more resources are invested in the first period, equal increments in investments engender successively smaller increases in future consumption; in short, it assumes society makes the best investments first.

The set of three curves labeled *SIC* in Figure 10-2 are social indifference curves. Each curve represents a combination of current and future consumption that provides society with an equal level of utility. For example, society is indifferent between points X and W on SIC_2. The negative slope of the *SICs* implies that society is only willing to give up some units of current consumption if future consumption is increased. The *social marginal rate of time preference* (SMRTP) is the *extra* amount of future consumption that society requires as compensation for giving up one unit of current consumption. At X, society requires at least $1 + p_x$ units in the future to give up one unit of current consumption, and the SMRTP equals p_x.

The First-Best Solution in the Two-Period Model

Society, of course, desires to reach the highest possible indifference curve. As can be seen in Figure 10-2, this curve is SIC_2 given the *CPF* and an initial endowment of *T* units. Although SIC_3 is preferable to SIC_2, the country's resources are insufficient to reach SIC_3. Indeed, the country's economy can only reach SIC_2 at a single point, *X*. At *X*, SIC_2 and the *CPF* curve are tangential and their slopes are equal. Consequently, at point *X*:

$$1 + p_x = 1 + r_x, \quad \text{or} \quad p_x = r_x$$

Accordingly, were the economy to operate at point *X*, the SMRTP would equal the marginal rate of return on investment. Furthermore, these rates would equal the economy-wide market rate of interest, denoted by *i*. In addition, if the rates of interest for borrowing and lending were equal and available to all individuals, then every member of society would have the same marginal rate of time preference, which would also equal the economy-wide market interest rate. As all of these rates would be equal, the choice of SDR at *X* would be both obvious and unambiguous. Point *X* is, therefore, the "first-best" solution.

To see why everybody would have the same MRTP, suppose that an individual initially had a MRTP in excess of *i*; that is, she wanted to consume more now. This person could borrow at *i*, a lower rate than she is willing to pay, and thereby increase her current consumption at the expense of her future consumption. This increase in current consumption would increase the relative value of future consumption, causing her MRTP to decline until it eventually equaled *i*. Analogously, another individual with an MRTP below *i* would willingly postpone some current consumption in exchange for increased future consumption. By doing so her MRTP would rise until it equalled *i*. Thus, at *X* every individual would have the same MRTP, equal to *i*.

Problems with Real Economies: The Second Best

Point *X* in Figure 10-2 is the socially optimal point in a perfectly competitive market with no taxes, no externalities and no transaction costs. Economies in real countries are unable to operate at point *X*. In practice, an actual economy with taxes and transaction costs would be more likely to function at point *Z*, which is a "second-best" outcome. Here, society would underinvest (actual investment $< I_t$); it would only be able to reach SIC_1, not SIC_2; and the marginal return on investment would exceed the marginal rate of time preference $(r_z > p_z)$.[12]

To illustrate the wedge between p_z and r_z, consider a firm that earns a one-year rate of return of 6 percent on an investment of $100 provided by a shareholder. In the presence of taxes and transaction costs, not all of the $6 earned by the firm would be returned to the shareholder. If the firm faced a corporate tax rate of 40 percent, then it would pay $2.40 to the government and give only $3.60 to the shareholder. But a shareholder facing a personal income tax rate of 30 percent would have to pay $1.08 of the $3.60 to the government, leaving her with only $2.52. Further, imagine that the shareholder faced transaction costs (searching for the investment opportunity, gathering information about its risks, taking steps to reduce the risk, etc.) of $0.52. The actual return realized by the shareholder would be only $2. Thus, the 6 percent rate of return on the investment would only elicit an investment from an individual with an MRTP of 2 percent or less.

Because different individuals and different firms have different preferences, face different tax rates, and the transactions costs associated with investments vary across investment projects and across individuals, numerous values exist for both the marginal rate of time preference and the marginal rate of return on investment. Thus, there is no obvious choice for the SDR that can be derived from these values.

An Infinite-Period Model: Discounting and the Optimal Growth Rate

In 1928, Frank Ramsey proposed a model with infinite periods in which society (or a single representative individual) attempts to maximize a social welfare function that reflects the values that society places on per capita consumption over time.[13] Through investment, consumption increases over time. Policy makers choose the amount of public investment in order to maximize the well-being of society now and in the future. Following Ramsey, a number of economists have shown that maximization of such a social welfare function implies that, on the optimal growth path, the SDR (i.e., society's marginal rate of time preference, p_x) would equal the sum of two components: one reflecting impatience and the other reflecting society's preference for smoothing consumption flows over time.[14] Specifically, p_x should equal the pure rate of time preference, d, plus a term multiplying the long-run rate of growth in per capita consumption, g, by a constant, e:

$$p_x = d + ge \qquad \qquad (10.6)$$

where $d, g, e \geq 0$.

Society discounts future consumption for two reasons. First, like the individuals that make up it, society is impatient and prefers to consume now rather than in the future, *ceteris paribus*. Suppose that there is no growth. Further suppose, as we did earlier, that the market is perfectly competitive (there are no taxes or transactions costs) and, for illustrative convenience, suppose that there are only two periods. Then, as shown in Figure 10-3, the *CPF* is symmetric and $OS = OT$. In this situation, society would discount the utility derived from its consumption of future goods using a "pure" rate of time preference, denoted by d. Because society is impatient, current consumption would exceed future consumption, such as at point X, which is below the 45° line.

This brings us to the second reason for discounting. Since this model assumes that there is economic growth, society can consistently enjoy higher per capita consumption in the future than it does today. This model further supposes that it is reasonable to assume that individuals have declining marginal utility of consumption. Societal welfare would be increased if consumption were "smoothed out" (made more equal) over time. Put another way, the future should have a lower weight than the present as incrementally higher levels of consumption are less valuable to them. The parameter e is an elasticity that measures how fast the social marginal utility of consumption falls as per capita consumption rises. Setting e equal to zero (with $d = 0$) implies no discounting of future consumption: society treats each unit of consumption received in

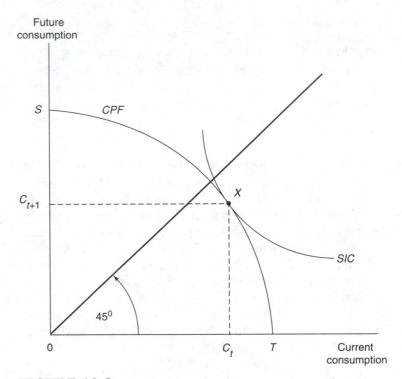

FIGURE 10-3 Optimal Levels of Consumption and Investment in a Two-Period Model without Growth

the future as identical to a unit of consumption in the present, signifying a complete lack of concern for our current lower wealth and, therefore, for intergenerational inequality. In contrast, as e approaches infinity, society completely discounts each unit of consumption received in the (richer) future, signifying an overwhelming desire to equalize per capita consumption over time. When e equals one, the relative weight on society's consumption in each time period equals the inverse of its relative per capita consumption. Thus, a 10 percent reduction in consumption today, for example, from $40,000 to $36,000, is an acceptable trade-off for a 10 percent increase in consumption at a richer, future time, for example, from $80,000 to $88,000. Society weighs the loss of $1 of consumption today as twice as important as a gain of $1 to its future self, because the future society is twice as rich.

It is possible to show that on the optimal growth path of the economy, the value of the marginal rate of return on investment must equal the value of the SMRTP, that is:

$$r_x = p_x = d + ge \tag{10.7}$$

As before, the x subscript indicates that this result holds for the first-best, or optimal, growth path.

DERIVING THE SOCIAL DISCOUNT RATE
FROM MARKET RATES: FOUR ALTERNATIVES

This section discusses four ways to derive the SDR based on observable, market rates, and it presents values of those rates for use in CBAs.[15] All four methods presume that a public-sector project should be undertaken if its benefits would exceed the opportunity cost of the resources; otherwise, it should not. This is essentially the CBA compensation test: is it better to invest in a government project or invest in the private sector and then use the returns to compensate the potential beneficiaries of the project?

The first way uses the marginal rate of return on private-sector investments, r_z. The second uses a value equal to the social marginal rate of time preference, p_z. The third uses a value equal to the government's real borrowing rate, i. The fourth uses a weighted average of p_z, r_z, and i, where the weights reflect the amount of the project's resources that are financed by consumption, investment, and foreign borrowing, respectively. We continue to use the subscript z on p and r to emphasize that we are discussing a real economy that is at a "second-best" point such as Z in Figure 10-2 (rather than at X), and as a consequence, the marginal rate of time preference is not equal to the marginal rate of return on investment.

Using the Marginal Rate of Return on Private Investment

The argument for using the marginal rate of return on private investment, r_z, as the SDR is that before the government takes resources out of the private sector, it should be able to demonstrate that society will receive a greater return in the public sector than it would have received had the resources remained in the private sector. The most compelling case for the use of r_z was made in an influential article by Arnold Harberger.[16] Harberger analyzed a closed domestic market for investment and savings, such as the one presented in Figure 10-4. In the absence of taxes and government borrowing, the demand curve for investment funds by private-sector borrowers is represented by D_0, and the supply curve of funds from lenders (savers) is represented by S_0.

Now consider the introduction of a corporate income tax and a personal income tax. The tax on corporate profits would shift the demand curve down to D_I because part of the returns from investments must now be paid to the government, whereas the tax on interest income would shift the supply curve up to S_S because part of the interest on savings must now be paid to the government. Thus, both taxes would reduce investment.

Given the initial demand and supply curves and these taxes, the market-clearing interest rate would be i. That is, investors would pay an interest rate of i to borrow funds, and savers would receive an interest rate of i prior to paying taxes. However, the marginal rate of return on investment before taxes (i.e., the opportunity cost of forgone private-sector investment) would be r_z, with the gap between r_z and i representing taxes paid by investors. The opportunity cost of forgone consumption or, equivalently, the marginal rate of time preference, p_z, would equal the marginal return on savings after taxes (i.e., there would be a gap between p_z and i representing taxes paid by savers on interest income). Thus, as previously discussed, taxes would cause r_z to exceed p_z.

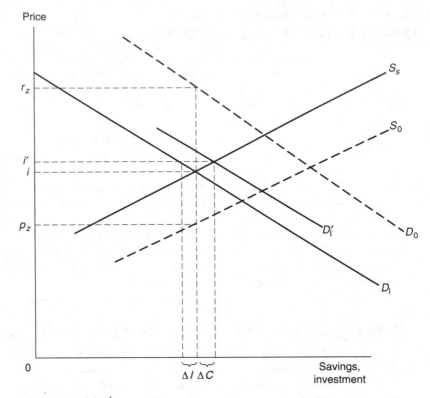

FIGURE 10-4   The Effects of Taxes and Government Borrowing on Savings and Investment

Now consider the effects of a government project *that is financed entirely by borrowing in a closed, domestic financial market.* Suppose the demand for funds for the new project shifts the market demand curve up to D_I'. The market rate of interest would rise from i to i'. Private-sector investment would fall by ΔI, and private-sector savings would increase by ΔC. Because the increase in private-sector savings would exactly equal the decrease in private-sector consumption, the project would "crowd out" both investment (by ΔI) and consumption (by ΔC).

Harberger suggests that the social discount rate should be obtained by weighting r_z and p_z by the respective size of the relative contributions that investment and consumption would make toward funding the project. That is, he suggests that the SDR should be computed using the weighted average cost of capital, WSOC:

$$\text{WSOC} = ar_z + bp_z \qquad (10.8)$$

where $a = \Delta I/(\Delta I + \Delta C)$ and $b = (1 - a) = \Delta C/(\Delta I + \Delta C)$.

Finally, Harberger asserts that savings are not very responsive to changes in interest rates. Some empirical evidence supports this assertion, implying that the S_S curve is close to vertical, and as a consequence, ΔC is close to zero.[17] This, in turn, suggests that the value of the parameter *a* is close to 1 and the value of *b* is close to 0. In other words, almost all of the resources for public-sector investment would be obtained by crowding out private-sector investment. Harberger, therefore, argues that the marginal rate of return on investment is a good approximation of the SDR.

Numerical Values of r_z. Probably the best proxy for the *marginal* rate of return on private investment, r_z, is the real, before-tax rate of return on corporate bonds, although some analysts argue for using an average return that also includes the rate of return on equities.

There are four reasons for using a bond rate rather than a measure of the average return on equities. The first is that doing so avoids the problem of having to estimate the effective marginal corporate tax rate. Because a firm can deduct the interest it pays to its bondholders before calculating its taxable income, it will equate (on the margin) its expected before-tax return on an investment with the before-tax rate it must pay on its bonds. So the real bond yield is a good direct proxy for r_z. Second, the measure should proxy the *marginal* pre-tax return on private investment. Using a measure based on average returns to equities would lead to too high a rate, as the return on a marginal investment is lower than the average return. The interest rate on bonds represents the marginal borrower's willingness-to-pay, and this should equal the return on the marginal investment. Third, bond yields are available contemporaneously, while the average return on equities must be calculated by looking back over some historical period (and will vary greatly according to the period chosen). Finally, as we discussed earlier, we want to use a risk-free rate of return, and returns to equity investments contain a risk premium, typically measured as the difference between the observed *ex post* real return to a diversified equity portfolio and the real return to a (default-risk free) government bond.[18] Although bond rates of return contain a risk premium, it is lower than the equity risk premium.

Taking the yields on Moody's AAA-rated corporate bonds or the yields on all Moody's rated corporate bonds and then adjusting for inflationary expectations suggests that the before-tax return on corporate bonds is approximately 4.5 percent. Based on this estimate, 4.5 percent is a reasonable value for r_z.

Criticisms of the Calculation and Use of r_z. Several factors suggest that use of an SDR of 4.5 percent is too high. Some of these criticisms pertain to the estimation of r_z while others pertain to the strong assumptions made by Harberger. First, private-sector rates of return may be pushed upward by market distortions caused by negative externalities and market prices that exceed social marginal cost.[19] Second, even low-risk private-sector bonds incorporate a small default risk premium that is not likely to apply to the government because it holds a broader, more diversified portfolio of projects.[20] In practice, therefore, actual government borrowing rates are lower.[21] Third, the project might be financed by taxes, rather than by loans, in which case consumption is more likely to be crowded out than investment. The reason is that most taxes are collected from individuals through income, payroll, and consumption taxes, which mainly affect consumption, especially if savings rates are fairly low. Fourth, the project may, in fact, be partially financed by borrowing from overseas. Fifth, there may not be a fixed pool of investment so that government investment may not replace private investment dollar-for-dollar. Indeed, government infrastructure projects can raise the private return to capital.[22] If the economy is not fully employing all its resources, then complete crowding out is unlikely. For all these reasons, using values of the SDR of about 4.5 percent should be viewed as close to the upper limit of the SDR.

Using the Social Marginal Rate of Time Preference

Many analysts hold that the SDR should be thought of as the rate at which individuals in society are willing to postpone a small amount of current consumption in exchange for additional future consumption (and vice versa), that is, at a consumption rate of interest (CRI). In principle, p_z represents this rate. Another way to justify using this rate is to assume that a project is financed entirely by domestic taxes and to assume that taxes reduce consumption but not investment. Then, it is appropriate to set $a = 0$ and $b = 1$ in equation (10.8), yielding a SDR equal to p_z.

Numerical Values of p_z. In practice, the best return that many people can earn in exchange for postponing consumption is the real, after-tax return on savings. Therefore, an obvious candidate for the p_z is the return to individuals from holding government bonds, the class of assets that have the lowest risk.

Two possible starting points to use to obtain a value of p_z are the average monthly yield on one-year U.S. government Treasury notes or that on medium-term (10-year) Treasury bonds.[23] These nominal, pre-tax average monthly yields must then be converted to real, after-tax rates by adjusting for taxes and inflation. In practice, it is difficult to know exactly what effective tax rate faces the marginal saver. John Shoven and Michael Topper argue that the personal tax rate on savings in the United States is 30 percent.[24] The rate of inflation that consumers and savers expected while holding these assets was obtained from the Livingston survey, which we discussed in Chapter 6. Based on these data, we estimate that the real, expected after-tax savings rates have typically fluctuated between 1 and 2 percent per annum. The real, after-tax returns to ten-year Treasury bonds, which employ explicit ten-year ahead inflation forecasts, probably provide the best estimate. *Given these estimates, tempered with the longer-term historical results, we recommend using 1.5 percent as the value of p_z, with sensitivity analysis at 1.0 percent and 2.0 percent (approximately plus or minus one standard deviation, given the most recent measures of volatility).*

Criticisms of the Calculation and Use of p_z. There are three main criticisms pertaining to the computation and use of p_z. First, as we discussed above, due to taxes and transaction costs, $p_z < r_z$. If we used p_z as the SDR then governments may engage in long-term investments that provide low returns at the expense of higher-return private projects, thereby harming allocative efficiency.

Second, individuals differ in their preferences and opportunities.[25] While some are saving at low rates, others are borrowing at high rates. Some save by reducing their debt. Because consumer borrowing rates exceed savings rates and because reducing some forms of debt is not taxed, consumers who save by reducing their debt earn a higher real, after-tax return than other savers. For example, the real after-tax return of paying down one's mortgage has historically been about 3 percent.[26] People who save by paying down the balance on their credit cards earn very high returns, often higher than 15 percent in real terms. It is not obvious how to aggregate these different individual rates into a single, social discount rate. Furthermore, some individuals are screened out of legitimate credit markets altogether due to informational asymmetries. Thus, their preferences are not reflected by market rates; in effect, they are not "counted."

Third, individuals are not always consistent and rational.[27] This weakens the normative argument for basing social choices on market behavior. There are three strands of behavioral evidence to support this assertion. First, some individuals simultaneously lend and borrow: they pay down mortgages, buy government and corporate bonds and stocks for retirement, borrow on their credit cards. It is unreasonable to assume that these individuals have a single marginal rate of time preference.[28] A study of retirement offers of annuities or lump-sum payments made to U.S. military personnel found implied rates of time preference averaging over 25 percent! These rates varied between 0 and 30 percent by age, race, number of children, education, and rank.[29] Second, individual preferences appear to be what is described as "time inconsistent." For example, individual rates of time preference and implied discount rates appear to decline over the horizon to which they are applied.[30] As a result, choices made at one time might be overturned later even if no new information becomes available. Similarly, projects that appear socially valuable at the time of an initial decision might later appear to be a mistake, even though nothing has changed except the passage of time. Third, there is a strand of evidence demonstrating that the framing of intertemporal choice affects individuals' implicit rates of time preference. Thus, individuals use different rates to discount large amounts versus small amounts, losses versus gains, choices involving the near future as against choices farther out in time, and choices between speeding up versus delaying consumption.

Using the Government's Borrowing Rate

Some economists argue that the government should discount projects using its long-term borrowing rate, i, because this rate reflects the actual cost of financing the marginal project.

Numerical Values of i.   To obtain a specific value of the government's borrowing rate, i, we begin with the average monthly yield on 10-year U.S. Treasury bonds for the period April 1953 to December 2001, which was 6.71 percent. Adjusting for inflation using the CPI, which increased at 3.89 percent per annum during this period, yields a real return on these bonds equal to 2.71 percent. *This suggests using a value of i equal to 2.7 percent with a plausible range for sensitivity analysis of 1.7 to 3.7 percent.*

Criticisms of the Calculation and Use of i.   Like r_z, i may be upwardly biased due to market failures. Also, government projects may be funded by taxes rather than borrowing, a point we discuss in more detail in the following section. Furthermore, even if projects were deficit financed, even open economies, such as the United States, may not be able to borrow at an unchanging real interest rate. We also expand on this point in the next section.

Using the Weighted Average Approach

Proponents of using r_z as the SDR assume that resources for government investment come from borrowing that crowds out domestic investment dollar-for-dollar. Advocates of p_z assume that resources come from taxes that crowd out current domestic consumption dollar-for-dollar. Others argue that projects are financed by government borrowing from foreigners.[31]

In practice, resources may come from all three sources. Some economists have proposed that the SDR should be calculated in terms of the social opportunity cost of the different sources weighted according to the relative contribution of each source. If a is the proportion of the project's resources that crowd out private domestic investment, b is the proportion of the resources that displace domestic consumption, and $1 - a - b$ is the proportion of the resources that are financed by borrowing from foreigners, then the weighted social opportunity cost of capital (WSOC) method computes the SDR as the weighted average of these rates:

$$\text{WSOC} = ar_z + bp_z + (1 - a - b)i \qquad (10.9)$$

As $p_z < i < r_z$, it follows that $p_z < \text{WSOC} < r_z$. Obviously, the previous methods are special cases of this more general approach.

Numerical Values of WSOC.   As previously discussed, reasonable U.S. values for r_z, p_z and i are 4.5 percent, 1.5 percent, and 2.7 percent, respectively. Values of a, b, and, hence, $(1 - a - b)$ may vary from project to project, depending on how it is financed.[32]

Proponents of the WSOC method tend to argue that a is large, b is small and $(1 - a - b)$ is something in-between. They tend to believe Harberger's argument that funding comes at the expense of private-sector investment, but recognize that some financing might come from consumption or by borrowing from overseas.

However, prior to the 2008–2009 financial crisis, governments and the public in most developed countries usually viewed new federal expenditures as necessitating additional taxes, and they viewed reductions in debt levels as enabling tax reductions (and vice versa). In the United States, almost all state governments are subject to requirements that they run balanced budgets. Thus, in most circumstances one can assume that government projects are tax financed. Furthermore, the majority of taxes are obtained from consumers.[33] And, there is fairly strong evidence that in "normal times," changes in consumers' disposable incomes lead to changes in consumption rather than changes in savings.[34] Hence, b would be large, a would be small, and $(1 - a - b)$ would be zero. Placing precise values on these parameters is difficult. However, it would be reasonable for a tax financed project to suppose that $a = 0.2$ and $b = 0.8$, suggesting that *the value of WSOC would be about 2.5 percent*.

When the government does resort to deficit financing, such as during the global financial crisis that began in 2008, it is likely to be when the economy is operating below full potential. In such circumstances, marginal public sector investments are unlikely to crowd out private investment.

Some specific projects are largely or completely deficit financed. A government may issue a bond to finance a specific project. Most developed countries are fairly open economies. Whether or not the economy is operating at its full potential, government can borrow from abroad at the government's borrowing rate. Increased borrowing may raise domestic interest rates, which would appreciate the exchange rate (under a flexible exchange rate regime). Net exports would fall, and given the supply of savings, some private-sector investment would be crowded out. Although there is little evidence on how responsive the supply of foreign funds is to the interest rate, analysts can probably assume that the effect on interest rates, the exchange rate, and investment are quite small, especially for a small project. The effect on consumption is likely to be even smaller because, as previously suggested, the balance of the evidence suggests that it is not very responsive to changes in market interest rates. Thus, for a specifically deficit financed project, $(1 - a - b)$ would be large, a would be small, and b would be very small. *Consequently, the value of WSOC would be about 2.75 percent.*

Criticisms of the Calculation and Use of the WSOC.   The criticisms pertaining to the use of p_z, r_z, or i as the social discount rate generally also apply to the WSOC. There is, however, one other consideration. The previous approaches each resulted in a single social discount rate. In contrast, the value of WSOC depends on the sources of a project's resources, which may vary from one project to another. In practice, governments prefer a single social discount rate because of the difficulty of monitoring assumptions about the sources of resources required for specific projects and of explaining why different discount rates are used on different projects.

THE SHADOW PRICE OF CAPITAL

As we discussed above, social welfare depends on consumption and the SDR should reflect society's willingness to trade off future consumption for present consumption. Thus, there is a strong theoretical justification for choosing a CRI as the social discount rate. However, resources invested in the private sector generally earn a higher return than the consumption rate of interest: $r_z > p_z$. If the government used a lower discount rate than the private sector, then it would undertake projects that the private sector would not undertake and it would grow undesirably large. Also, whether or not a project was undertaken would depend on whether the assets were state owned or privately owned and not exclusively on the merits of the project.

In order to overcome these problems, recall that, a public-sector project should be undertaken if its benefits would exceed the opportunity cost of the resources; otherwise, it should not. To ensure that government projects pass this test, changes in private-sector investment flows are weighted by a parameter, which is greater than 1, called *the shadow price of capital (SPC)* and denoted by θ. This parameter converts investment flows (in or out) into their *consumption equivalents*. In the SPC discounting method, these consumption equivalents, like consumption flows themselves, are then discounted at p_z.[35]

Consumption and investment are treated differently because consumption provides an immediate benefit while investment generates a stream of benefits that occur in future periods. To see this, suppose a dollar is invested in the private sector for an indefinite period. Suppose also that it earns a return of r_z each period and this return is consumed each period, while the original dollar is reinvested. Thus, r_z is consumed each period in perpetuity. The present value of this perpetual consumption flow, using the formula for a perpetuity introduced in Chapter 6, is:

$$\theta = \frac{r_z}{p_z} \qquad (10.10)$$

Because r_z is greater than p_z, the value of θ is greater than 1 reflecting the situation that, at the margin, *displaced private-sector investment is more costly to society than displaced consumption and that increments to private-sector investment are more beneficial than increments to consumption.* By multiplying flows into and out of private-sector investment by θ, we convert them into their consumption equivalents.

To explore the shadow price approach a bit further, suppose that a project yields real annual benefits of B per year indefinitely. If all of these benefits are consumed as they arise then the present value of this perpetual consumption flow discounted at p_z is B/p_z.

Now consider two extreme cases. If the project's capital cost, C, is paid in year 0 and all these funds are raised from consumption, then the *NPV* rule implies the project should be undertaken if $B/p_z > C$. Thus, in this extreme situation, the SPC method is equivalent to discounting benefits and costs at the SMRTP.

Next suppose instead that all the costs, which still occur in year 0, displace private investment. Under this assumption, the *NPV* rule implies the project should be undertaken if $B/p_z > \theta C = (r_z/p_z)C$ or, equivalently, if $B/r_z > C$. This condition is equivalent to discounting the benefits and costs at the rate of return on private investment, as Harberger suggested.

The expression for the SPC in equation (10.10) is based on several simplifying assumptions. One is that the investment will not depreciate. Another is that the entire return from the investment will be consumed when it occurs. More likely, some of the return will be consumed when it is generated and some will be reinvested. Consideration of these possibilities leads to a more general expression for the SPC:

$$\theta = \frac{(r_z + \delta)(1 - f)}{p_z - r_z f + \delta(1 - f)} \qquad (10.11)$$

where δ is the depreciation rate of the capital invested; f is the fraction of the gross return that is reinvested; and, as before, p_z is the SMRTP and r_z is the net return on capital after depreciation.[36] Note that in the absence of reinvestment and depreciation (i.e., if $f = 0$ and $\delta = 0$) this formula reduces to equation (10.10).

Numerical Values of θ

To apply equation (10.11), we need values for p_z, r_z, f, and δ. We have already discussed p_z and r_z; thus, we need consider only f and δ. To obtain a value for δ, the depreciation rate of capital, we rely on Charles Hulten and Frank Wykoff, who found that the annual depreciation rate for manufacturing equipment was 13.3 percent and for structures used in manufacturing was 3.4 percent.[37] Weighting these rates by the relative proportions of equipment (67 percent) and structures (33 percent) in U.S. capital stock (figures that are available from the *United States Statistical Abstracts*) gives an average annual depreciation rate of $[0.67 \times 0.133 + 0.33 \times 0.034] = 10$ percent.

The gross investment rate (the ratio of real gross fixed investment to real GDP) provides a rough estimate of f, the fraction of the gross return that is reinvested. It averaged 13.0 percent for 1947–2002, based on quarterly real GDP data with a range between 10.6 and 18.5 percent. A more recent five-year average was 17.6 percent. Based on these results, we choose 17 percent as our best estimate of f in the future.

Plugging these estimates into equation (10.11) yields a value of $\theta = 1.33$, implying that one dollar of private-sector investment would produce a stream of consumption benefits with an NPV equal to $1.33. If we had used equation (10.10) instead, then this would yield a value of θ equal to 3.0.

Earlier, we suggested using a range for r_z of 4.0 to 5.0 percent and a range for p_z of 1.0 to 2.0 percent. Using different combinations of these values, with $f = 17$ percent and $\delta = 10$ percent, results in values for θ of between 1.21 and 1.47. *For sensitivity analysis, the larger of these values ($\theta = 1.47$) should be used with $p_z = 1.0$ percent and the smaller ($\theta = 1.21$) with $p_z = 2.0$ percent.*

Using the Shadow Price of Capital with p_z

The SPC method requires that discounting be done in four steps. First, the costs and benefits in each period are divided into those that directly affect consumption and those that directly affect investment. Second, flows into and out of investment are multiplied by the SPC, θ, to convert them into consumption equivalents. Third, changes in consumption are added to changes in consumption equivalents. Fourth, the resultant consumption equivalents and the original consumption flows are discounted at p_z.

To illustrate how to apply the SPC, consider a project to improve the physical plant of a city's schools that is financed by a bond issue of $3 million.[38] We assume that the bonds would be purchased solely by city citizens and would be paid for by local residents at 4 percent (real) interest through five equal annual installments of $673,854. Benefits from the project are estimated to be $700,000 a year over a five-year period and $0 thereafter. Following Harberger, we assume that the entire amount borrowed, which would be repaid over five years, would displace private-sector investment.[39]

Given that the loan is repaid over five years at 4 percent interest, the equal annual installments are $673,854. For the first year, $120,000 ($0.04 \times 3,000,000$) is interest on the loan and $553,854 ($673,854 - 120,000$) is repayment of principal. Consequently, at the end of the first year, immediately after the first annual payment, the loan balance equals $2,446,146 ($3,000,000 - 553,854$). Extending this logic to the second and subsequent years, it follows that $576,008 ($673,854 - .04 \times 2,446,146$) is paid toward the capital portion of the loan at the end of the second year, and $599,048, $623,010, and

$648,080 are paid toward the loan at the end of years 3, 4, and 5, respectively. By the end of the fifth year the loan is completely paid off (553,854 + 576,008 + 599,048 + 623,010 + 648,080 = 3,000,000). Again, we assume that the full amount of each of the loan principal repayments goes toward increasing investment. In summary, under these assumptions, the net changes in investment each year are:

$$\Delta I_0 = -\$3,000,000, \ \Delta I_1 = \$553,854, \ \Delta I_2 = \$576,008,$$
$$\Delta I_3 = \$599,048, \ \Delta I_4 = \$623,010, \ \Delta I_5 = \$648,080.$$

There are three types of changes in consumption: the project benefits of $700,000 per year during each of the five years, the $673,854 loan repayment during each year, and the interest on the loan, which varies each year. The first year's interest on the loan is $120,000 as just discussed. For years 2, 3, 4 and 5, the interest equals $97,846, $74,806, $50,844, and $25,923, respectively. We assume that these amounts are entirely consumed, rather than reinvested. Thus, the net changes in consumption are:

$$\Delta C_0 = \$0$$
$$\Delta C_1 = \$700,000 - \$673,854 + \$120,000 = \$146,146,$$
$$\Delta C_2 = \$700,000 - \$673,854 + \$97,846 = \$123,992,$$
$$\Delta C_3 = \$700,000 - \$673,854 + \$74,806 = \$100,952,$$
$$\Delta C_4 = \$700,000 - \$673,854 + \$50,844 = \$76,146,$$
$$\Delta C_5 = \$700,000 - \$673,854 + \$25,923 = \$52,146.$$

Using $p_z = 1.5$ as the discount rate, the present value of the changes in consumption is $481,031 and the total present value of the changes in investment is −$134,571. With shadow pricing, the latter figure would be multiplied by $\theta = 1.33$ to convert it to its consumption equivalent and, hence, would equal −$178,979. Thus, with shadow pricing, the project's *NPV* would be $302,052 ($481,031 − $178,979). If shadow pricing were ignored, the *NPV* would increase to $346,460 ($481,031 − $134,571).

Although this method has strong theoretical appeal, it is somewhat difficult to use in practice and there are few examples of it actually being used to evaluate public-sector projects. One could certainly argue that there is no need to use the SPC if all of the impacts affect consumption, not investment. We argued above that in "normal times" most funds for government projects are obtained from taxes and that taxes tend to displace consumption, rather than investment, and therefore, as long as there are not other large effects on private-sector investments, one might be tempted to ignore the SPC. Sometimes, including during times of crisis, projects are deficit financed. However, in an open economy, deficit financing is not likely to have a big impact on domestic investment and so, again, one might discount using p_z, and ignore the SPC.[40]

The case for using the SPC is strongest for deficit-financed projects in a closed economy where the supply of savings and foreign funds are very unresponsive to the interest rate. It is also strong for CBAs of regulatory impacts. The social costs of abiding by a regulation are generally borne by firms and reduce the amount of resources available for investment.

Criticisms of Calculation and Use of θ

The SPC method accounts for increases and displacement of private investment and consumption in a theoretically appropriate fashion, which is an important advantage over other methods. Nonetheless, one can raise several objections. First, as opposed to just choosing a discount rate and using it in the *NPV* formula, it is difficult to explain to policy makers how the *NPV* calculations are made, let alone why. Second, the information requirements are more substantial than for the other discounting approaches. Third, as the previous example suggests, judgment plays an important role in deciding how to allocate benefits and costs between investment and consumption. Finally, as the *NPV* depends on θ, which in turn depends on r_z and p_z, the results are subject to the criticisms that pertain to the calculation of these parameters.

USING THE OPTIMAL GROWTH RATE APPROACH TO DISCOUNTING

Problems with Using Market Rates to Derive the SDR

Earlier we argued that the SDR should be based on the rate at which individuals are willing to trade current consumption for future consumption. We also showed that in some circumstances individual marginal rates of time preference, the marginal return on investment and the market rate of interest would all be equal and the choice of the SDR would be obvious. This has led some economists to argue that one can infer the SDR from market rates of interest. Also, as some market rates of return may reflect the opportunity cost of the resources used in a government project, it has been proposed that they can be used to infer the SDR. However, many economists now reject the notion that the SDR can be inferred from market interest rates. We discussed some of these reasons in the section on the calculation and use of p_z. One reason is that that there are many different market rates and it is not clear which rate to use or how to aggregate them. Also, evidence indicates that individuals do not behave rationally and consistently. Another reason is that market rates of return may overestimate the SDR due to market power and negative externalities, which we discussed in our critique of the use of r_z.

A final reason why analysts should not use market rates is that they only reflect the preferences of individuals currently alive, not those not yet born. This is especially problematic when a project's impacts span generations. Those yet unborn do not have a direct voice in current markets, yet we may believe that they should have standing in our (current) CBAs.[41] Members of the current generation may fail to account appropriately for the effects of long-term projects on the welfare of future generations. For these and other reasons, Nicholas Stern concluded that for projects addressing climate change it is "entirely inappropriate" to use market rates of return as a basis for the SDR.[42] The optimal growth rate method does not suffer from these problems.[43]

Numerical Values of the SDR Using the Optimal Growth Rate Method

We described the optimal growth rate model to determine the SDR earlier in this chapter. It implies that the SDR can be given by equation (10.6). To derive p_x by the optimal growth rate method, we need values of the elasticity of the social marginal utility of consumption with respect to per capita consumption, e, the pure rate of time preference, d, and the growth rate in per capita consumption, g.

Using annualized per capita quarterly data on real consumption expenditures for 1947–2002, we estimate that the average growth rate of consumption per head in the United States was 2.3 percent per annum.[44] It is difficult to predict the future long-run growth rate, especially as recent historical growth rates have varied substantially. *However, we think that future growth rates will fall somewhat and therefore recommend using g equal to 2.0 percent, with sensitivity analysis at 1.5 and 2.5 percent.*

There are a variety of ways to estimate or prescribe a value for e. Most proposed values range between 1 and 4.[45] Empirical estimates of e that are based on the progressivity built into the income tax schedule are about 1.5. *Based on a variety of considerations, we recommend setting e = 1.3, with sensitivity analysis at 1.0 and 2.0.*

There has been considerable debate about the value of d since Ramsey's original article. It may seem reasonable for society to discount consumption next year relative to consumption this year because of pure time preference, or impatience. However, when applied to long-term projects with intergenerational impacts, this would be equivalent to treating the utility of future generations as less valuable than the utility of the current generation. Ramsey himself thought that it is ethically indefensible to use a positive value. However, Kenneth Arrow shows that weighting all generations' welfare equally results in very high rates of savings being required of the current (or even of every) generation.[46] He demonstrates that, under reasonable parameter values, the current generation could be required to save approximately two-thirds of its income! To avoid this result, a positive pure rate of time preference should be employed. *Arrow suggests a figure of around 1.0 percent for d, which we use in the following calculations.*

With g = 2.0 percent, e = 1.3, and d = 1.0 percent, p_x is approximately equal to 3.5 percent. Sensitivity analysis with e ranging between 1.0 and 2.0 and with g varying between 1.5 and 2.5 percent implies p_x ranges from 2.5 percent and 6.0 percent. *Thus, we recommend using a value of p_x equal to 3.5 percent with sensitivity analysis at 2.0 and 6.0 percent.*[47]

Criticisms of the Optimal Growth Rate Method and Rate

There are several criticisms of this approach and of the estimated parameter values. First, as mentioned above, it is hard to predict the future long-run growth rate in consumption, g. Second, we use national income accounts to measure the growth rate in real (aggregate) consumption expenditure per person, but this may not accurately measure what economists mean by consumption. For example, this consumption measure includes purchases of consumer durables, which most analysts believe should be interpreted as investment. Also, it does not include the consumption of public goods. Third, the parameters e and d are based on value judgments about intergenerational equality.

The Shadow Price of Capital, θ, for Use with the Optimal Growth Rate Discount Rate

The optimal growth rate method derives a CRI. As mentioned above, if this rate is less than the rate that can be earned in the private sector, then society may underinvest in private-sector projects. To overcome this problem, private-sector investment flows should be converted to consumption equivalents by multiplying them by the shadow price of capital before discounting. In doing this, θ must be recomputed by replacing p_z in equation (10.10) or (10.11) with p_x. Using equation (10.11) with $p_x = 3.5$ percent, $r_z = 4.5$ percent, $f = 17$ percent, and $\delta = 10$ percent, then $\theta = 1.1$ approximately.[48] Given our recommended range for p_x of between 2 and 6 percent and for r_z of between 4 and 5 percent, θ can be as small as 1.0 and as large as 1.32. For sensitivity analysis, the smaller of these two values should be used with $p_x = 6$ percent and the larger value with $p_x = 2$ percent.

In summary, for intragenerational projects we recommend discounting using the optimal growth rate method with $p_x = 3.5$ percent and sensitivity analysis at 2 percent and 6 percent. Flows in or out of private-sector investment should first be multiplied by the shadow price of capital θ, equal to 1.1 with sensitivity analysis of θ equal to 1.0 when $p_x = 6$ percent and θ equal to 1.32 when $p_x = 2$ percent. These values are likely to be applicable in most developed countries.[49]

INTERGENERATIONAL DISCOUNTING

Reasons for Using a Time-Declining Discount Rate for Intergenerational Discounting

So far we have considered only constant (time-invariant) SDRs. We have assumed, for example, the same SDR is used to discount costs and benefits between years 401 and 400 as between years 1 and 0. There are at least four reasons to consider using a time-declining SDR (i.e., to use lower rates to discount costs and benefits that occur farther in the future). Most of these considerations become relevant when project effects cross-generational lines. However, there is no obvious way to decide when a project is intra-generational or intergenerational. In many circumstances, those as yet unborn when a project is initiated will live to be affected by it, whether as beneficiaries, taxpayers, or both. Those alive bear some of the startup costs, but may not live to reap the benefits. Nonetheless, both the serious ethical dilemmas and the practical differences that occur when considering long-term projects do not begin before a span of about 50 years. Thus, for discounting purposes, it is reasonable to define an intragenerational projects as one whose effects occur within a 50-year horizon.[50] Projects with significant effects beyond 50 years are considered intergenerational.

The first reason, which we briefly discussed earlier, is that individuals appear to be "time inconsistent."[51] Empirical behavioral evidence suggests that individuals apply lower rates to discount events that occur farther into the future, that is, they have decreasing time aversion. Exhibit 10-1 presents evidence that individual MRTPs for saving lives now versus saving lives in the future decline as the time horizon extends farther into the future. David Laibson cites evidence that individuals' discount functions are approximately hyperbolic, implying that they engage in *hyperbolic discounting*.[52] He explains that individuals recognize that, if they do not commit to saving, then on a day-to-day basis

---EXHIBIT 10-1---

Maureen Cropper and colleagues have conducted surveys to measure how participants are willing to trade off lives saved today with lives saved in the future. In round numbers, this research suggests that people are indifferent between one life saved today and two lives saved in 5 years' time, three lives saved in 10 years' time, six lives saved in 25 years' time, eleven lives saved in 50 years' time, and forty-four lives saved In 100 years' time. More precisely, and expressing the results in terms of marginal rate of time preference (MRTP), the research found an implicit marginal rate of time preference of 16.8 percent over a 5-year horizon, 11.2 percent over a 10-year horizon, 7.4 percent over a 25-year horizon, 4.8 percent over a 50-year horizon, and 3.8 percent over a 100-year horizon. These results suggest that individual MRTPs are significantly greater than zero, but they decline as the time horizon extends farther into the future.

Source: Adapted from Maureen L. Cropper, Selma K. Aydede, and Paul R. Portney, "Rates of Time Preference for Saving Lives," *American Economic Review: Papers and Proceedings* 82(2) 1992, 469–472.

(using a high short-term discount rate), they will never save as much for the future as they know they should (using a low long-term discount rate). Recognizing their lack of self-control, individuals may commit to savings plans with large penalties for early withdrawals, while using their available credit to otherwise maximize their current consumption. They may simultaneously save by purchasing an illiquid asset with a relatively low, after-tax real return (such as a government savings bond), make predetermined monthly mortgage payments, and borrow short-term on a credit card at a high real interest rate. These observed patterns of saving and borrowing simply reflect individuals' recognition of their lack of self-control and the time-declining discount rates that result from this.

The second reason pertains to evaluating decisions with impacts that occur far in the future, such as environmental effects, including reforestation, efforts to mitigate global warming by greenhouse gas abatement, preserving biodiversity through the protection of unique ecosystems, and the storage of radioactive waste. Discounting at a time-constant discount rate can pose ethical dilemmas. With a constant SDR the social discount factors decline geometrically. Even using a modest SDR, costs and benefits that occur sufficiently far in the future have a negligible value.[53] The use of a constant discount rate much in excess of 1.0 or 2.0 percent implies that it is not allocatively efficient for society to spend even a small amount today in order to avert a very costly environmental disaster, provided that the disaster occurs sufficiently far into the future. For example, if greenhouse gas buildup imposes a huge cost of say $1 trillion in 400 years' time, this has an *NPV* of less than $336 million today at a constant discount rate of 2 percent, and an *NPV* of less than $113,000 at a discount rate of 4 percent. Thus, if CBA used a discount rate of more than 2 percent, we would conclude that it is not worth spending $113,000 today to avert a major disaster with a cost of $1 trillion in 400 years. In contrast, with a time-declining SDR, the *NPV* may well imply that it is indeed worth averting the $1 trillion cost that will be incurred four centuries from now.

A third reason for using a time-declining SDR is to place greater weight on future generations than would otherwise occur. As we discussed above, some authors argue on ethical grounds that all generations should be weighted equally and that the SDR should be zero. Although the optimal growth rate method permits explicit consideration of the welfare of future generations, the most common social welfare function used with this method treats society as a single, representative individual whose well-being is equal to the discounted sum of the utility derived from present and future per capita consumption. This may make sense for evaluating 50-year investments; but it loses much of its relevance for evaluating 400-year or 10,000-year investments, such as for greenhouse gas abatement or the storage of radioactive waste.

The fourth reason for using a time-declining SDR is that the farther we look into the future, the greater is the inherent uncertainty as to the future growth rate of the economy and future market rates of interest. Allowing for this uncertainty means that lower and lower discount rates should be used to discount consumption flows that occur farther and farther in the future. To see why effective discount rates decline as they apply to benefits or costs that occur farther out in time when there is uncertainty about future discount rates, consider the following example. Suppose a project delivers a single benefit of $1 billion in 400 years. Suppose further that there is a 50 percent chance that the appropriate (constant) discount rate over this period will be 7 percent and a 50 percent chance that it will be 1 percent. One might imagine that we should average these two rates to obtain the expected discount rate, 4 percent, and then use this average rate to compute the expected *NPV* of the future benefit as $1 billion $\times e^{-(0.04) \times 400}$, which is approximately $110. However, this is incorrect. The expected *NPV* equals $1 billion $\times$ $[(0.5e^{-(0.07)400}) + (0.5e^{-(0.01)400})]$, which is approximately $9,157,800. This is equivalent to using a single, certain discount rate of approximately 1.2 percent. It is the discount factors of $e^{-(0.07)400}$ and $e^{-(0.01)400}$ that should be averaged. The values of these two discount factors are 6.9×10^{-11} percent, which is a very small number, and 0.183, respectively. In effect, the larger discount rate almost completely discounts itself out of the average. This effect grows as time horizons become longer, resulting in a time-declining schedule of discount rates. In the distant future, only the very lowest possible rate matters; all of the higher rates result in discount factors that approach zero. Note that this motivation for time-declining rates is due solely to uncertainty and does not imply time inconsistency in social choices.

Numerical Values of Time-Declining Discount Rates

Based on research by Richard Newell and William Pizer,[54] we suggest the following time-declining rate schedule based on the optimal growth rate model: *3.5 percent from year 0 to year 50, 2.5 percent from year 50 to year 100, 1.5 percent from year 100 to year 200, 0.5 percent from year 200 to year 300, and 0 percent thereafter.* For a single benefit in year 300, this schedule is equivalent to applying a single, constant rate of 1.67 percent. This schedule allow the effects on far future generations to be given more weight than time-invariant discount rates. After a given period of time, all future generations are essentially treated alike. Chapter 6 illustrates how this schedule would be used in practice.

THE SOCIAL DISCOUNT RATE IN ACTUAL PRACTICE

Current discounting practices in governments vary considerably. There is some evidence that many government agencies do not discount at all. For example, a survey of 90 U.S. municipalities with populations over 100,000 found that only 43 percent use discounting in evaluating projects.[55] At the federal level, U.S. government agencies appear to have less choice over whether to discount or not but there is considerable variation over the discount rate and procedure.[56]

The prescribed rates in the U.S. federal government have tended to be fairly high, but they have been trending lower. For example, in the 1970s and 1980s, the Office of Management and Budget (OMB) required most agencies to use a real discount rate of 10 percent.[57] More recently, the OMB has revised this rate downward to 7 percent.[58] The OMB advises agencies that wish to use either the consumption rate of interest with the shadow price of capital method or the optimal growth rate method to consult with the OMB prior to conducting their analyses.

In Canada, the pattern has been similar. In 1976, the Federal Treasury Board Secretariat (TBS) recommended the use of a real discount rate of 10 percent, with sensitivity analysis at 5 and 15 percent. In 1998, the TBS reaffirmed the 10 percent rate, but narrowed sensitivity analysis to plus or minus 2 percent.[59] In 2007 the TBS revised its guidelines and recommended an SDR of 8 percent, with sensitivity analysis using 3 percent and 10 percent.[60] Sometimes, however, the TBS allows much lower discount rates (0 to 3 percent) for health and environmental cost-benefit analyses, although this does not appear to be official policy. Some provincial government guidelines have led the federal guidelines in terms of adopting lower rates. For example, the British Columbia Crown Corporations Secretariat has recommended a real SDR of 8 percent since the early 1990s.[61]

These relatively high rates reflect the OMB's and TBS's preferences for basing the SDR on market rates. OMB's original 10% real rate was intended to approximate the opportunity cost of capital. The more recent 7 percent rate is based on low-yielding forms of capital (e.g., housing), as well as high-yielding corporate capital. The Canadian TBS's rates are based on the WSOC method with a high weight on the return to private sector investment. This was 75% in 1976 and 1998, but fell to 46 percent in 2007.

Even if one thinks that it is appropriate to discount using market-based methods reflecting the opportunity cost of capital, the rates proposed by the OMB and the TBS are too high. The private-sector does not achieve a real marginal before-tax return on investment of 10 percent, or even 7 percent. We estimate that this return is only about 4.5 percent, with sensitivity analysis at 4.0 and 5.0 percent.

Both the General Accountability Office (GAO) and the Congressional Budget Office (CBO) use a lower rate than the OMB. The CBO has estimated the real historical yield on U.S. government securities at 2 percent, and uses this rate plus or minus 2 percentage points. The GAO uses the average nominal yield on Treasury debt maturing between one year and the life of the project, less the forecast rate of inflation. GAO uses the same rate for all applications, while the CBO and OMB have a number of exceptions.[62]

A proposal by the U.S. Panel on Cost-Effectiveness in Health and Medicine recommends the use of a 3 percent discount rate for cost-effectiveness studies, with sensitivity analysis at rates between 0 percent and 7 percent.[63]

Guidelines published by the U.S. Environmental Protection Agency recommend using a SDR based on the optimal growth rate method. They propose a value of p_z of 2 to 3 percent.[64] They believe that because capital is relatively mobile and most environmental projects are relatively small, EPA projects are not likely to displace private-sector investment. Therefore, they do not suggest using the shadow price of capital, unless there are strong reasons to believe that private-sector investment is displaced. However, correspondence with the EPA indicates that they have commonly annualized the capital costs of an environmental rule using the marginal rate of return on private investment and then discounted this flow using p_z. This is equivalent to using the shadow price of capital under the simple assumptions of equation (10.10).[65] Using our point estimates and equation (10.10) would result in a shadow price of capital equal to 3.0. In contrast, using the more sophisticated approach in equation (10.11) would suggest that the shadow price of capital equals 1.33.

In 2003, the British Treasury issued recommendations for discounting that are similar to those recommended in this chapter. The specific recommendation is for a discount rate of 3.5 percent, which is based on the optimal growth rate method. They also suggest using a time-declining discount rate for projects with effects that occur after 30 years. After 300 years, the recommended discount rate reaches a minimum of 1 percent.[66] In France, a group of experts commissioned by the Ministry of Finance recommended a reduction in the SDR from 8% to 4% for most public-sector projects.[67]

CONCLUSION

There has been considerable debate as to the appropriate method of discounting, as well as the specific value of the SDR. There is now widespread agreement that the correct conceptual method of discounting is to shadow price investment flows and to discount the resulting consumption equivalents and the consumption flows using a consumption-based discount rate. We believe that the most appropriate method to determine the value of the SDR is the optimal growth rate method. We advocate the use of time-declining discount rates in projects with significant intergenerational impacts. Our discussion should have made it clear that analysts are unlikely to have complete confidence in whatever discount rate they use. It is almost always desirable, therefore, to test the sensitivity of ones results to changes in the parameters used in discounting. Nonetheless, in conducting CBA, choices must be made.

Our main conclusions are as follows. *First, flows in and out of private-sector investment during the first 50 years of a project should be weighted by the shadow price of capital, θ, which equals 1.1. Second, the resultant consumption equivalents and the consumption flows should be discounted, based on the optimal growth rate method, at a real SDR of 3.5 percent. Sensitivity analysis should be conducted with the SDR equal to 2 percent (and θ equal to 1.3) and with the SDR equal to 6 percent (and θ equal to 1.0). Intergenerational impacts, whether they affect investment or consumption, should be discounted at 2.5 percent (for years 50–100), 1.5 percent (for years 100–200), 0.5 percent (for years 200–300), and 0 percent (for years over 300).*

We do not recommend using a SDR derived from market-based interest rates (rather than using the optimal growth method). However, should you wish to do this, we suggest that, first, flows in and out of private-sector investment during the first 50 years of a project should be weighted by the shadow price of capital, θ, which equals 1.33. Second, the resultant consumption equivalents and the consumption flows should be discounted at a real SDR of 1.5 percent. Sensitivity analysis should be conducted with the SDR equal to 1 percent (and θ equal to 1.5) and with the SDR equal to 2 percent (and θ equal to 1.0). Intergenerational impacts, whether they affect investment or consumption, should be discounted at 1.0 percent (for years 50–100), 0.5 percent (for years 100–200), and 0 percent (for years over 300).

EXERCISES FOR CHAPTER 10

1. (Instructor-provided spreadsheet recommended.) The following table gives cost and benefit estimates in real dollars for dredging a navigable channel from an inland port to the open sea.

Year	Dredging and Patrol Costs ($)	Saving to Shippers ($)	Value of Pleasure Boating ($)
0	2,548,000	0	0
1	60,000	400,000	60,000
2	60,000	440,000	175,000
3	70,000	440,000	175,000
4	70,000	440,000	175,000
5	80,000	440,000	175,000
6	80,000	440,000	175,000
7	90,000	440,000	175,000

The channel would be navigable for seven years, after which silting would render it unnavigable. Local economists estimate that 75 percent of the savings to shippers would be directly invested by the firms or their shareholders, and the remaining 25 percent would be used by shareholders for consumption. They also determine that all government expenditures come at the expense of private investment. The social marginal rate of time preference is assumed to be 1.5 percent, the marginal rate of return on private investment is assumed to be 4.5 percent, and the shadow price of capital is assumed to be 1.33.

Assuming that the costs and benefits accrue at the end of the year they straddle and using the market-based interest rate approach, calculate the present value of net benefits of the project using each of the following methods.

a. Discount at the marginal rate of return on private investment, as suggested by the U.S. Office of Management and Budget.

b. Discount at the social marginal rate of time preference, as suggested by the U.S. Environmental Protection Agency.

c. Discount using the shadow price of capital method.

d. Discount using the shadow price of capital method. However, now assume that the social marginal rate of time preference is 2.0 percent, rather than 1.5 percent.

e. Discount using the shadow price of capital method. However, now assume that the shadow price of capital is 1.1, rather than 1.33. Again assume that the social marginal rate of time preference is 1.5 percent.

f. Discount using the shadow price of capital method. However, now assume that only 50 percent of the savings to shippers would be directly invested by the firms or their shareholders, rather than 75 percent. Again assume that the social marginal rate of time preference is 1.5 percent and that the shadow price of capital is 1.33.

2. An analyst for a municipal public housing agency explained the choice of a discount rate as follows: "Our agency funds its capital investments through nationally issued bonds. The

effective interest rate that we pay on the bonds is the cost that the agency faces in shifting revenue from the future to the present. It is, therefore, the appropriate discount rate for the agency to use in evaluating alternative investments." Comment on the appropriateness of this discount rate.

3. Assume the following: Society faces a marginal excess tax burden of raising public revenue equal to METB; the shadow price of capital equals θ; public borrowing displaces private investment dollar for dollar; and public revenues raised through taxes displace consumption (but not investment). Consider a public project involving a large initial capital expenditure, C, followed by a stream of benefits that are entirely consumed, B.
   a. Discuss how you would apply the shadow price of capital method to the project if it is financed fully out of current taxes.
   b. Discuss how you would apply the shadow price of capital method to the project if it is financed fully by public borrowing, which is later repaid by taxes.

4. Assume a project will result in benefits of $1 trillion in 500 years by avoiding an environmental disaster that otherwise would occur at that time.
   a. Compute the present value of these benefits using a time-constant discount rate of 3.5.
   b. Compute the present value of these benefits using the following time-declining discount rate schedule: 3.5 percent, years 1–50; 2.5 percent, years, 51–100; 1.5 percent, years 101–200; 0.5 percent, years 201–300; and 0 percent thereafter.

NOTES

1. This chapter draws on Mark A. Moore, Anthony E. Boardman, Aidan R. Vining, David L. Weimer, and David H. Greenberg, "'Just Give Me a Number!' Practical Values for the Social Discount Rate," *Journal of Policy Analysis and Management* 23(4) 2004, 789–812 and Anthony E. Boardman, Mark A. Moore and Aidan R. Vining, "The Social Discount Rate for Canada Based on Future Growth in Consumption," *Canadian Public Policy* 36(3), 2010 (forthcoming). We thank Mark Moore for his many contributions to this chapter.

2. Throughout this chapter we assume that impacts (costs and benefits) and discount rates are all measured in real dollars.

3. That is, $\Delta w / w_t = -i$.

4. In practice, analysts usually do not convert net benefits to certainty equivalents or option prices. Specifically, they use expected values rather than option prices because the former can be estimated from observable behavior, while the latter requires contingent valuation surveys. Unless strong assumptions are made about individuals' utility functions, even the sign, let alone the magnitude, of the difference between expected values and option prices is usually theoretically uncertain, except in the case of uncertainty about income (see Chapter 8, and the references therein). It is important, however, both conceptually and in practice, to treat risk and discounting separately. Nonetheless, in order to compensate for risk, analysts sometimes discount expected net benefits using a higher rate than they would in the absence of risk. Unfortunately, this procedure generally results in an incorrect estimate of the *NPV*. For example, suppose that a project has a relatively large expected terminal cost that is subject to risk. Using a higher rate to account for this risk will reduce, rather than magnify, the present value of this cost, making a positive *NPV* more, rather than less, likely. In contrast, the certainty equivalent for a negative net benefit is a more negative net benefit. As this example illustrates, it is inappropriate to attempt to take account of risk by adjusting the discount rate. For other reasons why doing this is problematic, see Coleman Bazelon and Kent Smetters, "Discounting Inside the Washington D.C. Beltway," *Journal of Economic Perspectives* 13(4) 1999, 213–228.

5. Nicholas Stern, *The Economics of Climate Change: The Stern Review* (New York: Cambridge University Press, 2007).

6. William D. Nordhaus, "A Review of the *Stern Review on the Economics of Climate Change*," Journal of Economic Literature 45(3) 2007, 682-702. See also Partha Dasgupta, "Commentary:

The Stern Review's Economics of Climate Change." *National Institute Economic Review* 199(1) 2007, 4–7 and Martin L. Weitzman, "A Review of the *Stern Review on the Economics of Climate Change*." *Journal of Economic Literature* 45(3) 2007, 703–724.

7. Assume here that, in order to reveal your true preferences, there is no arbitrage opportunity, that is, you could not borrow or lend money. Arbitrage means that you can simultaneously buy something in one market and sell it in another market and thereby make a guaranteed profit. If interest rates were less than 20 percent and arbitrage were allowed, you could say that you would rather have the $1,200 next year and then immediately borrow between $1,000 and $1,200 from the bank. Thus, you would say that you would prefer to have the $1,200 next year even though you would actually prefer to have $1,000 now.

8. It would make no conceptual difference if the consumer received income in both periods.

9. The (absolute value of the) slope of the budget constraint exceeds 1, indicating that the consumer earns positive interest (at rate i) on the part of income saved the first year.

10. To solve this problem formally we set up the following Lagrangian:

$$L = U(C_1, C_2) + \lambda \left[T - C_1 - \frac{C_2}{1 + 1} \right]$$

and then take derivatives with respect to C_1 and C_2:

$$L_{c_1} = \frac{\partial U}{\partial C_1} - \lambda = 0$$

$$L_c = \frac{\partial U}{\partial C_2} - \frac{\lambda}{1 + i} = 0$$

Consequently,

$$\frac{\partial U/\partial C_1}{\partial U/\partial C_2} = 1 + i$$

Now, by definition,

$$\text{MRS} \equiv \frac{\partial U/\partial C_1}{\partial U/\partial C_2} = 1 + p$$

where p = marginal rate of time preference. Therefore, $i = p$ at the optimum.

11. Formally, the result holds as long as the problem has an interior solution. A very impatient person

has an MRTP $> i$, which leads to a corner solution on the C_1 axis. For simplicity, we ignore this possibility.

12. At point Z, in Figure 10-2, the absolute value of the slope of the CPF, $(1 + r_z)$, exceeds the absolute value of the slope of the SIC, $(1 + p_z)$.

13. Frank P. Ramsey, "A Mathematical Theory of Saving," *Economic Journal* 38(152) 1928, 543–559.

14. Mathematically, they assume society (or a representative individual) maximizes social welfare which is given by:

$$\int_0^\infty e^{-\rho t} U(c_t)\, dt$$

Here, $U(c)$ is the utility that society (or a representative individual) derives from public and private per capita consumption at any moment in time, $e^{-\rho t}$ is the discount factor for utility of consumption at period t, e is the exponential function, and ρ is the rate at which future utility is discounted to the present. See Stephen A. Marglin, "The Social Rate of Discount and the Optimal Rate of Investment," *Quarterly Journal of Economics* 77(1) 1963: 95–111; James A. Mirrlees and Nicholas Stern, "Fairly Good Plans," *Journal of Economic Theory* 4(2) 1972: 268–288; W. R. Cline. *The Economics of Global Warming.* (Washington, D.C.: Institute for International Economics, 1992); Kenneth J. Arrow, "Intergenerational Equity and the Rate of Discount in Long-Term Social Investment." Paper presented at the IEA World Congress, 1995. Accessed 11 February 2008 at http://www-econ.stanford.edu/faculty/workp/swp97005.pdf; Nicholas Stern, *The Economics of Climate Change: The Stern Review* (New York: Cambridge University Press, 2007).

15. The estimated values of these rates, which were based on U.S. data, were obtained from Moore, Boardman, Vining, Weimer, and Greenberg, "'Just Give Me a Number!' Practical Values for the Social Discount Rate." For estimated values for Canada, see Boardman, Moore and Vining, "The Social Discount Rate for Canada Based on Future Growth in Consumption," *Canadian Public Policy* (forthcoming).

16. Arnold C. Harberger, "The Discount Rate in Public Investment Evaluation," *Conference Proceedings of the Committee on the Economics of Water Resource Development* (Denver, CO:

Western Agricultural Economics Research Council, Report No. 17, 1969).

17. See, for example, John Muellbauer and Ralph Lattimore, "The Consumption Function: A Theoretical and Empirical Overview," in M. H. Pesaran and M. R. Wickens, eds., *The Handbook of Applied Econometrics: Macroeconomics* (Cambridge, MA: Blackwell, 1995), 221–311.

18. Historical studies using U.S. data find this equity risk premium to be in the neighborhood of 6 to 7 percent; see R. Mehra and E. C. Prescott, "The Equity Premium in Retrospect," in G.M. Constantinides, M. Harris and R. Stulz, eds., *Handbook of the Economics of Finance* (Amersterdam: Elsevier, 2003). However, many researchers consider this amount is too high, a result known as the equity premium puzzle. Recent research by Glen Donaldson, Mark Kamstra and Lisa Kramer suggest that it is only about 3.5 percent; see R. Glen Donaldson, Mark J. Kamstra and Lisa A. Kramer, "Estimating the Equity Premium," *Journal of Financial and Quantitative Analysis* (forthcoming).

19. See P. Dasgupta, K. Maler, and S. Barrett, "Intergenerational Equity, Social Discount Rates, and Global Warming," in P. Portney and J. Weyant, eds., *Discounting and Intergenerational Equity* (Washington, D.C.: Resources for the Future, 1999), 51–78.

20. K. J. Arrow and R. C. Lind, "Uncertainty and the Evaluation of Public Investment Decisions," *American Economic Review* 60(3) 1997, 364–378.

21. However, Klein argues that the government pays a lower rate on its debt because it enjoys the coercive power of taxation and money creation, thus guaranteeing that it can always pay its debt Obligations; see M. Klein, "The Risk Premium for Evaluating Public Projects," *Oxford Review of Economic Policy* 13(4) 1997, 29–42.

22. C. J. Morrison and A. E. Schwartz, "State Infrastructure and Productive Performance," *American Economic Review* 86(5) 1991, 1095–1111.

23. Unless otherwise indicated, all our data are from the DRI Basic Economics macroeconomic database (formerly CITIBASE), viewed June 20, 2003.

24. J. B. Shoven and M. Topper, "The Cost of Capital in Canada, the United States and Japan," in J. B. Shoven and J. Whalley, eds., *Canada–U.S. Tax Comparisons* (Chicago: University of Chicago Press, 1992), 217–235. As high- income individuals

do most of the personal saving, their rates are likely the most appropriate.

25. If you think you have only a short time to live, then you will value the present very highly because, quite literally, there may be no tomorrow for you. Thus, it is reasonable to expect that older people have a higher MRTP rate than younger people. See Maureen L. Cropper, Sema K. Aydede, and Paul R. Portney, "Rates of Time Preference for Saving Lives." *American Economic Review* 82(2) (1992), 469–472, who found a positive relationship between age and the MRTP but found no significant relationship between respondents' MRTP and their sex, education, marital status, or income.

26. From April 1971 through December 2001, the average nominal primary conventional mortgage rate was 9.79 percent. Using the CPI-U (All Items) inflation rate of 4.85 percent and the tax rate of 30 percent, and accounting for the tax deductibility of interest paid on mortgages, the real, after-tax return to paying down a mortgage averaged 1.91 percent. Adjusting for the CPI overstatement of inflation and rounding yields an estimate of 3 percent. Similar calculations for 2001 and 2000 give estimates of 3.3 and 2.2 percent, respectively.

27. S. Frederick, G. Loewenstein, and T. O'Donoghue, "Time Discounting and Time Preference: A Critical Review," *Journal of Economic Literature* 40(2) 2002, 351–400.

28. Laibson explains that individuals may have pre-committed themselves to saving a certain amount of their income in an illiquid asset, while borrowing for current consumption from ready sources of credit. However, they are still not equating their marginal rates of time preference to a single market rate. See David Laibson, "Golden Eggs and Hyperbolic Discounting," *Quarterly Journal of Economics* 112(2) 1997, 443–477.

29. John T. Warner and Saul Pleeter. "The Personal Discount Rate: Evidence from Military Downsizing," *American Economic Review* 91(1) 2001, 33–53.

30. George Loewenstein and Drazen Prelec, "Anomalies in Intertemporal Choice: Evidence and an Interpretation," *Quarterly Journal of Economics* 107(2) 1992, 573–597.

31. See, among others, Robert C. Lind, "Reassessing the Government's Discount Rate Policy in Light

of New Theory and Data in a World Economy with a High Degree of Capital Mobility," *Journal of Environmental Economics and Management* 18(2) 1990, S8–S28.

32. For Canada, Jenkins and Kuo suggests $a = .46$, $b = .15$ and $1 - a - b = .39$. Glenn P. Jenkins and C.-Y. Kuo, "The Economic Opportunity Cost of Capital for Canada—An Empirical Update," Queen's Economics Department., February 2008).

33. In the United States, for example, since 1980 individual income tax provides about 46 percent of revenues while corporate income taxes provide about 10 percent of revenues; see http://www.gpoaccess.gov/usbudget/fy10/sheets/hist02z1.xls (accessed 13 Feb 2010).

34. Dynan and colleagues find that marginal propensities to save out of disposable income vary between 2.4 and 11 percent in the United States (K. E. Dynan, J. Skinner, and S. P. Zeldes, "Do the Rich Save More?" Federal Reserve Board, Financial and Economic Discussion Series, 2000). Souleles (2002) finds that the Reagan tax cuts of the 1980s had very strong effects on current consumption when enacted (rather than when announced), inducing marginal propensities to consume out of nondurables of between 0.6 and 0.9 (N. S. Souleles, "Consumer Response to the Reagan Tax Cuts," *Journal of Public Economics* 85(1) 2002, 99–120). Even predictable tax refunds are largely spent when received, indicating that consumption is very responsive to the actual, rather than the predictable, permanent level of income, contrary to standard economic theory. See N. S. Souleles, "The Response of Household Consumption to Income Tax Refunds," *American Economic Review* 89(4) 1999, 947–958.

35. This approach was first suggested by Otto Eckstein and systematically developed by David Bradford. See Otto Eckstein, *Water Resource Development: The Economics of Project Evaluation* (Cambridge, MA: Harvard University Press, 1958) and David F. Bradford, "Constraints on Government Investment Opportunities and the Choice of Discount Rate," *American Economic Review* 65(5) 1975: 887–899.

36. Understanding the derivation of equation (10.11) clarifies the meaning of f. Suppose an investment of \$1 yields a gross (before depreciation) return of ρ in the first period. Then, with a savings rate of f, $f\rho$ is reinvested and $(1 - f)\rho$ is consumed. With depreciation of d in this period, the total amount invested in the second period equals $1 + f\rho - \delta$. Similarly, in the second period the return is $\rho(1 + f\rho - \delta)$ of which $f\rho(1 + f\rho - \delta)$ is reinvested and $(1 - f)\rho(1 + f\rho - \delta)$ is consumed. With depreciation of $\delta(1 + f\rho - \delta)$ in the second period, the total amount invested in the third period equals $[1 + f\rho - \delta] + [f\rho(1 + f\rho - \delta)] - [\delta(1 + f\rho - \delta)] = (1 + f\rho - \delta)^2$. And so on. Consumption in period 1 is $(1 - f)\rho$, consumption in period 2 is $(1 - f)\rho(1 + f\rho - \delta)$, consumption in period 3 is $(1 - f)\rho(1 + f\rho - \delta)^2$, and so forth. This consumption stream is a perpetuity [with annual benefits of $(1 - f)\rho$] that grows at a constant rate, $f\rho - \delta$. Discounting this stream at p_z using the results in Chapter 6 gives:

$$\theta = \frac{\rho - f\rho}{p_z + \delta - f\rho}$$

In this formulation, r_z is the net return on capital after depreciation, that is,

$$\rho = r_z + \delta.$$

Substituting for ρ in the above equation yields equation (10.11). For more information see Randolph M. Lyon, "Federal Discount Policy, the Shadow Price of Capital, and Challenges for Reforms," *Journal of Environmental Economics and Management* 18(2) 1990, S29–S50, Appendix I.

37. Charles R. Hulten and Frank C. Wykoff, "The Measurement of Economic Depreciation" in R. Hulten, ed., *Depreciation, Inflation, and the Taxation of Income from Capital* (Washington, D.C.: Urban Institute Press, 1981), 81–125. See also B. M. Fraumeni, "The Measurement of Depreciation in the U.S. National Income and Product Accounts," *Survey of Current Business* 77(7) 1997, 7–23.

38. For a more detailed illustration see Mark A. Moore, Anthony E. Boardman, and David H. Greenberg, "The Social Discount Rate in Canada," in A. R. Vining and J. Richards, eds., *Building the Future: Issues in Public Infrastructure in Canada* (Toronto, ON: C. D. Howe Institute, 2001), 73–130.

39. If the loans for the project were obtained from persons residing outside the community instead of local citizens, one might believe that benefits and

costs accruing to these persons are irrelevant to its investment decisions and, therefore, ignore them in computing the project's net present value. Also, if there was the possibility of borrowing from abroad, then there will be less than complete crowding out of domestic private investment. Private investment may also be less than completely crowded out if there were unemployed resources in the local economy.

40. U.S. Environmental Protection Agency, *Guidelines for Preparing Economic Analyses* (Washington, D.C.: U.S. Government Printing Office, 2000), 48. See also R. C. Lind, "Reassessing the Government's Discount Rate Policy in Light of New Theory and Data in a World Economy with a High Degree of Capital Mobility."

41. For a discussion of this issue, see Daniel W. Bromley, "Entitlements, Missing Markets, and Environmental Uncertainty," *Journal of Environmental Economics and Management* 17(2) 1989, 181–194. Note, however, the willingness of people to pass inheritances to their children and to pay to preserve certain natural resources indicates indirect standing to future generations.

42. Nicholas Stern, 2008. "The Economics of Climate Change," *American Economic Review: Papers and Proceedings* 98(2) 2008, 1–37.

43. Otto Eckstein, *Water Resource Development: The Economics of Project Evaluation*; Edmund Phelps, "The Golden Rule of Accumulation: A Fable for Growthmen," *American Economic Review* 51(4) 1961, 638-643; Stephen Marglin, "The Social Rate of Discount and the Optimal Rate of Investment"; Kenneth J. Arrow, "Intergenerational Equity and the Rate of Discount in Long-Term Social Investment"; P. Dasgupta, K. Maler, and S. Barrett, "Intergenerational Equity, Social Discount Rates, and Global Warming."

44. This value was obtained by regressing the natural logarithm of real per capita consumption on time. Comparably, Prescott (p. 5) argues the secular growth rate of the U.S. economy in the twentieth century was 2 percent. See E. Prescott, "Prosperity and Depressions," *American Economic Review* 92(2) 2002, 1–15.

45. See Martin L. Weitzman, "A Review of the *Stern Review on the Economics of Climate Change*." Arrow et al. suggest that *e* is between 1 and 2.

K. J. Arrow, W. R. Cline, K. G. Maler, M. Munasinghe, R. Squitieri, and J. E. Stiglitz, "Intertemporal Equity, Discounting and Economic Efficiency," in J. P. Bruce et al., eds., *Climate Change 1995* (Cambridge, UK: Cambridge University Press, 1995), 128–144.

46. Kenneth J. Arrow, "Intergenerational Equity and the Rate of Discount in Long-Term Social Investment."

47. Kula estimates or argues g = 2.3 percent, e = 1.89, and d = 0.9, and therefore he suggests p_x = 5.2 percent. See E. Kula, "Derivation of the Social Time Preference Rates for the United States and Canada," *Quarterly Journal of Economics* 99(4) 1984, 873–882. Cline, assuming the likely future world growth rate is 1 percent, d = 0, and e = 1.5, estimates p_x = 1.5 percent. See W. R. Cline, *The Economics of Global Warming* (Washington, D.C.: Institute for International Economics, 1992).

48. Cline proposes using a value of θ equal to 1.56 and then discounting using p_x measured at 1.5 percent for all CBAs, including greenhouse gas abatement projects. His estimate of θ uses r_z 8.0 percent, assumes that all investments have 15-year lives, and that f = 0.2. See W. R. Cline, *The Economics of Global Warming*.

49. See also Evans and Sezer who provide theoretically grounded estimates of the SDR for a variety of countries. D. J. Evans and H. Sezer, "Social Discount Rates for Six Major Countries," *Applied Economic Letters* 11(9) 2004, 557–560, and D. J. Evans and H. Sezer, "Social Discount Rates for Member Countries of the European Union," *Journal of Economic Studies* 32(1) 2005, 47–60.

50. One rationale for this 50-year cutoff is that most equipment, structures, and buildings will not last much longer than 50 years. Depreciation rates appear to range between 3.4 and 13.3 percent per year, implying that between 80 percent and virtually everything has depreciated after 50 years. Thus, there are likely to be few public investments that are intergenerational in our sense. Another argument is that 50 years corresponds approximately to two generations—our generation and our children's—and that events beyond this time period truly belong to future generations. See C. R. Hulten and F. C. Wykoff, "The Measurement of Economic Depreciation"; and M. Nadir and I. Prucha, "Estimation of the

Depreciation Rate of Physical and R&D Capital" *Economic Inquiry* 34(1) 1996, 43–56. A third rationale is provided by Newell and Pizer, which we discuss later. R. G. Newell and W. A. Pizer, "Discounting the Distant Future: How Much do Uncertain Rates Increase Valuations?" *Journal of Environmental Economics and Management* 46(1) 2003, 52–71.

51. After reviewing the literature on counterexamples to constant discounting, George Loewenstein and Drazen Prelec conclude that "unlike the EU [expected utility] violations, which in many cases can only be demonstrated with a clever arrangement of multiple choice problems (e.g., the Allais paradox), the counterexamples to *DU* [constant discounting] are simple, robust, and bear directly on central aspects of economic behavior." See George Loewenstein and Drazen Prelec, "Anomalies in Intertemporal Choice: Evidence and an Interpretation," at p. 574.

52. David Laibson, "Golden Eggs and Hyperbolic Discounting."

53. With constant discounting, impacts that arise in year *n* are weighted by the discount factor $(1 + i)^{-n}$, which declines geometrically. Thus, impacts that occur far in the future have a low weight. For example, $1 in 100 years has an *NPV* of less than $0.01 using an SDR of more than 4 percent.

54. Newell and Pizer ("Discounting the Distant Future: How Much do Uncertain Rates Increase Valuations?") adopt an approach based on the historical behavior of interest rates. Their model captures the uncertainty in forecasting the rates that will prevail in the far future. They examine the U.S. government's real, long-term bond rate over the past 200 years and find the data do not clearly distinguish between a random-walk and a mean-reversion model. They prefer the random-walk version and use it to simulate the future path of the bond rate, from both a 4 percent and a 2 percent initial value. They generate thousands of different time paths and use these to construct expected discount factors. This results in a time-declining scale of effective discount rates. Hepburn, Koundouri, Panopoulou, and Pantelidis apply this method to four other countries. See C. Hepburn, P. Koundouri, E. Panopoulou, and T. Pantelidis, "Social Discounting Under Uncertainty: A Cross-Country Comparison,"
Journal of Environmental Economics and Management 57(2) 2009, 140–150. In an alternative approach, Weitzman surveyed almost 2,200 economists, asked each to provide a single, real rate to use in discounting the costs and benefits of global climate change, and found that the frequency distribution of the respondents' rates approximated a gamma distribution. His main finding is that even if every respondent believes in a constant discount rate, the widespread of opinion results in the SDR declining significantly over time. Based on the distribution of his respondents' preferred discount rates, Weitzman suggests a scale for SDRs that approaches zero after 200 years. See M. Weitzman, "Gamma Discounting," *American Economic Review* 91(1) 2001, 260–271. Newell and Pizer derive rates that are generally higher than Weitzman's rates and fall more slowly, with the declining rate kicking in after about 50 years.

55. Richard O. Zerbe Jr. and Dwight Dively, "How Municipal Governments Set Their Discount Rate: Do They Get It Right?" (manuscript, University of Washington, 1990).

56. Edward R. Morrison, "Judicial Review of Discount Rates Used in Regulatory Cost-Benefit Analysis," *The University of Chicago Law Review* 65(4) 1998, 1333–1363. For a review of discounting in various U.S. government agencies, see Coleman Bazelon and Kent Smetters, "Discounting Inside the Washington D.C. Beltway."

57. OMB (Office of Management and Budget, Circular A-94), 1972.

58. OMB, "Economic Analysis of Federal Regulations Under Executive Order 12866" (Office of Management and Budget: Washington, D.C.), 1996.

59. Treasury Board Secretariat, *Benefit-Cost Analysis Guide Regulatory Programs* (Ottawa, Ontario, March 1976), Chapter 11: Discounting. The 1998 Guidelines are no longer available.

60. Treasury Board of Canada Secretariat, *Canadian Cost-Benefit-Cost Analysis Guide: Regulatory Proposals (Interim)* (Ottawa, ON: Treasury Board Secretariat, 2007). Also available at http://www.regulation.gc.ca/documents/gl-ld/analys/analystb-eng.asp.

61. See British Columbia Crown Corporations Secretariat, *Multiple Account Evaluation Guidelines* (Victoria, BC, 1993).

62. Both the OMB and CBO use private-sector rates for asset divestitures. If they did not, they would be using a lower discount rate than the private sector, implying that the *NPV* of assets is higher in the public sector than in the private sector. Assuming no efficiency differences between public and private ownership, this would imply that the government should never divest any assets.

63. M. C. Weinstein, J. E. Siegel, M. R. Gold, M. S. Kamlet, and L. B. Russell, "Recommendations of the Panel on Cost-Effectiveness in Health and Medicine: Consensus Statement," *Journal of the American Medical Association* 276(15) 1996, 1253–1258.

64. U.S. Environmental Protection Agency, Guidelines for Preparing Economic Analyses, p. 48.

65. See Jeffrey A. Kolb and Joel D. Scheraga, "Discounting the Benefits and Costs of Environmental Regulations," *Journal of Policy Analysis and Management* 9 (1990), 381–390.

66. HM Treasury, *Green Book, Appraisal and Evaluation in Central Government: Treasury Guidance* (London: HM Treasury, 2003), Chapter 5 and Annex 6. Available at *www.hm-treasury. gov.uk/economic_data_and_tools/greenbook_ index.cfm.*

67. D. Lebegue, et al., "Révision Du Taux D'Actualisation Des Investissements Publics." Rapport du Groupe d'Experts Présidé par Daniel Lebegue, (Commissariat General du Plan 2005).

CHAPTER 11

Predicting and Monetizing Impacts

Cost-benefit analysis assesses the efficiency of alternative courses of action. It requires prediction of the impacts of the alternatives and their monetization. The first ten chapters lay out the conceptual foundations for predicting and monetizing. This chapter and the following five chapters provide methods and resources for actually completing these tasks in practice. This chapter provides a brief overview of the various approaches to prediction and monetization. The following five chapters describe these approaches in detail

Keep in mind that good CBA predicts and monetizes *all* the impacts of the alternative policies being considered. Some impacts, such as the use of real resources to implement policies, can usually be predicted with considerable confidence in fairly straightforward ways and monetized directly with market prices. Other impacts, especially those involving people changing their behaviors, can only be predicted indirectly, often based on statistical inference or perhaps even theory alone, and therefore they may be very uncertain. Furthermore, monetizing often requires analysts to use shadow prices, such as willingness to pay for reductions in mortality risk, that are not directly revealed in markets and thus also uncertain. CBA requires analysts to accept these uncertainties to produce a comprehensive assessment of alternative policies.

Imagine that you completed the first three steps in CBA set out in Chapter 1. You have identified the alternative policies, determined standing, and catalogued the relevant impacts with appropriate units of measure. Next you must predict the impacts of each alternative and monetize them. Much of the effort in a typical CBA goes into these two steps. Unlike most social science research, where one can choose to focus on some impacts, perhaps because data are available to support estimation of past effects as the basis for prediction, you do not have the luxury of focusing on some impacts and ignoring others. You must make predictions of all impacts even in the absence of strong supporting evidence. To do this, you should use policy research, relevant theory, and, when all else fails, learn about the subject and make informed guesses. By all means be self-conscious about your uncertainties and be forthright in presenting them. Because of these uncertainties, Monte Carlo simulation and the other forms of sensitivity analyses illustrated in Chapter 7 are essential components of almost any CBA for conveying the degree of certainty in the ultimate CBA prediction of net benefits.

PREDICTING IMPACTS

Prediction concerns impacts occurring in the future. Yet, the primary basis for prediction is usually what has happened in the past. Sometimes policy analysts, but more often policy researchers working in universities and research institutes, use observed data to assess the consequences of past policy changes. Their inferences about the effects of these prior policy changes drawn from evaluations can inform predictions about what is likely to happen if the policy were continued, terminated, expanded, or replicated. Obviously, analysts must move beyond this evaluation-as-the-basis-for-prediction approach when predicting the consequences of either novel policies or policies in place that have not been evaluated. Perhaps a similar policy intervention that has been evaluated can be found to provide at least some guidance for prediction. Or perhaps estimates of elasticities made in other contexts can be used to predict impacts.

Three major sources of error arise during the application of CBA.[1] First, *omission errors,* the exclusion of impacts with associated costs or benefits, prevent CBAs from being comprehensive. Sometimes impacts are not anticipated. Other times they are anticipated but not included in the analysis for lack of quantitative predictions of their magnitudes or plausible shadow prices for monetizing them. As discussed in Chapter 2, the inability or unwillingness to predict or monetize forces a retreat to qualitative CBA. In cases in which only one major impact cannot be predicted or monetized, the analyst may first calculate net benefits without it and then ask the question: how large would the monetized value of the excluded impact have to be to change the sign of net benefits?

Second, *forecasting errors* arise simply because we cannot predict the future with certainty. The past, which is the empirical focus of the social sciences, is an imperfect guide to the future. The larger and more novel is the policy being assessed, the greater the danger that the future will differ from the past. Much of the discussion that follows considers the ways that the past can be used as a basis for making predictions. As noted below, psychological biases of individuals tend to make some types of forecasts overly optimistic. There may also be unanticipated difficulties and adaptations that make actual experience deviate from forecasts. Forecasts of the real resources required for large and complex infrastructure projects are often too low because of the need for redesign as implementation reveals information about the site and the actual performance of the capital equipment employed. Forecasts of regulatory impacts are often too large because they fail to anticipate offsetting behaviors that reduce either risk reductions[2] or compliance costs.[3]

Third, *valuation errors* occur because we often do not have confident estimates of appropriate shadow prices for converting each predicted impact into an opportunity cost or a WTP. As with forecasting, the more novel is the impact being monetized, the greater is the challenge of finding an appropriate shadow price. Plausible shadow prices can often be gleaned from available research but sometimes they must be developed and defended by the analyst.

Analysts must often be clever and bold to complete comprehensive CBAs. They should also anticipate the errors inherent in their efforts and consciously assess them to the greatest extent possible.

Simplify by Predicting Incremental Impacts Relative to the Status Quo

Good policy analysis always keeps the status quo as a potential option in case none of the alternatives under consideration are superior to it. CBA also keeps the status quo as an alternative, albeit usually implicitly. It does so by *predicting the incremental impacts of policy alternatives relative to those that would occur under the status quo policy*. As discussed in Chapter 1, the most efficient alternative project has both the largest net benefits among the alternatives to the status quo and has positive net benefits to ensure that it offers larger net benefits than the status quo.

For example, imagine that the alternatives being assessed will have four types of impacts, Z_1, Z_2, Z_3, and Z_4. If an alternative policy and the status quo have logically identical impacts Z_1 and Z_2, then assessing the alternative relative to the status quo obviates the need to predict these impacts quantitatively because they net out when the predicted impacts of the status quo are subtracted from the predicted impacts of the alternative. The analyst would have to predict the difference in impacts Z_3 and Z_4 between the alternative and the status quo. For example, suppose an alternative criminal justice policy would use the same real resources as the status quo policy: the incremental resources required would be zero. However, if the alternative would reduce crime relative to the status quo, then it would be necessary to predict this difference quantitatively.

Predict Using Data from an Ongoing Policy

Policies often take the form of programs for specific populations, such as those in a particular geographic area or those with a particular condition. These existing policies may provide data useful for predicting the impacts of their own continuation or their replication for other populations. As discussed in Chapter 12, true experiments with random assignment of subjects into treatment and control groups, with the latter continuing under the status quo, generally provide the most confident inferences of the impacts that a policy has actually produced. Quasi-experiments with nonrandom assignment into treatment and control groups generally provide less confident assessment of impacts and often require statistical adjustments to account for nonrandom assignment. In any event, an evaluation of an existing program provides at least some basis for predicting its impacts in the future, or of the impacts likely to result from its replication.

Even in the absence of an experimental or quasi-experimental evaluation, investigation of the policy in place may prove useful in identifying the resources needed to implement it. Also, in the case of social programs, data may be available on relevant outcomes for at least program participants. To make use of these program measures, the analyst must find a relevant "comparison" group (sometimes also called a "control" group) to answer the question, "Compared to what?"

Consider, for example, an intervention aimed at supporting schizophrenics in community living situations that keeps track of the contacts of participants with the criminal justice system, their hospitalizations, their employment records, and their suicides. Absent an explicit control or comparison group as part of an experimental or quasi-experimental design, analysts may take population averages or reports from specific studies as a basis for comparison. With respect to hospitalizations, for instance, a study of California Medicaid recipients with schizophrenia found annual rates of psychiatric hospitalizations of 27 percent and medical hospitalizations of 11 percent.[4] A first cut at an estimate of the impact of the intervention on rates of hospitalizations would be to subtract the observed rates for those in the intervention from these reported rates for California. A more sophisticated approach might use the statistical model presented in the article to estimate what the hospitalization rates would have been for a group with the demographic characteristics of those in the intervention. It would also be important to consider if there are likely to be any systematic differences between California schizophrenics participating in the Medicaid program from 1998 to 2000 and the schizophrenics in the intervention. The estimate that results after taking account of these sorts of considerations would be the basis for predicting the effect of the intervention on hospitalizations if it were to be continued or replicated.

Predict Based on Single Evaluation of a Similar Policy

An evaluation of a policy similar to the one being analyzed may be available. Its value as a basis for prediction depends on how closely it matches the policy being considered and how well the evaluation was executed.

Policies can be similar in the sense of having the same underlying model, but differ in the intensity and type of inputs used and their target populations. Consider, for example, two visiting nurse programs aimed at reducing child abuse in at-risk families. One might involve one-hour visits every two weeks by public health nurses to families with adults who are suspected of having abused their children. The other might involve one-hour visits ever month by nurse's aids to families with adults who were formally found to have abused their children. Which of these differences are relevant in using the evaluation of one program to predict the consequences of the other? These two programs may have too many differences to allow confident prediction. Perhaps if they differed only in terms of the frequency of visits, the analyst could make various assumptions about the relationship between frequency of visits and impacts to get a range of plausible predictions. So, if a linear relationship were assumed, a program with half the frequency would be predicted to produce half the impact. Assumptions of nonlinear relationships would yield different predictions. Analysts must fall back on their substantive knowledge and theory to decide how to take account of such differences.

The quality of the evaluation design is especially important to consider when using a single study as the basis for prediction. In general, true experimental designs with random assignment of subjects to treatment and control groups are most desirable. However, randomization can fail to provide comparable treatment and control groups if the number of subjects is small or the mechanism for randomization is flawed. Quasi-experimental designs in which comparisons are made without random assignment to the treatment and control groups can produce poor inferences for a variety of reasons discussed in Chapter 12.

Even when its evaluation design is sound, basing prediction on a single study risks making incorrect predictions for several reasons. First, there is the bias of academic journals to publish studies with statistically significant results, while, in fact, there may be other unpublished studies that did not find statistically significant effects.[5] Consequently, the one published study may show an unrepresentative effect.

Second, people tend to bring cognitive biases to their decision making, including forecasting decisions, that tend to lead to overoptimistic predictions.[6] These cognitive biases, as well as more careful implementation when the evaluator is closely associated with the policy than is likely in replication, tend to make findings of positive effects somewhat overly optimistic.[7] Analysts should guard against this *optimism bias* when they are predicting the consequences of policies they favor. For the same reason, some analysts routinely discount the size of effects from studies in which the evaluator was closely associated with the design or implementation of the program.[8]

Third, although rarely taken into account in practice, the most appropriate statistical inference about what has happened may not correspond to the best prediction of what will happen. The common approach for analysts seeking to predict impact from evaluations is to interpret the estimated effect, perhaps a mean difference in an experiment or a coefficient in a regression analysis (see Chapter 13), as the predicted impact. However, when the sample size is small or the fit of the model to the data is poor, the estimated effect may give a prediction that is too large (in absolute value sense) from the perspective of being likely to be close to the impact that will actually result from a repetition of the experiment.[9] Consequently, a more reliable prediction may result if the estimated impact is "shrunk" in proportion to the poorness of the fit of the model to the data. In a regression context, for example, a recommended heuristic is to shrink the coefficient by $(F-1)/F$, where F is the F-statistic for the fit of the model to the data.[10]

Simply relying on standard statistical approaches can also lead to an underestimation of effects. It is common for social scientists to treat estimated impacts as zero if the probability of observing them if they were truly zero is more than 5 percent. In other words, impacts that are not statistically significant at conventional levels are treated as zero. This may be an appropriate approach in the social sciences where researchers wish to have overwhelming evidence before rejecting a null effect in favor of some alternative theory. However, it is generally not the right approach in CBA where the estimated effect, perhaps shrunk, is likely to be a better prediction than zero. The standard error of the estimated effect conveys the degree of uncertainty in its value and should be used in Monte Carlo simulations of net benefits. Indeed, the distribution of net benefits resulting from Monte Carlo simulations provides the basis for investigating the hypothesis of interest: predicted net benefits are positive.

Predictions Based on Meta-Analyses of Similar Policies

Some policy interventions are replicated in many locations and evaluated with experimental or quasi-experimental research designs. In some policy areas a sufficient number of these evaluations are made public to permit a statistical assessment of their combined results. This process, called *meta-analysis,* seeks to use the information in the studies to find an effect size and its variation.[11] Drawing information from multiple evaluations reduces the chances that the overall result will suffer from the limitations of any one of the evaluations.

Meta-analysis begins with an identification of the relevant evaluations that are the sources of its data. Social science researchers often limit the evaluations they consider to those found in articles published in refereed journals. Policy analysts seeking to apply CBA may choose to include unpublished evaluations of relatively new or unusual interventions, if there are few published evaluations. The quality of the source of the evaluation can itself be a variable in the meta-analysis, along with direct classifications of the quality of the research design. In general, published studies, which have undergone peer review, are more credible. However, the reviewing process tends to bias publication decisions toward articles showing statistically significant effects, which potentially makes the pool of available published articles overly optimistic.[12] In addition, the delay in the publishing process from initial submission of manuscripts to publication of articles may be several years, so that relying solely on published studies may miss the most recent, and perhaps most relevant, findings.

A standardized measure of effect size is determined and extracted from each study so that findings based on somewhat different measures can be combined. For example, different achievement tests may be used in evaluations of a classroom intervention. These results may be standardized in terms of their underlying distribution so that the units of measure become standard deviations. For example, an evaluation of the effect of tutoring on student performance measured the effect size as the difference between the test scores for the treatment and control groups divided by the standard deviation of scores for the control group.[13] Measures of the variation of effect size in each study are also extracted from the studies. In the simplest approach, the standardized effect sizes and their variances are combined to find an average effect size and its variance. More sophisticated approaches may use multivariate regression to estimate an average effect size and variance controlling for the qualities of the studies, variations in composition of subject populations in the studies, and differences in the details of implementation of the intervention.

The Washington State Institute for Public Policy (WSIPP), which does analysis at the request of the state legislature, makes exemplary use of meta-analysis to support its application of CBA to prospective policies.[14] For example, consider the efforts of a team of its analysts to assess the costs and benefits of interventions in K–12 schooling policies. The team conducted a meta-analysis of 38 evaluations of class size reductions and a meta-analysis of 23 evaluations of moving from half-day to full-day kindergarten.[15] Measuring effect size in standard deviations of test scores, the meta-analysis of class reduction evaluations found an effect size of reducing classes from 20 to 19 students of 0.019 standard deviations for kindergarten through grade 2, 0.007 standard deviations for grades 3 through 6, and no statistically significant effect for higher grades. The team used these effects as a starting point for their analysis, allowing for annual decay of effects in later grades. They then related improved test scores to lifetime earnings and other social effects.

When multiple evaluations relevant to predicting impacts for a CBA are available, it is worth considering whether to invest substantial resources to complete a competent meta-analysis. Even when only a few evaluations are available, it is worthwhile using meta-analysis methods to combine their effects. Indeed, with only a small number of available studies the costs of implementing the meta-analysis are likely to be low. Of course, analysts can take advantage of meta-analyses performed by others, whether they are directly related to CBA as are many of those done by the Washington

State Institute for Public Policy, or they summarize the research relevant to predicting a specific impact.

Predict Using Generic Elasticities

Evaluations of policies similar to the alternative being analyzed often provide evidence relevant to prediction of all or many of the impacts. In their absence, analysts must seek out a variety of evidence to support their predictions. One common approach is to search for relevant elasticities. Often policies or programs change the effective prices of goods, either directly through changes in their price or indirectly through changes in the convenience of consumption. In these cases the impact is the change in the quantity of the good consumed. If an estimate of the price elasticity of demand is available, then the methods set out in Chapter 13 can be used to translate the change in effective price to a change in consumption.

Consider, for example, a program that would lower the price seen by its participants for access to health care. Absent any available evaluation of this or similar policies, an analyst might predict a change in medical care utilization caused by the reduction in price based on a price elasticity of demand of −0.2 as estimated using data from the RAND Health Insurance Experiment.[16] Although finding a relevant elasticity or other empirical basis for prediction from experiments may seem somewhat fortuitous, it is often worth searching for them among the over 240 major social policy experiments that have been completed in the United States.[17]

Much empirical work in the social sciences, medicine, and many other fields makes use of observational data. In economics, for instance, price and quantity variation can be observed over time or across jurisdictions with different taxes. Researchers often take advantage of such natural (unplanned) variation to estimate elasticities and other parameters useful in prediction. Analysts can find these studies by searching in both general (e.g., ECONLIT, Google Scholar, JSTOR, and Proquest Digital Dissertations) and substantively specific (e.g., ERIC for education and PubMed for health) electronic databases of articles. The World Wide Web not only makes it easier to access these databases, but also provides a way of potentially finding unpublished studies that, although not vetted by referees or editors, might provide estimates of elasticities not available elsewhere.

Some of the common elasticities that have been estimated many times have been assessed in meta-analyses. For example, meta-analyses of the price elasticity of demand for gasoline,[18] electricity,[19] residential water,[20] and cigarettes[21] are available. Other meta-analyses review tax elasticities for corporate behavior and tax elasticities for economic development,[22] and price, service quality, income, gasoline price, and car ownership elasticities for the demand for public transportation.[23]

It may be possible to identify a chain of elasticities that link an immediate policy impact to other impacts, including some future impacts, that should also be valued. For example, high school completion has a variety of potentially relevant effects ranging from greater success in the labor market to reduced crime to better informed fertility choices.[24] Or consider an early childhood intervention that increases readiness for school. Although the increased readiness may have some direct value to children and parents, it may also have effects on the course of education, which in turn have other valued impacts—one can imagine the increased achievement in early grades contributing to a higher likelihood of high school completion and its relevant effects. Of course, the longer is the chain of causality linking the initial estimated impact to the predictions of future impacts, the less certain the predictions.

Guesstimate

Sometimes it is not possible to find any existing quantitative evidence to predict an impact. As a prediction must be made—excluding the impact is equivalent to predicting it is zero with certainty—one can turn to logic or theory to specify its plausible range. For example, if a policy will increase the price of some good, then it is almost certainly reasonable to assume that the amount consumed with not go up. You may be able to put an upper bound on reduction in consumption with an estimate of the price elasticity of demand of some other good that you can argue is likely to be more price elastic. The assumed range can be used in a Monte Carlo simulation to take account of your uncertainty of the magnitude of the impact. When your guesstimate has a very large range, you may also want to do sensitivity analysis in which, taking account of all other impacts first, you determine how large or small a value it would have to have to change the sign of net benefits.

If none of the above approaches is acceptable, you may obtain advice from experts who have developed tacit knowledge that allows you make guesstimates. An expert, such as a highway engineer, may be able to provide fairly confident ranges of predictions for project costs based on her experience in using the prevalent rules-of-thumb, without conducting a major and perhaps quite expensive study. In some circumstances, there may be value in consulting multiple experts in a systematic way. The best-known, approach for doing this is the Delphi Method, which was originally developed by the RAND Corporation to aid in the analysis of national defense issues. It requires participation by a number of experts. Each expert is consulted by the group coordinator in several rounds. In each round following the first, the coordinator provides feedback to the experts in the form of unattributed summaries of the answers provided by the fellow experts in the previous round. The final product is a statistical summary of the answers. The Delphi Method is sometimes used to generate input for economic analyses.[25]

MONETIZING IMPACTS

CBA requires that the quantitatively predicted policy impacts be valued in terms of a common money metric based on the relevant national or regional currency, such as the dollar or Euro. The fundamental principles of WTP and opportunity cost introduced in Chapter 2 provide the conceptual bases for monetizing. Depending on the impact being valued, monetization can be relatively straightforward and certain or, like much of prediction, indirect and uncertain.

Monetizing when Impacts Change Quantities Consumed in Markets

Policies that change consumption of market goods are relatively straightforward to monetize. As discussed in Chapters 3, 4, and 5, these changes should be monetized as the algebraic sum of the corresponding changes in social surplus, changes in government revenue, and the marginal excess tax burden of the changes in government revenue. In the simplest case, the policy involves purchasing an input in an undistorted market with a perfectly elastic supply schedule—the change in quantity of the input consumed in the market is monetized with the market price. Markets with less than perfectly elastic supply, distorted markets, or markets that exhibit both conditions, require careful accounting of changes in social surplus, including those external to the market, and changes in government revenue. In general, impacts occurring in such markets are not monetized by directly observed market prices but rather by *shadow prices* taking account of the all the relevant effects in the market. (We have already encountered several shadow prices: the marginal excess tax burden in Chapter 4 and the shadow price of capital in Chapter 10.) As long as the market supply and demand schedules and, if relevant, the social marginal benefit and social marginal cost schedules have been predicted, the monetization is still relatively straightforward. Further, the monetization itself in such cases does not add uncertainty beyond that inherent in the predictions of the relevant schedules.

Monetizing Impacts in Missing Markets

Most public policies, but especially those addressing social and environmental problems, have impacts that do not correspond to changes in consumption in well-functioning markets. Monetizing these impacts requires shadow prices. Researchers have to be clever in finding ways to estimate these shadow prices. As discussed in Chapter 14, hedonic pricing and asset valuation methods can often be used to make inferences about the social value of impacts from the indirect effects they have on observable behaviors. However, sometimes the impacts, such as changes in the availability of goods with an existence value, cannot be linked to observable behavior and therefore, as explained in Chapter 15, can only be estimated through contingent valuation surveys or other stated preference methods.

Fortunately, as reviewed in Chapter 16, researchers have estimated a number of shadow prices for commonly encountered impacts. Some shadow prices, such as the willingness to pay for reductions in mortality risk (a basis for estimating the value of a statistical life), the social cost of noise, or the opportunity cost of commuting time, have been estimated in a sufficiently large number of studies to make meta-analyses possible. Other shadow prices must be gleaned from smaller numbers of studies and often differ in terms of their comprehensiveness. For example, an important impact of many social policies is reduction in crime. A comprehensive shadow price would include not only the direct costs to victims and the use of resources in the criminal justice system, but also the costs that fear of crime imposes on potential victims. Improving these key shadow prices is an important project for social scientists wishing to promote the application of CBA.[26]

As with prediction, even a single relevant study can provide an empirical basis for determining a needed shadow price. For example, imagine that you faced the task of monetizing an impact that pertains to children. Perhaps you have a plausible shadow price for adults. If so, then you might use the findings from a study by Mark Dickie and Victoria L. Messman that parents appear willing to pay twice as much for reductions of flu symptoms for their young children as for themselves.[27] (Interestingly, the ratio falls to one by the time children reach the age of 18—a result probably very plausible for parents of teenagers!) Of course, the more the impact you are trying to monetize differs from flu symptoms, the less confident you should be about using ratios from this particular study.

More generally, empirically derived shadow prices should be treated as uncertain predictions. In calculating net benefits, analysts must usually multiply an uncertain prediction of effect by an uncertain shadow price. Again, the importance of Monte Carlo simulations to assess uncertainty in net benefits should be clear.

ILLUSTRATION: WSIPP CBA OF THE NURSE–FAMILY PARTNERSHIP PROGRAM

The Washington State legislature asked WSIPP to identify programs that could be implemented in Washington to reduce the number of children entering and remaining in the child welfare system. We briefly review the approaches to prediction and monetization used by the analysts to conduct a CBA of one particular intervention, the Nurse–Family Partnership for Low-Income Families (NFP).

Aside from providing a rich illustration of approaches to predicting and monetizing, familiarity with the work of WSIPP is valuable for CBA analysts for several reasons. First, WSIPP demonstrates how CBA can actually be conducted and presented to influence public policy.[28] Second, its CBAs are exemplary in their systematic use of empirical evidence through careful meta-analyses. Third, although the complicated methods it uses are sometimes difficult to follow as presented, it does strive to make them as transparent as possible. Finally, its meta-analyses are excellent resources for analysts assessing social policies.

The NFP is intended to promote child development and parenting skills through intensive visitation by nurses to low-income women during pregnancy and the two years following the birth of first children.[29] The following prediction strategy, summarized in Table 11.1, was employed by the analysts: First, a meta-analysis of the available evaluations of the implementation of the NFP in two sites was done to estimate the mean effect size for child abuse and neglect. That is, taking account of all the available studies, how much on average do NFP programs reduce abuse and neglect? This mean effect size is the predicted effect.

Second, the analysts conducted meta-analyses of studies linking child abuse and neglect to other impacts of interest. These meta-analyses provided estimates of the mean effect sizes of child abuse and neglect on the secondary impacts of crime, high school graduation, K–12 grade repetition, births and pregnancies for mothers under 18 years, test scores, illicit drug use, and alcohol abuse.

Third, the predicted effects of an NFP program on each of the secondary impacts was obtained by multiplying the effect size of an NFP on child abuse and neglect by the secondary impact mean effect size. So, following an example provided in the report, consider a target population with a lifetime child abuse and neglect rate of 13.7 percent and a high school graduation rate of 70 percent. Participation in an NFP program would reduce the lifetime child abuse and neglect rate by 2.7 percentage points.[30]

TABLE 11.1 Prediction and Monetization for the NFP Program

Impact per Participant	Prediction (Meta-Analyses)	Monetization
Child Abuse and Neglect (CAN)	Experimental evaluations of two NFP programs in Colorado and New York; lifetime prevalence of CAN in general population estimated from 10 studies (10.6 percent)	Welfare system costs: model of case processing and service use in Washington State Medical and mental health care costs and quality of life costs: based on estimates from study of juvenile violence in Pennsylvania[1]
Crime	10 studies of impact of CAN on crime	Criminal justice system costs: case processing model for Washington State Victim costs: personal expenses, property losses, mortality[2]
High School Graduation	3 studies of impact of CAN on high school graduation	Discounted lifetime money earnings gain from high school graduation based on data from Census Bureau's Current Population Survey
Test Scores	7 studies of impact of CAN on test scores	Rate of return per standard deviation of test score gain based on review article[3] multiplied by earnings of those with a high school degree but no college degree based on Current Population Survey
K–12 Grade Repetition	2 studies of impact of CAN on grade repetition	Cost of a year of schooling multiplied by the probability of high school completion to take account of elimination of year at end of schooling
Alcohol Abuse	4 studies of impact of CAN on alcohol abuse	After-tax lifetime earnings loss due to mortality and morbidity Treatment, medical, motor vehicle crashes, fire destruction, welfare administrative costs[4]
Illicit Drug Abuse	4 studies of impact of CAN on illicit drug abuse	After-tax lifetime earnings loss due to mortality and morbidity Treatment, medical, motor vehicle crashes, fire destruction, welfare administrative costs[5]
Program Costs	Based on program descriptions	Washington State wage and benefit rates

[1] Ted R. Miller, Deborah A. Fisher, and Mark A. Cohen, "Costs of Juvenile Violence: Policy Implications," Pediatrics 107(1) 2001, e3 (7 pages).

[2] Miller, Ted R., Mark A. Cohen and Brian Wiersema, *Victim Costs and Consequences: A New Look* (Washington, D.C.: National Institute of Justice, 1996).

[3] Eric A. Hanushek, "The Simple Analytics of School Quality," National Bureau of Economic Research Working Paper W10229, January 2004.

[4] Based on: Henrick J. Harwood, "Updating Estimates of the Economic Costs of Alcohol Abuse in the United States." Report prepare by Lewin Group for the National Institute on Alcohol Abuse and Alcoholism, 2000.

[5] Based on: Office of National Drug Control Policy, *The Economic Costs of Drug Abuse in the United States 1992–1998* (Washington, D.C.: Executive Office of the President, 2001).

Eliminating (that is, reducing the rate by 100 percentage points) child abuse and neglect would increase the rate of high school graduation by 7.9 percentage points. Multiplying these two percentage-point rate changes together yields a predicted increase in the probability of high school graduation of about 0.2 percentage points.

The analysts used a variety of approaches to monetize the predicted impacts. For example, the social cost of a case of child abuse and neglect was estimated in two major components. The first component was an estimate of the average cost to the Washington State child welfare system of a substantiated child abuse or neglect case. It was based on a model of the welfare system that took into account the real resource costs and probabilities of the steps in processing child abuse complaints and the possible services provided to victims. The second component was an estimate of the medical and mental health treatment costs and quality of life costs resulting from a case of child abuse. These costs were estimated from a study of adult on juvenile crime conducted by researchers using Pennsylvania data from 1993.[31] As usually the case when analysts gather data from published studies, the results must be translated into current dollars using the Consumer Price Index.

As the entries in Table 11.1 indicate, the analysts used a variety of sources for estimating shadow prices for the other predicted impacts: models of processes within Washington State, national economic data, and empirical findings reported in research articles. Along the way, they had to make many assumptions to move from available evidence to the needed shadow prices. Their efforts are commendable both in terms of their creativity and transparency.

CONCLUSION

The range of quality of available evidence to support the prediction and monetization of policy impacts is very wide. Very rarely, multiple evaluations employing rigorous experimental designs provide the basis for making fairly confident predictions of the magnitudes of the impacts that would result from continuation or replication of policies and these impacts can be monetized with readily available and widely accepted shadow prices. More often, analysts must piece together evidence to support predictions from a variety of sources and use shadow prices with varying degrees of provenance. Doing so well requires both a sound conceptual grounding in CBA and the courage to predict and monetize even when the supporting evidence is weak. It also demands that analysts make their assumptions and uncertainties transparent, both in presentation and through Monte Carlo and other methods to take account of uncertainties.

EXERCISES FOR CHAPTER 11

1. Review the following CBA: David L. Weimer and Mark A. Sager, "Early Identification and Treatment of Alzheimer's Disease: Social and Fiscal Outcomes," *Alzheimer's & Dementia* 5(3) 2009, 215–226. Evaluate the empirical basis for prediction and monetization.
2. Imagine that a project involves putting a high-voltage power transmission line near residential property. Discuss how you might predict and monetize its impact on residents.

NOTES

1. For more detail see Anthony E. Boardman, Wendy L. Mallery, and Aidan R. Vining, "Learning from *Ex Ante/Ex Post* Cost-Benefit Analysis Comparisons: The Coquihalla Highway Example," *Socio-Economic Planning Sciences* 28(2) 1994, 69–84.

2. For example, see Darren Grant and Stephen M. Rutner, "The Effect of Bicycle Helmet Legislation on Bicycling Fatalities," *Journal of Policy Analysis and Management* 23(3) 2004, 595–611 at 606.

3. Winston Harrington, Richard D. Morgenstern, and Peter Nelson, "On the Accuracy of Regulatory Cost Estimates," *Journal of Policy Analysis and Management* 19(2) 2000, 297–322

4. Todd P. Gilmer, Christian R. Dolder, Jonathan P. Lacro, David P. Folsom, Laurie Lindamer, Piedad Garcia, and Dilip V. Jeste, "Adherence to Treatment with Antipsychotic Medication and Health Care Costs among Medicaid Beneficiaries with Schizophrenia," *American Journal of Psychiatry* 162(4) 2004, 692–99. Note: rates calculated using data in article on hospitalization rates for drug compliance categories and the fraction of subjects in the categories.

5. David L. Weimer, "Collective Delusion in the Social Sciences," *Policy Studies Review* 5(4) 1986, 705–708.

6. Charles R. Schwenk, "The Cognitive Perspective on Strategic Decision Making," *Journal of Management Science* 25(1) 1988, 41–55.

7. Anthony Petrosino and Haluk Soydan, "The Impact of Program Developers as Evaluators on Criminal Recidivism: Results from Meta-Analysis of Experimental and Quasi-Experimental Research," *Journal of Experimental Criminology* 1(4) 2005, 435–450.

8. For example, analysts at the Washington State Institute for Public Policy routinely halve the intervention effects reported for programs in which the evaluator was closely involved in the design or implementation of the program. See, for instance, Steve Aos, Jim Mayfield, Marna Miller, and Wei Yen, *Evidence-Based Treatment of Alcohol, Drug, and Mental Health Disorders: Potential Benefits, Costs, and Fiscal Impacts for Washington State* (Olympia: Washington State Institute for Public Policy, 2006), Appendix A3.c.

9. For an intuitive introduction to this issue, see Bradley Efron and Carl Morris, "Stein's Paradox in Statistics," *Scientific American* 236 1977, 119–127.

10. Copas, J. B. (1997) Using Multiple Regression Models for Prediction: Shrinkage and Regression to the Mean. *Statistical Methods in Medical Research* 6(2), 167–183.

11. For an excellent introduction to doing meta-analysis, see Mark W. Lipsey and David B. Wilson, *Practical Meta-Analysis* (Thousand Oaks, CA: Sage Publications, 2001).

12. Weimer, "Collective Delusion in the Social Sciences."

13. Peter A. Cohen, James A. Kulik, and Chen-Lin C. Kulik, "Educational Outcomes of Tutoring: A Meta-Analysis of Findings," *American Educational Research Journal* 19(2) 1982, 237–248.

14. For an overview of the WSIPP approach, see Elizabeth K. Drake, Steve Aos, and Marna G. Miller, "Evidence-Based Public Policy Options to Reduce Crime and Criminal Justice Costs: Implications in Washington State," *Victims and Offenders* 4(2) 2009, 179–196. Analysts may find useful information in their own CBAs from those available on the WSIPP web page, www.wsipp.wa.gov.

15. Steve Aos, Marna Miller, and Jim Mayfield, *Benefits and Costs of K–12 Educational Policies: Evidence-Based Effects of Class Size Reductions and Full-Day Kindergarten* (Olympia: Washington State Institute for Public Policy, Document No. 07-03-2201, 2007).

16. Willard G. Manning, Joseph P. Newhouse, Naihua Duan, Emmitt B. Keeler, and Arleen Leibowitz, "Health Insurance and the Demand for Medical Care: Evidence from a Randomized Experiment," *American Economic Review* 77(3) 1987, 251–77.

17. David H. Greenberg and Mark Shroder, *Digest of Social Experiments* 3rd ed. (Washington, D.C.: Urban Institute Press, 2004).

18. Molly Espey, "Gasoline Demand Revisited: An International Meta-Analysis of Elasticities," *Energy Economics* 20(3) 1998, 273–95; Martijn Brons, Peter Nijkamp, Eric Pels, and Piet Rietveld, "A Meta-Analysis of the Price Elasticity of Gasoline Demand: An SUR Approach," *Energy Economics* 30(5) 2008, 2105–22.

19. James A. Espey and Molly Espey, "Turning on the Lights: A Meta-Analysis of Residential Electricity Demand Elasticities," *Journal of Agricultural and Applied Economics* 36(1) 2004, 65–81.

20. Jasper M. Dalhuisen, Raymond J. G. M. Florax, Henri L. T. de Groot, and Peter Nijkamp, "Price and Income Elasticities of Residential Water Demand: A Meta-Analysis," *Land Economics* 79(2) 2003, 292–308.

21. Craig A. Gallet and John A. List, "Cigarette Demand: A Meta-Analysis of Elasticities," *Health Economics* 12(10) 2003, 821–35.

22. Ruud A. de Mooij and Sjef Ederveen, "Corporate Tax Elasticities: A Reader's Guide to Empirical Findings," *Oxford Review of Economic Policy* 24(4) 2008, 680–97; Joseph M. Philips and Ernest P. Goss, "The Effects of State and Local Taxes on Economic Development: A Meta-Analysis," *Southern Economic Journal* 62(2) 1995, 320–33.

23. Johan Holmgren, "Meta-Analysis of Public Transport Demand," *Transportation Research: Part A, Policy and Practice* 41(10) 2007, 1021–35.

24. For demonstrations of this approach, see Robert Haveman and Barbara Wolfe, "Schooling and Economic Well-Being: The Role of Nonmarket Effects," *Journal of Human Resources* 19(3) 1984, 377–407 and Wolfe, Barbara and Robert Haveman, "Accounting for the Social and Non-Market Benefits of Education." In John F. Helliwell, ed., *The Contribution of Human and Social Capital to Sustained Economic Growth and Well Being* (Vancouver, BC: University of British Columbia Press 2001), 221–250.

25. Jon Landeta, "Current Validity of the Delphi Method in the Social Sciences," *Technological Forecasting and Social Change* 73(5) 2006, 467–482.

26. For a discussion of a number of shadow prices that would be useful in applying CBA to social programs, see David L. Weimer and Aidan R. Vining, *Investing in the Disadvantaged: Assessing the Benefits and Costs of Social Policies* (Washington, D.C.: Georgetown University Press, 2009).

27. Mark Dickie and Victoria L. Messman, "Parental Altruism and the Value of Avoiding Acute Illness: Are Kids Worth More than Parents?" *Journal of Environmental Economics and Management* 48:3 (2004), 1146–1174. For a general discussion of the issues, see Sandra Hoffmann, "Since Children Are Not Little Adults—Socially—What's an Environmental Economist to Do?" *Duke Environmental Law & Policy Forum* 17(2) 2006, 209–232.

28. For a discussion of WSIPP, see David L. Weimer and Aidan R. Vining, "An Agenda for Promoting and Improving the Use of CBA in Social Policy." In *Investing in the Disadvantaged*, 249–271.

29. Stephanie Lee, Steve Aos, and Marna Miller, *Evidence-Based Programs to Prevent Children from Entering and Remaining in the Child Welfare System: Benefits and Costs for Washington* (Olympia: Washington State Institute for Public Policy, Document No. 08-07-3901, 2008).

30. Effect size for a dichotomous variable (e.g., abuse/no abuse) is approximated by

$$ES = \ln\{[p_e(1 - p_c)]/[p_c(1 - p_e)]\}/1.65$$

where ES is the effect size, p_c is the frequency in the control group, and p_e is the frequency in the treated population. With an estimate of ES and p_c it is possible to solve for p_e, the predicted frequency for program participants.

A similar procedure can be used for continuous variables (e.g., test scores) to predict effects using the following formula

$$ES = (M_e - M_c)/[(V_e + V_c)/2]^{.5}$$

where M_c is the mean effect in the control group, M_e is the mean effect in the treatment group, V_e is the square of the standard deviation in the treatment group, and V_c is the square of the standard deviation in the control group. See Lipsey and Wilson, *Practical Meta-Analysis*.

31. Miller, Ted R., Mark A. Cohen, and Brian Wiersema, *Victim Costs and Consequences: A New Look* (Washington, D.C.: National Institute of Justice, 1996).

CHAPTER 12

Valuing Impacts from Observed Behavior: Experiments and Quasi Experiments

This chapter focuses on estimating the benefits and costs of program interventions by using experimental and quasi-experimental designs.[1] The chapter first describes experimental and quasi-experimental designs, indicating how they are used in estimating the impacts of social programs—for example, health, education, training, employment, housing, and welfare programs. The chapter then describes how these impacts are incorporated into CBA of employment and training programs. The chapter concludes by examining actual CBAs of employment and training programs that were targeted at welfare recipients. The chapter provides numerous illustrations of how concepts developed earlier in this book can be used in actual cost-benefit analyses.

ALTERNATIVE EVALUATION DESIGNS

CBAs of any intervention require comparisons between alternatives: the program or policy that is subject to the CBA is compared to the situation that would exist without the program (the so-called *counterfactual*), and impacts are measured as differences in outcomes (e.g., in health status or earnings) between the two situations. The term *internal validity* refers to whether this measured difference can be appropriately attributed to the program being evaluated. Internal validity, in turn, depends on the particular way in which the comparison between the program and the situation without the program is made. There are numerous ways in which this comparison can be made. Researchers usually refer to the specific scheme used for making comparisons in order to measure impacts as an *evaluation design*.

Diagrams that represent five commonly used evaluation designs,[2] as well as brief summaries of the advantages and disadvantages of each of these designs, appear in Table 12-1. In these diagrams, the symbol O represents an outcome measurement point, X represents a treatment point, and R indicates that subjects were assigned randomly to treatment and control groups.

The evaluation designs that are listed in Table 12-1 are not the only ones that exist. There are numerous others. But these designs provide a good sampling of the major alternatives. So that we can make our discussion of them as concrete as possi-

TABLE 12-1 Five Commonly Used Evaluation Designs

Type	Structure[1]	Major Advantages	Major Disadvantages
Design 1: Comparison of net changes between treatment and true control groups	$R: O_1 \; X \; O_2$ $R: O_3 \qquad O_4$	Random assignment guards against systematic differences between control and treatment groups so highest internal validity	Direct and ethical costs of random assignment; as with all evaluations external validity may be limited
Design 2: Comparison of post-treatment outcomes between true control and treatment groups	$R: X \; O_2$ $R: \qquad O_4$	Random assignment guards against systematic differences between control and treatment groups so high internal validity	Direct and ethical costs of random assignment; danger that a failure of randomization will not be detected
Design 3: Simple before/after comparison	$O_1 \; X \; O_2$	Often feasible and relatively inexpensive; reasonable when factors other than treatment are unlikely to affect outcome	Does not control for other factors that may cause change
Design 4: Comparison of post-treatment outcomes between quasi-control and treatment groups	$X \; O_1$ O_2	Allows for possibility of statistically controlling for factors other than treatment	Danger of sample selection bias caused by systematic differences between treatment and quasi-control groups
Design 5: Comparison of net changes between treatment and quasi-control group	$O_1 \; X \; O_2$ $O_3 \qquad O_4$	Allows for possibility of statistically controlling for factors other than treatment; permits detection of measurable differences between treatment and quasi-control groups	Danger of sample selection bias caused by systematic differences between treatment and quasi-control group in terms of nonmeasurable differences

O — observation
X — treatment
R — random assignment

[1]Draws on notation introduced by Donald T. Campbell and Julian Stanley, *Experimental and Quasi-Experimental Designs for Research* (Chicago: Rand McNally College Publishing Company, 1963).

ble, we assume that they all pertain to alternative ways in which a program for training the unemployed might be evaluated. In this context, "being in the treatment group" means enrollment in the training program.

Design 1: Classical Experimental Design

Design 1 is a classical experimental design. The symbols indicate that unemployed persons are randomly allocated between a treatment group and a control group. Members of the treatment group can receive services from the training program, while persons in the control group cannot. The way this might work in practice is that after the training program is put into place, unemployed persons are notified of its existence. Some of these persons apply to participate in it. A computer is used, in effect, to flip a fair coin: Heads the applicant is selected as a member of the treatment group and, consequently, becomes eligible to participate in the program; tails the applicant becomes a member of the control group. Control group members are not eligible to participate in the program but can receive whatever other services are available for the unemployed.

The procedure just described for establishing treatment and control groups is called *random assignment*.[3] Random assignment evaluations of social programs—for instance, a training program—are often called *social experiments*.

To see how well the training program works, data on outcomes are collected for both the treatment group and the control group, both before the treatment is administered and after. Using the collected data, members of the experimental and control groups are then compared.[4] For example, the earnings of the two groups can be compared sometime after the training is completed to measure the size of the program's impact on earnings.[5]

Although it is sometimes impractical or infeasible to use,[6] design 1 is the best of the five design schemes summarized in Table 12-1 for many types of evaluations. Its major advantage is the use of random assignment. Because of random assignment, the characteristics of people in the treatment and control groups should be similar, varying only by chance alone. As a result, random assignment helps ensure that the evaluation has internal validity; that is, members of the experimental groups can be directly compared in terms of such outcomes as earnings, and any differences that are found between them can be reasonably attributed to the treatment.

It is important to recognize, however, that although design 1 helps ensure internal validity, like the other evaluation designs discussed in this section, it may not provide *external validity*. That is, there is no assurance that findings from the evaluation, even though valid for the group of persons who participated in the evaluated program, can be generalized to any other group. The reason for this is that personal and community characteristics interact in complex ways with the services provided by a program. As a result, the program may serve some persons more effectively than others. For example, findings for a training program for unemployed, male, blue-collar workers who live in a community with low unemployment may provide little information concerning how well the program would work for unemployed female welfare recipients who live in a community with high unemployment. In addition, the findings may also not hold for future time periods.

Design 2: Classical Experimental Design without Baseline Data

Design 2 is similar to design 1 in that random assignment is also used to allocate individuals between the treatment and control groups, and both are referred to as *experimental designs*. The difference between the two designs is that collection of pretreatment, baseline information on members of the treatment and control groups is not part of design 2 but is part of design 1. The problem with not collecting pretreatment information is that there is no way of checking whether the treatment and control groups are basically similar or dissimilar.

For the comparison between the two groups to measure program effects accurately, the groups should, of course, be as similar as possible. Yet, as previously mentioned, they could be dissimilar by chance alone. This is more likely if each group has only a few hundred members, as is sometimes the case in social experiments. It is also possible that those running an experiment fail to implement the random assignment process correctly. If information is available on pretreatment status—for example, on pretreatment earnings—then statistical adjustments can be made to make the comparison between the treatment and the control groups more valid. Hence, there is less certainty concerning internal validity with design 2 than design 1.

Nonetheless, design 2 may be more appropriate than design 1 when it is possible that the collection of pretreatment information predisposes the participants to certain relevant behaviors. For example, pretreatment questions about knowledge of health risks may make the treatment group in a study of health education more prone to learning than the general public would be.

Design 3: Before and After Comparison

Design 3 is by far the worst of the five designs, relying as it does on a simple *before and after comparison* of the same group of individuals. For example, the earnings of a group of individuals that went through a training program are compared with their earnings before going through the program. The problem with this design is that there is no information on what would have happened without the program. Consequently, there is no way to ensure internal validity. For example, the average earnings of people going into a training program are likely to be very low if most of these people are unemployed at the time of entry. That, perhaps, is why they decided to go into the program in the first place. Even without the program, however, they might have found jobs eventually. If so, their average earnings would have gone up over time even if the program did not exist. With a before and after comparison, this increase in earnings would be incorrectly attributed to the program.

Before and after comparisons, however, do offer certain advantages. They provide a comparatively inexpensive way of conducting evaluations. Moreover, when valid information is not available for a comparison group, a before and after comparison may be the only feasible way of conducting an evaluation. Such a comparison is obviously most valid when nonprogram factors are not expected to affect the outcomes of interest (for example, earnings) or can be taken into account through statistical adjustments.

Design 4: Nonexperimental Comparison without Baseline Data

Design 4 is based on a comparison of two different groups: one that has gone through a program and the other that has not. Unlike design 2, however, membership in the two groups is not determined by random assignment. For example, the comparison group could be made up of people who originally applied for training but ultimately decided not to participate. Alternatively, the comparison group could be drawn from a geographical area where the program does not exist. Because such a comparison group is not selected through random assignment, it is sometimes called a *quasi-control group,* and design 4 is called a *quasi-experimental design.* Use of a quasi-control group may be necessary when obtaining a comparison group through random assignment is infeasible or impractical.

Unfortunately, with this design there is no means of controlling for those differences between the two groups that existed prior to the treatment and, hence, no way to ensure internal validity. Perhaps, for example, at the time of application for training, those who ultimately went through the program had been unemployed for a longer period of time than persons in the comparison group, suggesting that in the absence of training they would have fared worse in the job market than members of the comparison group. But if at the end of training it is observed that they actually did just as well as persons in the comparison group, this suggests the training had an effect: It pulled the trainees up even with the comparison group. However, with design 4, there is no way to know the difference in the length of unemployment prior to training. As a result, it would just be observed that, after training, members of the treatment group were doing no better than people in the comparison group. This finding is subject to a bias known as *sample selection bias* that results because systematic differences between the treatment and quasi-control group are not, and indeed cannot be, taken into account. In this instance, sample selection bias is important because it could lead to the incorrect conclusion that the training made no difference.

Design 5: Nonexperimental Comparison with Baseline Data

Design 5 utilizes both a treatment group and a control group. In addition, both pretreatment and posttreatment data are collected. This provides information on how the treatment group differed from the comparison group prior to the training (for example, in terms of length of unemployment). This information can be used in a statistical analysis to control for pretreatment differences between the treatment and control groups. For this reason, design 5 offers greater opportunity to obtain internal validity than either design 3 or 4.

Even so, because this design, which like design 4 is a quasi-experimental design, does not randomly assign individuals to the treatment and control groups, a major problem occurs if people in the treatment and the comparison groups differ from one another in ways that cannot be measured readily. Then it becomes very difficult to adjust statistically for differences between the two groups. Perhaps, for example, unemployed persons who enter training are more motivated than unemployed persons who do not. If so, they might receive higher earnings over time even without the training. If analysts cannot somehow take account of this difference in motivation—in practice, sometimes they can, but often they cannot—then they may incorrectly conclude that higher posttraining earnings received by the trainees are due to the training when, in fact, they are really due to greater motivation on the part of the trainees. In the evaluation literature, such a situation creates a threat to internal validity that is known as the *selection problem*.[7]

The occurrence of selection problems can be greatly reduced by using design 1 or 2. The reason is that when random assignment is used, people assigned to the treatment group should not differ from members of the control group in terms of characteristics such as motivation except by chance alone. Because of this advantage, an increasing number of evaluations of social programs that embody experimental designs have been conducted since the early 1960s.[8] However, large numbers of evaluations that utilize nonexperimental designs, such as designs 3, 4, and 5, also continue to be done either because costs or administrative factors prevent randomization or evaluations are initiated after the program has begun operating.

CBAs OF EXPERIMENTS AND QUASI EXPERIMENTS

Although numerous evaluations that have utilized the designs outlined above have been conducted, formal CBAs have been carried out for only a minority of them. Often the evaluations focus instead on only one or two outcomes of interest. For

────────────────**EXHIBIT 12-1**────────────────

How the consumption of medical care changes as a function of the cost of care to users is central to many public policy questions, especially those relating to universal health insurance. To address this question, the federal government funded a social experiment, the Rand Health Insurance Experiment, between 1974 and 1977. Analysis of the data from the six experimental sites by Willard Manning and colleagues suggests that the price elasticity of demand for health care services is in the range of −0.1 to −0.2.

Source: Adapted from Willard G. Manning, Joseph P. Newhouse, Naihua Duan, Emmett B. Keeler, Aileen Leibowitz, and Susan Marquis, "Health Insurance and the Demand for Medical Care: Evidence from a Randomized Experiment," *American Economic Review* 77(3) 1987, 251–277.

────────────────**EXHIBIT 12-2**────────────────

During the late 1960s and early 1970s, the U.S. government funded four income maintenance experiments. These experiments focused on how income transfers affected the supply of labor (equivalently the demand for leisure) of low-income persons. Data from these experiments were used to obtain estimates of wage and income elasticities. Based on averages of separate estimates from the numerous studies that have relied on data from these experiments, Gary Burtless derived a number of elasticity values. The compensated wage elasticities are 0.09 for married men, 0.24 for married women, and 0.14 for single women. The uncompensated wage elasticities are −0.02 for married men, 0.17 for married women, and −0.04 for single women. The income elasticities are −0.11 for married men, −0.07 for married women, and −0.18 for single women.

Source: Adapted from Gary Burtless, "The Work Response to Guaranteed Income: A Survey of Experimental Evidence," in Alicia Munnell, ed., *Lessons from the Income Maintenance Experiments* (Boston: Federal Reserve Bank of Boston, 1986), 22–52.

example, in the housing or health areas, they might focus on whether the evaluated program could be administered effectively or whether housing or health status improved, and not attempt to measure other benefits and costs. In relatively rare instances, social experiments have been used to estimate demand or supply relationships. Though these estimates can be used in CBAs, the experiments themselves were not subjected to CBA. Two especially important examples of such social experiments are described in Exhibits 12-1 and 12-2.

CBAs OF EMPLOYMENT AND TRAINING PROGRAMS: AN INTRODUCTION

Many of the evaluations of social programs that have been subjected to CBA have focused on programs that attempt to increase the employment or earnings of unemployed or low-skilled workers, especially the welfare population.[9] The services provided by these programs have varied considerably but have included job search assistance, remedial education, vocational training, subsidizing private-sector employers in exchange for hiring program participants, financial incentives to work, and the direct provision of public-sector jobs to participants. Although the individual programs that provide such services often differ greatly from one another, such programs are commonly referred to as *employment and training (E&T) programs.*[10]

E&T programs are often viewed as investments in the *human capital* of participants (i.e., attempts to improve their skills and abilities). Thus, the major economic rationale for funding them revolves around assertions that E&T programs help correct market or institutional failures that cause underinvestments in human capital. For example, low-income people may not have the resources to invest in certain kinds of training, such as classroom vocational training. Their access to private financing may be limited by a lack of collateral and a high risk of default. Moreover, public training may be justified as compensating for inadequacies in the public education system or as providing a second chance to those who prematurely terminate formal schooling because of imperfect foresight or a high subjective rate of time preference. In addition, E&T programs may help correct imperfect information among participants about human capital investment opportunities by guiding them into activities that yield the highest payoff for them.

A distinct rationale for E&T programs stems from a widely accepted value that, all else equal, it is better to receive income from employment than from transfer programs. To meet this goal, increasingly stringent requirements to participate in E&T programs have been imposed on welfare and unemployment insurance recipients since the early 1980s.

THE CBA FRAMEWORK IN THE EDUCATION AND TRAINING CONTEXT

The basic CBA accounting framework has been described in previous chapters. However, different policy areas have developed variations of the basic CBA framework that address issues specific to each area. The particular accounting framework that is used today in conducting most CBAs of E&T programs was originally developed during the late 1960s and refined in the early 1980s. A stylized version of this framework appears in Table 12-2. Although details concerning the specifics of the framework vary somewhat from one E&T CBA to another, depending upon the specific nature of the services provided, the table lists those benefits and costs that are typically measured.

This framework offers several advantages: It is readily understandable to policy makers; by displaying benefits and costs from the perspectives of both participants and nonparticipants, it suggests some of the distributional implications of the program being evaluated; and, possibly most important, because measures of each cost-benefit component listed can actually be obtained from data collected during the evaluation, it is operationally feasible. Indeed, despite shortcomings in the framework, it is difficult to find practical alternatives to it.

In Table 12-2, plus signs indicate anticipated sources of benefits and minus signs anticipated sources of costs from different perspectives. The first column (A) shows

TABLE 12-2   Stylized Cost-Benefit Framework Showing the Impacts of E&T Programs

	Society *(A)* *(B + C)*	*Participant* *(B)*	*Nonparticipant* *(C)*
Output produced by participant			
In-program output	+	0	+
Gross earnings	+	+	0
Fringe benefits	+	+	0
Participant work-related expenditures			
Tax payments	0	−	+
Expenditures on child care, transportation, etc.	−	−	0
Use of transfer programs by participants			
Welfare payments	0	−	+
Other transfer payments	0	−	+
Program operating costs	+	0	+
Use of support programs by participants			
Support services received by participants	−	0	−
Allowances received by participants	0	+	−
Program operating costs	−	0	−

aggregate benefits and costs from the perspective of society as a whole. The remaining columns show the distribution of benefits and costs to the two groups that are typically relevant in assessing E&T programs: participants or clients served by the evaluated program (B); and nonparticipants, including taxpayers who pay for the program (C).

Benefits and costs to society are simply the algebraic sum of benefits and costs to participants and to nonparticipants because society is the sum of these two groups. Hence, the table implies that if a program causes transfer payments received by participants (e.g., unemployment compensation or welfare payment receipts) to decline, then this should be regarded as a savings or benefit to nonparticipant taxpayers, a cost to program participants (albeit one that may be offset by earnings), and neither a benefit nor a cost to society as a whole but simply income transferred from one segment of the population to another.

This approach is consistent with the standard one used in CBA. As we have seen, in standard CBA "a dollar is a dollar," no matter to whom it accrues. Thus, in Table 12-2, a dollar gained or lost by an E&T participant is treated identically to a dollar gained or lost by a nonparticipant. Consequently, if an E&T program caused the transfer dollars received by participants to fall, then this would be viewed as not affecting society as a whole because the loss to participants would be fully offset by benefits to nonparticipants in the form of reductions in government budgetary outlays.

Typically, however, E&T participants have much lower incomes, on average, than nonparticipants. For reasons that will be discussed in detail in Chapter 19, a case can sometimes be made for treating the gains and losses of low-income persons differently from those of higher-income persons. This is almost never done in CBAs of E&T evaluations, however. Instead, as can be seen in Table 12-2, they simply lay out the results so that the distributional consequences of a particular program can be observed.

Table 12-2 divides the benefits and costs associated with E&T programs into four major categories. The first two categories pertain to effects that result if a program increases the work effort or productivity of participants—for example, by providing them work in a public-sector job where they perform useful services, providing them skill training, or helping them find private-sector employment through job search assistance. On the one hand, the value of the output they produce will rise, which in the private sector should be reflected by increases in earnings and fringe benefits. On the other hand, if hours at work rise, expenditures on child care and transportation will also increase. And if earnings rise, tax payments will increase. The third major cost-benefit category in Table 12-2 pertains to decreases in dependency on transfer payments that may result from an E&T program. Such reductions in dependency should cause both the amount of payments distributed under transfer programs and the cost of administering these programs to fall. The fourth major category refers to expenditures on the services received by program participants. Obviously, such expenditures increase when an E&T program is implemented. However, this increase will be partially offset because participants do not need to obtain similar services from other programs.

Three of the subcategories listed in Table 12-2 pertain to job-related expenditures and require clarification: participant expenditures on child care, transportation, and so forth; support services received by participants; and allowances received by participants. The first of these subcategories refers to total job-required outlays by E&T participants on such items as child care, transportation, and uniforms. The subcategory of support services pertains to the direct provision of such goods by a government agency, and the allowances subcategory refers to government reimbursement of job-required expenditures by participants. Table 12-2 reflects the philosophy that *all* program-induced increases in job-required expenditures should be treated identically, as resource costs to society engendered in producing goods and services. Of course, to the extent the government directly provides support services to participants, client outlays for this purpose will be smaller. In a CBA, this would be reflected by a smaller dollar amount appearing under the participant expenditures on job-related outlays and a larger dollar amount appearing under the subcategory of support services received by participants. Job-required expenditures are further discussed later in the chapter.

As previously indicated, all of the cost and benefit items listed in Table 12-2 would be measured as the difference between outcomes with and without the E&T program. In practice, many of the services offered by an E&T program may also be offered under other programs. For example, training provided by the programs may also be available through community colleges. Consequently, estimates of program effects on participants do not measure impacts of the receipt of service against the nonreceipt of services. Rather, such estimates attempt to determine the *incremental* effect of the program over the environment that would exist without the program. Similarly, the measure of program operating services is an estimate of the cost of running the program being evaluated less the cost of the services program participants would receive without the program.[11]

Benefits and costs that are sometimes referred to as *intangible effects* but are rarely, if ever, actually estimated in evaluations of E&T programs do not appear in Table 12-2. Examples of intangible effects include the values of leisure forgone and self-esteem from working. Almost by definition, intangible effects are difficult to measure, but they may be important. In fact, the nonmeasurement of important intangible costs and benefits is a key problem in conducing CBAs of most social programs.[12] In the next section, we examine the implications of not measuring certain intangible effects in conducting CBAs of E&T programs.

CONCEPTUAL ISSUES IN CONDUCTING CBAs OF EDUCATION AND TRAINING PROGRAMS

We now turn to a number of limitations of the accounting framework illustrated in Table 12-2. As will be seen, these arise from the fact that the framework is not completely consistent with the theoretical concepts discussed in Chapters 3, 4, and 5. Because these limitations can result in incorrect policy conclusions, comparing some of the operational measures of benefits and costs typically used in conducting CBAs of E&T programs with their conceptually correct counterparts appears useful. In doing this, it is helpful to examine measures of benefits and costs associated with E&T programs separately from the participant and the nonparticipant perspectives, keeping in mind that social benefits and costs are simply the algebraic sum of benefits received and costs incurred by these two groups.

The Participant Perspective

Two Alternative Measures. The standard E&T framework, as Table 12-2 suggests, estimates participant net benefits as net changes in the incomes of program clients—that is, as increases in earnings and fringe benefits minus increases in taxes, decreases in transfer payments, and increases in work-related expenditures that result from participation in the program. However, as Chapters 3 and 4 emphasize, the conceptually appropriate measure of participant net benefits is net changes in the surplus of program participants, not net changes in their incomes. As will be seen, the difference between these two measures can be substantial.

The extent to which the two measures diverge depends on the precise mechanism through which E&T programs influence earnings. For instance, E&T programs may either increase the hourly wage rates of participants (e.g., by imparting new skills) or increase the hours they work (e.g., by aiding in job search or increasing the obligations that must be met in exchange for transfer payments). Numerous E&T programs have been found to increase hours worked. Meaningful impacts on wage rates are rarer but have occurred. In the discussion that follows, we compare the two alternative measures of net benefits from the perspective of several different hypothetical E&T participants, each of whom is assumed to respond differently to the program.

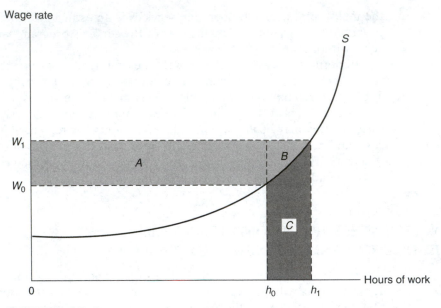

FIGURE 12-1 Social Surplus Change Resulting from an Induced
Wage Increase

The first participant is represented in Figure 12-1. Curve S is the labor supply schedule of this participant, an individual who is assumed to have successfully participated in an E&T program that increased her market wage from W_0 to W_1.[13] As a result, the individual increases her hours of work from h_0 to h_1. In the diagram, area A represents the increase in participant surplus (earnings) that would have resulted from the wage increase even if the participant had not increased her hours. Area $B + C$ represents an additional increase in participant earnings that resulting from the increase in hours that actually takes place at the higher wage. However, area C is fully offset by the individual's loss of leisure.[14] Consequently, although areas A, B, and C are counted as benefits when using the net income change measure of E&T effects, only A and B are counted in the conceptually correct (producer) surplus change measure.

In Figure 12-1, the first E&T participant was assumed to be in equilibrium both before entering the program and upon completing the program; that is, it was assumed that at both points she was able to work the number of hours she desired to work at her market wage. Many E&T participants, however, are not in equilibrium prior to entering a program. Indeed, many persons participate in E&T specifically because they are unemployed.

Such a situation is assumed to face the second participant, an individual who is represented in Figure 12-2. In this figure, the individual has a market wage of W_0 prior to entering E&T but is able to obtain only h_0 hours of work instead of the desired h_1 hours. Assume now that, although participating in E&T does not affect the participant's market wage, it does permit him to increase his hours of work from h_0 to h_1. As a result of this hours increase, the participant enjoys an earnings increase equal to areas $A + B$ but a (producer) surplus increase equal to only area A. Thus, once again,

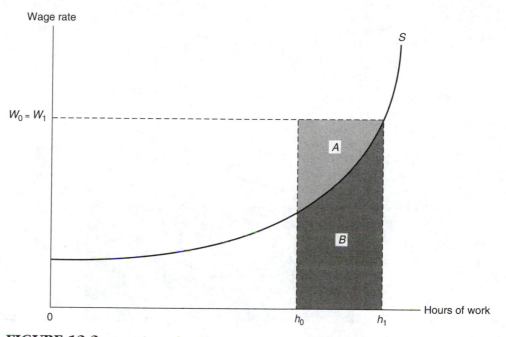

FIGURE 12-2 Social Surplus Change Due to an Induced Increase in Hours Worked

the net income change measure of E&T benefits is larger than the conceptually more appropriate (producer) surplus change measure.

Our findings for the first two E&T participants imply that while any earnings increases that result from wage increases should be fully credited to the program, only part of earnings increases resulting from increases in hours should be credited. In Figure 12-3, we turn to a more complex situation facing a third E&T participant: a welfare recipient who, as a condition for receiving her welfare grant, is required to work at a public-sector job for h^* hours each month, where h^* is determined by dividing her grant amount by the minimum wage. Similar arrangements, which are often referred to as *workfare*, have sometimes been used in administering welfare programs. The welfare recipient's market wage is assumed to equal W^m, the minimum wage, while curve S_0 represents her supply schedule in the absence of workfare. (Ignore curve S_1 for the moment.) Figure 12-3 implies that in the absence of workfare, W_0^r, the welfare recipient's reservation wage (i.e., the lowest wage at which she would be willing to work) would exceed her market wage. Thus, she would choose not to work.

Now imagine that the welfare recipient is enrolled in workfare in two distinct steps. In the first step, her welfare grant is withdrawn. This loss of income would cause her labor supply curve to shift to the right from S_0 to S_1. As a consequence, her reservation wage would fall from W_0^r to W_1^r, a value below the minimum wage. In the second step, she is offered the opportunity to work h^* hours at a public-sector workfare job at a wage of W^m. In other words, she is given the opportunity to earn back her welfare grant, which in the diagram corresponds to the rectangular area $W^m a h^* h_0$.[15] Because W^m exceeds W_1^r, the participant represented in Figure 12-3 would prefer workfare to not working at all.

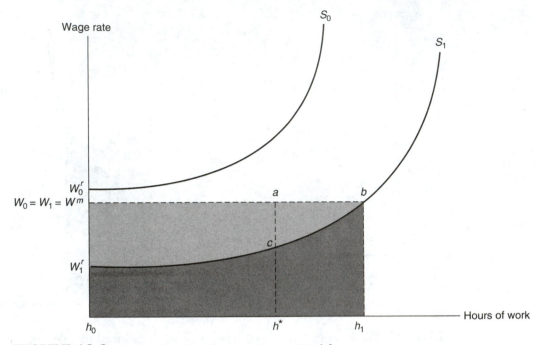

FIGURE 12-3   Social Surplus Change Due to Workfare

If the welfare recipient accepts the workfare offer, then the net income change and social surplus change measures of program impacts have quite different implications. Assuming she has no opportunities to work in addition to h^*, her net income would be unchanged from what it was prior to the program; consequently, the measure based on changes in net income would imply that she is no worse off. However, the social surplus change measure does imply that she is worse off. Specifically, her social surplus would decline by an amount represented by the area $W_1^r ch^* h_0$ an amount equal to the value that the recipient places on her lost leisure.[16]

So far, the focus has been on benefits received by and costs incurred by welfare recipients while they are participating in workfare. Now let us consider a different situation: The benefits and costs associated with a participant's move from welfare to a regular private-sector job. This is, of course, one of the major objectives of programs such as workfare, and Figure 12-3 implies that the program would in fact have the desired effect on the participant. Although in the absence of the workfare she would prefer not to work at all, given a choice between participating in workfare (point a) or working at a regular minimum-wage job (point b), the participant would select the latter. By restricting her hours to h^*, workfare causes the participant to be "off her labor supply curve." Only by finding a regular job can she work h_1 hours, the number of hours she would desire to work at the minimum wage. In actual practice, the participant might move directly from welfare to the job upon being confronted with the workfare requirement, or alternatively, she might first participate in workfare while seeking private-sector employment.

A comparison of the net income change measure of workfare's impact on a participant who moves directly to private-sector employment with the corresponding conceptually correct measure of the change in social surplus yields an interesting finding. On the one hand, the net income change measure implies that the participant represented in Figure 12-3 enjoys a net gain. Her transfer payments fall from $W^m ah^* h_0$ to zero, but her earnings increase from zero to $W^m bh_1 h_0$, resulting in a net increase in income of $abh_1 h^*$. On the other hand, the participant suffers a net social surplus loss because her gain in surplus from working, area $W^m bW_1^r$, is exceeded by the value of her lost transfer $W^m ah^* h_0$. Thus, under the circumstances represented in Figure 12-3, the net income change measure suggests a conclusion that is the diametrical opposite from that implied by the conceptually more correct social surplus change measure.

In measuring the impacts of E&T programs from the participant perspective, three rules can be drawn from the preceding analyses of the three illustrative E&T participants. First, *the full value of reductions in transfer payments should be counted as a cost to E&T participants.* Second, *the full value of increases in earnings that result from wage rate increases should be counted as a benefit to E&T participants.* Third, *only part of the value of earnings increases that result from hours increases should be counted as a benefit to E&T participants; namely, the part that represents an increase in participant surplus should be counted, while the part that is offset by reductions in leisure should not.*

In conducting CBAs of E&T programs, the first two of these rules are straightforward to implement. Implementing the third rule, however, requires an estimate of the percentage of earnings changes attributable to increases in hours that should be counted. The relatively few studies that have attempted to do this have found that the part of the earnings increase that should *not* be counted is potentially large and, if erroneously counted is likely to result in a substantial overstatement of estimated net benefits.[17]

Improvements in Self-Esteem. It is sometimes suggested that E&T programs can improve the self-esteem of E&T participants. For example, programs may impart skills that increase financial independence. If so, then this is a program benefit that should, in principle, be included in CBAs of E&T programs, although it is difficult to do so directly. However, to the extent an increase in the self-esteem of an E&T participant manifests itself as an increase in willingness to work (for example, because he or she is less concerned about rejection when seeking employment), the participant's labor supply curve will shift to the right. The resulting gain in surplus is represented graphically as the gap between the old and new supply curves below the market wage upon completion of training. Program benefits that are measured as increases in participant earnings, instead of as increases in surplus, will also be larger than if the curve does not shift. However, the increase in earnings will not correspond very well to the increase in surplus. Moreover, at most, only part of the benefits from an improvement in self-esteem is likely to be reflected by a shift in the labor supply curve. Indeed, it is easy to imagine E&T participants who enjoy increases in self-esteem as a result of participating in the program but whose willingness to work does not change.

Job-Required Expenditures. As discussed earlier, in the framework traditionally used in cost-benefit analyses of E&T programs, increases in job-related expenditures

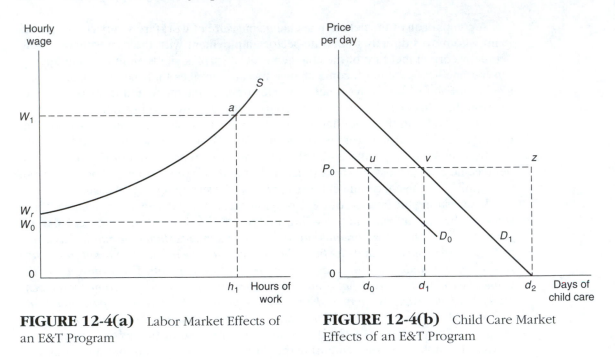

FIGURE 12-4(a) Labor Market Effects of an E&T Program

FIGURE 12-4(b) Child Care Market Effects of an E&T Program

such as child care and transportation that result from program participation are counted as a social cost of the program, regardless of whether paid for by E&T participants or the government. As discussed next, however, this approach can sometimes result in double counting.

For illustrative purposes, we focus on child care, although a similar analysis could be made for other work-related costs such as transportation. Figure 12-4(a) pertains to an individual who participated in an E&T program that increased her wage from W_0 to W_1. The supply curve, S, indicates the hours the individual would work if she must pay for child care. The diagram implies that, as a result of the program-engendered wage increase, she would go from not working to working h_1 hours. Thus the program would engender an increase in earnings equal to area $W_1 a h_1 0$ and a smaller surplus gain equal to area $W_1 a W_r$. Panel (b) illustrates the E&T participant's demand for child care. P_0 represents the market-set price for child care. As indicated in the figure, the demand curve for child care would shift out from D_0 to D_1 as a result of the wage increase and the increased hours worked resulting from the E&T.

As the reader may have noticed, Figure 12-4(b) is very similar to the diagrams of primary and secondary markets that appear in Chapter 5. This is hardly surprising. The direct effects of E&T programs typically occur in labor markets, while a complementary relationship exists between work effort and child care. Hence, the primary market is the labor market for E&T participants, while the market for child care is a secondary market.

As discussed in detail in Chapter 5, effects in undistorted secondary markets should usually be ignored if program benefits in primary markets are measured in terms of changes in surplus. Specifically, the individual represented in Figure 12-4 will presumably consider the child care expenses she will incur in determining the number of hours she would be willing to work at each wage rate. Thus, in using her labor supply curve to measure her surplus gain from participating in the E&T program, area W_1aW_r, her child care expenditures are already fully taken into account. Consequently, her increase in expenditures in the secondary market represented in panel (b)—that is, area uvd_1d_0—should be ignored, as should the area between the two demand curves in panel (b). Not doing so will result in double counting.

As emphasized earlier, benefits to E&T participants are traditionally measured as changes in net income, rather than as changes in surplus. To obtain this measure, increases in expenditures on child care would, of course, be subtracted from earnings increases. As indicated in Figure 12-4(a), the increase in earnings overstates the gain in surplus resulting from the E&T program by an amount represented by area W_rah_10. Subtracting the increase in day care expenditures, area uvd_1d_0, from the increase in earnings offsets this overstatement. However, area uvd_1d_0 could be either larger or smaller than area W_rah_10. Thus, the net income measure could be either larger or smaller than the more appropriate social surplus measure.

We next consider benefits and costs if the government directly provides child care or reimburses individuals for their expenditures on child care. A rather natural way to examine such a policy is to compare the earnings increases that result from the government subsidizing child care with the government's cost. As will be seen, however, this approach is incorrect.

For illustrative purposes, we assume that child care is provided free to subsidized individuals, but the government pays the market price of P_0. As previously discussed, at a market wage of W_1, the demand curve for child care for the individual represented in Figure 12-4 would be D_1. Thus, if child care was provided to her free, she would consume d_2 units of child care.

Because the direct effects of the government's subsidy occur in the market for child care, it should now be viewed as the primary market for purposes of analysis, while the labor market should be viewed as the secondary market. Thus, although the government's provision of subsidized child care would shift the labor supply curve to the right, and this, in turn, would affect earnings,[18] these effects should be ignored. Instead, the effects of the policy on individuals are best examined by measuring surplus changes in the primary market. For example, the individual represented in Figure 12-4 would enjoy a surplus gain corresponding to area d_1vd_2. However, the cost to the government, which is represented by area d_1vzd_2, would be considerably greater, resulting in dead-weight loss equal to area vd_2z.[19]

The Nonparticipants' Perspective[20]

Several categories of benefits and costs accrue to nonparticipants: intangible benefits, benefits from in-program output, and costs resulting from the displacement of public-sector and private-sector workers.

Intangible Benefits Received by Nonparticipants. The preceding section emphasized that in measuring the benefits and costs of E&T programs to participants it is changes in their surplus that should be estimated rather than changes in their money income. Thus, the effects on participant surplus of E&T-induced reductions in participant leisure time should be taken into account.

The same concept applies in measuring benefits and costs of E&T programs to nonparticipants. For example, if nonparticipants positively value the substitution of earnings for welfare payment in and of itself, then the increase in surplus they received will exceed any reductions in their tax obligations that might result from E&T programs targeted at welfare recipients. Thus, in principle, it is changes in the surplus of nonparticipants that result from E&T programs, rather than changes in their incomes, that should be measured. In view of the practical difficulty of doing this, however, it has never been attempted. An approach that might be used for this purpose, contingent valuation, is taken up in Chapter 15.

Changes in Taxpayer Excess Burden. As discussed in Chapter 4, taxes result in losses of economic efficiency that economists refer to as deadweight loss or excess burden. If taxes increase, excess burden also rises; but if they fall, excess burden also diminishes. A particular E&T program could cause taxes to either increase or decrease, depending on whether the program results in net costs or net benefits to the government. This would be determined as part of a CBA of the program. Once determined, the program's effect on deadweight loss—that is, its marginal excess tax burden—must be estimated. Doing this requires an estimate of the efficiency cost of one dollar more of taxes or of one dollar less. Such estimates can be found in Chapter 16. The value of this variable can be multiplied by the government's net benefits or net costs to determine the change in deadweight loss resulting from the E&T program.

Benefits from In-Program Output. Some E&T programs involve the provision of public-sector jobs. Perhaps the best-known example of this is the Works Projects Administration (WPA), which operated in the United States during the Great Depression and was intended to absorb some of the massive number of workers who were unemployed during this period. More recently, the Comprehensive Employment and Training Act provided as many as 750,000 public-sector jobs for unemployed persons during the late 1970s. In still more recent years, as discussed earlier, welfare recipients in some states have been required to perform work at government and nonprofit agencies in exchange for their payments.

How should the value to taxpayers of the in-program output produced by E&T participants be assigned to public-sector jobs? Ideally, this would be done by determining what taxpayers would be willing to pay for this output. Typically, this is infeasible, however, because the output is not purchased in market transactions. Consequently, an alternative approach is used that determines what the labor resources required to produce the output would have cost if purchased on the open market. Because agencies that "employ" E&T participants usually pay nothing for the services of these people, researchers use the wage rate that would have been paid to similar workers hired in the open market. Once an appropriate wage rate is determined, the basic calculation involves multiplying the number of hours E&T participants work by this wage and perhaps adjusting to account for differences between the average productivity of the E&T workers and workers hired in the open market.

This procedure can result in an estimate that either overstates or understates the true value of the in-program output produced by E&T participants. The reasons for this can be seen by examining a key assumption that underlies this valuation method: that the decisions of the public-sector agencies that employ E&T workers closely reflect the desires of taxpayers. More specifically, an analogy is drawn with the behavior of private-sector firms and consumers under perfect competition, and it is assumed that the amount that an agency would be willing to pay to employ an additional worker corresponds to the value that taxpayers would place on the additional output that the worker could potentially produce. Although this is not an appropriate place to assess the perfect competition analogy or discuss the extent to which bureaucratic behavior reflects taxpayer preferences, it should be obvious that a rather strong assumption is required to value output produced by E&T workers.[21]

The implications of this assumption can be explored by use of Figure 12-5, which depicts the demand curve for workers by a public-sector agency that might potentially be assigned E&T participants and the supply curve the agency faces in hiring workers in a competitive labor market. In using this diagram, we first examine a situation in which the assumption that bureaucratic behavior reflects taxpayer preferences is valid and then one where it is not.

In Figure 12-5, the horizontal line, S, represents the supply curve, which is set at the level of the market-determined wage, W, that must be paid to each regular worker hired by the agency; the downward-sloping line, D, represents the demand curve, which is assumed to slope downward as a result of diminishing returns and (as implied by the assumption about bureaucratic behavior) because the agency prioritizes its tasks so that, as its budget expands, successively less important services are performed. (Ignore curve D^* for the moment.) This demand curve reflects the willingness to pay for workers by the agency and, in keeping with the assumption concerning bureaucratic behavior, the area under this curve is presumed to measure the value to taxpayers of output produced by workers hired by the agency.

Figure 12-5 indicates that in the absence of E&T workers the agency would hire R regular workers; however, if P E&T participants were assigned to the agency, a total of $R + P$ workers would be employed. Thus, if the bureaucratic behavior assumption is valid, the value to taxpayers of the output added by the E&T workers would equal area A.

Unfortunately, however, area A typically cannot be directly measured. The reason for this is that the output produced by public-sector agencies is rarely sold in market transactions and, consequently, the agency's derived demand curve for labor, which is depicted in Figure 12-5, cannot actually be observed. However, even though government and nonprofit agencies that "employ" E&T participants pay nothing for the services of these people, the area under the supply curve between R and $R + P$ can be valued by simply determining the wages that would have to be paid to similar workers hired on the open

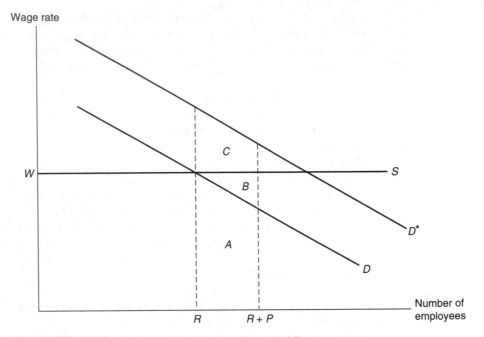

FIGURE 12-5   Demand for Workers by a Public-Sector Agency

market to do the work performed by E&T participants. Consequently, it is the area under the supply curve—that is, area *A* plus area *B*—that is usually used in practice as the measure of the value of in-program participant output. As a glance at Figure 12-5 suggests, the size of the resulting overstatement of the value of the output produced by E&T participation, which is represented by area *B*, depends upon the slope of the agency demand curve.

So far, we have assumed that agency behavior simply reflects the value that taxpayers would place on the agency's output. Let us now look at one of the numerous possible situations where this is not the case. The specific example we examine is one in which the agency, perhaps because of budget constraints resulting from the public goods characteristics of whatever services it provides, produces less output than taxpayers collectively desire. These circumstances are represented in Figure 12-5 by two demand curves. As before, curve *D* indicates *agency* willingness to pay for workers, but the value that *taxpayers* place on the output produced by the agency is now represented by the area under demand curve *D**. Consequently, the value of the additional output produced by the *P* E&T participants now equals area *A* plus area *B* plus area *C*. Thus, under these circumstances, the measure based on the supply curve of the output produced by E&T workers, which as previously indicated equals area *A* plus area *B*, understates the true value by an area equal to *C*.

Costs from Public-Sector Labor Displacement.   So far, our discussion has been based on the assumption that the E&T workers made available to a public-sector agency would simply be added to the regular workforce that the agency would hire in the absence of the program. However, the agency might instead substitute E&T workers for regular workers. In terms of Figure 12-5, this behavior on the part of the agency, which is usually referred to as *displacement,* would mean that agency employment would increase by less than the P workers provided by E&T. Indeed, with 100 percent displacement, the agency's workforce would remain at R, rather than increase to $R + P$. Consequently, at first blush, it would appear that displacement leads to overstatement of the value of output produced by E&T participants.[22]

The issue is actually a bit more subtle and complex, however. If the displaced workers have a similar risk of joblessness as E&T participants, then increases in output produced by E&T participants assigned to public-sector agencies may be entirely offset by losses in the output formerly produced by those workers who are displaced. This need not be the case, however, if the E&T participants are exceptional in terms of lack of skills or if they face exceptional barriers to labor market access. Moving such persons directly into jobs under these circumstances will change the characteristics of the general pool of unemployed in ways that may allow a reduction in the net incidence of joblessness, especially if local labor market conditions are tight. Thus, to the extent that E&T participants are unskilled relative to those they replaced, the labor market consequences will differ from a simple one-for-one replacement.

Costs from Private-Sector Labor Displacement.   A major objective of most E&T programs is to increase the unsubsidized private-sector employment of program participants. To the extent these efforts are successful, some participants undoubtedly end up in jobs that would otherwise have been held by nonparticipants. If, as a result, these nonparticipants become unemployed or accept lower-wage jobs, their earnings obviously fall. This earnings reduction, which is another type of displacement effect, is potentially a cost of E&T programs to nonparticipants. Because there is little agreement concerning the magnitude of private-sector labor displacement, it has rarely been taken into account in CBAs of E&T programs.[23]

The failure to take account of private-sector displacement may not be very serious, however. CBA usually assumes that full employment is maintained. If it is, then it should be relatively easy for displaced nonparticipants to find alternative job opportunities (although this may take some time), and E&T programs will raise the feasible employment level. Nonetheless, if E&T programs add workers with a particular set of skills to the workforce, they may still depress the wages of workers with similar skills. Private-sector displacement is a more serious issue if unemployment is high. Even then, however, it is possible that E&T programs may impart skills that allow trainees to leave slack occupational labor markets for tight ones. If they do, then they will decrease the competition for job vacancies in the slack labor markets, making it easier for unemployed workers who remain in these markets to find jobs. To the extent this occurs, E&T programs will again raise feasible employment levels.

CHOOSING PREDICTION PARAMETERS

In using the cost-benefit framework illustrated in Table 12-2, it is necessary to take account of the fact that some benefits and costs of E&T programs are likely to extend beyond the period for which postprogram data on outcomes are collected, which is typically only two or three years after participants leave the program. For example, as a result of having participated in an E&T program, some individuals could potentially enjoy increased earnings but pay higher taxes, incur greater job-required expenses, and receive fewer transfer payments over the remainder of their working lives. These streams of future benefits and costs must be incorporated into the CBAs of the program. Doing this requires that three important parameters be specified: the social discount rate, the discounting time horizon, and the decay rate of program effects. The social discount rate was discussed in detail in Chapter 10. The other two parameters are discussed in turn next. Because E&T programs are typically funded through taxes, as indicated in Chapter 10, the shadow price of capital does not have to be used.

The Discounting Time Horizon

As described in Chapter 6, the time horizon is the period over which benefit and cost streams are estimated. In CBAs of E&T programs, benefits and costs beyond the specified time horizon are assumed equal to zero. One procedure for determining the length of the time horizon in CBAs of E&T programs is to subtract the age of program participants at the time they entered the program from the age at which they are expected to retire from the workforce. Often, however, a shorter, somewhat arbitrarily selected time horizon—for example, five years—is used instead. Doing this is simply an acknowledgment on the part of analysts that because they do not possess crystal balls, uncertainty increases the further one attempts to extrapolate beyond the period for which evaluation data was collected. However, because most E&T operating costs are generally incurred shortly after program entry, basing a CBA of an E&T program demonstration on a short time horizon will understate E&T benefits relative to program operating costs if the key potential benefit, earnings improvements, persists well beyond the time horizon.

This understatement of benefits relative to costs could be substantial. Table 12-3 shows the present discounted value of an improvement of $1 in annual earnings under alternative assumptions about time horizons over which the improvement persists and for the value of the discount rate. The figures in the table have two important implications. First, it is evident that the magnitude of benefit and cost estimates are quite sen-

TABLE 12-3 The Sensitivity of a $1 Improvement in Annual Earnings to Alternative Time Horizons and Discount Rates

Time Horizon	Discount Rate	
	3%	5%
5 years	$4.58	$4.33
10 years	8.53	7.72
20 years	14.85	12.46
30 years	19.60	15.37

sitive to the choice of the time horizon. For example, if a 5 percent discount rate and a five-year time horizon are used for extrapolation purposes, the present value of an improvement of $1 in earnings equals $4.33. But if a 5 percent discount rate and a 20-year time horizon are used instead, the present value equals $12.46, almost a threefold increase. Second, the longer the time horizon that is used, the more sensitive are projections of benefits and costs to the choice of the discount rate. Hence, if a short time horizon is used, cost-benefit findings are less likely to be sensitive to the choice of a discount rate than if a long time horizon is used.

How long are program effects on earnings likely to last for actual E&T programs? While evidence on this topic is sketchy, a recent study that pooled findings from a large number of E&T evaluations indicates that program effects on earnings continue to exist for about six years for adult men and about four years for youth after they complete an E&T program, while program effects continue indefinitely for adult women.[24] However, results that are based on random assignment evaluations alone suggest that program earnings effects may last somewhat longer for adult men. Findings from a separate study that is based solely on random assignment evaluations of E&T programs targeted at female welfare recipients suggest that the effects of these programs on earnings continue for five to six years.[25]

Taken together, this evidence seems to suggest that, except for adult women participating in E&T programs, using fairly short time horizons in CBAs of these programs is probably appropriate. It is important to recognize, however, that these findings are based on averages for a variety of evaluated programs. The effects of a particular program could last for either a longer or a shorter period of time depending on its particular features.

The Decay Rate

A decay rate is necessary in extrapolating E&T effects that persist beyond the period over which postprogram data on outcomes are collected in order to take account of the possibility that the size of these effects may change over time. For example, it is usually argued that programs that provide training or job placement for low-wage workers initially may give them a competitive advantage in the labor market, but this advantage may decay over time. In the case of training, however, one could alternatively argue that doors are opened on the job that allow participants to obtain additional training after leaving an E&T program and, consequently, the program's effects on earnings will grow over time.

Unfortunately, only limited empirical evidence exists as to whether the earnings effects of E&T programs tend to grow or decay over time, let alone the magnitude of the actual rate of decay or growth. Because policy makers are often anxious for findings from evaluations of E&T programs, data on program outcomes are usually limited to three years or less, making predictions of decay rates highly subject to forecasting error, a common CBA problem discussed in Chapter 11.[26] However, one of the studies mentioned previously in discussing time horizons found that earnings effects for adult men, adult women, and youth who participated in E&T programs all initially grew after they completed training but only for a short period of time (perhaps a year or so). They then declined for the men and youth but remained constant for the women.[27]

The other study indicated that the earnings effects of programs targeted at welfare recipients increased for two or three years and then begin declining until they disappeared altogether after five or six years.[28] It is again important to recognize that these patterns pertain to a "typical" program and may not hold for a particular program that is being subjected to a CBA.

Once values for the discount rate, time horizon, and decay rate are chosen, equations (6A.5) and (6A.7) in Appendix 6A can be used to compute present values. In using these formulas, care must be taken to use a negative value for g if it is determined that the effects of the E&T program will decay over time and a positive value for g if it seems likely that these impacts will grow over time. For benefit and cost components that neither grow nor shrink over time, g should, of course, be set equal to zero.

CBAs OF WELFARE-TO-WORK EXPERIMENTS

Virtually every U.S. state operates programs that attempt to increase the employment of welfare recipients and thereby reduce their dependency on transfer payments. Similar to other E&T programs, the specific components of these *welfare-to-work* programs varied but included one or more of the following: assessment of basic skills, structured job search, training and education, financial incentives to work, and subsidized employment in the public or private sector.

CBA Results

Table 12-4 presents summary results from CBAs of 26 welfare-to-work programs.[29] These programs were all targeted at single parents who participated in the Aid for Families with Dependent Children (AFDC) program, which at the time the CBAs were conducted was the major cash welfare program in the United States. Most of the programs were mandatory in the sense that AFDC benefits could be reduced or even terminated if a parent did not cooperate. The CBAs were all conducted by MDRC, a well-known nonprofit research firm using a similar framework and the classical experimental design denoted as design 1 earlier in the chapter. The estimates in Table 12-4, which have been converted to 2006 dollar amounts using the U.S. Consumer Price Index, should be viewed as program impacts on a typical member of the treatment group in each of the listed programs.

The first three columns in the table present estimated benefits and costs from the participant perspective and the next four from the nonparticipant perspective. Columns A and D, respectively, report total net gains (or losses) from these two perspectives, while columns B, C, E, F, and G provide information on the benefit and cost components that together account for these gains (or losses). For example, column B reports the estimated *net* gain by participants from employment under each program, that is, estimates of the sum of increases in earnings, fringe benefits, and any work-related allowances paid under the program less the sum of tax payments and participant job-required expenditures on child care and transportation. Column C indicates changes in AFDC and other transfer benefits received by participants. Column E

TABLE 12-4 Summary of Cost-Benefit Estimates from MDRC's Evaluations of Selected Welfare-to-Work Experiments (in 2006 dollars)

	Participant Perspective			Nonparticipant Perspective				
	Net Present Value $A = B + C$ A	Changes in Income Attributable to Employment B	Changes in Transfer Payments C	Net Present Value $D = E + F + G$ D	Value of In-Program Output E	Changes Tax + Transfer Amounts F	Operating Costs G	Net Social Gain (or Loss) $H = A + D$ H
Mandatory Work Experience Programs								
Cook County WIN Demonstration ($n = 11,912$)	686	282	405	−183	182	−308	−57	503
San Diego ($n = 3,591$)	310	1,113	−804	1,411	409	1,142	−140	1,721
West Virginia CWEP ($n = 3,694$)	−163	−12	−151	1,424	1,752	177	−505	1,261
Mandatory Job-Search-First Programs								
Atlanta LFA NEWWS ($n = 4,433$)	−14	3,026	−3,040	−932	0	3,878	−4,809	−946
Grand Rapids LFA NEWWS ($n = 4,554$)	−2,867	2,434	−5,301	3,521	0	5,925	−2,405	653
Los Angeles Jobs-First GAIN ($n = 15,683$)	509	4,863	−4,354	3,044	0	4,765	−1,721	3,552
Riverside LFA NEWWS ($n = 8,322$)	−1,606	3,605	−5,211	1,870	0	5,888	−4,018	264
SWIM (San Diego) ($n = 3,227$)	−49	3,383	−3,432	2,599	333	3,958	−1,692	2,549
Mandatory Education-First Programs								
Atlanta HCD NEWWS ($n = 4,433$)	398	2,375	−1,977	−3,943	0	2,689	−6,632	−3,545
Columbus Integrated NEWWS ($n = 7,242$)	−1,975	2,537	−4,513	295	0	5,357	−5,062	−1,680

(*Continued*)

TABLE 12-4 (*Continued*)

Columbus Traditional NEWWS (*n* = 7,242)	−1,423	1,839	−3,263	−781	0	3,684	−2,204
Detroit NEWWS (*n* = 4,459)	196	1,674	−1,478	−401	0	2,084	−205
Grand Rapids HCD NEWWS (*n* = 4,554)	−2,443	1,226	−3,668	−374	0	4,192	−2,817
Riverside HCD NEWWS (*n* = 3,135)	−3,686	2,201	−5,888	735	0	6,268	−2,951
Mandatory Mixed-Initial-Activity Programs							
Butte GAIN (*n* = 1,234)	1,829	4,608	−2,778	197	120	4,129	2,026
Portland NEWWS (*n* = 4,028)	−1,167	6,371	−7,538	6,337	0	9,804	5,169
Riverside GAIN (*n* = 5,626)	2,117	7,115	−4,997	4,104	8	6,324	6,221
San Diego GAIN (*n* = 8,224)	1,026	3,895	−2,869	1,277	208	3,737	2,303
Tulare GAIN (*n* = 2,248)	2,020	2,189	−169	−3,162	−8	661	−1,142
Project Independence (Florida) (*n* = 18,237)	−579	902	−1,481	100	0	1,705	−478
Alameda GAIN (*n* = 1,205)	1,218	3,815	−2,597	−4,153	107	3,550	−2,935
Los Angeles GAIN (*n* = 4,434)	−2,229	800	−3,030	−4,811	−8	3,275	−7,041
Earnings Supplement Programs							
MFIP (Minnesota) (*n* = 3,208)	10,144	1,185	8,958	−10,958	0	−11,299	−814
SSP Applicants (Canada) (*n* = 2,371)	6,589	4,719	1,870	−580	0	817	6,009
SSP Long-Term Recipients (Canada) (*n* = 4,852)	4,614	1,828	2,786	−2,363	0	−1,123	2,251
WRP (Vermont) (*n* = 5,469)	241	−208	448	−228	0	−513	13

Source: Based on Appendix Table B-2 through Appendix Table B-16 in David Greenberg, Victoria Deich, and Gayle Hamilton, *Welfare-to-Work Program Benefits and Costs* (New York: MDRC, 2009).

presents MDRC's valuations of in-program output. Column F is the sum of tax increases paid by participants, reductions in transfer payments paid to participants, and reductions in transfer program operating costs, all of which may be viewed as benefits to nonparticipants. Column G shows the government's cost of operating the treatment programs. Finally, column H, which is computed by summing the benefit-cost components reported in columns B, C, E, F, and G, presents the overall CBA results.

As can be seen from column H, 15 of the 26 reported estimates indicate overall net gains and 11 imply net losses. Nonetheless, most of the total net gains and losses for either participants or nonparticipants that are implied by columns A and D are not especially large; all but six are well under $3,000 per program participant in 2006 dollars.

Table 12-4 distinguishes between five distinct types of welfare-to-work programs. As summarized below, the cost-benefit findings for different program types vary considerably and are quite relevant to policy.

- Mandatory work experience programs, which assigned welfare recipients to unpaid jobs, appear to be worthy of consideration as a component of a comprehensive welfare-to-work program. These program were implemented for persons who, after a period of time, could not find unsubsidized jobs through job search. These programs are not costly to the government and do little harm to participants. Moreover, society as a whole can reap some benefit from the output produced at work experience jobs.

- Mandatory job-search-first programs require individuals to look for jobs immediately upon being assigned to the program. If work is not found, then they are assigned other activities. Such programs appear worthy of consideration when governments want to reduce their expenditures. These programs tend to be less expensive than mandatory mixed-initial-activity programs and, thus, to have a more salutary effect on government budgets. However, they are unlikely to increase the incomes of those required to participate in them.

- The sorts of mandatory education-first programs that have been tested experimentally—ones that require individuals to participate in GED completion and Adult Basic Education prior to job search—do not appear to be cost-beneficial. They do little to either increase the incomes of participants or save the government money.

- Mandatory mixed-initial-activity programs require individuals to participate initially in either an education or training activity or a job search activity. The first six of these programs that are listed in Table 12-4 enrolled both short-term and long-term welfare recipients, while the last two enrolled only long-term welfare recipients. Four of the former were cost-beneficial from a societal perspective, but neither of the latter were.

- Earnings supplement programs provide individuals with financial incentives or earnings supplements intended to encourage work. As discussed in greater detail in Chapter 19, the CBA findings suggest that they are an efficient mechanism for transferring income to low-income families because participants gain more than a dollar for every dollar the government spends.

RANDOM ASSIGNMENT EXPERIMENTS IN HEALTH

Much of this chapter focuses on cost-benefit analyses of social programs, especially E&T programs, that have been based on random assignment experiments. Random assignment, of course, has also been used extensively to assess medicine and medical procedures. Health experiments, in fact, have been conducted for considerably longer than social experiments. And like social experiments, they sometimes provide the basis for CBAs, although they are used far more frequently in cost-effectiveness and cost-utility analyses (see Chapter 17).

Health experiments, especially those involving new drugs, differ from social experiments in an important respect. In experimentally testing new drugs, subjects in the control group are usually given a placebo and members of the treatment and control groups do not know whether they are receiving the new drug or the placebo. In fact, those administering the drug may not know either. If neither the patient nor the researchers know who is in the treatment and control groups, then the experiment is referred to as a "double-blind experiment." In social experiments, in contrast, it is rarely feasible to keep assignment to treatment and control groups hidden (placebo social programs are difficult to envision). Thus, there is the risk that the behavior of people in the control group may be affected by knowledge of the fact that they missed out in receiving the treatment. For example, in the case of an E&T experiment, some members of the control group may be discouraged, while others may be goaded into finding alternative sources of the services offered by the experimental program. It is also possible that some control group members are inappropriately provided some program benefits by sympathetic administrators.

CONCLUSION

The analysis presented in this chapter suggests that CBAs of E&T programs are more difficult both to conduct successfully and to interpret than they may first appear, even when the CBA is based on a classical experimental design. Nevertheless, as the findings drawn from Table 12-4 illustrate, they can provide useful insights. However, some uncertainty exists concerning the reported values, both because of uncertainty over how long the program impacts persisted and because of benefits and costs that were not estimated, such as the value of reductions in the leisure time of participants, changes in the self-esteem of program participants, possible labor displacement resulting from the programs, and society' preference for work over welfare.

EXERCISES FOR CHAPTER 12

1. Using the scheme shown in Table 12-1, diagram the evaluation design used in the CBA of each of the following programs.
    a. To evaluate a government training program that provides low-income, low-skilled, disadvantaged persons job-specific training, members of the target population are randomly assigned to either a treatment group that is eligible to receive services under the program or to a control group that is not. Data are collected on the earnings, welfare receipts, and so forth of both groups during the training period and for two years thereafter.

b. To evaluate a government training program that provides low-income, low-skilled, disadvantaged persons job-specific training, members of the target population who live in the counties in the eastern half of a large industrial state are assigned to a treatment group that is eligible to receive services under the program, while members of the target population who live in the counties in the western half of the state are assigned to a quasi-control group that is not. Information is collected on the earnings, welfare receipts, and so forth of both groups for one year prior to the beginning of training, during the training period, and for two years thereafter.

c. To evaluate a government training program that provides low-income, low-skilled, disadvantaged persons job-specific training, information is collected on the earnings, welfare receipts, and so forth of those persons who receive training. This information is collected for the year prior to the beginning of training, during the training period, and for two years thereafter.

2. Consider a government training program that provides low-skilled men job-specific training. To evaluate this program, members of the target population were randomly assigned to either a treatment group that was eligible to receive services under the program or to a control group that was not. Using this evaluation design, the following information was obtained:

   • Members of the treatment group were found to remain in the program an average of one year, during which time they received no earnings but were paid a tax-free stipend of $5,000 by the program to help them cover their living expenses. During the program year, the average annual earnings of members of the control group were $10,000, on which they paid taxes of $1,000. During the program year, the welfare and unemployment compensation benefits received by the two groups were virtually identical.

   • Program operating costs (not counting the stipend) and the cost of services provided by the program were $3,000 per trainee.

   • During the two years after leaving the program, the average annual earnings of members of the treatment group were $20,000, on which they paid taxes of $2,000. During the same period, the average annual earnings of members of the control group were $15,000, on which they paid taxes of $1,500.

   • During the two years after leaving the program, the average annual welfare payments and unemployment compensation benefits received by members of the treatment group were $250. During the same period, the average annual welfare payments and unemployment compensation benefits received by members of the control group were $1,250.

      a. Using a 5 percent discount rate, a zero decay rate, and a five-year time horizon, compute the present value of the net gain (or loss) from the program from the trainee, nonparticipant, and social perspectives. In doing this, ignore program impacts on leisure and assume that all benefits and costs accrue at the end of the year in which they occur.

      b. Once again ignoring program impacts on leisure, recompute the present value of the net gain (or loss) from the program from the trainee, nonparticipant, and social perspectives, assuming that at the end of the two-year follow-up period program impacts on earnings and transfer payments begin to decay at the rate of 20 percent each year.

3. Perhaps the most careful effort to measure the effects of compensatory preschool education was the Perry Preschool Project begun in Ypsilanti, Michigan, in 1962. Children, mostly three years old, were randomly assigned to treatment (58 children) and control (65 children) groups between 1962 and 1965. Children in the treatment group received two academic years of schooling before they entered the regular school system at about age five, while children in the control group did not. The project collected information on the children through age 19, an exceptionally long follow-up period. Using information generated by the

study, analysts estimated that two years of preschool generated social net benefits (1988 dollars) of $13,124 at a discount rate of 5 percent. (For a more complete account, see W. Steven Barnett, "Benefits of Compensatory Preschool Education," *Journal of Human Resources* 27(2) 1992, 279–312.)

    a. Before seeing results from the project, what would be your main methodological concern about such a long follow-up period? What data would you look at to see if the problem exists?

    b. Benefit categories beyond the age of 19 included crime reduction, earnings increase, and reductions in welfare receipts. If you were designing the study, what data would you collect to help measure these benefits?

4. Five years ago a community college district established programs in ten new vocational fields. The district now wants to phase out those programs that are not performing successfully and retain those programs that are performing successfully. To determine which programs to drop and which to retain, the district decides to perform CBAs.

    a. What perspective or perspectives should be used in the studies? Are there any issues concerning standing?

    b. Using a stylized cost-benefit framework table, list the major benefits and costs that are relevant to the district's decision and indicate how each affects different pertinent groups, as well as society as a whole. Try to make your list as comprehensive and complete as possible, while avoiding double counting.

    c. What sort of evaluation design should the district use in conducting its CBAs? What are the advantages and disadvantages of this design? Is it practical?

    d. Returning to the list of benefits and costs that you developed in part b, indicate which of the benefits and costs on your list can be quantified in monetary terms. How would you treat those benefits and costs that cannot be monetized?

    e. What sort of data would be required to measure those benefits and costs that can be monetized? How might the required data be obtained?

NOTES

1. For a detailed review of cost-benefit analyses of social policies, see David L. Weimer and Aidan R. Vining, eds. *Investing in the Disadvantaged: Assessing the Benefits and Costs of Social Policies* (Washington, D.C., Georgetown University Press, 2009).

2. This method of diagramming evaluation designs was developed a number of years ago by Donald Campbell and Julian Stanley, *Experimental and Quasi-Experimental Designs for Research* (Chicago: Rand-McNally, 1963).

3. On randomization, see Leslie L. Roos Jr., Noralou P. Roos, and Barbara McKinley, "Implementing Randomization," *Policy Analysis* 3(4) 1977, 547–559; and Larry L. Orr, *Social Experiments: Evaluating Public Programs with Experimental Methods* (Thousand Oaks, CA: Sage Publications, Inc., 1999).

4. Sometimes some members of the treatment group do not actually receive program services. For example, in the case of a training program, they may take a job before the training course begins. If so, then the comparison is said to estimate the effect of the program on the "intent-to-treat." If all members of the treatment group actually receive program services, then the comparison is said to estimate program effects on the treated.

5. Sometimes a problem occurs when some members of the two groups cannot be located for purposes of collecting postprogram information on outcomes or refuse to provide the information. This problem, which can occur with all five of the sample designs listed in Table 12-1 and is known as *sample attrition,* can bias the impact estimates if those who can and cannot be located systematically differ from one another in terms of the postprogram outcome measures. For example, those who can be located may have higher earnings, on average, than those who cannot be located.

6. For discussions of issues and problems that arise in conducting social experiments, see Gary Burtless, "The Case for Randomized Field Trials in Economic and Policy Research," *Journal of Economic Perspectives* 9(2) 1995, 63–84; James S. Heckman and Jeffrey A. Smith, "Assessing the Case for Social Experiments," *Journal of Economic Perspectives* 9(2) 1995, 85–110; and David H. Greenberg and Stephen Morris, "Large-Scale Social Experimentation in Britain: What Can and Cannot Be Learnt from the Employment Retention and Advancement Demonstration," *Evaluation* 11(2) 2005, 151–171.

7. The name stems from the fact that in the absence of random assignment people select themselves to participate or not participate in a program on the basis of such unobservable characteristics as motivation. If appropriate statistical adjustments cannot be made to control for this—as the text indicates, sometimes this is possible, but often it is not—then sample selection bias results. For further information on the selection problem and econometric techniques that are used to attempt to adjust for it, see William H. Greene, *Econometric Analysis,* 4th ed. (New York: Macmillan Publishing Company, 2000); Christopher H. Achen, *Statistical Analysis of Quasi-Experiments* (Berkeley: University of California Press, 1986); and Guido W. Imbens and Jeffrey M. Wooldridge, "Recent Developments in the Econometrics of Program Evaluation," *Journal of Economic Literature* 47(1) 2009, 5–86.

8. For a survey of the social experiments conducted between 1962 and 1996, see David Greenberg, Mark Shroder, and Matthew Onstott, "The Social Experiment Market," *Journal of Economic Perspectives* 13(3) 1999, 157–172. For two-to three-page summaries of each of the known 143 social experiments that were completed in the United States by the end of 1996, see David Greenberg and Mark Shroder, *The Digest of Social Experiments,* 3rd ed. (Washington, D.C.: The Urban Institute Press, 2004). For abstracts of more recent social experiments, see David Greenberg and Mark Shroder, editors, *Randomized Social Experiments eJournal,* Social Science Research Network.

9. In recent years, there has been increasing interest in using CBA to assess social programs for young people. For example, see E. Michael

Foster and E. Wayne Holden, "Benefit-Cost Analysis in the Evaluation of Child Welfare Programs," *Focus* 23(1) 2004, 44–49 and Robert Plotnick, "Using Benefit-Cost Analysis to Assess Child Abuse Prevention and Intervention Programs," *Child Welfare* 78(3) 1999, 381–407. Further examples appear in David L Weimer and Aidan R. Vining, eds., *Investing in the Disadvantaged: Assessing the Benefits and Costs of Social Policies.*

10. For summaries of findings from evaluations of E&T programs and methodological issues associated with these evaluations, see Robert J. LaLonde, "The Promise of Public Sector-Sponsored Training Programs," *Journal of Economic Perspectives* 9(2) 1997, 149–168; Daniel Friedlander, David H. Greenberg, and Philip K. Robins, "Evaluating Government Training Programs for the Economically Disadvantaged," *Journal of Economic Literature* 35(4) 1997, 1809–1855; James Heckman, Robert LaLonde, and Jeffrey Smith, "The Economics and Econometrics of Active Labor Market Programs," in Orley Ashenfelter and David Card, eds., *Handbook of Labor Economics, Volume 3A* (Amsterdam: North Holland, 1999), 1865–2097; and David H. Greenberg, Charles Michalopoulos, and Philip K. Robins, "A Meta-Analysis of Government Training Programs," *Industrial and Labor Relations Review* 57(1) 2003, 31–53. For summaries of evaluations of E&T programs specifically targeted at welfare recipients, see Judith M. Gueron and Edward Pauly, *From Welfare to Work* (New York: Russell Sage Foundation, 1991); and Karl Ashworth, Andreas Cebulla, David Greenberg, and Robert Walker, "Meta-Evaluation: Discovering What Works Best in Welfare Provision," *Evaluation* 10(3) 2004, 193–216.

11. For a detailed description of how the operating costs of E&T programs can be estimated, see David H. Greenberg and Ute Appenzeller, *Cost Analysis Step by Step: A How-to Guide for Planners and Providers of Welfare-to-Work and Other Employment and Training Programs*, New York: MDRC, 1998.

12. Several recent studies have discussed this problem in some detail and suggested possible ways of addressing the problem, especially by the use of contingent valuation (see Chapter 15). These studies include David L. Weimer and Aiden R. Vining, *Investing in the Disadvantaged: Assessing*

the Benefits and Costs of Social Policies; Brian Maskery and Dale Whittington, "Measuring What Works: The Feasibility and Desirability of Additional Cost-Benefit Analysis for Sixteen 'Social Programs that Work,'" Chapel Hill: University of North Carolina, 2007; and Lynn A. Karoly, "Valuing Benefits in Benefit-Cost Studies of Social Programs," Santa Monica, CA: Rand Corporation, 2008.

13. The supply curve in Figure 12-1 should be viewed as an equivalent variation supply curve — that is, it incorporates substitution, but not income, effects. For reasons discussed in Appendix 3A, this is the appropriate curve for measuring changes in worker surplus resulting from wage changes. However, as Exhibit 12-2 suggests, wage changes may engender substantial income, as well as substitution, effects.

14. The word *leisure,* as commonly used by economists and as used here, refers to all activities that take place outside the labor market. Many of these activities (e.g., child care, home repair, and education) may, of course, be quite productive.

15. Because the hours the recipient is required to work are computed by dividing her welfare grant by the minimum wage (i.e., $h^* = \text{grant}/W^m$), her grant equals $W^m h^*$, a value that in Figure 12-3 is represented by area $W^m ah^* h_0$.

16. Notice that because the supply curve first shifts from S_0 to S_1, and then, in response to this shift the participant adjusts the number of hours she works, the surplus loss is measured using S_1 rather than S_0.

17. Stephen H. Bell and Larry L. Orr, "Is Subsidized Employment Cost Effective for Welfare Recipients? Experimental Evidence from Seven State Demonstrations," *Journal of Human Resources* 19(1) 1994, 42–61. David H. Greenberg, "The Leisure Bias in Cost-Benefit Analyses of Employment and Training Programs," *Journal of Human Resources* 32(2) 1997, 413–439; and David H. Greenberg and Philip K. Robins, "Incorporating Nonmarket Time into Benefit-Cost Analyses of Social Programs: An Application to the Self-Sufficiency Project," *Journal of Public Economics,* 92(3) 2007, 766–794.

18. As with Figures 12-1, 12-2, and 12-3, the labor supply curve in Figure 12-4 should be viewed as an equivalent variation supply curve.

19. As mentioned earlier in the chapter, having as many able-bodied individuals work as possible is considered an important social goal by many U.S. citizens. Thus, even though subsidizing child care may be economically inefficient, it may still be justified if it helps meet this goal. Moreover, it is sometime argued that subsidies are needed to correct market failures in the market for child care that results in a lower quality of services than is socially optimal. For example, there may be information asymmetries because parents have difficulty in judging the quality of child care. In addition, viewing children as third parties, positive externalities may exist in the market for child care if parents are more concerned with convenience and price than with quality. See Suzanne W. Helburn and Barbara R. Bergmann, *America's Child Care Problem: The Way Out* (New York: Palgrave, 2002).

20. This section borrows heavily from David Greenberg, "Conceptual Issues in Cost-Benefit Analysis of Welfare-to-Work Programs," *Contemporary Policy Issues* 10(4) 1992, 51–63.

21. For a review of what bureaucrats actually maximize, see David L. Weimer and Aidan R. Vining, *Policy Analysis: Concepts and Practice,* 5th ed. (Upper Saddle River, NJ: Prentice Hall, 2011), 178–185.

22. A recent review of studies of public-sector labor displacement finds that these studies suggest that such displacement is fairly high, perhaps on the order of 30 to 60 percent. David Greenberg, "General Equilibrium Effects," (unpublished manuscript, 2009).

23. The review mentioned in the previous endnote found that most of these studies suggest that private-sector displacement is probably moderate, perhaps well under 20 percent. However, the findings from different studies vary greatly and the study methodologies are subject to important weaknesses.

24. David H. Greenberg, Charles Michalopoulous, and Philip K. Robins, "What Happens to the Effects of Government-Funded Training Programs Over Time?" *Journal of Human Resources* 39(1) 2004, 277–293.

25. David Greenberg, Karl Ashworth, Andreas Cebulla, and Robert Walker, "Do Welfare-to-Work Programmes Work for Long?" *Fiscal Studies* 25(1) 2004, 27–53.

26. The CBA of the Baltimore Options program provides an interesting example of this sort of forecasting error. A CBA from the participant perspective that was based on 42 months of data found that the net benefits of the program were nearly three times as large as an earlier CBA based on 18 months of data. The entire difference in these findings is attributable to the first study assuming that the program effect on earnings would decline between months 18 and 42, whereas the effect actually grew over these months. Daniel Friedlander, Gregory Hoerz, David Long, and Janet Quint, *Maryland: Final Report on the Employment Initiatives Evaluation* (New York: MDRC, 1985); and Daniel Friedlander, *Maryland: Supplemental Report on the Baltimore Options Program* (New York: MDRC, 1987).

27. See David H. Greenberg, Charles Michalopoulous, and Philip K. Robins, "What Happens to the Effects of Government-Funded Training Programs Over Time?" Greenberg, Michalopous, and Robins' findings for random assignment evaluations imply that the growth period may last well over a year. For a summary of the scant earlier evidence, see Friedlander, Greenberg, and Robins, "Evaluating Government Training Programs for the Disadvantaged," p. 1836.

28. David Greenberg, Karl Ashworth, Andreas Cebulla, and Robert Walker, "Do Welfare-to-Work Programmes Work for Long?"

29. A synthesis of the cost-benefit findings that are summarized in Table 12-4 appears in David Greenberg, Victoria Deich, and Gayle Hamilton, *Welfare-to-Work Program Benefits and Costs* (New York: MDRC, 2009), which also lists the individual reports from which the findings are drawn. These reports provide detailed descriptions of the programs to which the CBA findings pertain, as well as presenting the findings themselves. For a meta-analysis of the findings in Table 12-4, as well as those for other welfare-to-work programs, see David Greenberg and Andreas Cebulla, "The Cost-Effectiveness of Welfare-to-Work Programs: A Meta-Analysis," *Public Budgeting & Finance*, 28(2) 2008, 112–145.

CHAPTER 13

Valuing Impacts from Observed Behavior: Direct Estimation of Demand Curves

A key concept for valuing policy impacts is change in social surplus. As discussed in Chapters 3 and 4, changes in social surplus are represented by areas, often as triangles or trapezoids, bounded by supply and demand curves. Measurement of changes in social surplus is relatively straightforward when we know the shapes (functional forms) and positions of the supply and demand curves in the relevant primary market, before and after the policy change. In practice, however, these curves are usually not known. Analysts have to estimate them or find alternative ways to measure benefits and costs. In the previous chapter, we discuss how such information can be gathered from demonstrations. In this chapter, we discuss direct estimation of these curves.

We focus on estimating demand curves because, in practice, analysts are more interested in estimating changes in consumer surplus than estimating changes in producer surplus. There are three main reasons. First, changes in producer surplus are often offset by changes in consumer surplus, and thereby constitute transfers. Second, they are often negligible. Third, for *ex post* CBA, changes in producer surplus can usually be computed more easily from changes in profits, which can often be obtained directly from affected firms. There are, however, two major situations when it is important to estimate the supply curve. One pertains to unemployed labor, which we discuss in detail in Chapters 4 and 12. The second arises when the government intervenes in otherwise efficient markets for capital, foreign exchange, labor, and other productive assets. We discuss these issues in Chapter 17.

For goods traded in well-functioning markets, we can usually observe the market-clearing price. We may also observe the aggregate quantity bought and sold so that we have the point of intersection of the demand and supply curves. The task in this chapter is to estimate changes in social surplus where there is limited information. We consider three situations. First, we suppose that we have only one observation on the demand curve but previous research provides knowledge of its shape (functional form), and either its elasticity or slope. Second, we suppose that we have a few observations (points) on the demand curve. Third, we suppose that we have many observations of prices and quantities from different regions or from different time periods. In the first two situations we can make simple extrapolations. In the third situation we will apply standard econometric techniques to estimate the demand curve. Appendix 13A contains an introduction to multiple regression analysis and ordinary least squares estimation, which is applicable to demand curve estimation.

KNOWING THE SLOPE OR PRICE ELASTICITY OF DEMAND

Many municipalities charge annual fees for household refuse collection that do not depend on the quantity of refuse disposed of by households. In such communities, the marginal private cost (MPC) of an additional unit of garbage collected is effectively zero, whereas the marginal social cost (MSC) of collecting and disposing of it is shared equally among all households.[1] This divergence between MPC and MSC leads to free riding and a socially excessive amount of refuse disposal. Raising the price of refuse disposal would reduce the quantity of refuse disposed of by households and thereby reduce the social surplus loss from excess refuse disposal.

Imagine that you have been asked to measure the social benefits that would result if a town, Wasteville, which currently does not charge households by volume for refuse collection, imposes a fee of $1 for each 30-gallon container. That is, households would be charged $1 for each such container put at the curbside for emptying by the sanitation department. As a 30-gallon container holds about 20 pounds of waste, the new policy implies a price increase from zero to about $0.05/lb, assuming the containers were full.

From the sanitation department's records, you find that the current refuse disposal rate averages 2.60 pounds per person per day (lb/p/d), and the MSC of each ton of refuse collected is approximately $120 per ton, or $0.06/lb. (One ton equals 2,000 pounds in the United States.) This MSC is the sum of the marginal collection costs of $40 per ton and the tipping fee at the landfill of $80 per ton. Although the fee still leaves the MPC, the actual price, below the MSC, the socially optimal price, you expect it will produce a gain in social surplus by reducing the amount of waste generated.

To measure the social surplus gain, however, you need to know the demand curve for garbage collection. You know only one point on the demand curve: 2.60 lb/p/d of garbage at a price equal to zero. To progress any further, you must find a way of estimating the rest of the demand curve. Usually, demand curves are assumed to be linear or linear in logarithms. To begin, we assume the demand curve is linear.

Linear Demand Curve

A market demand curve for a good indicates how many units of the good consumers wish to purchase at each price. A linear functional form assumes that the relationship between the quantity demanded and the price is linear; that is, the (ordinary) demand curve can be written as:

$$q = \alpha_0 + \alpha_1 p \tag{13.1}$$

where q is the quantity demanded at price p, α_0 is the quantity that would be demanded if the price were zero (the intercept on the q axis), and α_1 indicates the change in the quantity demanded as a result of a one-unit increase in price (the slope).

For Wasteville, q is measured in terms of *quantity demanded per person* per day. Therefore, we can assume $\alpha_0 = 2.60$ (the amount of refuse disposed of daily by each person at a price of zero). Although we do not know the slope, α_1, we do know that other researchers have addressed this problem and have either estimated the slope or the price elasticity of demand.

Using a Slope Estimate. If you conducted some research, you might turn up a study that gave you an estimate of the slope of the demand curve for refuse disposal. Indeed, Robin Jenkins conducted such a study.[2] She based her estimate on data from nine U.S. communities that employed a variety of refuse fees, ranging from zero to $1.73 per 30- to 32-gallon container, over the period from 1980 to 1989. She estimated that each dollar increase in the price of a 30- to 32-gallon container reduced waste by 0.40 lb/p/d, that is, $\alpha_1 = -0.40$. Using this estimate leads to a prediction that if Wasteville imposed a fee of $1 (in 1985 dollars) per container ($0.05/lb), then residential waste disposal would fall by 0.40 lb/p/d from 2.60 lb/p/d to 2.20 lb/p/d.

Figure 13-1 shows the demand curve implied by Jenkins's slope estimate: $q = 2.60 - 0.4p$, drawn in the usual way with price on the vertical axis.[3] This curve goes through the status quo point of 2.60 lb/p/d at zero dollars per pound (point c) and the predicted point of 2.20 lb/p/d at $0.05 per pound (point d).

This curve can be used to estimate the change in social surplus. Remembering that the socially optimal price is $0.06 per pound, the area of the triangle abc, $0.5(2.60 - 2.12)(0.06 - 0.00) = 0.0144 per pound per day (p/d), is the social surplus loss per person at a price of $0, and the area of the small triangle aed, $0.0004/p/d, is the social surplus loss per person at the price of $0.05/lb. Thus, the area of trapezoid $debc$, $0.0140/p/d, is the gain in social surplus per person that would result from the price increase from

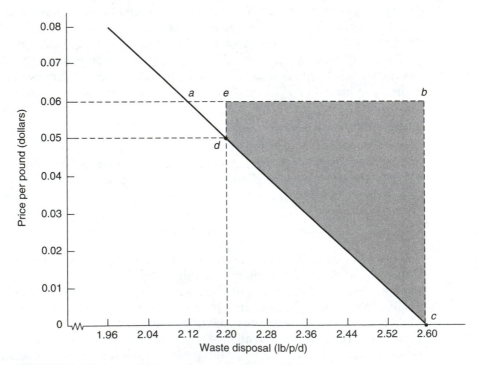

FIGURE 13-1 Social Surplus Gain from Refuse Fee

zero to $0.05/lb. If the population of Wasteville is 100,000 people, then the annual gain in social surplus from imposing a container fee of $1 is ($0.0140/p/d)(365 days)(100,000 persons) = $511,000. To obtain the net social benefit of this policy we would have to subtract the administrative cost of collecting the fee and take into account gains due to reducing taxation, if any.

Using a Price Elasticity Estimate.   Suppose now that the analyst has a valid estimate of the price elasticity of demand for garbage disposal in Wasteville and, as above, the demand curve is linear. As discussed in Chapter 3, the price elasticity of demand, E_d, measures the responsiveness of the quantity demanded to changes in price. For a linear demand curve as in equation (13.1), the price elasticity of demand equals:

$$E_d = \alpha_1 \frac{p}{q} \qquad (13.2)$$

It is *always* negative because $\alpha_1 < 0$ (demand curves slope down), and p and $q > 0$, and it is always nonconstant—it varies with both price and quantity. By rearranging equation (13.2) we can estimate the slope of an ordinary demand curve, α_1, if we have an estimate of its price elasticity and also know the price and quantity at which the elasticity was estimated:

$$\alpha_1 = E_d \frac{q}{p} \qquad (13.3)$$

Returning to our garbage example, suppose Jenkins had not provided an estimate of the slope but instead had reported an estimate of the price elasticity of demand for residential refuse disposal of −0.12, which had been estimated at the average price charged by those communities in her sample that had nonzero fees, $0.81/container, and at the average residential waste disposed of by the communities in her sample, 2.62 lb/p/d.[4] Substituting this information into equation (13.3) gives $\alpha_1 = (-0.12) (2.62)/(0.81) \cong -0.40$.

The general point is that construction of a linear demand curve to measure changes in social surplus requires either a direct estimate of the slope itself or an estimate of the price elasticity of demand and the price and quantity at which the elasticity was estimated.

Validity.   When using a slope or elasticity estimate from previous research, it is important to consider issues of *internal validity* and *external validity*. Internal validity involves the sort of evaluation design issues discussed in Chapter 12, as well as issues related to the proper use of econometric techniques, which we discuss later in this chapter. External validity concerns the appropriateness of using estimates derived from data collected at other times, in other places, and with different populations. Applying estimates to circumstances similar to those under which they were obtained has high external validity. Specifically, the closer Wasteville is in economic, policy, demographic, and geographic characteristics to the communities in Jenkins's sample, the more confident we can be in the accuracy of our estimated change in waste disposal following the introduction of a volumetric user fee in Wasteville. The fact that her estimate comes from the 1980s is of some concern because there has been considerable time for other unmeasured variables that affect people's behavior, such as the level of environmental awareness or recycling infrastructure, to have changed.

Constant Elasticity Demand Curve

The market demand curve may not be linear. Economists have found that many goods have a *constant elasticity demand curve,* that is:

$$q = \beta_0 p^{\beta_1} \tag{13.4}$$

where q denotes quantity demanded at price p, as before, and β_0 and β_1 are parameters. In order to interpret β_1 it is useful to take the natural logarithm, denoted by ln, of both sides of equation (13.4), which gives:

$$\ln q = \ln \beta_0 + \beta_1 \ln p$$

We see immediately that the constant elasticity demand curve is linear in logarithms.[5] Furthermore, β_1, the slope of this demand curve, equals E_d, the price elasticity of demand.[6] As E_d equals the slope of a linear curve, which is a constant, it follows that the price elasticity of demand is constant; hence the name of this demand curve—a constant elasticity demand curve.

   With quantity on the vertical axis and price on the horizontal axis, the slope of the constant elasticity demand curve is not constant; specifically, it equals $\beta_1 q/p$.[7] Similar to other demand curves, it slopes downward and $\beta_1 < 0$. It is also asymptotic to both the price and quantity axes, that is, as price becomes infinite, the quantity demanded approaches zero, and as price approaches zero, the quantity demanded approaches infinity. Because we are most often interested in the region of the demand curve where price is finite and greater than zero, and the estimates of elasticities are based on data in this range, these asymptotic extremes are usually not relevant to our analysis.

   As an illustration of how to use a constant elasticity demand curve, consider the following situation. A community (not Wasteville) currently charges a refuse collection

---

EXHIBIT 13-1

Erik Lichtenberg and David Zilberman wished to estimate the costs and benefits of government regulations that reduced pesticide use in agriculture. Their study covered three important crops: corn, cotton, and rice. There have been numerous empirical studies of price elasticities in agricultural markets. After reviewing this literature, they came up with "consensus values" for the elasticity of supply of 0.3 (corn), 0.5 (cotton), and 0.8 (rice), and for the elasticity of demand of −0.5 (corn), −0.41 (cotton), and −0.43 (rice). The supply and demand functions for all three crops were assumed to have constant elasticity forms.

Source: Adapted from Erik Lichtenberg and David Zilberman, "The Welfare Economics of Price Supports in U.S. Agriculture," *American Economic Review* 76(5) 1986, 1135−1141.

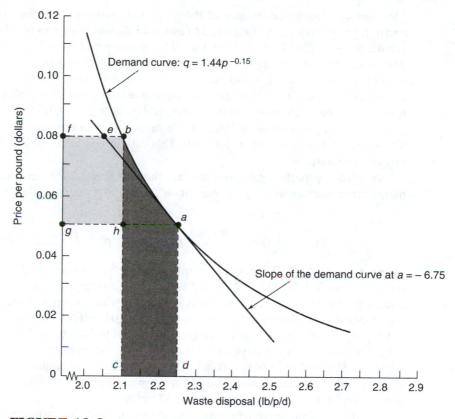

FIGURE 13-2 Constant Elasticity Demand Curve

fee of $0.05/lb, and waste disposal is 2.25 lb/p/d. This status quo point is labelled point *a* in Figure 13-2. We have been asked to estimate the change in consumer surplus that would result if the collection fee were raised to $0.08/lb, assuming that the demand for refuse collection and disposal has a constant elasticity functional form. This change in consumer surplus is represented by area *fbag* in Figure 13-2.

After some research we find an applicable study that reports an estimate of the price elasticity of demand of −0.15. Substituting this estimate of the price elasticity into equation (3.4) and setting $P^* = \$.05/lb$ and $X^* = 2.25$ lb/p/d suggests that the loss in consumer surplus is approximately $0.0645/p/d. For a town with a population of 100,000, the annual loss in consumer surplus would be approximately $2.35 million ($0.0645 \times 365 \times 100,000$).

It is possible to obtain a more exact estimate of the loss in consumer surplus, but it is a bit more complicated. For a constant elasticity demand curve, it can be shown that the change in consumer surplus is given by:

$$\Delta CS = (p_1 q_1 - p_0 q_0)/(1 + \beta_1) \qquad (13.5)$$

This formula requires estimates of the price and quantity after the price increase (p_1 and q_1). To estimate q_1 we first need to estimate β_0, which we can obtain from equation (13.4): $\beta_0 = (2.25)/(0.05)^{-0.15} \approx 1.44$. This gives $q = 1.44\, p^{-0.15}$ as the underlying demand curve for our application.[8] Consequently, if fees were raised to $0.08/lb, demand for waste disposal would fall to 2.10 lb/p/d ($1.44(.05)^{-0.15}$). This point is labelled as point b in Figure 13-2. Now, substituting into equation (13.5) implies that the reduction in consumer surplus would be $0.0653/p/d ($0.08 \times 2.1 - 0.05 \times 2.25)/(1 - .15$). For a town with a population of 100,000, the annual loss in consumer surplus would be $2.38 million ($.0653 \times 365 \times 100,000$). This estimate is very slightly higher than our original estimate.

A third approach begins with the fact that the area under a constant elasticity demand curve from quantity q_0 to quantity q_1, which is given (exactly) by:[9]

$$\text{Area} = \left(\frac{1}{\beta_0}\right)^{1/\beta_1}\left(\frac{q_1^\rho - q_0^\rho}{\rho}\right) \tag{13.6}$$

where $\rho = 1 + (1/\beta_1)$. This equation implies that the area under the demand curve where q ranges from 2.10 lb/p/d to 2.25 lb/p/d, which is equivalent to the dark-shaded area *badc*, equals $0.0097/p/d. If we now subtract area *hadc,* which measures the reduction in fee payments due to the reduction in quantity [($0.05/lb)(2.25 lb/p/d − 2.10 lb/p/d) = .0075/p/d], we obtain an estimate of area *bah* equal to $0.0022/p/d. Finally we add area *fbhg,* the increase in fee payments on the quantity remaining after the price increase [($0.08 − $0.05)(2.10 lb/p/d) = 0.063/p/d], to provide an estimate of overall loss in consumer surplus equal to $0.0652/p/d.[10] For a town with a population of 100,000, the consumer surplus lost annually would be $2.38 million.

A complication arises when we wish to use an elasticity estimated from a constant elasticity functional form to predict the effect of raising a price from zero to some positive level. As the constant elasticity demand curve is inconsistent with an observation of zero price, there is no fully satisfactory way to make use of the elasticity estimate. We are forced to postulate some other functional form that goes through the status quo point (price equals zero) and use the constant elasticity estimate as a rough guide for specifying its parameters. This expediency should be thought of as an informed guess that can serve as the starting point for sensitivity analysis.

EXTRAPOLATING FROM A FEW OBSERVATIONS

Recent policy or other fortuitous changes (at least from the analyst's perspective) often provide a basis for predicting the impacts of future policy changes. For example, imagine that we wish to predict the effect of a fare increase on bus ridership. If the last fare increase of $0.25 resulted in 1,000 fewer riders per day, then it may be reasonable to assume that a further increase of $0.25 would have a similar effect. Here we are treating the observations as if they resulted from a simple before and after quasi-experimental design.

Two considerations are important in determining the appropriateness of extrapolating from the effects of a previous change. The first consideration concerns the assumed functional relationship between the outcome and the policy variable or, specifically, the functional form of the demand curve. Linear functional forms can produce very

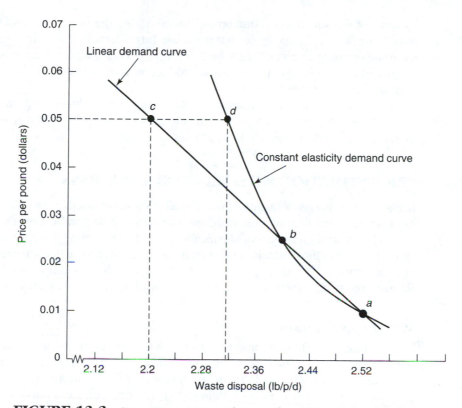

FIGURE 13-3 Imputing a Demand Curve from Two Points

different predictions than constant elasticity functional forms, for instance. This is illustrated in Figure 13-3. Suppose that another municipality, Twopointsville, has been experimenting with waste disposal charges. When these residents were charged $0.01/lb for refuse, they disposed of 2.52 lb/p/d (point *a*), and when the fee was raised to $0.025/lb, they disposed of only 2.40 lb/p/d (point *b*). We would like to know how much waste disposal would occur in Twopointsville if the fee were raised further to $0.05/lb. If we fitted a linear demand curve to the two known points (*a* and *b*), then we would predict that waste would fall by 0.20 lb/p/d to 2.20 lb/p/d (point *c*). If, instead, we fitted a constant elasticity demand curve to the two points, then we would predict that waste would fall by a smaller amount, 0.09 lb/p/d, to 2.31 lb/p/d (point *d*).[11] Note that each of these functional forms fits the two observed data points equally well—perfectly. In fact, there are an infinite number of curves that fit the two observed points perfectly.

Note also that Figure 13-3 illustrates an important point: *The further we extrapolate from past experience, the more sensitive are our predictions to assumptions about functional form.* In the absence of theoretical guidance or other empirical evidence, we have no basis for choosing between the two widely different predictions shown in Figure 13-3.

The second consideration concerns the validity of attributing the change in the outcome to the change in the policy variable. We are implicitly assuming that no other variable of relevance to the outcome changed during the time period under consideration. It is possible, for example, that the fall in bus ridership from *a* to *b* resulted in part from the opening of a major new highway. If this were the case, then it is unlikely that a similar further change in fare would produce as large a reduction in ridership as occurred after the earlier fare change.

One way to control for changes in other variables and to gain greater confidence about the appropriate functional form is to collect more observations and use econometric techniques to estimate key parameters.

ECONOMETRIC ESTIMATION WITH MANY OBSERVATIONS

If many observations of quantities demanded at different prices are available, then it may be possible to use econometric techniques to estimate demand curves or demand functions. The linear regression model typically serves as the starting point for such efforts. We assume here that the reader is familiar with the basic concepts of linear regression. Readers unfamiliar with these concepts, or desiring to review them, should read Appendix 13A. Readers requiring a fuller treatment should consult a basic econometrics text.[12]

Model Specification

The starting point for econometric estimation of demand functions is to specify the important explanatory (or independent) variables, such as price and income, that affect the quantity demanded and the functional form of the relationship.[13] For example, we may have theoretical reasons to believe that the demand for a particular good, *q,* is a function of the price of that good, *p,* income, *I,* and temperature, *T:*

$$q = f(p, I, T) \tag{13.7}$$

The functional form, represented by *f,* may be linear, linear in logarithms, or have some other form.

Sometimes the set of explanatory variables varies slightly from one study to another. *Remember, however, the discussion in Chapter 5 that suggests we should* not *include the prices of substitutes or complements as explanatory variables.* With this exception, the model should include all variables that affect demand in theory. Even though we may not have a substantive interest in some of the explanatory variables, such as temperature, they should be included to "control" for their effects on the dependent variable and thereby allow us to isolate the *independent effects* of the variables of interest, such as price and income. For example, and returning to waste disposal, a study by James Strathman, Anthony Rufolo, and Gerard Mildner assumed that the demand for waste disposal depended on the tipping fee, manufacturing income, and construction employment.[14] In this study, construction employment was included as a control variable.

In practice, the set of included explanatory variables is usually limited for three reasons. First, measures of variables may not be available at reasonable cost. For example, the demand for waste disposal may depend on attitudes toward recycling that we cannot measure without a costly specialized survey. Second, some variables may have relatively small expected effects. For example, temperature may be anticipated to have only a small effect on the demand for a good. Third, a variable may be excluded because it is too highly correlated with other explanatory variables—the problem of *multicollinearity,* which we discuss in Appendix 13A.

The seriousness of excluding a theoretically important variable depends on two factors. First, it depends on the degree to which the excluded variable is correlated with an included variable of interest—one whose coefficient we require for predicting policy effects.[15] The higher the correlation, the greater the bias in the estimated coefficient of the included variable.[16] Bias results because the estimated coefficient would incorporate part of the effect of the excluded variable with which it is correlated. Second, it depends on the true coefficient of the excluded variable if it were included. If this is very small, then the bias from excluding it is likely to be small.

After identifying the theoretically important and practically available variables, the next task is to specify the functional form of the model. As previously discussed, linear and constant elasticity forms are the most commonly used. Sometimes we have theoretical reasons for choosing between them; other times we simply see which fits the observed data better.

Assuming the model represented by equation (13.7) has a linear functional form gives the following model:

$$q = \alpha_0 + \alpha_1 p + \alpha_2 I + \alpha_3 T + \epsilon \qquad (13.8)$$

where ϵ denotes an error term. This model can be estimated by *ordinary least squares* (OLS), assuming no simultaneity (i.e., identification) problem, which we discuss later.

A linear model may still contain nonlinear functions of the explanatory variables. For example, by adding the square of temperature as an explanatory variable along with temperature itself, we allow for a nonlinear relationship between the quantity demanded and temperature. We can also allow for the possibility of different demand curves for different subgroups in our sample by introducing interaction terms. For example, if we have individual-level data and we suspect that men have a steeper demand curve than women, we could include a new variable that is the product of price and the dummy variable (or indicator variable) for gender (e.g., "0" for men and "1" for women). We would then interpret the coefficient of price as the slope of the demand curve for men, and the sum of the coefficient of the price variable and the coefficient of the price-gender interaction variable as the slope of the demand curve for women. The general point is that we can have quite complicated functional forms within the basic linear specification that can be estimated by OLS.

Assuming the model represented by equation (13.7) has a constant elasticity functional form gives the following model:

$$q = \beta_0 p^{\beta_1} I^{\beta_2} T^{\beta_3} e^{\epsilon} \qquad (13.9)$$

where the βs are parameters to be estimated, e is the base of the natural logarithm, and ϵ is the unobserved random error. Taking the natural logarithm of both sides of this equation gives:

$$\ln q = \ln\beta_0 + \beta_1 \ln p + \beta_2 \ln I + \beta_3 \ln T + \epsilon \qquad (13.10)$$

This linear model can be estimated by OLS with ln$q$ as the dependent variable and ln$p$, ln$I$, and ln$T$ as explanatory variables. The parameters, the βs, can be interpreted in the standard way, noting that the intercept is an estimate of lnβ_0 rather than β_0. The coefficient of the variable ln$p$ is the price elasticity of demand, and the coefficient of the variable ln$I$ is the income elasticity of demand.

Types of Data

Data availability is usually the limiting factor in estimating demand schedules. Researchers sometimes have sufficient resources to assemble their own data. More often, however, resource limitations force researchers to rely on *convenience samples,* that is, data that happen to be available at acceptable cost. These include previously published data, data collected by researchers for other purposes, and samples of administrative records or program clients. Nevertheless, it is worthwhile briefly reviewing the major considerations in the choice of data and their implications for demand function estimation.

Level of Aggregation.   The first major consideration is the level of aggregation. Individual-level data measure the behavior of persons, families, households, or other consuming units. Aggregate-level data measure the combined (aggregate) behavior of groups of consumers, usually organized by geographic jurisdictions or demographic characteristics.

Consumer theory is based on models of individual utility maximization. Individual-level data are generally preferable because they provide a close congruence between theory and data. Furthermore, theoretically important variables, such as income, can often be measured directly with individual-level data. In contrast, when using aggregate-level data, a mean or median typically serves as the measure of income.

In using aggregate data, there is a risk of making serious errors about the effects of policy-relevant variables on demand. For example, suppose that we use individual-level data from different states to estimate the price elasticity of demand for each state. Further suppose, as expected, each of these price elasticity estimates is negative. Now suppose that another less-fortunate researcher has only aggregate-level data that consist of one observation for each state (such as the average price and average quantity demanded in each state). He might hope that his estimated price elasticity is approximately a weighted average of the price elasticities of demand for each state and that his estimates of the effects of price changes are reasonably accurate. It is possible, however, that his estimated price elasticity is very different from the price elasticities that we estimate for each state. In fact, depending on the aggregate-level price and quantity observations, it could have the wrong sign.[17]

In practice, however, individual-level data are often not available. For example, in estimating the "demand" for criminal acts, an important theoretical variable is the "price," which depends on the perceived probability of arrest. We cannot directly observe the probability of arrest perceived by an individual, but we can assume that it is related to the objective (group) probability, which can be estimated as the fraction of crimes that result in arrest within a region or among a group of individuals.

Cross-Sectional Data versus Time Series Data.   The second major consideration in selecting data concerns the choice between cross-sectional data and time series data. A cross section involves observations on a number of comparable units at the same point in time, whereas a time series involves making repeated observations on the same unit at several points in time. For example, if we wished to determine the price elasticity of demand for wine, we might take advantage of different excise tax rates across different states. Using observations for each of the 50 states for a particular year, we would regress per capita consumption of wine on after-tax retail prices and other explanatory variables, such as average state levels of income and education. Alternatively, if the real price of wine has varied over time, we might estimate a price elasticity by regressing national per capita consumption in each year on the real price of wine in each year and other variables, such as real per capita income in each year. Cross-sectional and time series data are prone to different types of econometric problems and yield coefficient estimates that have somewhat different interpretations.

Cross-sectional data generally provide estimates of long-run elasticities, whereas time series data usually provide estimates of short-run elasticities. In estimating elasticities from cross sections, we usually assume that the variations in demands across units reflect long-run adjustments to previous price changes. Thus, we obtain estimates of long-run elasticities. Only if we make our observations shortly after a major price change would we interpret the elasticity obtained from a cross-section as a short-run elasticity. In estimating elasticities from time series data, we observe responses to price changes occurring as frequently as the time unit of the observations. Thus, annual data provide estimates of annual elasticities, and monthly data provide estimates of monthly elasticities. For most goods, monthly elasticities would be interpreted as short run. Annual elasticities, however, may be either short run or long run, depending on the extent to which full adjustment to price changes requires changes in capital goods, location, and other factors that consumers alter gradually.

We would expect short-run price elasticities to be smaller in absolute value than long-run price elasticities because, by definition, there is less time for consumers to adjust to price changes. Indeed, based on a review of 120 empirical studies, Molly Espy found an average short-run price elasticity of demand for gasoline of -0.26 and an average long-run price elasticity of -0.58, and an average short-run income elasticity of 0.47 and an average long-run income elasticity of 0.88.[18] P. B. Goodwin reviewed 120 empirical studies and reported average elasticities of the demand for automobile "traffic" with respect to motor fuel prices were -0.16 in the short run and -0.33 in the long run.[19]

Cross-section and time series data tend to suffer different econometric problems. Cross sections, especially when they consist of units of different sizes, often have error terms with different variances—the *heteroscedasticity* problem. For example, the variance in the number of accidental deaths from fire is likely to be larger among larger cities, such as New York City, than among smaller cities, such as Utica, New York. If the variances of the error terms are unequal, then the OLS estimates of the coefficients are unbiased but their calculated standard errors are smaller than the true standard errors. That is, the reported precision of OLS estimates would be overly optimistic. If the relative sizes of the variances of the error terms were known, then estimating the model by *generalized least squares* (GLS) would give more precise estimates of the coefficients.

Discussions of tests for detecting heteroscedasticity and for appropriate estimation procedures can be found in most econometrics texts.

Time series data also suffer from a common problem with the error term. Remember that the effects of excluded explanatory variables are incorporated into the error term. If an excluded variable tends to change gradually over time, then it may produce correlation between successive error terms. This is one example of the more general problem of *autocorrelation,* which often exists in one form or another in time series data. It has similar effects to heteroscedasticity: OLS coefficient estimates, though unbiased, are not as precise as reported. More precise estimates can be obtained by using GLS if the pattern of the autocorrelation is known. The most widely used test for autocorrelation is the Durbin-Watson statistic, which should always be a component of time series analysis. Again, discussions of methods for detecting autocorrelation and correcting for it can be found in econometrics texts.

It is also possible to pool cross-sectional and time series data, for example, by using data from each state for each of a number of years. Though modeling with pooled time series and cross-sectional data can be quite complex and cannot be discussed here, two points are worth noting. First, pooled data provide a rich source of information. Second, pooled data are vulnerable to the econometric problems encountered with both cross-sectional and time series data.

Identification

In a perfectly competitive market, price and quantity result from the simultaneous interaction of supply and demand. Changes in price and quantity can result from shifts in the supply curve, shifts in the demand curve, or both. In the absence of variables that affect only one side of the market, it may not be possible to estimate separately the supply and demand curves. Indeed, if quantity supplied and quantity demanded depended only on price, then the equation for both the demand curve and the supply curve would look identical. Determining whether we are estimating a demand curve or a supply curve is one example of the problem of *identification.* It occurs in multiple equation models in which some variables, such as price and quantity, are determined simultaneously. Such variables are called *endogenous variables.* In contrast, variables that are fixed or are determined outside of the model are called *exogenous variables.*

In order to identify a demand curve we need to have a variable that affects supply but not demand. Consider a competitive and unregulated market for wheat. If rainfall affects the supply of wheat but not the demand for wheat, then including rainfall in the supply equation but not in the demand equation identifies the demand equation. The reason is that changes in rainfall result in systematic shifts in supply but not demand, which will trace out the demand curve. Similarly, if income affects demand but not supply, then including income in the demand equation but not in the supply equation allows us to examine systematic shifts in the demand curve, which will trace out the supply curve. In general, a two-equation model will be identified if there is one exogenous variable that belongs in the first equation but not in the second equation, and another exogenous variable that belongs in the second equation but not in the first equation. By belong, we mean that it has a nonzero coefficient; by not belong, we mean that it has a zero coefficient. The zero coefficient conditions are most important. One cannot identify a model by excluding an exogenous variable from an equation that theoretically belongs in that equation.

Identification of demand curves tends to be less of a problem in the markets typically of interest to cost-benefit analysts than in markets generally. One reason is that CBA often deals with markets that are subject to exogenous government interventions. For example, the demand for cigarettes is probably easily identified in cross-sectional analysis because differences in state excise taxes shift the supply curve by a different amount in each state.

Another reason is that the identification problem does not arise in markets where the price is set exogenously. In some markets of interest to cost-benefit analysts, the government either provides the product or service, as is often the case with municipal waste disposal, or regulates the prices charged, as is the case with electricity. When government supplies a good or effectively sets price, there is no supply curve—price is exogenous, and we avoid the identification problem.

Confidence Intervals

The standard errors of the estimated coefficients of a model can be used to construct confidence intervals for the coefficients. A 95 percent confidence interval is commonly interpreted as there being a 95 percent chance that the true value of the coefficient lies within the interval. Strictly speaking, this is an incorrect interpretation. The correct interpretation is that if we were to repeat our estimation procedure many times, with a new data sample for each repetition, the estimated confidence intervals would contain the true value of the coefficient in about 95 percent of the repetitions. Nevertheless, confidence intervals provide some guidance for sensitivity analysis. Most analysts would consider it reasonable to treat the ends of a 95 percent confidence interval as best and worst cases.

Prediction versus Hypothesis Testing

As a final topic on estimating demand functions, it is important to keep in mind the distinction between hypothesis testing and estimation. Social scientists are typically interested in testing hypotheses about one or more coefficients in a regression model. If the estimated coefficients are not statistically significantly different from zero, then social scientists do not reject the null hypothesis that the variables have no effect on the dependent variable. In other words, there is not a statistically convincing case that the variables have any effect.

As cost-benefit analysts, however, we have to make a prediction. For such purposes we should use the estimated value of the coefficient, even if it is not statistically significant from zero at conventional levels. Although we may not be very confident that the true value of the coefficient is not zero, the estimated coefficient may be our best estimate of the true value. If so, it will give the best predictions. Sensitivity analysis should reflect the imprecision of our estimate. If we were to use only the statistically significant coefficients from an estimated model, we would bias our prediction. Eliminating statistically insignificant variables and reestimating the model may or may not be appropriate, depending on the theoretical strength of their inclusion in the original model.

CONCLUSION

Estimating the net social benefits of a policy requires estimates of the change in social surplus. Changes in social surplus require knowledge of the appropriate market demand and supply curves. This chapter concerns estimation of these curves, focusing on demand curves.

Sometimes, project revenues can be used as a measure of (gross) benefits. This has relatively limited requirements: It requires the existence of a market for the primary outcome of the project and knowledge of expenditures in this market. However, project revenues are often an inappropriate measure of benefits, and we may need to estimate consumer surplus. In these situations, we need to estimate the relevant market demand curve. Direct estimation of the demand curve is possible if we know at least one point on the demand curve, its functional form, and either its slope or the price elasticity of demand. In many practical situations we do not know the slope or the price elasticity of demand. We may be able to infer such information from a few observations. Preferably, there may be many observations, and the analyst can use econometric techniques to estimate the demand curve. It is important to consider the advantages and potential limitations of these different estimation methods.

An Introduction to Multiple Regression Analysis

Linear regression provides a manageable way to examine statistically the effects of one or more explanatory variables on a variable of interest—the dependent variable.[1] Its use requires us to assume that the effects of the various explanatory variables on the dependent variable are additive, that is, the model has the following functional form:

$$y = \beta_0 + \beta_1 x_1 + \beta_2 x_2 + \cdots + \beta_k x_k + \epsilon$$

where y is the dependent variable, $x_1, x_2, \ldots, x_k$ are k explanatory (or independent) variables, $\beta_0, \beta_1, \beta_2 \ldots, \beta_k$ are parameters (coefficients) to be estimated, and ϵ is an error term that incorporates the cumulative effect on y of all the factors not explicitly included in the model. The basic model assumes that the explanatory variables are nonrandom and are measured without error.

The intercept parameter, β_0, also called the *constant,* is the expected value of y if all of the explanatory variables equal zero. The other parameters, 1,2,...,k, which are called slope parameters, measure the marginal impact of an explanatory variable on the dependent variable. If, for instance, we were to increase x1 (NOTE: the 1 should be a subscript) by one unit while holding the values of the other explanatory variables constant, then y would change by an amount β_1.

Imagine that we set the values of all the explanatory variables except x_1 equal to zero. We could then plot y against x_1 in a two-dimensional graph. The equation $y = \beta_0 + \beta_1 x_1$ would represent the true regression line. The slope of this line is β_1; it measures the magnitude of the change in y that will result from a one-unit change in x_1. The actual observations will usually not lie exactly on the line. The vertical deviation between an observed point, and the line will equal the

random error, represented in our model by ϵ. If the values of ϵ are small in absolute value, then the true regression line fits the data well in the sense that the actual observations are close to it.

Estimating the Parameters of the Model

The most commonly used procedure for fitting a line to the data is the method of ordinary least squares (OLS). When we have only one explanatory variable so we can plot our data on a two-dimensional graph, the OLS procedure picks the line for which the sum of squared vertical deviations from the estimated line to the observed data is smallest.

Suppose we denote the OLS estimates of the $k + 1$ parameters by "hats": $\hat{\beta}_0, \hat{\beta}_1, \ldots, \hat{\beta}_k$. $\hat{\beta}_j$ provides an estimate of the change in y due to a small (one unit) change in x_j holding *all other variables constant.* For the ith observation $(y_i, x_{i1}, x_{i2}, \ldots, x_{ik})$, the predicted value of the dependent variable is

$$\hat{y}_i = \hat{\beta}_0 + \hat{\beta}_1 x_{i1} + \hat{\beta}_2 x_{i2} + \cdots + \hat{\beta}_k x_{ik}$$
$$i = 1, \ldots, n$$

and the ith *prediction error* or *residual* is

$$\hat{\epsilon}_i = y_i - \hat{y}_i \quad i = 1, \ldots, n$$

Thus, the residual is the observed value of the dependent variable minus the value we would predict for the dependent variable based on our estimated parameters and the values of our explanatory variables. OLS selects the parameter estimates to minimize the sum of squares of these residuals.[2]

The square of the correlation between the actual and predicted values of the dependent variable, R^2, is commonly used as a measure of the goodness-of-fit of a regression. The R^2, which ranges between 0 and 1, measures the percentage of variation in the dependent variable that is explained by the estimated model. It can be used to help select between alternative model specifications when theory is ambiguous, or to test alternative theories.

Multicollinearity

As long as the number of observations in our sample exceeds the number of coefficients that we want to estimate, computer regression software packages will usually enable us to obtain the OLS estimates. However, when one explanatory variable can be written as a linear combination of the others, we have a case of *perfect multicollinearity*. A less severe but more common form of the problem occurs when the explanatory variables in the sample are highly correlated. This condition is called *multicollinearity*. If two or more variables are highly correlated, OLS has difficulty identifying the independent effect of each explanatory variable on the dependent variable. As a result, these parameter estimates are not very reliable or, in the extreme case, they cannot be estimated. When two explanatory variables are highly correlated, the sum of their estimated coefficients will be closer to the sum of their true coefficients than will either individual coefficient estimate be to its true value. Often, researchers respond to a multicollinearity problem by excluding one or more explanatory variables, though this may lead to biased estimates of some parameters. Two alternative ways to deal with multicollinearity problems include using ridge regression or combining collinear variables into indices using principal components analysis.[3]

Properties of OLS Estimators

The OLS estimator will generally have a number of very desirable properties. (Note: An *estimator* is the formula we use to calculate a particular parameter from the data. The resultant specific value is an estimate.) If all of the explanatory variables are uncorrelated with the error term, ϵ, and if the expected value of the error term is zero, then the OLS estimators will be *unbiased*. To understand what it means for an estimator to be unbiased, we must keep in mind that a particular estimate depends on the errors in the actual sample of data. If we were to select a new sample, then we would realize different errors and, hence, different coefficient estimates. When an estimator is unbiased, the average of our estimates across different samples will be very close to the true coefficient value. For example, if the price of gasoline had no true effect on the quantity of gasoline demanded, then we would almost certainly estimate its coefficient to be positive or negative rather than exactly zero. Repeating OLS on a large number of samples and averaging our estimates of the coefficient of gasoline price, however, would generally yield a result very close to zero. Indeed, by adding more and more samples, we could get the average as close to zero as we wanted.

The OLS estimator is also consistent, which means that its variance approaches zero as we increase the sample size.[4] Consequently, as the sample size increases, we become more confident about the accuracy of our estimates—the confidence intervals become narrower.

A problem arises, however, if an important variable is excluded from the estimation and that variable is correlated with an included variable. Suppose, for example, that the weather (temperature) affects the quantity of gasoline demanded, and that temperature is also correlated with gasoline price, but that temperature is excluded from the model. Now, the coefficient of gasoline price will reflect both the effect of gasoline price on quantity demanded and the indirect effect of temperature for which it serves as a proxy. Other things being equal, the stronger the true effect of temperature on quantity demanded, and the higher the absolute value of the correlation between gasoline price and temperature, the greater will be the bias in the coefficient of gasoline price. This problem cannot be solved by increasing the sample size.

Statistical Significance and Hypothesis Testing

It is often important to determine whether an estimate deviates enough from zero for us to conclude that the true value of the parameter is not zero. If we make the reasonable assumption that the error term for each observation can be treated as a draw from a normal distribution with constant variance, σ^2, then we can show that the OLS estimators will be distributed according to the normal distribution.[5] Specifically, we can interpret the particular numerical estimate of a coefficient, $\hat{\beta}$, as a draw from a random variable having a normal distribution centered around the true value of the coefficient, β, with variance, $\sigma_{\hat{\beta}}^2$, which depends on σ^2. (The OLS estimator is the random variable; the actual estimate based on the data is a particular realization of that random variable.) Because we want to know how likely it is that we would observe a coefficient estimate as large as we did if the true value of the coefficient were zero, we now suppose that the true value of the coefficient is zero (the null hypothesis) so that the distribution of our estimator is centered around zero. We then standardize our distribution to have a variance of one by dividing our coefficient estimate by its *estimated standard deviation*. The resultant statistic, called a *t* statistic, or *t* ratio, has a *student's t distribution*, or *t* distribution.[6] The *statistical significance* of our coefficient estimate can be determined by comparing the *t* statistic to the critical values in a table of the *t* distribution, which can found in the appendix of almost any statistics text. For example, we might decide that we will reject the null hypothesis that the true value of the coefficient is zero if there is less than a 5 percent probability of observing a *t* ratio (in absolute value) as large as we did if the null hypothesis is true.[7] If the sample size is large we would reject this null hypothesis if the *t* statistic were larger in absolute value than 1.96.

The *t* distribution is tabulated by degrees of freedom. The OLS estimators have degrees of freedom equal to the total number of observations, denoted by *n*, minus the number of coeffi-

cients being estimated, $k + 1$. As the degrees of freedom increase, the student's *t* distribution looks more like a standardized normal distribution.

Returning to our gasoline example, suppose that the analyst wants to test whether gasoline price has a statistically significant effect on gasoline demand at the 5 percent level of significance. She may specify a one-tailed alternative hypothesis test or a two-tailed alternative hypothesis test. For example, she may test the null hypothesis that the true coefficient value is greater than or equal to zero (the one-tailed alternative is that it is less than zero), which means that the *critical region* consists of the entire 5 percent in the negative tail. Alternatively, she may test the null hypothesis that the true coefficient value is equal to zero (the two-tailed alternative is that it is less than *or* greater than zero), which means that the critical region consists of the 2.5 percent in the negative tail and the 2.5 percent in the positive tail. Now suppose that the *t* statistic for the coefficient of gasoline price equals -1.84. Further suppose that the sample size was 122, and there was only one explanatory variable, so that only two parameters were estimated (the intercept and slope) and there were 120 degrees of freedom. The absolute values of the critical values of the *t* distribution with 120 degrees of freedom are 1.658 for the one-sided alternative and 1.98 for the two-sided alternative. Thus, at the 5 percent level of significance, the analyst would reject the null hypothesis if she had specified a one-sided alternative, but she would accept the null hypothesis if she had specified a twosided alternative.

Most regression software saves us the trouble of looking up critical values in tables by directly calculating the probability under the null hypothesis of observing a *t* statistic as large as that estimated, assuming we want to test the null hypothesis that the true parameter equals zero against a two-sided alternative. To do this classical hypothesis test on the coefficient, we simply see if the reported probability is less than the maximum probability of falsely rejecting the null hypothesis that we are willing to accept. If it is smaller, then we reject the null hypothesis.

EXERCISES FOR CHAPTER 13

1. Consider the example presented in Figure 13-3. Imagine that the current price of waste disposal is $0.025/lb and the average waste disposal is 2.40 lb/p/d. As noted in the diagram, when the price was previously $0.01/lb, the average waste disposal was 2.52 lb/p/d. Assume that the marginal social cost of waste disposal is $0.06/lb, that marginal social costs are constant with respect to quantity, and that the town has a population of 100,000.

    a. Fitting a linear demand curve to the two observed points, calculate the annual net benefits of raising the price of waste disposal to $0.05/lb.

    b. Fitting a constant elasticity demand curve to the observed points, calculate the annual net benefits of raising the price of waste disposal to $0.05/lb.

2. (Regression software required; instructor-provided spreadsheet recommended.) An analyst was asked to predict the gross social benefits of building a public swimming pool in Dryville, which has a population of 70,230 people and a median household income of $31,500. The analyst identified 24 towns in the region that already had public swimming pools. He conducted a telephone interview with the recreation department in each town to find out what fee it charged per visit (Fee) and how many visits it had during the most recent summer season (Visits). In addition, he was able to find each town's population (Pop) and median household income (Income) in the most recent census. His data are as follows:

	Visits	Fee	Income	Pop
1	168,590	0	20,600	36,879
2	179,599	0	33,400	64,520
3	198,595	0	39,700	104,123
4	206,662	0	32,600	103,073
5	170,259	0	24,900	58,386
6	209,995	0.25	38,000	116,592
7	172,018	0.25	26,700	49,945
8	190,802	0.25	20,800	79,789
9	197,019	0.25	26,300	98,234
10	186,515	0.50	35,600	71,762
11	152,679	0.50	38,900	40,178
12	137,423	0.50	21,700	22,928
13	158,056	0.50	37,900	39,031
14	157,424	0.50	35,100	44,685
15	179,490	0.50	35,700	67,882
16	164,657	0.75	22,900	69,625
17	184,428	0.75	38,600	98,408
18	183,822	0.75	20,500	93,429
19	174,510	1.00	39,300	98,077
20	187,820	1.00	25,800	104,068
21	196,318	1.25	23,800	117,940
22	166,694	1.50	34,000	59,757
23	161,716	1.50	29,600	88,305
24	167,505	2.00	33,800	84,102

    a. Show how the analyst could use these data to predict the gross benefits of opening a public swimming pool in Dryville and allowing free admission.

    b. Predict gross benefits if admission is set at $1.00 and Dryville has marginal excess tax burden of 0.25. In answering this question, assume that the fees are used to reduce taxes that would otherwise have to be collected from the citizens of Dryville to pay for expenses incurred in operating the pool.

NOTES

1. More accurately, each household incurs a marginal private cost (MPC) of refuse disposal that is only $1/n$ of the marginal social costs (MSC); that is, $MPC = MSC/n$, where n is the number of households. The MPC approaches zero for large n.
2. Robin R. Jenkins, *The Economics of Solid Waste Reduction: The Impact of User Fees* (Brookfield, VT: Edward Elgar Publishing Company, 1993).
3. Rearranging equation (13.1) gives the following inverse market demand curve:

$$p = -\alpha_0/\alpha_1 + (1/\alpha_1)q$$

The slope of this curve equals $1/\alpha_1$. The intercept, $-\alpha_0/\alpha_1$, indicates the lowest price at which the quantity demanded equals zero; it is sometimes called the *choke price*. For the demand curve shown in Figure 13-1, the inverse demand curve is $p = 6.5 - 2.5q$, and the choke price is $6.50.
4. Jenkins, *The Economics of Solid Waste Reduction: The Impact of User Fees*, pp. 88–90, 101.
5. Some economists call this functional form a *log-linear demand curve;* others call it a *log-log demand curve* or a *double-log* demand curve. In order to minimize potential confusion, we will not to use any of these terms, but will refer to the curve as linear in logarithms.
6. Because β_1 is the slope of the linear in logarithms demand curve, $\beta_1 = \partial \ln q/\partial \ln p$. By definition, the price elasticity of demand $\epsilon_d = \partial \ln q/\partial \ln p$. Consequently, $\epsilon_d = \beta_1$.
7. The slope is given by:

$$\partial q/\partial p = \beta_1\beta_0 p^{\beta_1-1} = \beta_1\beta_0 p^{\beta_1}/p = \beta_1 q/p.$$

8. Note that our estimate of $\beta_0 = 1.44$ will generally differ from the original estimate of β_0 obtained by the researchers from whom we took our price elasticity estimate. This difference arises because we force the demand curve to pass through point *a,* our known data point, whereas the original, estimated equation probably will not pass through point *a.*
9. The area is calculated by integrating the inverse demand curve from q_0 and q_1, that is, as $\int p\,dq =$

$\int (q/\beta_0)^{1/\beta_1}\,dq$ with q_0 and q_1 as the limits of integration.
10. The change in consumer surplus is the area under the demand curve between p_0 and p_1, that is, $\int q\,dp = \int \beta_0 p^{\beta_1}\,dp$ with p_0 and p_1 as the limits of integration.
11. Solve for β_0 and β_1 as follows: $\beta_1 = \ln(q_0/q_1)/\ln(p_0/p_1) = -0.053$, and $\beta_0 = q_0/(p_0^{\beta_1}) = 1.97$.
12. For an excellent treatment of the econometric issues raised in this section, see William H. Greene, *Econometric Analysis,* 6th ed. (Upper Saddle River, New Jersey: Prentice Hall, 2008).
13. Thus far, this chapter has focused on demand curves that relate quantity demanded to price. Other variables also affect demand. A demand function relates the quantity demanded to price and other variables. Because a demand function is more general than a demand curve, this section focuses on demand functions. Sometimes we use the term *demand schedule* to refer to demand curves or demand functions.
14. They estimated an elasticity of disposal demand with respect to tipping fees of -0.11 for communities in the region around Portland, Oregon, over a seven-year period; see James G. Strathman, Anthony M. Rufolo, and Gerard C. S. Mildner, "The Demand for Solid Waste Disposal," *Land Economics* 71(1) 1995, 57–64.
15. If the estimated regression equation contains more than one explanatory variable, then the bias in the coefficient of a particular variable depends on the *partial correlation* between that variable and the omitted variable, controlling for all other variables in the regression.
16. If an excluded variable is not correlated with an included variable, then excluding it will not bias the estimated coefficient of the included variable. However, the overall fit of the model, measured by its R^2, will be poorer, and the precision of the estimated coefficients will be lower.
17. See, for example, Henri Theil, *Principles of Econometrics* (New York: Wiley, 1971), 556–557.
18. Molly Espey, "Gasoline Demand Revisited: An International Meta-Analysis of Elasticities," *Energy Economics* 20(3) 1998, 273–295.

19. P. B. Goodwin, "A Review of New Demand Elasticities with Special Reference to Short and Long Run Effects of Price Changes," *Journal of Transport Economics and Policy* 26(2) 1992, 155–170 at pp. 158–159. See also Tae Moon Oum, W. G. Waters II, and Jong-Say Yong, "Concepts of Price Elasticities of Transport Demand and Recent Empirical Estimates," *Journal of Transport Economics and Policy* 26(2) 1992, 139–154.

APPENDICES NOTES

1. For a clear introduction to regression analysis, see Jeffrey M. Wooldridge, *Introductory Econometrics: A Modern Approach* (Boston: South-Western Publishing, 2000).

2. Formally, OLS minimizes $\sum_{i=1}^{n} \hat{\epsilon}_i^2$.

3. See Greene, *Econometric Analysis*. For an application that presents both OLS and ridge regression estimates, see A. E. Boardman, S. Miller, and A. P. Schinnar, "Efficient Employment of Cohorts of Labor in the U.S. Economy: An Illustration of a Method," *Socio-Economic Planning Sciences* 13(6) 1979, 297–302.

4. The OLS estimators are also *efficient*. Here, efficiency means that among all estimators whose formulas are linear in the dependent variable, the OLS estimator has the smallest variance. It therefore has the greatest "power" for rejecting the null hypothesis that a coefficient is zero.

5. The *central limit theorem* tells us that the distribution of the sum of independent random variables approaches the normal distribution as the number in the sum becomes large. The theorem applies for almost any starting distributions with finite variances. If we think of the error term as the sum of all the many factors excluded from our model and, furthermore, we believe that these excluded factors are not systematically related to one another or to the included variables, then the central limit theorem suggests that the distribution of the error terms will be approximately normal.

6. Student is the pseudonym of William Gosset, a quality control engineer at the Guinness Brewery in Dublin, who originally derived the *t* distribution.

7. The probability we choose puts an upward bound on the probability of falsely rejecting the null hypothesis. Falsely rejecting the null hypothesis is referred to as Type I error. Failing to reject the null hypothesis when in fact the alternative hypothesis is true is referred to as Type II error. We usually set the probability of Type I error at some low level, such as 5 percent. Holding the sample size constant, the lower we set the probability of a Type I error, the greater the probability of a Type II error.

CHAPTER 14

Valuing Impacts from Observed Behavior: Indirect Market Methods

Generally, estimation of changes in social surplus requires knowledge of entire demand and supply schedules. The previous chapter discusses direct estimation of demand and supply curves, focusing on the demand curve for the purpose of measuring consumer surplus. It assumes that there is a market demand curve for the good in question, such as garbage collection or gasoline, and we can observe at least one point on this demand curve. In many applications of CBA, however, the markets for certain "goods," such as human life or pollution, do not exist or are imperfect for reasons discussed in Chapter 4. In these situations it may be impossible to estimate or inappropriate to use the market demand (or supply) curve directly. In the past, such goods were treated as "intangible," and their impacts were excluded or analysts were restricted to qualitative CBA or multigoal analysis. However, over the past 30 years, economists have devised methods to value these impacts, thus enabling analysts to conduct (comprehensive) CBA.

In practice, the change in social surplus can often be estimated from knowledge of the impact of a policy (e.g., number of affected persons) and the marginal social benefit or the marginal social cost of one more unit of the affected good or service. In a perfect market, the market price equals both the marginal social cost and the marginal social benefit of an additional unit of a good or service. When a market does not exist or market failure leads to a divergence between market price and marginal social cost, analysts try to obtain estimates of what the market price would be if the relevant good were traded in a market where the demand curve measured marginal social benefits and the supply curve measured marginal social costs. As we discuss in Chapter 4, such an estimate is called a *shadow price*.

When a market for the good of interest does not exist, one of two major methods of estimating shadow prices can be used.[1] This chapter recognizes that although there may not be a market for the good or service of interest, its value (shadow price) may be reflected indirectly in the market for a related good. Through statistical analysis of the related market, we can estimate the value of the nonmarketed good. The second way to estimate a shadow price is to use contingent valuation (survey) methods, which are discussed in the following chapter.

The indirect market methods discussed in this chapter are based on *observed behavior,* that is, *revealed preference.* Basing valuations on observed behavior is important because it means that people reveal their preferences without having to be asked. As we discuss in the following chapter, contingent valuation (survey) methods rely on stated preferences and are prone to a number of biases.

The chapter begins with a discussion of the market analogy method, which uses information from private-sector markets to value publicly provided goods. It then discusses estimation of shadow prices based on trade-offs, for example, the trade-off between time and wages to value leisure time or the trade-off between salaries and the risk of having a fatal accident to value a statistical life. Next, it discusses the intermediate good method, followed by the asset valuation method. All of these methods are subject to potential estimation biases, including the omitted variables problem and self-selection bias. After discussing these problems, we turn to the hedonic price method, which attempts to overcome them. We then discuss the travel cost method and, finally, the defensive expenditures method. Some of these methods involve estimation of the whole demand or supply curve, whereas others provide only an estimate of the shadow price. This chapter focuses on methods of estimating shadow prices; Chapter 16 presents and discusses specific estimates of them.

MARKET ANALOGY METHOD

Governments supply many goods that are also provided by the private sector. For example, housing, campsites, university education, home care, and adoption services are often provided by both the public and private sectors. The government usually provides these services free or at significantly below market prices. Thus, the actual price paid may not be on the market demand curve. However, it may be possible to obtain an estimate of the entire demand curve using data from a similar good provided by the private sector.

In some countries, the private-sector market may not be legal. For example, some countries have no legal private-sector adoption services. Nevertheless, analysts may turn to the *black market* to obtain an estimate of the value of such services.

Using the Market Price of an Analogous Good as a Shadow Price

Consider, for example, a local government project that provides housing for 50 families. The local government may charge a nominal rent of $200 per month so that government revenue equals $10,000 per month. Clearly, this expenditure underestimates (gross) benefits because all families would be willing to pay $200 per month or more.

Suppose that comparable units in the private sector charge rent of $500 per month. If we took this market price as the shadow price for the publicly provided units, then the estimated total monthly benefits of publicly provided housing would be $25,000 per month. *Using the market price would be an appropriate estimate of the value of the publicly provided good if it equals the average amount that users of the publicly provided good would be willing to pay.* In the case of government allocation at a lower-than-market price, however, occupants of public units typically have lower-than-average incomes and are probably willing to pay between $200 and $500 per month, that is, somewhere between $10,000 per month and $25,000 per month in aggregate.

The price of comparable private housing units might *underestimate* the value to families in public housing if it were poorly targeted. Specifically, if the units were allocated to moderately well-off people who, in the absence of obtaining publicly provided housing, would have purchased similar or better private-sector units at market prices, then the market price would be a lower bound for their willingness to pay (WTP) for the public housing. Ironically, from the CBA perspective (considering only the direct consumption benefits), the more poorly targeted public housing units are, the higher their benefits.

Using Information about an Analogous Private-Sector Good to Estimate the Demand Curve for a Publicly Provided Good

Suppose a municipal government wants to measure the gross benefits of a swimming pool that it owns and operates. Currently, the municipality does not charge an admission fee, and the pool receives 300,000 visitors per year, shown as point *a* in Figure 14-1. In a comparable municipality, a privately operated swimming pool charges $5 for admission and receives 100,000 visitors per year (point *b*). If these two municipalities and pools were comparable, it would be reasonable to assume that points *a* and *b* are both on the demand curve. Further, assuming the demand curve is linear implies that it is given (in both communities) by the line *abc* in Figure 14-1.

In these circumstances the consumer surplus for users of the municipal pool is the area under the entire demand curve, which equals $1,125,000 ($7.5 × 300,000/2). Using

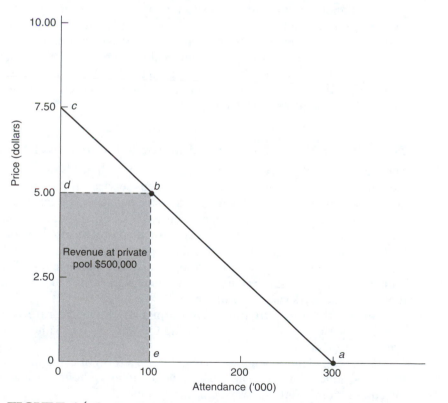

FIGURE 14-1 Demand Curve for Visits to a Municipal Swimming Pool

revenues at the private pool ($500,000) would underestimate the benefits of the public pool because it omits the consumer surplus of those willing to pay more than the $5, the area of triangle *cbd,* as well as of those willing to pay something less than $5, but more than $0, the area of triangle *bae.*

In order to regard the observed price and quantity at the private pool as a point on the demand curve for the municipal pool, the pools and their communities should be reasonably similar. For example, the pools should be similar in terms of changing room facilities, hours of business, the friendliness of the staff, and levels of crowding, and the two communities should be similar in terms of population, income, and tastes. If these assumptions do not hold, then adjustments should be made along the lines suggested later in the section on hedonic pricing.

THE TRADE-OFF METHOD

Economists may use the opportunity cost—the value of what one gives up to get something—as a measure of its value. For example, early CBAs used the after-tax wage as the value of travel time saved. The basic idea is that if you reduce your travel time by an hour then you can increase your income by the after-tax wage rate and vice versa. Put another way, people make trade-offs between time and money wages, and we can use the rate at which they make this trade-off to value time. Similarly the trade-off people are willing to make between changes in fatality risk, and wages can be used to measure the value of a statistical life. Analysts can examine the trade-off people are willing to make between cash expenditures and increased safety from air bags, smoke detectors, or other risk-reducing goods and can use this information to impute the value of a statistical life.

The Value of Time Saved, Including the Value of Travel Time Saved

Many government projects affect people's time, whether it is time spent traveling or in a queue waiting for provision of a government service. In the absence of market imperfections and taxes, the market-clearing wage equals the social value of an additional hour of work, and it equals the opportunity cost of an additional hour of work. If the inframarginal person would enjoy an additional hour of leisure if he or she worked one less hour, then the wage rate would indicate the value of an additional hour of leisure. Time saved in any other way would also be valued at the wage rate. The value of a government project that saves an hour for a person who earns $20 per hour is worth $20 to that person and to society as a whole.

Setting the value of time saved equal to the wage rate is relatively easy. However, serious problems exist in using the wage rate to value time saved by government projects.

First, wages ignore benefits. As benefits are a form of compensation for work, they should be added to wages. The social value of saving an hour of someone who is working equals their before-tax wage plus hourly benefits.

Second, we must take account of taxes. Although it is reasonable to view the value to society of an hour of work as the before-tax wage rate plus benefits, when deciding whether to work, individuals consider the after-tax compensation. Usually, this equals the after-tax wage rate only, because benefits are usually fixed and do not vary with time worked. Thus, when a government project increases or reduces someone's leisure time it should usually be valued at their after-tax wage rate, not the before-tax wage rate plus benefits.

Third, this approach assumes that people do not work while they are traveling or standing in line. In practice, some people multitask: They work and drive or fly at the same time. If they do so, then an hour of travel time saved is worth less than the wage rate. Of course, this does not apply truck drivers, who are obviously working while they are driving. For them, it does make sense to value their time saved at their before-tax wage rate plus benefits.

Fourth, people are willing to pay different amounts to save an hour doing different things. For example, the value of time saved while traveling may be worth less than the value of an hour saved while waiting in line. Some people like traveling, especially through spectacular scenery, such as along the highway from Banff to Jasper. These people derive consumption benefits from traveling and are willing to pay for the experience of traveling itself. (Consider, for example, the "busman's holiday.") In contrast, many people dislike waiting in line or in traffic jams and are willing to pay a lot to avoid it. Thus, the value of time saved depends on what one is doing. Because people generally do not dislike traveling, analysts value an hour of travel time saved for recreational travelers at a fraction (typically about 45 percent) of the *after-tax wage rate*.

Fifth, the wage rate may not be an appropriate shadow price for time saved because it assumes working hours are flexible. In practice, there are structural rigidities in the labor market. For example, some people involuntarily work overtime and, as a result, are "off their labor supply curve." Also, market failures or government failures, such as minimum wages and the monopoly power of unions, may distort the labor market. Consequently, everyone who wants to work at the market wage may not be able to find work at that wage. Indeed, for some people, such as retirees, no wage rate can be observed.

Finally, firms may not pay their employees the marginal social value of their output. For example, firms with market power may share their profits with employees in the form of higher-than-market wages. Of course, if an industry generated negative (positive) externalities, then the wage rate would exceed (be less than) the marginal social value of an hour saved.

Because of the serious nature of these problems, valuing time saved at the wage rate is only a first approximation to its social value. Later in this chapter, we present better methods for valuing time saved.

The Value of a Statistical Life

Valuing life is a contentious issue. Society often spends fortunes to rescue trapped miners or to give heart transplants to specific individuals. Yet it may not spend money to make obvious gains in mine safety or to reduce the risk of heart disease. In order to allocate resources efficiently in the health care sector or to determine the benefits of projects that save lives, analysts require a monetary value of a life saved.

Forgone Earnings: An Inappropriate Method.   Early efforts by economists to value life followed a similar method to the one discussed earlier concerning the value of time. Specifically, if one accepts that a person's value to society for one hour equals that person's wage, then one might reason that the value of that person to society for the rest of his or her lifetime equals the present value of his or her future earnings. One would thus conclude that the value of a life saved equals that person's discounted future earnings. This is the *forgone earnings method* of valuing a life saved.[2] It is still used by the courts in some U.S. states and in some other countries to award compensation in cases involving death due to negligence. This method generates a higher value of life for people with higher incomes than for people with lower incomes. On average, it also generates higher values for younger people than for older people and for men than for women.

The forgone earnings method provides unsatisfactory estimates of the value of a life saved for reasons similar to those discussed previously concerning the value of time saved. It assumes full employment, although the method can be adjusted to reflect expected lifetime earnings under average employment expectations. It also assumes people are paid their marginal social product, although often they are not. The lives of full-time homemakers and volunteers who are not paid for their services are unreasonably valued at zero.

A fundamental problem with the forgone earnings method is that it ignores individuals' WTP to reduce the risk of their own deaths. This point was made clearly by Thomas Schelling, who observed, "[t]here is no reason to suppose that a person's future earnings . . . bear any particular relation to what he would pay to reduce some likelihood of his own death."[3] Schelling also distinguished between the deaths of identifiable individuals and *statistical deaths*. A safety improvement to a highway, for example, does not lead *ex ante* to the saving of the lives of a few identifiable individuals, but rather to the reduction in the risk of death to all users: It leads to statistical lives saved. *In order to value the benefit of proposed safety improvements, analysts should ascertain how much people are willing to pay for reductions in their risk of death that are of the same magnitude as the reduced risk that would result from the proposed safety improvements.* Such reasoning has led to a series of consumer purchase and labor market studies that have attempted to compute the *value of a statistical life* (VSL).

Simple Consumer Purchase Studies.   Suppose airbags were not standard in new cars but, for $300, you could purchase and install an airbag at the time you purchased your new car.[4] The airbag would increase your survival rate from use of the car from p to $p + \omega$. Would you buy the airbag? This problem is represented as a decision tree in Figure 14-2.

If a person is indifferent between the two alternatives, then the expected value of the upper-branch alternative (spending the $300 more and increasing the probability of surviving by ω) and the expected value of the lower-branch alternative (not spending the $300 and surviving with probability p), that is

$$(p + \omega)V(\text{life}) - \$300 = pV(\text{life})$$
$$(p + \omega)V(\text{life}) - pV(\text{life}) = \$300$$
$$\omega V(\text{life}) = \$300$$
$$V(\text{life}) = \$300/\omega$$

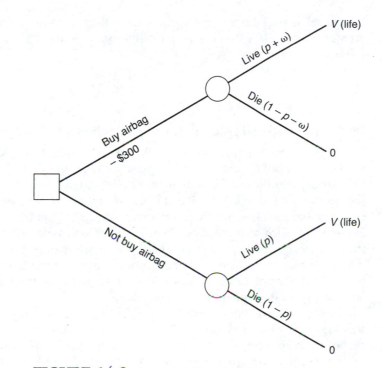

FIGURE 14-2 Decision Tree for Airbag Purchase

If we know that $\omega = 1/10,000$; that is, if 10,000 people buy airbags, then one statistical life will be saved, then, for a person who is indifferent between buying the airbag or not:

$$V(\text{life}) = (\$300)/(1/10,000) = \$3 \text{ million}$$

This method for estimating the *VSL* has been applied not only to the purchase of airbags but also to the purchase of other safety-enhancing devices, such as smoke detectors, safer cars, and fire extinguishers.

Simple Labor Market Studies.   Simple labor market studies examine the additional wage people require in compensation for exposing themselves to greater risk of death on the job (job fatality risk). Suppose, for example, one type of construction job has a 1/1,000 greater chance of fatal injury in a year than another type of construction job. Further suppose that the riskier job offers a salary that is \$3,500/year higher than the safer job. If workers are indifferent between these two types of job, then this implies:

$$(1/1,000)V(\text{life}) = \$3,500$$
$$V(\text{life}) = \$3.5 \text{ million}$$

In general, if $a is the amount workers are willing to accept in order to compensate for greater risk, and ω is the change in fatality risk, then the VSL is given by:

$$\text{VSL} = \frac{\$a}{\omega} \tag{14.1}$$

Problems with Simple Consumer Purchase and Wage-Risk Studies

One problem with simple consumer purchase and wage-risk studies is that they assume workers have full information concerning the risks, that is, ω. For example, in addition to knowing that the chance of dying in a risky job is 1/1,000 higher than in the less risky job, workers have to know what this means. Evidence that we discuss in Chapter 15 suggests that people suffer from cognitive biases that limit their ability to make rational judgments in such situations. For example, some studies suggest that people over-estimate the occurrence of low-probability "bad" events, while other studies suggest that people underestimate such events.[5] When people underestimate the fatality risk of a job (a bad event), then they will accept a lower risk premium to perform that job, and the VSL will be underestimated.

A second problem is that people who are relatively less risk averse (more risk seeking) self-select into more risky jobs. The mean fatality risk in recent VSL studies ranges from between about 3 in 100,000 to 22 in 100,000. However, the average U.S. fatality rate for all occupations is about 4 in 100,000.[6] Consequently, risk-averse individuals may be underrepresented in wage-risk studies, which would cause such studies to underestimate the VSL.

A third problem is that researchers may not have an accurate measure of the difference in fatality risk faced by different workers or consumers, the ω. Many U.S. wage-risk studies use aggregated, industry level data from the Bureau of Labor Statistics. These data do not reflect the difference in risk faced by workers in different occupations within the same industry. For example, a coal miner and a secretary in a coal mining company have quite different fatality risks. Furthermore, ω may be based on currently inaccurate historical data. Suppose that in a consumer purchase study $a equals $800 and ω equals 0.0002 so that the VSL equals $4 million. Now suppose that there was one more death among 5,000 people, then ω would equal 0.0004 and the VSL would equal $2 million.

In general, people experience diminishing marginal utility for safety; that is, the value of additional amounts of safety declines as the level of safety increases. The relationship between the WTP for increased safety and the level of safety (fatality risk) is probably convex. The WTP for additional amounts of safety depends on both the base level of safety and the magnitude of the change in the level of safety. A validity problem arises if the level of risk in the consumer purchase or wage-risk study used to obtain the VSL differs substantially from the level of risk applicable to where the policy is being applied.

Other problems with these methods are that they assume markets are efficient and that all other factors that influence prices or wages are held constant. In practice, wage differences may depend partially on the relative bargaining power of unions, on the different characteristics of the different jobs, or on different characteristics (skills) of workers in different jobs. For example, as Adam Smith noted,

---
EXHIBIT 14-1

Are estimates of the value of life that rely on wage premiums that workers receive for working in risky jobs systematically understated? Robert Frank and Cass Sunstein argue that they are understated by 18 to 75 percent *if* they are used to measure WTP for government safety regulations that improve the safety of *all* workers. According to Frank and Sunstein, the reason is that workers who decide to take relatively safe jobs pay for their additional safety by bearing two costs: they lose the wage premium they would receive if they took a more dangerous job and they are lower down in the wage distribution and thus lose status. Both factors affect their WTP for safety, although only the first is reflected in measures of the value of a statistical life that are based on wage premiums. However, a safety reg-

ulation that is universally applied reduces risk for everyone without affecting economic position. Thus, workers would be willing to pay more for such a regulation than the amount reflected by wage premiums alone.

Thomas Kniesner and Kip Viscusi take issue with this conclusion for several reasons. They point out that estimates of wage premiums for workplace risk differences are fairly small, on the order of a few hundred dollars a year, and thus are unlikely to have much of an effect on economic status. Kniesner and Viscusi further argue that, even if wage premiums do positively influence status, these gains may be offset because relatively risky jobs are likely to affect feelings of well-being adversely insofar as, by definition, health and safety are lower in such jobs.

Source: Adapted from Robert H. Frank and Cass R. Sunstein, "Cost-Benefit Analysis and Relative Position," *University of Chicago Law Review* 68(2) 2001, 323–374; and Thomas J. Kniesner and W. Kip Viscusi, "Cost-Benefit Analysis: Why Relative Economic Position Does Not Matter," *Yale Journal on Regulation* 20(1) 2003, 1–24.

"[t]he wages of labour vary with the ease or hardship, the cleanliness or dirtiness, the honourableness or dishonourableness of employment."[7] The omitted variables issue, which is illustrated by Exhibit 14-1, is discussed in more detail later in this chapter.

INTERMEDIATE GOOD METHOD

Some government projects produce intermediate goods, that is, goods that are used as inputs to some other *downstream* business. For example, a government irrigation project may provide water for farmers that is used in the production of avocados. If the intermediate good—water—is sold in a well-functioning market, it may be possible to directly estimate the market demand curve for water by using econometric methods. If it is not, we have to impute its value. The intermediate good method estimates the (gross) benefit of a project based on its *value added* to the downstream activity. Specifically, the value of the irrigation project can be measured by the increase in the incomes of avocado farmers. More generally, the intermediate good method measures the annual benefit of a project by the change in the annual incomes of the downstream businesses, thus:

Annual Benefit = Income (with the project) − Income (without the project)

The total benefit of a project can be computed by discounting these annual benefits over the project's life.

The intermediate good method can be used to value the benefits of education and training programs. Investment in the skills and abilities of human beings improves the stock of *human capital*. Much of the economic successes of Japan and Switzerland, for example, both of which are relatively poor in terms of physical natural resources, can be attributed to their investments in human capital. The intermediate good method measures the annual benefit of human capital programs by comparing the average incomes of those who have been enrolled in them and the average incomes of those who have not. For example, the benefit of a college education can be measured by comparing the before-tax incomes plus benefits of those with a college education and those who graduated from high school. The total benefit of such a program is found by discounting the annual benefits over the years people work after graduation and multiplying by the number of participants.

One problem with this method is that it assumes that differences in income capture all the benefits of a project. Some intermediate goods, such as college education, may be partially "final" goods. That is, they may have consumption value in addition to having investment value. Some people may enjoy their college education so much that they would pay for it even if it had no impact on their expected earnings. People's WTP for this consumption aspect should also be considered as a benefit of a college education. Also, those with more education may subsequently enjoy better working conditions (as well as higher salaries). Insofar as the intermediate good method excludes these consumption benefits, it underestimates the value of college education. On the other hand, this method does not control for other factors, such as ability or motivation. The higher income of those with a college education may be partially attributable to greater ability or motivation. Also, some employers may pay those with a college degree more simply because they have better "credentials," and may not necessarily have better skills. These latter effects tend to bias upward estimates of the benefit to higher education. Exhibit 14-2 discussed the returns to education in different countries.

EXHIBIT 14-2

Many studies have used the intermediate good method to value the social benefits from education. These studies usually measure the social benefits from a college education as the difference between the before-tax earnings of college graduates and those whose education stopped after graduating from high school. Some of these studies also estimate the cost of education—tuition fees, tax revenues, donations, and earnings that are forgone while in college. These estimates of benefits and costs can be used to compute the rate of return to different additional amounts of education.

George Psacharopoulos, for example, found that the average rate of return to society from secondary schooling is 10 percent in developed countries, 18 percent in sub-Saharan countries, and 11 to 13 percent in other developing countries. The estimated average rate of return to society from investments in higher education is 9 percent in developed countries and 11 to 12 percent in developing countries. The rate of return to private individuals is higher than these estimates because they capture the benefits, whereas the cost is often subsidized by the government or donors.

Source: Adapted from George Psacharopoulos, "Returns to Investment in Education: A Global Update," *World Development* 22(9) 1994, 1325–1343.

Also, care must be taken in the application of this method to avoid *double counting*. If the value of an intermediate good has been measured in some other way, then its contribution to the value of downstream production should not be counted as an additional benefit. For example, if the benefits of an irrigation project were estimated based on the estimated demand curve for water, then including the increased income of avocado farmers as an additional benefit would be double counting.

ASSET VALUATION METHOD

Government projects often affect the prices of assets such as land, housing, and stocks. The impacts are said to be *capitalized* into the market value of the assets. Observed increases (decreases) in asset values can be used to estimate the benefits (costs) of projects. For example, returning to the irrigation project to provide water to avocado farms, if the farms are the only users of the irrigation water and if the market for farm land is competitive, then the full value of the irrigation project will capitalize into the market value of avocado farms. Using the difference in the value of farms before and after the irrigation project is a relatively quick and easy way to estimate the benefits of a project.

A common application of the asset valuation method uses cross-sectional data on house prices to impute values of particular attributes of houses or of the environment, including negative externalities, such as noise or pollution. For example, the difference in market prices between houses with a view and houses with no view provides an estimate of how much households are willing to pay for a view. The difference between the average price of houses in a neighborhood with a park and the average price of houses in neighborhoods with no park provides an estimate of how much homeowners are willing to pay for a park. Of course, similar to other methods discussed earlier, this method assumes that house are similar in all other respects, and that no other factor affects the difference in prices. The section on hedonic prices discusses ways to control for other factors.

Event studies have now become an important method for estimating the costs or benefits to shareholders of new policies or regulations that affect firms.[8] Usually, researchers estimate the *abnormal return* to a security, which is the difference between the return to a security in the presence of an event and the expected return to the security in the absence of the event. These returns are calculated during an *event window,* that is, for the period during which the event is assumed to affect stock prices— often a few days. A main advantage of using stock prices is that new information concerning policy changes is quickly and, in theory, efficiently capitalized into stock prices. Because the return to the security in the absence of the event is unobservable, it is inferred from changes in the prices of other stocks in the market, such as the Dow Jones Index or the FTSE 100. The estimated daily abnormal returns during the event window can be aggregated to obtain the *cumulative abnormal return,* which measures the total return to shareholders that can be attributed to the event. Cumulative abnormal returns provide an estimate of the change in producer surplus due to some new policy.

PROBLEMS WITH SIMPLE VALUATION METHODS

The valuation methods discussed earlier in this chapter have several potential limitations, many of which were discussed earlier. This section focuses on the *omitted variable* problem and *self-selection* bias.

The Omitted Variable Problem

All of the methods discussed thus far in this chapter implicitly assume that all other explanatory variables are held constant, but this is unlikely in practice. Consider, for example, using the intermediate good method to value irrigation. Ideally, analysts would compare the incomes of farmers if the irrigation project were built with the incomes of the same farmers if the project were not built. In practice, if the project is built, analysts cannot directly observe what the farmers' incomes would have been if it had not been built. One way to infer what their incomes would have been without the project is to use the incomes of the same farmers before the project was built (a before and after design) or the incomes of similar farmers who did not benefit from an irrigation project (a nonexperimental comparison group design). The before and after design is reasonable only if all other variables that affect farmers' incomes remain constant, such as weather conditions, crop choices, taxes, and subsidies. If these variables change, then the incomes observed before the project may not be good estimates of what incomes would have been if the project had not been implemented. Similarly, the comparison group design is appropriate only if the comparison group is similar in all important respects to the farmers with irrigation, except for the presence of irrigation.

As mentioned in Exhibit 14-2, salary differences between those with a college degree and those with a high school degree may depend on ability, intelligence, socioeconomic background, and other factors in addition to college attendance. Similarly, in labor market studies of the value of life, differences in wages among jobs may depend on variations in status among jobs, the bargaining power of different unions or nonfatality accident risk in addition to fatality risk. In simple asset price studies, the price of a house typically depends on factors such as its distance from the central business district and size, as well as whether it has a view. Analysts should take account of all important explanatory variables. If a relevant explanatory variable is omitted from the model and if it is correlated with the included variable(s) of interest, then the estimated coefficients will be biased, as we discuss in Chapter 13.

Self-Selection Bias

Another potential problem is self-selection bias. Risk-seeking people tend to self-select themselves for dangerous jobs. Because they like to take risks they may be willing to accept lower salaries than other people in quite risky jobs. Consequently, we may observe only a relatively small wage premium for dangerous jobs. Because risk seekers are not representative of society as a whole, the observed wage differential may underestimate the amount that average members of society would be willing to pay to reduce risks and, hence, may lead to underestimation of the value of a statistical life.

The self-selection problem arises whenever different people attach different values to particular attributes. As another example, suppose we want to use differences in house prices to estimate a shadow price for noise. People who are not bothered much by noise, possibly because of hearing disabilities, naturally tend to move into noisy neighborhoods. As a result, the price differential between quiet houses and noisy houses may be quite small, which would lead to an underestimation of the shadow price of noise for the "average" person.

HEDONIC PRICING METHOD

The *hedonic pricing* method, sometimes called the *hedonic regression method,* offers a way to overcome the omitted variables problem and self-selection bias that arise in the relatively simple valuation methods discussed earlier. Most recent wage-risk studies for valuing a statistical life (also called labor market studies) apply the hedonic regression method. It can be used to value an attribute, or a change in an attribute, whenever its value is capitalized into the price of an asset, such as houses or salaries.

Hedonic Regression

Suppose, for example, that scenic views can be scaled from 1 to 10 and that we want to estimate the benefits of improving the (quality) "level" of scenic view in an area by one unit. We could estimate the relationship between individual house prices and the level of their scenic views. But we know that the market value of houses depends on other factors, such as the size of the lot, which is probably correlated with the quality of scenic view. We also suspect that people who live in houses with good scenic views tend to value scenic views more than other people. Consequently, we would have an omitted variables problem and self-selection bias.

The hedonic pricing method attempts to overcome both of these types of problems.[9] It consists of two steps. The first step estimates the relationship between the price of an asset and all of the *attributes* (characteristics) that affect its value.[10] From this it derives the marginal effect of an attribute (e.g., a better scenic view) on the value of the asset, while controlling for other variables that affect the value of the asset. The second step estimates the WTP for the attribute, after controlling for "tastes," which are usually proxied by socioeconomic factors. From this information, we can calculate the change in consumer surplus resulting from projects that improve or worsen the attribute.

Suppose we are interested in determining the hedonic price of a scenic view. The first step estimates the relationship between the price of a house, *P*, and all of its attributes, such as the quality of its scenic view, *VIEW*, its distance from the central business district, *CBD*, its lot size, *SIZE*, and various characteristics of its neighborhood, *NBHD*, such as school quality. A model of the factors affecting house prices can be written as follows:

$$P = f(CBD, SIZE, VIEW, NBHD) \tag{14.2}$$

This equation is called a *hedonic price function* or *implicit price function*.[11] The change in the price of a house that results from a unit change in a particular attribute (i.e., the slope) is called the *hedonic price, implicit price,* or *rent differential* of the attribute. In a well-functioning market, the hedonic price can naturally be interpreted as the additional cost of purchasing a house that is marginally better in terms of a particular attribute. For example, the hedonic price of scenic views, which we denote as r_v, measures the additional cost of buying a house with a slightly better (higher-level) scenic view.[12] Sometimes hedonic prices are referred to as *marginal hedonic prices* or *marginal implicit prices.* Although these terms are technically more correct, we will not use them in order to make the explanation as easy to follow as possible.

Usually analysts assume the hedonic price function has a multiplicative functional form, which implies that house prices increase as the level of scenic view increases but at a decreasing rate. Assuming the hedonic pricing model represented in equation (14.2) has a multiplicative functional form, we can write:

$$P = \beta_0 CBD^{\beta_1} SIZE^{\beta_2} VIEW^{\beta_3} NBHD^{\beta_4} e^\epsilon \tag{14.3}$$

The parameters, $\beta_1, \beta_2, \beta_3,$ and β_4, are elasticities: they measure the proportional change in house prices that results from a proportional change in the associated attribute.[13] We expect $\beta_1 < 0$ because house prices decline with distance to the *CBD*, but $\beta_2, \beta_3,$ and $\beta_4 > 0$ because house prices increase with increases in *SIZE, VIEW,* and *NBHD.*

The hedonic price of a particular attribute is the slope of equation (14.2) with respect to that attribute. In principle, it may be a function of all of the variables in the hedonic price equation.[14] For the multiplicative model in equation (14.3), the hedonic price of scenic views, r_v, is:[15]

$$r_v = \beta_3 \frac{P}{VIEW} > 0 \tag{14.4}$$

In this model, the hedonic price of scenic views depends on the value of the parameter β_3, the price of the house, and the view from the house. Thus, it varies from one observation (house) to another. Note that plotting this hedonic price against the level of scenic view provides a downward-sloping curve, which implies that the marginal value of scenic views declines as the level of the view increases.

The preceding points are illustrated in Figure 14-3. The top panel shows an illustrative hedonic price function with house prices increasing at a decreasing rate as the level of scenic view increases. The slope of this curve, which equals the hedonic price of scenic views, decreases as the level of the scenic view increases. The bottom panel shows more precisely the relationship between the hedonic price of scenic views (the slope of the curve in the top panel) and the level of scenic view.

In a well-functioning market, utility-maximizing households will purchase houses so that their WTP for a marginal increase in each attribute equals its hedonic price. Consequently, in equilibrium, the hedonic price of an attribute can be interpreted as the willingness of households to pay for a marginal increase in that attribute. The graph of the hedonic price of scenic views, r_v, against the level of scenic view is shown in the lower panel of Figure 14-3. Assuming all households have identical incomes and tastes, this curve can be interpreted as a household inverse demand curve for scenic views.

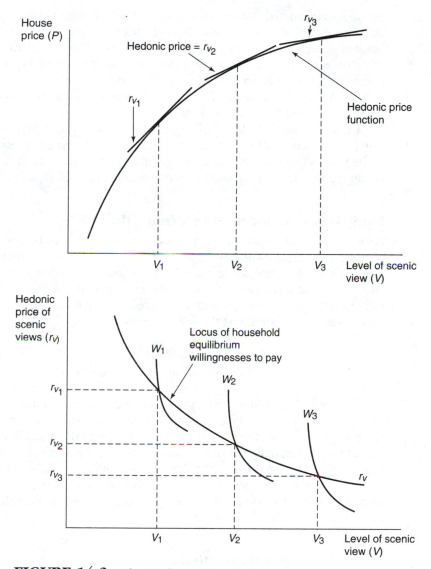

FIGURE 14-3   The Hedonic Price Method

Yet, households differ in their incomes and taste. Some are willing to pay a considerable amount of money for a scenic view; others are not. This brings us to the second step of the hedonic pricing method. To account for different incomes and tastes, analysts estimate the following willingness-to-pay (inverse demand) function for scenic views:[16]

$$r_v = W(VIEW, Y, Z) \qquad (14.5)$$

where r_v is estimated from equation (14.4), Y is household income, and Z is a vector of household characteristics that reflects tastes (e.g., socioeconomic background, race, age, and family size). Three willingness-to-pay functions, denoted W_1, W_2, and W_3, for three different households are drawn in the lower panel of Figure 14-3.[17] Equilibria occur where these functions intersect the r_v function. When incomes and socioeconomic characteristics differ, the r_v function is the locus of household equilibrium willingnesses to pay for scenic views.

Using the methods described in Chapters 3 and 4, it is straightforward to use equation (14.5) to calculate the change in consumer surplus to a household due to a change in the level of scenic view. These changes in individual household consumer surplus can be aggregated across all households to obtain the total change in consumer surplus.

Using Hedonic Models to Determine the VSL

As we mentioned above, the simple consumer purchase and labor market studies that we described previously may result in biased estimates of the value of a statistical life due to omitted variables. For example, labor market studies that focus on *fatality risk* (the risk of death) often omit potentially relevant variables such as *injury risk* (the risk of nonfatal injury). This problem may be reduced by using the hedonic pricing method and, for example, estimating the following nonlinear regression model:[18]

$$\ln(\text{wage rate}) = \beta_0 + \beta_1\ln(\text{fatality risk}) + \beta_2\ln(\text{injury risk}) + \beta_3\ln(\text{job tenure}) + \beta_4\ln(\text{education}) + \beta_5\ln(\text{age}) + \epsilon \qquad \textbf{(14.6)}$$

The inclusion of injury risk, job tenure, education, and age in the model controls for variables that affect wages and would bias the estimated coefficient of β_1 if they were excluded. Using the procedure demonstrated in the preceding section, the analyst can convert the estimate of β_1 to a hedonic price of fatality risk and then estimate individuals' WTP to avoid fatal risks, thereby controlling for self-selection problems. Most of the empirical estimates of the value of life that are reported in Chapter 16 are obtained from labor market and consumer product studies that employ models similar or analogous to the one described here.

Problems with Hedonic Models

In theory, the hedonic pricing method can be used to determine the shadow price of many goods that are not traded in well-developed markets, such as externalities and public goods.[19] It helps to overcome omitted variable and self-selection problems. However, it does not overcome all problems. Here we mention six problems.

First, people must know and understand the full implications of the externality or public good. For example, in order to use the hedonic pricing method to value pollution, families should know, prior to the purchase of their house, the level of pollution to which it is exposed and should also know the effect of different pollution levels on their health. Similarly, in hedonic wage-risk studies, workers must correctly perceive the actual risks. W. P. Jennings and A. Kinderman observe that the rate of occupational fatalities in most industries has fallen roughly 95 percent since 1920 and is now one-third of

---

EXHIBIT 14-3

Dean Uyeno, Stanley Hamilton, and Andrew Biggs used the hedonic pricing method to estimate the cost of airport noise in Vancouver, Canada. They estimated the following hedonic price equation:

$$\ln H = \beta_0 + \beta_1 \text{NEF} + \sum_{j=2}^{k} \beta_k \ln X_j + \epsilon$$

where $\ln H$ is the natural log of residential property value, NEF is a measure of noise level (ambient noise levels are in the NEF 15–25 range, "some" to "much" annoyance occurs in the NEF 25–40 range, and "considerable" annoyance occurs above NEFs of 40), the X_j are house characteristics $(j = 2, \ldots, k)$, and is an error term.

Their results show that Vancouver International Airport generates noise costs that capitalize into residential house and condominium prices. The estimated coefficient of the noise variable implies that detached houses very close to the airport with NEFs of 40 are 9.75 percent cheaper than houses far from the airport with NEFs of 25.

The estimated noise depreciation sensitivity is broadly consistent with previous studies, leading the authors to conclude that "the similarity of results spanning several decades and several Western countries would seem to suggest a broad and long-lived consensus on the issue (of the impact of airport noise on property values) ..." (p. 14). In aggregate, the social cost of noise from Vancouver International Airport amounts to about $15 million in 1987 Canadian dollars.

Source: Adapted from Dean Uyeno, Stanley W. Hamilton, and Andrew J. G. Biggs, "Density of Residential Land Use and the Impact of Airport Noise," *Journal of Transport Economics and Policy* 27(1) 1993, 3–18.

---

the rate of accidental deaths in the home.[20] They argue that "the current fatality rates are so low and their individual causes so often random that statistical attempts to measure how fatalities affect wages are unlikely to meet with success." Second, it is important that the hedonic equations, such as equation (14.3) or equation (14.6), include correctly measured variables, as opposed to more readily obtainable but incorrect proxies. For example, house values may depend on the quality of construction. As this variable is difficult to determine without inspection, the researcher may use the year of construction as a proxy for quality. In econometrics, this problem is referred to as the *errors in variables* problem. Third, if the hedonic pricing model is linear, then the hedonic price of each attribute is constant, which would make it impossible to estimate the inverse demand function, such as equation (14.5).[21] Fourth, the market should contain many different houses so that families can find an optimal "package," that is, a house with just the right combination of attributes. In other words, there should be sufficient variety so that families can find a house that permits them to reach an equilibrium. This would be a problem if, for example, a family wanted a small, pollution-free house, but all of the houses in pollution-free areas were large. Fifth, there may be multicollinearity problems in the data. To use the same example, if expensive houses were large and located mainly in areas free of pollution, but inexpensive houses were small and located mainly in polluted areas, it would be difficult to estimate separate hedonic prices for pollution and size. Sixth, the method assumes that market prices adjust immediately to changes in attributes and in all other factors that affect demand or supply.

TRAVEL COST METHOD[22]

Most applications of the travel cost method (TCM) have been to value recreational sites. If the "market" for visits to a particular site is geographically extensive, then visitors from different origins bear different travel costs depending on their proximity to the site. The resulting differences in total cost, and the differences in the rates of visits that they induce, provide a basis for estimating a demand curve for the site.

Suppose that we want to estimate the value of a particular recreational site. We expect that the quantity of visits demanded by an individual, q, depends on its price, p, the price of substitutes, p_s, the person's income, Y, and variables that reflect the person's tastes, Z:

$$q = f(p, p_s, Y, Z) \tag{14.7}$$

The clever insight of the TCM is that although admission fees are usually the same for all persons (indeed, they are often zero), the total cost faced by each person varies because of differences in travel costs. Consequently, usage also varies, thereby allowing researchers to make inferences about the demand curve for the site.

The *full price* paid by visitors to a recreational site includes the opportunity cost of time spent traveling, the operating cost of vehicles used to travel, the cost of accommodations for overnight stays while traveling or visiting, parking fees at the site, and the cost of admission. The sum of all of these costs gives the total cost of a visit to the site. *This total cost is used as an explanatory variable in place of the admission price in a model similar to equation (14.7).*

Estimating such a model is conceptually straightforward. First, select a random sample of households within the market area of the site. These are the potential visitors. Second, survey these households to determine their numbers of visits to the site over some period of time, their costs involved in visiting the site, their costs of visiting substitute sites, their incomes, and their other characteristics that may affect their demand. Third, specify a functional form for the demand schedule and estimate it using the survey data. For an application of the TCM see Exhibit 14-4.

It is important to emphasize that when total cost replaces price in equation (14.7), this equation is not the usual demand curve that gives visits as a function of the price of admission. However, as we show next, such models can be used to derive the usual market demand curve and to estimate the average WTP for a visit.

Zonal Travel Cost Method

With the *zonal travel cost method*, researchers survey actual visitors at a site rather than potential visitors. This is often more feasible and less expensive than surveying potential visitors. Also, the level of analysis shifts from the individual (or household) to the area, or zone, of origin of visitors, hence the name *zonal travel cost method*.

The zonal TCM requires the analyst to specify the zones from which users of the site originate. Zones are easily formed by drawing concentric rings or iso-time lines around the site on a map. Ideally, households within a zone should face similar travel costs as well as have similar values of the other variables that would be included in an individual demand function, including similar prices of substitutes, similar incomes, and

---EXHIBIT 14-4---

Kerry Smith and William Desvousges used the travel cost method to estimate the average household value of a trip to recreational sites along the Monongahela River and the average household value of improving water quality. Their estimates of travel costs assumed the marginal cost of operating an automobile was $0.08 per mile in 1976. For the time cost component of travel cost, they set the value of time equal to the wage rate in a person's particular occupation, which ranged from $2.75 per hour for female farmers to $7.89 per hour for male professional, technical, and kindred workers in 1977 dollars. Smith and Desvousges estimated many models including the following relatively simple travel cost model (*t*-statistics in parentheses):

$$\ln V = -3.928 - 0.051TC + 0.00001Y + 0.058DO \qquad (R^2 = 0.225)$$
$$\quad\;\; (-3.075) \quad (-2.846) \qquad (1.109) \qquad (3.917)$$

where V is the number of site visits, Y denotes income, and DO is the percent saturation of dissolved oxygen in the water. Based on this model, the authors estimated that the average annual value of improving the water quality from boat- able to game fishing would be $7.16 in 1981 dollars (about $15 in 2004 dollars), and the average annual value of improving the water quality from boatable to swimming would be $28.86 in 1981 dollars (about $60 in 2004 dollars).

Source: Adapted from V. Kerry Smith and William H. Desvousges, *Measuring Water Quality Benefits* (Boston: Kluwer Nijhoff Publishing, 1986), especially pp. 270–271.

similar tastes. If residents from different regions within a zone have quite different travel costs, then the zones should be redrawn. In practice, analysts often use local government jurisdictions as the zones because they facilitate the collection of data.

Assuming a constant elasticity functional form leads to the following model:

$$\ln\left(\frac{V}{POP}\right) = \beta_0 + \beta_1\ln\bar{p} + \beta_2\ln\bar{p}_s + \beta_4\bar{Y} + \beta_5\bar{Z} + \epsilon \qquad \textbf{(14.8)}$$

where V is the number of visits from a zone per period; POP is the population of the zone; and $\bar{p}, \bar{p}_s, \bar{Y}$, and $\bar{Z}$ denote the average values of p, p_s, Y, and Z in each zone, respectively. Again, when this equation is estimated, total cost replaces price.

Note that the quantity demanded is expressed as a visit rate. An alternative specification is to estimate the quantity demanded in terms of the number of visits, V, but to include population, POP, on the right-hand side of the regression equation. Although both specifications are plausible, the specification in equation (14.8) is less likely to involve heteroscedasticity problems (which we discuss in Chapter 13) and is, therefore, more likely to be appropriately estimated by OLS.

Using estimates of the parameters of equation (14.8), it is possible to estimate the change in consumer surplus associated with a change in the admission price to a site, the total consumer surplus associated with the site at its current admission fee, and the average consumer surplus per visit to the site. We illustrate how to do this using an example for a hypothetical recreational wilderness area, using the data presented in the first five columns of Table 14-1. This illustration assumes there are only five relevant

TABLE 14-1   Illustration of the Travel Cost Method

Zone	Travel Time (hours)	Travel Distance (km)	Average Total Cost per Person ($)	Average Number of Visits per Person	Consumer Surplus per Person	Consumer Surplus per Zone ($ thousands)	Trips per Zone (thousands)
A	0.5	2	20	15	525	5,250	150
B	1.0	30	30	13	390	3,900	130
C	2.0	90	65	6	75	1,500	120
D	3.0	140	80	3	15	150	30
E	3.5	150	90	1	0	0	10
Total						10,800	440

zones from which people travel to the recreational site. To avoid unnecessary complications, we assume that demand depends directly only on total price, not on income, the prices of substitutes, or any other variable.

In this example, the value of time for residents from different zones varies due to different income levels in different zones, as well as different travel times. Zone A is adjacent to the recreational area. Residents from zone A can, on average, pack up their equipment, drive to the site, park, and walk to the entrance in approximately one-half hour. Assuming the opportunity cost of their time is $9.40/hr and marginal vehicle operating costs are 15 cents/km, their total travel cost is $10 per round trip. Adding the admission fee of $10 per day yields a total cost of $20 per visit. Local residents make 15 visits each year, on average. Zone B is about 30 km away, requiring two hours of total travel time (including driving, parking, walking, and loading and unloading vehicles) for a round trip. Assuming the value of time for these residents is $5.50/hr and they travel individually, their total cost per visit is $30. Zone B residents make 13 visits per year on average. Zone C is about 90 km away and requires two hours of travel time in each direction. Assuming the value of these residents' time is $10.35/hr on average, and that their travel costs are shared between two people, the total cost per person is approximately $65 per visit. Zone C residents make six visits per year on average. Zone D residents live on the other side of the metropolitan area and, on average, make three visits each year. Assuming that their average wage rate is $8/hr and that two persons travel per vehicle, their per-person cost is $80 per visit. Zone E residents have to cross an international border. Though the distance is only slightly farther than from zone D, it takes almost one-half hour to get through customs and immigration. The average zone E wage is $8/hour. Assuming two persons per vehicle, the per-person cost is $90 per visit. On average, visitors from zone E make only one visit per year.

The data for average total cost per person visit (TC) and average visits per person (V), which are in columns 4 and 5 of Table 14-1, are represented graphically in Figure 14-4. The equation $TC = 95 - 5V$ fits these data perfectly. (In practice, ordinary least squares would be used to fit a line to data points that would not all lie exactly on the line.) This equation is the "representative" individual's inverse demand curve: it shows how much a typical visitor is willing to pay for a visit to the recreational area (specifically, $90 for the first visit, $85 for the second visit, . . . , $20 for the fifteenth visit).

Different individuals face different prices (costs) for their visits depending on their zone of origin. It is cheaper for those who live closer. Therefore, individuals' consumer surplus varies according to their zone of origin. The consumer surplus for a particular visit from a particular zone equals the difference between how much someone is willing to pay for that visit, given by the point on the "representative" individual's inverse demand curve, and how much the person actually pays for a visit *from that zone*. As mentioned previously, "representative" visitors are willing to pay $90 for their first visit, $85 for the second, . . . $65 for their sixth. People from zone C actually pay only $65 for each visit. Consequently, their consumer surplus equals $25 for the first visit, $20 for the second visit, $15 for the third visit, $10 for the fourth visit, $5 for the fifth visit, and $0 for the sixth visit.

The total consumer surplus for someone from zone C is obtained by summing the consumer surpluses associated with each visit across all visits, which amounts to $75. This amount is represented by the area of the shaded triangle in Figure 14-4.[23] Similarly, the consumer surplus is $525 per person for residents of zone A, $390 for residents of zone B, $15 for residents of zone D, and $0 for residents of zone E. These amounts are presented in the sixth column of Table 14-1. Clearly, people who live closer to the recreational site enjoy more consumer surplus from it than people who live farther away.

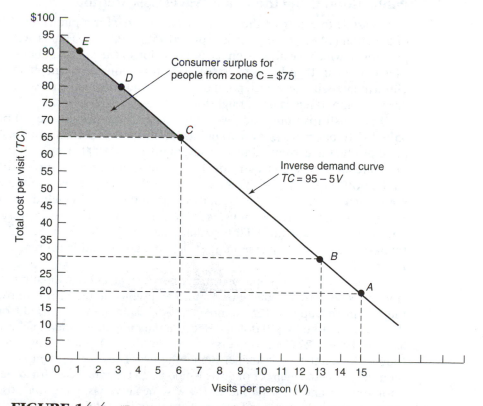

FIGURE 14-4 "Representative" Individual's Inverse Demand Curve for Visits to a Recreational Area as a Function of Total Cost per Visit

From this information and knowledge of the populations of each zone, we can calculate the total consumer surplus per year and the average consumer surplus per visit for the site. Suppose zones A, B, D, and E have populations of 10,000 people, while zone C has a population of 20,000 people. The consumer surplus per zone is obtained by multiplying the consumer surplus per person in a zone by the population of that zone, as shown in the fifth column in Table 14-1. Adding across all zones yields the total annual consumer surplus for the site of $10.8 million. Adding admission fees of $4.4 million indicates that the annual (gross) benefit of the site to all visitors equals $15.2 million. If the government decided to use the site for some completely different purpose, such as logging, this would be a measure of the lost annual benefits.

The total number of visits to the recreational area is 440,000, as shown in the last column of Table 14-1. Dividing the total consumer surplus by the total number of visits gives an average consumer surplus per visit of $24.55. If we now add the admission fee of $10, then we obtain the *average demand price* per visit, which is the average maximum amount a visitor would pay for a visit to the site. In this example, the average demand price is $34.55.

Estimating the Market Demand Curve for a Public Good Using the Zonal Travel Cost Method

It is possible to construct the *market demand curve* for a public good from estimation of equation (14.8) where price is replaced with total cost. That is, we can derive an expression in which the admission fee is a function of the *total* number of visits to the site. This curve can then be used to estimate total consumer surplus in the usual way. Unfortunately, because each point on the demand curve has to be estimated separately, precise computation is not straightforward.

For illustrative purposes, we continue with the previous example where $TC = 95 - 5V$. To begin, we know two points on the market demand curve. At an admission price of $10, the current admission fee, there are 440,000 visits, represented by point c in Figure 14-5. Now consider how high admission fees can be raised until demand is choked off (equals zero). We know from the representative individual's inverse demand curve ($TC = 95 - 5V$) that the maximum WTP (including all costs) is $95. Subtracting the travel cost of users from zone A (who have the lowest travel cost) implies that the maximum WTP for admission is $95 - $10 = $85. This is the intercept (choke price) of the inverse market demand curve and is represented by point a in Figure 14-5.

We can find other points on the market demand curve by assuming that the admission fee is increased or decreased and then predicting the visit rate from each zone at the new price. Suppose, for example, the admission fee were raised from $10 to $20, so that TC increased by $10 dollars. Because the *individual* demand curve can be written as $V = 19 - 0.2TC$ (the inverse of $TC = 95 - 5V$), a $10 increase in TC would reduce the number of visits per person by two. Thus, if the admission price were $20, then the predicted number of visits would be 13 for zone A, 11 for zone B, 4 for zone C, 1 for zone D, and -1 for zone E. Because negative visits are not possible, we set the number of visits per person for zone E to zero. The total number of visits demanded at the new price is computed by multiplying the predicted visit rate for each zone by its

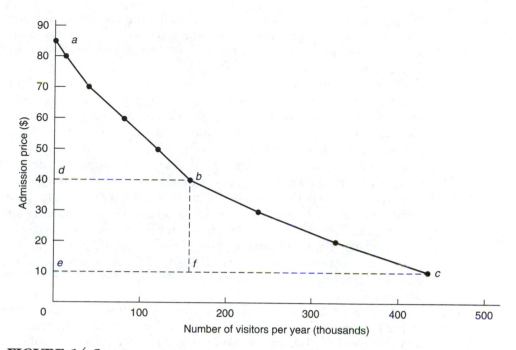

FIGURE 14-5   The Market Demand Curve for a Recreational Site Derived Using the Zonal Travel Cost Method

population and summing these products ($13 \times 10,000 + 11 \times 10,000 + 4 \times 20,000 + 1 \times 10,000 = 330,000$). Thus, at a price of $20 we would expect 330,000 visits. This is a third point on the market demand curve.

With a sufficient number of points, the market demand curve can be sketched to any desired level of accuracy. The market demand curve in Figure 14-5 is computed on the basis of $10 price increments. The annual consumer surplus for the site is the area between the curve and the current admission fee from zero visits to 440,000 visits. Assuming for simplicity that the demand curve is linear between points *a* and *b*, and between points *b* and *c*, we estimate the annual consumer surplus of the site equals $12.6 million, and the annual (gross) benefit of the site equals $17.0 million.[24] Due to the linear approximation and the relatively few points on the demand curve, we slightly overestimate the benefits.

Limitations of the TCM

The usefulness of the TCM is limited in a number of ways. One limitation is that the TCM provides an estimate of the WTP for the entire site rather than for specific features of a site. As we often wish to value changes in specific features of a site (e.g., improvements in the hiking trails), the basic TCM does not provide the needed information. However, if the residents of zones can choose from among a number of alternative recreational sites with different attributes, then it may be possible to use the *hedonic travel cost method* to find attribute prices.[25] This method treats the total cost of visiting a particular site from a particular zone as a function of both the distance from that zone to the site and various attributes of the site. Its application raises a number of issues beyond those previously discussed in the context of the basic hedonic pricing model. Therefore, before attempting to apply the hedonic travel cost method, we recommend consulting other sources.[26]

Measuring the cost of a visit to the site may be difficult.[27] Perhaps the most obvious problem is the estimation of the opportunity cost of travel time, which we have previously discussed.[28] Even defining and measuring travel costs raises some difficult issues. Some analysts include the time spent at the site, as well as the time spent traveling to and from it, as components of total price. If people from different zones spend the same amount of time at the site, and if the opportunity cost of their time is similar, then it does not matter whether the time spent at the site is included or not—both the height of the demand curve and total price shift by the same amount for each consumer so that estimates of consumer surplus remain unchanged. If, however, people from different zones have different opportunity costs for their time, or if they spend different amounts of time at the site, then including the cost of time spent at the site would change the price facing persons from different zones by different amounts and, thereby, change the slope of the estimated demand curve.

Another problem arises because recreation often requires investment in fairly specialized equipment such as tents, sleeping bags, wet-weather gear, canoes, fishing rods, and even vehicles. The marginal cost of using such equipment should be included in total price. Yet, estimating the marginal cost of using capital goods is usually difficult. As with time spent at the site, however, these costs can be reasonably ignored if they are approximately constant for visitors from different zones.

Multiple-purpose trips also pose an analytical problem. People may visit the recreational site in the morning and, for example, go river rafting nearby in the afternoon. Sometimes analysts exclude visitors with multiple purposes from the data. Including visitors with multiple purposes is usually desirable if costs can be appropriately apportioned to the site being valued. If the apportionment is arbitrary, however, then it may be better to exclude multiple users.

A similar problem results because the journey itself may have value. The previous discussion assumes implicitly that the trip is undertaken exclusively to get to the recreation site and travel has no benefit per se. If the journey itself is part of the reason for the visit to the site, then the trip has multiple purposes. Therefore, part of the cost of the trip should be attributed to the journey, not the visit to the recreation site. Not doing so would lead to overestimation of site benefits.

A more fundamental problem is that the travel cost variable may be endogenous, not exogenous. One neighborhood characteristic some people consider when making their residential choices is its proximity to a recreational area. People who expect to make many visits to a recreational area may select a particular neighborhood (zone) partially on account of the low travel time from that neighborhood to the recreational area. If so, the number of trips to a particular recreational area and the price of these trips will be determined simultaneously. Under these circumstances equation (14.8) may not be identified, a problem which we discuss in Chapter 13.[29]

Another econometric problem is that the dependent variable in the estimated models is *truncated*. Truncation arises because the sample is drawn from only those who visit the site, not from the larger population that includes people who never visit the site. Application of ordinary least squares to the truncated sample would result in biased coefficients. However, there are more complicated estimation methods that overcome this problem.

There may also be an omitted variables problem. If the price of substitute recreational sites varies across zones or if tastes for recreation varies across zones, then the estimated coefficients may be biased if the model does not control for these variables. As previously discussed, bias results when an excluded variable is correlated with an included variable.

Finally, derivation of the market demand curve assumes that people respond to changes in price regardless of its composition. Thus, for example, people respond to, say, a $5 increase in the admission price in the same way as a $5 increase in travel cost. This presumes that people have a good understanding of the impact of changes in the prices of fuel, tires, and repairs on their marginal travel cost.

DEFENSIVE EXPENDITURES METHOD[30]

If you live in a smoggy city, then you will probably find that your windows often need cleaning. If you hire someone to clean your windows periodically, the cost of this action in response to the smog is termed a *defensive expenditure*—it is an amount spent to mitigate or even eliminate the effect of a negative externality. Suppose the city passes an ordinance that reduces the level of smog so that your windows do not get as dirty. You would now have to spend less on window cleaners. The reduction in defensive expenditures—the defensive expenditures avoided—has been suggested as a measure of the benefits of the city ordinance. In other circumstances, the costs of a policy change might be measured by the increase in defensive expenditures.

This method is an example of a broad class of *production function methods*. In these methods, the level of a public good or externality (e.g., smog) and other goods (window cleaners) are inputs to some production process (window cleaning). If the level of the public good or externality changes, then the levels of the other inputs can be changed in the opposite direction and still allow the quantity of output produced to remain the same. For example, when the negative externality of smog is reduced, less labor is required to produce the same number of clean windows. The change in expenditures on the substitute input (window cleaners) is used as a measure of the benefit of reduction of the public good or externality.

Suppose that the demand curve for clean windows is represented by the curve labeled D in Figure 14-6. Let S_0 represent the marginal cost of cleaning windows initially, that is, prior to the new ordinance. The initial equilibrium price and quantity of clean windows are denoted by P_0 and Q_0, respectively. The effect of the new ordinance to restrict smog is to shift the marginal cost curve for clean windows down and to the right from S_0 to S_1: because there is less smog, windows are easier to clean, so more windows can be cleaned for the same price. At the new equilibrium, the price of clean windows is P_1 and the quantity of clean windows is Q_1. The change in consumer surplus is represented by the area of the trapezoid $P_0 ab P_1$.

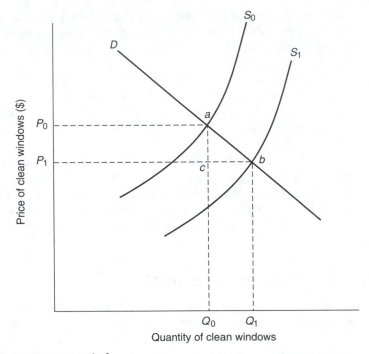

FIGURE 14-6 The Effect of an Ordinance Reducing
Smog on Expenditures for Window Cleaning

If households continued to consume the same quantity of clean windows after
the price shift as they did before the price shift, Q_0, then the benefit of the ordinance
would be represented by the rectangle $P_0 a c P_1$. This would be the amount by which
consumers reduce their defensive expenditure. Consumers, however, would not
maintain their consumption levels at Q_0, but would increase their consumption of
clean windows to level Q_1. Individuals would spend area $b Q_1 Q_0 c$ on the purchase of
$Q_1 - Q_0$ additional units of clean windows at a price of P_1. The net change in spending
on window cleaning services equals the area of rectangle $b Q_1 Q_0 c$ minus the area of
rectangle $P_0 a c P_1$. This net change in spending may be quite small. Indeed, if the demand curve were a constant elasticity demand curve, with an elasticity equal to 1,
there would be no change in total expenditure on window cleaning services at all. Yet
there are obviously positive benefits to consumers. In general, *the reduced spending
on defensive expenditures will underestimate the benefits of cleaner air or whatever
benefit is being estimated.*[31]

There are at least four additional problems with the defensive expenditures
method. First, it assumes implicitly that individuals quickly adjust to the new equilibrium. It may actually take some time for individuals to adjust their purchases and return to equilibrium. Second, a defensive expenditure may not remedy the entire damage so that reductions in this expenditure do not fully measure benefits. For example,

expenditures on window cleaning do not "avoid" the whole problem of smog. Smog also leads to dirtier shirts and to health problems. Defensive expenditures avoided on these items should also be included. Exhibit 14-5 illustrates that there may be many categories of defensive expenditures. It examines the costs of groundwater degradation and includes five categories of costs, not just the cost of new purchases of bottled water. Third, the defensive expenditures may have benefits other than remedying damage. For example, the

---

EXHIBIT 14-5

Charles W. Abdalla, Brian A. Roach, and Donald J. Epp measured the costs of groundwater degradation in the small Pennsylvania borough of Perkasie (population 7,877) using the defensive expenditures method. They conducted mail and telephone surveys to gather information from a sample of residents on the actions they took in response to trichloroethylene (TCE) contamination of one of the borough's wells between December 1987 and September 1989. They estimated the total costs to the community's residents, including both monetary costs and time expenditures, of each of five defensive actions:

Category of Cost	Cost Based on Value of Leisure Time Equal to Minimum Wage ($)[a]	Cost Based on Value of Leisure Time Equal to Individual Wage Rate ($)[a]
Increased purchases of bottled water	11,100	11,100
New purchases of bottled water	17,300	17,300
Home water treatment systems	4,700	4,700
Hauling water	12,500	34,000
Boiling water	15,600	64,100
Total	61,200	131,200

[a]Costs in original rounded to nearest hundred dollars.

Note that the costs of hauling and boiling water are very sensitive to the assumed opportunity cost of leisure. The researchers interpreted these total costs as a lower-bound estimate of the true cost of the contamination to residents because of the generally conservative nature of the defensive expenditures method.

A specific factor suggesting that these defensive expenditures represent a lower bound is that only 43 percent of residents were aware of the TCE contamination despite notification laws. Moreover, not all residents who knew about the contamination took defensive measures. Nevertheless, those who had more information about the contamination, those who perceived the cancer risk due to TCE to be higher, and those who had children between 3 and 17 years old in the household were generally more likely to take defensive action than other residents. Among those who took defensive action, having a child under 3 years of age seemed to be the most important factor influencing the intensity of the defensive actions taken.

Source: Adapted from Charles W. Abdalla, Brian A. Roach, and Donald J. Epp, "Valuing Environmental Quality Changes Using Averting Expenditures: An Application to Groundwater Contamination," *Land Economics* 68(2) 1992, 163–169.

cleaning necessitated by the smog may result in cleaner windows than one would otherwise achieve. Fourth, not all of the defensive measures are purchased in markets. Some people clean their own windows, and reductions in their opportunity costs should also be included as benefits.

CONCLUSION

This chapter describes the major indirect market methods used in CBA for estimating shadow prices. Some methods are not discussed because we believe that they are too advanced for this book. Perhaps most notably, we have not discussed the use of random utility models or probabilistic choice models to estimate demand, an approach that is quite important in the transportation area.[32] Also, we do not discuss recent methods that estimate demand curves by combining survey data with data on observed behavior.[33] Nevertheless, the methods covered here provide a rich set of tools for practical valuation of impacts.

EXERCISES FOR CHAPTER 14

1. Child care services in a small midwestern city cost $30 per day per child. The high cost of these services is one reason why very few mothers who are on welfare work; given their low potential wages, virtually no welfare mothers are willing to pay these high costs. To combat this problem, the city establishes a new program: in exchange for their welfare benefits, a group of welfare recipients is required to provide child care for the children of other welfare recipients who obtain private-sector employment. The welfare mothers who use these child care services are required to pay a fee of $3 per day per child. These services prove very popular; 1,000 welfare children receive them each day and an additional 500 welfare children are on a waiting list. Do the mothers of the 1,000 children who receive services under the program value these services at $30,000 ($30 × 1,000) a day, $3,000 a day ($3 × 1,000), or at a value that is greater than $3,000 but less than $30,000? Explain.

2. A worker, who is typical in all respects, works for a wage of $30,000 per year in a perfectly safe occupation. Another typical worker does a job requiring exactly the same skills as the first worker, but in a risky occupation with a known death probability of 1 in 1,000 per year, and receives a wage of $36,000 per year. What value of a human life for workers with these characteristics should a cost-benefit analyst use?

3. (Instructor-provided spreadsheet recommended.) Happy Valley is the only available camping area in Rural County. It is owned by the county, which allows free access to campers. Almost all visitors to Happy Valley come from the six towns in the county.

   Rural County is considering leasing Happy Valley for logging, which would require that it be closed to campers. Before approving the lease, the county executive would like to know the magnitude of annual benefits that campers would forgo if Happy Valley were to be closed to the public.

   An analyst for the county has collected data for a travel cost study to estimate the benefits of Happy Valley camping. On five randomly selected days, he recorded the license plates of vehicles parked overnight in the Happy Valley lot. (Because the camping season is 100 days, he assumed that this would constitute a 5 percent sample.) With cooperation from the state motor vehicle department, he was able to find the town of residence of the owner of each vehicle. He also observed a sample of vehicles from which he estimated that each vehicle carried 3.2 persons (1.6 adults), on average. The following table summarizes the data he collected.

Town	Miles from Happy Valley	Population (thousands)	Number of Vehicles in Sample	Estimated Number of Visitors for Season	Visit Rate (visits per 1,000 people)
A	22	50.1	146	3,893	77.7
B	34	34.9	85	2,267	65.0
C	48	15.6	22	587	37.6
D	56	89.9	180	4,800	53.4
E	88	98.3	73	1,947	19.8
F	94	60.4	25	666	11.0
Total				14,160	

In order to translate the distance traveled into an estimate of the cost campers faced in using Happy Valley, the analyst made the following assumptions. First, the average operating cost of vehicles is $0.36 per mile. Second, the average speed on county highways is 50 miles per hour. Third, the opportunity cost to adults of travel time is 40 percent of their wage rate; it is zero for children. Fourth, adult campers have the average county wage rate of $9.25 per hour.

The analyst has asked you to help him use this information to estimate the annual benefits accruing to Happy Valley campers. Specifically, assist with the following tasks.

a. Using the preceding information, calculate the travel cost of a vehicle visit (TC) from each of the towns.

b. For the six observations, regress visit rate (VR) on TC and a constant. If you do not have regression software available, plot the points and fit a line by sight. Find the slope of the fitted line.

c. You know that with the current free admission the number of camping visits demanded is 14,160. Find additional points on the demand curve by predicting the reduction in the number of campers from each town as price is increased by $5 increments until demand falls to zero. This is done in three steps at each price: first, use the coefficient of TC from the regression to predict a new VR for each town. Second, multiply the predicted VR of each town by its population to get a predicted number of visitors. Third, sum the visitors from each town to get the total number of predicted visits.

d. Estimate the area under the demand curve as the annual benefits to campers.

NOTES

1. When markets do exist but are imperfect due to government intervention, it is necessary to make adjustments to market prices in order to obtain the appropriate shadow prices.

2. The *net output method* of valuing a life subtracts the value of a person's own consumption from his or her forgone earnings. It measures the benefit or cost the individual contributes to or imposes on the rest of society. The courts' use of this method to measure the loss to survivors of someone's death is somewhat arbitrary but perhaps reasonable. However, it is clearly inappropriate to use this method in CBA to value a life saved. Although a typical person's net output will be slightly positive over his or her entire lifetime, it will be negative for a retired person.

3. Thomas C. Schelling, "The Life You Save May Be Your Own," in Robert Dorfman and

Nancy S. Dorfman, eds., *Economics of the Environment: Selected Readings,* 3rd ed. (New York: W. W. Norton, 1993), pp. 388–408 at p. 402.

4. Other examples of risk-reducing goods include detectors for smoke and carbon monoxide, fire extinguishers, and bicycle helmets.

5. See, for example, W. Kip Viscusi, "Prospective Reference Theory: Toward an Explanation of the Paradoxes," *Journal of Risk and Uncertainty,* 2(3) 1989, 234–264.

6. Jobs in finance, insurance, real estate, services, retail and government all have fatality rates below 3 in 100,000 according to the U.S. Department of Labor, Bureau of Statistics, Census of Fatal Occupational Injuries, 2002.

7. Adam Smith, *The Wealth of Nations* (New York: Modern Press, 1776 reprinted 1937), p. 12.

8. See, for example, Anthony E. Boardman, Ruth Freedman, and Catherine Eckel, "The Price of Government Ownership: A Study of the Domtar Takeover," *Journal of Public Economics* 31(3) 1986, 269–285; John C. Ries, "Windfall Profits and Vertical Relationships: Who Gained in the Japanese Auto Industry from VERs?" *Journal of Industrial Economics* 61(3) 1993, 259–276; Paul H. Malatesta and Rex Thompson, "Government Regulation and Structural Change in the Corporate Acquisitions Market: The Impact of the Williams Act," *Journal of Financial and Quantitative Analysis* 28(3) 1993, 363–379; Anthony Boardman, Ilan Vertinsky, and Diana Whistler, "Using Information Diffusion Models to Estimate the Impacts of Regulatory Events on Publicly Traded Firms," *Journal of Public Economics* 63(2) 1997, 283–300.

9. See Sherwin Rosen, "Hedonic Prices and Implicit Markets: Product Differentiation in Pure Competition," *Journal of Political Economy* 82(1) 1974, 34–55.

10. The basic idea behind hedonic regression was introduced in Kelvin L. Lancaster, "A New Approach to Consumer Theory," *Journal of Political Economy* 74(1) 1966, 132–157.

11. In general, the hedonic price function can be written: $P = p(C_1, C_2, \ldots, C_k, N_1, \ldots, N_m)$, where $C (i = 1, \ldots, k)$ denote k attributes of the house and $N_j (j = 1, \ldots, m)$ denote m neighborhood characteristics.

12. Formally, $r_v = \dfrac{\partial P}{\partial VIEW}$.

13. As we discussed in Chapter 13, in order to estimate the hedonic prices, analysts usually take the natural logarithms, ln, of both sides of equation (14.3) to obtain the hedonic regression model: $\ln P = \ln\beta_0 + \beta_1\ln(CBD) + C\beta_2\ln(SIZE) + \beta_3\ln(VIEW) + \beta_4\ln(NBHD)$. The parameters of this model, which is linear in logarithms, may be estimated by ordinary least squares.

14. The hedonic price of C_i may be a function of all of the variables in the hedonic price function. Given the general hedonic price function presented in note 11, $\partial P/\partial C_i = f(C_1, \ldots, C_k, N_1, \ldots, N_m)$.

15. Formally, $r_v = \dfrac{\partial P}{\partial VIEW}$
$$= \beta_3\beta_0 CBD^{\beta_1} SIZE^{\beta_2} VIEW^{\beta_3-1} NBHD^{\beta_4} e^\epsilon$$
$$= \beta_3 \frac{P}{VIEW}$$

16. The functional form of this model may be linear, multiplicative, or have some other form.

17. These functions indicate households' WTP, holding household characteristics constant.

18. Many researchers estimate linear models of the following form:

wage rate $= \beta_0 + \beta_1$fatality risk $+ \beta_2$injury risk $+ \beta_3$job tenure $+ \beta_4$education $+ \beta_5$age $+ \epsilon$

If the dependent variable is the hourly wage rate, fatality risk is measured as the number of deaths per 10,000 workers and $\beta_1 = 0.3$, then researchers estimate the VSL $= 0.3 \times 2,000$ hours/yr $\times 10,000 = 6$ million. However, linear hedonic models usually have identification problems as discussed below.

19. The seminal work on this topic, which actually preceded the formal development of the hedonic pricing method, is Ronald G. Ridker and John A. Henning, "The Determinants of Residential Property Values with Special Reference to Air Pollution," *Review of Economics and Statistics* 49(2) 1967, 246–257. For a review of studies that have attempted to use the hedonic method to estimate WTP for reductions in particulate matter in air, see V. Kerry Smith and Ju-Chin Huang, "Can Markets Value Air Quality? A Meta-Analysis of Hedonic Property Value Models," *Journal of Political Economy* 103(1) 1995, 209–227.

20. W. P. Jennings and A. Kinderman, "The Value of a Life: New Evidence of the Relationship be-

tween Changes in Occupational Fatalities and Wages of Hourly Workers, 1992–1999," *The Journal of Risk and Insurance* 70(3) 2003, 549–561.

21. For a discussion concerning identification and estimation of hedonic models, see Ivar Ekeland, James J. Heckman, and Lars Nesheim, "Identification and Estimation of Hedonic Models," *Journal of Political Economy* 112(1) 2004, S60–S109.

22. This method is often referred to as the Clawson method, or the Knetsch-Clawson method. However, it is now attributed to Harold Hotelling; see Harold Hotelling, "Letter," *An Economic Study of the Monetary Evaluation of Recreation in the National Parks* (Washington, D.C.: National Park Service, 1949).

23. Note that computing the area of the triangle using the formula ($95–$65)(6)/2 = $90 provides a slight overestimate of the consumer surplus, while using the formula ($90–$65)(6)/2 = $75 provides the correct answer. In effect, if we treat the intercept as $90 instead of $95, we obtain the correct answer. The problem arises because the number of visits is a discrete variable, while the equation for the inverse demand function is continuous.

24. Area *abc* ≈ $3.6 million, area *dbfe* = $4.8 million, area *bcf* = $4.2 million.

25. Gardner Brown Jr. and Robert Mendelsohn, "The Hedonic Travel Cost Model," *Review of Economics and Statistics* 66(3) 1984, 427–433.

26. For more detail, see Nancy G. Bockstael, Kenneth E. McConnell, and Ivar Strand, "Recreation," in J. B. Braden and C. D. Kolstad, eds., *Measuring the Demand for Environmental Quality* (Amsterdam: Elsevier, 1991), 227–270; and V. Kerry Smith and Yoshiaki Kaoru, "The Hedonic Travel Cost Model: A View From the Trenches," *Land Economics* 63(2) 1987, 179–192.

27. Alan Randall, "A Difficulty with the Travel Cost Method," *Land Economics* 70(1) 1994, 88–96.

28. See also John R. McKean, Donn M. Johnson, and Richard G. Walsh, "Valuing Time in Travel Cost Demand Analysis: An Empirical Investigation," *Land Economics* 71(1) 1995, 96–105.

29. Also, the travel cost variable may not be independent of the error term, thereby leading to ordinary least squares estimates that are biased and inconsistent.

30. This method is also referred to as the avoided cost method. For a review of the use of this method to measure groundwater values, see Charles Abdalla, "Groundwater Values from Avoidance Cost Studies: Implications for Policy and Future Research," *American Journal of Agricultural Economics* 76(5) 1994, 1062–1067.

31. The accuracy of using changes in defensive expenditures on a substitute to measure the benefits of changes in the levels of externalities or public goods depends on how these goods enter the individual's utility function and on the relationship between these goods and the market for the substitute. For more discussion of this issue, see Paul N. Courant and Richard Porter, "Averting Expenditure and the Cost of Pollution," *Journal of Environmental Economics and Management* 8(4) 1981, 321–329. Also see Winston Harrington and Paul Portney, "Valuing the Benefits of Health and Safety Regulation," *Journal of Urban Economics* 22(1) 1987, 101–112.

32. These models are also referred to as qualitative response models. See, for example, G. S. Maddala, *Limited-Dependent and Qualitative Variables in Econometrics* (Cambridge: Cambridge University Press, 1983); and Kenneth Train, *Qualitative Choice Analysis* (Cambridge, MA: MIT Press, 1986).

33. See, for example, David A. Hensher and Mark Bradley, "Using Stated Preference Response Data to Enrich Revealed Preference Data," *Marketing Letters* 4(2) 1993, 139–152.

CHAPTER 15

Contingent Valuation: Using Surveys to Elicit Information about Costs and Benefits

Economists generally are more comfortable observing individuals' valuations of goods and services through their behavior in markets than eliciting their valuations through survey questionnaires. They prefer to observe purchasing decisions because these decisions directly reveal preferences, whereas surveys elicit statements about preferences. Nevertheless, for some public goods there are simply no, or very poor, market proxies or other means of inferring preferences from observations. In such circumstances, many analysts have concluded that there is no viable alternative to asking a sample of people about their valuations.

Questionnaires designed to elicit preferences are normally referred to as *contingent valuation* (CV) surveys,[1] or sometimes hypothetical valuation surveys, because respondents are not actually required to pay their stated valuations of goods.[2] The primary use of CV is to elicit people's willingness to pay (WTP) for changes in quantities or qualities of goods. Many kinds of goods, including water quality at recreation sites, goose hunting, sports stadiums, and outdoor recreation, have been valued with CV surveys,[3] as have health outcomes.[4] Such agencies as the National Park Service and the U.S. Bureau of Reclamation use CV surveys to value recreation and wildlife opportunities. CV surveys are also used to value more complex and abstract goods, such as reductions in the volume of hazardous wastes, the value of archeological artifacts and sites, and the preservation of wetland ecosystems.[5] Valuing the use, or potential use, of goods with CV is relatively uncontroversial. Valuing passive use (nonuse) with CV is more controversial, both for the conceptual reasons discussed in Chapter 9 and the practical reasons related to gathering valid information from surveys discussed later in this chapter.

In spite of the controversy, the use of CV as a method for estimating costs and benefits is now widespread. Indeed, the federal courts have held that surveys of citizens' valuations have "rebuttable presumption" status in cases involving the assessment of damage to natural resources.[6] A blue-ribbon panel of social scientists convened by the National Oceanic and Atmospheric Administration (NOAA) further legitimized the use of CV by concluding that it could be the basis for estimating passive use values for inclusion in natural resource damage assessment cases.[7]

In this chapter we provide an overview of CV methods. We assess the major strengths and weakness of those methods most commonly used, emphasize the importance of informing respondents of how they would pay the costs of a project (the payment vehicle), review the major criticisms and problems related to CV use, discuss some of the survey issues most relevant to CV, and consider CV's accuracy. Finally, we present some heuristic checklists for analysts preparing or reviewing CV instruments.

OVERVIEW OF CONTINGENT VALUATION METHODS

The general approach of all CV methods is as follows. First, a sample of respondents from the population with standing is identified. Second, respondents are asked questions about their valuations of some good. Third, their responses provide information that enables analysts to estimate the respondents' WTP for the good. Fourth, the WTP amounts for the sample are extrapolated to the entire population. If, for instance, the respondents comprise a random sample of the population such that each member of the population had an equal chance of being in the sample, then the average WTP for the sample would simply be multiplied by the size of the population to arrive at the aggregate WTP.

As CV surveys are expensive to conduct, analysts may wish to extrapolate the results of existing surveys to different populations. However, the characteristics of these populations usually do not match those of the population previously sampled. For example, the populations may differ in terms of income, access to alternative goods, or other factors that may be relevant to their demands for the good. As discussed in Chapter 17, reasonable extrapolation requires that these differences be controlled for statistically.[8] Therefore, analysts increase the chances that their CV surveys will have use beyond their own CBAs by collecting and reporting information about the characteristics of their samples, including WTP amounts for subsets of the sample, even when such information is unnecessary for their own studies.

The remainder of this section introduces four specific methods that are used to elicit WTP amounts from survey respondents. We first briefly sketch three methods that have been used at various times: the *open-ended willingness-to-pay* method, the *closed-ended iterative bidding* method, and the *contingent ranking* method. We then turn to the *dichotomous choice, binary choice* or *referendum,* method, which was advocated by the NOAA blue-ribbon panel as the method of choice in most circumstances.[9]

Direct Elicitation (Nonreferendum) Methods

Several CV methods ask questions about preferences directly. The open-ended willingness-to-pay method and the closed-ended iterative bidding method seek to elicit the WPT amounts for each respondent. The contingent ranking method seeks to elicit a preference profile over a set of alternatives for each respondent. These methods contrast with the dichotomous choice method, which is indirect in the sense that it relies on patterns of responses across a large number of respondents to make inferences about the preferences of respondents with particular characteristics.

Open-Ended Willingness-to-Pay Method.   The earliest method to be used is the *open-ended willingness-to-pay* approach. Here respondents are simply asked to state their maximum WTP for the good, or policy, that is being valued.[10] The question might be formulated as follows: "What is the most that you would be prepared to pay in additional federal income taxes to guarantee that the Wildwood wilderness area will remain closed to development?" This method had dropped out of favor as analysts feared unrealistic responses because respondents needed some initial guidance on valuations.[11] Concerns that open-ended questions result in excessively large estimates of WTP seem unfounded; indeed, a more serious problem appears to be that respondents who have low valuations of the good often state a zero value.

Closed-Ended Iterative Bidding Method.   In the closed-ended iterative bidding method, respondents are asked whether they would pay a specified amount for the good or policy that has been described. If respondents answer affirmatively, then the amount is incrementally increased. The procedure continues until the respondent expresses an *unwillingness to pay* the amount specified. Similarly, if respondents answer negatively to the initial amount specified, the interviewer lowers the amount by increments until the respondent expresses a WTP that amount.

The initial question for determining WTP typically starts with something like the following: "Now suppose the costs to clean the Kristiansand Fjord were divided on [sic] all taxpayers in the whole of Norway by an extra tax in 1986. If this extra tax was 200 kronor for an average taxpayer, would you then be willing to support the proposal?"[12] In this CV survey the interviewer set the initial price at 200 kronor. If a respondent indicated a willingness to pay this initial price, then the interviewer raised the price by 200 kronor and asked the question again. The interviewer kept going until the respondent gave a negative answer. Similarly, if the initial response was negative, then the interviewer dropped the price by a 100-kronor increment and then 10-kronor increments until the respondent gave a positive response. Although iterative bidding was at one time the most common method in use, it is rarely used now because of considerable evidence that its results are highly sensitive to the initially presented value (the starting value).

Contingent Ranking Method.   In the contingent ranking, or ranked choice, method, respondents are asked to rank specific feasible combinations of quantities of the good being valued and monetary payments. For example, respondents choose on a continuum between a low level of water quality at a low tax price and a high level of water quality at a high tax price. The combinations are ranked from most preferred to least preferred.[13] The rankings provide a basis for estimating each respondent's WTP for various increments of quality. Contingent ranking implies an ordinal ranking procedure in contrast to the iterative bidding procedure, which requires cardinal evaluation. Typically, tasks that require only ordinal information processing, that is, a ranking rather than a precise specification of value, are considerably easier for respondents to perform coherently.[14] This is a valuable attribute in the CV context where complex information must often be processed by respondents. Of course, unlike the open-ended WTP method or the closed-ended iterative bidding method, the WTP of interest must be inferred from ordinal rankings rather than directly elicited. Additionally, responses appear to be sensitive to the order in which alternatives are presented to respondents.

Dichotomous Choice (Referendum) Method

In the dichotomous choice method, respondents are asked whether they would be willing to pay a particular specified price to obtain a good or policy.[15] Each respondent receives one randomly drawn price. Respondents are then asked to state whether they would be willing to pay for the good or policy (e.g., closing the Wildwood wilderness area to development) at that offered price ("yes" means willing to pay and "no" means not willing to pay); in other words, respondents are made a binary "take it or leave it" offer of the sort that they face in many markets for private goods. The choice situation is also like that faced by referendum voters—hence the label referendum method. The dollar amounts, often referred to as *bid prices,* that are presented to respondents vary over a range selected by the analyst.[16] The probability of respondents accepting the offer can then be calculated for each bid price.[17]

Figure 15-1 shows the distribution of responses to bid prices in the form of a histogram. Specific bid prices are shown on the horizontal axis ranging from the lowest dollar price offered ($X = \$0$) to the highest price offered ($X = \$100$) in \$5 increments. The vertical axis measures the percentage of respondents who answer "yes" to the bid price offered to them. In this example, almost all of the respondents who are offered the specified outcome at $X = \$0$ state they would accept it. About 75 percent of respondents who are offered the outcome for \$30 indicate that they would accept it at this price. We can interpret the response frequencies as estimates of the probability

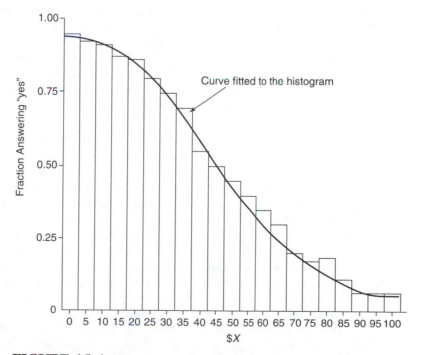

FIGURE 15-1   Histogram of Dichotomous Choice Responses

that a randomly drawn member of the sample of respondents is willing to pay a specific amount. For example, the probability a randomly drawn respondent would pay at least $30 for the specified outcome is about 0.75.

The fitted curve in Figure 15-1 may be viewed as the demand curve of a randomly drawn (i.e., average) member of the sample, while the histogram may be viewed as a rough approximation of this demand curve. The difference between the demand curve in Figure 15-1 and the more standard demand curve is that instead of the curve indicating the quantity of a good the individual would be willing to purchase at each price, it indicates the probability that the individual would be willing to pay for the specified outcome at each price.[18] As in the case of a standard demand curve, the area under the curve in Figure 15-1 provides an estimate of the individual's WTP.

If the values of X are evenly spread, then the histogram can be readily used to obtain a rough estimate of the average individual's WTP by applying a simple formula:

$$\text{WTP} = v \sum_{k=0}^{N} [\text{Probability of acceptance at price } kv] \qquad \textbf{(15.1)}$$

where v is the interval between prices (i.e., the width of the individual bars in the histogram) and N is the number of values of X (i.e., the number of bars). In other words, the area covered by the bars (the approximate WTP for an average member of the sample) can be computed by simply summing the heights of the bars and multiplying by the bar width.

Analysts rarely work directly from the histogram of accepted bids. Methods have evolved—from statistical models of the probability of acceptance to random utility models relating acceptance to the relationship between the bid price and an expression of WTP as a function of demographic characteristics.[19] Corrections are sometimes made to account for the finite range of bids[20] and other data limitations.[21] These statistical models can also be used to estimate WTP for each identified group within the sample. *To find the aggregate WTP for the entire population, multiply the mean for each group by the size of that group in the population with standing and then sum across groups.*[22]

Because this method only tells one whether a given respondent's valuation is greater or less than the offered amount, sample sizes have to be large in order to achieve reasonable levels of precision. For small samples, the true value of WTP may be considerably different from the observed value of WTP. On the other hand, "take it or leave it" questions are very easy for respondents to answer, and they are the closest approximation to market-like transactions.

Some analysts have now moved to *double dichotomous choice* (sometimes called *double-bounded dichotomous choice*) rather than single elicitation questions to reduce the need for large samples. In this version of the method, depending on the answer to the first offer, a follow-up offer is made that is either double (if yes) or half (if no) the first offer. This provides considerably more information than the standard single-offer version. However, there is danger that the respondent's exposure to the first offer may affect the probability that he or she will accept the follow-up offer.[23] Recognizing that follow-up bids provide information to respondents that may change their perceptions of the likely price or quantity of the good being valued,

Richard Carson and Theodore Groves suggest several ways that this information might affect their responses to the second bids.[24] First, those who initially rejected bids may take the lower follow-up bid as an indication that the bid price is negotiable and reject bids that they previously would have accepted. Second, those who initially accepted bids may believe that there is some possibility that the good could be provided at the lower price and reject the higher second bid even though it is below their WTP. Third, in responding to the follow-up bid price, respondents may base their responses not on that price but on some weighted average of the two bid prices they encountered.[25] Whether the greater amount of information generated by the double dichotomous choice method is worth the risk of such response behaviors remains an open research question.

As we discuss in detail in a subsequent section of this chapter (see *the Strategic Response (Honesty) Problem*), a major advantage of a binary choice formulation is that it meets the necessary condition for incentive compatibility—that is, the presence of an incentive for respondents to give truthful rather than strategic answers. The other methods we discuss are not incentive-compatible. The possibility that the referendum method is incentive compatible is an important reason that it is the most commonly used CV method.

PAYMENT VEHICLE

Almost all CV exercises specify a *payment vehicle,* which describes how the respondents', costs of providing the good will be paid. Payment vehicles include taxes paid into a fund specifically earmarked for the good, increased utility bills, higher income or sales taxes, and higher product prices. Specifying a payment vehicle, along with reminders that payments come at the expense of expenditures on other goods, helps ensure that respondents perceive the questions as real economic choices. In order to increase the realism of CV surveys, analysts generally try to specify a payment vehicle that is as close as possible to the actual one that would be used were supply of the good to proceed.

The choice of payment vehicle can make a difference in the estimated WTP. In a recent study, for example, researchers found that respondents appeared to value watershed management plans differently depending on whether there was a guarantee that taxes imposed to pay for them would not be used for other purposes.[26] The presence or absence of such a guarantee also affected respondents' valuations of specific attributes of watershed plans.

There has been considerable debate as to whether differences in the WTP of respondents that are attributable to differences in payment vehicles should be treated as a bias. Kenneth Arrow and others argue that respondents are being asked to value all elements of a project, which include the method of payment; therefore, respondent preferences about payment methods do not imply bias.[27] Other analysts argue that if specific payment vehicles, such as taxes, introduce "protest" valuations, then such outliers should be excluded from the estimation of aggregate WTP. Protest bidders can sometimes be screened out by their answers to specific questions designed to identify them.

GENERIC SURVEY ISSUES

Before turning specifically to CV surveys, it is useful to consider briefly some issues relevant to all survey contexts. One issue concerns the trade-offs among methods for administering surveys. Another issue is the extent to which the procedures for identifying and reaching respondents leads to an appropriate sample from which to estimate the distribution of attitudes within the population with standing.

Survey Administration: In-Person, Telephone, Mail, and Internet

Currently, there are four major technologies for administering surveys: in-person interviews, telephone interviews, mail questionnaires and Internet surveys. Each has strengths and weaknesses, and each raises different methodological issues. None of the four procedures is unequivocally superior to the others.

Table 15-1 summarizes the characteristics of the survey administration alternatives. In-person interviews involve interviewers meeting face-to-face with respondents. Especially relevant in the CV context, face-to-face interaction facilitates the provision of complex information to respondents through the presentation of maps, diagrams, photographs, and other visual aids by the interviewer. The interviewer can also clarify questions and provide additional information and otherwise interact directly with the respondent. This direct contact, however, also involves a high risk of interviewer bias, as respondents may react to the personal characteristics of the interviewer, perhaps slanting answers to gain the interviewer's approval. Unlike telephone interviews, which typically are conducted from a central location, in-person interviews are difficult to monitor. The greatest disadvantage, however, is that in-person interviews tend to be very expensive, especially for geographically disperse samples, because of the time

TABLE 15-1 Survey Administration Alternatives

	Cost per Completed Interview	Ease of Identifying and Reaching Respondents	Risk of Interviewer Bias	Maximum Complexity of Provided Information
In-Person	Very high—depends on questionnaire length and geographic spread	Medium—depends on availability of lists and access	High—personal presence, monitoring difficult	Very high—interactive communication and visual aids possible
Telephone	High—depends on questionnaire length and callbacks	Very high—random digit dialing	Medium—interviewer cues	Low—verbal communication limits complexity of content
Mail	Low—depends on number of follow-ups	High—depends on availability of appropriate lists	Low—uniform presentation	High—visual aids possible
Internet	Low—marginal costs very small	Low—"spamming" restrictions require panels of willing respondents	Low—uniform presentation	Very high—visual aids and interactive questions possible

spent traveling between interviews and the precautions that must be taken to ensure the security of the interviewers. As is the case with mail questionnaires, the capability for identifying a random sample of any population depends on the availability of lists of the individuals, families, or households that make up the population. In many locations, such as cities with guarded apartment buildings or suburbs with restricted-access housing developments, it may be difficult to reach respondents randomly selected to be in the sample.

Telephone interviews are a common method of administering CV surveys. Telephone interviews cost substantially less than in-person interviews, even with a large number of callbacks to reach persons who are not at home or who use answering machines. They also have the advantage of allowing researchers to draw reasonable random samples through random digit dialing, obviating the need for address lists in surveys of households. Unfortunately, verbal communication limits the complexity of information that can be provided. It also opens up the possibility of interviewer bias, as respondents react to voice cues and perceptions of the characteristics of the interviewer.

Several trends have made telephone interviews more costly and difficult to implement effectively. One trend is the greater prevalence of telemarketing, often masquerading as surveys. Many people refuse to participate in surveys to avoid unwanted telemarketing solicitations. Others use answering machines and caller identification to screen out calls from strangers. Another trend is the increasing number of individuals who do not have landlines, which makes it increasingly difficult to draw good random samples through random digit dialing. Some households also have multiple telephone lines, dedicated to home businesses or teenagers. Cellular telephones are breaking down area codes, making it more difficult to sample geographically. Dealing with these problems will likely raise the effective costs of telephone surveys in the future.

Mail questionnaires, which allow the provision of visual aids to respondents, have the advantage of very low cost. The ease of identifying samples depends on the availability of appropriate lists. Accurate lists also make it easy to identify a sample of respondents and contact them by mail, though response rates are typically low, often requiring multiple mailings to reach acceptable levels. As there are no interviewers, there is no interviewer bias.

As more U.S. adults become Internet users, the practicality of using the Internet for conducting surveys increases. Internet surveys have several advantages over the other methods. Because interviewers are not needed, Internet surveys have extremely low marginal costs, perhaps even lower than mail surveys. Unlike mail surveys, the actual data collection can often be fully automated and implemented within a very short time frame, an advantage when the CV survey is intended to inform a pending decision. Like mail surveys, they avoid the risk of interviewer bias, and they allow for the provision of complex information. Indeed, one can give respondents access to large quantities of information through menus and other interactive devices. Unfortunately, drawing random samples of populations remains a barrier. Not all members of most populations of interest are Internet users. This is changing, but even when Internet use has become ubiquitous, sampling is complicated by restrictions on spamming, which prevents procedures analogous to random digit dialing in telephone surveys. Firms have now developed databases of willing respondents that have become sufficiently large and representative of populations of interest to allow scientifically valid CV studies to be administered through the Internet.[28]

Sample and Nonresponse Biases

The essence of survey research is eliciting information about a population from a small sample drawn from that population. As summarized in Table 15-1, survey administration alternatives differ in terms of the ease with which they facilitate identifying and reaching respondents. How to identify individuals to be sampled from target populations is the topic of *sample design*.[29] The extent to which valid responses are obtained from those identified determines whether the sample design will actually produce data adequate for making valid inferences.

In almost all cases, the sample is selected by a probability mechanism, which produces a *random sample*. In a random sample, each individual has a known probability of being drawn from the population. *Simple random samples* give each individual in the target population the same probability of being sampled. *Stratified samples* give members of particular groups within a population the same probability of being sampled. In either case, knowing the selection probabilities allows researchers to base inferences about the characteristics of the population on the characteristics of the sample.

If a given sample is appropriately selected and administered, then sample biases can be avoided. Advances in probability sampling techniques have been such that findings based on samples of approximately a thousand people can be representative of the entire population of the United States. However, approximately the same sample size may also be necessary for much smaller populations—essentially, for large populations the sample size needed to achieve any desired level of precision does not depend on the size of the population being sampled. Additionally, there is considerable evidence that the observed distributions of WTP in CV are skewed toward extreme values. For this reason, *CV samples should be larger than samples drawn for many other purposes to obtain reliable estimates of population means*. This is especially true for the dichotomous choice method which provides less information (accept or not accept) per respondent than open-ended questions (willingness-to-pay amount).

For CV purposes, *the relevant target population is usually all individuals with standing who are affected by the policy*. Unfortunately, this heuristic begs the question of who is affected. For many projects it is apparent. But often it is not, especially in addressing environmental issues. In some contexts there is congruence between those who bear the cost of policies and those who are affected by them. In other contexts, however, these groups diverge, as when a state or province provides a wilderness area that is valued by people living in other jurisdictions. The greater such divergence, the more problematic it is to choose the correct population.[30]

Several major issues are involved in assessing who is affected. First, all those "users" directly affected by the project should be included. The term *users* is in quotes because we mean it in a specific way. Those who would directly utilize the good in question are, of course, users. But so are individuals who suffer direct negative impacts that they would pay to avoid. For example, nearby residents of a duck hunting reserve who dislike the noise are as much users as the duck hunters. Potential users should also be included. As discussed in Chapter 8, in situations involving uncertainty, the option price that an individual would be willing to pay for a good may differ from his or her expected surplus. So some people who never actually consume the good may value it.

Second, it is important for survey respondents to understand whether they are being asked to estimate WTP just for themselves or as a representative for their whole household. This distinction is important in extrapolating from the sample to the target population.

Third, an explicit decision should be made concerning the inclusion or exclusion of passive use benefits. As discussed in Chapter 9, either users or nonusers may derive existence value from a project. Conceptually, existence value should be included as a component of benefits. For environmental goods, CV surveys that either sample nonusers or estimate existence values of users typically yield much higher aggregate WTP estimates than do those that include only use benefits. However, there is considerable disagreement on the validity of using CV surveys to estimate nonuse benefits.

Fourth, the geographic *spread,* or *reach,* of the sample should be wide enough to capture all affected individuals. There is increasing recognition that decisions concerning the geographic footprint of the relevant market can drive the outcomes of many CBAs, especially if nonusers are included.[31]

An important sampling question relates to the exclusion of responses. It has been suggested that three categories of respondents should be excluded in estimating WTP: first, respondents who reject the whole notion of placing a value on the good in question, or of paying for the good in a certain way; second, respondents who refuse to take the exercise seriously; and third, respondents who clearly demonstrate that they are incapable of understanding the survey.[32] In the direct elicitation methods, all three types of respondents are usually assumed to provide either zero valuations or extremely high valuations. Sometimes such respondents can be directly identified by their answers to specific questions intended to screen them from the sample. Respondents who provide extreme values are known as *outliers.* Outliers are normally handled in CV by simply eliminating valuations that are above some specified threshold or that are above a specified percentage of the respondent's gross or discretionary income.

An appropriate sampling design can usually eliminate most sample bias if it is fully executed. Yet, bias can still remain if some individuals do not respond to the survey. Nonresponse bias is a serious problem in almost all survey research. Nonresponse problems have grown over the last 20 years as the public has been asked to give time to more surveys and has become suspicious of the motives of many who claim to be survey researchers. If nonresponse is purely random, then it can be dealt with by increasing the sample size. Unfortunately, however, nonresponse is often not random.

There are two major types of nonresponse problems: refusal to respond and unavailability to respond. In CV contexts, the primary approaches for dealing with refusal to respond are to highlight the legitimacy of the exercise (e.g., by stressing government or university affiliations) or to offer various response incentives, such as donations to charities or entries into prize lotteries. Where unavailability biases the sample, researchers typically account for underrepresentation and overrepresentation in the sample when extrapolating to the target population.[33]

EXHIBIT 15-1

As part of a court case, the plaintiffs conducted a CV survey to estimate the natural resource damage caused by a mine. They surveyed residents of both the county (Eagle County) and the state (Colorado) in which the mine was located. Based on their surveys, they estimated past damages were $50.8 million and future expected damages would be between $15 and $45 million. The defendants sampled a much smaller group within Eagle County that they believed had been directly affected by pollution from the mine; they assumed that residents in the rest of Colorado did not bear costs from the mine. Although the per-unit values of both sides were similar (for example, on the value of a day's fishing), the defendants' estimate of total past and future expected damage was approximately $240,000, less than 1 percent of the plaintiffs' estimate. "The discrepancies in these respective aggregate estimates arise from the plaintiff's assumption that . . . there would be a much larger number of people experiencing gains with the restoration" (p. 605).

Source: Adapted from Raymond J. Kopp and V. Kerry Smith, "Benefit Estimation Goes to Court: The Case of Natural Resource Damage Assessments," *Journal of Policy Analysis and Management* 8(4) 1989, 593–612.

CONTINGENT VALUATION PROBLEMS AND ISSUES

This section discusses specific problems relevant to CV surveys. The subsequent section discusses more general survey problems that are relevant to CV. Surveying opinions is not an exact science. The science of CV surveys is even less exact. Some critics argue that CV has such serious weaknesses that it should be used only as a last resort. Other critics contend that it is so seriously flawed when used to value either complex goods or passive use impacts that it should not be used at all for these purposes.[34] It has been pointed out that the summation of average valuations over a broad range of projects to improve the environment would exhaust the budget of average individuals.[35]

Specific CV survey difficulties stem from several sources. First, CV inevitably raises questions that are more novel and complex than those raised in other survey situations. This poses problems of *hypotheticality* (we use this as a catchall word to cover problems of understanding, meaning, context, and familiarity). Hypotheticality appears to be more severe when respondents have not, and will not, consume the good in some way. That is, hypotheticality tends to be most severe in the valuation of passive use. Second, CV raises questions of *neutrality* in the presentation of information to respondents. Third, for certain methods, *judgmental biases* may arise in response to certain kinds of questions (including whether the question is framed as willingness to pay or as willingness to accept). Not all these problems necessarily create biases (i.e., a systematic tendency to overvalue or undervalue the goods in question), but all of them do raise questions about the validity and reliability of CV as a procedure. Some specific CV methods appear to be more prone to biases than others. Fourth, CV asks questions about WTP, raising the potential for biases related to *strategic behavior* (misstatements intended to influence some outcome) and the specified payment vehicle.

Hypotheticality, Meaning, and Context Problems

A major concern in CV design is whether respondents are truly able to understand and place into context the questions they are being asked and, consequently, whether they can accurately value the good in question. Issues relating to the valuation of the supply of many publicly provided goods are complex and highly contextual. CV questions can be contrasted to many other types of questions for which meaning is not an issue (e.g., "For whom do you intend to vote in the next election?").

Questions of hypotheticality and meaning can be thought of as problems of specifying exactly what is the good in question. Understanding the good, or the policy that produces it, is difficult for respondents because they often are not familiar with either. When respondents are presented with questions about goods or projects that they do not understand, attitudes (and responses as expressed in the CV survey) are unlikely to correspond to the behavior that would occur if the project were actually implemented.[36] When a project (or the good itself) has multiple attributes, these all need to be explained to respondents: "Unless [an attribute is] specified explicitly (and comprehensively), evaluators must guess its value and, hence, what the offer really means. If they guess wrong, then they risk misrepresenting their values."[37]

This problem, however, has to be seen in context. Individuals also differentially value attributes of market goods: Some individuals may value a mountain bike mostly for prestige reasons and others for transportation purposes. The evidence also suggests that people find it somewhat difficult to value the attributes of new and unfamiliar products in market contexts.[38] As Richard Carson and his colleagues point out, "Many new products become available each year creating markets in which consumers regularly make purchase decisions . . . No standard microeconomics text has ever stated that prior experience is a precondition for rational decision making."[39]

Additional problems arise in CV if the perceptions of the good by respondents are not independent of the quality or quantity of the information provided. The possible information that could be provided when describing complex goods are unlimited. The quantity and quality of information, however, are limited in practice by the method of survey administration. Several commentators have argued that there is little evidence that hypotheticality per se introduces bias into CV.[40] But in the presence of hypotheticality certain kinds of bias may be more likely.

The potential for hypotheticality varies enormously across different CBA contexts. Unfortunately, CV is likely to be most useful in contexts in which goods are difficult to define, such as projects involving environmental impacts. When it is difficult to specify potential physical impacts, it is also likely to be difficult for respondents to understand what these impacts mean.

Hypotheticality and lack of realism can be reduced in a number of ways. *Clearly specifying the project and its impacts increases the likelihood of correspondence between attitudes and behavior; so too does providing explicit detail about the payment vehicle.* Visual aids such as photographs, maps, and diagrams often assist in understanding. One important class of visual aids useful in reducing hypotheticality is known as quality ladders. An example of a quality ladder is described in Exhibit 15-2. Quality ladders help respondents understand both what quality is under the status quo, and what particular increments of quality mean.

EXHIBIT 15-2

A "water quality ladder" has been used in several CBAs to help respondents understand how differing levels of toxins, dissolved solids, water clarity, and other factors affect water quality. In their CBA of water quality improvements to the Monongahela River, V. Kerry Smith and William Desvousges included a picture of a ladder with a 0-to-10 scale and the following interviewer instructions:

"(*Interviewer: Read the following.*) Generally the better the water quality the better suited the water is for recreation activities and the more likely people will take part in outdoor recreation activities on or near the water. Here is a picture of a ladder that shows various levels of water quality. (*Interviewer: Give respondent water quality ladder.*)

The top of the ladder stands for the best possible quality of water. The bottom of the ladder stands for the worst possible water quality. On the ladder you can see the different levels of the quality of the water. For example: (*Interviewer: Point to each level—E, D, C, B, A—as you read the statements that follow*).

Level E (*Interviewer: Point.*) is so polluted that it has oil, raw sewage, and other things like trash in it; it has no plant or animal life and smells bad.

Water at level D is okay for boating but not fishing or swimming.

Level C shows where the water is clean enough so that game fish like bass can live in it.

Level B shows where the water is clean enough so that people can swim in it safely.

And at level A, the quality of the water is so good that it would be possible to drink directly from it if you wanted to.

(*Interviewer: Now ask the respondent to use the ladder to rate the water quality in the Monongahela River on a scale of 0 to 10 and to indicate whether the ranking was for a particular site, and if so, to name it.*)"

Source: Adapted from V. Kerry Smith and William H. Desvousges, *Measuring Water Quality Benefits* (Boston, MA: Kluwer Academic, 1986), 87.

Baruch Fischhoff and Lita Furey have suggested a checklist for evaluating CV instruments in terms of the likelihood that respondents will understand the questions they are being asked.[41] It requires the analyst to assess the comprehensiveness of information with respect to the good, the specification of the payment vehicle, and the social context. In assessing the adequacy of information about the good, they stress the need to provide information on both substantive and formal components. The substantive aspect of the good deals with why someone might value it (basically its attributes), while the formal aspect of the good concerns how much they value it (once they understand its attributes).

In practice, *the only effective way to minimize hypotheticality and meaning problems in CV surveys is to devote extensive effort to developing detailed, clear, informative, and highly contextual materials and to pretest these materials extensively on typical respondents.*

Neutrality

While the previous section indicated that lack of clear meaning does not necessarily pose a bias problem, lack of neutrality is certain to do so. As CBA deals with increasingly controversial and complex topics, the neutrality of the CV questionnaire becomes an increasingly important issue. Neutrality has come to the fore as litigants in (especially environmental) court cases have conducted their own CV surveys.

Meaning and neutrality issues often intersect in ways that are extremely difficult to disentangle. For example, Daniel Hagen and colleagues surveyed 1,000 U.S. households by mail concerning the value of preserving the spotted owl.[42] Of the total, 409 questionnaires were returned. Some of the information that respondents were given included the following: " . . . a scientific committee concluded that logging should be banned on some forest lands to prevent the extinction of the Northern Spotted Owl . . ." and "a second group of independent scientists examined this study and agreed with these conclusions." The survey also included the comment that: "the well-being of the northern spotted owl reflects the well-being of the entire old-growth forest eco-system."

In a review of spotted owl CV studies in general, and the Hagen et al. study in particular, William McKillop criticized this framing of the issue. He argues that the survey did not include many relevant facts that respondents should have been told.[43] For example, the "committee of scientists" focused almost exclusively on old-growth habitat for spotted owls and largely ignored the fact that many are found in second-growth timber stands. Respondents were also not told that logging was already prohibited on considerable areas of old-growth timberland, and these acres were likely to increase in the course of normal national forest planning. In sum, McKillop argues that the spotted owl issue was not presented accurately or neutrally to respondents. He further argues that this issue is simply too complicated to be addressed by CV surveys.

There are no simple answers to the neutrality problem. But an inevitable conclusion is that one has to be especially cautious in interpreting the results of CV surveys that have been prepared by either parties to litigation or advocacy groups. At a practical level, *neutrality can best be ensured by pretesting the survey instrument with substantive experts who have "no axe to grind" in terms of the specific project that is being considered.* If neutral experts cannot be found, then pretesting with opposing advocates can be an alternative, perhaps enabling researchers to avoid the most serious challenges from those with positions not supported by the results.

Decision Making and Judgment Biases

Although it is reasonable to assume that individuals can make rational judgments about their valuations of goods in most market situations, evidence suggests that in certain circumstances they may not be able to do so readily. This is even more likely to occur in the context of CV surveys, because judgment rather than decision making is involved and because there are not opportunities to learn from mistakes (we discuss the evidence on this issue later in the chapter). More formally, in such circumstances, there is a tendency for individuals to behave as if they are not maximizing utility, especially with respect to choices involving uncertainty. In the context of functioning markets, these behaviors appear as decision-making biases that can result in irrational purchases (or lack of purchases). These decision-making errors can be thought of as a type of market failure.[44] In the context of CV, the term *judgment bias* rather than *decision-making bias* is applicable because the respondent is not actually purchasing the good in question.

Both decision-making and judgment biases appear to be most serious for activities or projects that would generate small changes in the probabilities of (already) low-probability events that have "catastrophic" costs if they occur (for example, activities that might cause a marginal change in the probability of a nuclear power plant accident).[45] As WTP depends on how likely respondents perceive such events will be, their perception of changes in probabilities is important in CV studies. Fortunately, researchers and analysts rarely rely solely on CV estimates in such contexts. For example, they can use value-of-life estimates derived from other methods in which these biases are less endemic (see Chapter 16).

Some of the major types of judgmental biases to which individuals are particularly prone include *availability bias,* whereby individuals estimate the probabilities of events by the ease with which occurrences can be recalled—more salient instances, such as those covered by the media, are more likely to be recalled; *representativeness,* or *conjunction bias,* whereby individuals judge the probabilities of events on the basis of their plausibility—people perceive the probability of an event as being higher as more detail is added, even though the detail is irrelevant; *optimism bias,* whereby people believe that they can beat the objective odds; *anchoring bias,* whereby individuals do not fully update their probability assessments as new information becomes available; *hindsight bias,* whereby individuals believe, after an event occurs, that it was more predictable than it actually was; *status quo bias,* whereby individuals stick with the status quo even when it is inexpensive to experiment or when the potential benefits from changing are large; and *probability assessment bias,* whereby people tend to overestimate small probabilities and underestimate large probabilities.

Many of these violations of the expected utility hypothesis can be explained by the fact that, when dealing with complex information, people tend to use simplifying (nonutility-maximizing) heuristics, or "rules of thumb." Essentially, people frame problems consistently, but the framing does not correspond to maximization of expected utility.

One conceptual framework for explaining violations of the expected utility hypothesis is *prospect theory.*[46] Prospect theory, which is particularly relevant to CV issues, suggests that individuals deviate from expected utility maximization in several ways. They value gains and losses from a reference point rather than valuing net wealth. Moreover, people are risk averse toward gains and risk seeking toward losses (known as *loss aversion*)—a loss and a gain of the same size would leave a person who is loss averse worse off. This may stem from an *endowment effect,* whereby individuals have a greater psychological attachment to things they currently possess.[47]

Several of these effects can be summarized in a prospect theory value function, which is illustrated in Figure 15-2. In this figure, the vertical axis measures value, and the horizontal axis measures losses and gains. The figure is drawn to show three things. First, people start from a reference point from which changes are measured as losses or gains. Second, individuals are risk averse with respect to potential gains (i.e., they prefer a smaller certain gain over a larger probable gain, when the expected values of the two alternatives are the same). Individuals are also risk seeking with respect to potential losses (i.e., they prefer a larger probable loss to a smaller certain loss, when the expected values of the two alternatives are the same). This is represented in the

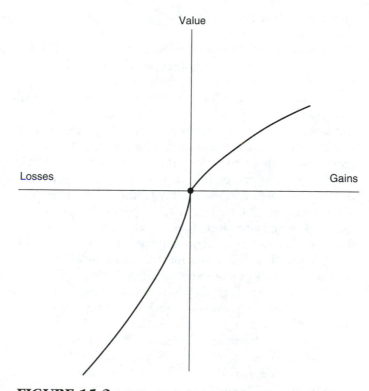

FIGURE 15-2 A "Loss Aversion" Value Function Value

figure by the concave gain function and the convex loss function. Third, losses loom larger than gains of equal size. This is represented in the figure as the loss function being steeper for losses than for gains from the reference point.

The biases suggested by prospect theory are particularly relevant to CV for a number of reasons. Anchoring via reference points is always a potential problem. Even if open-ended questions are used to eliminate starting point bias, payment vehicles and other descriptive detail may introduce anchoring indirectly. Furthermore, detailed descriptions may evoke availability bias. Finally, as we discuss later, CV questions can sometimes be plausibly framed as either involving gains or losses.

Empirical research suggests that the most serious judgment problems actually found in CV results relate to *noncommitment bias, order effects* (sometimes described as sequencing effects), *embedding effects* (sometimes described as whole/part effects or inclusiveness effects), and *starting point bias.*

Noncommitment Bias.[48] It is well recognized in the marketing literature that respondents to surveys tend to overstate their willingness to purchase a product that is described to them.[49] This may be a strategic response (an issue discussed later), but can also be thought of as either a form of anchoring bias (e.g., "this product must be valuable because they are asking me about it and describing it in such detail") in a context in which potential consumers do not engage in any learning. It is likely to be quite unconscious. The bias can flourish, of course, because the respondent does not actually have to commit money.

One set of experiments has attempted to test for noncommitment bias. The researchers conclude that "hypothetical WTP is consistently and significantly higher than the WTP that reflects real economic commitments."[50]

It is difficult to test for noncommitment bias when dealing with passive use values. One indirect way of testing for the bias is to introduce elements to the survey that encourage respondents to think more carefully about their income and their budget constraints. Michael Kemp and Christopher Maxwell have developed a "top-down disaggregation method" to do just this.[51] Top-down disaggregation attempts to mitigate noncommitment bias by raising awareness of budget constraints. After asking respondents to state initially their total WTP, they were questioned specifically about comparative valuations. For example, after respondents were asked about their WTP to avoid a specified oil spill, they were then asked about their valuations of environmental protection versus reduction in crime, homelessness, and other social problems. They were also asked about their valuations for different kinds of environmental protection (wilderness areas versus groundwater quality, rainforest protection, and other environmental goals). At the next level, they were asked to evaluate various kinds of wilderness area protection (reduction in harm from human-caused problems versus natural degradation and other destructive processes). At the end of this top-down disaggregation process, respondents were again asked their WTP. The result was WTP values several hundred times smaller than the WTP values from the initial open-ended questions.

This finding suggests that it may be desirable to ask questions that require respondents to think more carefully about the budget constraints that they face.[52] For example, asking questions that encourage respondents to think about how much of their income is discretionary may help avoid noncommitment bias. The answers may also be useful in helping to assess whether the WTP values provided are subject to noncommitment bias.

Order Effects. George Tolley and Alan Randall found that survey respondents' statements of the value of improved visibility in the Grand Canyon were greatly affected by the order in which the issue was raised.[53] Other studies have also found important order, or sequence, effects. Consider, for example, a study that asked some respondents to value preserving seals and then whales, while others were asked to value preserving whales and then seals. Seal values were considerably lower when the seal question was asked after the whale question.[54]

These findings could be explainable in terms of either an income effect, a substitution effect, or a combination of both. The rationale for an income effect is as follows: If someone has expressed a positive WTP to pay for the first good in a sequence of goods, then that person has less income to spend on the second good in the sequence. Critics of CV, however, have observed that the steep declines in WTP as a good moves down in order cannot be fully explained by income effects because these should be relatively small.[55]

Substitution effects, such as between seals and whales, could be quite large, and consequently they can be important in CBA, especially in terms of assessing the aggregate impacts of projects. (That is, respondents may view one environmental improvement as a substitute for another quite different environmental improvement.) If people engage in extensive substitution, then the net aggregate benefits from a project may be smaller than predicted. For example, if a resident of Chicago agrees to contribute to a project that cleans the air in Chicago and is then offered a project that preserves visibility in the Grand Canyon, the value of the Grand Canyon project may be decreased because of the substitution effect.

The issue of whether substitution effects could account for much of the order inconsistency in CV surveys of passive use values is still undecided.[56] Critics argue that the phenomenon is explained neither by income nor by substitution effects, but it instead demonstrates that respondents cannot really understand these kinds of questions. Hence, they inevitably engage in judgment heuristics that usually cause them to overstate valuations. Thus, it is uncertain that income and substitution effects provide a complete explanation for order effects.[57]

Embedding Effects.   A fundamental axiom in the standard economic description of preferences is that individuals value more of a good more highly than less of it. This is sometimes referred to as a *scope test*. If CV respondents' valuations are only slightly higher for large changes in the amount of the good offered than for small changes, then the validity of their responses becomes a concern. But research indicates that individuals often do not readily distinguish between small and large quantities in their valuations of a good when the different quantities are *embedded* in one another. For example, William Desvousges and colleagues found that different samples of respondents value 2,000 migratory birds approximately the same as 200,000 birds, and small oil spills much the same as much larger oil spills (given that these are different samples, it does not directly test whether given individuals prefer more to less).[58] Two additional examples of embedding are described in Exhibit 15-3. It is unlikely that declining marginal utility can explain all or even most of the absence of different valuations for different quantities of goods.

When dealing with passive use values, embedding is probably the most worrisome problem identified by critics of CV. It goes to the very heart of welfare economics. Critics argue that the empirical evidence suggests that in these contexts respondents are not actually expressing their valuations but instead are expressing broad moral attitudes to environmental issues—a "warm glow" or "moral satisfaction."[59] However, Carson and colleagues have argued that most studies that manifest embedding problems, or scope insensitivity, are poorly designed and executed, and well-designed CV instruments do not manifest the problem.[60]

Starting Point Bias.   Prospect theory identifies anchoring as a common behavioral response to being asked to make complex judgments. A problem arises in CV when starting values are presented to respondents. The iterative bidding method is particularly prone to this problem because this method provides respondents with a specific initial starting "price."[61] Consider, for example, the Kristiansand Fjord study mentioned earlier in the chapter. It was found that a range starting at 200 kronor and progressing to 2,000 kronor produced different valuations than a range starting at 0 kronor and progressing to 2,000 kronor, even when there were no bids between 0 and 200 kronor.[62]

The dichotomous choice question format is intended to eliminate starting point bias. It has been argued, however, that "responses to dichotomous choice questions are

---

EXHIBIT 15-3

Daniel Kahneman and Jack L. Knetsch report that residents of Toronto expressed a willingness to pay increased taxes to prevent a drop in fishstocks in all Ontario lakes that was only slightly larger than their expressed WTP to preserve fish stocks in a small area of the province. This is implausible.

The same researchers studied the impact of embedding. They did so by specifying a good: (1) very broadly to one sample of respondents (environmental services that included "preserving wilderness areas, protecting wildlife, providing parks, preparing for disasters, controlling air pollution, insuring water quality, and routine treatment and disposal of industrial wastes") (2) considerably more narrowly to a second sample of respondents (to improve preparedness for disasters" with a subsequent allocation to go to "the availability of equipment and trained personnel for rescue operations"), and (3) more narrowly still to a third sample ("improve the availability of equipment and trained personnel for rescue operations"). Respondents in each sample were asked to express their willingness to pay for their "good." The differences in WTP among the three samples were not large.

Source: Adapted from Daniel Kahneman and Jack L. Knetsch, "Valuing Public Goods: The Purchase of Moral Satisfaction," *Journal of Environmental Economics and Management* 22(1) 1992, 57–70. (For a critique of this study, see V. Kerry Smith, "Comment: Arbitrary Values, Good Causes, and Premature Verdicts," *Journal of Environmental Economics and Management* 22(1) 1992, 71–89.)

---

very strongly influenced by starting-point bias, because respondents are likely to take initial cues of resource value from the solicited contribution amount (e.g., assuming it to be his/her share of the needed contribution)."[63] Moreover, there is at least some empirical evidence to support the contention that the dichotomous choice method is subject to starting point bias,[64] although WTP estimated from dichotomous choice responses appears to be less affected by the provision of information about the total cost of providing a good or the size of the group receiving it than does WTP estimated from open-ended surveys.[65]

Hypotheticality Bias versus Judgment Bias. In the last resort it is almost impossible to disentangle hypotheticality issues from various forms of judgment bias in nonuse contexts because they are essentially two different sides of the same coin. Hence, the same approach is required to minimize both: an effort to present the project or good in question as concretely as possible, at the lowest level of disaggregation as possible, and with as much realism concerning budget constraints as possible. Neutrality problems also appear to be generic to CV. But this problem is less worrisome because it can be made reasonably transparent with good research protocols.

WTP versus WTA

Economic theory implies that if individuals behave rationally, and if markets are working efficiently, then in most circumstances it should make little difference whether respondents to a CV survey are asked their WTP for receiving a good or their willingness to accept (WTA) the loss of a comparable good.[66] Similarly, it should make little difference whether they are asked their WTP to prevent a loss or their WTA for a comparable loss.

As we have already discussed, considerable evidence suggests that individuals demand greater monetary compensation to give up things that they already possess than they are willing to pay to acquire the same exact item. In experiments that actually require people to trade goods for money, as well as in other contexts, it has been found that required WTA amounts range from a ratio of four to fifteen times greater than WTP amounts.[67] Similar differences have also been found in CV studies, even with a well-specified market good. There is some evidence that this difference between WTP and WTA is attributable to loss aversion.[68]

There is also considerable evidence, however, that as the subjects in experiments become more experienced, differences between WTP and WTA shrink considerably, usually as a result of decreases in WTA amounts.[69] Other experimental evidence suggests that for nonmarket goods with imperfect substitutes the divergence between WTP and WTA persists even with experience.[70] In any event, CV survey contexts, which are typically one-shot events for respondents, do not present opportunities for learning. Moreover, they often involve nonmarket goods with no close substitutes.

Some commentators have argued that stated preferences are preferences and that, if respondents are actually being asked to give up something, then the relevant formulation is WTA. But even in a context in which something is being given up, analysts still have to decide whether to treat WTA as involving a judgment bias problem that requires adjustments. In view of the fact that experiments show learning effects in some contexts and, as discussed later, WTP amounts are much closer to estimates derived from methods based on revealed preferences, the usual procedure is to use WTP estimates.[71] This procedure is typically followed even in cases in which WTA questions fit the facts better than WTP questions—for example, as when the project involves the respondent giving up a good, such as a scenic view, that he or she currently consumes. The heuristic is, therefore, *that WTP question formats rather than WTA question formats should be used in CV in almost all cases.*

In thinking about WTP and WTA, one additional point should be kept in mind: We are concerned only about differences between the two *for the same individual.* The fact that different individuals have differing WTPs and WTAs is what makes markets work and presents no problem to CV.

The Strategic Response (Honesty) Problem

Will respondents answer honestly when asked about their WTP? It is frequently argued that respondents in CV surveys have incentives to behave *strategically,* that is, to misrepresent their true preferences in order to achieve a more desired outcome than would result if they honestly revealed their preferences. An analogy is often drawn between strategic behavior in CV studies and free riding in the provision of public goods.[72] The potential for strategic behavior in CV, however, is actually more varied than the free-riding characterization suggests.[73]

The Carson and Groves Framework.   Carson and Groves assess the nature of strategic responses to CV questions likely to be encountered in use of the major CV methods.[74] They begin by making the point that we should not expect respondents' answers necessarily to be consistent with economic theory, and hence appropriate for inclusion in

CBA, unless respondents believe that the survey is *consequential* in the sense that it could potentially influence some outcomes about which they care. In contrast, if respondents believe that the survey will have absolutely no influence on outcomes about which they care, then it is *inconsequential,* and economic theory offers no predictions about the nature of responses.

They next note that the design of consequential CV surveys falls under the theory of *mechanism design,* which deals with the problem of creating rules for collective choice based on signals sent by individuals. Mechanisms that provide incentives for individuals to reveal their preferences truthfully are called *incentive compatible.*

One of the central theorems of mechanism design is that, in the absence of restrictions on the domain of preferences,[75] mechanisms involving more than binary signals will always be incentive compatible.[76] Mechanisms employing binary signals will not always be incentive compatible, but depending on the specific circumstances of choice, they may be (in other words, a binary signal is a necessary, but not necessarily sufficient, condition). More complex signals provide an opportunity for individuals to misstate their preferences in order to obtain a more desirable outcome.

As a brief illustration, return to the choice situation presented Chapter 2. Table 2-2 shows how the mechanism, pair-wise majority rule voting, could result in an intransitive social ordering. Consider a case in which the mechanism is being implemented by first putting X against Y in round one and then, in round two, Z against the winner of round one. Note that the signal sent by the voters in this situation is not binary—it consists of *two* binary signals, one for each round. If the voters send truthful signals about their preferences, then X beats Y in round one and Z beats X in round two, so that the mechanism selects Z as the social choice, which is voter 1's least preferred outcome. Anticipating this, voter 1 has an incentive to misrepresent his preferences by voting for Y in round one, so that Y would win and be put against Z in round two and win. This misrepresentation of preferences in round one would result in Y, an outcome more desirable to voter 1 than the one that resulted from sending a truthful signal about his preferences in round one. Once the voters reach round two, it is as if they are facing a new choice situation in which they send only a binary signal. In this last round, there is no incentive to misrepresent preferences.

One immediate implication of this theorem is that continuous response formats, as used in the open-ended WTP method, or multiple response formats, as used in the contingent ranking method, will always be vulnerable to strategic responses that misstate true preferences.

Consider the open-ended WTP method. We can imagine two types of misrepresentation of preferences. First, assume that respondents perceive having to make payments that do not depend on their stated WTPs, that they have true WTPs above their anticipated payments, and that they anticipate that the likelihood of the good being provided depends on the aggregate of stated WTPs. They would then have an incentive to overstate their WTPs, so that the estimated aggregate WTP would be too high. The possibility of such overstatement was widely anticipated by economists. Yet, at least in comparison with the dichotomous choice method, which, as we will discuss, can be incentive compatible, it does not appear that such overstatement is a major problem in the open-ended WTP method.[77] One explanation is that the assumptions that make overstatement a desirable strategy for respondents may not often hold. For example, respondents may fear that their shares of the cost of providing the good will be a positive function of their stated WTPs and, hence, state WTPs that are as small as possible. However, they may also believe that the likelihood of provision depends on the fraction of respondents who state WTPs at or above the average cost of provision, rather than on aggregate WTP. If both of these assumptions hold, then a strategic respondent with a true WTP above the anticipated cost would state a WTP that is only slightly above the anticipated cost—above anticipated cost to increase the chances of provision but as little above as possible to minimize cost share.

Second, now consider respondents with true WTPs that are less than the costs that they anticipate would be imposed on them if the good were to be provided. Assume that they believe that the likelihood of provision depends on aggregate WTP. As they do not want the good provided, they have an incentive to state the smallest possible WTP, usually set to zero for goods researchers believe to be desirable. These strategic responses in the open-ended WTP method should lead to many zeros, and few WTP amounts under the respondents' perceived costs of provision. The larger the fraction of respondents following this strategy, the greater will be the underestimation of aggregate WTP.

As it involves a binary response, the dichotomous choice method *may* be incentive compatible. Carson and Groves note that incentive compatibility requires that payment for the good can be compelled and that the question deals only with a single issue. Table 15-2 summarizes the incentive properties of several circumstances in which the dichotomous choice method has been used.

Using the dichotomous choice method to elicit WTP for a new public (nonexcludable) good that will be funded with coercive payments by respondents meets the requirements for incentive compatibility. Respondents have no incentive to vote against their true preferences. Because CV is often the only way analysts can estimate WTP for public goods, this is reassuring. Incentive compatibility also holds for comparisons between two mutually exclusive public goods with the same cost. As long as respondents place a positive value on both goods, they have no incentive to misstate their preferred good.

Incentive compatibility is lost in cases in which payment is voluntary because it introduces a second issue, whether to donate or to purchase, into the choice situation. In the case of a public good to be funded by contributions, respondents who place any positive value on the good have an incentive to accept bids above their WTPs to increase the chances that the good is provided because they do not actually have to make a donation in that amount.[78] Similarly, respondents who have any probability of actually wanting a

TABLE 15-2 Incentive Properties of Dichotomous Choice Questions Applied to Types of Goods

Type of Good	*Incentive Property*
New public good with coercive payment	Incentive compatible
New public good with voluntary payment	Not incentive compatible
Introduction of new private good	Not incentive compatible
Choice between two new public goods	Incentive compatible
Choice between an existing and an alternative private good	Incentive compatible, but choice does not reveal information about quantity demanded

Source: Adapted from Richard T. Carson and Theodore Groves, "Incentive and Informational Properties of Preference Questions," *Environmental and Resource Economics* 37(1) 2007, p. 192.

new private (excludeable) good have an incentive to accept bids above their WTP to increase the chances that it will actually be provided because they can decline to purchase it if they decide that they do not want it. The problem is so severe for new private goods that dichotomous choice CV has largely been abandoned for this purpose.

Questions that ask respondents to choose between an existing private good and an alternative are incentive compatible about that choice as long as only potential users are surveyed. (The question will not be consequential for those who are not potential users.) Answers to the questions, however, do not reveal information about how much of the selected private good will actually be demanded. For example, a town may ask a sample of residents to choose between the existing skating rink, which is available only during daylight hours and has a small entrance fee, and a new skating rink with electric lighting, which would be available evenings and would have a higher entrance fee. The respondents have no incentive to misstate their true preferences over the choices, but the answers do not tell the town about how often residents will use the new facility.

Conclusion About the Importance of Strategic Responses.   The danger that strategic responses to CV questions will bias estimates of aggregate WTP cannot be assessed without considering both the elicitation method and the nature of the good being valued. The dichotomous choice method applied to the valuation of new public goods to be funded by taxes or other coercive payments can be designed to avoid strategic response bias. It is subject to an upward bias, however, if payments are voluntary. The open-ended WTP method will generally be subject to strategic response bias, most likely leading to aggregate WTP estimates that are too small if payments are coerced and too large if payments are voluntary.

HOW ACCURATE IS CONTINGENT VALUATION?

It is possible to test the accuracy of CV WTP estimates in a number of ways.[79] The first method is to compare CV values to those generated by other indirect methods. CV values have been found to be approximately the same as those derived from travel cost studies.[80] They have also been found to be reasonably similar to prices derived from hedonic price regressions[81] and to the market prices of substitutes.[82] Wesley Magat and Kip Viscusi tested whether respondents' WTP for risk reductions associated with an insecticide and toilet bowl cleaner were consistent with standard economic theory or subject to the kinds of judgment biases described earlier. In general, they did not find strong evidence of bias.[83]

The second type of comparison, one that is more common and more appropriate, is between respondents' CV statements and their actual behavior when they participate in an experiment that utilizes a simulated or constructed market for the good in question.[84] Results from studies that have used experimental techniques to examine CV accuracy typically suggest that CV valuations of WTP relying on open-ended and dichotomous choice methods approximate actual market transactions, although there is some tendency for overvaluation.[85] In assessing these experiments, it is useful to keep in mind that the simulated market only approximates the workings of a real market; for example, there is only one opportunity to buy the good. In addition, the experiments have only been conducted in contexts in which respondents clearly derive use value from the good.

Richard Bishop and Thomas Heberlein have conducted a number of experiments along these lines. The example presented in Exhibit 15-4 is typical of these experiments.

John Loomis has investigated how consistent household CV valuations are over time. Though not a direct test of accuracy, his investigation is relevant because consistency is a prerequisite for accuracy. He surveyed both visitors and the general public's WTP for recreational, option, existence, and bequest values derived from Mono Lake in California. Identical surveys were administered to the same individuals eight or nine months apart. The results were virtually identical.[86]

Though the evidence tends to suggest that CV is plausible in use contexts, the jury is still out in terms of nonuse values, given the ordering, embedding, noncommitment, and starting point problems discussed previously. Obviously, given the nature of nonuse values, it is much more difficult to elicit WTP from observed behavior. Nonetheless, with sufficient cleverness researchers may be able to find ways to do so. For example, as noted in Chapter 9, voluntary contributions to environmental causes might serve as the basis for estimation. Market-like experiments might also be used.[87] For example, individuals who have expressed WTP for nonuse could be given the option of returning none, part, or all of the checks sent to them by experimenters (as described in Exhibit 15-4), thus testing noncommitment bias. Successfully implementing

---

EXHIBIT 15-4

A wildlife area in Wisconsin is periodically opened to hunting. Hunters require a special permit to participate in these hunts. The permits are issued free to the winners of a lottery. For the 1984 lottery, a large number of applications were received. As a result of the lottery, 150 permits to hunt were issued.

To measure WTA, half of these hunters also received a letter explaining the study and a check made out in their name. To cash these checks, the hunters had to relinquish their permits. The denominations of the checks, which ranged randomly from $18 to $518, corresponded to the dichotomous choice method described earlier. The other half of the hunters received a similar letter with a hypothetical payment offer drawn from the same range as the first half. They were asked if they would have been willing to give up their permits for the hypothetical amounts stated in their letters.

To measure WTP, 150 unsuccessful lottery participants were selected at random. Again, 75 received a letter explaining that a hunting permit was available if they paid the amount specified in the letter. The amounts covered the same range as described previously. The other 75 were asked the same question hypothetically. That is, they were asked the CV question rather than given the opportunity to reveal their preferences through purchases.

Looking first at WTP, the results indicated that the CV valuations ($35) were only slightly higher than those measured through revealed preference ($31), a difference that was not statistically significant. These results suggest that noncommitment bias was not a major problem in this context. But, consistent with the findings discussed earlier, WTA valuations were much higher than WTP valuations. Furthermore, the CV valuations ($420) were considerably higher than those actually revealed by check cashing ($153).

Source: Adapted from Richard C. Bishop and Thomas A. Heberlein, "The Contingent Valuation Method," in Rebecca L. Johnson and Gary V. Johnson, eds., *Economic Valuation of Natural Resources: Issues, Theory, and Application* (Boulder, CO: Westview Press, 1990), 81–104.

such experiments would be extremely difficult with current levels of knowledge and typically available resources, however.

The Potential for Calibration

It has long been recognized in marketing research that it may be necessary to *calibrate* respondents' valuations of goods in various ways to obtain more accurate estimates of their WTP. As noted earlier, noncommitment bias, which may also be interpreted as strategic response bias, is a well-recognized problem in marketing research when individuals are asked to express their valuations of market goods. Kenneth Arrow has concluded, "A hypothesis to be explored is that, if the results of CVs for nonuse values were suitably calibrated, they would provide useful and reliable estimates."[88] Testing Arrow's hypothesis may be one of the most valuable areas of future research on CV.

The Accuracy of Different CV Methods and Proneness to Biases

Richard Bishop and Thomas Heberlein have conducted experiments comparing the size of valuations from different elicitation formats (again, this is in a use context). They conclude that:

> These experiments indicate that contingent values for willingness to pay may be somewhat high, but for open-ended and dichotomous choice questions the difference was not large enough to be statistically significant. . . . Bidding seems to introduce a substantial upward bias. . . . Contingent compensation demanded tended to produce excessive values when an open-ended question was asked and values that were biased substantially upward compared to values obtained from actual cash transactions when dichotomous choice questions were used.[89]

Other researchers have also addressed this issue. V. Kerry Smith and William Desvousges compared the valuations from several CV methods in their study of improvements in the quality of water in the Monongahela River. Their analysis suggests that starting point bias is important with iterative bidding: A low starting point ($25) generated lower valuations than other methods, while a high starting point ($125) produced valuations higher than other methods. Open-ended questions produced fairly similar valuations. Overall, mean valuations from different CV methods ranged from $7 to $36 for one water quality change, from $4 to $31 for another change, and from $11 to $51 for a third change.[90]

William Desvousges and his colleagues have compared open-ended question responses with dichotomous choice responses to the same questions. They found that in some contexts the differences in the mean WTP valuations were not statistically significant, but in other contexts they were. They also found the dichotomous choice method generated a considerable number of very high valuations.[91] This is consistent with the likely relative importance of strategic response bias discussed previously, as well as with the relatively lower precision of the dichotomous choice method relative to direct elicitation methods for given sample sizes.

HEURISTICS FOR THE DESIGN AND USE OF CV SURVEYS

Several experts in CV have suggested overall criteria for evaluating CV instruments. Ronald Cummings, David Brookshire, and William Schulze, for example, suggest five criteria for evaluating instruments. First, respondents should understand and be familiar with the good that is being valued. Second, respondents should have, or be given, experience in both valuation and the choice procedure. Third, there should be as little uncertainty as possible about the details of the project. All three of these concerns can best be addressed by attempting to reduce hypotheticality—for example, by employing quality ladders, by stressing realistically and concretely the substitution possibilities, and by presenting gains (benefits) in percentage terms as well as in absolute terms. Fourth, WTP rather than WTA should be used for valuation purposes. Fifth, attempts should be made to avoid anchoring and starting point bias.[92]

Heuristics for Using Estimates from Previous CV Studies

Because CV surveys are inevitably complex and expensive, many analysts are more concerned with using values derived from existing CV studies than they are in going out and doing CV surveys themselves. In an examination of alternative environmental regulatory policies for dealing with water pollution, Ralph Luken illustrates how existing CV estimates can be "plugged in" to a CBA. Specifically, he extrapolates previous CV valuations of benefits from the Monongahela River studies discussed earlier in this chapter. His analysis provides a useful example of how to use plug-in values and is described more fully in Chapter 16.[93] He is careful to specify which studies and which specific estimates he is using, the specific assumptions he makes in the extrapolations, the quality changes that are involved, the distinction between use and any nonuse components, and any potential remaining biases. He also performs sensitivity analysis.

Environment Canada, in cooperation with several international organizations, has developed a database of CV and other studies that value environmental impacts.[94] In order to facilitate the use of findings from these studies in CBA, it provides an abstract for each study describing the study area and its population characteristics, the environmental asset being valued, the research methods employed, and the monetary values that were estimated. Access to the online database is by subscription.[95]

CONCLUSION

Contingent valuation is now relatively uncontroversial in contexts involving use values, although it may overestimate them. Its accuracy in nonuse contexts is more controversial, yet it is in this context where its potential usefulness is likely to be the greatest. Doubts about the accuracy of CV in nonuse contexts stem from the problems of hypotheticality and the attendant judgment biases that appear to flourish in the nonuse context. Strategic response bias, on the other hand, does not appear to be a major problem in the use of the dichotomous choice method to value public goods with coercive payments, and neutrality bias can be minimized by use of appropriate survey techniques. Probably the most important topics for future CV research are the directional biases in particular methods and the development of techniques that allow reliable calibration.

EXERCISES FOR CHAPTER 15

1. The construction of a dam that would provide hydroelectric power would result in the loss of two streams: one that is now used for sport fishing, and another that does not support game fish but is part of a wilderness area.

   a. Imagine that a CV method is used to estimate the social cost of the loss of each of these streams. Would you be equally confident in the two sets of estimates? Why?

   b. Consider two general approaches to asking CV questions about the streams. The first approach attempts to elicit how much compensation people would require to give up the streams. The second approach attempts to elicit how much people would be willing to pay to keep the streams. Which approach would you recommend? Why?

2. A number of residents of Dullsville have complained to the mayor that the center of town looks shabby compared to the centers of many other nearby towns. At the mayor's request, the Parks Department has put together a proposal for converting the town square parking lot into a sitting park with flower displays—it modeled the design on a similar park in the neighboring town of Flowerville. The annualized cost of installing and maintaining the park, and relocating parking to nearby Short Street, would be about $120,000. With about 40,000 households paying property taxes, the project would cost an average household about $3 per year.

   You have been asked to give advice about conducting a survey to measure the benefits of the project.

   a. The Parks Department proposes conducting a telephone survey. Does this seem like an appropriate survey vehicle?

   b. How might a random sample be drawn for a telephone survey?

   c. Write a statement that could be read by the interviewer to describe the project.

   d. Write questions to implement the open-ended WTP method.

   e. Propose a procedure for implementing the dichotomous choice method.

3. Consider a project that would involve purchasing marginal farmland that would then be allowed to return to wetlands capable of supporting migrant birds. Researchers designed a survey to implement the dichotomous choice method. They reported the following data.

Stated Price (annual payment in dollars)	Fraction of Respondents Accepting Stated Price (percent)
0	98
5	91
10	82
15	66
20	48
25	32
30	20
35	12
40	6
45	4
50	2

What is the mean WTP for the sampled population?

NOTES

1. Most observers attribute the origins of CV to Robert K. David, "Recreation Planning as an Economic Problem," *Natural Resources Journal* 3(2) 1963, 239–249.

2. Two helpful CV overviews are Ian J. Bateman and Kenneth G. Willis, eds., *Valuing Environmental Preferences: Theory and Practice of the Contingent Valuation Method in the U.S., EU, and Developing Countries* (Oxford and New York: Oxford University Press, 1999) and Timothy C. Haab and Kenneth E. McConnell, *Valuing Environmental and Natural Resources: The Econometrics of Non-Market Valuation* (Cheltenham, UK: Edward Elgar Publishers, 2003).

3. William H. Desvousges, V. Kerry Smith, and Ann Fisher, "Option Price Estimates for Water Quality Improvements: A Contingent Valuation Study for the Monongahela River," *Journal of Environmental Economics and Management* 14(3) 1987, 248–267; and Richard C. Bishop and Thomas A. Heberlein, "Measuring Values of Extra-Market Goods: Are Indirect Measures Biased?" *American Journal of Agricultural Economics* 61(5) 1979, 926–930.

4. Alan Diener, Bernie O'Brien, and Amiram Gafni, "Health Care Contingent Valuation Studies: A Review and Classification of the Literature," *Health Economics* 7(4) 1998, 313–326.

5. For example, see David Maddison and S. Mourato, "Valuing Different Road Options for Stonehenge," *Conservation and Management of Archeological Sites* 4(4) 2001, 203–212; Peter C. Boxall, Jeffrey Englin, and Wiktor L. Adamowicz, "Valuing Aboriginal Artifacts: A Combined Revealed-Stated Preference Approach," *Journal of Environmental Economics and Management* 45(2) 2003, 213–230; Richard T. Woodward and Yong-Suhk Wui, "The Economic Value of Wetland Services: A Meta-Analysis," *Ecological Economics* 37(2) 2001, 257–270; and Bruce K. Johnson and John C. Whitehead, "Value of Public Goods from Sports Stadiums: The CVM Approach," *Contemporary Economic Policy* 18(1) 2000, 48–58.

6. Raymond J. Kopp, Paul R. Portney, and V. Kerry Smith, "The Economics of Natural Resource Damages after *Ohio v. U.S. Dept. of the Interior,*" *Environmental Law Reporter* 20(4) 1990, 10, 127–10, 131.

7. Kenneth Arrow, Robert Solow, Paul Portney, Edward Leamer, Roy Radner, and Howard Schuman, "Report of the NOAA Panel on Contingent Valuation," *Federal Register* 58(10) January 15, 1993, 4601–4614.

8. On this point, see Daniel McFadden and Gregory Leonard, "Issues in the Contingent Valuation of Environmental Goods: Methodologies for Data Collection and Analysis," in J. A. Hausman, ed., *Contingent Valuation: A Critical Assessment* (New York: North-Holland, 1993), 165–208.

9. Arrow et al., "Report of the NOAA Panel on Continent Valuation," p. 4608.

10. For an example of this approach, see J. C. Horvath, *Southeastern Economic Survey of Wildlife Recreation* (Atlanta, GA: Environmental Research Group, Georgia State University, 1974).

11. One compromise between the open-ended format and the provision of "guidance" that has been used in in-person interviews is the *payment card* with a range of prices. For example, in the Nestucca oil spill CV survey, respondents were asked to specify the maximum amount their households would pay for programs to prevent oil spills. They were then shown a payment card with dollar amounts ranging from $0 to $5,000 and asked to circle the amount closest to their evaluation. Robert Rowe, William D. Schulze, W. Douglas Shaw, David Schenk and Lauraine G. Chestnut, "Contingent Valuation of Natural Resource Damage Due to Nestucca Oil Spill," prepared for the Department of Wildlife, Ministry of the Environment, BC, and Environment Canada, by RCG/Hagler, Bailly Inc., June 1991.

12. James L. Regens, "Measuring Environmental Benefits with Contingent Markets," *Public Administration Review* 51(4) 1991, 345–352.

13. For an example, see V. Kerry Smith and William H. Desvousges, *Measuring Water Quality Benefits*

(Boston, MA: Kluwer Nijhoff Publishing, 1986), Chapter 6.

14. Baruch Fischhoff and Louis A. Cox Jr., "Conceptual Framework for Regulatory Benefits Assessment," in Judith D. Bentkover, Vincent T. Covello, and Jeryl Mumpower, eds., *Benefits Assessment: The State of the Art* (Boston, MA: D. Reidel Publishing Co., 1986), 51–84.

15. For an example that uses this method, see John Loomis, *Integrated Public Lands Management* (New York: Columbia University Press, 1993), 276–279.

16. Selecting appropriate bid prices is one of the most difficult tasks analysts face in applying the dichotomous choice method. The bid prices must be spaced sufficiently far apart so that they show a range of acceptance rates, ideally from about .85 to about .15. Simply spreading bid prices over a very wide range, however, is unsatisfactory because, for a given sample size, statistical efficiency in estimating WTP from the pattern of acceptances is greater for fewer bid prices. This suggests the importance of conducting pre-test surveys to determine an appropriate set of bid prices. (Of course, in any survey study, pre-tests are important for ensuring that respondents understand questions.) See Barbara J. Kanninen, "Bias in Discrete Response Contingent Valuation," *Journal of Environmental Economics and Management* 28(1) 1995, 114–125.

17. On the technical issues relating to interpreting the function as utility and how to deal with truncation, see W. Michael Hanemann, "Welfare Evaluations in Contingent Valuation Experiments with Discrete Responses," *American Journal of Agricultural Economics,* 66(3) 1984, 332–341.

18. The formula for computing the WTP of the average member of the sample can be derived more formally if some additional notation is introduced. (Note that this derivation involves approximating the expected value of WTP.) Assume that the offer prices are $0, v, 2v, 3v, \ldots Nv$, where v is the interval between prices, and Nv is the maximum price offered. For example, if the offer prices were 0, $10, $20, $30, \ldots, $200, then $v = \$10$ and $N = 20$. Let $\mathbf{F}[X]$ be the fraction of respondents offered price X who accept the offer—this is the height of the bar in the histogram that sits above X. In order to calculate the expected value of WTP, we require the probability that each offer price is the *maximum* amount that a respondent would be willing to pay. We can approximate this for offer amount $\$kv$ with the expression: $\mathbf{F}[kv] - \mathbf{F}[(k+1)v]$ for $k = 0, 1, \ldots, N - 1$, which is roughly the probability of a respondent accepting $\$kv$ minus the probability of accepting a larger offer price, $\$(k + 1)v$. The mean WTP (that is, the WTP of a randomly selected respondent) is then approximately the sum of the products of maximum payments times their probabilities:

$$\mathbf{E}[\text{WTP}] = Nv\mathbf{F}[Nv] + (N-1)v\{\mathbf{F}[(N-1)v] - \mathbf{F}[Nv]\} + (N-2)v\{\mathbf{F}[(N-2)v] - \mathbf{F}[(N-1)]\} + \cdots + 0\{\mathbf{F}[0] - \mathbf{F}[v]\}$$

Collecting terms yields the simple expression:

$$\mathbf{E}[\text{WPT}] = v\sum_{k=0}^{N}\mathbf{F}[kv]$$

19. For a treatment of estimation issues, see W. Michael Hanemann and Barbara Kanninen, "The Statistical Analysis of Discrete Response CV Data," in Ian J. Bateman and Ken G. Willis, eds., *Valuing Environmental Preferences: Theory and Practice of the Contingent Valuation Method in the U.S., EC, and Developing Countries,* 302–441; and Haab and McConnell, *Valuing Environmental and Natural Resources.*

20. A complication arises because the statistical model usually assumes an infinite range for x. In practice, surveys use offer prices with a finite range, usually bounded from below at zero. Averaging over this finite range will miss some of the probability assumed by the statistical model. A correction to help account for this truncation bias involves rescaling the distribution to account for the missing areas in the tails of the distribution. See Kevin J. Boyle, Michael P. Welsh, and Richard C. Bishop, "Validation of Empirical Measures of Welfare Change: Comment," *Land Economics* 64(1) 1988, 94–98.

21. See Haab and McConnell, *Valuing Environmental and Natural Resources*, for a systematic and comprehensive treatment of the WTP modeling issues.

22. For an overview of the statistical issues in estimating aggregate WTP from such models, see Timothy Park, John B. Loomis, and Michael Creel, "Confidence Intervals for Evaluating Benefits Estimates from Dichotomous Choice Contingent Valuation Studies," *Land Economics* 67(1) 1991, 64–73.

23. Joseph A. Herriges and Jason F. Shogren, "Starting Point Bias in Dichotomous Choice Valuation with Follow-Up Questioning," *Journal of Environmental Economics and Management* 30(1) 1996, 112–131.

24. Richard T. Carson and Theodore Groves, "Incentive and Informational Properties of Preference Questions," *Environmental and Resource Economics* 37(1) 2007, 181–210.

25. Empirical work supports this weighted averaging explanation; see Anthony C. Burton, Katherine S. Carson, Susan M. Chilton, and W. George Hutchinson, "An Experimental Investigation of Explanations for Inconsistencies in Responses to Second Offers in Double Referenda," *Journal of Environmental Economics and Management* 46(3) 1996, 472–489.

26. Robert J. Johnston, Stephen K. Swallow, and Thomas F. Weaver, "Estimating Willingness to Pay and Resource Tradeoffs with Different Payment Mechanisms: An Evaluation of a Funding Guarantee for Watershed Management," *Journal of Environmental Economics and Management* 38(1) 1999, 97–120.

27. See "The Review Panel's Assessment," 180–204.

28. See Robert P. Berrens, Alok K. Bohara, Hank Jenkins-Smith, Carol Silva, and David L. Weimer, "The Advent of Internet Surveys for Political Research: A Comparison of Telephone and Internet Samples," *Political Analysis* 11(1) 2003, 1–22; and Robert P. Berrens, Alok K. Bohara, Hank C. Jenkins-Smith, Carol L. Silva, and David L. Weimer, "Information and Effort in Contingent Valuation Surveys: Application to Global Climate Change Using National Internet Samples," *Journal of Environmental Economics and Management* 47(2) 2004, 331–363.

29. For issues specifically relevant to CV, see Steven F. Edwards and Glen D. Anderson, "Overlooked Biases in Contingent Valuation Surveys: Some Considerations," *Land Economics* 63(2) 1987, 168–178.

30. Richard T. Carson, "Constructed Markets," in John B. Braden and Charles D. Kolstad, eds., *Measuring the Demand for Environmental Quality* (New York: Elsevier Science Publishers, 1991), 152.

31. For an example of an attempt to estimate the extent of a recreational market, see V. Kerry Smith and Raymond J. Kopp, "The Spatial Limits of the Travel Cost Recreational Demand Model," *Land Economics* 56(1) 1980, 64–72.

32. Desvousges, Smith, and Fisher, "Option Price Estimates for Water Quality Improvements."

33. For a review, see John B. Loomis, "Expanding Contingent Value Sample Estimates to Aggregate Benefit Estimates: Current Practices and Proposed Solutions," *Land Economics* 63(4) 1987, 396–402.

34. The most comprehensive criticisms of CV can be found in Hausman, ed., *Contingent Valuation: A Critical Assessment.*

35. William D. Schulze, Ronald G. Cummings, and David S. Brookshire, *Methods Development in Measuring Benefits of Environmental Improvements, Vol. II* (Washington, D.C.: Report to U.S. EPA, 1983).

36. For an extensive discussion of the attitude-behavior nexus, see Robert C. Mitchell and Richard T. Carson, *Using Surveys to Value Public Goods: The Contingent Valuation Method* (Washington D.C.: Resource for the Future 1989), 175–187.

37. Baruch Fischhoff and Lita Furey, "Measuring Values: A Conceptual Framework for Interpreting Transactions with Special Reference to Contingent Valuation of Visibility," *Journal of Risk and Uncertainty* 1(2) 1988, 147–184, at 179–180.

38. In marketing, the technique called *conjoint analysis* is used to elicit consumer valuations for new, unfamiliar goods. For a review, see Daniel McFadden, "The Choice Theory Approach to Market Research," *Marketing Science* 5(4) 1986, 275–297.

39. Richard T. Carson, Nicholas E. Flores, and Norman F. Meade, "Contingent Valuation:

Controversies and Evidence," *Environmental and Resource Economics* 19(2) 2001, 173–210, at 178.

40. For a discussion of this point, see Ronald G. Cummings, David S. Brookshire, and William D. Schulze, *Valuing Environmental Goods: An Assessment of the Contingent Valuation Method,* (Totawa, NJ: Rowman & Allenhead, 1986) at 43, 253. For the case that hypothetical bias is real and endemic, although variable across locations, see Mariah D. Ehmke, Jayson L. Lusk, and John A. List, "Is Hypothetical Bias a Universal Phenomenon? A Multinational Investigation," Land Economics 84(3) 2008, 489–500.

41. Fischhoff and Furey, "Measuring Values: A Conceptual Framework for Interpreting Transactions with Special Reference to Contingent Valuation of Visibility," Table 1, 156. Effectively implementing contingent valuation surveys in developing countries is especially difficult. See Dale Whittington, "Improving the Performance of Contingent Valuation Studies in Developing Countries," Environmental and Resource Economics 22(1&2) 2002, 323–367.

42. Daniel A. Hagen, James W. Vincent, and Patrick G. Welle, "The Benefits of Preserving Old-Growth Forests and the Northern Spotted Owl," *Contemporary Policy Issues* 10(2) 1992, 13–16.

43. William McKillop, "Use of Contingent Valuation in Northern Spotted Owls Studies: A Critique," *Journal of Forestry* 90(8) 1992, 36–37.

44. See David L. Weimer and Aidan R. Vining, *Policy Analysis: Concepts and Practice,* 5th ed. (Upper Saddle River, NJ: Pearson Prentice Hall, 2011), 122–123.

45. For an extensive review of this issue and other biases, see Colin F. Camerer and Howard Kunreuther, "Decision Processes for Low Probability Events: Policy Implications," *Journal of Policy Analysis and Management* 8(4) 1989, 565–592.

46. Daniel Kahneman and Amos Tversky, "Prospect Theory," *Econometrica* 47(2) 1979, 263–292. Many of the violations of expected utility hypothesis that can be explained by prospect theory can also be explained by assuming people maximize expected utility but employ Bayesian updating of probabilities; see W. Kip Viscusi,

"Prospective Reference Theory: Toward an Explanation of the Paradoxes," *Journal of Risk and Uncertainty* 2(3) 1989, 235–263.

47. Richard H. Thaler, "Towards a Positive Theory of Consumer Choice," *Journal of Economic Behavior and Organization* 1(1) 1980, 39–60. For some empirical evidence on loss aversion in housing markets, see David Genesove and Christopher Mayer, "Loss Aversion and Seller Behavior: Evidence from the Housing Market," *Quarterly Journal of Economics* 116(4) 2001, 1233–1260.

48. It may seem somewhat artificial to separate hypotheticality from noncommitment bias. However, as emphasized earlier, hypotheticality does not appear to generate upward or downward bias, whereas, as we will see, noncommitment does appear to bias valuations upward.

49. See, for example, Linda F. Jamieson and Frank M. Bass, "Adjusting Stated Intention Measures to Predict Trial Purchase of New Products: A Comparison of Models and Methods," *Journal of Marketing Research* 26(3) 1989, 336–345.

50. Helen R. Neill, Ronald G. Cummings, Philip T. Ganderton, Glenn W. Harrison, and Thomas McGuckin, "Hypothetical Surveys and Economic Commitments," *Land Economics* 70(2) 1994, 145–154; and Kalle Seip and Jon Strand, "Willingness to Pay for Environmental Goods in Norway: A Contingent Valuation Study with Real Payment," *Environmental and Resource Economics* 2(1) 1992, 91–106.

51. Michael A. Kemp and Christopher Maxwell, "Exploring a Budget Context for Contingent Valuation Estimates," 217–265, in Hausman, ed., *Contingent Valuation: A Critical Assessment.*

52. I. J. Bateman and I. H. Langford, "Budget-Constrained, Temporal, and Question-Ordering Effects in Contingent Valuation Studies," *Environment and Planning A* 29(7) 1997, 1215–1228.

53. George Tolley and Alan Randall, "Establishing and Valuing the Effects of Improved Visibility in the Eastern United States," Report to the U.S. EPA, Washington, D.C., 1983.

54. Karl C. Samples and James R. Hollyer, "Contingent Valuation of Wildlife Resources in the Presence of Substitutes and Complements," in Rebecca L. Johnson and Gary V. Johnson, eds., *Economic Valuation of Natural Resources: Issues,*

Theory, and Application, (Boulder, CO: Westview Press, 1990), 177–192.

55. See Peter A. Diamond, Jerry A. Hausman, Gregory K. Leonard, and Mike Denning, "Does Contingent Valuation Measure Preferences? Experimental Evidence," in Hausman, ed., *Contingent Valuation: A Critical Assessment,* 43–85.

56. See the heated argument between Peter Diamond and Richard Carson, in Hausman, ed., *Contingent Valuation: A Critical Assessment,* 87–89.

57. The case that these effects adequately explain the empirical findings is made in Carson, Flores, and Meade, "Contingent Valuation: Controversies and Evidence," 186–189; see also Richard T. Carson, Nicholas E. Flores, and Michael Hanemann, "Sequencing and Valuing Public Goods," *Journal of Environmental Economics and Management* 36(3) 1998, 314–323.

58. William H. Desvousges, F. Reed Johnson, Richard W. Dunford, Sara P. Hudson, and K. Nicole Wilson, "Measuring Natural Resources Damages with Contingent Valuation: Tests of Validity and Reliability," in Hausman, ed., *Contingent Valuation: A Critical Assessment,* 91–159.

59. Daniel Kahneman and Jack L. Knetsch, "Valuing Public Goods: The Purchase of Moral Satisfaction," *Journal of Environmental Economics and Management* 22(1) 1992, 57–70, at 64–68.

60. Carson, Flores, and Meade, "Contingent Valuation: Controversies and Evidence," *Environmental and Resource Economics.*

61. Kevin J. Boyle, Richard C. Bishop, and Michael P. Walsh, "Starting Point Bias in Contingent Valuation Bidding Games," *Land Economics* 16(2) 1985, 188–194.

62. Regens, "Measuring Environmental Benefits with Contingent Markets," 347–348.

63. Walter J. Mead, "Review and Analysis of State-of-the-Art Contingent Valuation Studies," in Hausman, ed., *Contingent Valuation: A Critical Assessment,* 305–332.

64. See Trudy A. Cameron and D. D. Huppert, "Referendum Contingent Valuation Estimates: Sensitivity to the Assignment of Offered Values," *Journal of the American Statistical Association* 86(416) 1991, 910–918.

65. Alok K. Bohara, Michael McKee, Robert P. Berrens, Hank Jenkins-Smith, Carol L. Silva, and David S. Brookshire, "Effects of Total Cost and Group-Size Information on Willingness to Pay Responses: Open Ended vs. Dichotomous Choice," *Journal of Environmental Economics and Management* 35(2) 1998, 142–163.

66. However, Michael Hanemann in "Willingness to Pay and Willingness to Accept: How Much Can They Differ?" *American Economic Review* 81(3) 1991, 635–647 points out that there is no reason why WTA should not be considerably larger than WTP in certain circumstances. For example, one cannot pay more than one's income year after year to save one's own life, but there may be no finite offer that could make one willingly give up one's life.

67. Jack Knetsch and J. S. Sinden, "Willingness to Pay and Compensation Demanded: Experimental Evidence of an Unexpected Disparity in Measures of Value," *Quarterly Journal of Economics* 99(3) 1984, 507–521; Shelby Gerking, Menno De Haan, and William Schulze, "The Marginal Value of Job Safety: A Contingent Valuation Study," *Journal of Risk and Uncertainty,* 1(2) 1988, 185–199; and Wesley Magat and W. Kip Viscusi, *Informational Approaches to Regulation* (Cambridge, MA: MIT Press, 1992).

68. Timothy McDaniels, "Reference Points, Loss Aversion, and Contingent Values for Auto Safety," *Journal of Risk and Uncertainty* 5(2) 1992, 187–200.

69. Don L. Coursey, John J. Hovis, and William D. Schulze, "The Disparity between Willingness to Accept and Willingness to Pay Measures of Value," *Quarterly Journal of Economics,* 102(3) 1987, 679–690; Jason F. Shogren, Seung Y. Shin, Dermot J. Hayes, and James B. Kliebenstein, "Resolving the Differences in Willingness to Pay and Willingness to Accept," *American Economic Review* 84(1) 1994, 255–270; and Wiktor L. Adamovicz, Vinay Bhardwaj, and Bruce McNab, "Experiments on the Difference Between Willingness to Pay and Willingness to Accept," *Land Economics* 64(4) 1993, 416–427.

70. Shogren, Shin, Hayes, and Kliebenstein, "Resolving the Differences in Willingness to Pay and Willingness to Accept."

71. Arrow et al., "Report of the NOAA Panel on Continent Valuation," 4608.

72. On free riding in the provision of public goods, see Oliver Kim and Mark Walker, "The Free Rider Problem: Experimental Evidence," *Public Choice* 43(1) 1984, 3–24 and Linda Goetz, T. F. Glover, and B. Biswas, "The Effects of Group Size and Income on Contributions to the Corporation for Public Broadcasting," *Public Choice* 77(2) 1993, 407–414.

73. Mitchell and Carson, *Using Surveys to Value Public Goods: The Contingent Valuation Method.*

74. Carson and Groves, "Incentive and Informational Properties of Preference Questions."

75. On the domain of preferences, see the discussion of Arrow's Possibility Theorem in Chapter 2.

76. Alan Gibbard, "Manipulation of Voting Schemes: A General Result," *Econometrica* 41(4) 1973, 587–601; and Mark A. Satterthwaite, "Strategy-Proofness and Arrow's Conditions: Existence and Correspondence Theorems for Voting Procedures and Social Welfare Functions," *Journal of Economic Theory* 10(2) 1975, 187–217.

77. See Kevin J. Boyle, F. Reed Johnson, Daniel W. McCollum, William H. Desvousges, Richard W. Dunford, and Sara P. Hudson, "Valuing Public Goods: Discrete versus Continuous Contingent Valuation Responses," *Land Economics* 72(3) 1996, 381–396.

78. A number of studies have found a large divergence between WTP as expressed in contingent choice CV and actual donations. For a review, including a discussion of using follow-up questions on the certainty of donation to adjust contingent donations, see Patricia A. Champ, Richard C. Bishop, Thomas C. Brown, and Daniel W. McCollum, "Using Donation Mechanisms to Value Nonuse Benefits from Public Goods," *Journal of Environmental Economics and Management* 33(2) 1997, 151–162.

79. For an overview and a listing of relevant studies, see V. K. Smith, "Nonmarket Valuation of Environmental Resources: An Interpretive Appraisal," *Land Economics* 69(1) 1993, 1–26, at 8–14, and Table 1.

80. See William K. Desvousges, V. Kerry Smith, and Matthew P. McGivney, "A Comparison of Alternative Approaches for Estimating Recreation and Related Benefits of Water Quality Improvements," Report to U.S. EPA, Research Triangle Institute, 1983; and Christine Sellar, John R. Stoll, and Jean-Paul Chavas, "Validation of Empirical Measures of Welfare Change: A Comparison of Nonmarket Techniques," *Land Economics* 61(2) 1985, 156–175. Smith and Desvousges, *Measuring Water Quality Benefits,* compare CV to "simple" travel cost methods.

81. David S. Brookshire, Mark A. Thayer, William D. Schulze, and Ralph C. d'Arge, "Valuing Public Goods: A Comparison of Survey and Hedonic Approaches," *American Economic Review* 72(1) 1982, 165–177.

82. Mark A. Thayer, "Contingent Valuation Techniques for Assessing Environmental Impacts: Further Evidence," *Journal of Environmental Economics and Management* 8(1) 1981, 27–44.

83. Magat and Viscusi, *Informational Approaches to Regulation,* Chapter 7.

84. For a listing of such studies, see Carson, "Constructed Markets," at 121–126.

85. Coursey, Hovis, and Schulze, "The Disparity Between Willingness to Accept and Willingness to Pay Measures of Value"; Mark Dickie, Ann Fisher, and Shelby Gerking, "Market Transactions and Hypothetical Demand Data: A Comparative Study," *Journal of the American Statistical Society* 82(398) 1987, 69–75; Craig E. Landry and John A. List, "Using Ex Ante Approaches to Obtain Signals for Value in Contingent Markets: Evidence from the Field," *American Journal of Agricultural Economics,* 89(2) 2007, 420–429.

86. John Loomis, "Test-Retest Reliability of the Contingent Valuation Method: A Comparison of General Population and Visitor Responses," *American Journal of Agricultural Economics* 71(1) 1989, 76–84.

87. For a discussion of this possibility, see Douglas M. Larson, "On Measuring Existence Value," *Land Economics* 69(3) 1993, 377–388.

88. Kenneth Arrow, "Contingent Valuation of Nonuse Values: Observations and Questions," in Hausman, ed., *Contingent Valuation: A Critical Assessment,* 479–483.

89. Bishop and Heberlein, "The Contingent Valuation Method," 97.

90. Smith and Desvousges, *Measuring Water Quality Benefits,* Table 105, 271.

91. Desvousges, Johnson, Dunford, Hudson, and Wilson, "Measuring Natural Resources Damages with Contingent Valuation: Tests of Validity and Reliability."

92. Summarized from "Comparison Studies: What Is Accuracy," 71–109, and "reference operating conditions," Table 13-1, p. 230, in "Summary and Conclusions," 205–236 in Cummings, Brookshire, and Schulze, *Valuing Environmental Goods: An Assessment of the Contingent Valuation Method.*

93. Ralph A. Luken, *Efficiency in Environmental Regulation: A Benefit-Cost Analysis of Alternative Approaches* (Boston, MA: Kluwer Academic Publishers, 1990), 45–53.

94. Richard T. Carson, "Contingent Valuation: A User's Guide," *Environmental Science and Technology* 34(8) 2000, 1413–1418.

95. The database address is http://www.evri.ec.gc.ca/evri/.

CHAPTER 16

Shadow Prices from Secondary Sources[1]

Policy analysts typically face time pressure and resource constraints. They naturally wish to do cost-benefit analysis as efficiently as possible and without getting into estimation issues beyond their competence. Anything that legitimately lowers the cost of doing CBA increases the likelihood that any particular CBA will be worth doing—in effect, it increases the chance that a CBA of doing a CBA will be positive.

In order to evaluate existing or proposed policies and projects, analysts require credible measures of the social values of the impacts. As we saw in Chapter 4, where these impacts occur in efficient markets, the value of these impacts can be estimated from changes in social surplus. Estimating social surplus requires knowledge of the appropriate demand and supply curves. When knowledge of these curves is not readily available, we may use the methods in Chapters 12 through 15 to value impacts. Most of these methods, however, are expensive and time consuming. What else could the analyst do? Two situations are worth discussing in more depth.

In the first situation, the analyst believes that it is necessary to estimate the demand curve in order to measure consumer surplus. As we discuss in Chapter 13, this is relatively easy if we know one point on the demand curve and we have an estimate of its elasticity or slope at that point. Fortunately, economists have estimated price elasticities of demand, cross-elasticities, and income elasticities for a range of specific goods. Many elasticities have been summarized in survey articles.[2] Because these elasticities are based on the responses of people to similar price changes in the past, they provide an empirically grounded basis for predicting the responses to proposed price changes. For example, how consumers responded to a price increase for water in New Mexico can be reasonably used to estimate how they will respond to a similar price increase in Arizona. In addition to own-price elasticities, estimates of cross-price elasticities, which identify changes in the demand for a good that are likely to result from changes in the prices of other goods, though less often available, are frequently useful. For example, are transportation and various forms of communications (such as telecommuting and teleconferencing) complements or substitutes?[3] These cross-elasticities are important to transport planners and policy analysts who are estimating the costs and benefits of transport capital investments, assessing expected consumers' responses to price changes, or forecasting changes in demand for transportation. Existing estimates of income elasticities can also be useful, especially when policies have strong distributional effects. Elasticity estimates are scattered widely throughout the academic literature, usually in the topic-specific journals. Therefore, analysts often garner them from the relevant economic and policy journals on an ongoing basis, and we will not discuss them further here.

In the second situation, analysts need to only predict the project's impacts, which we discuss in Chapter 11, and multiply them by the appropriate market prices or shadow prices. Many CBAs involve some impacts that can be valued at current market prices and other impacts that can be valued using shadow prices. Transportation and infrastructure project analyses, for example, often use current market prices for construction resources (materials, land, labor, and equipment) and ongoing operational costs (labor and maintenance materials), but require shadow prices for the value of lives saved, injuries avoided, crashes avoided, time saved, air quality changes, and noise level changes, to name only some. In order to obtain a shadow price, analysts might conduct their own valuation study using one of the methods discussed in Chapters 14 or 15. However, employing any of these methods is generally time consuming and resource intensive. The most straightforward, least-cost approach would be to use a previously estimated shadow price. Such estimates can be "plugged into" a cost-benefit analysis. Consequently, we refer to such estimates as *plug-ins*. More formally, using plug-ins in a CBA is known as *benefit transfer* or sometimes *information transfer*.

The main purpose of this chapter is to survey the relevant literature and provide a "best estimate" for a number of frequently used shadow prices. It focuses on impacts that occur in many CBAs: the value of a statistical life, the cost of various kinds of injuries (including those resulting from road crashes), the cost of crime, and the value of time.[4] We also review per-unit values of recreational activities, the environment, and water and air pollution. Finally, we briefly discuss empirical estimates of the marginal excess tax burden. Many of these plug-ins are particularly useful in the evaluation of transportation projects, such as construction of new roads, better road lighting, altered speed limits, or new vehicle safety features. They are also applicable in a host of other areas including criminal justice, the environment, health, education, and training.

Most of the plug-ins discussed in this chapter are estimates of marginal values. For example, we provide estimates of the marginal social cost of one ton of particulate matter pollution or the value of one additional hour saved. The marginal value is usually the most useful value for policy purposes. However, some plug-ins are more accurately thought of as average values. For example, the value of a life saved is the average value in a population consisting of many people with different ages, incomes, and other characteristics.

In practice, marginal values are not likely to remain constant as output levels change. For example, the value of time saved is likely to increase as the time stuck in traffic increases. Similarly, the marginal cost of pollution is likely to increase with the level of pollution. When marginal costs are increasing or decreasing, it would be incorrect to estimate total costs by multiplying the output level by our plug-in estimate of the marginal cost.

The plug-ins we discuss are summarized in tables throughout this chapter. In order to facilitate comparability and for ease of use, plug-in values are usually expressed in 2008 U.S. dollars. The units of each impact are usually in "dollars per person" or in "dollars per event." Other values are reported in terms of units produced, such as "per ton." We also report the relevant time unit, such as "per day" or "per year."

Different people have different opportunities and different preferences. Consequently, our plug-in values should ideally be adjusted to take account of the preferences and characteristics of the affected population in a particular CBA. After discussing the plug-ins, we briefly address some of the information transfer issues related to adjusting plug-ins to different situations or to new CBAs.

During the past two decades there have been an increasing number of *meta-analyses*. These studies summarize the existing evidence about a particular topic, though they do not necessarily attempt to determine a best estimate. Often, their primary purpose is to explain why different studies obtain different estimates.[5] For example, do certain estimation techniques provide larger estimated values than other estimation techniques or are valuations larger for some populations than for others? Answers to such questions assist benefit transfer. The usual approach in a meta-analysis is to estimate the statistical relationship between the plug-in estimate from each study and a number of characteristics of that study, such as the methodology employed (e.g., contingent valuation study), data source, and characteristics of the population (e.g., income).

THE VALUE OF A STATISTICAL LIFE

Researchers have used several techniques to estimate the value of a statistical life(VSL). Market-based techniques observe the "price" people are willing to pay (or accept) in order to decrease (increase) the risk of a fatality in markets that embody this risk, as we discuss in Chapter 14. Contingent valuation (CV) methods elicit these amounts with hypothetical survey questions, as we discuss in Chapter 15. The most widely accepted market-based techniques are those that examine how much of a wage premium people working in risky jobs must be given to compensate them for the additional fatality risk. Our purpose here is not to revisit methodological issues, but to summarize the empirical estimates of the VSL.

The range in the VSL varies considerably across studies, sometimes between $0 and $30 million. Even when the outliers are discarded, the range is quite large. A number of important reviews were published around 1990.[6] Most of the reliable estimates of the VSL at that time ranged between $1.4 million and $4 million in 1990 dollars. More recent estimates have been trending higher, even after adjusting for inflation. Here we briefly review four relatively recent meta-analyses, one by Ted Miller, a second by Janusz Mrozek and Laura Taylor, a third by W. Kip Viscusi and Joseph Aldy, and a fourth by Ikuho Kocki, Bryan Hubbell, and Randal Kramer.[7]

The Miller Analysis of VSL Estimates

Ted Miller undertook a meta-analysis of 68 international studies of the VSL. He notes that studies that do not use occupational-specific mortality risk or that do not use variables to control for occupational differences tend to overestimate the VSL. Studies that use all-mortality risk (from employment and all other sources) tend to underestimate the value of statistical life. Estimates of the VSL based on wage-risk studies and those based on CV studies produce similar estimates to each another but are significantly higher than those based on consumer behavior because consumers often underperceive the risks to which they are exposed. Miller estimates that the VSL in the United States is $4.88 million in 2008 U.S. dollars, with a range of $4.4 to $6.1 million.

The Mrozek and Taylor Analysis of VSL Estimates

Janusz Mrozek and Laura Taylor undertook a meta-analysis of 33 international VSL studies. The mean VLS was roughly $7.7 million in 2008 U.S. dollars. The explanatory variables in their regression analyses include study design characteristics (model equation specifications, control of other risk factors), occupation (dummy variables for occupational attributes), and sample characteristics (blue-collar workers, sex, unionized environment, and actual versus perceived risk levels). Also included are variables that reflected the sources of the wage and risk data. Basic regression results for their full dataset produce a mean VSL of $7.2 million U.S. dollars.

However, Mrozek and Taylor are suspicious of VSL estimates from labor market studies that propose values in excess of $2.6 million to $3.8 million because they think that previous research has not controlled well for unobservable factors that occur at the industry level. To address this problem, Mrozek and Taylor include seven broad industry classification dummy variables in a regression analysis in addition to the usual labor market variables. These industry classification variables capture the effect of interindustry wage differentials separately from the effect of occupational risks. For instance, a secretary working for an oil firm in an urban environment may earn a higher wage than a secretary in the same environment working for a nonprofit organization, even though their job risk profiles would be very similar. Imposing this adjustment on studies that did not do so originally yielded a predicted VSL of $3.3 million in 2008 U.S. dollars for the "average worker."

The Viscusi and Aldy Analysis of VSL Estimates

In their meta-analysis, W. Kip Viscusi and Joseph Aldy examine 49 wage-risk studies published over the past 30 years. More than half of the studies were specific to the U.S. labor market, and the remaining studies were international. Roughly half of the U.S. labor market studies obtained estimates of the VSL that range between $6.22 million and $14.92 million (2008 U.S. dollars). The median value of these studies is near $8.7 million.[8] Viscusi and Aldy have most confidence in studies with estimates from $6.6 million to $7.8 million dollars.

Viscusi and Aldy conduct a number of meta-analysis regressions, replicating the models used in previous meta-analyses. Their explanatory variables reflect whether the workplace was unionized, the level of education, income, the mean risk, the type of risk, and the type of study. They omit studies that did not contain an income measure. Viscusi and Aldy use their regressions analyses to predict values of the VSL for each study. The mean predicted VSL for the U.S. population ranges between $6.8 million and $9.4 million. They also note that for most of the regression models the upper bound of the 95 percent confidence interval is roughly two times greater than the lower bound of the 95 percent confidence interval, or more.

The Kochi, Hubbell, and Kramer Analysis of VSL Estimates

Ikuho Kochi, Bryan Hubbell, and Randall Kramer conducted a recent meta-analysis on a sample of 31 hedonic wage-risk studies and 14 contingent valuation studies that were published between 1990 and 2002. These studies were carefully selected to minimize bias in computing the mean VSL—for example, they only include studies conducted in high-income countries, and they excluded contingent valuation studies with samples of under 100 and hedonic wage-risk studies that were based entirely on individuals who worked in extremely risky jobs, such as policemen, who may have risk preferences that are very unrepresentative of the general population. In addition, in computing the mean VSL, they give greater weight to VSL estimates with greater levels of statistical significance than to studies with smaller levels of statistical significance. Although doing this is commonplace in meta-analysis, it apparently had not been done previously in meta-analyses of VSL estimates.

After making this adjustment, Kochi, Hubbell, and Kramer compute a mean VSL of $6.8 million in 2008 U.S. dollars with a standard deviation of $3.0 million. Interestingly, they find that there is a considerable difference between estimates produced by hedonic wage-risk studies and those resulting from contingent valuation studies, with the former having a mean value of $12.0 million and the latter having a mean value of $3.5 million.

Conclusion on the VSL

These four comparatively recent analyses produce different VSL estimates. Mrozek and Taylor are lowest at $3.4 million; Miller is next with a best point estimate of $4.9 million with a range between $4.4 million and $6.1 million; Kochi, Hubbell, and Kramer are next at $6.8 million; and Viscusi and Aldy are highest with a mean estimated VSL for the U.S. population of between $6.8 million and $9.4 million.[9] Many authors suggest figures at the lower end of this range for policy purposes, partially due to the methodological problems discussed in Chapters 14 and 15. In our opinion, the best point estimate of the VSL for policy purposes in the United States is currently $5 million, with sensitivity analysis at around $3 million and $7 million, as shown in Table 16-1.

TABLE 16-1 The Value of a Statistical Life, Injury Costs, and Crash Costs (in 2008 U.S. dollars)

Plug-In Category (Impact)	Shadow Price Value	Comments
Value of a Statistical Life (VSL)	Best point estimate $5 million (sensitivity analysis at $2.4 million to $7.2 million per life saved)	Based on Miller (2000), Mrozek and Taylor (2002), Viscusi and Aldy (2003), and Kochi, Hubbell and Kramer (2006). Should adjust for risk level.
Value of a Life-Year (VLY)	$234,100 per person per year	Based on a VSL of $5 million, 40 year life expectancy, and a discount rate of 3.5%.
Monetary Injury Costs		
1. Eventually fatal	1. $623,441 per injured person	Based on Rice, MacKenzie, and Associates (1989). Includes monetary costs only, not pain and suffering.
2. Hospitalized (nonfatal)	2. $67,298 per injured person	
3. Nonhospitalized (nonfatal)	3. $1,015 per injured person	
4. Average cost of an injury	4. $5,460 per injured person.	
A. Motor vehicle injury	A. $17,777 per injured person	
B. Falls	B. $5,968 per injured person	

(Continued)

TABLE 16-1 (*Continued*)

Plug-In Category (Impact)	Shadow Price Value	Comments
C. Firearm injuries	C. $105,773 per injured person	
D. Poisonings	D. $9,900 per injured person	
E. Fire injuries and burns	E. $5,080 per injured person	
F. Drownings and near drownings	F. $127,740 per injured person	
G. Other	G. $2,286 per injured person	
Cost of Work-Related Occupational Injuries		
A. Fatal injury	A. $4.1 million per injured worker	Based on Miller and Galbraith (1995). Includes quality-of-life losses.
B. Nonfatal injury with compensable lost work	B. $2,640 per injured worker	
C. Nonfatal injury with worker non-compensable lost work	C. $1,093 per injured worker	
D. Nonfatal injury, no lost work	D. $21,040 per injured worker	
E. Average injury cost	E. $21,040 per injured worker	
F. Average motor vehicle work-related injury cost	F. $123,750 per injured worker	
Cost of Work-Related Injuries		
Value of one year of work impairment due to injury	$160,204 to $248,946 per year	Based on Dillingham, Miller, and Levy (1996).
Social Cost of Motor Vehicle Crash Injuries		
1. Spinal cord	1. $3.5 M per victim ($1.2M–$5.3M for AIS 3–5)	Based on Zaloshnja, Miller, Romano, and Spicer (2004). All means are arithmetic and do not reflect the distribution of injury severity within each body region. M = million.
2. Brain	2. $1.4M per victim ($0.15M–$4.2M for AIS 1–5)	
3. Lower extremity	3. $0.55M per victim ($0.01M–$1.32M for AIS 1–5)	
4. Upper extremity	4. $0.18M per victim ($0.01M–$0.36M for AIS 1–3)	
5. Trunk/abdomen	5. $0.34M per victim ($0.01M–$0.73M for AIS 1–5)	
6. Other face, head, or neck	6. $0.46M per victim ($0.01M–$1.3M for AIS 1–4)	
7. Minor external	7. $0.01M per victim	
8. Burn	8. $0.64M per victim ($0.08M–$1.07M for AIS 1–5)	
Motor Vehicle Accident Costs		
1. PDO (Property damage only)	1. $3,150 per vehicle	Based on Blincoe et al. (2002). These figures reflect the per-person costs related to motor vehicle accidents of varying severity. AIS = Abbreviated Injury Scale.
2. AIS 1	2. $18,670 per injured person	
3. AIS 2	3. $196,350 per injured person	
4. AIS 3	4. $390,576 per injured person	
5. AIS 4	5. $909,404 per injured person	
6. AIS 5	6. $2,987,090 per injured person	
7. AIS 6 (Fatal)	7. $4,184,651 per fatality	

THE VALUE OF A LIFE-YEAR

The value of a life-year (VLY) is the constant annual amount, that, taken over a person's remaining life span, has a discounted value equal to his or her VSL. We can think about the average VSL as the discounted value of the remaining life-years of the average member of society. Thus, assuming the VLY is constant, it can be computed from an estimate of the average VSL, denoted $V\hat{S}L$:

$$VLY = \frac{V\hat{S}L}{A(T - a, r)} \tag{16.1}$$

where $A(T - a, r)$ is the annuity factor based on the expected number of remaining years of life $(T - a)$ and the appropriate discount rate (r). Thus, using an average VSL of $5 million (as indicated in Table 16-1), a discount rate of 3.5 percent, and a life expectancy of 40 years implies the VLY equals $234,136. This estimate is higher than many other estimates. For example, Eduard Zaloshnja, Ted Miller, Eduardo Romano, and Rebecca Spicer suggest the VLY equals $114,000 based on a VSL of $3.7 million.[10] Peter Abelson suggests the VLY for use by public agencies in Australia should be $95,640 in 2008 U.S. dollars.[11]

Given the VLY, one can now compute the VSL for a person aged a as the discounted sum of the value of the remaining life-years; specifically:

$$VSL(a) = \sum_{t=0}^{T-a} \frac{VLY}{(1 + r)^t} \tag{16.2}$$

where a is current age, T is the expected age at death and $T - a$ is life expectancy. According to this model, the VSL declines with age.

The above formulation implies that the VLY is constant and the VSL declines with age. There is considerable discussion in the literature about whether the VLY (or the VSL) changes with age. One might expect that the VLY increases with age: if you expect you have only a few more years to live, then life-years are becoming scarcer and you might be willing to pay more for an additional life-year than when you were younger. The Science Advisory Board of the U.S. Environmental Protection Agency points out that economic theory is inconclusive about the issue, and recent reviews of the empirical literature differ considerably in their findings.[12]

A quality-adjusted life-year (QALY) weights the VLY by the quality of health during that year:

$$QALY_t = w_t VLY \tag{16.3}$$

where the weight (w_t) equals 1 in perfect health, 0 in death, and is something else inbetween.[13] The purpose of a QALY is to account for the fact that not all years are lived with the same vigor and enthusiasm. Some years are spent in better health than others. For many ill people the weights decline over time as their condition becomes more severe. In order to compare one intervention or policy with another, analysts compute the discounted sum of future expected QALYs under each alternative, that is, VLY in equation (16.2) is replaced with $QALY_t$. We discuss QALYs in more depth in Chapter 18.

THE COST OF CRASHES AND THE COST OF INJURIES

Table 16-1 also summarizes five sets of estimates of the cost of injuries or the cost of crashes in the United States, again standardized to 2008 dollars. The first set is based on a major report prepared for Congress by Dorothy Rice, Ellen MacKenzie, and Associates.[14] It provides detailed estimates of the monetary costs of injuries from different causes and for three levels of severity. The second set, produced by Ted Miller and Maury Galbraith, focuses on the cost of occupational injuries.[15] The third set is based on a wage-risk study by Alan Dillingham, Ted Miller, and David Levy that estimates the value of an impaired work year.[16] The fourth set, produced by Eduard Zaloshnja, Ted Miller, Eduardo Romano, and Rebecca Spicer, focuses on motor vehicle crash injuries.[17] The fifth set is based on a report by Lawrence Blincoe et al. prepared for the National Highway Safety Administration.[18] It provides unit cost estimates for seven categories of motor vehicle crashes with varying levels of personal injury to occupants.

For relatively minor crashes, the cost of a motor vehicle crash per victim is higher than the cost of a personal injury because motor vehicle crashes typically result in additional costs, particularly property damage (vehicle) costs. However, for relatively severe crashes, the cost of pain and suffering from injury is the largest component of crash costs, often greater than half the total.

The Rice, McKenzie, and Associates' Estimates of the Cost of Injuries

Dorothy Rice, Ellen MacKenzie, and their associates focus on the direct monetary cost of injuries. Their estimates incorporate medical and rehabilitation costs and forgone earnings (including an imputed value for household labor). Because these estimates focus on monetary costs, they do not include pain and suffering and other dimensions of unhappiness that people would pay to avoid. Also, these estimates do not include property damage losses and other related social costs, such as court costs. Thus, the study leads to very conservative estimates of the social cost of injuries. However, the methodology and estimates are still widely cited.

The Miller and Galbraith Estimates of the Cost of Occupational Injuries

Ted Miller and Maury Galbraith estimate the cost of occupational injuries in the United States using a methodology similar to that of Rice, MacKenzie, and Associates. However, they include a measure of the willingness to pay (WTP) to avoid the disutility associated with injury. Using incidences of injuries reported in the United States, predominantly through state worker's compensation systems, the authors use a top-down national accounting framework to estimate the cost of injury for all injuries, for fatal injuries, and for three subclasses of nonfatal injuries (compensable lost work, noncompensable lost work, and nonlost work). As the authors acknowledge, using a top-down accounting method is less accurate than using incidence-based bottom-up estimation techniques.

The estimated costs include the costs of medical and emergency services (hospital/home care, physician services, rehabilitation services, ancillary items, police, fire/paramedic response, and emergency transportation), wage and household work (lost wages, household work, and fringe benefits), administrative and legal costs (investigation, insurance processing, record keeping, limited litigation costs), workplace disruption (overtime pay, loss of specialized skills, recruitment and training associated with long-term disability) and quality of life (reduced quality of life to workers and their families who bear the nonmonetary losses associated with injury). Quality-of-life losses account for 43 percent of workplace injury costs, and the average cost per occupational injury is $21,040 (2008 U.S. dollars), but note the large range between specific injury categories as shown in Table 16-1.[19]

The Dillingham, Miller, and Levy Estimates of the Cost of Injuries

One problem with estimating the cost of injuries is that injuries come in a wide range of severities, affect different parts of the body, and cause differe levels of pain and disability. Alan Dillingham, Ted Miller, and David Levy attempted to measure the cost of injuries through a wage-risk study, looking at the implied WTP in order to avoid one year of impairment to an individual's work life.

They estimate that individuals are willing to pay around $160,200 to $249,000 per year to avoid one year of impairment. However, there is no specific level of severity to which to apply this measure. One important assumption is that a work-life shortened by a fatal injury is equivalent to one that is shortened by a nonfatal but permanent total disability. A specific advantage of their estimates is that they are transferable to non-work-related injuries, allowing for the estimation of the WTP for safety improvements in other markets, such as recreational activities.

The Zaloshnja, Miller, Romano, and Spicer Estimates of the Cost of Motor Vehicle Crash Injuries

Eduard Zaloshnja, Ted Miller, Eduardo Romano, and Rebecca Spicer estimate the social cost of motor vehicle crash injuries for the year 2000, updating the estimates made by Miller in 1993.[20] The main purpose of this study is to provide a relatively comprehensive estimate of the social cost of damage to a large spectrum of body parts injured in motor vehicle crashes, such as the spinal cord or the brain. These cost estimates include medical and emergency services, household and workplace productivity losses, insurance and legal costs, property damage, and quality-of-life losses. Monetary costs are supplemented by the addition of the WTP to avoid pain and suffering for each type of injury, based on a VSL of $3.7 million (2008 U.S. dollars) and a VLY of $114,000.

Injuries to each body part are also broken down by level of severity, based on the most severe ("maximum") injury sustained by a person according to the Abbreviated Injury Scale (AIS), sometimes referred to as the Maximum Abbreviated Injury Scale (MAIS). This scale ranges from one (minor) to six (fatal); see Table 16-2.[21] Following Miller, the pain and suffering or the lost quality of life for an injury of a particular level of severity is expressed as a fraction of the WTP to avoid a fatal injury, less the lost human capital.[22] The particular fractions proposed by Miller for each level of severity are also shown in Table 16-2. This approach is not ideal because the fractions are somewhat arbitrary, but we are not aware of a better approach, and it has been adopted by many regulatory bodies.[23]

TABLE 16-2 AIS Classification System, Including Equivalent Proportion of VSL

AIS Code	Injury Severity	Fraction of VSL	Description of Common Injury
PDO	None	0.00	No injury
AIS 1	Minor	0.0020	Superficial abrasion or laceration of skin, sprain, first-degree burn, head trauma with headache or dizziness but no other symptoms
AIS 2	Moderate	0.0155	Significant abrasion or laceration of skin, concussion with less than 15 minutes of lost consciousness, closed fracture with or without dislocation, digit crush/amputation
AIS 3	Serious	0.0575	Major nerve injury, multiple rib fracture without chest collapse, bruise of internal organ, hand/arm or foot crush/amputation
AIS 4	Severe	0.1875	Spleen rupture, leg crush/amputation, concussion with loss of consciousness 15 minutes to 24 hours, chest wall perforation
AIS 5	Critical	0.7625	Permanent spinal cord injury, extensive burns (second or third degree), concussion with severe neurological signs
AIS 6	Fatal	1	Injuries which, if not immediately fatal, ultimately result in death

Source: Adapted from Stephan Hoffer, Frank Berardino, Jack Smith, and Stuart Rubin, *Economic Values for Evaluation of FAA Investment and Regulatory Decisions,* US DOT FAA-APO-98-8, Federal Aviation Administration, June 1998.

Table 16-1 presents the average cost of a motor vehicle crash injury to the spinal cord, brain, lower extremities, upper extremities, trunk/abdomen, and other head/face/neck, as well as minor external injuries, burns, and fatal injuries. It also reports in parentheses a range for each body part according to level of severity. For example, the average cost of a motor crash that causes a brain injury is $1.44 million, but it ranges from $148,800 for a brain injury of AIS 1 to $4.2 million for one of AIS 5. Injury costs range from approximately $12,000 for a minor injury to a leg or foot to $5.3 million to a critical injury (AIS 5) to the spinal cord. Note that the cost of the latter injury slightly exceeds the VSL.

The Blincoe and Colleagues Estimates of the Cost of Motor Vehicle Crashes

Lawrence Blincoe and his colleagues provide fully allocated costs for motor vehicle crashes. These comprehensive estimates include property damage, the costs of emergency and medical services, productivity losses, pain and suffering, and travel time delay to other motorists. Blincoe and his colleagues present estimates of the cost of a crash based on the maximum AIS to an injured person. At the lowest level (property damage only, PDO), there is no personal injury, but there is property damage, insurance administrative costs, and police costs. The figures that are shown in Table 16-1 are per (maximally) injured person, except for PDO (property damage only) crashes, which are per vehicle.

Transportation economists often distinguish between direct costs, indirect costs, and intangible costs. Direct costs include emergency treatment, initial medical costs (including physician, hospital, prescription costs, and ancillary costs, such as administration costs of processing medical payments to providers), rehabilitation costs, long-term care costs (if required), legal costs, and employer/workplace costs. Other direct costs are property damage to vehicles, cargo, and personal property. Indirect costs include productivity losses due to temporary and permanent disability and decreases in household productivity. Intangible costs relate to pain and suffering or lost quality of life. The individual components of crash costs for each level of severity appear in Table 16-3. These components may be applicable to other settings where injuries occur at similar severity levels.

Conclusion on the Cost of Injuries

The Rice, MacKenzie, and Associates study provides estimates of the monetary costs of a wide range of injuries. However, these estimates are not particularly useful as measures of social costs, especially for injuries that eventually prove fatal, as monetary costs are likely to be only a fraction of total social costs. If injury costs are

TABLE 16-3   The Cost of Components of Crashes by Level of Severity (2008 U.S. dollars)

AIS Level	PDO	1	2	3	4	5	6 (Fatal)
Medical	0	2,959	19,423	57,796	163,222	413,268	27,466
Emergency	38	120	263	457	1,032	1,058	1,036
Market Productivity	0	2,174	31,098	88,822	132,311	545,341	740,070
Household Productivity	59	712	9,102	26,197	34,818	185,600	238,099
Insurance Admin	145	922	8,588	23,485	40,195	84,773	46,144
Workplace Costs	64	313	2,428	5,303	5,839	10,182	10,817
Legal Costs	0	187	6,192	19,650	41,873	99,266	126,964
QALYs	0	5,538	113,290	159,246	476,650	1,624,488	2,969,915
Property Damage	1,846	4,778	4,915	8,452	12,223	11,742	12,770
Travel Delay	998	966	1,051	1,169	1,242	11,371	11,371
Total	**3,150**	**18,670**	**196,350**	**390,576**	**909,404**	**2,987,090**	**4,184,651**

Source: Adapted from Lawrence J. Blincoe, Angela G. Seay, Eduard Zaloshnja, Ted R. Miller, Eduardo O. Romano, Stephen Luchter, and Rebecca S. Spicer, *The Economic Impact of Motor Vehicle Crashes 2000*, National Highway Traffic Safety Administration, U.S. Department of Transportation, May 2002, p. 9 and p. 62. Available at www.nhtsa.dot.gov.

underestimated, then the benefits of safety-enhancing road improvements are reduced relative to the benefits of time-saving road improvements. It may thus appear that it is better to be dead than to be stuck in traffic![24] This is usually not the case when the numbers are estimated correctly.

The Miller and Galbraith and the Dillingham, Miller, and Levy studies focus on the cost of work-related injuries, but the two studies focus on different measures. The Zaloshnja and colleagues study provides comprehensive estimates of injuries sustained in a motor vehicle crash. Blincoe and colleagues adopt a similar methodology to measure the total social cost of an accident.

THE COST OF CRIME

Many criminal justice and training programs have reduction of crime as one of their goals. In order to estimate the benefits of crime reduction, it is necessary to estimate the number of crimes of each type that will be avoided during each time period and the social cost of each type of crime.[25] Table 16-4 provides evidence on the cost of violent crimes from three sources. Ted Miller, Mark Cohen, and Brian Wiersema estimate the victim costs of crime in a report prepared for the National Justice Institute; Cohen estimates the cost of the criminal justice system; and Cohen and three colleagues estimate WTP to reduce crime.[26] Each set of estimates excludes criminal justice system costs and prevention costs.

TABLE 16-4 The Cost of Crime and the Willingness to Pay for Crime Reduction (2008 U.S. dollars)

| Plug-In Category | Shadow Price Value | | | |
	Victim Cost Per Incident *Based on Miller et al. (1996)*	*Criminal Justice Cost Per Incident* *Based on Cohen (1998)*	*Total Cost Per Incident* *Sum of First Two Columns*	*Willingness to Pay Per Incident* *Based on Cohen et al. (2004)*
Burglary	$2,225	$3,225	$5,450	$31,250
Armed robbery	$30,125	$9,663	$39,788	$87,500
Serious assaults	$38,100	$6,438	$44,538	$290,000
Rape and sexual assaults	$138,113	$4,063	$142,175	$296,250
Murder	$4,625,000	$228,750	$4,853,750	$12,125,000
Drunk driving resulting in death	$4,500,000	NA	NA	NA
Drunk driving, no death	$25,440	NA	NA	NA
Arson resulting in death	$3,876,000	NA	NA	NA
Arson, no death	$53,040	NA	NA	NA
Child abuse, nonfatal	$84,000	NA	NA	NA
Larceny (or attempt)	$480	NA	NA	NA
Motor vehicle theft (or attempt)	$5,280	NA	NA	NA

NA: Not available

The Miller, Cohen, and Wiersema Estimates of the Cost of Crime

Ted Miller, Mark Cohen, and Brian Wiersema examine the consequences and cost of crime. They focus on victims' costs and ignore society's response to victimizations, including the real costs to the criminal justice system and other social costs, such as fear. They examine rape, robbery, child abuse/neglect, assault, drunk driving (DWI), arson, larceny, burglary, and motor vehicle theft. They further examine the number of deaths resulting from these crimes and, if not fatal, whether there was injury.

Miller and colleagues include pain and suffering as well as direct costs. Direct costs include lost productivity, medical/emergency care, mental health care, police/fire services, social victim services, and property damage. The lost quality of life for a fatality was based on a VSL of $3.82 million (2008 U.S. dollars). For nonfatal consequences, intangible costs are based on jury awards to crime victims and burn victims. In the case of multiple incidents of crime occurring to single individuals, the intangible costs of a single incident were multiplied by the average number of victimizations per individual.

Miller and colleagues exclude criminal justice system costs and the cost of actions taken to reduce the risk of becoming a crime victim. These are two of the largest costs associated with criminal behavior. Other omitted impacts include expenses for processing insurance or welfare payments to totally disabled victims of crime, long-term effects on earnings resulting from psychological injury, and "second-generation costs," which are described as crimes committed by persons who themselves are victims of crime. Some "second-generation costs" are likely to be included implicitly, for example, property crime or assault that results from drug abuse (i.e., victimless drug offenses).

As is often the case in social cost estimates involving personal injury, the intangible costs are the largest component for all crime categories, except burglary, larceny, and motor vehicle theft, where the likelihood of personal injury is low. The Miller, Cohen, and Wiersema costs are presented per criminal incident. Their estimates are similar to those from other studies conducted in the past 25 years.

The Cohen Estimates of Criminal Justice Costs

Mark Cohen uses administrative data to estimate criminal justice-related costs. These costs are based on the probability that an offender will be detected and punished. As Table 16-4 indicates, at least in the case of crimes involving a high risk of injury, these costs are generally much smaller than the victim cost of crime.

The Cohen, Rust, Steen, and Tidd Estimates of WTP for Crime Control Programs

Mark Cohen, Roland Rust, Sara Steen and Simon Tidd conducted a contingent valuation study with a nationally representative sample of 1,300 households using the dichotomous choice method discussed in Chapter 15.[27] Each household was asked if they would be willing to pay a particular price for a program that would reduce a particular crime (e.g., burglaries) by 10 percent. This was then converted into an estimate of total WTP using the methods described in Chapter 15. The resulting dollar figure was then multiplied by the number of household in the United States and divided by the national number of crimes of the type under consideration (e.g., burglaries) that would be prevented by a 10 percent reduction. Thus, the estimates in Table 16-4 represent total national WTP for a reduction in one crime of each type.

In principle, these estimates should incorporate any reductions in costs that respondents consider in answering the questions—potentially reductions in direct costs, pain and suffering, criminal justice system costs (if respondents considered tax savings from reduced load within the system), costs resulting from actions taken to prevent crime (e.g., time spent locking doors, purchases of alarms, and hiring more police), psychological costs resulting from worry over being a crime victim, and so forth. However, it is difficult to know what respondents had in mind when they responded. It should also be kept in mind that respondents probably answered on the basis of their personal judgment about the risk of being a crime victim, rather than their actual risk. For example, if they believed their risk of being murdered is larger than it really is, they may have indicated a larger WTP for a reduction in the murder rate than if they knew the actual rate.

The WTP estimates for a reduction in crime shown in fourth column in Table 16-4 are markedly larger than the total cost figures shown for the same crimes in the third column. Moreover, the WTP to reduce murders is considerably larger than the point VSL estimates we earlier suggested using in CBAs. The reasons for the rather large estimates of WTP for crime reduction are not entirely clear. The contingent valuation study from which they were derived was carefully executed. One possible explanation is, as already suggested, that WTP estimates capture some costs, such as crime prevention costs, that are missed by the cost estimates. A second possible explanation, as also previously suggested, is that individuals tend to inflate the risk of being a crime victim above the actual risk.

Conclusion on the Cost of Crime

As can be seen in Table 16-4, the cost of crime varies depending on the nature of the crime. Crimes with high personal injury rates, especially death, are much more costly than less-violent criminal activity.

THE VALUE OF TIME

Time is a valuable commodity; as the saying goes, "time is money." Change in travel time is an important component of many CBAs, most obviously those concerned with transportation. Though rarely a dominating cost or benefit, change in waiting time can also be important in many nontransportation projects. For example, queuing time is an important cost component of policies that ration goods or affect access to services, such as motor vehicle registration, medical care, or social services.

Most of the empirical literature on the value of time has been concerned with estimating the value of travel time. This is normally referred to as the *value of travel time savings* (VTTS), reflecting the fact that many government projects expect to save travel time. Recently, attention has been devoted to the value of saving time in other activities, recognizing that it may differ from the VTTS. For example, people usually experience considerably greater disutility from waiting time than from "pure" travel time.[28] Even the value of travel time saved depends on the travel conditions themselves, for example, whether traffic has just slowed down or is stop-and-go. Often the value of time saved in different activities or in different conditions is expressed as a multiple of the VTTS.

One might think that time saved simply reflects time saved, but it actually reflects several related, but separable, entities. To begin, one should ask why drivers slow down as traffic flow increases or density increases.[29] Presumably drivers slow down because they want to prevent or reduce the risk of an accident. Thus, one can think of increases in travel time as reducing the *ex ante* cost of an accident. Another way to reduce one's expected private cost of an accident is to buy a larger, sturdier car.

The VTTS reflects not only the benefits of travel time savings (or reduced risk of accident) but also the reliability of those time savings (the variance of travel time savings).[30] This is one reason why the VTTS is higher during congested periods, where there is more uncertainty, than under free-flow conditions.

The large empirical literature on VTTS has been reviewed by several authors, mostly on a country-specific or regional basis. Typically, these estimation exercises have been commissioned by the governments of individual countries and have led to the adoption of a standard VTTS for use in analysis in that country.[31] In most cases, as we will discuss, VTTS is expressed as a proportion of the before-tax or after-tax wage rate. This allows analysts to readily estimate travel time costs using local wage rates, although they should be adjusted for income and other factors, as we discuss near the end of this chapter.

Table 16-5 contains estimates of the VTTS for road transportation, based on literature reviews by William Waters, and by Markus von Wartburg and William Waters.[32] The latter study also presents estimates of the value of time saved in other activities, such as walking and waiting, expressed as multiples of the VTTS.

The Waters Estimates of VTTS

William G. Waters reviewed estimates of the VTTS from 56 empirical studies conducted between 1974 and 1990. These studies use revealed preference or CV methods. Revealed preference studies include a wide range of situations: route choice decisions in which there are different costs (e.g., toll roads versus nontoll roads), mode choice

TABLE 16-5   The Value of Time

Plug-In Category	*Shadow Price Value*	*Comments*
VTTS for Road Transportation		
1. Commuting or leisure travel time	1. 50% of the average after-tax wage rate per hour saved	Based on Waters (1996) and von Wartburg and Waters (2004).
2. Travel time paid for by employers	2. 100% of the before-tax wage rate plus benefits per hour saved	
Time in Other Activities		
1. Walking	1. 2 × VTTS	Common convention in many jurisdictions (von Wartburg and Waters, 2004).
2. Waiting	2. 2.5 × VTTS	
3. Congestion	3. 2 × VTTS	

decisions (bus or car travel versus faster, but more costly, airline travel), speed choice decisions (in which faster speeds involve higher operating costs), and location choice decisions (hedonic methods that isolate the impact of commuting time on land values). Survey methods are also used to estimate VTTS because they allow researchers to gather data of direct relevance to determining WTP.

As is the standard in the VTTS literature, Waters presents the VTTS as a percentage of the after-tax hourly wage rate, rather than as a dollar figure. He found as much as a tenfold variation in estimates from the literature. As with other estimates described in this chapter, the studies cover a wide range of circumstances. Waters partitions previous studies in a number of ways. He aggregates the 32 studies that focus on commuting trips (after eliminating some outliers) and calculates the mean value at 48 percent of the after-tax wage rate with a median of 40 percent. When using only the 15 of the 22 studies that are North American automobile commuting studies, Waters calculates a mean of 59 percent (54 percent with the elimination of outliers) and a median of 42 percent. The 17 non–North American auto commuting studies generate a mean of 38 percent. Waters concludes that a shadow price of between 40 to 50 percent of the after-tax wage rate is the appropriate VTTS for auto commuting.

The von Wartburg and Waters Estimates of the VTTS and Time in Other Activities

Markus von Wartburg and William Waters review more recent advances in the study of the VTTS. They note that the establishment of toll roads is particularly useful for examining the components of VTTS (time saved and reduced variance in time saved). They also note that there is still considerable heterogeneity of results depending on the parameters of the study designs.

Von Wartburg and Waters recommend that the VTTS should be set at 50 percent of the average after-tax wage rate for commuting or leisure nonwork trips. They also suggest that there should be no distinction based on the reason for these trips (i.e., vacation time saved and commuting time saved should be valued at the same percentage even though some people enjoy traveling in cars on their vacations).[33] The VTTS for business trips in which the time required is paid for by the employer should be valued at 100 percent of the gross (before-tax) wage plus labor-related overheads (e.g., employer-paid benefits); no other adjustments should be made for the socioeconomic characteristics of travelers.

They also suggest that commuting and leisure travel time savings in congested traffic should be weighed at twice the uncongested (free-flow) rate.[34] Finally they recommend a weighing factor of two times the VTTS for time spent walking and two and one-half times for waiting time.[35] The authors maintain that these multipliers are in line with convention.

THE VALUE OF RECREATION

The value of recreation is important for assessing damage to rural areas, whether this damage is caused by fire or by development. The National Park Service, the Fish and Wildlife Service, the Bureau of Reclamation, and the Forest Service require this information to assess damage. This information is also helpful in assessing the benefits of new recreational opportunities and for determining whether to develop wilderness areas.

Studies that estimate the value of various kinds of recreation generally rely on the travel cost method or the CV method. Recreational facilities almost always provide both use benefits and nonuse benefits. Within the category of use benefits, we include rivalrous consumption (such as hunting), direct nonrivalrous consumption (such as hiking), and indirect nonrivalrous consumption (such as watching a movie about hiking in the wilderness). Within the category of nonuse benefits, which are discussed in more detail in Chapter 9, we include pure existence value (valuing the "natural order") and altruistic existence value (such as valuing other people's use or nonuse value of wilderness).

Reviews of the value of recreational activities have built upon one another over the past 20 years. An early review of 93 studies was conducted by Cindy Sorg and John Loomis in 1984.[36] Richard Walsh, Donn Johnson, and John McKean updated and extended this earlier study, incorporating studies that had been conducted through 1988.[37] In 2001, Randall Rosenberger and John Loomis merged the results of two more recent reviews.[38] This study focused on recreational activities that are of importance to the Forest Service. Most recently, Pam Kaval and John Loomis extended the survey; it now encompasses a study period from 1967 to 2003, covering 1,239 observations from 593 individual studies.[39]

Kaval and Loomis report the mean net WTP for 30 separate outdoor recreation activities, which are shown in Table 16-6. They report their findings by "activity day,"

TABLE 16-6   The Value of Recreational Activities (in 2008 U.S. dollars)

Backpacking	$57.84	Pleasure driving	$65.75
Bird-watching	$32.87	(including sightseeing)	
Camping	$41.28	Rock climbing	$62.45
Cross-country skiing	$34.84	Scuba diving	$35.93
Downhill skiing	$37.18	Sightseeing	$40.90
Fishing	$52.36	Snorkeling	$33.65
Boating	$112.02	Snowmobiling	$40.28
(nonmotorized)		Swimming	$47.39
General recreation	$38.96	Visiting an environmental	$6.67
Going to the beach	$43.78	education center	
Hiking	$34.24	Visiting an arboretum	$15.02
Horseback riding	$20.11	Visiting an aquarium	$31.43
Hunting	$52.08	Waterskiing	$54.42
Motor boating	$51.36	Wildlife viewing	$47.03
Mountain biking	$81.90	Windsurfing	$439.01
Off-road vehicle	$25.44	*Average value of a*	*$52.88*
driving		*recreational day*	
Other recreation	$54.06		
Picnicking	$46.02		

All figures are per activity day.
Source: Adapted from Pam Kaval and John Loomis, "Updated Outdoor Recreation Use Values with Emphasis on National Park Recreation," Final Report to National Park Service, Fort Collins, CO (Colorado State University, Department of Agricultural and Resource Economics: Fort Collins, CO, 2003).

which is the typical amount of time pursuing an activity within a 24-hour period. This unit is easily converted to other visitation/participation units (e.g., recreation visitor days, trips, or seasons). Across all recreational activities, the average value of a recreational day is about $53.

THE VALUE OF NATURE (SPECIFIC SPECIES OR HABITATS)

Interest in the environment has increased considerably in recent years. At the same time, scientists have developed a better understanding of the relationship between the environment, human intervention, and human well-being.[40] However, valuing most environmental impacts is difficult. One reason is that each environmental area is generally used for multiple purposes—commercial (e.g., timber and fish), recreation, and other purposes. Moreover, environmental areas can affect the value of neighboring areas. For example, using a hedonic pricing model, Elena Irwin found that the marginal benefit per household of preserving open space in the rapidly suburbanizing region of Central Maryland ranges from $1,213 to $4,035 for each acre of neighboring farmland that is preserved.[41] Consequently, there are potential problems of aggregation and double counting.

This section focuses on valuing aspects of nature and biodiversity. It concerns the value of specific species of flora and fauna and, more broadly, of habitats and ecosystems. Given the increasing interest in the environment, it is perhaps surprising that relatively few studies have attempted to value such goods, at least relative to the number of studies that value recreation. This has begun to change in the last decade, however.

Studies that value elements of nature often use the contingent valuation method. Such studies usually incorporate both option price (e.g., for bird-watching, and possibly for hunting) and existence value. The option price typically varies according to proximity. For example, Bateman and colleagues found that people living near the Norfolk Broads (a wetland site in eastern England that covers three National Nature Reserves and offers opportunities for bird-watching, sailing, and coarse fishing) were willing to pay about three times as much as people living elsewhere in the United Kingdom to preserve these recreational opportunities afforded by the Broads.[42] Some authors have conducted longitudinal studies, which are particularly useful for examining the effects of changes in urban areas on ecosystem services and the value of those services.[43]

In 1993, Johan Loomis and Douglas White surveyed the value of specific species.[44] They summarized estimates from different CV studies of 18 threatened or endangered species and conducted a meta-analysis using these estimates. Respondents to the CV questions were usually either the residents of an area in which the species was found or visitors to the area or both. Occasionally, however, a national sample was used. The estimates of the public's WTP to preserve an endangered animal species, which appear in Table 16-7, are presented on a per person basis and the amounts pertain either to WTP each year or to willingness to make a single one-time payment. When more than one estimate is available for a single species, the amounts are averaged.

TABLE 16-7 The Value of Environmental Impacts (in 2008 U.S. dollars)

Plug-In Category	Shadow Price Value	Comments
Specific Species		
Annual WTP		
Northern spotted owls	$104 per person	Based on Loomis and White
Grizzly bears	$69 per person	(1996)
Whooping cranes	$52 per person	
Red-cockaded woodpeckers	$19 per person	
Sea otters	$43 per person	
Gray whales	$39 per person	
Bald eagles	$36 per person	
Bighorn sheep	$31 per person	
Sea turtles	$19 per person	
Squawfish	$12 per person	
Striped shiner	$9 per person	
Pacific salmon/steelhead	$94 per person	
Atlantic salmon	$12 per person	
One-time lump sum		
Bald eagle	$322 per person	
Humpback whale	$258 per person	
Monk seal	$179 per person	
Gray wolf	$100 per person	
Arctic graying/Cutthroat trout	$22 per person	
Existence Value of Habitats		
Terrestrial	$32–$122 per household per year	Based on Nunes and van den Bergh (2001)
Coastal	$11–$62 per household per year	
Wetland	$10–$116 per household per year	
Wetland Habitats		
Overall	$3,948 ($212) per hectare per year	Based on Brander, Floran, and Vermaat (2006). Mean
Woodland	$4,512 ($282) per hectare per year	values with median values in parentheses
Freshwater marsh	$4,935 ($169) per hectare per year	
Salt/brackish marsh	$3,666 ($240) per hectare per year	
Unvegetated sediment	$12,690 ($494) per hectare per year	
Mangrove	$564 ($113) per hectare per year	
Water Quality Improvements		
1. From unusable to boatable	1. $10.20 to $70.80 per year per household	Based on Luken, Johnson, and Kibler (1992)
2. From boatable to rough fishing	2. $15.24 to $61.20 per year per household	
3. From rough fishing to game fishing	3. $20.28 to $50.40 per year per household	
4. From game fishing to superior game fishing	4. $24 to $42 per year per household	
5. From unusable to superior game fishing	5. $50.40 to $182.40 per year per household	

(Continued)

TABLE 16-7 (*Continued*)

Plug-In Category	Shadow Price Value	Comments
Water Values by Use		
Waste disposal	$4.15 ($1.38)	Based on Frederick, van den
Recreation/fish and wildlife	$66.50 ($6.92)	Berg, and Hanson (1996). Mean
Navigation	$202.26 ($13.85)	values with median values
Hydropower	$34.63 ($29.09)	in parentheses. Values are per
Irrigation	$103.91 ($55.42)	acre-foot
Industrial processing	$390.67 ($182.87)	
Thermoelectric power	$47.10 ($40.18)	
Domestic	$287.96 ($134.38)	

Paulo Nunes and Jeroen van den Bergh survey various measures of biodiversity.[45] As shown in Table 16-7, they find that the existence value of different habitats ranges from $9.6 to $122.4 per household per year in 2008 U.S. dollars.

Luke Brander, Raymond Floran, and Jan Vermaat conducted a meta-analysis using 190 studies of the value of wetlands that provided 215 value observations.[46] The studies were from 25 countries, but a little over a half of these studies valued wetlands in North America. A wide variety of methods were used to value wetlands, including the travel cost method, hedonic pricing, and the replacement cost method; but the most important were market prices, which accounted for nearly 40 percent of the value observations, and contingent valuation, which accounted for 16 percent. The market price approach simply computed the total revenue obtained from the wetland being valued. Thus it ignores the costs of producing the goods and services derived from the wetland and, unlike the CV studies, misses any nonuse value associated with wetlands.

Averaging over all 215 available observations, the annual wetland value was found to be a little under $4,000 U.S. dollars per hectare per year. However, the median value was only $212 per hectare per year, indicating that some extremely large estimates drove up the mean. The mean and median for the North American studies are about 50 percent and 40 percent larger, respectively, than the overall mean and median. The mean and median values produced by the market price method are about $550 and $140, respectively, while those resulting from CV studies are around $11,000 and $60, respectively. Thus, extreme values produced by some of the CV studies helped pull up the overall mean. Table 16-7 displays mean and median values for different types of wetlands. As can be seen, the median values vary much less than the mean values.

THE VALUE OF WATER AND WATER QUALITY

Fresh water is a necessity and is becoming scarcer. As there generally is no well-functioning market for fresh water in most locations, analysts have to estimate its shadow price. CV surveys, the market analogy method, the intermediate good method, defensive expenditures, and the travel cost method have all been used to estimate the value of water of different quality levels or the benefits of improvements in water quality for various purposes.[47]

The fourth section in Table 16-7 summarizes annual household WTP amounts for water quality improvements for recreational purposes by Ralph Luken, Reed Johnson, and Virginia Kibler.[48] These authors drew on previous studies of the Monongahela River, near Pittsburgh. Luken, Johnson, and Kibler argue for distances of 30 miles as an upper bound in defining the relevant markets for such recreational sites. They also recommend using visitation rates for households within this distance that range from 50 percent for sites with few substitutes to 10 percent for sites with numerous substitutes.

EXHIBIT 16-1

Ralph Luken wished to estimate the costs and benefits of (technology-based) water pollution standards introduced by the Clean Water Act of 1972. However, there were no existing estimates of WTP for improvements in the water quality of the rivers in question. Therefore, he utilized WTP estimates from existing studies as a basis for his estimates of the value of improvements in water quality.

He initially considered eight existing studies that might provide plug-in values. Five of the existing studies used the contingent valuation method, two studies used the travel cost method, and the eighth study was a user participation study. Luken eliminated five of the studies because their focus was not similar to the sites he was considering. These five studies dealt with water systems, such as those on a large western lake and a western river basin. His sites, in contrast, were generally eastern rivers with local recreation usage. Therefore he focused on three studies: one on the Charles River in Boston and two on the Monongahela River in Pennsylvania. The Monongahela studies estimated benefits for three levels of improvement in water quality (from boating to fishing, from fishing to swimming, and from boating to swimming), whereas the Charles River study only examined improvements in water quality from boating to swimming (i.e., the biggest "jump" in quality). The summarized values as annual WTP per household (1984 dollars) are as follows:

	Water Quality Change		
River	*Boat-Fish*	*Fish-Swim*	*Boat-Swim*
Monongahela (contingent valuation)	$25–40	$14–23	$40–64
Monongahela (travel cost)	$8	$10	$18
Charles (contingent valuation)	—	—	$74

Unfortunately, these benefit categories did not directly map into the benefit categories Luken was using, which covered five quality improvement levels: U = Unusable, B = Boatable, R = Rough fishing, G = Game fishing, and G^* = Superior game fishing. Luken assumed that the travel cost method provided lower-bound estimates (because they include only use valuations) and the contingent valuation estimates provided upper-bound estimates (as they include nonuse as well as use valuations). As shown next, he also included

(Continued)

intrause estimates to reflect smaller benefit improvements. His plug-in values for water quality benefits (WTP per household per year in 1984 dollars) follow:

Initial Water Quality	Final Water Quality	Lower Bound	Upper Bound
U	U	$1–3	$9–18
U	B	$5	$35
U	R	$15	$50
U	G	$20	$80
U	G*	$25	$90
B	B	$2–4	$8–15
B	R	$8	$30
B	G	$15	$50
B	G*	$20	$60
R	R	$3–5	$6–13
R	G	$10	$25
R	G*	$15	$35
G	G	$3–6	$5–10
G	G*	$12	$20

Although the purpose of this exhibit is to illustrate the use of secondary sources, it is interesting to note that in using these values, Luken generally found that costs exceed benefits.

Sources: Adapted from Frederick W. Gramlick, "The Demand for Clear Water: The Case of the Charles River," *National Tax Journal,* 30(2) 1977, 183–195; Ralph A. Luken, *Efficiency in Environmental Regulation* (Boston: Kluwer Academic Publishers, 1990), 45–50, 88–90; V. Kerry Smith and William H. Desvousges, *Measuring Water Quality Benefits* (Boston: Kluwer-Nijhoff Publishing, 1986); V. Kerry Smith, William H. Desvousges, and Ann Fisher, "A Comparison of Direct and Indirect Methods for Estimating Environmental Benefits," Working Paper No. 83–W32, Vanderbilt University, Nashville, TN, 1984.

Kenneth Frederick, Tim van den Berg, and Jean Hanson summarize plug-in values for different uses of water based on a survey of 41 earlier studies.[49] The authors provide estimates of the cost of water in eight uses: waste disposal, recreation/fish and wildlife habitat, navigation, hydropower, irrigation, industrial processing, thermoelectric power generation, and domestic uses. Values are expressed in terms of dollars per acre-foot (one acre-foot equals 325,851 gallons, the volume of water required to cover one acre at a depth of one foot).

Water used for industrial processing and domestic use have the highest mean and median values. However, recreation/fish and wildlife habitat and irrigation account for nearly 80 percent of all the estimates and the highest values of any individual studies. We report both the median and mean values in Table 16-7 due to the lack of weighting in the final estimates. The authors point out that median values may be most applicable to national level assessment and likely reflect normal hydrologic conditions.

The authors note several caveats. Water quality is important in most uses, but this factor is not reflected in the estimates. The timing of rainfall and levels of the water table play a large role in the cost of water, and values vary among regions (as water value is inversely related to availability). They also note that supply and demand conditions change over time (due to seasonal variation, technological changes, and weather conditions), thereby affecting the value of water.

THE COST OF NOISE

The cost of noise is mostly relevant in the evaluation of transportation projects. The dominant method for estimating the cost of noise is the hedonic pricing method. Property values (usually those of private residences) are regressed on noise, structural characteristics of the houses (numbers of rooms, square footage), neighborhood characteristics (number of lots or broken windows per block), accessibility characteristics (to downtown or local waterfront), and other environmental characteristics (air pollution). It is important to control for air quality because it is correlated with noise pollution from automobiles.

The U.S. Federal Aviation Agency has developed a measure of the level of noise called the Noise Exposure Forecast (NEF).[50] One NEF is equal to a mean exposure over time to one decibel of noise. Ambient noise is in the 15–25 NEF range, "some" to "much" annoyance occurs in the 25–40 NEF range, and "considerable" annoyance occurs above 40 NEFs.

The sensitivity of house prices to changes in the noise level is measured by the noise depreciation sensitivity index (NDSI), which is also called the noise sensitivity depreciation index (NSDI). Either way, it represents the percentage reduction in the value of a house that results from a unit increase in the noise level, measured in NEFs.[51] One way to obtain the NDSI is to specify a semilog hedonic price function in which the price of a house (in logarithms) is a linear function of noise and various control variables. The NDSI equals the slope of this function with respect to noise multiplied by -100.[52]

Ian Bateman, Brett Day, Ian Lake, and Andrew Lovett conducted a review of "noise" studies published after 1970.[53] Perhaps somewhat surprisingly, consensus estimates of the NDSI have remained fairly stable over several decades. As shown in Table 16-8, noise pollution has two primary sources—air traffic and road traffic. The

TABLE 16-8   The Cost of Noise Pollution

Plug-In Category	*Shadow Price Value*	*Comments*
Cost of Noise		
Airline noise pollution	0.65 percent reduction in property value per NEF	Based on Schipper (1996) and Bateman, Day, Lake, and Lovett (2001).
Roadway noise pollution	0.64 percent reduction in property value per NEF	
Cost of Noise		
1. Residential properties	1. 0.65 percent reduction in value per NEF	Based on Uyeno, Hamilton, and Biggs (1993).
2. Condominiums	2. 0.90 percent reduction in value per NEF	
3. Vacant land	3. 1.66 percent reduction in value per NEF	

best estimate of the NDSI for air traffic noise in the U.S. is 0.65 percent.[54] Recall that the NDSI measures the percentage change in house prices for a change in ambient noise level of one NEF. In other words, if the noise level increases by one NEF, then the price of an affected house will decreases in value by 0.65 percent on average. Thus, houses adjacent to an airport with NEFs of 40 are priced 9.75 percent lower than houses farther from the airport with NEFs of 25. For roadway noise pollution, Bateman and his colleagues suggest that the NDSI is 0.64 percent.

The estimated NDSIs discussed thus far pertain to residential properties. Dean Uyeno, Stan Hamilton, and Andrew Biggs recognize that the NDSI may differ according to land use.[55] They estimate a semilog hedonic price function where the price of a house (in logarithms) is a linear function of noise (in NEFs) and other house quality characteristics. Using Canadian data, they estimate that the NDSI is 0.65 percent for detached houses with NEFs of 25 or higher (exactly the same as mentioned previously); they estimate it is 0.90 percent for condominiums and 1.66 percent for vacant land.

THE COST OF AIR POLLUTION

Air pollution results in both health and nonhealth costs. Health costs include the costs of premature death and the costs of morbidity (illness).[56] Nonhealth costs include environmental costs, such as those associated with rising sea levels, coastal erosion, river floods, deforestation, retarded plant growth, and reduced agricultural output. Other nonhealth costs include corrosion to buildings, cars, and materials (such as rubber), as well as loss of views.

Air pollutants are emitted from many sources, especially motor vehicles, industrial plants, and power plants.[57] Important pollutants are volatile organic compounds (VOCs), nitrogen oxides (NO_x), sulfur oxides (SO_x), carbon oxides (CO_x), and particulate matter of less than 10 microns in diameter (PM_{10}). VOCs combine with NO_x to produce ozone, which is a primary contributor to morbidity. Through chemical reactions SO_x, VOCs, and NO_x produce PM_{10}s, which cause both premature death and morbidity, especially respiratory diseases. The solution of SO_x and NO_x in cloud and rain droplets causes acid rain, which is known to damage pine and spruce forests and is thought to damage tobacco, wheat, and soya crops. Acid rain also damages buildings, increases the acidification of lakes, and affects fish populations.[58] The accumulation of greenhouse gas emissions, especially, carbon dioxide (CO_2), causes global warming.[59]

Analysts estimate the cost of pollution using two main approaches. One is the hedonic property value method.[60] The more widely used approach is called the *dose response function* or *damage function* approach. A dose response function (or damage function) relates unit increases in a pollutant to various health effects, such as the probability of premature death and increases in different types of important effects such as on visibility, materials deterioration, damage to the natural environment, and health. For example, in the case of health, an increase in a ton of particulate matter might be related to the increased probability of premature death and increases in different types of respiratory problems. These effects would then be weighted by dollar valuations of these effects, which themselves would usually be based on CV estimates of WTP.

TABLE 16-9   The Social Cost of One Ton of Air Pollutants (in 2008 U.S. dollars)

Plug-In Category	Number of Studies	Shadow Price Value (Dollars per ton of air emissions)			
		Minimum	*Median*	*Mean*	*Maximum*
Carbon monoxide (CO)	2	$2	$796	$796	$1,607
Nitrogen oxides (NO$_x$)	9	$337	$1,622	$4,284	$14,535
Sulfur dioxide (SO$_2$)	10	$1,178	$2,754	$3,060	$7,191
Particulate matter (PM$_{10}$)	12	$1,454	$4,284	$6,579	$24,786
Volatile organic compound (VOC)	5	$245	$2,142	$2,448	$6,732
Global warming potential (in CO$_2$ equiv)	4	$3	$21	$20	$35

Source: Adapted from Table 1 of Matthews and Lave (2000).

H. Scott Matthews and Lester Lave have derived estimates of the cost of key air pollutants based on a number of damage function studies that were conducted in the early and mid 1990s.[61] These estimates, with the cost figures updated to 2008 dollars, are summarized in Table 16-9. They indicate the costs resulting from a one-ton increase in each pollutant. As indicated by the wide ranges between the minimum and maximum values, there is a great deal of uncertainty related to the actual costs associated with various types of air pollution. As pointed out by Matthews and Lave, much of this uncertainty relates to the damage functions used to obtain the values. For example, it is difficult to isolate the extent to which premature death results from a one-ton increase in particulate matter from increases in premature death due to other pollutants. The wide range of values also occurs because air pollution varies considerably across areas and time. In addition, some studies only consider health effects, while other studies also incorporate other effects, such as on visibility and the natural environment. According to Matthews and Lave, monetization plays a comparatively minor role.

Probably the most important aggregate air pollution cost is the cost of carbon, the major source of global warming. Given its importance, it is not surprising that there has been considerable effort in recent years to estimate the social cost of carbon emissions. Richard Tol has recently conducted a meta-analysis of 211 estimates of the social cost of carbon from 47 different studies and found that, for peer-reviewed estimates that were based on a 3 percent discount rate, the mean social cost per ton of carbon is $35 in 2008 U.S. dollars, with a median of $28 per ton.[62] After carefully reviewing previous studies and adding considerable analysis of his own, David Pearce concluded that the marginal social cost of carbon is between $10 and $65 per ton of carbon.[63] Finally, in a less-formal examination of the literature, Ian Parry, Margaret Walls, and Winston Harrington settle on a value of $22 per ton of carbon.[64] They also point out that the social cost of carbon emissions is likely to rise in the future because of growth in the value of world output and because marginal damage will increase as temperature levels rise. Thus, they suggest the social cost will be $92 per ton of carbon by 2050 and $297 per ton of carbon by 2100.

All of the estimates of the current social cost of carbon emissions that appear above, including the mean estimate provided by Mathews and Lave, are roughly of the same magnitude. However, the well-known *Stern Review* contains a much larger estimate of over $300 per ton.[65] William Nordhaus suggests that the major reason for this high estimate is that carbon dioxide emissions have an expected atmospheric life of 100 years or so and, hence, estimates of the cost of emissions are very sensitive to the assumed discount rate.[66] The estimate in the *Stern Review* is based on a low social discount rate of 1 percent, while Chapter 10 of this book, in contrast, suggests a rate of 3.5 percent (and Nordhaus prefers an even higher rate). In addition, the *Stern Review* assumes that the damage of a current emission of carbon will continue into perpetuity. The fairly wide range for the cost of carbon emissions suggested by Pearce is also largely (although not entirely) attributable to discount rate assumptions, with the lower end of the range based on a constant discount rate and the upper end resulting from the use of a time-declining discount rate.

THE SOCIAL COSTS OF AUTOMOBILES

Ian Parry, Margaret Walls, and Winston Harrington review numerous studies that estimate negative externalities resulting from the operation of automobiles. Based on this review, they present their "very tentative" assessment of social costs resulting from each mile traveled by lightweight vehicles in the United States.[67] These estimates are shown in Table 16-10.[68] Perhaps surprisingly, the largest item in the table, at 6 cents per mile, is costs that result from congestion, much of which is attributable to wasted time. The second largest item at 3 cents per mile is costs resulting from accidents. These costs include injuries and property damage, but exclude injuries to the driver and other passengers as these are assumed to be internalized. Interestingly, Parry, Walls, and Harrington estimate that the costs associated with global warming that result from driving a mile is only about one-quarter of a penny. This is because a gallon of gasoline contains 0.0024 tons of carbon and they assume that an automobile can drive 21 miles with each gallon, which was the national average at the time of their study. Thus, given their conclusion that the social cost of one ton of carbon is $22, the cost per mile works out to 0.25 cents $((.0024 \times \$22)/21)$. Of course, there are many automobiles in the United States and many of them travel a substantial number of miles each year. Parry, Walls, and Harrington point out that, in aggregate, light-duty vehicles account for about 20 percent of carbon dioxide emissions in the U.S.

TABLE 16-10 The Social Cost of Automobiles
(in 2008 U.S. dollars)

Plug-In Category	*Shadow Price Value (Cents per mile)*
Greenhouse warming	0.3¢
Local pollution	2.0¢
Oil dependency	0.7¢
Congestion	6.0¢
Accidents	3.0¢
SUM	10.9¢

Source: Adapted from Table 2 of Parry, Walls, and Harrington (2007)

THE COST OF TAXATION: MARGINAL EXCESS TAX BURDEN

Government projects often involve expenditures that have to be financed through taxes. As discussed in Chapter 3, taxes typically result in a deadweight loss: the marginal excess tax burden (METB). This loss, or "leakage," occurs whenever there is a behavioral response to a tax—for example, an excise tax on a good causes purchases to fall or a tax on earnings causes workers to reduce their work hours. The marginal social value of the lost consumption or lost work is the deadweight loss of the tax. Important manifestations of the deadweight loss include the inefficient substitution of leisure for work, of barter for legal trade, and the search for tax loopholes. METBs vary according to the type of tax. In general, METBs are greater when the taxed activity is more demand elastic. The METBs from income taxes are higher than the METBs from property taxes and sales taxes.

There are numerous empirical estimates or the value of the marginal excess tax burden and the estimates vary for a number of reasons. For example, each type of tax (e.g., income taxes, sales taxes, and property taxes) has a different marginal excess tax burden. With respect to federal projects, however, it is probably reasonable to view income taxes as the marginal tax source. Thus, we focus on METB estimates that pertain to income taxes.

The major distortions caused by the individual income tax occur in labor markets. Therefore, estimates of the marginal excess tax burden of the income tax utilize estimates of labor supply elasticities. Although most estimates of the METB of the income tax are based on compensated labor supply elasticities, a few are based instead on uncompensated elasticities. It can be reasonably argued that unless a policy or program sufficiently benefits those who fund it through their taxes so that it essentially compensates them, which is unlikely in the case of most projects and programs, a METB that is based on uncompensated labor supply elasticities should be used in CBA.[69]

Daniel Fujiwara has assembled estimates of the METB that are based on both compensated and uncompensated labor supply elasticities. The estimates he collected of the marginal excess tax burden that are based on uncompensated labor supply elasticities appear in Table 16-11.[70] The average of the five mid-point estimates is 23 cents per dollar. The average of the low estimates is 18 cents per dollar and the average of the high estimates is 28 cents per dollar. The mean for the twenty studies based on compensated

TABLE 16-11   Plug-Ins for the Marginal Excess Tax Burden per Dollar of Revenue from Income Taxes

Study	Country	METB as a percentage	Mid-Point of METB Estimate (country dollars)
Dahlby (1994)	Canada.	0.09–0.38	0.235
Stuart (1984)	USA	0.43	0.430
Fullerton and Henderson (1989)	USA	0.06 – 0.17	0.115
Ballard et al. (1985)	USA	0.12 – 0.23	0.185
Campbell and Bond (1997)	Australia	0.19	0.190

Source: Correspondence with Daniel Fujawara.

labor supply elasticities that Fujiwara collected is 26 cents per dollar, with a range between 21 cents and 32 cents per dollar once the more extreme values are eliminated. METBs that are based on compensated labor supply elasticities tend to be larger than those based on uncompensated labor supply elasticities because the reduction in hours worked resulting from a given increase in taxes is greater with a compensated elasticity.

Although an estimate of 23 cents per dollar appears to provide a reasonable value for the METB for federal projects that are funded by income taxes, this estimate may not be appropriate for local government projects that are more likely to be funded through property taxes. For these projects, a METB of 17 cents per dollar, which Charles Ballard, John Shoven, and John Whalley estimated for property tax, might be used instead.[71]

TRANSFERRING AND ADJUSTING PLUG-IN VALUES

For the most part, the estimates discussed here are based on U.S. research. Differences in incomes, tastes, and other factors bring into question the appropriateness of using these estimates to analyze projects in other countries. Wherever possible, plug-in values should be adjusted to reflect the particular characteristics of a specific application, whether that is a different country or a nonrepresentative region of the United States.[72] Here, we briefly review four sets of factors that one might consider as a basis for adjustment: (1) differences in socioeconomic and other personal characteristics of the population (e.g., income and age), (2) differences in physical and other characteristics of the jurisdiction (e.g., geographic characteristics), (3) differences in the characteristics of the project itself (e.g., project quality), and (4) temporal changes.

Income, Tastes, and Other Socioeconomic Factors

It is often important to make adjustments due to socioeconomic differences or preference differences among different populations. Perhaps the most important variable is income. Most of the "goods" discussed here, including a statistical life, time, recreation, and the environment, are likely to be normal goods. People place higher values on them as their incomes rise. Some of them might be luxuries (sometimes called superior goods) (i.e., people might be willing to spend a higher proportion of their incomes on these goods as their income increases).

Preferences may also differ from one region to another or from one occupational group to another. People who live near airports may object less than others to aircraft noise; people who live in polluted areas may not value changes in air quality as much as people who live in areas with better air quality; and people who work in dangerous jobs may have greater propensity for risk than the average worker. Such differences in preferences affect how much people are willing to pay for particular policy effects.

Adjusting the VSL for Income and Other Factors. The VSL rises with income. Thus, U.S. estimates should be adjusted before they are applied to other countries. Although one might suspect that a statistical life is a luxury and thus has an income elasticity greater than 1, numerous researchers have obtained estimates of the income elasticity for the VSL of less than 1.[73] For example, Miller finds a range of income elasticity from 0.85 to 0.96, Mrozek and Taylor obtain estimates of 0.46 to 0.49, and Viscusi and Aldy find that it is between 0.52 and 0.61.[74]

Using the estimated VSL for the United States of $5 million to obtain the VSL for some other country, such as Canada, requires two steps. The first step is to convert the U.S. estimate into Canadian dollars. At mid-2008 exchange rates, for example, one Canadian dollar was equivalent to US$0.978. Consequently, US$5.0 million was equivalent to approximately C$5.1 million, where C$ represents Canadian dollars.[75] The second step is to adjust for income differences.

By definition, the income elasticity of the VSL, E_I, is given by:

$$E_I = \frac{\%\Delta VSL}{\%\Delta I} \qquad\qquad (16.4)$$

where $\%\Delta VSL$ represents the percentage change in VSL and $\%\Delta I$ represents the percentage change in income. Consequently, to convert a VSL based on U.S. data to an appropriate figure for Canada, we use the following formula:

$$V_{CAN} = V_{US} + E_I V_{US}(I_{CAN} - I_{US})/I_{US} \qquad\qquad (16.5)$$

Adjusting for purchasing power, Canadian incomes are currently approximately 15 percent lower than U.S. incomes and have maintained this average difference over the past several decades.[76] Setting $(I_{CAN} - I_{US})/I_{US} = -0.15$, the Canadian VSL equals C$4.62 million if E_I equals 0.50, C$4.44 million if E_I equals 0.75, and C$4.25 million if E_I equals 1.00. It seems reasonable to pick the midrange, thus giving a VSL for Canada in 2008 equal to C$4.44 million or US$4.34. Thus, it is roughly about 90 percent as high as the U.S. VSL. Further support for this estimate comes from Canadian-specific VSL studies.[77]

Earlier we mentioned that, in theory, the WTP to reduce fatality risk declines as the risk level declines. Therefore, the VSL should be adjusted for fatality risk. Air carrier fatality rates are lower than motor vehicle fatality rates, which suggests that the VSL for air travel should be lower than the VSL for road travel, holding everything else constant. At the same time, road travel is approximately 20 times more risky than working on a per-hour basis.[78] This suggests that the VSL for improvements in road safety should be valued more than the VSL computed from wage-risk studies. However, there are at least two problems with adjusting the VSL for the level of fatality risk. First, the appropriate size of the adjustment is not known. Second, contrary to theory, some studies have found that the VSL declines as fatality risk increases.[79] More research is needed before adjusting the VSL for fatality risk.

A third potentially important factor is sense of control. M. W. Jones-Lee and colleagues found that the average WTP to reduce death on the London underground is 50 percent higher than on roads.[80] This difference may be due to many factors, including incorrect estimation of the risks, loss of sense of control, or the method of death (people may think that dying in an underground crash is more traumatic than dying in a car crash). The loss of sense of control may be associated with the feeling that when one gives up control to a train driver or pilot, then that person may not fully internalize the externality associated with one's own death.

Adjusting the VTTS for Income and Other Factors. W. G. Waters examined how estimates of the VTTS vary with income, time (year of study), country, and trip purpose (interurban versus commuting or "other").[81] He finds that VTTS increases with income, but less than proportionately:

$$\text{VTTS}_Y = \left(\frac{Y}{\overline{Y}}\right)^{0.5} \overline{\text{VTTS}} \tag{16.6}$$

where VTTS_Y is the VTTS of a traveler with income Y, $\overline{Y}$ is the average income level, and $\overline{\text{VTTS}}$ is the average VTTS. He suggests that a convenient rule of thumb for the relationship is a square root rule. For example, if income goes up fourfold from the average, the VTTS doubles. Using such a rule, the VTTS rises more slowly than does income; it is a normal good but not a luxury. Subsequently, von Wartburg and Waters suggested using an income elasticity of 0.75; that is, the exponent in equation (16.6) would be 0.75, rather than 0.5.[82]

The relationship between VTTS and other variables appears to be weak. Waters found that VTTS increases over time (drifting upward at one percentage point per year) and that interurban travel has a slightly higher value than trips for other purposes. Von Wartburg and Waters suggest using a positive distance elasticity of 0.3.

Physical and Other Regional Characteristics

The second set of factors that may affect the transferability of plug-in values are the physical and other characteristics of a region. For example, the impact of air pollution varies widely geographically, depending on population density, climate, and topography. More people are affected in more densely populated areas. Other things held constant, greater precipitation in Vancouver than in Los Angeles means that the morbidity costs of NO_x or particulate matter are lower there.

The current level of consumption of a good in a region may also affect the value of changes in the amount of that good. In general, holding all other factors constant, people are willing to pay more (less) for safety-improving projects as the level of safety decreases (increases). Consequently, the VSL used in a project in a "high-risk" area should be higher than the VSL used in a project in a "low-risk" area, holding all other relevant factors constant.

Project Differences

The third set of factors pertains to the similarity between the policy under evaluation and the projects in the studies used to derive the plug-in values. For example, the value of water quality improvement obtained from studies involving small improvements in quality levels may not apply to a proposed policy that would involve a large change in the level of water quality. The magnitude of the error in the generalization depends on the degree of nonlinearity in the relationship between water quality improvements and WTP. Additionally, there may be important differences in the price and availability of substitutes which, if not accounted for, can cause biases.[83] In sum, policies or projects under evaluation should ideally be similar to the projects in the studies used to derive the plug-in values in terms of the availability and quality of alternatives.

Temporal Changes

The final set of factors includes those relating to the fact that valuations may change over time. For example, health costs per vehicle mile traveled are declining over time as heavily polluting vehicles are replaced. Technological change, as well as temporal changes in population characteristics or jurisdictional characteristics, may affect the plug-in estimates. For example, increasing incomes and declining supply of accessible recreational areas might increase the value of such activities, while increasing congestion at the sites might decrease the value of recreational activities. Updating original estimates using the composite CPI or the GDP deflator implies no change in the relative value of a recreational activity.

CONCLUSION

By making use of the plug-in values presented in this chapter, analysts can apply CBA to a wider range of policies than would be feasible if all shadow prices had to be estimated firsthand.

EXERCISES FOR CHAPTER 16

1. A 40-mile stretch of rural road with limited access is used primarily by regional commuters and business travelers to move between two major interstate highways. The legal speed limit on the road is currently 55 miles per hour (mph), and the estimated average speed is 61 mph. Traffic engineers predict that if the speed limit were raised to 65 mph and enforcement levels were kept constant, the average speed would rise to 70 mph.

    Currently, an average of 5,880 vehicles per day uses the stretch of road. Approximately half are commuters and half are business travelers. Traffic engineers do not expect that a higher speed limit will attract more vehicles. Vehicles using the road carry, on average, 1.6 people. Traffic engineers predict that raising the speed limit on this stretch of road would result in an additional 52 vehicle crashes involving, on average, 0.1 fatalities annually. They also predict that operating costs would rise by an average of $0.002 per mile per vehicle. The average hourly wage in the county in which the majority of users of the road work is $18.30/hour.

    Estimate the annual net benefits of raising the speed limit on the road from 55 mph to 65 mph. In doing this, test the sensitivity of your estimate of annual net benefits to several alternative estimates of the value of time savings and the value of life that you have selected from this chapter.

2. Analysts estimate that expanding the capacity of the criminal courts in a city would require about 7,200 additional hours of juror time. The average wage rate in the county is $20/hour. A recent survey by the jury commissioner, however, found that the average wage for those who actually serve on juries under the present system, who are also currently employed, is only $15/hour. The survey also found that about one-third of those who actually serve on juries under the existing system do not hold jobs—for example, they are homemakers, retirees, or unemployed.

    a. What shadow price should the analysts use for an hour of jury time?

    b. About one-fourth of the jurors do not receive wages from their employers while on jury duty. How does this affect your choice of the shadow price?

3. (Instructor-provided spreadsheet recommended.) Assuming that the elasticity of the value of a statistical life with respect to income is between 0.4 and 0.9 and that the value of a

statistical life in the United States is between $2 million and $7 million, ranges of values of a statistical life for Australia, Portugal, and Brazil are found in the spreadsheet. Data on per capita income were obtained from the Quick Reference Tables section of the World Bank site: http://siteresources.worldbank.org/DATASTATISTICS/Resources/GNIPC.pdf, using the Atlas method figures. Using the same source of data on per capita income, calculate ranges of the value of a statistical life for Norway, New Zealand and Croatia.

NOTES

1. This chapter draws upon Anthony E. Boardman, David H. Greenberg, Aidan R. Vining, and David L. Weimer, "Plug-In Shadow Price Estimates for Policy Analysis," *Annals of Regional Science* 31(3) 1997, 299–324; and Anming Zhang, Anthony E. Boardman, David Gillen and William G. Waters II, *Towards Estimating the Social and Environmental Costs of Transportation in Canada: A Report for Transport Canada* (Vancouver, Canada: Centre for Transportation Studies, University of British Columbia, August 2004) also available on Transport Canada's Web site. We would like to thank Diane Forbes for research assistance in preparing this chapter.

2. For example, Tae Hoon Oum, W. G. Waters II, and Jong-Say Yong surveyed over 60 studies of own-price elasticities of transport demand, "Concepts of Price Elasticities of Transport Demand and Recent Empirical Estimates: An Interpretative Essay," *Journal of Transport Economics and Policy* 26(2) 1992, 139–154. A companion survey reviews empirical estimates of public transit and auto usage; see Philip Goodwin, "A Review of New Demand Elasticities with Special Reference to Short and Long Run Effects of Price Changes," *Journal of Transport Economics and Policy* 26(2) 1992, 155–169.

3. For example, one study suggests that transportation and communications are substitutes; see E. A. Selvanathan and Saroja Selvanathan, "The Demand for Transport and Communication in the United Kingdom and Australia," *Transportation Research–B* 28(1) 1994, 1–9.

4. For our purpose, *value* and *cost* can be used interchangeably, but we stick with common nomenclature—that is, we refer to "the value of life saved (or lost)" and "the cost of injury."

5. For example, on gasoline demand, see Molly Espey, "Explaining the Variation in Elasticity Estimates of Gasoline Demand in the United States: A Meta-Analysis," *Energy Journal* 17(3)1996, 49–60.

6. Ted R. Miller, *Narrowing the Plausible Range Around the Value of Life* (Washington, D.C.: The Urban Institute, 1989); Ann Fisher, Lauraine G. Chestnut, and Daniel M. Violette, "The Value of Reducing Risks to Death: A Note on New Evidence," *Journal of Policy Analysis and Management* 8(1) 1989, 88–100; and W. Kip Viscusi, "The Value of Risks to Life and Health," *Journal of Economic Literature* 31(4) 1993, 1912–1946. See also Arianne de Blaeij, Raymond J. G. M. Florax, Piet Rietveld, and Erik Verhoef, "The Value of Statistical Life in Road Safety: A Meta-Analysis," *Accident Analysis and Prevention 35*, 2003, 973–986.

7. Ted R. Miller, "Variations Between Countries in Values of Statistical Life," *Journal of Transport Economics and Policy* 34(2) 2000, 169–188; Janusz R. Mrozek and Laura O. Taylor, "What Determines the Value of Life? A Meta-Analysis," *Journal of Policy Analysis and Management* 21(2) 2002, 253–270; W. Kip Viscusi and Joseph Aldy, "The Value of Statistical Life: A Critical Review of Market Estimates Throughout the World," *Journal of Risk and Uncertainty* 27(1) 2003, 5–76; and Ikuho Kochi, Bryan Hubbell, and Randall Kramer, "An Empirical Bayes Approach to Combining and Comparing Estimates of the Value of a Statistical Life for Environmental Policy Analysis," *Environmental & Resource Economics* 34 2006, 385–406.

8. Based on a meta-analysis of 22 U.S. wage-risk studies, Francois Bellavance and his colleagues obtained a slightly smaller median value of $7.63 million. Francois Bellavance, Georges Dionne, and Martin Lebeau, "The Value of a Statistical Life: A Meta-Analysis with a Mixed Effects Regression Model," Working Paper 06-12, Montreal: Canada Research Chair in Risk Management, 2006.

9. In addition, a recent empirical study in which Viscusi was involved with others found virtually identical values to these for the lower and upper bounds of the VSL. Thomas J. Kniesner, W. Kip Viscusi, Christopher Woock, and James P. Zillak, "Pinning Down the Value of Statistical Life," Discussion Paper No. 3107, Bonn: The Institute for the Study of Labor, 2007.

10. Eduard Zaloshnja, Ted Miller, Eduardo Romano, and Rebecca Spicer, "Crash Costs by Body Part Injured, Fracture Involvement, and Threat to Life Severity, United States, 2000," *Accident Analysis and Prevention 36*(3) 2004, 415–427.

11. Peter Abelson, "The Value of Life and Health for Public Policy," *The Economic Record* 79 (Special Issue) 2003, 2–13. This estimate is based on a VSL of $3 million, life expectancy of 40 years, and a discount rate of 3 percent.

12. EPA Science Advisory Board, *SAB Advisory on EPA's Issues in Valuing Mortality Risk Reduction*, (Washington, D.C.: U.S. Environmental Protection Agency, 2007); Joseph E. Aldy and W. Kip Viscusi, "Age Differences in the Value of a Statistical Life Revealed Preference Estimates," *Review of Environmental Economics and Policy* 1(2) 2007, 241–260; and Alan Krupnick, "Mortality Risk Valuation and Age: Stated Preference Evidence," *Review of Environmental Economics and Policy* 1(2) 2007, 261–282.

13. As we discuss in Chapter 18, the weights can be determined in a variety of ways including, for example, the standard gamble method, time trade-off value measurements, or estimated by physicians. Scores on indirect utility assessment instruments, such as the Health Utilities Index Mark 2 and 3, the EuroQol, and the Short-Form 6-D, can also be used as weights.

14. Dorothy P. Rice, Ellen J. MacKenzie, and Associates, *Costs of Injury in the United States: A Report to Congress* (San Francisco, CA: Institute for Health and Aging, University of California and Injury Prevention Center, The Johns Hopkins University, 1989)

15. Ted R. Miller and Maury Galbraith, "Estimating the Costs of Occupational Injury in the United States," *Accident Analysis and Prevention 27*(6) 1995, 741–747.

16. Alan E. Dillingham, Ted Miller, and David T. Levy, "A More General and Unified Measure for Valuing Labour Market Risk," *Applied Economics* 28 1996, 537–542.

17. Zaloshnja, Miller, Romano, and Spicer, "Crash Costs by Body Part Injured, Fracture Involvement, and Threat to Life Severity, United States, 2000."

18. Lawrence J. Blincoe, Angela G. Seay, Eduard Zaloshnja, Ted R. Miller, Eduardo O. Romano, Stephen Luchter, and Rebecca S. Spicer, *The Economic Impact of Motor Vehicle Crashes 2000*, National Highway Traffic Safety Administration, U.S. Department of Transportation. Available at http://www.nhtsa.dot.gov.

19. Note the high cost of motor vehicle crashes that cause workplace injuries. Although they account for only 3 percent of workplace injuries, they represent 6 percent of total costs, nearly six times the average cost of $21,040. This is partly explained by the high rate of fatalities from these crashes and by litigation with nonemployees over crashes involving multiple vehicles.

20. Ted R. Miller, "Costs and Functional Consequences of U.S. Roadway Crashes," *Accident Analysis and Prevention 25*(5) 1993, 593–607.

21. There is an AIS 0 category, but we ignore this level because it is very similar to property damage only (PDO).

22. Ted Miller, "Costs and Functional Consequences of U.S. Roadway Crashes."

23. The Federal Aviation Authority, the Office of the Secretary of Transportation for the Department of Transportation, American Road & Transportation Builders Association, and the Texas Transportation Institute commonly use these fraction of VSL figures to determine the WTP for avoiding an injury caused by an accident.

24. Ascribed by Miller, *Narrowing the Plausible Range Around the Value of Life,* 1989, p. 605, to Ezra Hauer (no cite).

25. For an excellent example see David A. Long, Charles D. Mallar, and Craig V. Thornton, "Evaluating the Benefits and Costs of the Jobs Corps," *Journal of Policy Analysis and Management* 1(1) 1981, 55–76.

26. Ted R. Miller, Mark Cohen, and Brian Wiersema, *Victim Costs and Consequences: A New Look,* NCJ 155282, National Institute of Justice, Washington, D.C., 1996; Mark A. Cohen, "The Monetary Value of Saving a High Risk Youth, *Journal of Quantitative Criminology* 14(1) 1998, 5-33; and Mark A. Cohen, Roland T. Rust, Sara Steen, and Simon T. Tidd, "Willingness-to-Pay

for Crime Control Programs," *Criminology* 42(1), 2004, 89–108.

27. For a CV study of the economic value of reducing violent crime in the United Kingdom, see Giles Atkinson, Andrew Healey, and Susana Mourato, "Valuing the Costs of Violent Crime: A Stated Preference Approach," *Oxford Economic Papers* 57(4) 2005, 559–585.

28. Herbert Mohring, John Schroeter, and Paitoon Wiboonchutikula, "The Values of Waiting Time, Travel Time, and a Seat on a Bus," *Rand Journal of Economics* 18(1) 1987, 40–56.

29. The relationship between speed and flow and between speed and density has been well documented. For example, see Anthony E. Boardman and Lester B. Lave, "Highway Congestion and Congestion Tolls," *Journal of Urban Economics* 4(3) 1977, 340–359.

30. The value of reliability (VOR) has been estimated between 50 to 140 percent of the wage rate, a variation larger than for recent estimates of VTTS. See Terence C. Lam and Kenneth A. Small, "The Value of Time and Reliability: Measured from a Value Pricing Experiment," *Transportation Research Part E* 37(2–3) 2001, 231–251.

31. United Kingdom: C. Sharp, "Developments in Transport Policy: The Value of Time Savings and of Accident Prevention," *Journal of Transport Economics and Policy* 22(2) 1988, 235–238; Mark Wardman, "The Value of Travel Time: A Review of British Evidence," *Journal of Transport Economics and Policy* 32(3) 1998, 285–316; Canada: J. J. Lawson, *The Value of Passenger Travel Time for Use in Economic Evaluation of Transport Investments* (Ottawa, Ontario: Transport Canada, 1989); New Zealand: Ted Miller, "The Value of Time and the Benefit of Time Saving," presented to the National Roads Board, New Zealand, and the Federal Highway Administration, U.S. Dept. of Transportation (Washington, D.C.: Urban Institute, 1989); The Netherlands: H. F. Gunn and C. Rohr, "The 1985–1996 Dutch Value of Time Studies," paper presented at PTRC International Conference on the Value of Time, Wokingham, UK, 1996; Norway: Farideh Ramjerdi, Lars Rand, and Kjartan Saelensminde, *The Norwegian Value of Time Study: Some Preliminary Results* (Oslo: Institute of Transport Economics); United States: Texas Transportation Institute, "Value of Time and Discomfort Costs, Progress Report on Literature Review and Assessment of Procedures and Data," Technical Memorandum for NCHRP, pp. 7–12; Ted R. Miller, "The Value of Time and the Benefit of Time Saving," Report prepared for the U.S. Department of Transportation; Developing countries: John Bates and Stephen Glaister, "The Valuation of Time Savings for Urban Transport Appraisal for Developing Countries: A Review," Report prepared for the World Bank, 1990.

32. William G. Waters II, "Values of Travel Time Savings in Road Transportation Project Evaluation," in David A. Hensher, Jenny King, and Tae Hoon Oum, eds., *World Transport Research: Proceedings of the 7th World Conference on Transport Research*, vol. 3 (New York: Elsevier, 1996) and Markus von Wartburg and William G. Waters II, "Congestion Externalities and the Value of Travel Time Savings," Chapter 2 in Anming Zhang, Anthony E. Boardman, David Gillen, and William G. Waters II, *Towards Estimating the Social and Environmental Costs of Transport in Canada: A Report for Transport Canada*.

33. Richard G. Walsh, Larry D. Sanders, and John R. McKean, "The Consumptive Value of Travel Time on Recreation Trips," *Journal of Travel Research* 29(1) 1990, 17–24. These authors found that travelers express a positive WTP for up to three hours of scenic driving in the Rockies on weekends.

34. See also David A. Hensher, "The Valuation of Commuter Travel Time Savings for Car Drivers: Evaluation Alternative Model Specifications," *Transportation* 28(2) 2001, 101–118.

35. See also Mark Wardman, "A Review of British Evidence on Time and Service Quality Valuations," *Transportation Research Part E* 37(2) 2001, 107–128. Wardman concluded that the multiplier for waiting time is 1.47 in Great Britain.

36. Cindy F. Sorg and John B. Loomis, *Empirical Estimates of Amenity Forest Values: A Comparative Review*, General Technical Report RM-107 (Fort Collins, CO: Rocky Mountain Forest and Range Experiment Station, Forest Service, USDA, 1984).

37. Richard G. Walsh, Donn M. Johnson, and John R. McKean, "Benefit Transfer of Outdoor Recreation Demand Studies, 1968–1988," *Water Resources Research* 29(3) 1992, 707–713.

38. Randall Rosenberger and John B. Loomis, *Benefit Transfer of Outdoor Recreation Use Values: A Technical Report Supporting the Forest Service's Strategic Plan* (2000 Revision). General Technical Report RMRS-GTR-72 (Fort Collins, CO: Rocky Mountain Research Station, 2001). This report was based on Doug MacNair, *1993 RPA Recreation Values Database,* RPA Program Contract 43-4568-3-1191 (Washington, D.C.; USDA Forest Service, 1993) and John Loomis, Randall S. Rosenberger, and Ram Shrestha, *Updated Estimate of Recreation Values for the RPA Program by Assessment Region and Use of Meta-Analysis for Recreation Benefit Transfer,* Final Report RJVA 28-JV7-962 (Fort Collins, CO: Colorado State University, Department of Agricultural and Resource Economics, 1999).

39. Pam Kaval and John Loomis, *Updated Outdoor Recreation Use Values with Emphasis on National Park Recreation*, Final Report to National Park Service, Fort Collins, CO (Colorado State University, Department of Agricultural and Resource Economics: Fort Collins, CO, 2003).

40. See, for example, the reports produced by the Millennium Ecosystem Assessment (www.millenniumassessment.org/en/index.aspx).

41. Elena G. Irwin, "The Effects of Open Space on Residential Property Values," *Land Economics* 78(4) 2002, 465–480.

42. I. J. Bateman, K. G. Willis, G. D. Garrod, P. Doktor, I. Langford, and R. K. Turner, "Recreation and Environmental Preservation Value of the Norfolk Broads: A Contingent Valuation Study," Report to the National Rivers Authority, Environmental Appraisal Group, University of East Anglia, 1992.

43. See, for example, Urs P. Kreuter, Heather G. Harris, Marty D. Matlock, and Ronald E. Lacey, "Change in Ecosystem Service Values in the San Antonio Area, Texas," *Ecological Economics* 39(3) 2001, 333–346.

44. John B. Loomis and Douglas S. White, "Economic Benefits of Rare and Endangered Species: Summary and Meta-Analysis," *Ecological Economics* 18 1996, 197–206.

45. Paulo A. L. D. Nunes and Jeroen C. J. M. van den Bergh, "Economic Valuation of Biodiversity: Sense or Nonsense?" *Ecological Economics* 39(2) 2001, 203–222.

46. Luke M. Brander, Raymond J. G. M. Floran, and Jan E. Vermaat, "The Empirics of Wetland Valuation: A Comprehensive Summary and a Meta-Analysis of the Literature," *Environmental & Resource Economics* 33(2) 2006, 223–250.

47. For a CV survey example, see Jeffrey L. Jordan and Abdelmoneim H. Elnagheeb, "Willingness to Pay for Improvements in Water Drinking Quality," *Water Resources Research* 29(2) 1993, 237–245. Charles W. Abdalla, Brian A. Roach, and Donald J. Epp, "Valuing Environmental Quality Changes Using Averting Expenditures: An Application to Groundwater Contamination," *Land Economics* 68(2) 1992, 163–169, use both the market analogy method (observations of bottled water expenditures) and defensive expenditures (expenditures incurred in boiling or hauling water or installation of household treatment systems). For a study that estimates the benefits of water quality improvements on river segments using the travel cost method, see V. Kerry Smith and William H. Desvousges, *Measuring Water Quality Benefits* (Boston, MA: Kluwer-Nijhoff Publishing, 1986).

48. Ralph Luken, F. Johnson, and V. Kibler, "Benefits and Costs of Pulp and Paper Effluent Controls Under the Clean Water Act," *Water Resources Research* 28(3) 1992, 665–674.

49. Kenneth D. Frederick, Tim van den Berg, and Jean Hanson, "Economic Values of Freshwater in the United States," Discussion Paper 97-43 (Resources for the Future: Washington, D.C., 1996).

50. Other measures, which were proposed in the U.K., are the Noise and Number Index (NNI), which measures aircraft noise, and the Traffic Noise Index (TNI), which measures motor vehicle noise.

51. Specifically, NSDI = $(D/\text{property value}) \times 100$, where D = reduction in property value from a unit increase in noise exposure that is, D = -100 $(\partial H/\partial \text{NEF})/H)$, where H represents house prices.

52. NDSI = $-100\dfrac{\partial \ln H}{\partial \text{NEF}}$. In contrast, the hedonic price of noise or marginal implicit price of noise is the slope of the function relating house prices, H, to noise level, that is, $\dfrac{\partial H}{\partial \text{NEF}}$.

53. Ian Bateman, Brett Day, Iain Lake, and Andrew Lovett, "The Effect of Road Traffic on Residential Property Values: A Literature

Review and Hedonic Pricing Study," Report to the Scottish Executive Development Department (Scottish Executive: Edinburgh, 2001).

54. See Y. J. J. Schipper, "On the Valuation of Aircraft Noise: A Meta-Analysis," unpublished paper, Titenberg Institute, Free University of Amsterdam, 1996.

55. Dean Uyeno, Stanley Hamilton, and Andrew J. G. Biggs, "Density of Residential Land Use and the Impact of Airport Noise," *Journal of Transport Economics and Policy* 27(1) 1993, 3–18.

56. Dallas Burtraw, Alan Krupnick, Erin Mausur, David Austin, and Deirdre Farrell, "Costs and Benefits of Reducing Air Pollutants Related to Acid Rain," *Contemporary Economic Policy* 16(4) 1998, 379–400.

57. For more on the sources of emissions in the United States, Germany, and the United Kingdom, see David W. Pearce and R. Kerry Turner, *Economics of Natural Resources and the Environment* (Baltimore: The Johns Hopkins University Press, 1990), 192. Also see Alan J. Krupnick and Paul R. Portney, "Controlling Urban Air Pollution: A Benefit-Cost Assessment," *Science* 252(26) 1991, 522–528.

58. Pearce and Turner, *Economics of Natural Resources and the Environment.*

59. Thomas C. Schelling, "Some Economics of Global Warming," *American Economic Review* 82(1) 1992, 1–14 and Intergovernmental Panel on Climate Change, *Climate Change 2001: Synthesis Report* (Cambridge: Cambridge University Press, 2001).

60. For example see Kenneth Y. Chay and Michael Greenstone, "Does Air Quality Matter? Evidence from the Housing Market," *Journal of Political Economy* 113(2) 2005, 376–424.

61. H. Scott Matthews and Lester B. Lave, "Applications of Environmental Valuation for Determining Externality Costs," *Environmental Science & Technology* 34(8) 2000, 1390–1395.

62. Richard S. J. Tol, "The Social Cost of Carbon: Trends, Outliers and Catastrophes," *Economics: The Open-Access, Open-Assessment E-Journal* 2 2008, 1–22.

63. David Pearce, "The Social Cost of Carbon and Its Policy Implications," *Oxford Review of Economic Policy* 18(3) 2003, 362–382.

64. Ian W. H. Parry, Margaret Walls, and Winston Harrington, "Automobile Externalities and Policies," *Journal of Economic Literature* 45(2) 2007, 373–399.

65. Nicholas Stern, *The Economics of Climate Change: The Stern Review* (New York: Cambridge University Press, 2007).

66. William D. Nordhaus, "A Review of the Stern Review on the Economics of Climate Change," *Journal of Economic Literature* 45(3) 2007: 682–702.

67. Ian W. H. Parry, Margaret Walls, and Winston Harrington, "Automobile Externalities and Policies."

68. Parry, Walls, and Winston also discuss costs that cannot be estimated, such as U.S. vulnerability to oil price volatility and military costs associated with protecting access to foreign oil.

69. We are indebted to Daniel Fujiwara for suggesting the argument in favor of using estimates based on uncompensated labor supply elasticities to us.

70. The original sources of these estimates are as follows. B. Dahlby (1994), "The Distortionary Effect of Rising Taxes", in W. Robson and W. Scarth (eds), *Deficit Reduction: What Pain, What Gain,* Toronto: C. D. Howe Institute 1994; Charles E. Stuart, "Welfare Costs per Dollar of Additional Tax Revenue in the United States," *American Economic Review* 74(3) 1984, 452–462; D. Fullerton and Y.K. Henderson (1989), "The Marginal Excess Burden of Different Capital Tax Instruments, *Review of Economics and Statistics* 71 1989, 435–42; Charles L. Ballard, John B. Shoven, and John Whalley, "General Equilibrium Computations of the Marginal Welfare Costs of Taxes in the United States," *American Economic Review* 75(1) 1985, 128–138; Charles L. Ballard, John B. Shoven, and John Whalley, "The Total Welfare Cost of the United States Tax System: A General Equilibrium Approach," *National Tax Journal* 38(2) 1985, 125–140; Harry F. Campbell and K. Bond, "The Costs of Public Funds in Australia," *Economic Record* 73 1997, 28–40.

71. Charles L.Ballard, John B. Shoven, and John Whalley, "General Equilibrium Computations of the Marginal Welfare Costs of Taxes in the United States."

72. For further discussion of these issues, see Kevin J. Boyle and John C. Bergstrom, "Benefit Transfer Studies: Myths, Pragmatism and Idealism," *Water*

Resources Research 28(3) 1992, 657–663; William H. Desvousges, Michael C. Naughton, and George R Parsons, "Benefit Transfer: Conceptual Problems in Estimating Water Quality Benefits Using Existing Studies," *Water Resources Research* 28(3) 1992, 675–683; Kenneth E. McConnell, "Model Building and Judgment: Implications for Benefit Transfers with Travel Cost Models," *Water Resources Research* 28(3) 1992, 695–700; John B. Loomis "The Evolution of a More Rigorous Approach to Benefit Transfer: Benefit Function Estimation," *Water Resources Research* 28(3) 1992, 701–705; Mark Downing and Teofilo Ozuna Jr. "Testing the Reliability of the Benefit Function Transfer Approach," *Journal of Environmental Economics and Management* 30(3) 1996, 316–322; and Martin van Bueren and Jeff Bennett, "Towards the Development of a Transferable Set of Value Estimates for Environmental Attributes," *The Australian Journal of Agricultural and Resource Economics* 48(1) 2004, 1–32. The van Bueren and Bennet article investigates the validity of transforming WTP values that were estimated for a national sample in Australia to regions within the country.

73. In Brad J. Bowland and John C. Beghin, "Robust Estimates of Value of a Statistical Life for Developing Economies: An Application to Pollution and Mortality in Santiago," *Journal of Policy Modeling* 23(4) 2001, 385–396. The authors find a median income elasticity of 1.95 and a range of income elasticity from 1.7 to 2.3.

74. Ted R. Miller, "Variations Between Countries in Values of Statistical Life," *Journal of Transport Economics and Policy* 34(2) 2000, 169–188; W. Kip Viscusi and Joseph Aldy, "The Value of Statistical Life: A Critical Review of Market Estimates Throughout the World," *Journal of Risk and Uncertainty* 27(1) 2003, 5–76; and Janusz R. Mrozek and Laura O. Taylor, "What Determines the Value of Life? A Meta-Analysis," *Journal of Policy Analysis and Management* 21(2) 2002, 253–270.

75. See PACIFIC Exchange Rate Service, University of British Columbia at *http://fx.sauder.ubc.ca/*.

76. Over the past 25 years Canadian incomes (measured by GDP/capita) have varied between 80 and 90 percent of U.S. incomes according to the Centre for the Study of Living Standards, Table 3 at http:// www.csls.ca/data/iptjune2009.pdf (accessed 20 Feb 2010), and are currently at about 85 percent.

77. For more discussion see Anthony E. Boardman and Steve Yong, "The Value of Statistical Life," Chapter 3 in Anming Zhang, Anthony E. Boardman, David Gillen, and William G. Waters II, *Towards Estimating the Social and Environmental Costs of Transport in Canada: A Report for Transport Canada.*

78. See Anthony E. Boardman and Steve Yong, "The Value of Statistical Life," p. 185.

79. See, for example, W. Kip Viscusi and Joseph Aidy, "The Value of Statistical Life: A Critical Review of Market Estimates Throughout the World" However, de Blaeij, Florax, Rietveld, and Verhoef, "The Value of Statistical Life in Road Safety: Meta-Analysis," and others, find WTP declines as the risk level declines.

80. M. W. Jones-Lee, G. Loomes, S. Jones, P. Rowlatt, M.. Spackman, and S. Jones, "Valuation of Deaths from Air Pollution," *NERA and CASPAR,* report prepared for the Department of the Environment, Transport and the Regions and the Department of Trade and Industry, London, 1998.

81. W. G. Waters II, "The Value of Travel Time Savings and the Link with Income: Implications for Public Project Evaluation," *International Journal of Transport Economics* 12(3) 1994, 243–253.

82. von Wartburg and Waters, "Congestion Externalities."

83. Stephanie Kirchhoff, Bonnie G. Colbey, and Jeffrey T. LaFrance, "Evaluating the Performance of Benefit Transfer: An Empirical Inquiry," *Journal of Environmental Economics and Management* 33(1) 1997, 75–93.

CHAPTER 17

Shadow Prices: Applications to Developing Countries[1]

Why does this book contain a separate chapter on cost-benefit analysis in developing countries? CBA in developing countries has much in common with CBA in industrialized countries. The major distinguishing characteristic of CBA in developing countries is the need to place greater emphasis on shadow pricing, that is, adjusting the market prices of project outputs and inputs so that they more accurately reflect their value to society. This topic is obviously important for those who actually will apply CBA in developing countries. However, it also provides insight into shadow pricing in developed countries.

The reason for the emphasis on shadow pricing is that markets in some developing countries are much more distorted than in most developed countries. Analysts suggest, for example, that labor markets are segmented and labor mobility is limited by systems of land tenure; that official exchange rates do not accurately reflect the value of the national currency; that the prices of goods exchanged in international markets are distorted by trade taxes, import controls, and high tariffs; and that credit markets are divided between formal and informal sectors. Consequently, experts advocate that shadow prices, which are often and rather confusingly called *accounting prices,* be used instead of market prices in conducting CBAs in developing countries. Similar to shadow price adjustments used in industrialized countries for CBA, accounting prices may incorporate adjustments for market failures such as monopoly and externalities. Particular emphasis in developing countries, however, is placed on adjustments for taxes (especially tariffs), subsidies, and quotas that affect the market prices of imports and exports.

Surprisingly, perhaps, there is not only agreement among the experts on using shadow prices, but also on the basic methods to use in determining the values of these shadow prices. Nonetheless, considerable variation remains in the details of how these methods are applied in practice. These methods, which received much of their impetus from international organizations involved in the funding of projects in developing countries, were developed in the early 1970s by the United Nations Industrial Development Organization[2] and by Ian Little and James Mirrlees.[3] The ideas contained in these two publications were then synthesized by Lyn Squire and Herman G. van der Tak,[4] two employees of the World Bank, who emphasized the concepts developed by Little and Mirrlees. As a consequence, the resulting approach, which with some modification continues to enjoy wide acceptance, is sometimes called the *LMST accounting price method.* This chapter describes this method and discusses some of the key issues it raises.[5]

THE LMST METHODOLOGY

The LMST methodology makes a basic distinction between tradeable goods and nontradeable goods. *Tradeable goods* include consumption goods and productive factors that are exported or imported, as well as products for which there might potentially be an international market—for example, close substitutes of the goods that are traded internationally. Thus, traded goods affect, or potentially can affect, a nation's balance of payments. *Nontradeable goods* include all other consumption goods and productive factors such as local transportation, electricity, services, and (most importantly) local labor. The key to LMST project evaluation is in using *world prices,* the prices at which goods are actually bought and sold internationally, to shadow price all project inputs and outputs that are classified as tradeable.[6] Nontradeable goods are often produced with inputs that are tradeable so that world prices can also be used to value them. Even the labor for a project may be drawn from other sectors of the economy where it was previously producing tradeable goods so that world prices can once more be used.[7]

The rationale for using world prices is not that free trade prevails or that world prices are undistorted—although they are less distorted than the domestic market prices in many developing countries and are probably less distorted today than they were when the LMST methodology was initially developed—but that they more accurately reflect the opportunities that are available to a country, and these opportunities should be recognized in evaluating projects. For example, if a project input has to be imported, it is reasonable to value it at its import price. Similarly, if project output is to be exported, it is reasonable to value it on the basis of its export price because this indicates what it would contribute to the nation's foreign exchange. Thus, the methodology is based on the principle of *trade opportunity costs.*

To see the rationale for using world prices to value project outputs and inputs more clearly, consider a developing country that is conducting a CBA of a proposal to build a steel plant with government funds. Although the country currently has a high tariff on imported steel, it nonetheless is dependent on steel produced in other countries. Because the tariff is incorporated into the domestic market price of steel, it can be viewed as a transfer between domestic steel buyers and the government. However, world prices do not incorporate tariffs. Thus, the world price for an export is often considerably lower than its market price in a developing country. Consequently, a CBA that is based on domestic market prices could indicate that the steel plant project should proceed, when, in fact, the real resource cost of importing steel (that is, the cost net of the tariff) is smaller than the resource cost of producing it domestically. Similarly, if a project uses a locally produced (but potentially importable) input that has an artificially inflated price because of high tariffs or import quotas, the potential to purchase the input more cheaply on the world market should be recognized in determining the project's cost. As a third example, consider a project to increase the production and foreign sales of an agricultural crop. In some developing countries, national policies keep the domestic market prices of some agricultural crops artificially low. When this occurs, a crop production project might not pass the cost-benefit test if domestic market prices are used, but could pass it if the analysis is based instead on world prices. Thus, the LMST method argues that the values of imports and exports on the world market should be the basis for decisions about domestic projects.

ILLUSTRATIONS OF THE LMST METHOD IN PRACTICE

To describe how this kind of shadow pricing is done in practice, we discuss three examples for an import, for an export, and for a nontradeable good (electricity).[8] All three examples are assumed to pertain to a project being considered in a small, developing country with a distorted economy. For simplicity, it is also assumed that the amounts of imports and exports involved would not be large enough to affect world prices. This last assumption, which is sometimes called the "small country assumption," is the one usually made in conducting CBAs of projects in developing countries and is realistic except when a project will substantially affect a country's export of a good and the country has a large share of the world market for that good.[9]

Shadow pricing in all three cases involves multiplying each market price by an *accounting price ratio* (APR). An APR can be defined as follows:

$$\text{APR for good } i = \frac{\text{accounting price of good } i}{\text{market price of good } i}$$

$$= \frac{\text{shadow price of good } i}{\text{market price of good } i} \qquad (17.1)$$

Because the accounting price of a good or a productive factor is essentially synonymous with its shadow price, multiplying the market price of a good by its APR converts it to its shadow price. That is,

$$\text{shadow price for good } i = \text{APR for good } i \times \text{market price for good } i$$

The ways in which APRs are obtained in practice are described as we work through the examples.

An Import

Determination of the accounting price for an import that is being used as an input to our hypothetical project (or, alternatively, an output from the project that substitutes for a good that otherwise would have to be imported) is shown in Table 17-1. The *CIF*

TABLE 17-1 Accounting Price for Imported Good

Item	Dollars (U.S. $)	Market Value (Pesos)	APR	Accounting Value (Pesos)
CIF price	40	80	1.00	80
Tariff	—	10	0.00	—
Transport	—	8	0.50	4
Distribution	—	5	0.80	4
All components	—	103	0.85	88

Exchange rate: 2 pesos = US$1

Source: Adapted from Terry A. Powers, "An Overview of the Little-Mirrlees/Squire-van der Tak Accounting Price System," in Terry A. Powers, ed., *Estimating Accounting Prices for Project Appraisal* (Washington, D.C.: Inter-American Development Bank, 1981), Table 1-1.

price of a unit of the good on the world market, that is, the cost of the item (*C*) plus insurance (*I*) and freight expenses to the port of destination (*F*), is US$40. This $40 price is sometimes called a *border price* because it corresponds to the amount of foreign currency needed to pay for the good at the border. To translate the $40 amount into the local currency, pesos, it would be multiplied by the country's exchange rate. In the example, a dollar is assumed to equal 2 pesos. Thus, the $40 CIF price is equivalent to 80 pesos. Because the 80 peso price is already a world price, its shadow price is also 80 pesos. Hence, the accounting price ratio equals 1.

As just indicated, an exchange rate is needed to translate foreign currency, such as U.S. dollars, into the local currency. Usually, the official exchange rate is used for this purpose. However, as the existence of black markets in currency exchange in many developing countries attests, a nation's official exchange rate may not accurately reflect the actual value of its currency. This would occur, for example, if the official exchange rate is that a dollar is convertible into 2 pesos, but a dollar can, on average, actually be used to purchase domestic output worth 3 pesos. This latter value is called the *shadow exchange rate.* In practice, the official, rather than the shadow, exchange rate, is normally used in determining accounting prices because it is more easily obtained. This choice is not very important for CBA, however. In conducting a CBA using the LMST method, *all* project benefits and costs must be expressed in accounting prices. As just seen, some, such as imports, already are. As discussed later, others, such as nontradeables, must be converted into accounting prices. As a result, all benefits and costs are made commensurable. Moreover, each is the multiplicative product of its value in dollars (or some other foreign currency) and a constant that equals whatever exchange rate is being used. Consequently, the choice between the official and the shadow exchange rates affects the absolute size of benefits and costs—the shadow rate is usually larger than the official rate—but not their relative size. Thus, the choice neither determines whether net benefits are positive or negative nor the relative ranking of projects.[10]

As indicated in Table 17-1, in addition to its CIF price of 80 pesos, the domestic market price of the import also reflects a tariff of 10 pesos, local transportation costs of 8 pesos, and distribution costs of 5 pesos. Thus, a unit of the import would cost 103 pesos in the local market. However, only part of these additions to the market price reflect real resource costs to the economy. For example, the revenue from a tariff is simply a transfer between buyers and the government. Thus, its accounting price ratio is set equal to zero. Transportation and distribution do involve the use of real resources, but in this example, their accounting price ratios are less than 1. Consequently, their shadow or accounting prices are less than their market prices. (The reasons for this divergence will be discussed later.) Hence, the shadow price of the import equals 88 pesos (80 + 4 + 4), considerably less than its market price of 103 pesos. The import's overall APR is, therefore, less than 1 (0.85 = 88/103), which is typically the case for imports.

An Export

Table 17-2 describes the determination of the shadow price of an export that is produced by the project (or, alternatively, a project input that otherwise would have been exported). The price of the export at the port of origin, before insurance and freight charges to its ultimate destination are added (its so-called *free on board [FOB] price),* is

TABLE 17-2 Accounting Price for Export

Item	U.S. Dollars (U.S. $)	Market Value (pesos)	APR	Accounting Value (pesos)
FOB price	100	200	—	—
Export tax	25	50	1.0	50
Transport for export	1	2	0.5	1
Factory gate price	74	148	1.0	148
Transport for domestic sale	—	4	0.5	2
Distribution in domestic market	—	10	0.8	8

Exchange rate: 2 pesos = U.S. $1
Source: Adapted from Terry A. Powers, "An Overview of the Little-Mirrlees/Squire-van der Tak Accounting Price System," in Terry A. Powers, ed., *Estimating Accounting Prices for Project Appraisal* (Washington, D.C.: Inter-American Development Bank, 1981), Table 1-2.

assumed to equal $100 or 200 pesos. Because the $100 is the amount of foreign currency received at the border, it is the border price for an export. The FOB price includes the cost of producing a unit of the good (148 pesos), as well as an export tax (50 pesos) and transportation costs to the port of origin (2 pesos). Only half the transportation costs are assumed to reflect real resource costs to the economy (i.e., the APR equals 0.5). The export tax is a transfer between foreign purchasers and the domestic government, but because foreigners typically would not be given standing in evaluating the project, the tax amount would be included in the shadow price. Therefore, if the good were produced by the project and exported, its shadow price would equal 199 pesos (148 + 50 + 1). Thus, the overall accounting price ratio for the export is slightly less than 1 (0.99 = 199/200).

It is useful to point out that by shadow pricing the export, it is valued on the basis of each unit's contribution to the nation's foreign exchange. Thus, for example, although a tax on an export increases its shadow price, possibly decreasing sales, a subsidy on an export, perhaps, to encourage sales, decreases its shadow price.

Now, suppose that rather than being a product for export, the good in question is a project input that would be exported if the project were not undertaken. Under these circumstances, the shadow price must include the additional costs incurred by diverting the good to domestic use, as well as revenue forgone and costs saved by not exporting the product. Thus, the net effects of not exporting the good must be determined. The revenue forgone is the 200 peso FOB price, while the cost saved is the 1 peso of transportation cost to the port of origin. The additional costs incurred by diverting the good to the project include local transportation costs of 4 pesos and distribution costs of 10 pesos. As previously discussed, because only part of these additional costs reflect real resource costs to the economy, they must be adjusted to their shadow price equivalents by multiplying them by their accounting price ratios. Thus, the shadow price of the export when it is diverted to domestic use is 209 pesos (200 − 1 + 2 + 8).

A practical problem arises when project inputs are potential exports, such as the case just described, and also when project outputs are substituted for potential imports. The problem involves selecting the appropriate world price to use in shadow pricing because often there will be several alternative world prices that are candidates because similar products may vary along different dimensions such as quality and ease of access.

Obviously, a CBA that selects an export price from the low end or an import price from the high end of such a range is more likely to show that net benefits are positive than one that selects from the opposite end of the range. One reasonable approach is simply to use a value from the middle of the range if the good cannot be priced in terms of its specific characteristics.

A Nontradeable Good (Electricity)

Table 17-3 lists the costs of the various inputs needed to produce the additional electricity required by the project. These inputs would presumably be diverted by the project from other uses and, thus, represent opportunity costs associated with the project. The electricity itself is assumed to be produced domestically and, hence, is an example of a nontraded good. However, for CBA purposes, it must be made commensurable with traded goods, which, as already discussed, are valued in terms of their world prices.

To make tradeable and nontradeable goods commensurable, the LMST approach involves determining the equivalent value of nontradeables in world prices. To do this, it exploits the fact that the production of nontradeables involves inputs that are tradeable. As the table indicates, many of the inputs required to produce the

TABLE 17-3 Accounting Price for Electricity Value at Marginal Cost of Supply (in thousands of pesos)

Item	Cost in Domestic Prices	APR	Cost in Accounting Prices
Capital costs	**3,000**	0.89[c]	**2,678**
Thermal generating unit (CIF)	1,800	1.00	1,800
Building and site construction	1,200	0.73	878
Imported materials (CIF)	500	1.00	500
Labor	250	0.60[a]	150
Industry taxes and tariffs	200	0.00	0
Other expenses	250	0.91	228
Imported materials (CIF)	180	1.00	180
Labor	40	0.60[a]	24
Other expenses	30	0.80[b]	24
Annual operating costs	**1,000**	0.83[c]	**831**
Fuel oil (CIF)	800	1.00	800
Maintenance	40	0.78	31
Parts (CIF)	15	1.00	15
Labor	20	0.60[a]	12
Other	5	0.80[b]	4
Taxes and tariffs	160	0.00	0

[a]The accounting price ratio of labor is discussed later; here it is assumed to equal 0.6 for purposes of the example.
[b]The standard conversion factor (SCF), which is assumed to have a value of 0.8 for purposes of the example, is used to convert the domestic value to its accounting price.
[c]Rounded to two significant digits.
Source: Adapted from Terry A. Powers, "An Overview of the Little-Mirrlees/Squire-van der Tak Accounting Price System," in Terry A. Powers, ed., *Estimating Accounting Prices for Project Appraisal* (Washington, D.C.: Inter-American Development Bank, 1981), Table 1-3.

needed electricity—for example, the material required to construct the generating plant—are tradeable. Thus, using the LMST method to shadow price a nontraded good involves breaking down the cost of the good into its traded, nontraded, and labor components. The nontraded components can then be further broken down into *their* traded, nontraded, and labor components, and so forth. These components and subcomponents are listed in the table. By multiplying each of these components and subcomponents by their accounting price ratio, the opportunity cost of supplying an additional amount of a nontraded good to the project can be evaluated in terms of the tradeable goods required to produce the additional amount. Although this example pertains to electricity, the same procedure would be used in the case of other nontraded goods such as the transport and distribution costs items listed in Tables 17-1 and 17-2.

The different APRs listed in Table 17-3 are derived by several different methods. As previously indicated, the APR of a tradeable component that is expressed in CIF prices (for example, imported materials) is 100, although the ratio for a domestic transfer (for example, tariffs on tradeables and taxes on nontradeables) is zero. The APR for domestic labor is complex to derive and will be discussed in some detail later. Those for nontradeable components are simply weighted averages of the APRs of their components, where the weights are the cost of each component expressed in shadow prices as a fraction of total cost. Sometimes these weighted averages are derived from calculations made by the project evaluators. For example, the APR for annual operating costs of 0.83, shown in Table 17-3, is computed as follows: 1.0 (800/1000) + 0.78(40/1000) + 0(160/1000). However, the weighted APRs that are used to obtain shadow pricing for fairly small subcomponents (for example, other maintenance expenses) are often *conversion factors* (CFs), which are obtained from previous studies and pertain to entire industries or national economic sectors, such as the electricity and gas industry, rather than to one specific input, such as the fuel oil used to produce the electricity needed by the project.

Except for pertaining to a broader segment of the economy, conversion factors are similar to APRs that are developed for a specific project evaluation. Like project-specific APRs, they are weighted averages of their components. Because conversion factors can be plugged into more than one CBA, they are obviously an example of shadow prices from secondary sources, the topic covered in Chapter 16. Because the use of conversion factors saves time for evaluators, the extent to which they are used in a particular CBA depends on the resources available for the study and the accuracy required. In practice, the role of conversion factors is often of considerable importance.

A technique called *semi-input-output (SIO) analysis* is often used to derive conversion factors. SIO analysis utilizes national input-output tables, national censuses, household expenditure surveys, and other national data, such as information on tariffs, quotas, and subsidies. SIO analysis is particularly difficult to conduct if input-output tables are not already available, because then the analyst must piece together the equivalent information. Using the available data, an SIO table is constructed that divides the economy into as many productive sectors as the data allow (for example, corn and corn products, fishing, mining, hotels, electricity and gas, real estate, etc.). Often fifty or more productive sectors are listed. Part of the output produced in each sector will be directly consumed, and part will be used as inputs in the other sectors. The table indicates the percentage contribution of the output produced in each sector to the total market value of the output produced in all the other sectors. In addition, primary factor inputs such as labor, capital, foreign exchange, and taxes and subsidies are also listed, and their percentage contributions to the total market value of the output produced in each of the productive sectors is also indicated. Deriving conversion factors from the table constructed for SIO analysis essentially involves solving a set of simultaneous equations using matrix algebra.[11] In doing this, SIO analysis treats interdependence between different sectors of the economy consistently; for example, coal may be used to produce electricity and electricity may be used in mining coal.

In addition to being used to obtain CFs for individual industries, SIO can be used to obtain CFs for skilled and unskilled labor and aggregate CFs. One such aggregate CF is the *consumption conversion factor* (CCF), which is a weighted average of the APRs for a nationally representative market basket of goods. The CCF plays several roles in shadow pricing that are mentioned later. Another aggregate CF is the *standard conversion factor* (SCF), which is the ratio of the value of all production at accounting prices to the value of all production at market prices. In other words, the SCF is the weighted average of the CFs for the productive sectors of the economy, where the weights are the contribution that each sector makes to total national output. The SCF is used in computing the shadow prices of minor components of nontraded goods when more specific CFs are not available.

Although nowadays the SCF is usually derived by actually computing a weighted average of the CFs for the productive sectors of an economy, it is instructive to examine briefly the following formula, which has been used in the past to obtain a crude approximation of the SCF:

$$\text{SCF} = \frac{M + X}{M(1 + T_m - S_m) + X(1 - T_x + S_x)} \tag{17.2}$$

where, M is the total value of imports in market prices, X is the total value of exports in market prices, T_m is the total effective tariff rate on imports, T_x is the total effective tax rate on exports, S_m is the total effective subsidy rate on imports, and S_x is the total effective subsidy rate on exports. The numerator of this expression values imports and exports at their domestic market prices, while the denominator values them at their world prices. This expression is only a crude approximation because it ignores nontraded goods in the economy and because it assumes that distortions in domestic market prices are entirely due to tariffs and import taxes and subsidies (thereby ignoring other distortions such as taxes on nontraded goods and import quotas, monopoly power, and externalities). What is interesting about this expression is that it implies that tariffs and export subsidies cause market prices to be larger than world prices, while taxes on exports and import subsidies have the opposite effect. As the former are usually more important in developing countries than the latter, the SCF, most CFs for specific sectors of the economy, and most APRs for specific goods have values that are less than 1.[12] For example, Steve Curry and John Weiss examined separate studies of 13 different countries and found that estimates of the SCF range between 0.59 and 0.96, with an average value of about 0.8.[13]

SHADOW PRICING WHEN GOODS ARE IN FIXED SUPPLY

As previously indicated, the LMST approach normally relies on the shadow prices of inputs required to produce a good to convert its market price to a shadow price. An important exception to this procedure occurs when the supply of a good is fixed, however. This could happen, for example, if there is a quota on imports or the government exercises a monopoly over providing a particular good or service and has run out of funds needed to supply more.

A situation in which supply is fixed is illustrated in Figure 17-1, which pertains to the electricity that would be required for our project. The production of electricity is often characterized as having constant marginal costs up to a capacity constraint. Consistent with this, the supply curve in the figure is perfectly elastic prior to Q_1 and then becomes completely inelastic when the nation's generating capacity is exhausted. Let D_a represents the demand curve for electricity without the project and D'_a represents the demand curve with the project. Under these circumstances, the electricity capacity constraint is not binding. As a result, the project would not affect the current consumers of electricity. However, it would require that additional inputs be used to produce the additional electricity needed by the project. Consequently, the method

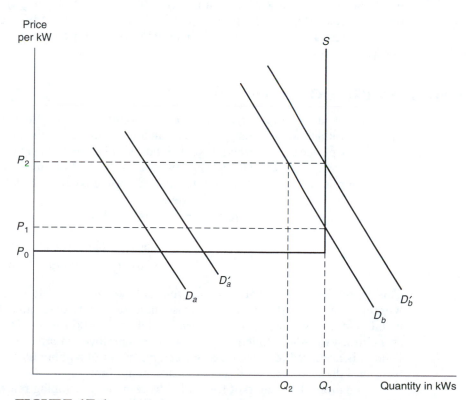

FIGURE 17-1 Shadow Pricing when Electricity Supply Is Either Completely Elastic or Completely Inelastic

outlined earlier for deriving the shadow cost of the electricity used on the project would be appropriate.

Now assume that without the project the demand curve for electricity is D_b and with the project it is D'_b. Thus, the project would increase the market price of electricity from P_1 to P_2 and reduce the consumption of electricity by current consumers from Q_1 to Q_2. Because of the price increase, current consumers lose surplus, while the producers of electricity gain surplus. As explained in Chapter 4, these changes in surplus can be appropriately taken into account in determining the cost of electricity to the project by simply using the average of the old and new prices, $(P_1 + P_2)/2$, as the market price. Thus, measured in market prices, the cost of electricity for the project would equal $[(P_1 + P_2)/2](Q_1 - Q_2)$.

To use the LMST method, however, this cost must be converted to its shadow price equivalent. In doing this, account must be taken of the fact that when the supply of electricity is fixed the opportunity cost of diverting some electricity from current consumers to the project is not additional inputs but the consumption forgone by current consumers. One way of doing this is to ask what consumers would purchase with $[(P_1 + P_2)/2](Q_1 - Q_2)$ of additional income and then determine the shadow prices of each of these goods using the techniques discussed earlier. Of course, it is highly unlikely that the specific items that consumers would purchase would actually be known. Thus, in practice, $[(P_1 + P_2)/2](Q_1 - Q_2)$ would probably be converted to its shadow price equivalent by multiplying it by the CCF, which as previously mentioned is a weighted average of APRs for a nationally representative market basket of goods.

THE SHADOW PRICE OF LABOR

A project in any country will use labor. In developing countries, increasing the employment of unskilled workers may, in fact, be an important part of the motivation for initiating many projects. Even when it is not, labor is still likely to be a major nontradeable input used in the project. Hence, shadow pricing the cost of employing workers is of critical importance in conducting CBA in developing counties. Shadow pricing labor raises some difficult special issues, however.

Like any input used in a project, labor has an APR:

$$\text{APR of type } j \text{ labor} = \frac{\text{shadow wage of type } j \text{ labor}}{\text{the market wage of type } j \text{ labor}} \qquad (17.3)$$

This expression implies that different types of labor (for example, skilled and unskilled workers) may have different APRs. It also indicates that to determine the shadow price of labor it is first necessary to determine labor's market wage. Doing this is fairly straightforward when skilled workers who are employed at a nation's business establishments are hired to work on a project, but it is not so apparent when the project hires unskilled workers. We discuss the easier case first.

If a nation's labor market for skilled workers is functioning reasonably well—for example, unemployment among such workers is not high—then, as seen in Chapter 4, the wage at which they are hired by a project provides a reasonable approximation of their market wage. Consequently, the project wage provides a reasonable approximation of their productivity elsewhere and, hence, represents the social opportunity cost (expressed in domestic prices) of hiring them for the project.[14] If a conversion factor is available for skilled workers, then the shadow wage can be obtained by multiplying it by the project wage. Alternatively, but less satisfactorily, the project wage can be multiplied by sector-specific conversion factors to convert it to its foreign exchange equivalent. For example, if carpenters are hired, then the project wage for carpenters can be multiplied by the conversion factor for the construction industry. Still less satisfactory if neither a conversion factor for skilled workers nor an appropriate sector-specific conversion factor is available, then an estimate of the standard CCF can be used.

A special case occurs when a developing country does not have sufficient skilled workers for the project and the required workers must be hired from abroad. These foreign workers would typically not be given standing. Nonetheless, they would spend some of their earnings within the country, while sending or taking the remainder out of the country. Thus, to determine the shadow cost of hiring foreign labor, the fraction of earnings sent abroad would have to be estimated. As these earnings would be a direct loss of foreign exchange, they would have an APR of 1. In principle, the value of each item purchased within the country should be multiplied by its APR. Because the information to do this would probably not be available, however, all earnings that remain in the country would probably be multiplied by the economy-wide CCF.[15] Hence, the shadow wage for foreign workers, SW_f, would be computed as follows:

$$SW_f = [h + (1 - h)(CCF)](PW) \qquad (17.4)$$

where, PW is the project wage, h is the fraction of the project wage sent or taken home, and $(1 - h)$ is the fraction spent domestically.

A substantial fraction of the unskilled workers for a project in a developing country are ultimately likely to be drawn from the countryside. This will be true not only of projects in rural areas, but also of projects in cities, even if the workers who are directly hired by the project currently reside in urban areas. The reason is that as employment increases in urban areas in developing countries, workers in rural areas are induced to migrate to the areas where employment has increased.

Why this migration occurs is suggested by a well-known model developed by John Harris and Michael Todaro.[16] Their model is based on two observations about developing countries: unemployment is often very high in urban areas, and earnings are typically considerably higher in urban than in rural areas. Although Harris and Todaro do not explain the reasons for the higher urban wages, they could be due to minimum wage laws that are enforced in urban areas but not rural areas, the role of unions, decisions by foreign corporations that are under pressure in their home countries to pay wages that exceed subsistence levels, or a belief on the part of employers that higher wages result in higher productivity because higher paid workers are healthier, less likely to leave the firm, and more motivated.[17] The key point for purposes of the Harris-Todaro model is that urban wages are above their equilibrium level and, consequently, result in urban unemployment.[18]

Rural wages, in contrast, are at their equilibrium level and, consequently, lower than urban wages.

Harris and Todaro suggest that because of the higher urban wages, workers will migrate from the countryside to the cities, even though some of them will not be able to find jobs. More specifically, they postulate that the probability that a rural worker will obtain employment upon migrating to a city equals $(L - U)/L$, where L is the size of the workforce in the city, U is the number of unemployed persons, and $E = (L - U)$ is the number of employed workers. Therefore, the model implies that workers will have an incentive to migrate from the countryside to the city as long as:

$$RW < UW(E/L) \qquad \qquad \textbf{(17.5)}$$

where RW is the rural wage, UW is the urban wage, and $UW(E/L)$ is the wage that migrating workers will receive on average (in other words, $UW(E/L)$ is their expected wage). Thus, according to the model, rural-urban migration will cease when:

$$RW = UW(E/L) \qquad \qquad \textbf{(17.6)}$$

Two important implications of this model are that even when there is no incentive for further migration urban unemployment may continue to be high, and urban wages may continue to exceed rural wages.

We now use the Harris-Todaro model to examine the effects of locating a new project in a city. Assume that prior to initiating the project the equilibrium condition specified in equation (17.6) is being met. Now assume that ΔE unskilled workers are hired to work on the project. If ΔE is fairly small relative to the size of the workforce, then wage rates are unlikely to be affected. Moreover, urban wage rates may also be unaffected because they are already above their equilibrium level. However, because of the increase in the number of available urban jobs, the expected urban wage facing rural workers will increase to $UW[(E + \Delta E)/L]$, inducing some rural workers to migrate. Consequently, the equilibrium can only be reestablished if:

$$E/L = (E + \Delta E)/(L + \Delta L) \qquad \qquad \textbf{(17.7)}$$

where ΔL is the number of workers added to the urban labor force.

There are two things to notice here. First, if there are no changes in urban wage rates, then current residents of the city who are presently outside the labor force (that is, not already employed or seeking employment) will not be induced to join it, except perhaps by the increase in the number of available jobs. Therefore, many, if not most, of the workers added to the urban labor force will be migrants from rural areas. Second, according to the model, the number of migrants is likely to exceed the number jobs created by the project. This can be seen by first rearranging the terms in equation (17.7) to obtain:

$$L + \Delta L = L(E + \Delta E)/E \qquad \qquad \textbf{(17.8)}$$

and then by subtracting $L = L(E)/E$ from equation (17.8) and rearranging the terms to obtain:

$$L + \Delta L - L = L(E + \Delta E)/E - L(E)/E$$

or

$$\Delta L/\Delta E = L/E \tag{17.9}$$

Because the urban labor force consists of both workers and the unemployed (that is, $L = E + U$), the ratio L/E must exceed 1 and, thus, as equation (17.9) implies, so will the ratio $\Delta L/\Delta E$.

The implications of this simple model can be illustrated with an example. If the urban wage is 50 percent higher than the rural wage (that is, if $RW(L/E) = 1.5RW = UW$), then equation (17.6) implies that E/L equals 0.67. Hence, one-third of the urban workforce will be unemployed. Moreover, equation (17.9) implies that for each job created by a project, 1.5 persons will enter the urban labor force (that is, $\Delta L = \Delta E(L/E) = 1(3/2) = 1.5$). For reasons already stressed, many, if not most, of these persons are likely to be rural migrants.

Because most of the unskilled workers added to the workforce as a result of a government project would probably be drawn from the countryside, the output that is forgone is production in rural areas. If the project is located in a rural area, then rural-urban migration is not a consideration, and the shadow wage would be obtained by simply multiplying the rural wage by the most appropriate conversion factor that is available. (Some of the possible conversion factors that might be used were listed earlier when the shadow wage of skilled workers was discussed.) However, if the project is located in an urban area, then account must be taken of the number of workers who would leave the countryside for each job created. According to the Harris-Todaro model, if *all* the workers added to the workforce as a result of the project are rural migrants, then this can be accomplished by multiplying the product of the rural wage and the conversion factor by the ratio, L/E. Notice, however, that equation (17.6) indicates that $RW(L/E) = UW$. In other words, the Harris-Todaro model implies that an *upper-bound* estimate of the shadow wage rate for evaluating projects in urban areas can be obtained by multiplying the urban wage rate by the appropriate CF.[19]

The product of the urban wage rate and the CCF should be viewed as an upper bound because fewer than L/E rural workers may migrate in response to each job created by an urban project. First, as previously mentioned, some urban residents may be induced into the labor force as jobs are created by the project. Second, the actual number of migrants could be less if workers are risk averse or there are monetary or psychic costs associated with migrating. Third, if the project is sufficiently large, then the migration of rural workers could cause rural wages to rise, thereby reducing the ultimate number of migrants. If fewer than L/E workers migrate, then the appropriate market wage to use in determining the shadow wage rate would be less than the urban wage. Thus, Caroline Dinwiddy and Francis Teal demonstrate that, under a wide variety of assumptions, the appropriate market wage to use is likely to fall somewhere between the rural and the urban market wage.[20] Consequently, *if large numbers of unskilled workers will be employed on an urban project in a developing country, and there are wide differences between rural and urban wages, a sensitivity test should be conducted in determining the shadow wage rate by first using the rural market wage and then using the urban wage.*

While urban wage rates for unskilled workers can be obtained from survey data—for example, the average manufacturing wage can be used[21]—many rural workers produce crops for their own consumption. Hence, the effective wage rate of these workers is more difficult to ascertain. One way to construct an estimate of the rural market wage is to first determine how a typical rural worker who is likely to be affected by the project being evaluated allocates his or her productive time and then estimate the value of the worker's output. For instance, suppose that the typical worker is employed on a cacao plantation for half the year and receives a daily wage of 40 pesos and food and transportation valued at 10 pesos a day, for a total of 50 pesos. Because the worker is only needed at the plantation for six months, he or she works at home during the remainder of the year, growing corn for three months and bananas for the remaining three months. Although the corn and bananas are mostly grown for home consumption, if they were brought to the local market they could be sold for 910 pesos and 1,365 pesos, respectively. Dividing market value of corn and bananas by the 91 days during which the work to grow each was performed suggests that the worker earned a daily market wage of 10 pesos from growing corn and a daily market wage of 15 pesos from growing bananas. Given this information, the worker's daily wage can be computed as a weighted average of his or her daily return from each endeavor, where the weights are the fraction of time he or she devoted to each activity. That is:[22]

$$RW = .5(50) + .25(10) + .25(15) = 31.25 \text{ pesos} \qquad (17.10)$$

In principle, at least two additional factors should be taken into account in determining the shadow wage rate of rural, unskilled workers, although in practice they rarely are because of the lack of adequate information.

First, it is possible that moving to the city requires the worker to work longer hours, places the worker under greater stress, and results in a less-satisfactory lifestyle. If so, then the shadow wage rate should, in principle, be adjusted upward to account for the resulting loss of utility.

Second, many rural workers live in large extended families. If a project induces a rural worker to migrate to the city, then the effects on the remaining family members should, in principle, be taken into account. The remaining family members lose the migrating worker's output, of course, but they gain because the worker no longer consumes the income available to the family. These two amounts are not necessarily entirely offsetting; it is possible that the gain exceeds the loss. This would occur, for example, if the family shares its income (the total value of the output produced by all family members) equally among its members. Under these circumstances, each family member's consumption level would be equal to the average value of the output produced by the family. The family member's contribution to family output, however, would correspond to his or her marginal product. Because rural families typically produce much of their output at home on a fixed amount of land, it is likely that the family would be producing on the declining segment of its marginal product curve. If so, the value of a family member's marginal product will be smaller than the value of

---
EXHIBIT 17-1

In 1974, the World Bank led an international effort to eradicate onchocerciasis (river blindness) in West Africa. The project, which extended over more than two decades and covered 11 countries, used insecticides to kill the blackfly, the carrier of the parasite that causes onchocerciasis. The benefits of the program stem from the reduction in the number of cases of river blindness. A CBA of a similar program in a developed country would likely have measured benefits by monetizing the morbidity and mortality effects with shadow prices. However, estimating the necessary shadow prices in these very poor countries was impractical. Instead, the CBA of the project conducted by the World Bank in 1995 measured benefits in terms of the value of increased agricultural output resulting from increased labor and land. As the average person who develops blindness lives with it for 8 years and dies 12 years prematurely, each avoided case adds about 20 years of productive life. Assuming that these years are employed in agriculture, the percentage increase in the rural labor supply resulting from the project was projected and multiplied by an estimated output elasticity of labor of 0.66 to obtain the predicted percentage increase in agricultural output. The increase in agricultural output was in turn valued using an accounting price, the agricultural value-added, which is estimated by the World Bank. A similar procedure was used to value the additional agricultural land made available through eradication. Overall, the project offered net positive benefits, even when assuming labor force participation rates and land utilization rates of only 70 percent.

Source: Adapted from Aehyung Kim and Bruce Benton, "Cost-Benefit Analysis of the Onchocerciasis Control Program," World Bank Technical Paper Number 282, May 1995.

the output that he or she consumes. Thus, if a family member is induced by a project to migrate in such circumstances, the consumption levels of the remaining family members will increase.

ADDITIONAL TOPICS

As previously mentioned, with the exception of using world prices to shadow price benefits and costs, conducting CBAs in developing countries is similar to CBA in industrialized countries. However, the literature concerning CBA in developing countries has evolved somewhat separately from the main body of CBA literature. As a result, there are a few additional topics that are treated somewhat differently in the former than in the latter. In this section, we briefly review these topics. The discussion is brief because these differences are mainly conceptual in nature; they appear to have had little effect on the actual conduct of CBA.

Budget-Constrained CBA and Discounting

The points discussed in Chapters 6 and 10 concerning discounting are generally applicable to CBA in developing countries as well as industrialized countries. Chapter 10, however, presumes that funding for government projects would come from taxes, which would reduce consumption or private-sector investment, or by borrowing from foreigners. In contrast, a government in a developing country may be reluctant or unable to borrow additional funds or to increase tax revenues. In other words, government expenditures cannot, or will not, be increased even if such an increase would greatly benefit the public. By the same token, they cannot or will not be decreased even if the funds could be better used in the private sector. Given a fixed public-sector budget, therefore, a new project can be undertaken only if the funds are diverted from a current government project or program.[23] In these circumstances, the opportunity cost of undertaking that project is not forgone consumption or private-sector investment, but forgone public-sector investment.

We are skeptical, however, that a government's budget would ever really be fixed, at least over the long run. Nonetheless, if this were the case, then the appropriate social discount rate should be obtained by conducting CBAs of current government projects and determining their internal rates of return. Analysis should focus on projects that would be terminated if the proposed project went ahead. These projects should have relatively low internal rates of return as government should terminate the worst projects. The very worst project might have a negative internal rate of return, which indicates, of course, that it should be terminated. One should never use a negative rate of return to evaluate a new project.

If government budgets are reasonably flexible, then the social discount rate may be based on observed market interest rates. The practical problems in doing this, however, are considerably more formidable in developing than in developed countries because of the high degree of fragmentation in lending markets in developing countries. For example, Karla Hoff and Joseph Stiglitz cite evidence that lending rates in the informal economy in some developing countries vary considerably and are up to six times higher than rates in the formal sector.[24]

It is also important to remember that where governments have expenditure constraints, new projects should be selected on the basis of their benefit-cost ratio, as we discussed in Chapter 2.

Multiple Goals and Social Project Appraisal

The literature on CBA in developing countries suggests that public expenditures have three somewhat conflicting goals: (1) increasing economic efficiency (that is, maximizing net economic worth), (2) encouraging economic growth, and (3) redistributing income from the rich to the poor. A sharp distinction is made between CBAs that focus solely on the first goal, economic efficiency, and analyses that attempt to assess the contribution of projects to all three goals. This chapter has so far discussed only CBA. The second type of analysis is sometimes called *social project appraisal*.

In the LMST approach, social project appraisal is based on the following general framework:

$$SW = NSB + C(W/\theta - CCF) \tag{17.11}$$

where *SW* is the social welfare gain from a project, *NSB* is the present value of net social benefits as they are usually estimated in CBA using appropriate accounting prices, *C* is the present value of the net change in private-sector consumption resulting from the project and is measured in domestic market prices, *W* is a *distributional weight* parameter with a value that is greater than 1 if the change in consumption disproportionately accrues to persons with below-average incomes and a value smaller than 1 if the consumption change disproportionately accrues to persons with a with above-average incomes. The value of W would be 1 if the per capita consumption of all income groups changed by the same amount. Methods for obtaining values for the parameter, W, are described in Chapter 19. θ is the shadow price of capital and is defined in Chapter 10, and CCF is, again, the economy-wide consumption conversion factor.

The first term on the right-hand side of equation (17.11), *NSB*, reflects only the first of the goals listed above: economic efficiency. Most actual CBAs in developing, as well as in industrialized, countries simply stop at this point, thereby implicitly setting the second term equal to zero. The second term is meant to incorporate the other two goals: economic growth and income redistribution. It implies that while a reduction in investment is a social cost, an increase in consumption is a social benefit. For example, it is often suggested that savings rates are especially low in developing countries and result in insufficient investment to sustain economic growth. Thus, $C \times$ CCF is subtracted to reflect the notion that an increase in consumption has less social value than an equal increase in investment. In other words, the intent is to bias choices among projects toward those that increase investment the most. Because the benefits and costs that comprise the *NSB* estimate are all measured in shadow prices, but C is measured in domestic market prices, the CCF is used to make the two terms commensurable. The ratio, W/θ, indicates that social welfare increases as a greater part of the increase in consumption accrues to persons with incomes below the national average (that is, as W becomes larger) but decreases as the amount of forgone investment becomes greater (that is, as θ becomes larger).[25]

To get some flavor for how use of the framework summarized by equation (17.11) might affect a CBA in practice, consider a project that increases the per capita consumption of higher income groups more than lower income groups, so that $W = 0.5$. Chapter 10 suggests that a reasonable value for θ is 1.1. Finally, Steve Curry and John Weiss have assembled 14 different estimates of the value of CCF from 12 studies of different developing countries.[26] These estimates range between 0.74 and 1.12, but all but four are between 0.79 and 0.94. For illustrative purposes, we assume that CCF = 0.85. Given these values, $(W/\theta - \text{CCF}) = (0.45 - 0.85) = -0.40$. This implies that a one-peso increase in consumption as a result of a government project is around 40 percent as valuable as a one-peso increase in investment. Notice, however, that if the consumption from the project is spread more evenly across income groups, it is conceivable that $(W/\theta - \text{CCF})$ will have a positive value, implying that an increase in consumption has greater social value than a similar increase in investment. This would occur, for example, if $W = 1$.

Although the LMST framework for social project appraisal addresses important issues, it is somewhat ad hoc. In our view, the method that is described in Chapter 10 for incorporating the shadow price of capital into social discounting, which results in a direct adjustment of the *NPV* estimate, provides a more appropriate way of taking account of the opportunity cost of consuming project output, rather than investing it. The use of the parameter, W, in equation (17.11) represents one particular approach to taking account of the possibility that an increase in the consumption of low-income persons is of greater social value than an equal increase in the consumption of higher-income persons. Alternative, and perhaps preferable, approaches that can be used to do this are described in some detail in Chapter 19, where we discuss distributional weighting. These alternative approaches also directly adjust the net present value estimate.

Using Plug-In Values

Many of the plug-in values that we discussed in Chapter 16 can be used in CBAs in developing countries. However, when we engage in benefits transfer (i.e., use a shadow price estimate obtained in one country at one time to estimate the shadow price in another country at another time), we should adjust for differences in incomes, tastes, and other factors. In Chapter 15, we illustrated how to compute an appropriate value of a statistical life (VSL) for Canada based on a VSL for the United States. The same procedure can be used to compute a VSL for use in a developing country, adjusted for income.

The estimated VSL does control for income differences between the two countries. However, this is only a partial adjustment because, as we discussed in Chapter 14, the VSL may vary with other factors. For example, it generally increases with the level of fatality risk: people are willing to pay more to avoid fatality risk as the fatality risk level increases. If the level of fatality risk is higher in a developing country than in the United States, then the estimated VSL should be adjusted upward, holding everything else constant. Furthermore, one should also adjust for other factors that affect the VSL, such as age, attitudes, or culture. In practice, however, adjustments are rarely made for these other factors.

IS THE LMST METHOD ACTUALLY USED FOR PROJECT EVALUATION?

Not surprisingly, international organizations such as the World Bank make regular use of the shadow pricing procedures discussed in this chapter in conducting CBA. However, the governments of many developing countries do not. Some time ago, the World Bank surveyed 27 developing countries about the project evaluations that they conduct.[27] All but three of these countries had one or more offices with specific responsibility for project evaluation. None of these offices conducted social project appraisals; that is, their formal analyses were concerned solely with whether the evaluated projects increased economic efficiency. However, some of the offices were not using appropriate methods to determine this. Although information was not available for several of the surveyed countries, only eight of the countries surveyed were found to use shadow pricing regularly in conducting project evaluations. In fact, seven of the remaining countries not only failed to shadow price, but they also did not discount benefits and costs.

CONCLUSION

A large fraction of economic activity in developing countries typically occurs outside efficient markets. Consequently, the application of CBA in developing countries requires extensive use of shadow prices. The LMST accounting price method is the most commonly used framework for determining a consistent set of shadow prices. Implementing it often requires considerable skill in working with available information.

Finding appropriate shadow prices for unskilled labor poses a particularly difficult problem. Thus, although the principles of CBA are readily transferable to developing countries, their application requires familiarity with a variety of complex shadow pricing issues.

EXERCISES FOR CHAPTER 17

1. A developing country is considering building a steel plant in its largest city. The estimated construction costs of this plant in domestic prices are listed in the following table.
   a. Compute the weighted APR for the imported materials that would be used in constructing the plant.
   b. Compute the total construction cost of the plant in accounting prices.

Accounting Price for Steel Plant Construction (in Thousands of Dubyas)			
Item	*Cost in Domestic Prices*	*APR*	*Cost in Accounting Prices*
Imported materials			
CIF price	500		
Taxes and tariffs	100		
Transportation	50	0.60	
Distribution	20	0.80	
Local materials	600	0.90	
Labor			
Skilled	300	0.95	
Unskilled	800	0.55	
Capital costs			
Equipment	250	0.75	
Other	100	0.90	

2. A certain developing country currently imports all its wheat but is considering funding an irrigation project that would allow domestic farmers to grow and sell wheat. The domestically grown wheat would be sold in competitive markets at an estimated price of 15 dubyas per bushel. The wheat the nation currently imports has a CIF price of US$3 per bushel. The official exchange rate is 4 dubyas per dollar. The nation's tariff on imported wheat is 2 dubyas per bushel. Transportation and distribution charges from the port to a typical market are 2 dubyas and 1 dubya per bushel, respectively. The APR has been estimated to be 0.6 for transportation and 0.8 for distribution.
   a. Calculate the market price of imported wheat.
   b. Calculated the shadow price of imported wheat.
   c. Should the irrigation project proceed?
3. Assume that a typical unskilled rural worker in a developing country would be paid 2 dubyas a week if he migrates to the city and finds a job. However, the unemployment rate for unskilled workers is 40 percent in the city.
   a. What does the Harris-Todaro model predict the worker's rural wage is?
   b. Assume now that the government is considering funding a project in the city that would use substantial numbers of unskilled workers. Using your answer to part a, suggest a reasonable upper-bound and lower-bound estimate of the market wage rate for unskilled workers that the government might use in conducting a CBA of the proposed project.

NOTES

1. We are indebted to Tim Gindling for suggestions on this chapter.
2. *United Nations Industrial Development Organization, Guidelines for Project Evaluation* (New York: United Nations, 1972).
3. I. M. D. Little and J. A. Mirrlees, *Project Appraisal and Planning for Developing Countries* (London: Heinemann Educational, 1974).
4. Lyn Squire and Herman van der Tak, *Economic Analysis of Projects* (Baltimore: Johns Hopkins University Press, 1975).
5. An excellent concise summary of the approach can be found in Terry A. Powers, "An Overview of the Little-Mirrlees/Squire-van der Tak Accounting Price System," in Terry A. Powers, ed., *Estimating Accounting Prices for Project Appraisal* (Washington, D.C.: Inter-American Development Bank, 1981), 1–59. Recent book-length treatments include Caroline Dinwiddy and Francis Teal, *Principles of Cost-Benefit Analysis for Developing Countries* (Cambridge, UK: Cambridge University Press, 1996); Robert J. Brent, *Cost-Benefit Analysis for Developing Countries* (Cheltenham, UK: Edward Elgar Publishing, 1998); and Steve Curry and John Weiss, *Project Analysis in Developing Countries* (London: Macmillan, 1993). The book by Curry and Weiss provides a particularly clear exposition of how to use the approach in practice. The Dinwiddy and Teal book focuses on the economic principles that underlie the approach.
6. There is an alternative to this approach, which is known as the UNIDO approach and is based on the United Nations Industrial Development Organization's 1972 guidelines. Instead of using world prices to shadow price project inputs and outputs, it uses domestic prices to do this. In practice, the major focus of the LMST method is in adjusting nontradeables to world prices, whereas the major focus of the UNIDO approach is in adjusting tradeables to domestic prices. CBA can be conducted using either approach and, as demonstrated by Curry and Weiss, *Project Analysis in Developing Countries,* Chapter 6, the two approaches will produce similar results if equivalent assumptions are made in conducting analyses under them. Because the LMST method is more widely used than the UNIDO approach, we focus on it in this chapter.
7. What is the world price? The purchasing power parity (PPP) theory predicts that "the nominal exchange rate between two currencies should be equal to the ratio of aggregate price levels between the two countries, so that a unit of currency of one country will have the same purchasing power in a foreign country" (Alan M. Taylor and Mark P. Taylor, "The Purchasing Power Parity Debate," *Journal of Economic Perspectives* 18(4) 2004, 135–158 at 135). The PPP theory suggests that the world price can be measured in any free-floating currency. However, the PPP appears not to hold fully in the short run, so the choice of a currency for the world price may make a difference. The best strategy is probably to choose a widely traded currency such as the U.S. dollar.
8. These examples are all adapted from Terry A. Powers, "An Overview of the Little-Mirrlees/Squire-van der Tak Accounting Price System," 20–28.
9. If a project increases a country's exports of a good, and the increase reduces the world price for the good, then a CBA must not only take account of the benefits to the country from the increased sales of the product but also the cost that results because previous exports of the product must now be sold at a lower price.
10. For a detailed discussion, see Dinwiddy and Teal, *Principles of Cost-Benefit Analysis for Developing Countries,* 128–131; or Curry and Weiss, *Project Analysis in Developing Countries,* 130–137.
11. For an introduction to using the semi-input-output approach to derive conversion factors, see Curry and Weiss, *Project Analysis in Developing Countries,* Chapter 11. For a detailed description of methods for computing CCFs either directly with input-output tables or using the semi-input-output approach, as well as four studies in which these methods are used to compute conversion factors for developing countries, see Terry A. Powers, ed., *Estimating Prices for Project Appraisal.*
12. The major exceptions usually occur among APRs for goods that are exported.
13. Curry and Weiss, *Project Analysis in Developing Countries,* 264–266.

14. This will not be the case, of course, if labor markets are highly distorted by union contracts, government wage controls, or for other reasons. Under these circumstances, the method described in Chapter 4 for determining the opportunity cost of hiring the unemployed to work on a project may have to be used.

15. Because the spending patterns of domestic and foreign workers are likely to differ, a CCF that is specific to foreign workers should ideally be used. Such a CCF is unlikely to be available, however. Thus, the CCF for the overall population would probably be used in practice.

16. John. R. Harris and Michael. P. Todaro, "Migration, Unemployment, and Development," *American Economic Review* 60(1) 1970, 126–142. This model is quite simple, making no attempt to capture all important labor market phenomena in developing countries, yet it provides some very useful insights.

17. See Dinwiddy and Teal, *Principles of Cost-Benefit Analysis for Developing Countries,* 145–147 and 151. Higher living costs could also contribute to higher urban wages but, unlike the factors listed in the text, would not induce workers to migrate from rural to urban areas.

18. The urban wage is still equal to the marginal product of labor because urban employers hire workers until the point where the marginal product of labor equals the marginal cost of hiring an additional worker.

19. The conclusion that the urban wage should be used was also reached by Christopher J. Heady ("Shadow Wages and Induced Migration," *Oxford Economic Papers* 33[1] 1981, 108–121) on the basis of a model that incorporated more general and complex assumptions than the Harris-Todaro model. However, Heady also discussed

certain circumstances under which a lower wage, but one that is probably higher than the rural wage, should be used.

20. Dinwiddy and Teal, *Principles of Cost-Benefit Analysis for Developing Countries,* Chapter 9.

21. This particular measure is suggested by Heady, "Shadow Wages and Induced Migration."

22. If the rural market wage rate is being used to determine the shadow wage rate and a conversion factor exists for each crop, then the shadow wage can be directly computed by multiplying each of the terms in equation (17.10) by its conversion factor.

23. Little and Mirrlees, *Project Appraisal and Planning for Developing Countries,* in particular, emphasize this possibility. The alternative possibility that is often also mentioned in the CBA literature on developing countries is that government investment will be funded through foreign borrowing. This latter possibility is discussed in Chapter 10.

24. Karla Hoff and Joseph E. Stiglitz, "Imperfect Information and Rural Credit Markets: Puzzles and Policy Perspectives," *World Bank Economic Review* 4(3) 1990, 329–351.

25. In the framework represented in equation (17.11), the *NPV* would not be estimated by using the shadow price of capital method described in Chapter 10. Instead, the shadow price is incorporated into the third term of the equation.

26. Curry and Weiss, *Project Analysis in Developing Countries,* Table 11-5.

27. The findings are reported in Lyn Squire, "Project Evaluation in Theory and Practice," in Hollis Chenery and T. N. Srinivasan, eds., *Handbook of Development Economics,* Volume II, (Amsterdam: North Holland, 1989), 1126–1127.

CHAPTER 18

Cost-Effectiveness Analysis

Cost-effectiveness analysis (CEA) is a widely used alternative to CBA, especially in areas such as health and defense policy. Analysts seeking efficient policies but facing constraints that prevent them from doing CBA may find it useful. In particular, CEA circumvents three common constraints. First, analysts may be unwilling or unable to monetize the most important policy impact. Relatedly, clients may not want monetization. This constraint arises frequently in the evaluation of alternative health policies; for example, many people are willing to predict the numbers of lives saved by alternative public health programs but are unwilling to place a dollar value on a life saved. Second, analysts may recognize that a particular effectiveness measure does not capture all of the social benefits of each alternative, and some of these other social benefits are difficult to monetize. In using CBA, analysts face the burden of monetizing all impacts. If the effectiveness measure captures most of the benefits, then it may be reasonable to use CEA to avoid the burden of conducting a CBA. Third, analysts may be dealing with intermediate goods whose linkage to preferences is not clear. For example, the exact contribution of different types of weapon systems to overall national defense is often unclear. In such situations, CBA is not possible, but CEA may give useful information concerning the relative efficiency of alternatives.

CEA compares (mutually exclusive) alternatives in terms of the ratio of their costs and a single quantified, but not monetized, effectiveness measure. For example, alternative highway safety programs may each involve different costs and numbers of lives saved. The cost-effectiveness ratios of the programs would be expressed as dollars per life saved, and the program that costs the least per life saved would be assessed as the most efficient. In many circumstances such an assessment is valid; in other circumstances, however, the assessment would not be valid because cost-effectiveness ratios ignore scale effects, ranking policies that produce small impacts at a relatively low cost per unit above policies that produce much larger impacts at a somewhat higher cost per unit. Consequently, care must be taken in interpreting cost-effectiveness ratios as measures of efficiency.

In some applications, especially in health policy, it may be possible to construct an outcome measure that serves as a direct proxy for changes in individuals' utilities. In such applications, CEA is referred to as cost-utility analysis (CUA). For example, the benefit measure may be quality-adjusted life-years, which combines both the number of additional years of life and the quality of life during those years. If a CUA employs a perfect proxy for changes in utility, then use of the marginal utility of money would enable the analyst to move directly to CBA; this would not be the case for a CEA that excludes some dimension of utility, such as quality of life.

The presentation that follows addresses the following questions: How should cost-effectiveness ratios be computed and used to compare policy alternatives? How should costs and excluded benefits be handled? How should sensitivity analysis be conducted? How can health outcome measures be made proxies for utilities? How reliable are league tables for comparing large numbers of policies?

COST-EFFECTIVENESS RATIOS AND POLICY CHOICE

CEA involves computing cost-effectiveness ratios and using these ratios to choose policies that promote efficiency. These apparently simple tasks typically involve several complications. The analyst must choose an appropriate basis from which to compute the effects and costs of alternatives. Once cost-effectiveness ratios for alternative policies have been specified, the analyst must also take account of relevant resource constraints in choosing among them.

Cost-Effectiveness Ratios: Incremental Costs and Benefits

As CEA does not monetize benefits, it inevitably involves two different metrics: Costs are measured in dollars, whereas effectiveness may be measured in units such as lives saved, tons of carbon dioxide reduced, or children vaccinated. Because noncommensurate metrics cannot be added, it is impossible to obtain a single measure of net social benefits from the two metrics. However, it is possible to compute the ratio of the two measures, which can be used as a basis for ranking alternative policies. Obviously, the ratio can be expressed in two ways: either as a *cost-effectiveness ratio* (CE ratio), computed by dividing the costs of an alternative by the measure of its effectiveness, or as an *effectiveness-cost ratio* (EC ratio), computed by dividing the effectiveness measure of an alternative by its costs. The discussion that follows focuses on the cost-effectiveness ratio, which is by far the more commonly used ratio.

Costs and effectiveness are always measured *incrementally.* Consider two policies, labeled i and j. The cost-effectiveness ratio of policy i relative to policy j, CE_{ij}, is given by the following formula:

$$CE_{ij} = \frac{C_i - C_j}{E_i - E_j} \qquad (18.1)$$

where C_i is the cost of alternative i, C_j is the cost of alternative j, E_i is the number of effectiveness units produced by alternative i, and E_j is the number of effectiveness units produced by alternative j. The simplest application of the formula occurs when a single policy, i, is being assessed as an addition to the status quo, j, and both the cost and effectiveness of i can be expressed as increments to the status quo, $C_i = C + C_j$ and $E_i = E + E_j$. The cost-effectiveness ratio then becomes C/E. For example, imagine that in addition to the highway safety program already in place, it is possible to add an additional program that would cost $2 million more than the current program and avoid an additional 4 fatalities. The cost-effectiveness ratio would then be ($2 million)/(4 avoided fatalities), or $500,000 per avoided fatality. By itself, this ratio does not indicate whether the program is efficient. Rather, it indicates that the program should be adopted before other safety programs that avoid the same number of fatalities and cost more than $500,000 per avoided fatality.

TABLE 18-1   Working with Cost-Effectiveness Ratios

	C (dollars per student)	E (average test score)	C/E (relative to no schooling)	S_j (basis for comparison)	ΔC (relative to S_j)	ΔE (relative to S_j)	ΔC/ΔE (incremental cost-effectiveness ratio)
S_{30}	2000	60	33.3	—	—	—	—
S_{25}	2400	68	35.3	S_{30}	400	8	50
S_{20}	3000	74	40.5	S_{25}	600	6	100
S_{15}	4000	76	52.6	S_{20}	1000	2	500
S_c	3000	72	41.7	S_{30}	1000	12	83.3

The application of the cost-effectiveness ratio becomes more complicated when choosing among multiple policy alternatives. As an illustration, consider alternatives for improving student achievement scores. Imagine that a school currently assigns 30 students per classroom at a total marginal cost per classroom of $60,000 and achieves an average achievement score of 60. Label this alternative S_{30}. Alternatively, the school could reduce class size to 25 students (S_{25}), 20 students (S_{20}), or 15 students (S_{15}). Obviously, these are mutually exclusive alternatives because there can only be one class size. Imagine that an alternative to reducing class size below 30 students is to enhance 30-student classrooms with computer support (S_c). The costs and effects of each of these alternatives are displayed in the columns of Table 18-1, which are labeled C and E, respectively. The third column, labeled C/E, presents the ratio of costs to effects. It can be thought of as the incremental cost-effectiveness ratio where the comparison alternative, S_j, is no schooling, with zero costs and zero effectiveness. This ratio is referred to as the *average cost-effectiveness ratio*. Not surprisingly, relative to no schooling, a 30-student classroom offers the smallest cost-effectiveness ratio of $33 (per student) per point increase in average test.

No schooling, however, is not a realistic alternative. Rather, the current classroom size of 30 students should be thought of as the status quo policy and, therefore, the starting point for comparisons. The column labeled S_j makes clear the alternative used as the basis for calculating the *incremental cost-effectiveness ratio,* $\Delta C/\Delta E$, shown in the last column. It is appropriate to compare the reduced class size of 25 (S_{25}) as well as the computerized classroom (S_c) to the status quo. Further reductions in class size, however, are more appropriately assessed relative to the previous reduction, so that S_{20} is assessed relative to S_{25} and S_{15} is assessed relative to S_{20}. Note that the smallest incremental cost-effectiveness ratio arises in moving from S_{30} to S_{25}. The next smallest incremental cost-effectiveness ratio results from moving from S_{30} to S_c, suggesting that S_c should be selected over S_{20} if the decision maker wants to achieve a higher average test score than that provided by S_{25}. Yet a comparison of S_{20} and S_c in terms of costs and effects in the first two columns of Table 18-1 makes clear that this would be an incorrect choice because S_{20} and S_c have the same total cost, but S_{20} offers a larger gain in average test score. S_{20} *strictly dominates* S_c; thus it would never make sense to choose S_c over S_{20}.

The dominance of S_{20} over S_c is shown graphically in Figure 18-1, which plots the cost of each alternative on the vertical axis and its effect on the horizontal axis. Holding cost constant, one should always prefer an alternative that has a larger effect. In other words, one would always like to make possible moves due east—S_{20} is due east of S_c and

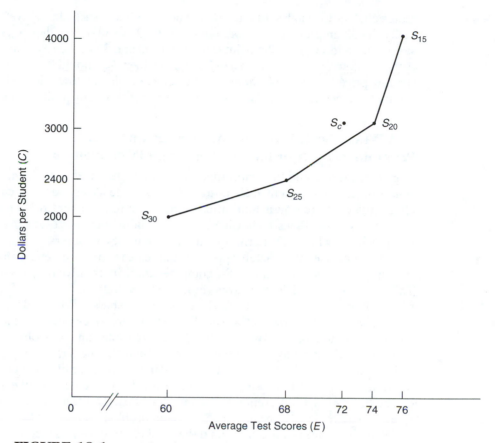

FIGURE 18-1   Graphical Representation of Costs and Effectiveness

therefore should always be preferred. In addition, holding effect constant, one should also prefer an alternative with a smaller cost. In other words, one should always want to make possible moves due south because they give the same effect at lower cost.

The lines shown connecting S_{30} to S_{25} to S_{20} to S_{15}, which have slopes equal to their incremental cost-effectiveness ratios, map out a frontier of the best possible outcomes—those that push as far to the southeast as possible. Points to the northwest of this frontier are subject to what is called *extended dominance*.[1] For example, if S_c costs a few dollars less, then it no longer is strictly dominated by S_{20}. Yet, as long as it still falls to the northwest of the frontier, it will be subject to extended dominance. *The first step in comparing alternatives using cost-effectiveness ratios should always be to remove from further consideration all alternatives that are dominated, either strictly or by extension.* Plotting costs and effects as in Figure 18-1 facilitates the identification of dominated alternatives.

Frontiers like the one shown in Figure 18-1 narrow the set of alternatives to consider, but in the absence of information about the decision maker's preferences there is no way to select a particular alternative on the frontier. In contrast, CBA leads to a specific choice.[2] In the example presented in Table 18-1, assigning a shadow price to average test scores enables the analyst to estimate the net benefits of each alternative. One can easily verify that, if an average test score point is valued at $50 or less, then S_{30} should be chosen. If the shadow price of a point is between $50 and $100, then S_{25} should be selected. If the shadow price is between $100 and $500, then S_{20} should be selected. Only if the shadow price is over $500 should S_{15} be selected. No shadow price exists at which S_c should be selected because S_{20} has larger net benefits for any positive shadow price.

CEA Where Scale Problems Are Irrelevant: Identical Program Budgets or Identical Program Effectiveness

In general, absent additional information about preferences or the context of the decision problem, cost-effectiveness ratios do not provide a clear basis for choosing among alternatives. The reason is that ratios do not take into account the different scales of projects, a reason discussed in Chapter 2 for avoiding benefit-cost ratios. The major exception arises when one alternative clearly dominates all others.

Dominance is immediately apparent, and scale is not a problem, if all of the alternatives have the same cost. Table 18-2 compares three alternative projects for saving lives. The only costs are budgetary costs (in millions of dollars), and the effectiveness criterion is the number of lives saved. The cost-effectiveness ratio reveals the average cost per life saved. Of course, in this simple example one does not even have to compute cost-effectiveness ratios: By "eyeballing" the table, one can easily observe that alternative C saves the most lives. Computing the cost-effectiveness ratio simply confirms this. It does not matter whether the ratio is calculated as cost per life saved or as lives saved per (million) dollars. Because all alternatives involve the same level of expenditure, they can be thought of as different ways of spending a *fixed budget*. In this case, CEA corresponds to a simple effectiveness maximization problem (maximize lives saved).

Similarly, scale is not a problem if the level of effectiveness is constant across all alternatives. Obviously, the alternative that offers the lowest cost dominates the others because it provides the same level of outcome at a lower cost. Situations in which the level of effectiveness is constant across alternatives can be thought of as different ways of achieving a *fixed effectiveness*. In this case, CEA corresponds to a simple cost-minimization problem (minimize dollars).

In the fixed budget and fixed effectiveness cases, dominance is readily apparent. It is possible, however, that one alternative can dominate another even if they have neither

TABLE 18-2   Cost-Effectiveness Analysis with Fixed (Identical) Costs

	Alternatives		
Cost and Effectiveness	*A*	*B*	*C*
Cost measure (budget cost)	$10M	$10M	$10M
Effectiveness measure (number of lives saved)	5	10	15
CE ratio (cost per life saved)	$2.0M	$1.0M	$0.67M[a]
EC ratio (lives saved per million dollars)	0.5 life	1.0 life	1.5 lives[a]

[a]CE ratio or EC ratio of the most cost-effective alternative.

the same cost nor the same effectiveness, as long as it is superior on both dimensions. Clearly, dominated alternatives should not be selected. If an alternative dominates all others, then it should be selected.

Imposing Constraints to Deal with Scale Differences

Scale differences among alternatives may distort choice as illustrated in Table 18-3. If we used a cost-effectiveness ratio, then we would choose alternative A. Yet, if we look more closely at alternative B, we see that it would save a large number of lives at the relatively low "price" per life saved of $0.5 million, which is much less than the shadow prices reviewed in Chapter 16. It is, therefore, likely that a CBA would show that alternative B has larger net social benefits. As CEA was probably proposed in the first place because an analyst, client, or decision maker was unwilling to monetize lives saved, how can CEA be used sensibly as a decision rule without monetizing lives saved?

Before answering this question, it is helpful to remind ourselves that if we could replicate project A in 49 other locations (50 in total), the total cost would be $50 million and 200 lives would be saved. This alternative, which we will call project C, would dominate project B. However, project C is not feasible. If it were feasible, then it should have been included in Table 18-3 as one of the alternatives in an *exhaustive* (i.e., complete) set of mutually exclusive alternatives.

In order to use CEA for decision making, a common practice is to impose a constraint, either a minimum acceptable level of effectiveness, denoted $\overline{E}$, or a maximum acceptable cost, denoted $\overline{C}$.

If we impose a minimum level of effectiveness, we may either minimize costs, C_i, or the cost-effectiveness ratio, CE_i. Thus, we could select the project that meets a minimum level of effectiveness at the lowest cost:

$$\text{Minimize } C_i$$
$$\text{Subject to } E_i \geq \overline{E} \tag{18.2}$$

In this specification, the decision maker is acting as if he or she does not value additional units of effectiveness. This might apply, for example, to alternative ways of ensuring that children receive minimum amounts of fluoride to protect their teeth. It might also apply to some national defense activities, such as sea lift capability. Even in these

TABLE 18-3 The Problem with the CE Ratio When Scale Differs

	Alternatives	
Cost and Effectiveness	*A*	*B*
Cost measure (budget cost)	$1M	$100M
Effectiveness measure (number of lives saved)	4	200
CE ratio (cost per life saved)	$250,000[a]	$500,000
EC ratio (lives saved per million dollars)	4.0 lives[a]	2.0 lives

[a]CE ratio or EC ratio of the most cost-effective alternative.

examples, however, additional units of effectiveness above $\overline{E}$ are probably worth something to decision makers. Alternatively, we could select the most cost-effective alternative that satisfies the effectiveness constraint:

$$\text{Minimize } CE_i$$
$$\text{Subject to } E_i \geq \overline{E} \qquad\qquad (18.3)$$

This rule generally leads to higher levels of effectiveness and higher costs than the first rule.

If we specified a maximum budgetary cost, $\overline{C}$, then we might select the project that yields the largest number of units of effectiveness, subject to the budget constraint:

$$\text{Maximize } E_i$$
$$\text{Subject to } C_i \leq \overline{C} \qquad\qquad (18.4)$$

The problem with this rule is that it ignores incremental cost savings. In other words, cost savings beyond $\overline{C}$ are not valued. Alternatively, we could select the project that most cost-effectively meets the imposed budget constraint:

$$\text{Minimize } CE_i$$
$$\text{Subject to } C_i \leq \overline{C} \qquad\qquad (18.5)$$

This rule places some weight on incremental cost savings and is more likely to result in the selection of a project with less than the maximum cost.

An Illustration of the Different CE Rules

Imagine that each of the ten mutually exclusive and exhaustive projects shown in Table 18-4 are intended to save lives. The expected number of lives saved for each project is given in column 2, and the expected budgetary cost in millions of dollars for each project is in column 3. Dominated projects can be eliminated from the choice set at the outset to simplify the analysis: Project D can be eliminated because it is dominated by project C, and projects C and F can be eliminated because they are dominated by project A.

The cost-effectiveness ratio (cost per life saved) appears in column 4. The projects can be ranked from most cost-effective to least cost-effective using this ratio. Project E is the most cost-effective alternative with an average cost per life saved of $2.0 million. The next most cost-effective alternative is project B, followed by J, then I and A, which have equal cost-effectiveness, then G, and then H.

Note, however, that Project E saves the fewest lives. Project B saves twice as many lives as project E and costs only $24 million more. Which project is better? This question illustrates the problem of different scales. Preferably, we would like the option of performing project E 2.2 (or more) times, but this option is not feasible because the list of projects was constructed to be exhaustive.

Suppose the decision maker is willing to specify that she wants to adopt only projects that save at least 50 lives. Which alternative that satisfies this constraint is preferable?

TABLE 18-4 Cost-Effectiveness Analysis with Constraints

				$E \geq 50$		$C \leq 250$	
Projects (1)	Lives Saved (2)	Budget Cost ($M) (3)	CE Ratio (cost per life saved) ($M/life saved) (4)	Budget Cost of Projects That Save at Least 50 Lives (5)	CE Ratio of Projects That Save at Least 50 Lives (6)	Lives Saved of Projects That Cost No More than $250M (7)	CE Ratio of Projects That Cost No More than $250M (8)
A	100	250	2.5	250	2.5[a]	100[a]	2.5
B	20	44	2.2	—	—	20	2.2
C	100	300	3.0	300	3.0	—	—
D	50	300	6.0	300	6.0	—	—
E	10	20	2.0[a]	—	—	10	2.0[a]
F	100	900	9.0	900	9.0	—	—
G	60	210	3.5	210	3.5	60	3.5
H	50	200	4.0	200[a]	4.0	50	4.0
I	40	100	2.5	—	—	40	2.5
J	45	110	2.4	—	—	45	2.4

[a]CE ratio, budget cost, or effectiveness of the most preferred alternative.

The least costly of the acceptable alternatives is project H, whereas the most cost-effective acceptable alternative is project A. Note that project A costs $50 million more than project H, but it saves 50 more lives. The incremental cost-effectiveness ratio of project A relative to project H is $1 million per life saved, on average, which is very low. Indeed, spending the additional $50 million would be even more cost-effective than project E. However, the choice depends on the decision maker's willingness to trade additional lives saved for additional budgetary cost. Even though CEA is often proposed as a way of avoiding monetization of an important benefit category, analysts or decision makers must often make trade-offs between costs and a nonmonetized benefit to rank alternatives. In doing so, they implicitly consider the value of an additional saved life.

The same type of problem arises if a budget constraint is imposed. Suppose, for example, the decision maker indicates that she cannot spend more than $250 million. Subject to this constraint, project A saves the most lives, but project E is the most cost-effective. Again, to choose between projects A and E, the decision maker must consider trade-offs between additional lives saved and additional budgetary costs.

Sensitivity Analysis: The Problem of Ratios

We rarely predict either costs or effects of policy alternatives with great certainty. Conveying the level of uncertainty in projected cost-effectiveness ratios provides important information to decision makers. The methods of sensitivity analysis for CBA presented in Chapter 7—partial sensitivity analysis, worst- and best-case analysis, and Monte Carlo simulations—can also be applied to CEA. The problem posed by ratios, however, makes Monte Carlo simulations particularly attractive in cost-effectiveness analysis.

If we were to add or subtract normally distributed random variables, then the resulting random variable would also be normally distributed. In contrast, dividing one

normally distributed random variable by another does not produce a normally distributed ratio. More generally, the ratio of any two random variables generally does not
have the same distribution as either of the random variables that make it up.

   Figure 18-2 illustrates this property of cost-effectiveness ratios. The cost of the project is estimated to be $20 million with a standard deviation of $2 million. The number
of lives saved is estimated to be 20 with a standard deviation of 2. The estimates might
be based on data from similar projects that have been implemented elsewhere, in
which case the standard deviations might be a by-product of the estimations, or the estimates might be constructed from shadow prices and elasticities, in which case the

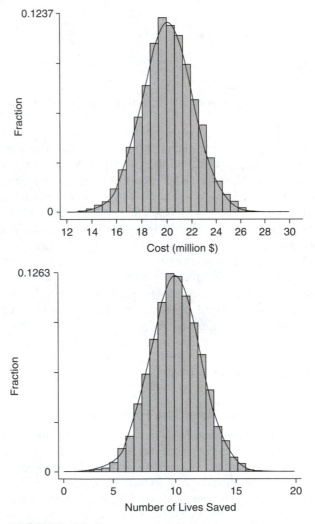

FIGURE 18-2   Monte Carlo Analysis of a Cost-
Effectiveness Ratio

(Continued)

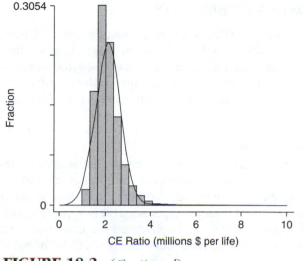

FIGURE 18-2 *(Continued)*

standard deviations would be based on their ranges. The Monte Carlo simulation presented in the figure assumes that cost and lives saved are each normally distributed. The simulation involves generating 10,000 pairs of values of cost and lives saved based on draws from their respective normal distributions. The top two histograms show the resulting distributions of draws for costs and lives saved separately, with theoretical normal distributions superimposed to show that they are approximately normal. The simulation next computes a cost-effectiveness ratio for each pair of costs and lives saved. The distribution of the resulting 10,000 cost-effectiveness ratios is displayed in the third histogram in the figure. Note that the distribution of cost-effectiveness ratios does not correspond nearly as closely to the normal distribution, again superimposed on the histogram, as did the variables used to construct it. It is considerably skewed with a longer tail to the right of the mean of $2.1 million per life saved. In other words, the most likely outcome is a cost-effectiveness ratio slightly below the mean but with some probability of substantially larger ratios. The distribution of the ratios can also be used to provide other information, such as the probability of the ratio being above, say, $3 million (5.6 percent).[3]

Note that the skew shown in the figure would be even more dramatic if the distribution of effectiveness were spread more evenly over some range rather than having a central mode like the normal distribution. Also note that one could compare the distributions of cost-effectiveness ratios for two alternatives by superimposing their Monte Carlo distributions. A thicker left-hand tail, showing a higher probability of lower CE ratios, would tend to favor that alternative. To make a more systematic comparison, one would construct a cumulative distribution for each alternative and, if one cumulative distribution lay consistently to the left of the other, select it as *stochastically dominant*. That is, it would consistently offer higher probabilities of achieving more desirable outcomes.

OMITTED COSTS AND BENEFITS

As should be clear from the previous chapters, CBA seeks to include *all* social costs and benefits. For CEA to be an appropriate guide for the more efficient allocation of resources, given its inherent limitations, it too should seek to be as comprehensive as possible in measuring valued impacts. Most fundamentally, it should be based on social costs and take account of social benefits not captured in the effectiveness measure.

Measurement of Costs

The measurement of costs in actual CEA studies varies enormously. In the health care area, costs might include only the costs of treatment, perhaps even just the costs of medication. More broadly, costs might include other treatment costs, such as doctors' time or hospitalization expenses. This is important, for example, in assessing drugs for schizophrenia that, although expensive, may reduce the time patients spend in hospitals, which may be even more expensive. Costs might also include waiting time or time lost from work, which are borne by patients or employers—effects on members of society that would be included in CBA.

If CEA is to be a guide to the more efficient use of resources, then it should include all social costs. Costs that are constant across all alternatives can be omitted without changing the CE rankings of the alternatives under consideration. Their exclusion, however, generally changes the magnitude of the computed CE ratios, which may be relevant in using these context-specific CE ratios as a basis for making general comparisons across types of alternatives.[4]

In practice, when CEA is conducted for a particular government agency, costs are often measured as that agency's budgetary costs.[5] In the regulatory area, for example, analysts might measure only the agency's cost of enforcing compliance. From an efficiency perspective, the costs should also include firms' costs of complying with the regulations. Of course, even when looking at agency costs, the guiding principle should be opportunity cost.

Omitted Benefits: Technical versus Allocative Efficiency

CEA almost invariably omits impacts that would be included in CBA. CEA considers only one measure of effectiveness. In practice, however, projects often have multiple benefits. For example, regulations that save lives almost always also reduce injuries or illnesses. Similarly, new drugs may effectively cure a disease and also have fewer harmful side effects than current drugs. To measure allocative efficiency, all costs and benefits should be taken into consideration. One way to get closer to doing this—that is, to reach a "halfway house" between standard CEA and CBA—is to compute the following *adjusted CE* ratio:

$$CE^* = \frac{\text{Social Cost} - \text{Other Social Benefits}}{\text{Effectiveness}} \qquad (18.6)$$

If the numerator can be fully valued and monetized, then this adjusted CE ratio incorporates all the impacts that would be included in a CBA. The omission of a particular category of social cost or benefit from the numerator could very well alter the ranking of alternatives, however. The danger of obtaining an arbitrary ranking increases as alternatives become less similar in terms of the inputs they require and the various impacts they produce. Moreover, the transparency of CEA is also reduced because costs may no longer have a simple interpretation, such as budgetary dollars. For these reasons, moving all the way to CBA with extensive sensitivity analysis is often a better analytical strategy than expanding the scope of measured costs and benefits within a CEA framework.

It is important to emphasize that in CEA a weak link may exist between the measure of effectiveness and things that individuals value. It is quite reasonable to presume that individuals would be willing to pay for incremental units of "lives saved," an often-used measure of effectiveness. But now consider the "number of addicts treated." This intermediate output may or may not be a good proxy for the final consumption good that individuals value, such as reductions in street crime. Analysts cannot avoid estimating the value of final consumption goods when doing CBA, even if they must rely on shadow prices from secondary sources. However, in CEA they may not make an explicit connection between the effectiveness measure used and benefits that individuals value. When analysts use an intermediate output as a measure of effectiveness, they should establish a link between the effectiveness measure and a final consumption good or at least show that the intermediate output indeed has some value.[6]

COST-UTILITY ANALYSIS

The most common use of *cost-utility analysis* occurs in the evaluation of health policies. In CUA the incremental costs of alternative policies are compared to the health changes, usually measured in *quality-adjusted life-years* (QALYs) or *disability-adjusted life-years* (DALYs), that they produce.[7] CUA is most useful when alternative programs or treatments embody a trade-off between quality of life (morbidity) and length of life (mortality). It can be thought of as a form of CEA that employs a more complex effectiveness measure that more directly corresponds to changes in utilities. All of the previous discussion about cost-effectiveness ratios and decision rules thus applies. The rationale for looking specifically at CUA is that considerable analytical effort has gone into the measurement of QALYs, which not only serve as a common effectiveness measure in CEA but also can be directly monetized for CBA through application of a shadow price for life-years.

The Meaning of Life—Quality-Adjusted Life-Years, That Is!

QALYs involve two distinct dimensions: quality and quantity. The analyst must decide how to define, measure, and combine these dimensions. Consider, for example, the effects of three mutually exclusive prenatal programs. Under the status quo, no babies with a particular condition are born alive. Prenatal alternative A will result in five babies being born alive per year, but with permanent, serious disabilities. Prenatal alternative B will result in only two live births, but with only low levels of disability. Before we can compare the costs of these alternatives to their effectiveness, we first have to make quantity and quality commensurate.

TABLE 18-5   The Basic QALY Format

Health Status (H)	Additional Years of Life (Y)				
	Y_1	Y_2	Y_3	Y_4	Y_5
H_1	$Y_1H_1{}^{SQ}$	Y_2H_1	Y_3H_1	Y_4H_1	Y_5H_1
H_2	Y_1H_2	Y_2H_2	Y_3H_2	$Y_4H_2{}^{B}$	Y_5H_2
H_3	Y_1H_3	Y_2H_3	$Y_3H_3{}^{A}$	Y_4H_3	Y_5H_3
H_4	Y_1H_4	Y_2H_4	Y_3H_4	Y_4H_4	Y_5H_4
H_5	Y_1H_5	Y_2H_5	Y_3H_5	Y_4H_5	Y_5H_5

The general form of the problem is shown in Table 18-5. The columns show additional years of life ranging from a low of Y_1 to a high of Y_5. The rows show health status ranging from the worst (health state H_1) to the best (health state H_5). For simplicity, assume that alternatives A and B and the status quo involve the same costs and that there is no uncertainty about the longevities and health statuses they will yield. Suppose that the status quo (denoted SQ) gives Y_1H_1 (the fewest years of life in the worst health status), while alternative A achieves Y_3H_3 and alternative B achieves Y_4H_2. Clearly, the status quo is dominated, but how should we choose between alternatives A and B? In order to make the comparison, alternatives A and B must be expressed in a common metric.

Before discussing the various methods for putting health statuses into a common metric, QALYs, a prior question of relevance must be asked: Whose preferences should be the basis for assessing health-related quality of life (HRQoL)? Researchers have used three groups of people as respondents to questions designed to elicit valuations of health statuses: medical experts, patients who have experience with similar statuses, and the general population.

Medical experts typically bring to the valuation exercise relevant experience and knowledge, especially with respect to the physical implications of various health statuses. They also are likely to be sophisticated respondents who can answer more complex questions. Nonetheless, their medically informed assessments may not be consistent with the holistic assessments made by patients or the general public.

The appropriate choice between patients and the general public as respondents is not clear. Some commonly made arguments in favor of patients as respondents include: Patients are likely to be more knowledgeable than the general public about what it is like to experience illnesses and disabilities; researchers need not provide as much description about health statuses to patients as respondents from the general public in order to obtain informed valuations; and, in some circumstances, the general public may be biased against certain conditions, such as those that result from risky behavior or unhealthy lifestyles. Commonly made arguments in favor of the general public as respondents include: The preferences of the general public are most relevant in making decisions concerning the allocation of scarce resources through public policy; patients may overstate their HRQoL relative to the general public because of cognitive dissonance or psychological adaption or actual adaptation to their conditions; and the general public is less likely than patients to offer strategic responses to influence public policy.[8]

Although valuations based on patients and the general public tend to provide similar rankings of health statuses, and no systematic differences related to demographic characteristics other than health status appear to exist,[9] patients tend to place higher valuations on conditions that they are experiencing.[10] The difference implies an asymmetry in the valuation of losses and gains: The loss in utility from moving from perfect health to some impaired condition is greater than the gain in utility in moving from the same impaired condition back to perfect health. It can be explained either as a consequence of loss aversion (discussed in Chapter 15) or costly adjustments to changes in health status.[11] If the policy being analyzed just involves gains in the HRQoL, then patients would be the appropriate group to survey. In contrast, if it involves just losses, then the general public should be surveyed. The choice between patients and the general public is not clear, however, when policies involve both gains and losses in HRQoL.

The basic approach for constructing QALYs involves assessing HRQoL for different health statuses. The HRQoL is usually measured on a scale in which the value 1 is assigned to perfect health and the value 0 to death. The HRQoL measures can then be used to weight life-years to produce QALYs. Researchers have used four approaches, three direct and one indirect, to assess HRQoL: the health rating method, the time trade-off method, the standard gamble method, and the health index method.[12]

Health Rating Method.   Generally, researchers derive a *health rating* (HR) from questionnaires or interviews with health experts, potential subjects of treatment, or the general public. They present scales with well-defined endpoints to respondents, typically with death assigned a value of 0 and perfect health a value of 1. Intermediate health states are described in detail to the respondents, who are then asked to locate each state between the end points, 0 and 1. For example, if three intermediate health states described to an individual correspond to "seriously disabled," "moderately disabled," and "minimally disabled," then an individual might assign values of 0.15, 0.45, and 0.90 to these states, respectively.

Respondents often have difficulty assigning numerical values to the various health states, however. An alternative version of the health rating method uses a bisection process to obviate the need for respondents to provide numerical values. It provides respondents with a list of health states from which they are asked to find the one that falls midway between the end points on a visual display, such as a thermometer scale.[13] The respondents are then asked to find the health state that falls midway between the initially placed health state and the upper and lower endpoints, respectively. The process continues until respondents have placed the various health states on the scale. It yields an interval scale for HRQoL, but one without a clear basis in revealed preferences.

The Time Trade-Off Method.   In the *time trade-off* (TTO) method, respondents are asked to compare different combinations of length and quality of life.[14] The typical comparison is between a longer life of lower health status and a shorter life with a higher health status. Figure 18-3 illustrates such a comparison. The horizontal axis measures additional years of life (Y), and the vertical axis measures health status (H). Respondents might be asked to compare some status quo point, say R, representing health status H_2 and additional years of life Y_1, with an alternative point, say S, representing health status H_1 and additional years of life Y_2. If a respondent is indifferent between the two points, then he or she is willing to give up $H_2 - H_1$ units

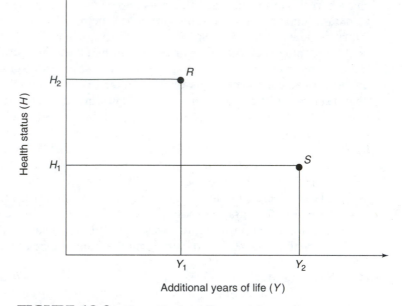

FIGURE 18-3   Time Trade-Off Example

of health quality in return for $Y_2 - Y_1$ additional years of life. Assuming that health status H_2 is perfect health and assigning it a utility of 1, the utility assigned to H_1 is then Y_1/Y_2.

For example, imagine that one wanted to assign a utility to the health status of twice-weekly severe lower back pain that prevented strenuous physical activity. The severity and consequences of the back pain would be carefully described to a number of respondents. Then each would be asked to compare living 10 additional years with the back pain to living some number of years in perfect health. If a respondent were indifferent between living 10 years with the back pain and 9 years in perfect health, then the analyst would assign a utility of 9/10 for the health state of back pain. Thus, in comparing medical interventions, an additional year of life with back pain would be valued at 0.9 instead of at 1 for an additional year in perfect health.

A complication arises if a person views the health status being valued as worse than death. In such cases, respondents are asked to compare immediate death as one alternative with t_1 additional years of life in the extremely undesirable health status followed by t_2 years in full health as the other. Holding the total of t_1 and t_2 constant, the values that make the respondent indifferent between the alternatives would assign a utility to the extremely undesirable health status of $-t_2/t_1$. The resulting negative value is consistent with the health status being valued as worse than death, which is assigned a utility of 0.

In order for the TTO values to be valid utilities, a strong assumption must be met: Individuals must be willing to give up constant proportions of their remaining life-years to attain an improvement in health status, no matter how many additional life-years remain. For example, if a person expecting to live 10 years with a disability were willing to give up 5 years to attain perfect health, then when the person has only 8 years of expected life, he or she should also be willing to give up 4 of the 8 remaining years to obtain perfect health. The assumption of constant proportional time trade-off implies that the person has a zero marginal rate of time preference. A particularly serious violation of the constant proportions assumption occurs when a person's preferences for life-years in some health status exhibit *maximum endurable time* (MET): There is a limit to the number of years people want to live with the health status.[15] The stringency of the constant proportions assumption suggests caution in interpreting TTO values as utilities. Nonetheless, the TTO method continues to be used to place relative values on health statuses for the construction of QALYs.

The Standard Gamble Method.   In the *standard gamble* (SG) approach, respondents are presented with a decision tree like those described in Chapter 7.[16] Respondents are offered a choice between two alternatives. Alternative A has two possible outcomes: either a return to normal health for n additional years (occurring with probability p) or immediate death (occurring with probability $1 - p$). Alternative A might be an operation that has probability $1 - p$ of failure (death), but which, if successful, will return the patient to normal health for n years. Alternative B guarantees the patient n additional years with a specified level of health impairment. This choice is shown in Figure 18-4. The probability p is varied until a respondent is indifferent between alternatives A and B. When using a health status index ranging from 0 (death) to 1 (normal health for n years), the p at which a respondent is indifferent can be interpreted as that respondent's utility from alternative B.

For example, consider again the assignment of a utility to the health status of twice-weekly severe lower back pain that prevented strenuous physical activity. There are two approaches to finding the probability of perfect health that would make the respondent indifferent between the gamble and the back pain. First, we could simply

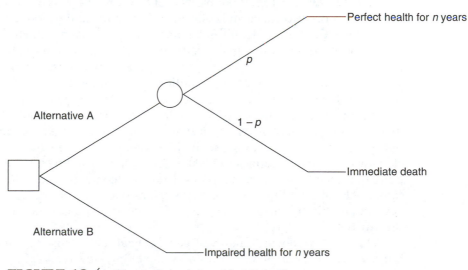

FIGURE 18-4   The Standard Gamble Method

ask the respondent to state the probability. Second, we could offer an initial probability, and then raise or lower it until the respondent expresses indifference. The former approach might falter with respondents who are not used to thinking in terms of probabilities. To avoid this problem, it may be desirable to engage the respondent in some valuations of other health statuses before turning to the one of interest. The latter approach risks the sort of starting point bias that was discussed in connection with contingent valuation in Chapter 15. Starting points should be varied across respondents to allow for the possibility of detecting any starting point bias. Imagine that the method used reveals that the respondent is indifferent between the back pain for certain and a gamble with a probability of perfect health of 0.95 and a probability of death of 0.05. The SG method would assign a utility to the health status of lower back pain of 0.95.

The SG method assumes that individuals make choices consistent with the expected utility hypothesis. To the extent that they do follow the expected utility hypothesis, then the utilities resulting from the SG method are valid utilities. Deviations from the expected utility hypothesis, such as the judgmental biases discussed in Chapter 15, challenge the validity of the utilities derived from the SG method. Although direct comparisons of the TTO and SG methods generally conclude that they provide similar utilities at least in terms of ordinal rankings,[17] a majority of studies find that the SG method yields higher values.[18]

Health Index Method.   Clinicians have developed a variety of scales to assess variations in health, whether in relationship to particular diseases, injuries, or mental states, or to health in general. The *health index* (HI) method uses one of the direct methods (HR, TTO, or SG) to assign utilities to points on the health scales, which can then be used to construct QALYs in a variety of applications. The HI method provides utility weights that can be applied to standard health scales, thus offering analysts utilities akin to the shadow prices discussed in Chapter 16.

A widely used HI method evolved out of a health classification system introduced by George Torrance and colleagues[19] and further developed by the McMaster University's Centre for Health Economics and Policy Analysis. Heath Utilities, Inc., currently offers several copyrighted versions to researchers.[20] Its Health Utility Index Mark 3, for instance, is comprised of eight attributes: vision, hearing, speech, ambulation, dexterity, emotion, cognition, and pain. Each attribute has clearly defined levels. For example, the levels for pain are "free of pain and discomfort," "mild to moderate pain that prevents no activities," "moderate pain that prevents a few activities," "moderate to severe pain that prevents some activities," and "severe pain that prevents most activities." With either five or six levels for each attribute, this classification system defines 972,000 different health statuses.[21] Standardized questionnaires enable researchers to assess health outcomes for individuals or population samples. Health Utilities, Inc., provides tables derived from general population surveys and multiattribute utility scaling that convert responses into utilities for each of the attributes.

The most widely used index of general health status is the Short Form Health Survey (SF-36), which was originally developed by researchers at the RAND Corporation as part of the Medical Outcomes Study.[22] Constructed to conform to psychometric standards for making group comparisons, the SF-36 uses 35 items to construct eight scales: physical functioning, role limitation due to physical problems, bodily pain, general health, vitality, social function, role limitation due to emotional problems, and mental health. The first four of these scales combine to form a summary measure of physical health, and the latter four combine to form a summary measure of mental health. The SF-36 is licensed through Quality Metric, Inc.,[23] and has been made available in many languages through the International Quality of Life Assessment Project.[24]

Efforts are underway to create a mapping from scales derived from the SF-36 to utilities. For example, John Brazier and his colleagues have created a simplified version of the SF-36, the SF-6D, which reduces the number of scales (dimensions) from eight to six by excluding the general health scale and combining the physical and emotional role limitations into a single index.[25] Each of the six dimensions has five or six levels of response, enabling them to define 18,000 different health statuses. The researchers next selected 49 representative health statuses and employed the SG method in interviews with a general population sample of UK respondents. They next estimated econometric models with utilities as the dependent variable and the various levels on the six dimensions as explanatory variables. The coefficients estimated for the various levels can then be used to assign utilities to any one of the possible health statuses.[26] Researchers who can classify outcomes in terms of the SF-6D scale can thus obtain utilities for these outcomes. Of course, the utilities are based on the preferences of the UK general public and might not be appropriate in other national contexts. In the future, however, the estimates are likely to be replicated for other populations.

Other health status indexes have been created and related to population preferences. For example, European researchers organized as the EuroQol association have developed the EQ-5D index to supplement existing indexes.[27] Utilities have been assigned to EQ-5D health status through general population surveys using the TTO method.[28] Researchers have begun to compare the utilities and the sensitivity of these utilities to changes in health statuses across the various health indexes. For example, a recent comparison of EQ-5D and SF-6D utilities for liver transplant patients found that the SF-6D does not describe health statuses at the lower end of the utility scale well but is more sensitive than EQ-5D in detecting small changes toward the top of the scale.[29] A comparison of the HUI Mark 3, the SF-6D, and the EQ-5D for patients with rheumatological conditions suggested broad agreement, but it also showed a number of specific differences that make the particular choice of index potentially relevant to constructing QALYs.[30]

QALYs: Caveats and an Extensions

The construction of QALYs using health status utilities requires a strong assumption: The utility of being in a particular health status is proportional to the time spent in that status. For example, consider a person who has an expected life of Y years in health status H. The number of QALYs accruing to this person would be $YU(H)$, the product of the number of years in the health status and the utility of the health status, $U(H)$.

EXHIBIT 18-1

Researchers recently conducted a study comparing various utility elicitation methods for gastroesophageal reflux disease with heartburn. Samples of patients with a history of heartburn were recruited in Germany and Sweden. After asking respondents about the severity of their heartburn in a typical week, the researchers administered the EQ-5D health index and then applied the health rating (HR), time trade-off (TTO), and standard gamble (SG) methods. For example, the SG alternatives were presented as follows:

> Alternative 1 is that you know for certain that you will live for another 10 years in your current health state. During these 10 years, your heartburn as well as symptoms of any other health problems that you may have will be exactly as you have experienced them over the last 12 months. After these 10 years you will die.
>
> Alternative 2 is that there is a treatment that either is successful or fails. If the treatment is successful, you will recover perfect health and remain perfectly healthy during 10 years, that is, the same period of time as in alternative 1.

Perfect health means that you are free from all health problems, that is, you are free from heartburn as well as symptoms of any other health problems that you may have. After these 10 years you will die. If treatment fails, you will die immediately. (p. 43)

After giving respondents randomly assigned starting points of either 0.95 or 0.70 for the probability of success, probabilities were raised or lowered until the respondent was indifferent between the alternatives. Over one-third of respondents were unwilling to accept any risk of death for the chance of perfect health (or accept any reduction of years in the TTO method). The mean values from the SG method were 0.92, 0.88, and 0.86 for mild, moderate, and severe heartburn, respectively. The TTO values for the three levels of severity were 0.90, 0.87, and 0.85. In contrast to these relatively high utilities, the HR method produced utilities of 0.75, 0.67, and 0.49, while the EQ-5D based utilities were 0.78, 0.67, and 0.49. Thus, the SG and TTO methods showed much smaller losses in utility from chronic heartburn than the HR or the EQ-5D methods.

Source: Adapted from Bernt Kartman, Gudrun Gatz, and Magnus Johannesson, "Health State Utilities in Gastroesophageal Reflux Disease Patients with Heartburn: A Study in Germany and Sweden," *Medical Decision Making* 24(1) 2004, 40–52.

A number of conceptual issues about how to measure utilities remain.[31] A particularly important issue is discounting for time. From a CBA perspective, it is problematic to discount costs but not to discount health years. The reason is that if costs but not QALYs were discounted, the cost-effectiveness ratio of a policy that involved the accrual of costs and QALYs over substantial periods of time would improve if we delayed the health expenditure until the following year.[32] As discussed in Chapter 10, the basic idea that individuals have positive discount rates relating to additional years is widely accepted, but considerable controversy over the theory, measurement, and level of the appropriate discount rate exists.[33]

The use of QALYs is not limited to CEA, but can also be used in CBA. The basic procedure would be to monetize QALYs using a value of a life-year. For example, imagine that a public health intervention would save 10 QALYs this year and 20 QALYs next year. If the analyst values a life-year (VLY) at $200,000, then the benefits in the first year of the intervention would be $2 million, and the benefits in the second year would be $4 million. These yearly benefits would then be discounted to produce a present value of benefits. As noted in Chapter 16, however, moving from the value of a statistical life (VSL) to a VLY is especially controversial as it implies a VSL that is lower for older people with shorter life expectancies.

THE USE OF LEAGUE TABLES

CEA usually compares mutually exclusive projects. By definition, this means that the alternative projects address the same problems, for example, alternative methods of breast cancer screening. Yet, CEA has been used to make rankings *across* policies that have the same broad purpose (e.g., saving lives) but are not necessarily mutually exclusive. *League tables* rank multiple CEAs that share the same cost-effectiveness measure. Tammy Tengs and her colleagues, for example, have developed a league table of 587 interventions intended to avert premature death (i.e., to save lives).[34] They found that, on average, the United States spent about $433,500 per life saved or $41,600 per year of life saved (in 1999 dollars). They also asked the question: How many lives would be saved if the same investment were focused on the most cost-effective interventions? They conclude that an additional 60,200 lives could be saved, or about twice as many lives as under the status quo allocation. In a similar study, John Morrall III, updating an earlier review he conducted, assessed the cost-effectiveness of 76 regulations issued by the U.S. federal government between 1967 and 2001. He found that the cost-effectiveness ratios differed by six orders of magnitude and that regulations aimed at reducing safety and cardiovascular risks have been much more cost-effective than regulations aimed at reducing cancer risks.[35]

How useful are league tables? Comparisons of mutually exclusive projects inherently control for some of the differences in the measurement of cost and effectiveness. There can be no such presumption when comparing studies across different authors, using different data, and somewhat different methodologies. Different studies may measure costs differently, they may omit different costs, and they may differ considerably in scale. These problems apply even more so to CUA league tables because different methodologies are used to calculate QALYs and, as discussed earlier, these

---

EXHIBIT 18-2

The Cost-Utility Registry housed in the Center for the Evaluation of Value and Risk in Health at Tufts University provides a comprehensive listing of cost-effectiveness studies in the health area. The registry currently includes over 1,700 cost-effectiveness studies of health-related interventions that provide a rich source of QALY estimates for cost-benefit analysts who do not have the resources to develop their own estimates. More generally, analysts planning to conduct their surveys may find it useful to review studies that used similar methods. The Cost-Utility Registry can be accessed at research.tufts-nemc.org/cear/overview/.

Source: Adapted from CEA Registry, Center for the Evaluation of Value and Risk in Health, Tufts University, research.tufts-nemc.org/cear/.

methodologies do not necessarily produce similar results. Therefore, Karen Gerard's caution on the use of league tables is appropriate:

> [A]s more and more studies were read in the course of the investigation, it became striking how many not only placed their results in some standard QALY league table . . . but also purported to present their results as "favourable." It is unlikely to be the case that all of these studies can have "favourable" results.[36]

Other critics have noted the absence of information on uncertainty in most league tables.[37] Thus, caution is warranted in using league tables as guides for policy choice.

Conclusion: When Is CEA Close to CBA?

CEA measures technical efficiency, not allocative efficiency. It can rank alternative policies is terms of technical efficiency but cannot indicate whether something is worth doing. CEA is closest to CBA when all social costs are measured, when the effectiveness measure captures all of the social benefits, and when alternative projects are of similar scales. Under these circumstances the most cost-effective alternative is the most allocatively efficient alternative. However, this does not necessarily imply that it should be adopted because it may not be worth doing. Unless we can monetize units of effectiveness, we cannot answer the latter question.

When significant nonbudgetary social costs or other categories of benefits exist, CEA is not close to CBA. Analysts have three options. First, they can try to incorporate significant nonbudgetary social costs and other categories of benefits into an adjusted cost-effectiveness measure, such as is done in the construction of QALYs. Second, if they can also monetize effectiveness, then they should do CBA. Third, they can move to a more qualitative evaluation method such as multigoal analysis.

Exercises for Chapter 18

1. A public health department is considering five alternative programs to encourage parents to have their preschool children vaccinated against a communicable disease. The following table shows the cost and number of vaccinations predicted for each program.

Program	Cost ($)	Number of Vaccinations
A	20,000	2,000
B	44,000	4,000
C	72,000	6,000
D	112,000	8,000
E	150,000	10,000

   a. Ignoring issues of scale, which program is most cost-effective?

   b. Assuming that the public health department wishes to vaccinate at least 5,000 children, which program is most cost-effective?

   c. If the health department believes that each vaccination provides social benefits equal to $20, then which program should it adopt?

2. Analysts wish to evaluate alternative surgical procedures for spinal cord injuries. The procedures have various probabilities of yielding the following results.

> Full recovery (FR)—the patient regains full mobility and suffers no chronic pain.
> Full functional recovery (FFR)—the patient regains full mobility but suffers chronic pain that will make it uncomfortable to sit for periods of longer than about an hour and will interfere with sleeping two nights per week, on average.
> Partial functional recovery (PFR)—the patient regains only restricted movement that will limit mobility to slow-paced walking and will make it difficult to lift objects weighing more than a few pounds. Chronic pain is similar to that suffered under full functional recovery.

> Paraplegia (P)—the patient completely loses use of legs and would, therefore, require a wheelchair or other prosthetic for mobility and suffers chronic pain that interferes with sleeping four nights per week, on average. Aside from loss of the use of his or her legs, the patient would regain control of other lower body functions.

a. Describe how you would construct a quality-of-life index for these surgical outcomes by offering gambles to respondents. Test your procedure on a classmate, friend, or other willing person.

b. Assume that the index you construct on the basis of your sample of one respondent is representative of the population of patients. Use the index to measure the effectiveness of each of three alternative surgical procedures with the following distributions of outcomes.

	Surgical Procedures		
	A	*B*	*C*
FR	0.10	0.50	0.40
FFR	0.70	0.20	0.45
PFR	0.15	0.20	0.10
P	0.05	0.10	0.05

c. Imagine that the surgical procedures involved different life expectancies for the various outcomes. Discuss how you might revise your measure of effectiveness to take account of these differences.

3. (Instructor-provided spreadsheet recommended.) Two alternative mosquito control programs have been proposed to reduce the health risks of West Nile disease in a state over the next five years. The costs and effectiveness of each program in each of the next five years are provided in the following table.

	Alternative A		*Alternative B*	
	QALYs Saved	*Incremental Cost (millions of dollars)*	*QALYs Saved*	*Incremental Cost (millions of dollars)*
Year 1	1.0	3.8	0.5	1.0
Year 2	0.5	0.0	0.5	1.0
Year 3	0.3	0.0	0.5	1.0
Year 4	0.1	0.0	0.5	1.0

    a. Calculate CE ratios for each program without discounting.

    b. Calculate CE ratios discounting cost but not effectiveness assuming a discount rate of 4 percent.

    c. Calculate CE ratios discounting both costs and effectiveness at 4 percent.

    d. Assume that the uncertainty range for each of the yearly effectiveness estimates is plus or minus 20 percent and the uncertainty in each of the yearly cost estimates is 10 percent. Assuming uniform distributions of errors, produce Monte Carlo distributions of CE ratios for each program and compare them.

NOTES

1. See Alan M. Garber, "Advances in Cost-Effectiveness Analysis," in Anthony J. Culyer and Joseph P. Newhouse, eds., *Handbook of Health Economics* 1A (New York: Elsevier, 2000), 181–221 at 193–194.

2. Economists have attempted to determine the circumstances under which CEA is consistent with the assumptions of welfare economics that underlie CBA. Overall, strong assumptions are required for consistency. For overviews, see Werner B. F. Brouwer and Marc A. Koopmanshap, "On the Economic Foundations of CEA: Ladies and Gentlemen, Take Your Positions!" *Journal of Health Economics* 19(4) 2000, 439–459; and Paul Dolan and Richard Edlin, "Is It Really Possible to Build a Bridge Between Cost-Benefit Analysis and Cost-Effectiveness Analysis?" *Journal of Health Economics* 21(5) 2002, 827–843.

3. Monte Carlo simulations can be used to construct cost-effectiveness acceptability curves that give the probability of a particular alternative being optimal for different shadow prices of effect. See Elisabeth Fenwick, Karl Claxton, and Mark Sculpher, "Representing Uncertainty: The Role of Cost-Effectiveness Acceptability Curves," *Health Economics* 10(8) 2001, 779–787.

4. Christopher J. L. Murray, David B. Evans, Arnab Acharya, and Rob M. P. M. Baltussen, "Development of WHO Guidelines on Generalized Cost-Effectiveness Analysis," *Health Economics* 9(3) 2000, 235–251.

5. Karen Gerard found that approximately 90 percent of the health studies she reviewed only looked at direct budgetary costs; see Karen Gerard, "Cost-Utility in Practice: A Policy Maker's Guide to the State of the Art," *Health Policy* 21(3) 1992, 249–279 at 263.

6. See Michael Drummond, Greg L. Stoddart, and George W. Torrance, *Methods for the Economic Evaluations of Health Care Programmes* (Oxford, UK: Oxford University Press, 1987), especially page 76.

7. DALYs were developed primarily to quantify the mortality and morbidity burdens of various diseases in populations. See Christopher J. L. Murray and Arnab K. Acharya, "Understanding DALYs," *Journal of Health Economics* 16(6) 1997, 703–730. For a critique, see Sudhir Anand and Kara Hanson, "Disability-Adjusted Life Years: A Critical Assessment," *Journal of Health Economics* 16(6) 1997, 685–702.

8. These arguments are taken from Peter A. Ubel, Jeff Richardson, and Paul Menzel, "Societal Value, the Person Trade-Off, and the Dilemma of Whose Values to Measure for Cost-Effectiveness Analysis," *Health Economics* 9(2) 2000, 127–136 at 128.

9. David L. Sackett and George W. Torrance, "The Utility of Different Health States as Perceived by the General Public," *Journal of Chronic Diseases* 31(11) 1978, 697–704; and Debra Froberg and Robert L. Kane, "Methodology for Measuring Health-State Preferences—IV: Progress and a Research Agenda," *Journal of Clinical Epidemiology* 42(7) 1989, 775–685.

10. Paul Dolan, "The Measurement of Health-Related Quality of Life for Use in Resource Allocation in Health Care," in Anthony J. Culyer and Joseph P. Newhouse, eds., *Handbook of Health Economics* 1B (New York: Elsevier, 2000), 1723–1760 at 1738–1739 and 1748.

11. Rajiv Sharma, Miron Stano, and Mitchell Haas, "Adjusting to Changes in Health: Implications for Cost-Effectiveness Analysis," *Journal of Health Economics* 23(2) 2004, 335–351.

12. In addition to these methods, which attempt to elicit individual valuations of health states, the *person trade-off* (PTO) method seeks to assess

societal values for different distributions of health outcomes. For example, if respondents were indifferent between a policy that would move five people from extremely poor health to moderate health and an alternative that would move fifteen people from moderate health to perfect health, then the social value of the unit effect of the first policy is three times that of the unit effect of the second. See Erik Nord, Jose Luis Pinto, Jeff Richardson, Paul Menzel, and Peter Ubel, "Incorporating Societal Concerns for Fairness in Numerical Valuations of Health Programs," *Health Economics* 8(1) 1999, 25–39.

13. For an overview of this and the other methods for assessing HRQoL, see Dolan, "The Measurement of Health-Related Quality of Life for Use in Resource Allocation in Health Care."

14. The TTO method was first proposed by G. W. Torrance, W. H. Thomas, and D. L. Sackett, "A Utility Measurement Method for Evaluation of Health Care Programs," *Health Services Research* 7(2) 1972, 118–133.

15. Paul Dolan and Peep Stalmeier, "The Validity of Time Trade-Off Values in Calculating QALYs: Constant Proportional Time Trade-Off versus the Proportional Heuristic," *Journal of Health Economics* 22(3) 2003, 445–458.

16. The general SG method was introduced by John von Neumann and Oskar Morgenstern, *Theory of Games and Economic Behavior* (Princeton, NJ: Princeton University Press, 1944).

17. See, for example, J. L. Read, R. J. Quinn, D. M. Berrick, H. V. Fineberg, and M. L. Weinstein, "Preferences for Health Outcomes: Comparisons of Assessment Methods," *Medical Decision Making* 4(3) 1984, 315–329; and George W. Torrance, "Social Preferences for Health States: An Empirical Evaluation of Three Measurement Techniques," *Socio-Economic Planning* 10(2) 1976, 129–136.

18. See, for example, Han Bleichrodt and Magnus Johannesson, "Standard Gamble, Time Trade-Off and Rating Scale: Experimental Results on Ranking Properties of QALYs," *Journal of Health Economics* 16(2) 1997, 155–175.

19. George W. Torrance, Michael H. Boyle, and Sargent P. Horwood, "Application of Multi-Attribute Utility Theory to Measure Social Preferences for Health Status," *Operations Research* 30(6) 1982, 1043–1069.

20. Additional information, including a bibliography of studies that have used the health utilities indices, can be found at, www.healthutilities.com.

21. John Horsman, William Furlong, David Feeny, and George Torrance, "The Health Utilities Index (HUI®): Concepts, Measurement Properties, and Applications," *Health Quality and Life Outcomes* 1(1) 2003, 54–67.

22. John E. Ware Jr. and Cathy D. Sherbourne, "The MOS 36-Item Short Form Health Survey: I. Conceptual Framework and Item Selection," *Medical Care* 30(6) 1992, 473–483.

23. See www.qualitymetric.com/products/descriptions/sflicenses.shtml for additional information.

24. John E. Ware Jr. and Barbara Gandek, "Overview of the SF-36 Health Survey Instrument and the International Quality of Life Assessment (IQOLA) Project," *Journal of Clinical Epidemiology* 51(11) 1998, 903–912.

25. John Brazier, Jennifer Roberts, and Mark Deverill, "The Estimation of a Preference-Based Measure of Health from the SF-36," *Journal of Health Economics* 21(2) 2002, 271–292; and John Brazier, Tim Usherwood, Rosemary Harper, and Kate Thomas, "Deriving a Preference-Based Single Index from the UK SF-36 Health Survey," *Journal of Clinical Epidemiology* 51(11) 1998, 1115–1128.

26. John Brazier, Jennifer Roberts, and Mark Deverill, "The Estimation of a Preference-Based Measure of Health from the SF-36," Tables 5 and 6.

27. Richard Books and EuroQol Group, "EuroQol: The Current State of Play," *Health Policy* 37(1) 1996, 53–72. For current information about EuroQol and the EQ-5D index, see www. euroqol.org/

28. See, for example, Paul Dolan, "Modelling Valuations for Health States: The Effect of Duration," *Health Policy* 38(3), 189–203.

29. Louise Longworth and Stirling Bryan, "An Empirical Comparison of EQ-5D and SF-6D in Liver Transplant Patients," *Health Economics* 12(12) 2003, 1061–1067.

30. Barbara Conner-Spady and Maria E. Suarez-Almazor, "Variation in the Estimation of Quality Adjusted Life-Years by Different Preference-Based Instruments," *Medical Care* 41(7) 2003, 791–801.

31. For more on the debate over how well different methods get at utility, see A. J. Culyer and Adam Wagstaff, "QALYs versus HYEs," *Journal of*

Health Economics 11(3) 1993, 311–323; and Amiram Gafni, Stephen Birch, and Abraham Mehrez, "Economics, Health and Health Economics: HYEs versus QALYs," same issue, 325–329.

32. Emmett B. Keeler and Shan Cretin, "Discounting of Life-Saving and Other Nonmonetary Effects," *Management Science* 29(3) 1983, 300–306. However, this is not a paradox per se because, as we have shown, a CE ratio never tells us whether a project has positive social value and hence, should be implemented—whether this year or next year.

33. Amiram Gafni, "Time in Health: Can We Measure Individuals' 'Pure Time Preference'?" *Medical Decision Making* 15(1) 1995, 31–37; Donald A. Redelmeier, Daniel N. Heller, and Milton C. Weinstein, "Time Preference in Medical Economics: Science or Religion?" *Medical Decision Making* 13(3) 1993, 301–303; and Magnus Johannesson, Joseph Pliskin, and Milton C. Weinstein, "A Note on QALYs, Time Trade-off and Discounting," *Medical Decision Making* 14(2) 1994, 188–193.

34. Tammy O. Tengs, Miriam E. Adams, Joseph S. Pliskin, Dana Gelb-Safran, Joanna E. Seigel, Michael C. Weinstein, and John D. Graham, "Five-Hundred Life-Saving Interventions and Their Cost-Effectiveness," *Risk Analysis* 15(3) 1995, 369–390. For more on their methodology and policy implications, see Tammy O. Tengs and John D. Graham, "The Opportunity Costs of Haphazard Social Investment in Life-Saving," in Robert W. Hahn, ed., *Risks, Costs, and Lives Saved: Getting Better Results from Regulation* (New York and Oxford: Oxford University Press; Washington, D.C.: The AEI Press, 1996).

35. John F. Morrall III, "Saving Lives: A Review of the Record," *Journal of Risk and Uncertainty* 27(3) 2003, 221–237.

36. Gerard, "Cost-Utility in Practice," 274.

37. Josephine Mauskopf, Frans Rutten, and Warren Schonfeld, "Cost-Effectiveness League Tables: Valuable Guidance for Decision Makers?" *Pharmacoeconomics* 21(14) 2003, 991–1000.

CHAPTER 19

Distributionally Weighted Cost-Benefit Analysis

Government policies, programs, and projects typically affect individuals differently. Thus, in conducting CBAs, analysts often report benefits and costs for separate categories of people. The relevant classification of individuals into groups for this purpose depends on the specific policy under evaluation. Some examples include consumers versus producers versus taxpayers, program participants versus nonparticipants, citizens (of a nation or a state or a city) versus noncitizens, and high-income groups versus low-income groups. This chapter focuses on the most common form of distributionally weighted CBA, which that involves high-income versus low-income groups.

Once individuals are divided into categories, the first issue that must be decided is whether each group will be given standing in the CBA.[1] For example, in conducting a CBA of U.S. regulatory policy on acid rain, a decision must be made as to whether to give standing to Canadians affected by acid rain resulting from manufacturing in the United States. Similarly, when evaluating a policy that impacts foreign-based and owned companies, one must decide whether to give standing to foreign shareholders.

Given a decision on standing, costs and benefits may be reported separately for each group with standing. This idea was introduced in Chapter 3 and expanded on in Chapter 4 in the context of a *social accounting ledger*. The usefulness of showing the impacts on each group separately is illustrated by the following hypothetical example. Here, it is assumed that the government is considering proposals from three different (national) companies for constructing and operating a pipeline that would transport oil from inside the country to customers in another country. Consider, for example, a pipeline from Northern Canada into the United States. The benefits and costs associated with each proposal may be presented in two ways.

Table 19-1 exemplifies "traditional" CBA, which ignores distributional considerations. Impacts are categorized as benefits or costs from the perspective of society as a whole. Society would be better off if it adopted Company A or B's proposals than no pipeline (the NPV of the net social benefits are positive) and would be best off by adopting Company B's proposal. In contrast, Table 19-2 indicates how three different groups would be affected by each proposal. It shows that all firms would enjoy net benefits as their profits (producer surplus) would be positive. Some (firms A and B), however, would enjoy more profits than others (firm C). Government would also benefit as government surplus (tax revenues) would be positive. However, a third party

TABLE 19-1   Social Cost-Benefit Analysis of Alternative Pipeline Proposals

	Company A	*Company B*	*Company C*
Social benefits			
Revenues	4.00	4.00	4.00
Total benefits	4.00	4.00	4.00
Social costs			
Construction cost	1.88	1.98	2.36
Operating costs	1.20	1.25	1.50
Environmental cost of construction	0.20	0.20	0.20
Expected subsequent environmental costs	0.29	0.13	0.08
Total costs	3.57	3.56	4.14
Net social benefits	0.43	0.44	−0.14

TABLE 19-2   Social Cost-Benefit Analysis of Alternative Pipeline Proposals
(Net Benefits to Each Affected Group)

	Company A	*Company B*	*Company C*
COMPANY			
Benefits			
Revenues	4.00	4.00	4.00
Costs			
Construction cost	1.88	1.98	2.36
Operating costs	1.20	1.25	1.50
Taxes	0.24	0.20	0.05
Expected firm environmental costs	0.18	0.08	0.05
Costs	3.50	3.51	3.96
Expected profit	**0.50**	**0.49**	**0.04**
RESIDENTS' COSTS			
Environmental cost of construction	0.20	0.20	0.20
Expected subsequent environmental costs	0.15	0.07	0.04
Less compensation received	−0.04	−0.02	−0.01
Cost to residents	**0.31**	**0.25**	**0.23**
GOVERNMENT REVENUES (TAXES)	**0.24**	**0.20**	**0.05**
Net social benefits	**0.43**	**0.44**	**−0.14**

composed of individuals who live near the pipeline would be worse off under all three proposals. (There is no consumer surplus in this illustration because it is assumed that the oil is exported and foreigners do not have standing.) Table 19-2 also indicates that, although net social benefits would be similar under the proposals from Company A and B, there is a trade-off between them because the government would receive greater tax revenues under Company A's proposal, but residents would be better off under the proposal from Company B. Thus, Table 19-2 provides richer information than Table 19-1. But how can this information to be utilized in making a decision concerning the three proposals?

Throughout this book, we have emphasized use of the Kaldor-Hicks potential compensation test in reaching such decisions. In using this test, benefits and costs are simply summed across all groups that have standing to determine whether total benefits are larger than total costs and, hence, whether the policy should be adopted. Thus, this test examines benefits and costs from the perspective of society as a whole. Indeed, an implicit result of using the Kaldor-Hicks potential compensation test is that, with standing, it does not matter who receives the benefits from a government program or who pays the costs ("a dollar is a dollar regardless of who receives or pays it"), as long as there is a net gain to society as a whole—in other words, as long as the program is efficient in terms of potential Pareto improvement. Thus, regardless of whether Table 19-1 or 19-2 is used to make a decision, the decision would be in favor of Company B's proposal.

In making actual policy decisions, however, the way in which benefits and costs are distributed among various groups is sometimes important. For instance, this consideration can have an influence over whether a policy is politically acceptable. For example, effects on local residents may have more influence than the same amount of funds added to government revenue. Hence, a dollar received or expended by a member of one group may not be treated as equal to a dollar received or expended by a member of another group.

In this chapter, we focus on the role of the distribution of benefits and costs among groups in using CBA for decision making.[2] We first examine the economic rationale for treating dollars received or expended by various income groups differently in CBA. We then consider approaches for doing this in practice.

DISTRIBUTIONAL JUSTIFICATIONS FOR INCOME TRANSFER PROGRAMS

The rationale suggested by economists for treating dollars received or expended by various groups differently in CBA is mainly limited to situations in which low-income persons are helped (or hurt) by a program more than other persons.[3] Political decision makers may treat dollars received or expended by various other groups differently, even if their income levels are similar. They may, for example, be influenced by differences among groups in voting behavior or campaign contributions. Economists, however, typically argue for treating dollars received or expended by various groups similarly unless they differ in terms of income or wealth.[4] Consequently, in the remainder of this chapter, we focus on CBAs of policies that have differential effects on groups that differ by income—for example, projects that are located in underdeveloped regions or programs that are targeted at disadvantaged persons.

To illustrate such policies, consider a program that taxes high-income persons in order to provide income transfers to low-income persons. The tax component of this program is illustrated in Figure 19-1. For purposes of discussion, assume that the market represented in this graph is for a luxury good, such as yachts, that is purchased only by the rich. In the absence of the tax, equilibrium in this market would occur at a price of P_1 and a quantity of Q_1. If an excise tax of t is levied on each unit of output, then the supply curve would shift up by this amount as suppliers attempt to pass along to consumers the additional cost the tax imposes upon them.

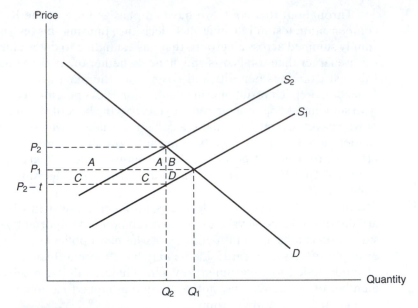

FIGURE 19-1   An Excise Tax on a Luxury Good

Source: Adapted from Arnold C. Harberger, "On the Use of Distributional Weights in Social Cost-Benefit Analysis," *Journal of Political Economy* 86(2) 1978, S87–S120; Figure 1, p. S89.

Using the approach implied by the Kaldor-Hicks rule, a distributional analysis of the costs and benefits associated with this tax would look like this:

	Benefits	*Costs*
Producers		$C + D$
Consumers		$A + B$
Transfer recipients	$A + C$	
Society		$\overline{B + D}$

Thus, a deadweight loss equal to areas $B + D$ would result from the tax. In addition to this deadweight loss, two off-graph social costs also result from our transfer program:

1. Administering both the tax and the transfer parts of the program requires the use of social resources.
2. Some of those receiving the transfer will probably work less or stop working entirely, thereby reducing the goods and services available to society. In fact, there is considerable evidence that this is what occurs under existing welfare programs.[5] Only part of this loss would be offset by the gains in leisure to transfer recipients (see Chapter 12). The remaining residual is a second source of deadweight loss.

It is obvious that this program does not pass the Kaldor-Hicks test. It must instead be justified on distributional grounds. In other words, one would have to argue that giving a low-income person a dollar warrants taking more than a dollar away from a higher-income person. Apparently, this distributional argument has some force because programs such as Temporary Assistance to Needy Families (TANF) and food stamps, which transfer income from higher-income to lower-income persons, do in fact exist. Hence, it appears that society is willing to sacrifice some efficiency in order to provide assistance to low-income persons.

The importance of this for CBA analysis is that it implies that, in practice, a dollar of benefits received or a dollar of costs incurred by a low-income individual is sometimes given greater weight in assessing government programs than a dollar of benefits received or a dollar of costs incurred by a higher-income individual. How can this be justified?

THE CASE FOR TREATING LOW- AND HIGH-INCOME GROUPS DIFFERENTLY IN CBA

There are at least three arguments for giving dollars received or paid by low-income persons greater weight in CBA than dollars received or paid by higher-income persons:

1. Income has diminishing marginal utility.
2. The income distribution should be more equal.
3. The "one person, one vote" principle should apply.

We discuss each of these arguments in turn.

Diminishing Marginal Utility of Income

The first argument is based on the standard assumption in economics that each additional dollar an individual receives provides less utility than the preceding dollar. A corollary of this assumption is that a dollar received or a dollar of cost incurred by a high-income person has less of an impact on his or her utility than it would on a low-income person's utility. For that reason, the argument suggests, it should count less in a CBA.[6] This argument can be summarized algebraically as follows:

$$\Delta u_l / \Delta y_l > \Delta u_h / \Delta y_h \tag{19.1}$$

where $\Delta u_i / \Delta y_i$ is the marginal private utility of income of individual i, l indicates a low-income person, and h a high-income person.

Income Distribution Should Be More Equal

The second argument for giving dollars received or paid by the poor greater weight in CBA than dollars received or paid by the rich is premised on the assertion that the current income distribution is less equal than it should be and social welfare would be higher if it were more equal.[7] There are several possible bases for such an assertion. The first is that a highly unequal distribution of income may result in civil disorder, crime, and riots. More equality in income may reduce these threats to the general social welfare. Second, it can be argued that some minimum threshold of income exists that is so low that no one can (or, to preserve human dignity, should have to) live below it. Third, some relatively well-off persons may receive utility if the circumstances facing the worse-off members of society at the bottom of the income distribution improve. Certain types of charitable giving, such as contributions to the Salvation Army, provide evidence for the existence of this form of altruism. Finally, it is possible that some persons value greater income equality in and of itself.[8]

If for any of these reasons society prefers greater income equality than currently exists, then a dollar increase in the income of a low-income person would result in a larger increase in the welfare of society as a whole than would a dollar increase in the income of a high-income person. Note that this would still be true even if the marginal utility of income was not diminishing and, consequently, a dollar increase in the income of high- and low-income persons resulted in equal increases in the utilities of these persons. Each of the justifications listed in the previous paragraph suggests that society as a whole (or at least some relatively well-off members of society) becomes better off if those at the bottom of the income distribution gain relative to those in the rest of the distribution. Thus, the first and second arguments are distinct from one another.

Stated algebraically, the second argument implies that:

$$\Delta SW/\Delta y_l > \Delta SW/\Delta y_h, \text{ even if } \Delta u_1/\Delta y_l = \Delta u_h/\Delta y_h \qquad (19.2)$$

where ΔSW refers to the change in aggregate social welfare and $\Delta SW/\Delta y_i$ is the marginal effect on social welfare of a change in income that is received by individual i.[9]

This argument confronts the Kaldor-Hicks test quite directly. It implies that some projects or programs that fail the Kaldor-Hicks test should nonetheless be adopted if they redistribute income in a way that makes the income distribution more equal. In other words, the argument suggests that some programs that are inefficient should be undertaken if they increase income equality sufficiently. This also implies that some projects that make the income distribution less equal should not be undertaken, even though the Kaldor-Hicks test implies that they are efficient.

The "One Person, One Vote" Principle

This argument begins by noting that the benefits and costs of government programs to consumers are appropriately measured as changes in consumer surplus. Then it goes on to point out that because high-income persons have more income to spend than low-income persons, the measured impacts of policies on their consumer surplus will typically be larger and, hence, will be of greater consequence in a CBA based strictly on the Kaldor-Hicks rule.

This is illustrated by Figure 19-2, which compares the demand schedules of a typical high-income consumer and a typical low-income consumer for a good. If the good is a *normal good,* that is, if demand for the good increases as income increases, then the demand schedule of the high-income consumer will be to the right of that of the low-income consumer, as the diagram shows. If a government policy increases the price of the good, say from P_1 to P_2, both consumers will bear the cost of that increase in the form of a loss in consumer surplus. However, the loss suffered by the high-income consumer (areas $A + B$) will be greater than the loss borne by the low-income consumer (area A

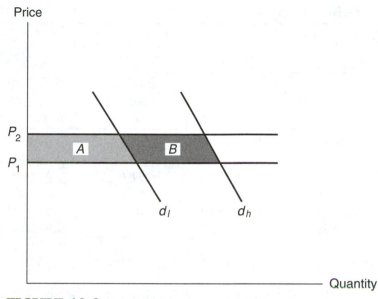

FIGURE 19-2   Changes in Consumer Surplus for High- and Low-Income Consumers

alone). As a result, a CBA will give more weight to the impact of the policy on the high-income consumer than on the low-income consumer.

The final part of the argument suggests that in a democracy low-income persons should have as much influence over decisions on whether to undertake public projects as high-income persons. In other words, it is argued that "since the principle of 'one person, one vote' is deeply embedded in the concept of democracy," measures of changes in consumer surplus for different persons should be adjusted to what they would be if everyone had the same income.[10] For example, we would count the impact of the price change on the low-income person represented in the diagram at about double what we would count the impact on the high-income person, in effect, equalizing the "votes" of the two individuals.[11]

DISTRIBUTIONAL WEIGHTS

In principle, various groups can be treated differently in a CBA by using *distributional weights*. Distributional weights are just numbers—such as 1, 2, or 1.5—that are intended to reflect the value placed on each dollar paid out or received by each group. Table 19-3 compares standard and distributionally weighted CBA for two projects affecting two income groups. In standard CBA, as shown in the upper panel of the table, both groups receive an equal weight of 1. In distributionally weighted CBA, Group B (the higher-income group) is given a value of 1, while Group A (the lower-income group) is given a value of 3, implying that a dollar received by a member of the low-income group is valued in the CBA at three times that of a dollar received by a member of the high-income group. Given this weighting, as shown in the lower panel, project selection switches from Project I to Project II.

TABLE 19-3   Standard versus Distributionally Weighted CBA

1. Standard CBA

Projects	Net Benefits		Aggregate Net Social Benefits
	Group A	*Group B*	
I	10	50	60
II	20	30	50
Weights	1	1	Selection: Project I

2. Distributionally Weighted CBA

Projects	Net Benefits		Aggregate Net Social Benefits
	Group A	*Group B*	
I	$10 \times 3 = 30$	50	80
II	$20 \times 3 = 60$	30	90
Weights	3	1	Selection: Project II

More formally, distributional weights can be incorporated into a CBA through a slight modification of the net present value (*NPV*) formula:

$$NPV = \sum_{j=1}^{m} \left[W_j \sum_{t=0}^{\infty} \frac{B_{t,j} - C_{t,j}}{(1 + s)^t} \right] \qquad \textbf{(19.3)}$$

where W_j is the distributional weight for group j, $B_{t,j}$ are the benefits received by group j in period t, $C_{t,j}$ are the costs incurred by group j in period t, m is the number of groups, and s is the social discount rate.

EXHIBIT 19-1

Proposed mergers that appear likely to result in price increases are not allowed in the United States, but they are permitted in Canada if the potential gains in efficiency are deemed sufficient. Viewed somewhat differently, mergers are permitted in Canada if potential gains in producer surplus seem to offset potential losses in consumer surplus resulting from price increases, but such mergers are not permitted in the United States. Thomas Ross and Ralph Winter point out that this is equivalent to giving producer and consumer surplus equal distributional weights in Canada, but giving consumer surplus a greater weight than producer surplus in the United States. Indeed, producer surplus is, in effect, given a weight of zero in the United States. One rationale for the U.S. approach might be that producers (e.g., corporative stockholders) tend to be wealthier than consumers, but Ross and Winter argue that this need not always be the case (e.g., consider the markets for luxury goods) and, even if it is, distributional weights should be based on the actual wealth or income of individuals, not on whether they happen to be classified as "producers" or "consumers" in the case of a particular merger.

Source: Adapted from Thomas W. Ross and Ralph A. Winter, "The Efficiency Defense in Merger Law: Economic Foundations and Recent Canadian Developments," *Antitrust Law Journal* 72 2004–5, 471–503.

The idea behind this formula is simple. The persons affected by the government policy are divided into as many groups as appropriate. Each group is then given a distributional weight. The *NPV* for each group is then computed and multiplied by its weight. These weighted *NPV*s are then added together to obtain an overall *NPV*. Note that in CBAs that rely strictly on the Kaldor-Hicks rule, W_j is implicitly set equal to 1 for all groups. On the other hand, W_j is set to 0 for any group that is not given standing.

DETERMINING DISTRIBUTIONAL WEIGHTS

The obvious difficulty with implementing this approach is determining appropriate weight for each group. The weights should, of course, be consistent with the rationale for using them. However, of the three arguments for using weights presented earlier, only the one based on the "one person, one vote" principle suggests an approach that could potentially be used in practice for valuing the weights of various groups, and even in this case, the information requirements are substantial. Among the required information is the average income level of each relevant group, an estimate of the *income elasticity of demand* for each good affected by the government policy being evaluated (i.e., the percentage change in the quantity demanded of each good that results from a 1 percent increase in income), and an estimate of the market demand curve for each affected good. Given this information, the consumer surplus of the average member of each group can then be computed. These estimates can, in turn, be used to derive distributional weights for each group that are consistent with the one person, one vote principle.[12]

To develop weights that are consistent with the remaining two arguments, information is needed on $\Delta u/\Delta y$ (the marginal private utility of income) and $\Delta SW/\Delta y$ (the marginal effect on social welfare of a change in income) for a typical member of each group of interest. For example, a set of distributional weights could be developed that is consistent with the diminishing marginal utility of income argument if we knew that a $100 increase in income increased the utility of rich people by two units and the utility of poor people by three units by simply computing weights on the basis of the ratio of the marginal utility values. Thus, W_j would be set equal to 1 for rich persons and to 1.5 for poor persons. Similarly, a set of distributional weights that is consistent with the argument that the income distribution should be more equal could be developed if we knew that a $100 increase in the income of a typical poor person increased social welfare by two units, but the same increase in the income of a typical rich person increased social welfare by only one unit.

Unfortunately, such information is not available, nor is there any known way to obtain it. First, utility is a subjective concept that defies cardinal measurement.[13] Indeed many economists eschew any explicit interpersonal comparisons of utility for this reason. But in the absence of interpersonal comparisons of utility, it is not possible to develop a system of distributional weights that is consistent with the diminishing marginal utility of income argument. Second, no general consensus among members of society exists concerning the specific relationship between a given change in the income levels of individuals and social welfare, except that most persons would, perhaps, agree that the relation is positive and its magnitude is larger for low-income than for high-income persons. Without such a consensus, however, it is not possible to develop distributional weights that are consistent with the greater income equality argument.

EXHIBIT 19-2

Whether a dollar of benefits or costs is valued higher in poor developing countries than in a richer developed countries has important implications for international environmental agreements. For example, in the absence of weighting, the per capita benefits of an agreement to reduce global climate change by restricting emissions of fossil fuel would be smaller in a poor country than in a rich country. One reason for this is that when based on willingness to pay the value of a statistical life is smaller in the poor country simply because of differences in ability to pay. Without weighting, the per capita dollar costs of restricting emissions in a poor country (for example, job losses) would also be smaller than in a rich country. A recent analysis by Christian Azar, which uses a CBA framework, found that, compared to a situation in which weighting is not used, the use of weighting greatly reduces emissions that rich countries should be allowed relative to those that poor countries should be permitted.

Source: Adapted from Christian Azar, "Weight Factors in Cost-Benefit Analysis of Climate Change," *Environmental and Resource Economics* 13(3) 1999, 249–268.

A PRAGMATIC APPROACH TO WEIGHTING

Given the practical difficulties with obtaining a defensible set of distributional weights,[14] we suggest that their use be limited to only those CBAs where distributional issues are of central concern (for example, CBAs of programs targeted at disadvantaged groups or at impoverished areas within countries, states, or cities) or CBAs of policies that explicitly treat different income groups differently (for example, a CBA of a plan to store radioactive waste in a low-income area). It may then be possible to use an approach that highlights the importance of the distributional implications associated with the policy being analyzed without requiring that any particular set of distributional weights be selected as the "correct" set.

To illustrate the particular approach that we suggest using to do this, we return to the CBA of welfare-to-work programs, first discussed in Chapter 12. These programs provide various combinations of job search, education, training, financial incentives, and subsidized jobs for welfare recipients. Because these programs are targeted at welfare recipients—an especially disadvantaged low-income group—both their distributional effects and their effects on economic efficiency are relevant. Thus, in principle, CBAs of welfare-to-work programs should take both types of effects into account.

Displaying Unweighted Cost and Benefit Estimates

The first step in taking account of both the efficiency and distributional effects of welfare-to-work programs is simply to display unweighted program impacts on society as a whole, as well as on pertinent subgroups. This is accomplished in the first three columns in Table 19-4, which simply duplicate the total net present value estimates for the programs that were originally reported in Table 12-4. Column 1 reports these estimates from the perspective of program participants, column 2 from the perspective of nonparticipants, and column 3 (which is computed by summing the first two columns) from the perspective of society as a whole.

TABLE 19-4   Sensitivity of MDRC's Evaluations of Selected Welfare-to-Work Experiments to the Use of Distributional Weights (in 2006 dollars)

	NPV from Participant Perspective (1)	*NPV from Nonparticipant Perspective* (2)	*Unweighted Social NPV* [Col 1 + Col 2] (3)	*NPV If Participant Weight = 2* [2 × Col 1 + Col 2] (4)	*Estimates of Internal Weights for Participants* [Col 2/Col 1] (5)
Mandatory Work Experience Programs					
Cook County WIN Demonstration (*n* = 11,912)	686	−183	503	1,190	NA
San Diego (*n* = 3,591)	310	1,411	1,721	2,030	NA
West Virginia CWEP (*n* = 3,694)	−163	1,424	1,261	1,098	8.74
Mandatory Job-Search-First Programs					
Atlanta LFA NEWWS (*n* = 4,433)	−14	−932	−946	−960	NA
Grand Rapids LFA NEWWS (*n* = 4,554)	−2,867	3,521	653	−2,214	1.23
Los Angeles Jobs-First GAIN (*n* = 15,683)	509	3,044	3,552	4,061	NA
Riverside LFA NEWWS (*n* = 8,322)	−1,606	1,870	264	−1,342	1.16
SWIM (San Diego) (*n* = 3,227)	−49	2,599	2,549	2,500	52.59
Mandatory Education-First Programs					
Atlanta HCD NEWWS (*n* = 4,433)	398	−3,943	−3,545	−3,147	9.91
Columbus Integrated NEWWS (*n* = 7,242)	−1,975	295	−1,680	−3,656	NA
Columbus Traditional NEWWS (*n* = 7,242)	−1,423	−781	−2,204	−3,628	NA
Detroit NEWWS (*n* = 4,459)	196	−401	−205	−9	2.05
Grand Rapids HCD NEWWS (*n* = 4,554)	−2,443	−374	−2,817	−5,259	NA
Riverside HCD NEWWS (*n* = 3,135)	−3,686	735	−2,951	−6,638	NA
Mandatory Mixed-Initial-Activity Programs					
Butte GAIN (*n* = 1,234)	1,829	197	2,026	3,855	NA
Portland NEWWS (*n* = 4,028)	−1,167	6,337	5,169	4,002	5.43
Riverside GAIN (*n* = 5,626)	2,117	4,104	6,221	8,339	NA
San Diego GAIN (*n* = 8,224)	1,026	1,277	2,303	3,329	NA
Tulare GAIN (*n* = 2,248)	2,020	−3,162	−1,142	878	1.57

(Continued)

TABLE 19-4 *(Continued)*

	NPV from Participant Perspective (1)	NPV from Nonparticipant Perspective (2)	Unweighted Social NPV [Col 1 + Col 2] (3)	NPV If Participant Weight = 2 [2 × Col 1 + Col 2] (4)	Estimates of Internal Weights for Participants [Col 2/Col 1] (5)
Project Independence (Florida) (*n* = 18,237)	−579	100	−478	−1,057	NA
Alameda GAIN (*n* = 1,205)	1,218	−4,153	−2,935	−1,717	3.41
Los Angeles GAIN (*n* = 4,434)	−2,229	−4,811	−7,041	−9,270	NA
Earnings Supplement Programs					
MFIP (Minnesota) (*n* = 3,208)	10,144	−10,958	−814	9,329	1.08
SSP Applicants (Canada) (*n* = 2,371)	6,589	−580	6,009	12,599	NA
SSP Long-Term Recipients (Canada) (*n* = 4,852)	4,614	−2,363	2,251	6,865	NA
WRP (Vermont) (*n* = 5,469)	241	−228	13	253	NA

NA=Not Applicable
Source for columns 1–3: Table 12.4

None of the estimates reported in the first three columns of Table 19-4 are weighted. *Even when distributional weighting is used, unweighted estimates of benefits and costs for society as a whole should always be provided in CBAs. In addition, whenever distributional considerations are important, benefit and cost estimates for relevant subgroups should also be provided* if it is feasible to do so.

The unweighted *NPV* estimates reported in the first three columns of Table 19-4 have two especially important implications. First, they indicate that just over half of the reported programs pass the Kaldor-Hicks test. Specifically, 14 of the 26 unweighted *NPV* estimates for society as a whole, which appear in column 3, are positive, and 12 are negative. Second, in 5 of the 14 cases that pass the Kaldor-Hicks test, program participants were apparently made worse off by the tested program, while nonparticipants—a group who, on average, enjoys substantially higher incomes than participants—were made better off; but in 5 of the 12 cases that failed the Kaldor-Hicks test, program participants were made better off, while nonparticipants were made worst off. In these instances, a trade-off occurs between economic efficiency and distributional considerations. *It is only when a policy or program change results in a trade-off between efficiency and equality in the income or wealth distribution that distributional weighting is relevant. It is not needed in the case of a "win-win change" (i.e., both efficiency and progressivity improve) or a "lose-lose change" (both efficiency and progressivity decline).*[15] Table 19-4 displays nine win-win changes and seven lose-lose changes, as well as the ten trade-off changes.

Conducting Sensitivity Tests

Column 4 tests the degree to which the estimates reported in column 3 of Table 19.4 are sensitive to the choice of distributional weights. In contrast to the unweighted figures appearing in column 3, which are based on the assumption that society values the gains and losses of welfare recipients and nonrecipients equally, those appearing in column 4 assume that the gains and losses of welfare recipients are valued by society at twice those of nonrecipients. In other words, participants are given a distributional weight of 2 and nonparticipants a weight of 1. Although these weights are obviously arbitrary—as previously stressed, we do not know the actual relative values that society places on dollars received and paid out by participants and nonparticipants—in our judgment, it seems likely that they overstate society's generosity toward welfare recipients and thus test whether the social *NPV* estimates are sensitive to a rather extreme assumption.

A comparison of columns 3 and 4 indicates, as expected, that this assumption causes changes in magnitude in all of these estimates. More importantly, however, only four change sign. Two of these sign changes are from positive to negative, thereby turning a net gain into net loss, while the other two are from negative to positive, turning a net loss into a net gain. Because the remaining 22 *NPV*s do not change sign even when a rather large distributional weight is used, it seems apparent that conclusions as to whether most of the programs listed in Table 19-4 are cost-beneficial are not very sensitive to taking account of distributional considerations.

Computing Internal Weights

Column 5 in Table 19-4 is based on the computation of *internal weights,* an alternative to the approach used in column 4 for computing distributional weights. This scheme works best if there are just two pertinent groups, one of which is relatively disadvantaged (e.g., participants in welfare-to-work programs) and the other relatively advantaged (e.g., nonparticipants in these programs).

Internal distributional weights are derived by first setting the weight for the advantaged group equal to unity and then computing the weight for the disadvantaged group by dividing the estimated *NPV* for the advantaged group by the estimated *NPV* for the disadvantaged group. The idea is similar to that behind the computation of internal rates of return. Instead of somehow selecting weights, one finds the weights at which the program being analyzed would just break even; in other words, the weights at which the *NPV* for society as a whole would equal zero. Viewed a bit differently, the internal weight for the disadvantaged group indicates the dollars of costs incurred by the advantaged group per dollar of benefits received by the disadvantaged group if the former is made worse off by the program and the latter better off, or the dollars of benefits received by the advantaged group per dollar of costs incurred by the disadvantaged group if the former is made better off and the latter worse off.

In Table 19-4, we compute internal weights for Work/Welfare Demonstration participants by dividing column 2 by column 1. We do this, however, only when the program results in a trade-off between efficiency and distribution (that is, when column 1 and column 3 are of the opposite sign). In the case of win-win or lose-lose changes, a trade-off between efficiency and distribution does not exist and, consequently, distributional weighting is not germane. As trade-off changes occurred in only ten instances in the estimates presented in Table 19-4, only ten internal weights for program participants appear in column 5.

Each of these ten values indicates the weight at which a demonstration program would just break even. Thus, if the "true" weight for participants is larger than their internal weight, programs with positive unweighted (or standard) social *NPV*s would fail to break even once their distributional implications were taken into account, and programs with negative unweighted social *NPV*s would more than break even. However, because the "true" weight for participants is unknown, policy makers would have to make a judgmental decision as to whether dollars of benefits or costs to participants should be given a higher or lower value than that implied by the computed internal weights. Indeed, a major advantage of internal weighting is that it makes the trade-off between efficiency and distribution explicit for policy makers.

For example, in five of the cases for which internal weights are computed in Table 19-4, program participants were worse off under the demonstration programs, but the unweighted (standard) social *NPV* estimate was positive. Thus, these five programs pass the Kaldor-Hicks test, even though it make the distribution of income less equal. If policy makers believed that dollars lost to participants in the programs listed in Table 19-4 should be valued at, say, 25 percent more than dollars gained by nonparticipants, then this would imply that one of these five programs failed to break even and, hence, should be discontinued even though they passed the Kaldor-Hicks test. If they instead valued dollars lost to participants at a little over two times more than dollars gained by nonparticipants, then this would imply that three of the five programs failed to break even. Thus, they would conclude that three of the programs that passed the Kaldor-Hicks test actually had a negative payoff once their adverse effects on the income distribution were taken into account. But is a weight for participants of over two plausible? We consider this issue next.

Obtaining Upper-Bound Values for Distributional Weights

It was pointed out earlier in this chapter that pure transfer programs inevitably fail the Kaldor-Hicks test because each dollar of transfer benefits costs nonrecipients more than a dollar. However, it has been argued that transfer programs can be used as a standard to which other types of programs that redistribute income can be compared.[16] Specifically, the argument suggests that *if a nontransfer program makes the disadvantaged better off but results in a loss of efficiency, then it should not be accepted if a transfer program that results in a smaller loss in efficiency can potentially be used instead.* By the same token, *if a nontransfer program makes the disadvantaged worse off but results in gains in efficiency, then it should be accepted if there is a transfer program that can potentially compensate the disadvantaged for their losses without fully offsetting the gains in efficiency from the nontransfer program.*

This approach requires that internal weights that are derived similarly to the ten values that appear in the last column of Table 19-4 be obtained for transfer programs. Along these lines, Edward Gramlich, estimates that it costs taxpayers approximately $1.50 to $2.00 to transfer a dollar to a recipient under a transfer program.[17] As Gramlich suggests, although these estimates should be considered approximate and tentative, if one accepts them as being of the right order of magnitude, then it can be argued that distributional weights for the disadvantaged should never be set above one and a half to two times the weight for the advantaged.

Consider, for example, a nontransfer program that has a negative unweighted net present value, although it makes the poor better off. More specifically, assume the program costs the advantaged $2.50 for every dollar of benefits received by the disadvantaged. Gramlich's estimates imply that every dollar received by the disadvantaged under a transfer program would cost the advantaged only $1.50 to $2.00. Thus, in principle, the transfer program could be used instead to make the disadvantaged just as well off as under the nontransfer program but at a lower cost to the advantaged. Thus, not only does the nontransfer program have a negative unweighted social *NPV,* but it is also inferior to a simple transfer program for redistributing income to the disadvantaged.

Now consider a different program that provides the advantaged $2.50 of benefits for every dollar of costs incurred by the disadvantaged. Under these circumstances, each dollar lost under the program by the disadvantaged could, in principle, be reimbursed through a transfer program at a cost to the advantaged of only $1.50 to $2.00. Hence, this program not only has a positive unweighted social *NPV,* but the disadvantaged also can be compensated for their losses without completely offsetting the gains in efficiency from the program.

The argument just presented implies that *distributional weights assigned to the disadvantaged should not exceed 1.5 or 2 in value if the value for the advantaged is set to 1.* Larger weights would imply acceptance of inefficient programs that are also inferior to simple transfer programs for redistributing income and rejection of efficient programs that allow the advantaged to enjoy net gains even when the disadvantaged could be fully compensated through income transfers for losses they suffer. Thus, the argument suggests that the three programs in Table 19-4 that have internal weights well in excess of 2 and positive unweighted (standard) social *NPV*s should definitely be accepted, even though they have adverse effects on the income distribution. In contrast, the three programs that have internal weights that exceed 2, but negative unweighted social *NPV*s, should probably be rejected, even though they improve the income distribution.

Note, however, that this argument is very similar in spirit to the one underlying the Kaldor-Hicks rule. Both are based on the *potential* use of transfer payments to compensate losers under a policy, while leaving winners better off than they would be in the absence of the policy. Nothing, however, requires that these income transfers actually be made.

CONCLUSION

This chapter focuses on the use of distributional weighting to take account of the fact that many policies have divergent impacts on different income groups. Given the absence of generally accepted sets of distributional weights, we suggest that the use of distributional weights should be limited to policies that meet both of the following conditions: (1) they are targeted at the disadvantaged or treat the advantaged and the disadvantaged differently, and (2) they result in reductions in overall social efficiency but make low-income persons better off, or they increase social efficiency but make low-income persons worse off.

There may, in fact, be relatively few policies that meet both of these conditions. Those policies that do might be subjected to sensitivity tests based on a plausible range of weights. Or alternatively, internal weights might be computed, thereby providing policy makers with information on which to base their choice of distributional weights.

In either case, however, a cogent argument can be made for not allowing the distributional weights for low-income groups to be set much more than 50 to 100 percent above those for higher-income groups.

EXERCISES FOR CHAPTER 19

1. A city is about to build a new sanitation plant. It is considering two sites, one located in a moderately well-to-do neighborhood and the other in a low-income neighborhood. Indeed, most of the residents in the latter neighborhood live below the poverty line. The city's sanitation engineer is adamant that "the city needs the new plant and it has to go somewhere." However, he is indifferent as to which neighborhood it is located in. The plant would operate at the same cost and as efficiently in either neighborhood, and about as many people would be affected by the air pollution emitted by the plant. The city hires an economist to study the two sites. The economist finds that the plant would cause a considerably larger fall in average property values in the well-to-do neighborhood than in the low-income neighborhood, given the more expensive homes that are located in the former. Consistent with this, a contingent valuation study that the economist conducts finds that willingness to pay to avoid the sanitation plant is substantially higher in the well-to-do neighborhood than in the low-income neighborhood.

    The residents of the poor neighborhood strongly prefer that the plant be built in the well-to-do neighborhood. In the face of the economist's findings, what sort of arguments might they make?

2. CBAs have been conducted for six proposed projects. None of these projects are mutually exclusive, and the agency has a sufficient budget to fund those that will make society better off. The following findings from the CBAs are summarized in millions of dollars:

	Net Social Benefits	Net Group I Benefits	Net Group II Benefits
Project A	$2	$2	$0
Project B	6	8	−2
Project C	4	12	−8
Project D	−1	−3	2
Project E	−2	−1	−1
Project F	−2	4	−6

Group I consists of households with annual incomes over $25,000, whereas Group II consists of households with annual incomes under $25,000.

a. According to the net benefit rule, which of these projects should be funded?

b. For which of the projects might distributional considerations be an issue?

c. Compute internal distributional weights for the projects you selected in part b. Using these weights, indicate the circumstances under which each project might actually be undertaken.

d. Recompute social net benefits for the six projects using a distributional weight of 1 for Group I and a distributional weight of 2 for Group II. Using these weight-adjusted net social benefit estimates, indicate the circumstances under which each project might actually be undertaken. In doing this, assume that the distributional weight for Group II is an upper bound—that is, it probably overstates society's true generosity toward low-income households.

NOTES

1. For a further discussion of standing in CBA, see Chapter 2.

2. For a more general discussion of the role of distributional considerations in assessing policy initiatives, see Alphonse G. Holtmann, "Beyond Efficiency: Economics and Distributional Analysis," in David L. Weimer, ed., *Policy Analysis and Economics* (Boston, MA: Kluwer Academic Publishing, 1991), 45–64.

3. It would be better to distinguish among the persons or families affected by government programs in terms of their wealth (i.e., the value of their stock of assets), rather than in terms of their income (the observed flow of payments they receive in exchange for the labor, capital, and land that they provide the production process). For example, two households may have similar incomes, but if one owns a house and the other does not, their standard of living may be quite different. However, income normally is used instead of wealth in categorizing individuals or families because it is more readily measured.

4. As discussed in Chapter 17, however, an exception sometimes occurs in the case of less-developed countries. Because of the paucity of funds for investment in such countries, some economists argue that each reduction in savings that results from a project should count more heavily in conducting a CBA of the project than each dollar of increase or reduction in consumption. In principle, however, the relative importance of savings and consumption can be taken into account by using the shadow price of capital approach to discounting, which is described in Chapter 10.

5. See Robert Moffitt, "Incentive Effects of the U.S. Welfare System: A Review," *Journal of Economic Literature* 30(1) 1992, 1–61, and the references cited therein.

6. Martin Feldstein's discussion of technical issues in computing distributional weights is premised on this argument. See Martin S. Feldstein, "Distributional Equity and the Optimal Structure of Public Prices," *The American Economic Review* 62(1) 1972, 32–36.

7. Arnold Harberger's classical examination of distributional weighting ("On the Use of Distributional Weights in Social Cost-Benefit Analysis," *Journal of Political Economy* 86(2) 1972, S87-S120.) can be viewed as a critical assessment of whether this assertion provides a basis for conducting distributionally weighted CBA.

8. These points are discussed in greater detail by Aidan R. Vining and David L. Weimer, "Welfare Economics as the Foundation for Public Policy Analysis: Incomplete and Flawed but Nevertheless Desirable," *The Journal of Socio-Economics* 21(1) 1992, 25–37. John Rawls, *A Theory of Justice* (Cambridge, MA: Harvard University Press, 1971), and others have provided a more philosophical basis than the reasons listed here for greater income equality.

9. The first two arguments can be derived more formally by specifying a social welfare function. To illustrate, we specify a very simple social welfare function in which individual utility depends upon income, total social welfare depends upon a linear combination of individual utilities, and the possibility of interdependent utility (i.e., one person's utility being affected by the gains or losses of others) is ignored:

$$SW = f[u_1(y_1)\ldots,u_i(y_i)\ldots,u_n(y_n)]$$

where n is the total number of individuals in society. Totally differentiating the social welfare function yields the following expression:

$$dSW = \sum_{i=1}^{n}[(\partial SW/\partial u_i)(\partial u_i/\partial y_i)dy_i]$$

where dy_i represents the change in income resulting from a government policy. The first argument implies that $\partial u_l/\partial y_l > \partial u_h/\partial y_h$, while the second argument implies that $\partial SW/\partial u_h > \partial SW/\partial u_l$. Thus, together the two arguments imply that $(\partial SW/\partial u_l)(\partial u_l/\partial y_l) > (\partial SW/\partial u_h)(\partial u_h/\partial y_h)$.

10. D. W. Pearce, *Cost-Benefit Analysis,* 2nd ed. (New York: St. Martin's Press, 1983), 64–66. An example, of using this approach is found in Richard S. J. Tol, Thomas E. Downing, Samuel Frankhauser, Richard G. Richels, and Joel B. Smith, *Progress in Estimating the Marginal Costs of Greenhouse Gas Emissions,* Working Paper SCG-4 (Hamburg: Centre for Marine and Climate Research, Hamburg University, 2001) www.uni-hamburg.de/wiss. They find that

because the countries that are worst affected by global warming are located near the equator and tend to be relatively poor, the costs of global warming from a global perspective appear much worst if aggregation across countries is based on population size rather than on dollars of income.

11. From the perspective of social choice theory, this is a somewhat naive view of democracy. See William H. Riker, *Liberalism Against Populism* (San Francisco: Freeman, 1982).

12. For an illustration of how this might be done in practice, see Pearce, *Cost-Benefit Analysis,* p. 71.

13. For a brief overview, see Amartya Sen, *On Ethics and Economics* (New York: Basil Blackwell, 1987). For a more detailed discussion, see Robert Cooter and Peter Rappoport, "Were the Ordinalists Wrong About Welfare Economics?" *Journal of Economic Literature* 22(2) 1984, 507–530.

14. Although several attempts have been made to develop distributional weights based on political decisions concerning taxes or public expenditures, there has been limited acceptance of any of these weights. Examples of these attempts can be found in Otto Eckstein, "A Survey of the Theory of Public Expenditure Criteria," in James M. Buchanan, ed., *Public Finances: Needs, Sources and Utilization* (Princeton, NJ: Princeton University Press, 1961), 439–494; . Robert H. Haveman, *Water Resource Investment and the Public Interest* (Nashville, TN: Vanderbilt University, 1965); V. C. Nwaneri, "Equity in Cost-Benefit Analysis: A Case Study of the Third London Airport," *Journal of Transport Economics and Policy* 4(3) 1970, 235–254; and Burton A. Weisbrod, "Income Redistribution Effects and Benefit-Cost Analysis," in S. B. Chase, ed., *Problems in Public Expenditure Analysis* (Washington, D.C.: The Brookings Institution, (1968), 177–208. In addition, Shlomo Yitzhaki has developed a method for deriving distributional weights from inequality indices commonly used by economists such as the Gini coefficient. He argues that doing this is appropriate because inequality indices are explicitly or implicitly based on a set of axioms concerning distribution and, hence, "by choosing an inequality measure the economist implicitly assumes distributional weights" (p. 326). Thus, Yitzhaki relies on the behavior of economists, rather than that of politicians. See Shlomo Yitzhaki, "Cost-Benefit Analysis and the Distributional Consequences of Government Projects," *National Tax Journal* 56(2) 2003, 319–336.

15. Shlomo Yitzhaki coined the terms "win-win reforms," "trade-off reforms," and "lose-lose reforms" to distinguish among the three types of reforms described in the text. See Shlomo Yitzhaki, "Cost-Benefit Analysis and the Distributional Consequences of Government Projects."

16. This argument was apparently first made by Arnold C. Harberger, "On the Use of Distributional Weights in Social Cost-Benefit Analysis," *Journal of Political Economy* 86(2) 1978, S87–S120.

17. Edward M. Gramlich, *A Guide to Benefit-Cost Analysis,* 2nd ed. (Englewood Cliffs, NJ: Prentice Hall, 1990), 123–127. Gramlich bases his conclusion on his own "simple analysis" and on findings from a general equilibrium computer simulation conducted by Edgar Browning and William Johnson ("The Trade-Off between Equality and Efficiency," *Journal of Political Economy* 92(2) 1984, 175–203). Both analyses are examples of attempts to compute the marginal excess burden associated with taxes, which is discussed in Chapters 3 and 16.

CHAPTER 20

How Accurate Is CBA?

C hapter 1 emphasizes that CBA can be useful as a public-sector decision-making tool. In practice, its usefulness depends on its accuracy. One way to examine the accuracy of CBA is to perform analyses of the same project at different times and to compare the results. In Chapter 1 we called such studies *ex ante/ex post* comparisons or *ex ante/in medias res* comparisons. We now return to this topic in more detail.[1]

An *ex ante* CBA is performed when the decision is made about whether to proceed with a proposed project. We refer to this time as year 0 or $t = 0$. An *ex post* analysis is performed after all the impacts of the implemented project have been realized. This may take many years, even centuries. Suppose that all impacts have occurred by year T; then an *ex post* analysis is one performed in year t, where $t \geq T$. Although an *ex post* analysis is conducted too late to influence a decision about the particular project, it offers insight into similar projects. An *in medias res* analysis is performed in some year t, where $0 < t < T$. An *in medias res* analysis may provide information about similar projects or about whether to continue or to terminate a particular project if not yet completed. Both *in medias res* and *ex post* analyses are performed in the same way as *ex ante* analysis but use data actually revealed from the project.

The accuracy of a CBA depends on how well the analyst performs the nine steps presented in Chapter 1. Each step is subject to errors. The most important ones relate to specifying the impact categories, predicting the impacts, valuing the impacts and, for *in medias res* or *ex post* studies, incurring measurement error. Difficulties associated with the other steps, while they occur frequently enough, should be avoidable by analysts with a good training in CBA. In this chapter, then, we consider only omission errors, forecasting errors, valuation errors, and measurement errors.

In general, these errors decline as CBAs are performed later, but they never reach zero. Thus, CBAs performed toward the end of a project are more accurate than those performed earlier, but even later studies contain errors. This chapter illustrates these errors in CBA by providing a detailed example of the highway project discussed in Chapter 1. This project has been the subject of three separate CBAs performed at different times—one *ex ante,* one *in medias res,* and one *ex post.*

The estimates of net benefits differ considerably across the studies. Contrary to what might have been expected, the largest source of the difference was not errors in forecasts or differences in evaluation of intangible benefits, but major differences in the actual construction costs of the project. Thus, the largest errors arose from what most analysts would have thought were the most reliable figures entered into the CBA.

SOURCES OF ERROR AND THEIR EFFECTS ON
CBA STUDIES AT DIFFERENT TIMES

Errors in CBA studies may arise for many reasons. They may result from the manager's bureaucratic lens, as we discussed in Chapter 1.[2] Some errors in CBA studies appear to be disingenuous or strategic, that is, resulting from self-interest. There is considerable evidence that managers systematically overestimate benefits and underestimate costs; see, for example, Exhibit 20-1.[3] Strategic bias of this sort is widespread among managers and does not appear to be limited to the public sector.[4] For example, Nancy Ryan found that nuclear power projects experienced "awe-inspiring" cost overruns, some attributable to strategic underestimation of costs.[5]

When CBAs are performed by truly independent analysts, as was the case for our highway example, one would not expect to encounter strategic bias. However, as we discussed in Chapter 11, prediction is subject to omission errors and forecasting errors, and monetization is subject to valuation errors. In addition, there may be measurement errors. Exhibit 20-2 summarizes the view of Steven Popper, Robert Lempert and Steven Bankes that, due to uncertainty in long-term projects, policy makers should "satisfice" under all possible contingencies rather than selecting the alternative with the largest expected net social benefits.

Over time, the net effect of these errors will generally decline and the estimated NPV will converge to the true value. This point is illustrated in Figure 20-1. Suppose NB_t denotes the present value (in year 0 dollars) of the net benefits of a project at time t. NB_t is a random variable with a probability density function, $f_t(NB_t; \mu_t, \sigma_t)$, where μ_t is the mean and σ_t is the standard deviation. *Ex ante,* the distribution of the present value of net benefits, NB_0, typically has quite a large variance. In Figure 20-1 it is shown with a normal distribution, which is a reasonable assumption for any project with many impacts. Over time some impacts are realized—nature "rolls the dice" on some impact variable, for example, the initial volume of traffic. Consequently, the distribution of net benefits changes over time. The mean of the distribution may increase or decrease relative to the *ex ante* mean, but it will tend to approach the true value, denoted NB_T, and highlighted by the vertical line. At the same time, the variance decreases over time, although it never equals zero.

─────────────── **EXHIBIT 20-1** ───────────────

Political and bureaucratic actors not only directly underestimate costs and overestimate benefits of their favored alternative, but they also overestimate the costs and underestimate the benefits of alternatives they do not favor. John Kain documents the use of such "straw men" alternatives by Houston's regional transit authority in its consideration of a new urban light rail system. He shows how it made its preferred rail alternative appear better by "goldplating" the all-bus alternatives. For example, it overestimated the capital costs of the bus-way alternatives in one report by 70 percent.

Source: Adapted from John F. Kain, "The Use of Straw Men in the Economic Evaluation of Rail Transport Projects," *American Economic Review: Papers and Proceedings* 82(2) 1992, 487–493.

─────EXHIBIT 20-2─────

Steven Popper, Robert Lempert, and Steven Bankes are sufficiently concerned about forecasting errors resulting from uncertainty in the case of long-term, complex projects that they are attempting to develop an alternative to conventional cost-benefit analysis. As discussed in Chapter 7, when there is uncertainty about which of several contingencies will be realized, one approach in CBA is to compare alternative policies by first estimating the benefits and costs of each under each contingency, then estimating the expected value for each alternative policy by using predicted probabilities of each contingency being realized, and finally selecting the alternative with the largest net expected values. Popper, Lempert, and Bankes suggest, in contrast to selecting the most optimal policy in terms of its net expected value, which under some contingencies may result in outcomes that are unsatisfactory, choosing a policy that yields "satisfactory" outcomes under all possible contingencies, even if this policy has a smaller expected value than another alternative. One reason they promote their approach is that they believe that under many circumstances the probabilities for each contingency cannot be accurately forecast. Thus, they suggest computing what the probability of each possible contingency being realized would have to be to justify selecting one policy alternative over another and then letting policy makers assess whether the actual probabilities are larger or smaller than these estimates.

Source: Adapted from Steven W. Popper, Robert J. Lempert, and Steven C. Bankes, "Shaping the Future," *Scientific American* 292(4) 2005, 66, 6p.

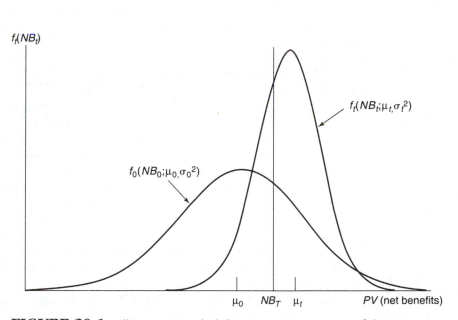

FIGURE 20-1   Illustrative Probability Density Functions of the Present Value of Net Benefits at Time 0, Time *t*, and the Actual Net Benefits, *NB_T*.

Source: Anthony E. Boardman, Wendy L. Mallery, and Aidan R. Vining, "Learning from *Ex Ante/Ex Post* Cost-Benefit Comparisons: The Coquihalla Highway Example," *Socio-Economic Planning Sciences* 28(2) 1994, 69–84. Reprinted with kind permission from Elsevier Science Ltd, The Boulevard, Langford Lane, Kidlington OX5 19GB, UK.

Omission errors will certainly decline over time as more is known about the project. Similarly, forecasting errors are likely to be reduced or eliminated as impacts are realized. Of course, even an *ex post* CBA may contain some forecasting errors due to difficulties associated with predicting the counterfactual events. Valuation errors are also likely to decline over time due to methodological improvements in valuing impacts. While measurement errors may not change over time, this type of error is likely to be relatively small. Thus, in aggregate, as *t* increases, the variance of the estimate of the present value of net benefits will decrease. It will never equal zero: uncertainty is reduced but never completely eliminated.

Whether estimates of the present value of net benefits are consistently above or below NB_T, that is, whether estimators are systematically positively or negatively biased, depends on whether omission, forecasting, valuation, or measurement errors are systematically biased (as well as on the size of these biases relative to other errors). Obtaining and comparing estimates of net benefits at different times provides clues about the magnitude of the different types of errors in a CBA and about the presence of systematic biases. With such knowledge, analysts may be able to provide better information about the precision of their estimates in similar situations.

THREE CBAs OF THE COQUIHALLA HIGHWAY

The Coquihalla Highway is a four-lane toll road, which improves access to the interior of British Columbia (B.C.) from Vancouver. Alternate routes are generally two-lane, with occasional sections of passing lanes. Congestion and safety concerns were important factors in the decision to build the highway. Construction was performed in three phases. Phase I goes from the town of Hope to Merritt, Phase II goes from Merritt to Kamloops, and Phase III goes from Merritt to Kelowna.

Three CBAs of the Highway are summarized in Table 20-1.[6] They show the benefits and costs of the highway relative to the status quo (no new highway in this region). These studies are similar in many respects. All three were performed by independent analysts; they took a global perspective, that is, everyone had standing, including foreigners; they assumed that there would be tolls at the levels that were implemented initially; they used a 7.5 percent real social discount rate and a 20-year horizon value. Benefits and costs were expressed as present values in 1984 Canadian dollars. One important difference is that the *ex ante* study was performed on the first two phases only, whereas the other two studies were performed on all three phases.

The first CBA was conducted by Bill Waters and Shane Meyers (henceforth WM) in 1986.[7] This is essentially an *ex ante* study, although Phase I was just opening at that time. The authors used "information and forecasts developed before the highway was built as this is more relevant to assessing the original decision to build the highway."[8] The impact categories, which are listed in Table 20-1, are self-explanatory. Because all three CBAs were performed from the global perspective, there is no impact category for toll revenues, which are transfers. WM calculated the present value of the net benefit of the project to be $40.2 million in 1984 dollars.

The second study was conducted by Wendy L. Mallery (hereafter MLY) in late 1987.[9] At that time, Phases I and II had been completed, but Phase III had not. MLY

TABLE 20-1   Three CBAs of the Coquihalla Highway

	Waters and Meyers Phases I and II Ex Ante	*Mallery Phases I, II, and III In Medias Res*	*Boardman, Mallery, and Vining Phases I, II, and III Ex Post*
PROJECT BENEFITS:			
Time and operating savings	$290.7	$417.6	$900.3
Safety benefits	36.5	51.5	203.1
Reduced congestion on alternative routes	14.1	29.7	56.6
Terminal value after 20 years	53.3	140.6	147.8
Total Benefits	$394.6	$639.4	$1,307.8
PROJECT COSTS:			
Construction	$338.4	$702.6	$837.2
Toll collection	8.4	8.4	8.4
Maintenance and snow removal	7.6	56.6	67.9
Total Costs	$354.4	$767.6	$913.5
NET BENEFITS	$40.2	($128.2)	$394.3

Note: All figures are present values expressed in millions of 1984 Canadian dollars, discounted at 7.5 percent, assuming a project life of 20 years.
Source: Anthony E. Boardman, Wendy L. Mallery, and Aidan R. Vining, "Learning from *Ex Ante/Ex Post* Cost-Benefit Comparisons: The Coquihalla Highway Example," *Socio-Economic Planning Sciences* 28(2) 1994, 69–84, Table 2, p. 77. Reprinted with kind permission from Elsevier Science, Ltd., The Boulevard, Langford Lane, Kidlington OX5 19GB, UK.

had access to actual traffic data (for sixteen months for Phase I and for one month for Phase II) and published estimates of actual construction costs. Thus, MLY's study is an early *in medias res* CBA.

The final study by Anthony Boardman, Wendy Mallery, and Aidan Vining (hereafter BMV) was completed in 1993, although some impacts were estimated earlier.[10] Despite the fact that this study was conducted before the end of the project's life, we will follow conventional practice and treat it as an *ex post* CBA.

Omissions

It could be argued that there were omission errors in all three analyses. None considered the opportunity cost of the land occupied by the highway. This land was owned by the provincial government. Even analysts have a tendency to treat publicly owned land as "free," which, of course, is incorrect. In fact, the land did not have a high oppor- tunity cost, so excluding it did not have a large impact on the *NPV*s.

There is considerable controversy over the highway's environmental impacts. Though there is no separate impact category for environmental damage in any of the studies, the cost of constructing underpasses, which allow animals to safely cross underneath the highway, careful timing of construction activity, and special efforts to repair any encroachment of rivers were included in construction costs. All three analyses assumed implicitly that, after taking these actions, environmental impacts would be negligible. Environmentalists, however, contend the actual environmental impacts (e.g., wild animal road kills, wildlife and fish habitat destruction) are quite large.

None of the CBAs includes benefits associated with regional development. Such indirect, local benefits are generally viewed in CBA as transfers from other areas, rather than real benefits. Yet, analysis of indirect effects becomes complicated in the presence of *network externalities*. In the years since the construction of the highway, there has been an unexpected economic boom in Kelowna. These positive network externalities or agglomeration effects may be partially attributable to the highway.[11] If so, it would be legitimate to treat part of the regional development benefits as real benefits.

Forecasting Differences

Traffic Volume Data on the Coquihalla and Other Routes. Estimates of traffic volume are likely to be the most crucial forecast in a highway CBA because they directly affect many of the benefit categories. Future traffic levels are difficult to predict. Furthermore, they may change over the life of the project as potential consumers "learn" about the advantages and disadvantages of the highway and alternative routes, as population distributions change, and as consumer tastes change.

WM obtained aggregate annual traffic forecasts by applying traffic growth patterns around the time of their study to a British Columbia Ministry of Transportation forecast for 1986 and allowing for an EXPO 86 traffic bulge. They then disaggregated the data into different origin-destination groups for three categories of vehicles (trucks, passenger vehicles—work, and passenger vehicles—leisure). For each group, they estimated the proportion of diverted, undiverted, and generated traffic.[12] Price-sensitive diversion rates were used to account for the impacts of tolls on the Coquihalla Highway.

MLY used actual Coquihalla traffic counts from May 1986 (when Phase I opened) to September 1987 (when Phase II opened). For subsequent years, MLY produced three different *NPV*s, assuming a 1, 3, and 5 percent annual traffic growth. The 3 percent rate is used in Table 20-1. Under this assumption, total vehicle traffic (at the toll booth) in the years 2000 and 2005 was projected to be 2.85 million and 3.65 million, respectively. MLY estimated the annual average daily traffic allocations on alternative routes for 1984–1987 based on actual average summer daily traffic counts.[13] This historical information was used to estimate a diversion rate of 30 percent for Highway 3 traffic to the Coquihalla after the completion of Phase III.

BMV draw on four sources of data: (1) Toll booth receipts for the years 1986–1990, which were broken out by the following vehicle classes: motorcycles, passenger vehicles, and trucks with two axles, three axles, four to five axles, or six axles or more;[14] (2) perusal of April 1991 traffic counts at the Coquihalla toll booth and on the Okanagan Connector (Phase III), which shows that completion of Phase III increased Coquihalla traffic by about 40 percent; (3) counters on all alternative routes for 1985–1989 (the summer traffic counts for each highway section were then adjusted to account for seasonality: summer traffic was 1.25 to 1.9 times the annual average daily traffic); and (4) Ministry of Transportation origin-destination surveys, which suggested 90 percent of passenger vehicles were leisure travelers, while 10 percent were business travelers. Based on these data, and assuming a 5 percent annual growth rate (after completion of Phase III), BMV project annual Coquihalla traffic volumes of 4.03 million and 5.14 million vehicles for the years 2000 and 2005, respectively.

It is impossible to determine the accuracy of the traffic volume forecasts of WM's *ex ante* study because they did not present them explicitly, nor did they specify the growth rate. Backward induction suggests that WM only slightly overestimated initial use but seriously underestimated future traffic volumes. MLY used actual data for the initial year and then estimated a growth rate of 3 percent, while actual growth has been about 5 percent. WM predicted that the opening of Phase III would increase the traffic base by 20 percent, but it actually increased by around twice as much. BMV's *ex post* study projections for the years 2000 and 2005 are 41 percent higher than MLY's estimates.

Time and Distance Savings on the Coquihalla.   One would expect that time and distance savings per trip would not vary by much among the analyses. In fact, they did vary, as shown in Tables 20-2 and 20-3. Differences in distance are due to changes in the final design as well as the use of different data to measure distance. Differences in time saved are due to differences in distance saved and different assumptions about the speeds traveled on different routes.

Reduced Congestion on Alternative Routes.   WM estimated that, due to the Coquihalla, through traffic on the old routes would save 20 minutes during congested periods. They assumed local traffic would save less time, proportional to the number of cars diverted to the new highway. MLY also used the 20-minute saving. BMV followed

TABLE 20-2 Distance Saved per Coquihalla Trip (Kilometers)

Trip	Waters and Meyers Ex Ante	Mallery In Medias Res	Boardman, Mallery, and Vining Ex Post
Phase I: Hope to Merritt	N/A[a]	87	112
Phases I and II: Hope to Kamloops	72	83	107
Phases I and III: Hope to Peachland	N/A	77	53

[a]N/A = Not available or not applicable.
Source: Anthony E. Boardman, Wendy L. Mallery, and Aidan R. Vining, "Learning from *Ex Ante/Ex Post* Cost-Benefit Comparisons: The Coquihalla Highway Example," *Socio-Economic Planning Sciences* 28(2) 1994, 69–84, Table 3A, p. 79. Reprinted with kind permission from Elsevier Science, Ltd., The Boulevard, Langford Lane, Kidlington OX5 19GB, UK.

TABLE 20-3   Time Saved per Coquihalla Trip (Minutes)

Trip	Waters and Meyers Ex Ante	Mallery In Medias Res	Boardman, Mallery, and Vining Ex Post
Phase I: Hope to Merritt	N/A[a]	102	108
Phases I and II: Hope to Kamloops	72	89	120
Phases I and III: Hope to Peachland	N/A	100	79

[a]N/A = Not available or not applicable.
Source: Anthony E. Boardman, Wendy L. Mallery, and Aidan R. Vining, "Learning from *Ex Ante/Ex Post* Cost-Benefit Comparisons: The Coquihalla Highway Example," *Socio-Economic Planning Sciences* 28(2) 1994, 69–84, Table 3B, p. 79. Reprinted with kind permission from Elsevier Science, Ltd., The Boulevard, Langford Lane, Kidlington OX5 19GB, UK.

a different approach, assuming users of alternative routes would save 2 kilometeres per hour in 1986 and 5 kilometeres per hour from 1987 onward.

Accident Rates.   WM calculated safety benefits resulting from both reduced distance traveled and from traveling on a safer highway. To estimate safety benefits from reduced distances, they multiplied the predicted 130 million vehicle-kilometers saved by the accident rates for fatal, injury, and property-damage-only accidents on two-lane highways determined by Radnor Pacquette and Paul Wright.[15] To estimate benefits resulting from a safer road, WM multiplied the estimated 313 million vehicle-kilometers traveled on the Coquihalla by one-third of the accident rate—their estimate of the accident rate reduction due to using a four-lane divided highway versus the existing highway. MLY followed a similar approach but, for benefits due to a safer road, she used the higher accident rate reductions implied by Pacquette and Wright, which ranged from 35 to 50 percent, depending on the severity of accident. BMV obtained accident rate data by severity from the ministry.

The Coquihalla Highway does save lives. The fatal accident rate of the Coquihalla is about 50 percent lower than on alternate routes, a higher reduction than WM assumed but similar to MLY's estimate. Furthermore, actual fatal accident rates on all routes in British Columbia are higher than WM or MLY assumed. Consequently, more lives are saved due to reduced distance driving than either WM or MLY predicted. Relative to other routes, the Coquihalla has a lower injury rate but a higher property-damage-only rate. Nonetheless, because both of these types of accident rates are also higher in British Columbia than anticipated, the shorter Coquihalla generates much higher safety benefits than projected.[16]

Valuation Differences

Value of Vehicle Operating Cost Savings and Value of Time Saved.   The three CBAs were similar in terms of how they valued time savings. Specifically, each assumed that business travelers value an hour of their time at the average gross wage for British Columbia hourly and salaried employees, whereas leisure travelers value their time at 25 percent of this rate. All three studies also made similar assumptions about the number of passengers in each vehicle. Based on a perusal of estimates from the ministry, BMV assumed 2.2 passengers per leisure vehicle and 1.2 passengers per business vehicle. As far as we know, the other studies used similar estimates.

The three analyses differed, however, in the estimated gross wage rates and in the vehicle operating costs. Consider, for example, the estimates pertaining to a trip from Hope to Kamloops. WM estimated vehicle operating cost savings per Coquihalla trip at $7.00 for automobiles and $33.50 for large trucks. Estimated time savings were $8.00, $14.40, and $16.80 per trip for leisure vehicles, business vehicles, and trucks, respectively. MLY calculated vehicle operating cost savings at $9.66 per automobile trip and at $46.73 per truck trip. Time savings were calculated as $6.58 per leisure trip, $20.25 per business-auto trip, and $22.35 per truck trip.[17] BMV's estimates were considerably higher. Based largely on data provided by Trimac Consulting Services, BMV estimated time *and* vehicle operating cost savings at $27.50 per leisure trip, $46.80 per business trip, and $86.50 for a five-axle semitrailer trip in 1987 Canadian dollars.[18]

Value of Safety Benefits.   WM valued fatalities, injuries, and property-damage-only accidents at $500,000, $11,000, and $2,000, respectively. MLY used slightly higher valuations: saved fatalities, injuries, and property-damage-only accidents were valued at $550,000, $12,000, and $2,000, respectively. Since 1984 there has been considerable research on this topic. As discussed in Chapter 15, current valuations are considerably higher in real dollars than was thought appropriate in 1984. Based on the most recent research at the time of their study, BMV used $2.2 million (1984 Canadian dollars) for the value of an avoided fatality.

Terminal Value.   As discussed in Chapter 6, with a discounting period of 20 years, the terminal value conceptually equals the present value of the net benefits of the project from the 21st year to infinity. The obvious difficulty is in making projections that far into the future. Future costs, for example, will depend critically on the actual depreciation rate of the highway, which is partially endogenous insofar as it varies with use.

The method used in all three studies was to base the terminal value on the initial construction cost. WM assumed the terminal value in the 21st year was 75 percent of the initial construction costs. MLY used 85 percent of initial construction costs, due partially to the high proportion of Coquihalla construction costs, such as rock cutting and sand blasting, that needed to be done only once. BMV used 75 percent.

Estimation/Measurement Differences

Maintenance Expenses.   At the time of the *ex ante* study, the Maintenance Services Branch estimated the cost of annual maintenance and snow removal ranged between $2,500 and $7,500 per lane-kilometer. WM selected a number near the low end of this range but interpreted the figures as per kilometer rather than per lane-kilometer, resulting in an estimate of $2,600 per kilometer. In contrast, MLY estimated $7,000 per lane-kilometer for Phase I, and $5,000 per lane-kilometer for Phases II and III. Because the highway was 80 percent a four-lane highway and 20 percent a six-lane highway, MLY's maintenance and snow removal estimates are far higher than WM's estimates. BMV made a largely unsuccessful attempt to isolate actual maintenance expenses. One problem was that the ministry maintained appropriate data by district, not by highway. To complicate matters, in 1988 the ministry privatized highway maintenance. The two major contractors for the Coquihalla were reluctant to reveal their costs because they were bidding on new tenders. They did admit, however, that, due to poor quality control in construction, ditch cleaning costs were higher than expected and some older sections of the highway already required resurfacing. Ultimately, BMV used an estimate of $6,000 per lane-kilometer, the average of the two figures used by MLY. There was one difference, however, stemming from the record-breaking snowstorms over the 1990–1991 winter. To account for the "once in 10-, 20-, or 50-year" snowstorms that can severely affect the Coquihalla, maintenance and snow removal costs were arbitrarily increased in each of two randomly chosen years. Overall, this approach is not entirely satisfactory, but it highlights that, like *ex ante* analyses, *ex post* analyses can suffer from prediction error.

Construction Costs.   WM performed their study after Phase I was completed. Consequently, forecasting construction costs was not an issue, but they still encountered measurement problems. Based on the best available estimates, WM estimated the present value of construction costs for Phases I and II were equal to $338.1 million (in 1984 dollars).

Soon after completion of the highway, rumors circulated of higher costs. On November 7, 1987, the *Vancouver Sun* published estimates of undiscounted total costs of $570 million for Phases I and II and $270 million for Phase III. MLY discounted these estimates to obtain construction costs of $507.9 million for Phases I and II and $194 million for Phase III. BMV's construction cost estimates are based on the MacKay Commission, a commission of inquiry that was formed when it became publicly known that the Coquihalla had cost much more than originally anticipated.[19] MacKay concluded that "differences between costs and estimates of the Coquihalla Highway . . . are due to . . . lack of proper budgeting, monitoring cost-control and reporting systems" (p. xi), and observed "[t]he current method of reporting highway capital spending . . . by individual contracts, by Electoral Districts, and on an annual basis . . . has served to disguise the true cost of major projects" (p. xi). MacKay also commented that "The Ministry's cost reporting system for capital works is fragmented and inconsistent" (p. xx). Based on the MacKay Commission report, BMV estimated that the present value of construction costs of the Coquihalla was $837 million, which is $135 million higher than MLY. The difference between BMV's estimate and the estimates in the earlier studies is probably mostly due to strategic biases.

During BMV's enquiries on actual construction costs, one ministry official estimated that MacKay's total Coquihalla construction cost figures were "out" (underestimated) by as much as 300 percent. Uncertainties undoubtedly remain even after the events. Doubling construction costs would be a rough way of accounting for work that was hidden or lost in general accounts and for increases in indirect ministry overhead costs due to the Coquihalla.

EXHIBIT 20-3

Richard Anguera conducted both an *ex post* financial analysis and an *ex post* cost-benefit analysis of the Channel Tunnel (between England and France). He did not conduct or present an *ex ante* cost-benefit analysis and did not conduct an *ex ante-ex post* CBA comparison, but he had access to many *ex ante* forecasts and was able to make *ex ante-ex post* comparisons of these forecasts. His main conclusions are

1. *Ex ante* forecasts overestimated the total size and growth of the cross-Channel passenger and freight markets. While the Channel Tunnel's market share was predicted accurately, this was only achieved by price cutting. Eurotunnel's forecasts of freight increased over time, concurrently with cost estimate increases. In fact, its early estimates of freight traffic were lower than actual. In contrast, its passenger traffic forecasts were extremely optimistic—between 2 and 3 times the actual traffic.

2. Costs were significantly underestimated: they ended-up being twice the expected amount. The major reason was regulatory risk, mainly attributable to the Independent Safety Authority that had responsibility for the safety design standards. Brent Flyvbjerg, Nils Bruzelius, and Werner Rothengatter also identified lack of clear ownership and control as another major reason.[20] In addition, and probably not totally unexpectedly, there were unforeseen problems in the works program.

3. The net social benefit of the Tunnel for the 1987–2003 period was −£10 billion in 2004 pounds, using a real social discount rate of 3.5 percent. While this is a substantial amount, it is important to note that it does not include a terminal value.

4. In terms of distributional implications, the main beneficiaries were users who benefitted from lower prices. The main losers were producers, both the Tunnel operator and ferry operators (competitors). Most of the users gain was a transfer from producers.

Adapted from Richard Anguera, "The Channel Tunnel–An Ex Post Economic Evaluation," *Transportation Research Part A* 40(4) 2006, 291–315.

Overall Underestimation of the Differences

In fact, simply looking at the aggregate differences understates the actual differences in the earlier studies. First, some benefits and costs erred in the same direction, thereby tending to cancel each other. For example, the *ex post* study had higher construction costs but also had higher time and operating savings benefits than the previous studies. Second, some errors offset one another within an impact category. For example, concerning safety benefits, the Coquihalla accident rate was higher than predicted, but highway ridership and accident rates elsewhere were also higher than forecast.

CONCLUSION

Contrasting an *in medias res* or *ex post* analysis with earlier CBAs of the same project provides an opportunity to assess the predictive capability of earlier analyses. This is a critical element in determining the value of *ex ante* CBAs. In the Coquihalla Highway example this exercise was somewhat humbling. *Ex ante* CBA is hard to do precisely.

One comparison study alone cannot tell us everything about the general accuracy of CBA. Are such aggregate prediction errors prevalent in other CBAs? If they are, it is troubling. One might argue that this particular project raises more problems than is typical, but we think not. This project is *relatively* straightforward; after all, it is a highway, not a high-tech, mega project. Another possibility is that the cost underestimation problem (partly due to regional rather than project-specific budgeting) is specific to "wild and woolly" British Columbia. Again, we do not think so. Several non–British Columbia bureaucratic readers acknowledge that their agencies routinely hide project budget items in other accounts.

In conclusion, the main lesson illustrated here is the importance of periodically conducting *ex ante/ex post* comparisons. This may seem trivial, but it is almost totally ignored in the cost-benefit analysis literature. If *ex ante* studies were mandatory, should one in ten be subject to *in medias res* or *ex post* follow-up and comparison to the *ex ante* analysis? If so, this chapter provides a template for how to do such comparisons.

NOTES

1. The chapter draws upon Anthony E. Boardman, Wendy L. Mallery, and Aidan R. Vining, "Learning from Ex Ante/Ex Post Cost-Benefit Comparisons: The Coquihalla Highway Example," *Socio-Economic Planning Sciences* 28(2) 1994, 69–84.
2. See Anthony Boardman, Aidan Vining, and W. G. Waters II, "Costs and Benefits Through Bureaucratic Lenses: Example of a Highway Project," *Journal of Policy Analysis and Management* 12(3) 1993, 532–555.
3. For example, see Bent Flyvbjerg, Mette K. Skamris Holm, and Soren L. Buhl, "How (In)accurate Are Demand Forecasts in Public Works Projects? The Case of Transportation," *Journal of the American Planning Association* 71(2) 2005, 131–146; and, by the same authors, "Cost Underestimation in Public Works Projects: Error or Lie?" *Journal of the American Planning Association* 68(3) 2002, 279–295.
4. This bias has been found in a wide range of corporations by Stephen W. Pruitt and Lawrence J. Gitman, "Capital Budgeting Forecast Biases: Evidence from the Fortune 500," *Financial Management* 16(1) 1987, 46–51. See also Charles R. Schwenk, "The Cognitive Perspective on Strategic Decision Making," *Journal of Management Studies* 25(1) 1988, 41–55, and J. E. Russo and P. J. Schoemaker, "Managing Overconfidence," *Sloan Management Review* 33(2) 1992, 7–17.

5. Nancy E. Ryan, "Policy Formation in a Politically Charged Atmosphere: An Empirical Study of Rate-Base Determination for Recently Completed Nuclear Power Plants," paper presented at the 14th Annual APPAM Research Conference, 1992, at p. 3.
6. For various reasons the summary benefit and cost figures of the *ex ante* CBA in Table 20-1 are not exactly the same as those presented in Table 1-3.
7. W. G. Waters II and Shane J. Meyers, "Benefit-Cost Analysis of a Toll Highway—British Columbia's Coquihalla," *Journal of the Transportation Research Forum* 28(1) 1987, 435–443.
8. Ibid.
9. Wendy L. Mallery, "A Cost-Benefit Analysis of the Coquihalla Highway," course paper for J. M. Munro, Simon Fraser University, December 1987.
10. Boardman, Mallery, and Vining, "Learning from Ex Ante/Ex Post Cost-Benefit Comparisons." Using a similar approach, Winston Harrington, Richard D. Morgenstern, and Peter Nelson ("On the Accuracy of Regulatory Cost Estimates," *Journal of Policy Analysis and Management* 19[2] 2000, 297–322) compared *ex ante* cost estimates of the direct cost of regulations with *ex post* estimates of the same regulations and found that the former were overestimated much more often than they were underestimated.
11. A positive network externality arises where the utility one person derives from the consumption of a good increases with the number of other

people consuming the good. For example, the benefit of having a cell phone increases with the number of other people who have cell phones that are connected to the same network. In the context of regional development, positive externalities may arise when a region reaches a critical mass, or agglomeration, in terms of the nature, depth, and breadth of its economic activity.

12. Diverted traffic refers to traffic that would have gone on the old routes but now travels on the Coquihalla. Undiverted traffic refers to traffic that continues on the old routes despite the existence of the Coquihalla. Generated traffic refers to traffic that would not have made the trip by road at all without the Coquihalla but now does so because the effective price is lower. These travelers may have gone by air or train or done something completely different.

13. These numbers were then adjusted by the estimated ratio of average summer to average annual traffic.

14. Total traffic data were obtained for 1986 to 1990. Traffic data by vehicle class were obtained for the period April 1987 to March 1991 and estimated for 1986 and part of 1987. The traffic data thus cover three full years of Phase II operation from Hope to Kamloops and a few months of Phase III operation from Hope to Peachland.

15. Radnor J. Pacquette and Paul H. Wright, *Highway Engineering* (New York: Wiley & Sons, 1979), at p. 73.

16. MLY based her projections on Pacquette and Wright (p. 73), who estimated the accident rates on a divided highway are 0.0155, 0.168, and 0.304 (per million vehicle-kilometers) for fatalities, injuries, and property damage only, respectively.

17. MLY used the average April 1986 gross wage for all B.C. industries for hourly and salaried employees, from the Statistics Canada publication, *Monthly Employment Earnings and Hours,* as the business hourly wage.

18. Trimac Consulting Services Limited, *Operating Costs of Trucks in Canada,* 1986 and 1988 editions, prepared for the Motor Carrier Branch, Surface Transport Administration, Transport Canada (Ottawa, Ontario: Minister of Supply and Services, 1986, 1988).

19. Douglas L. MacKay, Commissioner, *Report of the Commission Inquiry into the Coquihalla and Related Highway Projects,* Province of British Columbia, December 1987.

20. Brent Flyvbjerg, Nils Bruzelius, and Werner Rothengatter, *Megaprojects and Risk: An Anatomy of Ambition,* (New York: Cambridge University Presss 2003).

Name Index

Page numbers followed by "n" and number denote "note number"; page numbers followed by "t" show tables.

A

Aaron, Henry J., 24n4
Abdalla, Charles W., 367
Abelson, Peter, 438n11
Acharya, Arnab, 486n4
Achen, Christopher H., 317n7
Adams, Miriam E., 488n34
Aldy, Joseph, 409, 437n7, 442n74
Alston, Julian M., 77n7
Anand, Sudhir, 486n7
Anderson, Glen D., 401n29
Anderson, Robert J., Jr., 222n18
Anderson, Roy M., 201n15
Anguera, Richard, 517
Aos, Steve, 286n15, 287n29
Appenzeller, Ute, 317n11
Arrow, Kenneth, 50n4, 201n18, 223n24, 268n13,
    269n20, 271n46, 377, 396, 399n7
Ashenfelter, Orley, 317n10
Ashworth, Karl, 26n25, 318n25, 319n28
Atkinson, Giles, 439n27
Austin, David, 441n56
Aydede, Selma K., 262
Azar, Christian, 498

B

Ballard, Charles L., 441n71
Baltussen, Rob M. P. M., 486n4
Bankes, Steven, 509
Barrett, S., 269n19
Bateman, Ian J., 236n8, 399n2, 402n52,
    440n42, 441n50
Becht, Marco, 77n8
Becker, Gary S., 113n20, 222n8
Behn, Robert D., 25n21, 199n6
Bell, Stephen H., 318n17
Bellavance, Francois, 437n8
Bengochea-Morancho, Aurelia, 236n13
Benton, Bruce, 457
Bergson, Abram, 50n9
Berliant, Marcus C., 51n21
Berrens, Robert P., 403n65
Biggs, Andrew J. G., 357, 441n55
Bishop, Richard C., 395, 403n61
Blackorby, Charles, 50n5, 50n6

Blais, André, 25n17
Blau, Julian H., 50n4
Blincoe, Lawrence, 415–416, 438n18
Boadway, Robin W., 77n7
Boardman, Anthony E., 25n10, 25n14, 26n28, 67,
    201n20, 267n1, 437n1, 511, 518n10
Bohara, Alok K., 403n65
Books, Richard, 487n27
Borins, Sanford, 25n15
Boskin, Michael J., 164n15
Boulding, Kenneth E., 11
Bowland, Brad J., 442n73
Boyle, Kevin J., 403n61
Braden, John B., 236
Bradford, David, 270n35
Bradley, Cathy J., 200n14
Brander, Luke M., 440n46
Brazier, John, 487n25, 487n26
Bromley, Daniel W., 51n17, 271n41
Brookshire, David S., 401n35, 403n65, 404n81
Brown, Gardner, Jr., 371n25
Browning, Edgar K., 66
Bruce, Neil, 77n7
Bruzelius, Nils, 519n20
Bryan, Stirling, 487n29
Buhl, Soren, 25n23
Burnett, Jason K., 26n32
Burtless, Gary, 293
Burtraw, Dallas, 441n56

C

Camerer, Colin F., 221n2
Campbell, Donald, 316n2
Carson, Richard T., 377, 383, 389, 391–394, 400n24,
    400n30, 401n39, 403n60, 404n73, 405n93
Castle, Barbara, 20
Cebulla, Andreas, 26n25, 317n10, 318n25, 319n28
Cicchetti, Charles J., 222n17
Cockburn, Iain, 165n18
Cohen, Linda R., 188
Cohen, Mark, 287n31, 418–419, 438n26
Cohen, Peter A., 286n13
Colbey, Bonnie G., 442n83
Conner-Spady, Barbara, 487n30
Conrad, Jon M., 201n19

Subject Index

Page numbers followed by "n" and number denote "note number"; page numbers followed by "t" show tables.